Foreword

This course handbook is one of about 150 published each year by the Practising Law Institute.

Its primary function is to serve as an educational supplement to each program. It may also be used as a reference manual by attorneys and related professionals unable to attend the sessions.

The method of reproduction utilized has been chosen to insure that registrants receive these materials as quickly as possible and in the most usable form practical.

The Practising Law Institute wishes to acknowledge its debt and extend its sincere appreciation to the authors who have rendered this valuable service. They exemplify the finest tradition of our profession by sharing their expertise with their colleagues.

CORPORATE LAW AND PRACTICE
Course Handbook Series
Number B-1046

Securities Law & The Internet

Doing Business In a Rapidly Changing Marketplace

Co-Chairs

Brandon Becker
Stephen J. Schulte
Michelle C. Wallach

To order this book, call (800) 260-4PLI or fax us at (800) 321-0093. Ask our Customer Service Department for PLI Order Number B0-003H, Dept. BAV5.

Practising Law Institute
810 Seventh Avenue
New York, New York 10019

"This publication is designed to provide information in regard to the subject matter covered. It is sold with the understanding that the publisher is not engaged in rendering legal, accounting or other professional service. If legal advice or other expert assistance is required, the services of a competent professional person should be sought."

—from Declaration of Principles jointly adopted by Committee of American Bar Association and Committee of Publishers and Associations

 ISBN 0-87224-444-X

Prepared for distribution at the
SECURITIES LAW & THE INTERNET: DOING BUSINESS IN A RAPIDLY CHANGING MARKETPLACE
Program
April 1998

Contents:

1

DISCLOSURE PRACTICE IN THE ELECTRONIC AGE: THE WEB SITE – OPPORTUNITIES AND PITFALLS

Steven E. Bochner
Anita S. Presser

CORPORATE DISCLOSURE PRACTICES IN THE ELECTRONIC AGE: THE WEB SITE - OPPORTUNITIES AND PITFALLS

Advice for companies disclosing information on a web site

By Steven E. Bochner
and Anita S. Presser[1]

INTRODUCTION

Notwithstanding the passage of the Private Securities Litigation Reform Act of 1995 (the "Reform Act"), the rate of securities lawsuits has not declined and remains a concern of every public company.[2] The increasingly pervasive use of the World Wide Web (the "WWW") by public companies as a disclosure vehicle has created a new dimension of potential risk. This article analyzes current utilization of web sites by certain corporations. It identifies inconsistencies and vulnerabilities that may facilitate the goals of securities plaintiffs, and suggests ways to reduce the risk of a securities lawsuit.

A great majority of public companies maintain a web site and use it to communicate information to current and potential investors.[3] The benefits of using a web site to communicate information are considerable. A web site provides companies with a low cost means of disseminating information to a wide audience of current and potential investors and analysts. Information posted on a web site also reaches the public faster and is easier to update, search, organize and analyze than written communication. Further, information distributed via a web site allows small and large investors equal access to information, and small and large companies equal ability to widely disseminate information.[4]

While web sites offer companies and their investors significant benefits, web site disclosures can be a potential source of liability in securities lawsuits and have already been cited in securities class action complaints.[5] Many companies that have rigorous clearance procedures with respect to

---

[1] Steven E. Bochner is a partner and Anita S. Presser is an associate in the law firm of Wilson Sonsini Goodrich & Rosati in Palo Alto, California. The views expressed are the authors' own and do not necessarily represent the views of their firm. They can be reached at SBOCHNER@WSGR.COM and APRESSER@WSGR.COM.

[2] The Private Securities Litigation Reform Act of 1995 (the "Reform Act") (Pub. L. No. 104-67, 109 Stat. 737 (1995)) This legislation "seeks to protect investors, issuers and all who are associated with our capital markets from abusive securities litigation." H.R. Conference Report No. 369, 104th Cong., 1st Sess. at 38, n.26. (1995).

[3] See Table 1 for a study by the National Investor Relations Institute concerning the type and frequency of certain data available on corporate web sites.

[4] See SEC Report to Congress: *The Impact of Recent Technological Advances on the Securities Markets,* at http://www.sec.gov/news/studies/techrp97.htm/apps.

[5] *See* Howard Gunty v. Quantum Corporation, Amended Complaint No. CV760370, (CA Super. Ct. Santa Clara Cty., March 20, 1997).

press releases and other formal disclosure may not have similar policies with respect to the posting of information on corporate web sites. In addition to the hazards of public disclosures generally, online disclosures create vulnerabilities specific to the web site setting and require additional measures to reduce potential exposure to a securities lawsuit. Moreover, web sites often contain extensive information, conveniently contained in one place, providing securities plaintiffs with one-stop shopping in their search for incriminating evidence against potential defendants.

THE SECURITIES LITIGATION ENVIRONMENT IN THE POST REFORM ACT ERA

The concern over abusive private securities lawsuits culminated with the enactment of the Reform Act. The Reform Act and the safe harbor provisions contained therein were designed to limit abusive securities litigation, through pleading reforms and other measures, and to encourage the use of forward-looking information (historically the riskiest of all public disclosures). By following the Reform Act safe harbor provisions companies that disclose forward-looking information can protect themselves in most contexts from liability under the federal securities laws.

Despite its good intentions, since the adoption of the Reform Act there have been no meaningful reduction in cases filed overall.[6] A study conducted by Professors Grundfest and Perino of the Stanford Law School indicated that in the year following the Reform Act, the number of cases filed in federal court declined. However, these were offset by securities lawsuits filed in state court, presumably to circumvent the enhanced pleading and stay of discovery provisions of the Reform Act.[7] Further, according to testimony by the Securities and Exchange Commission (the "SEC") chairman Arthur Levitt, a study conducted by the staff of the SEC indicated that securities lawsuits filed in federal courts in 1997 returned to pre-Reform Act levels.[8]

In addition to curtailing abusive securities lawsuits, another stated purpose of the Reform Act was to encourage forward-looking disclosure, through the enactment of the safe harbor for forward-looking information. While certain companies have increased the amount of forward-looking information disseminated to the public, it is questionable whether the safe harbor has fostered an overall increase in the disclosure of forward-looking information.[9] Many companies that utilize the

---

6 Joseph A. Grundfest and Michael A. Perino, *Securities Litigation Reform The First Years's Experience*, Working Paper Series Release 97.1, Feb. 27, 1997 (hereinafter "Grundfest and Perino, *Securities Litigation Reform.*"). *See also* Testimony of Arthur Levitt, Chairman of the SEC concerning the implementation of the Reform Act Before the Subcommittee on Finance and Hazardous Materials Committee on Commerce, U.S. House of Representatives, October 21, 1997 (hereinafter "Levitt Testimony").

7 *See* Grundfest and Perino, *Securities Litigation Reform.*

8 *See* Levitt Testimony.

9 *See* Levitt Testimony (Reform Act safe harbor provision has not resulted in significantly higher amount of forward-looking statements by officers and directors); *But See* Marilyn Johnson, Ron Kasznik & Karen Nelson, *The Impact of Securities Litigation Reform on the Disclosure of Forward-Looking Information by Technology Firms*, Research Paper No. 1471, Graduate School of Business, Stanford University, January 1998 (A study conducted by authors found an increase in "long horizon forecasts of good news and short horizon forecasts of bad news" among a sample of 547 firms in high tech industries).

safe harbor do so primarily with respect to prophylactic, cautionary forward-looking statements, such as those typically found in the Management's Discussion and Analysis of Financial Condition and Results of Operations sections of quarterly and periodic SEC reports and registration statements.

Because the Reform Act has not yet succeeded in its primary goal of reducing securities lawsuits, public companies must remain vigilant when issuing forward-looking statements to qualify for the Reform Act safe harbor.

OPPORTUNITIES AND PITFALLS CONCERNING WEB SITE DISCLOSURE

Unfortunately, many companies that make efforts to protect their disclosures through clearance procedures, the safe harbor and other means in more formal disclosures do not do the same with respect to more informal, but equally risky, disclosures such as those on web sites or conveyed in discussions with analysts. A web site survey conducted by the authors examined the web sites of the 50 largest public companies in Silicon Valley as listed in the August 1997 edition of The San Jose and Silicon Valley Business Journal (the "Survey"). The Survey analyzed information regarding the types of disclosures found on corporate web sites as a percentage of companies surveyed.

Use the Safe Harbor For Web-Based Forward-Looking Statements

One of the major risks concerning web site disclosures today is the inconsistent or ineffective use of the safe harbor by companies making risky forward-looking statements. The Survey results demonstrate the inconsistent use of the safe harbor among companies. For example, almost all of the web sites surveyed post press releases, however, only sixteen percent of these web sites used some cautionary language for non-financial press releases containing forward-looking information. Also, twenty-nine percent of the web sites surveyed posted either company presentations to analysts and investors or speeches by officers of the company. However, less than half of these web sites accompanied such presentations or speeches with any cautionary language.

In addition to not using the safe harbor when appropriate, many of the companies surveyed accompanied forward-looking statements with boilerplate or "generic" risk factors that change little over time and are seemingly applicable to almost any company. The legislative history accompanying the Reform Act makes it clear that boilerplate risk factors do not suffice, and the statute provides that the cautionary language accompanying the forward-looking statement must be "meaningful." In other equally ineffective cases, forward-looking statements may reference entire risk factor sections instead of matching the specific forward-looking statement with its risk disclosure counterpart. In addition, the risk factor sections of documents containing the cautionary disclosure which must "accompany" the forward-looking disclosures are often far removed from the forward-looking statements to which they are meant to apply. All of these problems provide plaintiff's lawyers with strong arguments as to why the Reform Act's safe harbor protection should not apply to the forward-looking statements that did not come true.

All forward-looking statements should be <u>accompanied</u> by <u>meaningful</u> cautionary language. While the underlined terms in the preceding sentence have not been tested in court, cautionary language far removed from the forward-looking statement creates substantial risk that safe harbor protection will not apply. Hyperlinks may also be used to link forward-looking statements to risk factors tailored to the particular statement, although the efficacy of hyperlinks in meeting the "accompanied by" requirement of the safe harbor has not yet been confirmed by the SEC or tested in court.

Another problem encountered frequently is attempts to cross reference cautionary language found in filed documents to information posted on web sites. While the Reform Act allows disclosers of oral forward-looking information to reference "readily ascertainable" documents (such as documents filed with the SEC) with respect to the cautionary language, no such flexibility is afforded written communications. Accordingly, companies making forward-looking disclosures on web sites, in press releases and in other forms of written communications must include the cautionary language in the written disclosure itself - cross referencing is not permitted (As noted above, hyperlinks may satisfy the "accompanied by" requirement, however, this has not yet been confirmed by the courts or the SEC). In this regard, a trap for the unwary exists with respect to converting oral forward-looking information (such as the presentation delivered at the last analyst teleconference) to a written script format on the web site. Posting transcripts of speeches of company presentations on the web site triggers the requirement to accompany forward-looking statements with cautionary language. Some companies have successfully circumvented this problem by posting audio or visual clips of speeches thereby maintaining their audio or video format, thus avoiding the more rigorous safe harbor requirements for written disclosure.

To ensure safe harbor protection, companies should adopt clear and consistent internal corporate policies and procedures to govern disclosure on a web site. Web site policies should include a system for monitoring and updating information posted on the site. As is the case with press releases, a company should designate a "web site clearance person" familiar with the hazards of public disclosures and the need for safe harbor protection of forward-looking statements to review all materials before they are posted on the web site.

Potentially Enhanced Duty to Update

In addition to reviewing materials prior to their posting on a web site, information already posted should be periodically examined for continued accuracy. Unlike press releases which are issued as of a particular date, plaintiffs may argue that because web site disclosures are republished constantly, an ongoing duty to update is created. Thus, out of date information should be updated or deleted.

The Survey results illustrate the failure to address a duty to update among companies that post timely information. For example, among the companies that posted time-sensitive presentations or speeches on their web sites, only one web site disclaimed the duty to update such posted information.

Ideally, all posted material should include a notice providing that the material disclosed is accurate as of its particular date, and the company disclaims any duty to update the information subsequently. This precaution is especially important with respect to more aggressive assertions or forward-looking statements, such as those concerning earnings forecasts, anticipated product introductions or competitive positioning. However, these disclosures are probably unlikely to negate a duty to update or correct prior material disclosures which are still alive in the market, but are no longer accurate.[10]

"Entanglements" with Analysts Reports.

Another potential source of liability are analyst's reports posted on the company web site or links to analyst reports from a company web site. These practices create the risk that a court will view the analyst report as sufficiently entangled with the company to treat the report as if it had come directly from the company, thereby triggering the duty to correct information which is materially inaccurate in the report.[11] A safer approach is to avoid posting analyst reports on web sites or any links to analyst reports or other sites that contain analyst reports. Instead, companies may list the names, addresses, telephone or fax numbers and E-mail addresses of the firms and analysts that cover the company.

Although none of the web sites in the Survey were linked directly to analyst reports on the company, most web sites did provide the names, phone and fax numbers, and respective companies of analysts covering the company. However, less than a third of these web sites accompanied such information with any disclaimers or cautionary language.

SUMMARY

Most public companies today utilize a web site to make information available to analysts, investors and potential investors in a timely and cost-effective manner. However, the widespread use of this electronic media, combined with the lack of formal procedures for posting web site information by many companies and the uncertainties concerning the application of certain securities law principles, such as aspects of the safe harbor to online disclosures, may increase the risk of a securities lawsuit. Companies should view web site disclosures in the same manner as press releases and adopt clear and consistent corporate policies and procedures to govern disclosure on a web site.

---

10 For a thorough discussion on the duty to update *see* Carl W. Schneider, *The Duty to Update: Time Requires a Reevaluation of Basics*. Insights, Vol. 8, No. 4, pg. 2 (April 1994).

11 *See* In re RasterOps Corp. Sec. Litig., [1994-1995 Tr. Binder] Fed. Sec. L. Rep. [CCH] P. 98,467, at 91,195 (N.D. Cal. Oct. 31, 1994), (Company passed out favorable analyst reports and as a result was held responsible for the contents of such reports). *See also* Boris Feldman & Ignacio Salceda, *Shareholder and Investor Relations in the Electronic Age*, at 5-14 in *Securities in the Electronic Age: A Practical Guide to the Law and Regulation,* John F. Olson & Harvey L. Pitt, Glasser LegalWorks, 1998.

TABLE 1

CORPORATE INFORMATION AVAILABLE ON HOME PAGE [Web Site]*

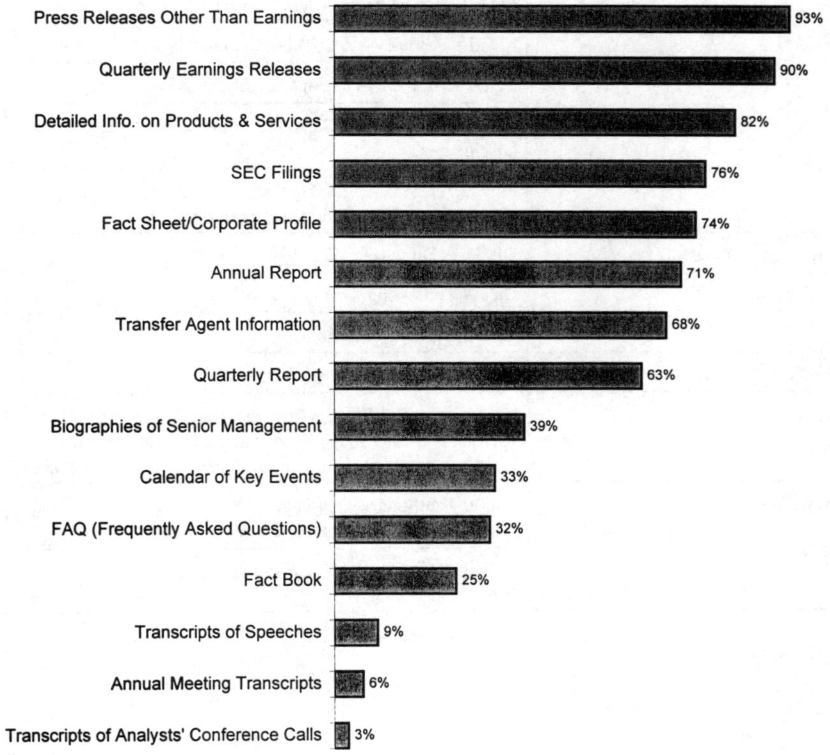

* Based on 96% of the respondents who either have a web site (85%) or plan to have one within a year (10%)
Source: National Investor Relations Institute – 1998 Utilizing Technology in the Practice of Investor Relations Survey

TABLE 2

The table below summarizes procedures to be considered with respect to the posting of information on corporate web sites.

ITEM	RECOMMENDATION
Review All Documents Before Posting	Adopt Clearance Procedure
	Safe Harbor Effectively and Consistently Used
	Identify All Forward-Looking Statements
	Tailor Risk Factors to Forward-Looking Statements
	Keep Risk Factors in Close Proximity to Forward-Looking Disclosures
	Force Web Site Visitor Through Risk Section and Duty to Update Disclaimer Before Accessing Information
Update Information	Disclaim Duty to Update
	Date Web Posting
	Update Stale Information
Analyst Reports	No Direct Link to Analyst Reports
Company Presentations	If Transcribed to Written Format - Add Appropriate Risk Factors, If Audio/Video Format-Include Reference to Written Document With Appropriate Cautionary Language
Hyperlinks	Link to Cautionary Language - Probably Okay But Not Tested in Court
	Do not Link to Analyst Reports or Other Sites Creating "Entanglement" Risks

NOTES

NOTES

2

AVOIDING SPIDERS ON THE WEB: RULES OF THUMB FOR ISSUERS USING WEB SITES AND E-MAIL

Harvey L. Pitt
Dixie L. Johnson

Avoiding Spiders on the Web: Rules of Thumb for Issuers Using Web Sites and E-Mail

by Harvey L. Pitt
and Dixie L. Johnson*

In the current frenzy to take advantage of computerized communications, and with an almost prurient fascination with the Web, many companies are embarking upon a journey into cyberspace without fully comprehending the potential mischief that can await them, and the potential obligations they may be assuming. While this development is still in its nascent stages, there are some useful rules of thumb that issuers and others can follow to minimize, if not avoid, adverse legal and regulatory scrutiny under the federal securities laws.

Many of these rules of thumb are easily recognizable – they are rooted in practices developed over the years in familiar contexts other than Web sites. They also derive from the limited regulatory forecasts of how the government intends to operate in the new technological environment. To protect the company, potential private litigants and government investigators alike should be viewed as potential "spiders" on the Web, ready to take legal or regulatory action fueled by the new technology. Combining a focus on these rules of thumb with some wariness in light of an uncertain legal environment will enable companies to take advantage of the opportunities afforded by the Web with cautious confidence and enthusiasm.

1. Make Your Web Site an Attraction, Not an Attractive Nuisance!

When a company contemplates the creation of a Web site, the focus of attention is on the positive aspects of such a development. The ability to advertise a firm's products or services and the potential to attract clientele at little cost are some of the fundamental benefits offered by the Web. But there is a double edge to the use of Web sites. More and more frequently, companies are becoming painfully aware of the possibility that their Web sites can be used against them in litigation or regulatory investigations.

No one source can provide definitive guidance in the current environment. The SEC has made admirable strides in providing guidance to those who now navigate this new environment. The Commission has issued several releases within the past couple of years that were crafted to assist issuers in grappling with questions regarding how the SEC would apply its own rules to Web-related circumstances.[1] But SEC policies are not binding on other regulators or private

---

* Mr. Pitt and Ms. Johnson are partners in the law firm of Fried, Frank, Harris, Shriver & Jacobson, resident in the Washington, D.C. office. Mr. Pitt also is resident in the firm's New York office. The authors express their appreciation to Mark J. Dorsey, Michael J. Rivera, Edward B. Whittemore, Deborah L. Box and Mary Pelletter for their helpful contributions to this article.

1 *See* Use of Electronic Media for Delivery Purposes, Securities Act Release No. 7233, 60 SEC Docket (CCH) 1091 (Oct. 6, 1995) ("Interpretive Release"); Use of Electronic Media for Delivery Purposes, Securities Act Release No. 7289, 61 SEC Docket (CCH) 2179 (May 9, 1996) (containing technical amendments to the Interpretive Release); and Use of Electronic Media by Broker-Dealers, Transfer Agents, and Investment Advisers for Delivery of Information; Additional Examples Under the Securities Act of

litigants, so issuers cannot rely exclusively on those pronouncements. Other regulators, including state securities officials, have provided less guidance about how they will interpret statements made on the Web, but they have demonstrated an alarming degree of enthusiasm for enforcement actions involving the new technology.[2] Private litigants cannot be expected to forecast their moves, but they can be counted upon to scan all available sources for statements made by company personnel, and the company's Web site is sure to be included in that search.

In order to minimize problems, issuers should assign to one or more persons, either within or outside the company, the responsibility for monitoring the legal environment for regulatory and litigation developments.

2. Avoid Entanglement in the Web of a Securities Law Violation.

When an issuer plans to issue securities, it sends a preliminary prospectus to potential investors. The SEC's rules require that the issuer's offer of securities be made only by use of this preliminary prospectus, until the prospectus has become effective. As a result, companies generally cannot include marketing materials in the prospectus envelope, because those materials typically are not drafted to meet the criteria assigned to prospectuses by the SEC. The liability imposed upon issuers by the federal securities laws inspires issuers to screen information in the prospectus, and to include only essential, and tested, information.

Some issuers currently post their preliminary prospectuses on their Web sites. Recognizing this, the SEC's releases were written to clarify the circumstances under which issuers could credit those postings as "delivery." The SEC Staff currently analyzes the regulatory compliance of electronic communications, including Web sites, by analogy to this paper standard.[3] A potential problem arises, however, when considering a company's potential liability for information posted on its Web site during periods when a preliminary prospectus is in effect.

The Staff has shown at least a modicum of flexibility on this point in two recent no-action letters, in which the SEC Staff confirmed that:

> the identification of the Company's web site in the registration statement and the statement "our SEC filings are also available to the public from our web site" will not, by itself, include or incorporate by reference any information into the registration statement which is included or hot linked to the Company's regular

---

1933, Securities Exchange Act of 1934 and Investment Company Act of 1940, Securities Act Release No. 7288, 61 SEC Docket (CCH) 2167 (May 9, 1996).

2 To date, these actions appear to have focused on the issuance and marketing of unregistered securities. *See, e.g., In re Octagon Tech. Group, Inc.*, No. 9500578, 1995 Il. Sec. LEXIS 284 (Nov. 2, 1995) (Illinois temporary cease and desist order).

3 Interpretive Release, 60 SEC Docket (CCH) 1094 n. 22 and accompanying text.

> web site but is not otherwise incorporated by reference into the registration statement.[4]

While this is welcome news, issuers have little comfort that private litigants or state regulators will take the same approach. As a result, until more guidance has evolved, issuers may prefer to avoid steps, such as including the company's Web site address in a written preliminary prospectus, that might be construed as incorporating their Web sites into their offering materials.

3. Use Disclaimers, the Corporate Version of "That's Not What I Meant!"

A company should consider creating disclaimers that clarify the extent to which Web site visitors can rely on the information in the site. A general disclaimer might be sufficient, but a tailored disclaimer for each page that needs one probably is more effective. By use of these devices, companies can clarify that their statements are forward-looking, and can include meaningful cautionary language. Companies also may disclaim any duty or intention to update the information provided on the site. The disclaimer need not appear in full text on the page, but instead can be accessible by "hyperlink."[5] Circumstances where disclaimers can be particularly useful are mentioned below.[6]

4. Guard the Gate to the Web.

Who could forget the nightmare experienced by two Apple Computer Inc. officers earlier this decade? A jury found them *personally liable* for securities fraud in connection with marketing statements the company had made regarding a new product during the early 1980s. Their total personal liability was estimated at $100 million. Although the verdict was reversed, and the case settled (for $16 million paid by Apple), the case continues to ring cautionary bells in the ears of corporate officers and their lawyers.

Had Apple made these marketing statements a decade later, chances are they would have been made on the Web. To guard against corporate missteps on the Web, all of the elaborate screening systems issuers have established for reviewing advertisements, marketing pitches and press releases before they are released into the public domain also should be applied to the issuers' Web sites. Lawyers who are accustomed to reviewing corporate pronouncements before they are circulated should be included in reviewing proposed Web site additions.

---

4 *See* ITT Corporation, SEC No-Action Letter, 1996 SEC No-Act. LEXIS 895 (Dec. 6, 1996); Baltimore Gas and Electric, SEC No-Action Letter, 1997 SEC No-Act. LEXIS 14 (Jan. 6, 1997).

5 A "hyperlink" is a path which associates an object on a Web page, such as a button or highlighted text, with another Web address, allowing the user to move to the desired location by "clicking" the button or text. *See* Morgan Stanley & Co., Inc., *The Internet Advertising Report* (Dec. 1996) at 11-3.

6 *See also* Steven E. Bochner, *Finding the Harbor: Advice for Companies on Navigating Federal Securities Litigation Reform,* THE EMERGING LAW OF SECURITIES IN THE ELECTRONIC AGE, (Feb. 1997).

5. Keep It Current!

Just as it is important to monitor items proposed to be *added* to the Web site, so also it is important to monitor existing postings for items that should be *deleted.* The ideal approach would be to review the site *regularly and frequently* to ensure that all available information is current. Even if constant and thorough review is not possible, however, issuers with Web sites should adopt a system for archiving and/or deleting stale and inaccurate information.

Developing an archiving system on the Web site helps to clarify that certain information remains posted not because it is current, but because it may be of historical interest. With an appropriate disclaimer, an archive section of a Web site can store "old" information, and even inaccurate or obsolete information, without leaving the impression that the information is current. For example, archiving press releases, as discussed below, might provide a useful history of the company's accomplishments.

Instead of, or in addition to, an archiving system, issuers may choose to delete stale information after a set period of time. The current practice employed by many companies' Web sites of dating information as of the date it is posted is particularly useful when monitoring stale information. A company could presume all information stale after a period of time and then automatically delete it. Most issuers would find this impractical, given the effort necessary to construct an attractive and useful site. Another approach would be to review unrevised pages regularly (monthly, for example) for stale information that should be deleted. In either event, it would be prudent to note on the Web site's disclaimer that although the company regularly purges the site for stale information, readers should assume that information is current only as of the day it is posted to the site.

Incorrect information that is not clearly identified as archived (with an appropriate disclaimer) should be deleted promptly upon discovery. Again, a disclaimer confirming that information is reliable only as of the date it is posted will be useful in arguing that those accessing the Web site had no right to rely on any incorrect information inadvertently posted on the site. But a company should not knowingly allow unarchived, incorrect information to remain posted. One method for minimizing that possibility would be to require persons who post information to the Web site to be responsible for reviewing that information for accuracy periodically (weekly, for example) and whenever potential inaccuracies come to their attention.

6. Archive or Delete Stale Press Releases.

Some issuers view their Web pages as opportunities to circulate, in one location, all information available about a company. It is tempting to focus this opportunity only upon positive information about the company, but doing so is fraught with risk, particularly if the Web site is deemed incorporated by reference into a company's securities filings. Thus, either posting all press releases, with those over a day or two old segregated in an Archives section, or strictly following a practice of deleting press releases a day or two after they are released, should avoid the argument that a company was selectively posting only positive releases. Under these constraints, of course, some companies may prefer not to post press releases at all.

In any event, a special disclaimer would be useful. The disclaimer should state:

- that the information in these press releases should not be deemed accurate or current except as of the date the release was posted;

- that the company has no intention of updating, and specifically disclaims any duty to update, the information in the press releases; and

- that, to the extent the information is forward-looking, it is intended to fit within the safe harbor for forward-looking information, and is subject to material risk factors.

7. Keep Analysts at Arms' Length on the Web.

Companies with Web sites find them very useful for distributing to shareholders and potential shareholders information that otherwise would be made available by the company's investor relations office. However, those reviewing these postings to determine whether they should be included on the Web page should not be lulled by the thought that the information would otherwise be made available. For example, should a company use its Web page to direct visitors to analysts who cover the company? This question illustrates the tensions that can arise in this arena.

In a telephone call, a corporate officer may find it appropriate, for example, to provide the name of only one analyst to a potential shareholder seeking information about the company. She might even decide to fax the analyst's most recent report about the company to the potential shareholder. Most likely, she would be enthusiastic about doing this only if the report were favorable. While a regulator might second-guess that choice later, possibly accusing the officer of pointing the potential investor only to positive information, proving such an accusation and tying it to a violation of the federal securities laws would be problematic.

Contrast that with a hypothetical set forth by the SEC in a recent release:

> Company XYZ places a preliminary prospectus on its Internet Web site and provides direct access via a hyperlink to a research report on the Company written by ABC Corporation, a registered brokerage firm. The investor reviewing the preliminary prospectus can click on a box marked "ABC's research report" and the investor will be linked to the brokerage firm's Web site where the research report is available.[7]

The SEC Staff's response to this hypothetical stresses the potential pitfalls of including analyst reports on a Web site:

---

7 Interpretive Release, 60 SEC Docket (CCH) 1100 at example 16.

> The hyperlink function provides the ability to access information located on another Web site almost instantaneously. This direct and quick access to ABC's research report would be similar to the Company including the paper version of the research report in the same envelope that it is using to mail the paper version of the preliminary prospectus to potential investors. During the waiting period, the Company may make offers only through the use of a preliminary prospectus, whether in paper or electronic format; therefore, its use of the research report under these circumstances would not be permissible.[8]

To guard against this result, companies would be wise to avoid quoting, citing or hyperlinking to any analyst's statements about the company.

But what about merely notifying Web page visitors of the analysts who cover the company's securities? Even this practice can be problematic. One commentator flatly advises against including analysts' names in Web sites at all, citing no potential economic benefit and significant litigation risk.[9] At best, if a company lists the analysts that cover the securities, the list should be complete, in alphabetical order (as opposed to listing first the most prominent, friendly analyst), and with no quotes, cites or hot links to the analysts' Web pages. The list also should be accompanied by a disclaimer clarifying that the company in no way endorses or incorporates by reference any statements by the analysts.

8. Guard the Home Site and Surf for Attacks on Other Sites.

In August 1996, the United States Justice Department temporarily closed down its Web site because a hacker had infiltrated the system, creating a mock Justice Department site including "[a]ntigovernment diatribes, a swastika, a nude photo and other graffiti."[10] Sites for the CIA, the United States Air Force, NCAA and the Social Security Administration have fallen victim to hackers as well.[11] An NCAA spokesman was quoted as saying, "It's like somebody breaking into your house and painting graffiti all over it."[12]

---

8 *Id.*

9 Statement by Joseph Grundfest at *The Emerging Law of Securities in the Electronic Age*, San Francisco, California (Feb. 10, 1997).

10 Steve Ulfelder, *Arm the Firewall, Here Comes a 14-Year Old Boy*, COMPUTERWORLD, Jan. 6, 1997, at 97 (analogizing the Web to a frog pond as a magnet for mischief).

11 *Id.; Social Security Reveals Internet Insecurity*, INTERNET ALERT, Apr. 16, 1997; David Hayes, *"I Screwed Up," Teen Hacker Says,* KANSAS CITY STAR, Mar. 12, 1997, at A1.

12 David Hayes, *"I Screwed Up," Teen Hacker Says*, KANSAS CITY STAR, Mar. 12, 1997, at A1 (statement of Wally Renfro, who oversees the NCAA Web site).

Another hackers' practice, "Web spoofing," also threatens companies with W
Spoofers create a "shadow copy" of the original site and channel user access through their
computers. By this means, the hacker can pose as the company and can monitor, alter, capture o
redirect all information to and from a particular user. Certain short-term security provisions, such as authentication software, can reveal the presence of such an attacker.

These frightening stories suggest at least two lessons for issuers with Web sites. First, all available technology should be used to secure the issuer's Web site from hackers.[13] Second, an employee or team of employees should monitor the company's Web site daily, to make sure it still says what the company intends.

A related lesson involves monitoring Web sites that are not the issuer's. Just as companies often have clipping services or public relations experts assigned to monitor press references to the company and its key personnel, so should companies assign someone to "surf" the Web for such references. Issuers can become the subject of discussion in newsgroups, or so-called chat rooms, or can be improperly classified in lists or reports presented on-line. While companies may decide not to correct misstatements made by others, they will not be able to decide whether to make such corrections if they are not aware of their occurrence.

9. Sensitize Web Participants.

With increasing frequency, company employees or members of their families post personal or family home pages that are intended to be separate from their work. For example, news reports last December highlighted families who posted personal Web pages rather than sending holiday cards. Employees and their families also may post messages in news rooms or on bulletin boards.

In most cases, such sites and postings would be of no relevance to the company, and restricting them would be impractical, difficult if not impossible to enforce and possibly counterproductive. But in some cases, employees might reveal personal predilections or corporate activities that would be of interest to persons hostile to the company. For example, if a manager posted, on his personal Web page, statements or pictures that could be interpreted as hostile to members of another gender, race or religion, those statements or pictures could surface later in a litigation alleging that the manager discriminated against members of those groups.

Personal Web pages and other Web postings are part of the public domain, and therefore may be reviewed by the company just as a news article profiling an employee might be reviewed. Nevertheless, a company may want to minimize the potential for conflict with employees by notifying them that such a review might occur. In any event, workers should be cautioned that statements they make on the Web can be just as discoverable in litigation or in a governmental investigation as company press releases are. Circulating notices of corporate officials whose

---

13 *See generally* Kelly J. Higgins, *Under Attack – What Hackers Know Will Harm You*, COMMUNICATIONS WEEK, Mar. 10, 1997 at 47 (citing concerns expressed by Princeton University research report on Web spoofing, available at <www.cs.princeton.edu>).

ed embarrassing upon disclosure would sensitize employees to the arise in this context.

he Evils of E-Mail.

executive of a high-tech issuer apparently sent an electronic memo, or "e-mail message," to ... company's employees. The message was leaked outside the company, and was posted to an on-line service with 10,000 subscribers. This forced the issuer to terminate a planned initial public offering, because the posting occurred during the pre-offering "quiet period" imposed by SEC rules.[14]

Thus, corporate lawyers join the ranks of defense lawyers who, for years, have had nightmares over the contents of e-mail messages of their clients. People tend to say things on e-mail that they would say aloud only in private, whispered conversations — if they would say them aloud at all. Although some lawyers might prefer that employee use of e-mail be limited to situations that ordinarily would be reduced to writing anyway, companies that have incorporated e-mail into their working culture would not be able to function without free and frequent correspondence among employees via e-mail.

Employers with Web sites should consider the following steps to minimize the likelihood that employee e-mails will come back to haunt the company:

- engage in e-mail sensitivity training, cautioning employees to write nothing on an e-mail message that they would not want to see on the front page of local and national newspapers, and circulating news articles citing embarrassing examples of private messages gone public;

- warn employees that the government, in investigations, and private parties, in litigation, routinely subpoena e-mail messages, which are not easily deleted from the company's system, and which will be used against the employee and/or the company;

- require privileged and confidential messages to be marked as such on the message so that later, if the message is subpoenaed, it is more likely that the claim will be identified and supported;

- install a mechanism designed to delete all archived messages after they have been stored for a sufficient period of time to be helpful for business use (e.g., 90 days), but recognize that, once a memo has been sent, it is very difficult to ensure that all copies have been deleted;

---

14 *See* Deborah Lohse, *Wired Kills IPO Amid Mishap With E-Mail*, THE WALL ST. J., Oct. 25, 1996, at C-1.

- caution employees that the e-mail addresses assigned to them by the company are for business use only, to minimize arguments that messages should be protected by a privacy claim;

- create a company forum for solicitations and notices, organized by one department in the company, and require that all such messages be posted in this forum, to minimize e-mail "noise" and to allow company review before notices and solicitations are posted;

- adopt a policy regarding e-mail, warning that e-mail messages are company property, that employees have no privacy protections on the company's e-mail system, and that employees should expect that the company will save, monitor and/or seize messages at any time;

- include in the policy a warning that e-mail must not be used to transmit ethnic jokes or to make statements that foster a hostile environment for any race, religion or gender;

- post the policy periodically as a greeting screen when employees log onto the company's e-mail system, and require employees to confirm that they understand the policy before they are allowed to log on; and

- discipline employees who abuse the e-mail system, with notices to all employees who witnessed the abuse (for example, for an inappropriate joke circulated within a division of the company, an employee should be reprimanded in accordance with normal company practices, but in addition, notice of the reprimand should be circulated to all recipients of the prior message, along with the relevant company policy statement).

Conclusion

The Web is full of spiders, some potentially poisonous to public companies. The SEC's Division of Enforcement has developed a Cyberforce of enforcement attorneys who surf the Web for several hours each week looking for potential securities law violations. While they currently appear to be preoccupied with blatant frauds such as pyramid schemes and unregistered offerings of securities, issuers should prepare for the day that these enforcers examine issuer Web sites for possible disclosure violations. State securities enforcers also are policing the Web with frequency. And plaintiffs' lawyers and disgruntled company enemies are sure to examine the company's Web site for support for their complaints.

In a few years, more regulatory guidance and lessons learned through litigation will provide more guidance. But for now, issuers are forging ahead in this new environment, taking risks every day that the spiders will attack. Following these rules of thumb can help minimize the likelihood of a poisonous encounter on the Web.

Washington D.C.

Harvey L. Pitt
Dixie L. Johnson

NOTES

3

CURRENT ISSUES AND RULEMAKING PROJECTS: DIVISION OF CORPORATION FINANCE, SECURITIES AND EXCHANGE COMMISSION

Brian J. Lane

Mr. Lane is the Director, Division of Corporate Finance, Securities and Exchange Commission.
The Commission, as a matter of policy, disclaims responsibility for any private publication or statement by any of its employees. The views expressed herein do not necessarily reflect the views of the Commission or its staff.

February 9, 1998

CURRENT ISSUES AND RULEMAKING PROJECTS

DIVISION OF CORPORATION FINANCE

Securities and Exchange Commission
Washington, D.C. 20549

* As a matter of policy, the Securities and Exchange Commission disclaims responsibility for any private publication or statement of any of its employees. The views expressed do not necessarily represent the views of the Commission or its staff.

TABLE OF CONTENTS

February 9, 1998

CURRENT ISSUES AND RULEMAKING PROJECTS
DIVISION OF CORPORATION FINANCE

I. DIVISION ORGANIZATION

With the appointment in March 1996 of Brian J. Lane as Director of the Division, a program was commenced to streamline the Division's operations by reducing the number of support offices and directing this staff to the primary work of the Division -- the review and processing of disclosure documents filed by public companies.

The Division's organizational structure follows:

Division Director - Brian Lane (202) 942-2929

Operations

Associate Director (Disclosure Operations)
- Martin P. Dunn (202) 942-2890

Associate Director (Small Business)
- Albert Dandridge (202) 942-2880

Disclosure Support

Senior Associate Director (Legal)
- William Morley (202) 942-2820

Associate Director (Regulatory and EDGAR Policy, Mergers & Acquisitions)
- Mauri Osheroff (202) 942-2840

Associate Director (International)
- David Sirignano (202) 942-2870

Associate Director (Chief Accountant)
- Robert Bayless (202) 942-2850

Chief Economist
- Jennifer Bethel (202) 942-2800

Assistant Directors

Health Care and Insurance
- Shelley Parratt (202) 942-1840

Consumer Products
- H. Christopher Owings (202) 942-1900

Communications and Computers
- James Daly (202) 942-1800

Natural Resources
- Roger Schwall (202) 942-1870

Transportation and Leisure
- William L. Tolbert, Jr. (202) 942-1850

Manufacturing and Construction
- Steven Duvall (202) 942-1950

Banking and Leasing
- Peggy Fisher (202) 942-1760

Structured Financing and Real Estate
- Paula Dubberly (202) 942-1960

Small Business
- Richard Wulff (202) 942-2950

Other Offices

Office of Chief Counsel
- Catherine Dixon, Chief (202) 942-2900

Office of Mergers and Acquisitions
- Dennis O. Garris, Chief (202) 942-2920

Office of International Corporate Finance
- Paul Dudek, Chief (202) 942-2990

Office of Information and Analysis
- Herbert Scholl, Chief (202) 942-2930

Office of EDGAR Policy
- Ruben Gechter, Acting Chief (202) 942-2940

II. REEXAMINATION OF THE REGULATION OF OFFERINGS

A. Report of the Advisory Committee on the Capital Formation and Regulatory Processes

On July 24, 1996, the Advisory Committee on the Capital Formation and Regulatory Processes (the "Advisory Committee") presented its report to the Commission recommending the adoption of a "company registration" system. The Advisory Committee recommended that the Commission take the steps necessary to shift the focus of the regulatory process for public offerings of securities by these companies from a transactional registration system to a company registration system, beginning with a pilot system. The basic features of a company registration system as the Advisory Committee envisioned it are as follows:

1. Scope

The Advisory Committee suggested that participation in a company registration pilot be voluntary and be limited to issuers with a $75 million public float, two years of reporting history, and a class of securities listed on a national securities exchange or traded on the National Market System of the Nasdaq Stock Market.

Under the type of pilot recommended by the Advisory Committee, participating companies could elect to continue to conduct offerings not registered under the Securities Act. Under a "full" company registration system envisioned for the future by the Advisory Committee, all issuances by a participating company or its affiliates, other than straight debt securities (if an issuer so chooses), would be registered under the Securities Act.

2. The Offering Process

Under the system the Advisory Committee envisioned, an eligible company would file a core registration statement, and would continue to file Exchange Act reports which would be incorporated into the core registration statement. (A nominal fee would be paid when the company is registered. A full registration fee would be paid at the time of sale.)

At the time of each offering, the issuer would file with the Commission material information relating to the specific offering, as well any material updates to the company-related information contained in Exchange Act reports. In non-convertible debt and de minimis equity offerings, a Form 8-K or a prospectus supplement would be used. In an equity offering over a de minimis threshold, a Form 8-K would be filed no later than the date of the first sale. If a Form 8-K would contain material undisclosed company-related disclosure, it would be required to be filed some period of time before the sale to provide an adequate opportunity for the market to absorb the information. In all offerings of voting equity amounting to 40% or more of the existing public float, the Advisory Committee suggested that the Commission be able to review the prospectus prior to its use.

3. Prospectus Delivery

In all offerings of voting equity that amount to 20% or more of existing public float, the Advisory Committee suggested requiring traditional final prospectus delivery prior to sale, except for sales to accredited investors. In all other offerings, the Advisory Committee suggested requiring that the issuer either continue traditional final prospectus delivery or incorporate by reference such filed information into a delivered document such as the confirmation of sale or selling materials.

4. Disclosure Enhancements

The Advisory Committee recommended that the Commission mandate the following for any company opting into a company registration system.

- Certification to the Commission by senior executive officers that they have reviewed the periodic reports and are not aware of any misleading disclosures or omissions.

- A report by management to the audit committee describing procedures followed to ensure the integrity of periodic reports and procedures instituted to avoid potential insider trading abuses (filed as an exhibit to the Form 10-K).

- Disclosure on Form 8-K of:

    - Material modifications to security holders' rights;
    - Resignation or removal of top executive officers;
    - Defaults of senior securities;
    - Sales of a significant percentage of stock; and
    - Auditor advice that reliance on audit report in previous filings is no longer permissible.

    (The Advisory Committee recommended that the Form 8-K filing due date be accelerated to 5 business days for those events where it currently is 15 calendar days.)

- Disclosure of risk factors in the Form 10-K.

5. Disclosure Committee

To expand the role of the outside directors in ensuring the integrity of corporate disclosure, the Advisory Committee recommended that the Commission encourage creation of a separate board committee of one or more outside directors to review the issuer's disclosure.

6. Due Diligence

The Advisory Committee recommended that the Commission provide interpretive guidance to underwriters and directors as to more effective methods of satisfying the "reasonable investigation" and "reasonable care" standards, respectively, of Sections 11 and 12(a)(2) of the Securities Act.

B. Securities Act Concept Release

The Commission currently is engaged in a broad reexamination of the regulatory framework for the offer and sale of securities under the Securities Act of 1933. As part of that effort, the Commission issued a concept release (Securities Act Release No. 7314 (July 25, 1996)) soliciting comment on the best means of improving the regulation of the capital formation process while maintaining or enhancing investor protection. The concept release noted that the continuing challenge for the Commission is in adapting the statutory disclosure framework to developments in the capital markets while ensuring that investors receive full and fair disclosure in a manner and at a time that allows informed decision-making.

The concept release solicited comment regarding conceptual issues that are integral to the regulatory framework for offerings. Among them were:

- whether investors in registered offerings are receiving prospectus information (including prospectus supplements) in sufficient time to enable them to make informed investment decisions;

- the extent to which constructive delivery, rather than physical delivery, of certain prospectus information provides adequate protection for investors;

- whether greater flexibility to inform investors by means of written materials other than the traditional prospectus, such as profile or simplified prospectuses or selling materials, should be permitted during the offering process;

- whether investors in the secondary markets are receiving information about registered offerings, particularly offerings from a shelf registration statement, on a timely basis;

- whether independent gatekeepers (such as underwriters, independent accountants and others) that share responsibility for the quality of disclosure are able to function effectively in that role, particularly in light of issuers' desire to have quick access to capital;

- whether improvement of ongoing periodic disclosure of companies reporting under the Exchange Act (upon which investors in primary offerings and secondary markets rely) is needed; and

- whether Commission staff review practices with respect to filings should be changed.

In the concept release, the Commission sought comment on the best methods for eliminating unnecessary obstacles to capital formation while improving the quality and timing of disclosure. Comment was requested on a number of different approaches that had been the subject of public discourse, including: a "company registration" approach (such as the Advisory Committee recommended); modifications to the existing shelf registration system; an approach that would involve deregulation of offers; and reforms that would change the treatment of unregistered securities. The Commission also asked for others' ideas about possible approaches to regulatory reform.

The comment period on the concept release ended October 31, 1996. The Commission has received 54 comment letters, which reflect a variety of views on the subject matter.

III. TASK FORCE ON DISCLOSURE SIMPLIFICATION

In August 1995, Chairman Arthur Levitt created a staff Task Force on Disclosure Simplification to review rules and forms relating to capital raising transactions, periodic reporting pursuant to the Exchange Act, proxy solicitations, and tender offers and beneficial ownership reporting under the Williams Act. The goal was to streamline and simplify the disclosure process and to make regulation of securities transactions more effective and efficient where consistent with investor protection. On March 5, 1996, the Commission published the Report of the Task Force on Disclosure Simplification (the "Task Force Report"). Some of the more significant recommendations include:

- Elimination and streamlining of rules and forms that have become outdated or duplicative, or impose unnecessary burdens.

- Using a plain English format for the opening pages of disclosure documents, such as prospectuses and tender offer documents, so that investors can understand them more easily.

- Reducing the costs of securities offerings by increasing the flexibility of both smaller and seasoned companies to raise capital.

- Creating an integrated regulation for mergers, tender offers and other extraordinary transactions.

- Various recommendations for adapting Securities Act requirements to current market conditions, including providing companies with greater flexibility in switching between the public and private markets.

At the time it authorized publication of the Task Force's Report, the Commission initiated implementation of certain Task Force recommendations by proposing for public comment the elimination of 45 rules and four forms that were viewed as redundant or otherwise no longer necessary. A number of minor and technical amendments also were proposed (Securities Act Release No. 7271 (March 5, 1996)). Most of these changes were adopted as proposed on May 31, 1996 (Securities Act Release No. 7300).

At the same time that the Commission adopted the first round of proposals, the Commission published proposals to implement additional recommendations made by the Task Force to eliminate unnecessary requirements and streamline the disclosure process. See Securities Act Release No. 7301 (May 31, 1996). The Commission adopted most of these proposals on July 18, 1997 (Securities Act Release No. 7431). The following summarizes the principal form and rule changes that were adopted:

- Elimination of Form SR, the use of proceeds report for initial public offerings, and the inclusion of the information currently required by Form SR in Exchange Act periodic reports;

- Elimination of Form 8-B, which pertains to the registration of the securities of successor issuers, and the amendment of Exchange Act Rule 12g-3 to cover situations formerly covered by Form 8-B;

- Amendment to Form 8-A, the short-form Exchange Act registration statement, to provide automatic effectiveness for <u>all</u> securities that are registered on that Form, and to eliminate certain exhibit requirements,

- Exemption of American Depositary Receipts that are listed on a national securities exchange and registered on Form F-6 under the Securities Act from the registration requirements of Section 12(b) of the Exchange Act, although the Section 12(b) registration requirements would still apply to the underlying class of securities;

- Amendment of Rule 401(c) under the Securities Act to permit an issuer to switch to a shorter Securities Act form at the time <u>any</u> amendment is filed if the issuer has become eligible to use the shorter form;

- Elimination of the special filing requirements for radio and television broadcast prospectuses, so that such prospectuses will be filed according to the same requirements applicable to all other prospectuses; and

- Automatic effectiveness upon filing of post-effective amendments to Securities Act registration statements filed solely to add exhibits.

A number of other Task Force recommendations have been implemented, at either the proposing or adopting stage, and are reflected in this Outline. Still others are being considered and may be implemented as part of the Commission's rulemaking agenda in the future.

IV. PLAIN ENGLISH INITIATIVE

A. Final Rules

One of the Task Force on Disclosure Simplification's major concerns was the lack of readability of prospectuses and other disclosure documents. They noted that issuers, underwriters and their lawyers draft defensively written documents that place a premium on legal jargon and over-inclusive disclosures. The Task Force recommended requiring plain English disclosure to improve the readability of the prospectus.

To implement the Task Force recommendations, the SEC issued proposed rules for public comment (Securities Act Release No. 7380 (January 14, 1997)). On January 22, 1998, the Commission adopted the final plain English rules (Securities Act Release No. 7497). These rules apply to public companies and mutual funds.

1. Phase-In Period for Public Companies

To ease the transition to plain English and to avoid delaying public companies' access to the capital markets, we will phase in the plain English rules as follows:

- If you first file a registration statement on or after October 1, 1998, you must comply with the new requirements. If you file a registration statement before October 1, 1998, but it is not yet effective on that date, you do not have to amend it to comply with the new requirements before it is effective.
- On or after October 1, 1998, any supplement you file to a prospectus in an effective registration statement that relies on Rule 415(a)(1)(x) must comply with the new requirements.
- If you file a post-effective amendment on or after October 1, 1998, either to include the company's latest audited financial statements in the registration statement or to update the prospectus under Section 10(a)(3), you must comply with the new requirements.

2. Phase-In Period for Mutual Funds

Mutual funds must comply with the plain English rules for new registration statements filed on or after October 1, 1998. When we act on the proposed changes to the mutual fund disclosure requirements, we may change the compliance date for mutual funds so they may comply with these new requirements with one filing.

3. New Rule 421(d) - The Plain English Rule

This rule requires public companies and mutual funds to prepare the front portion of their prospectuses in plain English. They must use plain English principles in the organization, language, and design of the front and back cover pages, the summary, and the risk factors section. Also, when writing these portions of the prospectus, they must comply substantially with six basic principles:

- Short sentences;
- Definite, concrete, everyday language;
- Active voice;
- Tabular presentation or bullet list for complex material, whenever possible;
- No legal jargon or highly technical business terms; and
- No multiple negatives.

In addition, public companies and mutual funds must design the cover page, summary, and risk factors section to make them easy to read. They must format the text and design the document to highlight important information for investors. The rule also permits them to use pictures, charts, graphics, and other design features throughout the prospectus to make it easier to read.

4. Amended Rule 421(b) - The Clear, Concise, and Understandable Rule

Rule 421(b) currently requires that the *entire* prospectus be clear, concise, and understandable. To provide guidance on this rule, we adopted amendments that set out four general writing techniques that public companies and mutual funds must use throughout their prospectuses:

- Present information in clear, concise sections, paragraphs, and sentences. Whenever possible, use short explanatory sentences and bullet lists;
- Use descriptive headings and subheadings;
- Avoid frequent reliance on glossaries or defined terms as the primary means of explaining information in the prospectus. Define terms in a glossary or other section of the document only if the meaning is unclear from the context. Use a glossary only if it facilitates understanding of the disclosure; and
- Avoid legal and highly technical business terminology.

We also added a new note to Rule 421(b) that lists writing conventions to avoid because they make prospectuses harder to read:

- Legalistic or overly complex presentations that make the substance of the disclosure difficult to understand;
- Vague boilerplate explanations that are readily subject to differing interpretations;

- Complex information copied directly from legal documents without any clear and concise explanation of the provision(s); and

- Repetitive disclosure that increases the size of the document but does not enhance the quality of the information.

5. Amendments to Regulation S-K and Regulation S-B

To implement the changes we made to Rule 421, we also adopted amendments to Regulations S-K and S-B.

B. Pilot Program

Until the final rules go into effect on October 1, 1998, the Division of Corporation Finance will continue its pilot program for those public companies that want to voluntarily write plain English disclosure documents. Although the plain English rules apply only to documents filed under the Securities Act, the staff will work with volunteers on the techniques for preparing plain English documents filed under either the Securities Act or the Exchange Act.

In these "hands on" drafting sessions, companies that volunteer can draft plain English documents and submit them to the staff for their suggestions and comments in a nonpublic forum. However, the staff will no longer expedite the review of volunteers' filings. If you want to participate or would like to know more about the program, contact Carolyn Miller, Attorney Adviser, at (202) 942-2890.

C. Plain English Handbook

When we released the proposed plain English rules in January, 1997, the Office of Investor Education and Assistance simultaneously released a draft of A Plain English Handbook: How to Create Clear SEC Disclosure Documents. Based on suggestions received from the public, the staff revised the handbook and will be publishing it in final form within the next several weeks. To request a copy, call (800) SEC-0330. It will also be available on our Internet site but, because the web version will not contain all of the handbook's graphic elements, we suggest you order a hard copy. The draft version of the handbook is currently available on our Internet site (http://www.sec.gov).

V. ELECTRONIC FILING AND TECHNOLOGY

A. EDGAR

The Commission's Electronic Data Gathering, Analysis, and Retrieval ("EDGAR") system has been operational since 1992, with mandated electronic filing by those subject to the Division's review beginning in April 1993. See Securities Act Release Nos. 6977 (February 23, 1993) and 7122 (December 19, 1994). The following events are of current interest:

1. Rule Changes

a. The Commission has adopted a new electronic filing rule (Rule 14 of Regulation S-T) to make it clear that it will no longer accept filings made in paper that should have been filed electronically. See Release No. 33-7472 (October 24, 1997). The rule is effective January 1, 1998. After that date, if a filer submits a paper document required to be filed electronically, and does not follow the appropriate procedures for a temporary or continuing hardship exemption outlined in Rules 201 and 202 of Regulation S-T, the filing will not be accepted or processed. If the filing desk receives a document by courier it will be given back to the courier, and if received through the mail or other delivery service, it will be returned by mail.

b. On July 1, 1997, the Commission adopted a number of minor and technical amendments to its rules governing electronic filing, including the elimination of the transition rules used during the EDGAR phase-in period. See Release No. 33-7427 (July 1, 1997). The release codifies several staff interpretations and adds new rules and clarifies others to outline issuers' electronic filing obligations. For example, the release adds new Rule 100 for domestic issuers and third party filers and Rule 600 for foreign private issuers and foreign governments. These new rules outline who is subject to the electronic filing requirements; these provisions formerly were in the EDGAR transition rules. The Commission also eliminated the requirement to send the staff a copy of the performance graph required in connection with proxy statements. The tabular presentation of the graph in the electronic filing is all that now needs to be sent to the Commission. The rules became effective August 7, 1997.

2. Rule Amendments -- Regional Office Filings

On December 16, 1996, the Commission issued a release amending Forms SB-1, SB-2 and Regulation A to require registrants to file these materials at the Commission's Headquarters in Washington, D.C. rather than in the Commission's Regional Offices as of January 21, 1997. See Securities Act Release No. 7373 (December 16, 1996) and Section VI for further discussion. Regulation S-T also was revised to reflect the elimination of filing with the Regional Offices. As a result, all Forms SB-1 and SB-2, including those relating to initial public offerings, are required to be filed via EDGAR. Regulation A filings will continue to be filed in paper.

3. EDGAR RFP released

On October 30, 1996, the Commission released a Request for Proposals (RFP) soliciting offers for the construction and operation of a new, modernized, privatized EDGAR electronic filing system. This RFP was the first phase of a two-phase approach. The Commission issued an amended RFP (Phase Two) on October 10, 1997. An award is expected in early 1998.

4. Phase-in completed

Registrants were brought onto the EDGAR system in a series of discrete groups over a three-year period. Phase-in for all domestic registrants was completed on May 6, 1996. As a result, all filings made by domestic issuers (including registration statements for initial public offerings) must be submitted electronically except in cases of hardship or where the rules otherwise provide for paper filing. Persons or entities making filings jointly with domestic issuers or with respect to such issuers, such as those filing beneficial ownership reports under the Williams Act, must file electronically as well. Foreign private issuers generally are not required to file registration statements or periodic reports electronically, but may do so voluntarily.

5. **Forms 3, 4, 5 and 144**

As of December 18, 1995, Forms 3, 4 and 5, for reporting securities transactions of corporate insiders under Section 16 of the Exchange Act, and Form 144, the notice of proposed sale of securities pursuant to Securities Act Rule 144, may be filed electronically via EDGAR on a voluntary basis. See Securities Act Release No. 7241 (November 13, 1995). Forms 144 may be filed electronically only if the issuer of the securities is a public company. These forms previously could not be filed on the EDGAR system.

6. **Internet web site**

On September 28, 1995, the Commission initiated the agency's World Wide Web site on the Internet. See News Release No. 95-195. One of the most important features of the Web site is its ability to make EDGAR available to the public through the Commission's home page on a 24-hour delayed basis. The Commission's Web site is located at *http://www.sec.gov*.

B. **Electronic Delivery of Information**

The Commission has issued interpretive releases and rules addressing the use of electronic media to deliver or transmit information under the federal securities laws. These initiatives reflect the Commission's continuing recognition of the benefits that electronic technology provides to the financial markets. These releases are premised on the belief that the use of electronic media should be at least an equal alternative to the use of paper delivery.

The first interpretive release (Securities Act Release No. 7233 (October 6, 1995)) provides guidance to issuers who use electronic media in complying with the applicable delivery requirements of the federal securities laws. Information distributed through electronic means may be viewed as satisfying the delivery requirements of the federal securities laws if it results in the delivery to the intended recipients of substantially equivalent information as they would have had if the information were delivered in paper form. The interpretive release advises issuers to consider the following:

- Has timely and adequate notice been provided to the investor that the information is available?
- Does the investor have access to the information? Specifically:
    - is it practically accessible?
    - is it available on-line for as long as a delivery requirement applies?
    - does the investor have the opportunity to retain the information or have ongoing access equivalent to personal retention?
    - is it available in paper upon request?
- Does the selected distribution method provide reasonable assurance that it will result in delivery? Examples for consideration by persons with delivery obligations include:

- an investor has given an informed consent to receive the information through a particular electronic medium and been provided appropriate notice and access;

- there is evidence that the investor actually received the information (e.g., electronic mail return receipt or confirmation of downloading);

- the information is provided by facsimile to an investor who has provided a fax machine number;

- the investor has accessed an electronic document with hypertext linking to a document required to be delivered; or

- an investor returns an order form available only through an electronically delivered document.

The release also contains numerous examples applying these concepts to specific fact situations.

On May 9, 1996, the Commission issued a second interpretive release primarily addressing issues associated with the electronic delivery of information by broker-dealers, transfer agents, and investment advisers under certain Exchange Act and Advisers Act rules (Securities Act Release No. 7288). This release also contains a section following up the 1995 release with additional examples.

On May 9, 1996, the Commission also adopted a number of technical amendments to its rules and forms intended to codify some interpretations set out in the interpretive release (Securities Act Release No. 7289). Most changes relate to rules that require distribution of information by mail, or rules that require presentation of information in a specified type size or font, or in red ink or bold-face type. For example, if a rule requires presentation of a legend using a specified type size and font, the rule now provides that if an electronic medium is used, the legend must be presented using any means reasonably calculated to draw attention to it.

Guidance in this area also is provided by interpretive letters addressing particular issues regarding electronic dissemination. See Sections XII.A and XII.C. In addition, the staff has issued two letters addressing the identification of an issuer's web site in a prospectus: ITT Corporation (December 6, 1996) and Baltimore Gas and Electric Company (January 6, 1997).

In October 1997, the Commission submitted to Congress a report addressing the use of electronic media in the context of the federal securities laws. This report, The Impact of Recent Technological Advances on the Securities Markets, is available on the Commission's web site.

C. No-Action Requests by Internet E-Mail

The Division has established an Internet e-mail address to receive requests for interpretive or no-action letters. Persons seeking such letters from the Division may submit their requests either in paper or electronically at *cfletters@sec.gov*. At this time, electronic requests must be in standard e-mail text or ASCII format so the staff can easily read and print the letters. The letters will be processed by the staff in the same manner as requests submitted in paper. The requests should comply with all of the procedures set forth in Release No. 33-6269 (December 5, 1980), except that multiple copies are not needed. The letter should include the telephone number of the requestor. If there is confidential information in the requests, remember that it may be possible for others to intercept and read e-mail.

This electronic mailbox is only for interpretive and no-action requests from the Division, not for other correspondence. In addition to the interpretive and no-action letter process, the Division responds to many interpretive questions over the telephone. Persons with these questions should continue to call the Division's Office of Chief Counsel at (202) 942-2900.

VI. SMALL BUSINESS ISSUES

A. Recent Small Business Initiatives

The Commission has undertaken several recent initiatives to assist small businesses, including the following:

- A special Corporation Finance headquarters unit specializes in small company filings and the needs of small businesses, including crafting rules to lessen the burden of Commission's regulation on these issuers. The telephone number for the unit is (202) 942-2950.

- Effective January 21, 1997, small business issuers are required to file their Forms SB-1, SB-2, and Regulation A materials at the Commission's Headquarters rather than in the Commission's Regional Offices. See Securities Act Release No. 7373 (December 16, 1996). The Commission's forms and rules, including Regulation S-T, also were revised to reflect the elimination of filing with these offices. See Section V for a discussion of the requirement that registrants file these forms via EDGAR.

- The Web site of the Commission (http://www.sec.gov) has been enhanced to provide information specifically designed for small business and access to such Commission publications as "Q & A: Small Business and the SEC."

- Since 1996, a number of town hall meetings between the Commission and small businesses have been conducted throughout the United States. These town hall meetings convey basic information to small businesses about fundamental requirements that must be addressed when they wish to raise capital through the public sale of securities. In addition, the Commission hopes to learn more about the concerns and problems facing small businesses in raising capital so that programs can be designed to meet their needs, consistent with the protection of investors. The most recent town hall meeting was held in Austin, Texas, on January 30, 1998, and drew over 200 persons.

- The 16th annual Government-Business Forum on Small Business Capital Formation was held in San Francisco on September 18-19, 1997. This platform for small business is the only governmentally-sponsored national gathering for small business, which offers annually the opportunity for small businesses to let government officials know how the laws, rules and regulations are affecting their ability to raise capital. Questions regarding the 1998 annual Forum, which will be held in Chicago, may be directed to Barbara Jacobs at the telephone number noted above.

B. 1997 Rulemaking

On February 20, 1997, the Commission issued a release (Securities Act Release No. 7393) proposing an amendment to Securities Act Rule 430A to permit certain smaller companies, including small business issuers, to delay pricing of securities offerings after registration in order to provide them flexibility in the marketplace. By being able to go to market more quickly, these companies could take advantage of favorable market conditions to meet their capital needs. This increased flexibility should result in smaller issuers raising more capital through the public markets rather than through exempt offerings conducted in the domestic and offshore markets.

The proposed "delayed pricing" procedure would permit a company to have its registration statement declared effective without the name of the managing underwriter or specified price-related information, such as the price and certain terms of the securities to be offered. This information would be furnished when the company decided to price the securities. The current, more limited procedure afforded by Rule 430A also would continue to be available.

Significant conditions to the use of the proposed delayed pricing procedure include the following:

- The company would have to have been subject to the reporting provisions of the Exchange Act during the most recent 12 months, have filed all required reports, and have satisfied specified electronic filing requirements.
- The company would have to be a U.S. company, or a foreign private issuer filing the same Exchange Act reports as domestic issuers.
- The company would have to deliver a preliminary prospectus to investors 48 hours prior to sale.
- The company could not be a blank check company or a company that issues penny stock.
- The company would be required to file a post-effective amendment with a new prospectus each year to provide updated audited financial statements. Post-effective amendments also would be required under other circumstances, such as for significant acquisitions.
- Whenever a prospectus was delivered, it would be accompanied by the latest quarterly report on Form 10-Q and any current reports on Form 8-K except for those filed voluntarily. Alternatively, the company could choose to put the quarterly and 8-K information in a supplement to the prospectus.

These safeguards are designed to assure that investors have adequate and current disclosure available to them to be able to make informed investment decisions at the time the securities are offered and sold. The release solicits comment on whether additional or alternative conditions are appropriate. The comment period ended on April 29, 1997.

VII. INTERNATIONALIZATION OF THE SECURITIES MARKETS

A. Foreign Issuers in the U.S. Market

Foreign companies raising funds from the public or having their securities traded on a national exchange or the Nasdaq Stock Market are generally subject to the registration requirements of the Securities Act and the registration and reporting requirements of the Exchange Act. The Commission has provided a separate integrated disclosure system for foreign private issuers that provides a number of accommodations to foreign practices and policies. These accommodations include:

- interim reporting on the basis of home country and stock exchange practice rather than quarterly reports;
- exemption from the proxy rules and the insider reporting and short swing profit recovery provisions of Section 16;
- aggregate executive compensation disclosure rather than individual disclosure, if so permitted in an issuer's home country;
- acceptance of three International Accounting Standards relating to cash flow statements (IAS # 7), business combinations (IAS # 22) and operations in hyperinflationary economies (IAS # 21);
- offering document financial statements updated principally on a semi-annual, rather than a quarterly basis; and
- an exemption from Exchange Act registration under Section 12(g) for foreign private issuers that have not engaged in a U.S. public offering or whose securities are not traded on a national exchange or the Nasdaq Stock Market.

Additionally, the Commission staff has implemented procedures to review foreign issuers' disclosure documents on an expedited basis and in draft form, if requested by the issuer. This helps to facilitate cross-border offerings and listings in light of potentially conflicting home-country schedules and disclosure requirements.

Over the last five years, the number of foreign companies accessing the U.S. public markets has increased dramatically. As of February 1, 1998, there were over 1000 foreign companies from 55 countries filing periodic reports with the Commission.

B. Abusive Practices under Regulation S and Proposed Amendments

The Commission adopted Regulation S in 1990 to clarify how the Securities Act registration requirements apply to offshore transactions. Since the adoption of Regulation S, a number of abusive practices have developed involving unregistered sales of equity securities by U.S. reporting companies purportedly in reliance upon Regulation S. These transactions result in indirect distributions of those securities into the United States without the investor protection provided by registration.

These transactions are effected in circumstances that indicate that securities are in essence being placed offshore temporarily to evade registration requirements, with the result that the incidence of ownership of the securities never leaves the U.S. market, or that a substantial portion of the economic risk is left in or is returned to the U.S. market during the restricted period, or that there was no reasonable expectation that the securities could be viewed as coming to rest abroad.

In June 1995, the Commission issued an interpretive release that described certain abusive practices under Regulation S and requested comment on whether the regulation should be revised to limit its vulnerability to abuse, Securities Act Release No. 7190 (June 27, 1995). Because these practices continued, in February 1997, the Commission published for comment a proposal to amend Regulation S, Securities Act Release No. 7392 (February 20, 1997).

The proposed amendments are designed to eliminate these abusive practices, while preserving the benefits of Regulation S for capital formation. The amendments also would level the playing field for U.S. investors by subjecting resales of unregistered offshore Regulation S offerings of equity securities by U.S. companies to the same requirements as unregistered onshore private placements.

These proposals would:

- Treat equity securities of covered issuers placed offshore pursuant to Regulation S as "restricted securities" within the meaning of Rule 144 (with the result that unregistered public resales into the United States generally could not be made for at least one year);

- Align the Regulation S restricted period during which persons relying on the Regulation S safe harbor may not sell these equity securities to U.S. persons (unless pursuant to registration or an exemption) with the Rule 144 holding periods by lengthening the restricted period from 40 days to two years;

- Impose certification, legending and other requirements currently only applicable to sales of equity securities by non-reporting issuers;

- Require purchasers of these securities to agree not to engage in hedging transactions with regard to such securities unless such transactions are in compliance with the Securities Act;

- Prohibit the use of promissory notes as payment for these securities;

- Make clear that offshore resales of any equity securities of covered issuers that are "restricted securities" under Rule 144 will not "wash off" the restrictions; and

- Revise the recently adopted Form 8-K reporting requirement for unregistered sales of securities issued in reliance on Regulation S to permit such sales to be reported on a quarterly basis, as is now permitted for unregistered sales of equity securities made other than in reliance on Regulations S.

The proposed changes to Regulation S would affect offshore offerings of common stock and other types of equity securities (including convertible securities) by U.S. publicly traded companies. The proposed changes also would apply to offerings by foreign companies where the principal market (more than 50% of worldwide trading) for their equity securities is in the United States. The comment period regarding the proposals ended on April 29, 1997.

C. <u>International Accounting Standards</u>

The Commission has been working with the International Accounting Standards Committee (IASC) through the International Organization of Securities Commissions (IOSCO) since 1987 in an effort to develop a set of accounting standards for cross-border offerings and listings. The IASC is an independent, private sector body that was formed in 1973 by the professional accounting bodies in the U.S. and eight other industrialized countries to improve and harmonize accounting standards.

In July 1995, IOSCO and the IASC joined in an announcement that the IASC had developed a four-year work program focusing on a core set of standards previously identified by IOSCO as being the necessary components of a reasonably complete set of accounting standards. The announcement noted that completion of comprehensive core standards that are acceptable to the IOSCO Technical Committee would allow the Technical Committee to recommend endorsement of the standards for cross-border capital raising and listing purposes in all global markets.

In April 1996, the IASC announced that, in response to strong demand from international companies and with significant encouragement from the members of IOSCO, it had accelerated its work program in order to complete work on the core standards by March 1998. The Commission responded with a press release expressing support for the IASC's objective. The Commission's statement noted that the standards should include a core set of accounting pronouncements that constitute a comprehensive, generally accepted basis of accounting; that the standards be of high quality, <u>i.e.</u>, they must result in comparability and transparency, and they must provide for full disclosure; and that the standards must be rigorously interpreted and applied.

D. <u>International Disclosure Standards</u>

For a number years the Commission has been working with other members of IOSCO to develop a set of international standards for non-financial statement disclosures that could be used in cross border offerings and listings. The international disclosure standards are intended to facilitate cross border capital raising and listing by letting companies comply with one set of non-financial disclosure requirements for offerings in several jurisdictions. The disclosure project grew out of an IOSCO Technical Committee report on International Equity Offers published in 1989. One of the report's recommendations encouraged regulators to facilitate the use of single disclosure documents in order to enhance the efficiency of the capital raising process. The first stage of the project was a report on the disclosure requirements then in effect in the major capital markets, titled "Comparative Analysis of Disclosure Regimes," which was published by the Technical Committee in 1991.

The next stage of the project involved the development of a set of international disclosure standards that reflect a consensus among securities regulators in the major capital markets as to the types of disclosures that should be required for cross border offerings and listings. A draft of the international disclosure standards has been circulated to the regulators involved in this project, and they are reviewing the standards and, in some cases, consulting with representatives of outside groups involved in the capital raising process.

The draft standards currently would apply only to offerings and listings of common equity securities and only to listings and transactions for cash; they would not cover the additional disclosures that may be required by the host country in tender and exchange offers, business combinations or going private and other affiliated transactions. These issues, as well as disclosure requirements for companies in specific industries such as banking or insurance and disclosure requirements for annual reports, may be covered in future stages of the project. After completion of the standards and IOSCO action on them, Commission rulemaking would be undertaken relating to this project.

E. Safe Harbors for Offshore Press Activities

In some foreign countries, it is common practice for companies to conduct press conferences, issue press releases, and meet with members of the press when offering securities or conducting a tender offer. U.S. journalists, and journalists for foreign publications with a significant U.S. circulation, have had difficulty obtaining direct access to these offshore press activities due to uncertainty whether allowing such access would violate the U.S. federal securities laws.

On October 10, 1997, the Commission adopted two new safe harbors under the Securities Act and the Williams Act that should eliminate perceived grounds for the exclusion of any journalist from access to offshore press activities. The safe harbors are intended to reflect existing offering practices in certain foreign countries, and level the playing field between U.S. and foreign journalists with respect to accessing these press activities. Securities Act Release No. 7470.

Securities Act Safe Harbor

Under Rule 135e under the Securities Act, a foreign private issuer or foreign government issuer, selling security holder, or their representatives would not be deemed to have: (i) made an offer for the purposes of Section 5; (ii) engaged in a general solicitation under Regulation D; or (iii) engaged in "directed selling efforts" under Regulation S, by allowing journalists access to offshore press activities that discuss a present or proposed offering of securities, provided the following conditions are met:

- First, at least part of the offering must be conducted outside the United States, i.e., the offering cannot be conducted solely in the United States. Issuers cannot claim the protections of the safe harbor for offshore press activities if there is no apparent reason for conducting these press activities offshore.

- Second, the access must be provided to both foreign and U.S. journalists, i.e., whatever is made available to U.S. journalists also must be made available to foreign journalists. In this way, issuers and other offering participants cannot use offshore press activities to channel publicity regarding the offering solely into the United States.

- Third, in certain offerings where there is likely to be a significant interest in the offering by U.S. investors (i.e., any offering by a foreign issuer where part of the offering will be conducted in the United States), any written materials released to journalists under the safe harbor must contain a cautionary legend and not attach any form of purchase order or coupon that could be returned to express interest in the offering. These additional procedural safeguards are intended to alert U.S. investors that these materials are not to be considered an offer of securities for sale in the United States, and that when and if an offer is made in the United States, the appropriate required disclosure will be made at that time.

Tender Offer Safe Harbor

The Commission also adopted a tender offer safe harbor to make it clear that a foreign or domestic bidder for the securities of a foreign private issuer, as well as the foreign target company itself, their representatives, and any other person who may have a filing obligation under the Williams Act, would not be deemed to have triggered the filing and procedural requirements of the Williams Act by allowing journalists access to offshore press activities that discuss the tender offer. The safe harbor for tender offers is subject to the conditions that:

- First, the target must be a foreign private issuer. The safe harbor is not available for any tender offers for the securities of domestic companies because there appears to be no need in that case to accommodate foreign offering practices.

- Second, just as with the Securities Act safe harbor, access to the offshore press activity must be provided to both U.S. and foreign journalists.

- Third, in tender offers for the equity securities of a foreign issuer that are registered under the Exchange Act, any written materials must contain a cautionary legend and not attach any means to tender securities, or coupons that could be returned to indicate interest in the tender offer. These additional procedural safeguards only apply where the written materials discuss a tender offer for equity securities registered under Section 12 of the Exchange Act because that is the only type of tender offer where a mandated disclosure document is required to be filed under the U.S. federal securities laws.

VIII. OTHER PENDING RULEMAKING AND RECENT RULE ADOPTIONS

A. Adoption of Amendments to Beneficial Ownership Reporting Under Exchange Act Section 13(d)

On January 12, 1998, the Commission adopted amendments to its beneficial ownership disclosure rules under Section 13(d) of the Exchange Act of 1934 to reduce the reporting obligations of certain investors. See Exchange Act Release No. 39538 (January 12, 1998). The rules had been published for comment in Exchange Act Release No. 37403 (July 3, 1996). The new provisions include the following:

- Unless they were qualified institutional investors, most investors previously were required to file a long-form Schedule 13D disclosing detailed information about the "investor and the purpose and background of the acquisitions. The revised rules now allow passive investors (those that do not have the purpose or effect of changing or influencing control of the issuer) to report their greater than 5% ownership on the short-form Schedule 13G if they do not own 20% or more of the outstanding securities.
    - The initial schedule must be filed within 10 days.
    - The schedule must be amended annually to reflect any changes in the information.
    - The schedule must be amended promptly if ownership increases by more than 10% and thereafter promptly upon increasing or decreasing by more than 5%.
    - If the reporting person no longer has a passive investment purpose or increases his or her ownership to 20% or more, a Schedule 13D must be filed within ten days. Upon those events, the person may not vote the securities or acquire additional equity securities of the issuer until 10 days after the Schedule 13D is filed.
    - A reporting person may re-establish its Schedule 13G-eligibility and switch from Schedule 13D to Schedule 13G once it becomes a passive investor and its ownership decreases below 20%.
- The list of qualified institutional investors who are eligible to file on Schedule 13G, regardless of their percentage ownership, is expanded to include the following:
    - employee benefit plans maintained primarily for the benefit of state or local government employees;
    - savings associations;
    - church employee benefit plans;

- control persons of qualified institutional investors who have a passive investment purpose and do not own directly, or indirectly through an ineligible entity, more than 1% of the issuer's stock;

- investment advisers prohibited from registering under the Investment Advisers Act of 1940 pursuant to Section 203A of that Act.

- Copies of Schedule 13G are no longer required to be sent to the exchanges on which the securities trade.

- Under interpretive guidance provided by the Commission in adopting the amendments, the Commission clarified that beneficial ownership by a subsidiary or other business unit may not have to be attributed to the subsidiary's parent entity if the voting and investment powers over the subsidiary's shares are exercised independently from the parent. This determination is based on the facts and circumstances.

  - One circumstance in which beneficial ownership may not be required to be attributed to the parent is when these entities have in place certain informational barriers that ensure that the voting and investment powers are exercised independently.

  - If informational barriers are relied upon, written policies and procedures should be used, annual independent assessments of the informational barriers should be made, and the entities should not share common officers, directors or employees that are involved in the exercise of the voting and investment powers.

- The Commission also provided guidance regarding the impact of soliciting activities by a shareholder with respect to shareholder proposals on the use of Schedule 13G by that shareholder. Soliciting activity that does not have the purpose or effect of changing or influencing control does not prevent the use of Schedule 13G. That determination is based on the facts and circumstances. The release highlights five relevant factors to consider in assessing the purpose and effect of the proposal and related soliciting activity.

B. Shareholder Proposals

On September 18, 1997, the Commission issued a release (Exchange Act Release No. 39093) proposing amendments to Rule 14a-8, the shareholder proposal rule, and related amendments to Rules 14a-4, 14a-5, 14a-2 and 13d-5. The proposals represent a package of reforms to address a range of concerns raised by both shareholder and corporate participants in the proposal process. If adopted, the proposals are expected to make it easier for shareholders to include a broader range of proposals in companies' proxy materials. They are also expected to provide companies with clearer ground rules and more flexibility to exclude proposals that failed to attract significant shareholder support in prior years.

There are seven principal proposals:

- Rewrite the shareholder proposal rule so that it is more understandable to individual shareholders. As proposed, the rule would be in a Question & Answer format.

- Reverse the Cracker Barrel position on employment-related shareholder proposals that raise significant social policy matters. Those types of proposals would no longer be automatically excludable from companies' proxy materials under the "ordinary business" exclusion;

- Introduce a new route onto a company's proxy materials for a shareholder able to muster support from the holders of 3% of a company's shares to put the proposal to a vote. That is, 3% of the company's share ownership could override two bases for omitting proposals, Rules 14a-8(c)(5) and (c)(7);

- Modify the "relevance" exclusion under Rule 14a-8(c)(5) to include a more objective test for excluding proposals that are economically insignificant to a company's business;

- Amend the exclusion under Rule 14a-8(c)(12) make it more difficult for shareholders to repeat proposals that failed to receive certain levels of support from fellow shareholders in previous years. This would involve raising the resubmission thresholds in the rule;

- Amend Rule 14a-4(c) to establish a clearer, more predictable, framework for management's ability to exercise discretionary voting authority when a shareholder notifies the company that it intends to present a proposal without invoking Rule 14a-8's mechanisms; and

- Modify the Commission staff's administration of Rule 14a-8(c)(4), the "personal grievance" exclusion, so that the staff would henceforth express "no view" on the excludability of a proposal under that rule if the proposal (including any supporting statement) is neutral on its face.

Finally, the Commission authorized the issuance of a report on shareholder proposals as required by Section 510(b) of the National Securities Markets Improvement Act.

C. **<u>Revision of Rule 144 Holding Period and Rule 144 Rule Proposals</u>**

Securities Act Rule 144 provides a safe harbor for the resale of securities by persons who hold either "restricted" securities, or securities of a company of which they are affiliates. The rule permits persons who hold such securities to publicly sell them without registration and without being deemed underwriters, if certain conditions are satisfied.

The Commission issued a release (Securities Act Release No. 7390 (February 20, 1997)) adopting amendments to the holding period requirements contained in Rule 144(d) and (k) to permit limited resales of restricted securities after a one-year holding period, and unlimited resales by non-affiliates after a two-year holding period. Parallel changes were made to the resale provisions of Securities Act Rule 145. The revised holding periods apply to all securities, whether acquired before or after the effective date. The amendments became effective on April 29, 1997.

On the same date, the Commission issued a companion release (Securities Act Release No. 7391 (February 20, 1997)) proposing changes to make Rule 144 easier to understand and apply. The proposals would reorganize and rewrite the text of the rule in a more succinct and straightforward fashion, provide a bright-line exclusion from the Rule 144 definition of affiliate, eliminate the manner of sale requirements, increase the threshold requirements for filing Form 144 to reflect inflation since their initial adoption, and amend Securities Act Rule 145 to eliminate the resale limitations that are based on a "presumptive underwriter" approach.

The proposing release also solicits comment on the need to further revise the Rule 144 holding periods, revise the volume limitation standard by eliminating the two trading volume tests, and address the application of the Securities Act to hedging activities. The comment period for the proposals ended on April 29, 1997.

D. <u>Expansion of Short-Form Registration to Include Companies with Non-Voting Common Equity</u>

On May 8, 1997, the Commission issued a release (Securities Act Release No. 7419) adopting amendments to Forms S-3 and F-3 under the Securities Act to include non-voting as well as voting common equity in the computation of the required $75 million aggregate market value of common equity held by non-affiliates of the registrant. The Commission also adopted conforming amendments so that the aggregate market value of non-voting as well as voting common equity would be included in the calculation of the amount of the required public float for issuers to qualify to use Form F-2 and to be small business issuers and in stating the amount of the public float on Forms 10-K and 10-KSB.

E. <u>Auditor Reporting Requirements under Exchange Act Section 10A</u>

The Commission adopted rule amendments (Exchange Act Release No. 38387) to implement the reporting requirements in Section 10A of the Exchange Act, which was added by Title III to the Private Securities Litigation Reform Act of 1995. Section 10A codifies certain professional auditing standards and imposes expanded obligations on auditors to report in a timely manner certain uncorrected illegal acts to a registrant's board of directors. It further requires the registrant, or the auditor if the registrant fails to do so, to provide information regarding the illegal act to the Commission.

Under the final rules, which went into effect on April 17, 1997, the Office of the Chief Accountant is designated as the office to receive Section 10A reports. The reports can be provided by submission of a facsimile, telegraph or personal delivery or any other means assuring receipt within the statutory time period. The report is required to be in writing, and is required to identify the registrant and the auditor, state the date the auditor made its report to the board, and provide a summary of the report. The summary should describe the act and the potential impact of that act on the registrant's financial statements. The registrant is permitted to provide additional information regarding its view of, and response to, the Section 10A report it has received from the auditor.

The final rule provides that the reports of both the board and the auditor are non-public and exempt from disclosure under the Freedom of Information Act to the same extent as the Commission's investigative records. However, disclosures to the public should continue to be made in modified audit reports or, when the auditor has resigned, been dismissed, or elected not to stand for re-election, on Form 8-K.

Rule 1-02(d) of Regulation S-X was also amended to conform the definition of "audit (or examination)" with Section 10A, by noting that audits of the financial statements of Commission registrants should be performed in accordance with generally accepted auditing standards as may be modified or supplemented by the Commission.

F. <u>Derivatives and Market Risk Disclosure</u>

On January 28, 1997, the Commission adopted amendments to Regulation S-K, Regulation S-X, and various forms (Securities Act Release No. 7386) to clarify and expand existing requirements for disclosures about derivatives and market risks inherent in derivatives and other financial instruments. Derivative financial instruments are defined in FASB Statement No. 119 to include futures, forwards, swaps, and options. Derivative commodity instruments are defined in the Release to be commodity contracts that are permitted by contract or business custom to be settled in cash or with another financial instrument (e.g., commodity futures, commodity forwards, commodity swaps, and commodity options). Other financial instruments are defined in FASB Statement No. 107 to include, for example, investments, including structured notes, loan receivables, debt obligations, and deposit liabilities.

In general, the release:

- requires enhanced descriptions of accounting policies for derivatives in the footnotes to the financial statements;
- requires quantitative and qualitative disclosures about market risk inherent in derivatives and other financial instruments outside the financial statements; and
- provides a reminder to registrants to supplement existing disclosures about financial instruments, commodity positions, firm commitments, and other anticipated transactions with related disclosures about derivatives.

Disclosure of accounting policies

The release amends Rule 4-08 of Regulation S-X and requires enhanced disclosure in the footnotes to the financial statements of accounting policies for derivatives, including a description of (i) each method used to account for derivatives; (ii) the criteria to be met for the accounting method used, and (iii) other disclosures that will assist investors in understanding how derivatives impact the financial statements.

Quantitative disclosures about market risk

To allow investors to assess the magnitude of market risk, the release adds a new item (Item 305(a)) to Regulation S-K that requires registrants to provide quantitative disclosures about market risk. In essence, the release requires disclosure of information that is encouraged, but not required, by FASB Statement No. 119.

The release requires quantitative disclosure outside the financial statements for market risk of market risk sensitive instruments. Registrants have the flexibility to choose from of the following three disclosure alternatives of presenting quantitative information:

(i) *Tabular Presentation* of fair value information and contract terms relevant to determining future cash flows, categorized by expected maturity dates;

(ii) *Sensitivity Analysis* expressing the potential loss in future earnings, fair values, or cash flows of market risk sensitive instruments due to hypothetical changes in interest rates and other relevant market rates or prices; or

(iii) *Value at Risk* disclosures expressing the potential loss in future earnings, fair values, or cash flows from market movements with a selected likelihood of occurrence.

Registrants also are required to disclose (i) the modeling technique and key assumptions used to measure market risk; (ii) limitations that may cause the information not to reflect fully the overall market risk of the entity, including a description of leverage, option, or prepayment features that may enhance market risk; and (iii) the reasons for material changes in the amount of reported market risk when compared to information reported in the previous year.

Qualitative disclosures about market risk

Qualitative disclosures about market risk help place the registrant's market risk management activities in context and, therefore, are useful in understanding the quantitative disclosures about market risk. The release (through the addition of Item 305(b) to Regulation S-K) requires registrants to disclose material information about (i) their primary market risk exposures; (ii) how those exposures are managed (e.g., description of objectives, strategies, and instruments, if any, used); and (iii) actual or expected material changes in their primary market risk exposures and actual or expected material changes in how those risks are managed.

Additional disclosures

The release also reminds registrants of their current obligation to disclose all material information necessary to prevent required disclosures from being misleading (e.g., Rules 12b-20 and 408). This reminder is included to ensure that registrants provide disclosures about derivatives that affect directly or indirectly reported financial items when such disclosure is material and will prevent the disclosures about the reported item from being misleading. For example, when information about interest rates and repricing characteristics of debt obligations is required to be disclosed in the footnotes to the financial statements, registrants also should include, when material, disclosure of the effects of derivatives. Similarly, summary information and disclosures in Management's Discussion and Analysis about the cost of debt obligations also should include, when material, disclosure of the effects of derivatives.

Safe Harbor

The safe harbors for forward looking statements provided in Section 27A of the Securities Act and Section 21E of the Exchange Act apply to market risk information outside the financial statements. The Commission deems all information required by paragraphs (a), (b)(1)(i), (b)(1)(iii) and (c) of Items 305 and 9A to be "forward looking statements" for purposes of the safe harbor rules, except for historical facts such as the contract terms and number of market risk sensitive instruments held during or at the end of the reporting period. To the extent that information provided pursuant to paragraph (b)(1)(ii) of Items 305 and 9A includes forward looking statements, those statements would be eligible for safe harbor protection.

"Meaningful cautionary statements" necessary under the safe harbor rules will be satisfied with respect to the Item 305(a) and 9A(a) disclosures if a registrant satisfies the requirements of those items. Registrants desiring to qualify for the "meaningful cautionary statements" prong of the safe harbor for the remainder of the new items will need to consider what information should be given to alert investors to important factors that could cause actual results to differ materially from the information given in the forward looking statements.

Dates Effective

The effective dates for the quantitative and qualitative disclosures about market risk are phased in over the next few years. For banks, thrifts, and registrants with market capitalization in excess of $2.5 billion, the rules become effective for filings that include audited financial statements for fiscal years ending after June 15, 1997 (e.g., large commercial companies with December 31 year-ends will need to provide the required information for the year ended December 31, 1997). For other registrants the rules become effective one year later. Accounting policy disclosures should be included in reports with the Commission that include financial statements for periods ended after June 15, 1997.

The requirements for quantitative and qualitative information about market risk apply to all registrants except registered investment companies and small business issuers.

Q & A

On July 31, 1997, the staff released Questions and Answers about the New "Market Risk" Disclosure Rules. The interpretive answers were prepared by the staffs of the Office of the Chief Accountant and the Division of Corporation Finance. This publication is posted at the Commission's internet site: http://www.sec.gov.

G. Definition of "prepared by or on behalf of the issuer" for purposes of determining whether an offering document is subject to state regulation

The National Securities Markets Improvements Act of 1996 revised Section 18 of the Securities Act. The revised section reallocates regulatory responsibility relating to securities offerings between the federal and state governments based on the nature of the security or offering. Among other things, the revised statute prohibits states from directly or indirectly prohibiting, limiting or imposing any conditions on the use of any offering document for a covered security if the offering document is "prepared by or on behalf of the issuer."

Pursuant to a statutory mandate, the Commission adopted a definition of the term "prepared by or on behalf of the issuer," on April 30, 1997 (Release No. 33-7418). The definition has been added as Rule 146 under the Securities Act. It provides that if an issuer or an agent or representative authorizes an offering document's production and approves the document before its use, it is "prepared by or on behalf of the issuer" and is therefore not subject to state regulation.

H. Amendments to forms and schedules to remove voluntary provision of Social Security numbers

On June 25, 1997, the Commission issued a release adopting revisions to Form 144, Schedule 13D, Schedule 13G, Schedule 14D-1, Form 3, Form 4, Form 5, Form MSD, Form TA-1 and Form T-2 to eliminate the portion of those forms and schedules that requests filers who are natural persons to furnish their Social Security numbers. The Commission has taken this action in response to increasing concern about the improper use of Social Security numbers for access to otherwise non-public information. The changes became effective on July 1, 1997. The Commission's printing unit has prepared new versions of most of these forms. The current forms will continue to be valid, but filers using those forms are requested not to include their Social Security numbers.

IX. STAFF LEGAL BULLETINS

The Division of Corporation Finance has begun issuing Staff Legal Bulletins to provide advice to the public on frequently recurring issues. Copies of the bulletins may be obtained from the Commission's Web site (http://www.sec.gov) or by writing to, or making a request in person at, the Public Reference Room, Securities and Exchange Commission, 450 5th Street, N.W., Room 1024, Washington, DC, 20549 ((202) 942-8090).

A. Staff Legal Bulletin No. 1 (CF) - Confidential Treatment Requests

On February 28, 1997, the Division announced the publication of Staff Legal Bulletin No. 1. Staff Legal Bulletin No. 1 sets forth views of the Division of Corporation Finance regarding the requirements a registrant must satisfy when requesting confidential treatment pursuant to Rule 406 under the Securities Act of 1933 or Rule 24b-2 under the Securities Exchange Act of 1934.

In recent years, the number of confidential treatment requests (CTRs) processed by the Division has increased steadily from approximately 540 in fiscal year 1992 to more than 1,000 in fiscal year 1996. CTRs as initially filed often lack the information and analysis necessary for the staff to evaluate compliance with the requirements of the rules. The purpose of the bulletin is to help issuers prepare complete CTRs and so reduce the time and costs incurred by issuers and the Division in processing confidential treatment applications. The bulletin provides guidance on the substantive and procedural requirements contained in Rules 406 and 24b-2. The bulletin also suggests procedures that, while not required, facilitate the staff's processing of CTRs.

B. Staff Legal Bulletin No. 2 (CF) - Modified Exchange Act Reporting for Companies in Bankruptcy

On April 15, 1997, the Division announced the publication of Staff Legal Bulletin No. 2. Staff Legal Bulletin No. 2 sets forth the factors that the Division of Corporation Finance considers when acting on "no-action" requests for modified Exchange Act reporting for companies in bankruptcy. The bulletin provides guidance as to the information regarding the following issues that must be provided in order for the staff to evaluate a request, and the substantive standards on which the evaluation will be made:

- Disclosure of the issuer's financial condition;
- The trading market for the issuer's securities; and
- The timing of the issuer's request for modified reporting.

The bulletin also provides guidance as to:

- The reports required while bankruptcy proceedings are pending;
- The reports required upon emergence from bankruptcy;
- The effect of modified reporting on satisfaction of Rule 144 and Regulation S, and eligibility for short-form registration under the Securities Act; and
- The availability of Rule 12h-3.

C. Staff Legal Bulletin No. 3 (CF) - Reliance on the Section 3(a)(10) exemption from the Securities Act of 1933 registration requirements

The Division announced the publication of CF Staff Legal Bulletin No. 3 (CF) on July 25, 1997. The bulletin provides the Division's views regarding the Section 3(a)(10) exemption from the Securities Act of 1933 registration requirements. The Bulletin also expresses the Division's views regarding the Securities Act resale status of securities that are received in transactions exempt from registration pursuant to Section 3(a)(10).

Section 3(a)(10) of the Securities Act is an exemption from Securities Act registration for offers and sales of securities in specified business combinations. The exemption is available without any action by the Division. Issuers that are not sure whether the exemption is available for a specific contemplated transaction have sought the Division's views by requesting a "no-action" position from the Division. The bulletin discusses the issues that commonly arise in those "no-action" requests. The Division believes that, by making its views on these issues more widely known, it will enhance issuers' understanding of when the exemption is available. By making the Division's views more widely known, the bulletin should decrease those situations in which an issuer is uncertain whether the exemption is available for a contemplated transaction.

D. Staff Legal Bulletin No. 4 (CF) - Spin-Offs

The Division announced the publication of CF Staff Legal Bulletin No. 4 (CF) on September 16, 1997. The bulletin states the Division's views regarding whether Section 5 of the Securities Act of 1933 applies to spin-offs. The bulletin also addresses related matters, including how securities received in spin-offs may be resold under the Securities Act.

In a spin-off, a parent company distributes shares of a subsidiary to the parent company's shareholders. Even though companies do not have to request the Division's views on a proposed spin-off, many companies do. The bulletin discusses the issues that commonly arise in those requests.

The Division believes that, by making its views on these issues more widely known, the bulletin should decrease those situations in which companies seek the Division's views. The Division no longer will respond to requests for its views on issues it addresses in the bulletin. The Division will, however, respond when a company asks for the Division's views on novel or unusual issues in a proposed spin-off.

E. Staff Legal Bulletin No. 5 (CF/IM) - Year 2000 Disclosure Issues

On January 12, 1998, the Divisions of Corporation Finance and Investment Management announced the publication of revised Staff Legal Bulletin No. 5 (originally issued on October 8, 1997). Staff Legal Bulletin No. 5 sets forth views of the Divisions regarding companies' disclosure obligations relating to anticipated costs, problems, and uncertainties associated with the Year 2000 issue. Companies may be undertaking major research and development projects in order to address this problem. They also must coordinate with other entities with which they electronically interact. To the extent the problem is not successfully addressed, material adverse consequences could follow, depending on the extent of the problem, the nature of the industry and the computer software. Companies should review their disclosure obligations on an ongoing basis.

In particular, consideration should be given to whether either the costs of addressing the problem or the consequences of incomplete or untimely resolution of the problem represent a known material event or uncertainty that would affect future financial results, or cause reported financial information not to be necessarily indicative of future operating results or future financial condition. As such, appropriate disclosure should be made in "Management's Discussion and Analysis of Financial Condition and Results of Operations" (Item 303 of Regulation S-K and S-B) in the company's reports on Form 10-K (10-KSB) and 10-Q (10-QSB).

If a company determines that it should make Year 2000 disclosure, the applicable rules or regulations should be followed. If a company has not made an assessment of its Year 2000 issues or has not determined whether it has material Year 2000 issues, the staff believes that disclosure of this known uncertainty is required. In addition, the staff believes that the determination as to whether a company's Year 2000 issues should be disclosed should be based on whether the Year 2000 issues are material to a company's business, operations, or financial condition, without regard to related countervailing circumstances (such as Year 2000 remediation programs or contingency plans). If the Year 2000 issues are determined to be material, without regard to countervailing circumstances, the nature and potential impact of the Year 2000 issues as well as the countervailing circumstances should be disclosed. As part of this disclosure, the staff expects, at the least, the following topics will be addressed:

- the company's general plans to address the Year 2000 issues relating to its business, its operations (including operating systems) and, if material, its relationships with customers, suppliers, and other constituents; and its timetable for carrying out those plans; and

- the total dollar amount that the company estimates will be spent to remediate its Year 2000 issues, if such amount is expected to be material to the company's business, operations or financial condition, and any material impact these expenditures are expected to have on the company's results of operations, liquidity and capital resources.

The disclosure must be reasonably specific and meaningful, rather than standard boilerplate.

Companies also should consider other disclosure requirements, such as "Description of Business" (Item 101 of Regulation S-K and S-B) and rules requiring disclosure of any additional material information, beyond information specifically required to be disclosed, that is necessary to make the required statements not misleading (Securities Act Rule 408 and Exchange Act Rules 12b-20 and 14a-9). The Staff Legal Bulletin also addresses Form 8-K, accounting considerations, disclosure by foreign private issuers, and disclosure by investment companies and investment advisers.

X. CURRENT DISCLOSURE, LEGAL AND PROCESSING ISSUES

A. Disclosure Issues

1. Disclosure Issues Arising in Tender Offers for Limited Partnership Units

Several tender offers for limited partnership interests have commenced where the price offered is significantly below the amount originally paid for the units, prices paid for the interests in the secondary markets, and/or recent appraisals of the assets owned by the partnership. Some of these tender offers have been conducted by the general partner of the limited partnership, while others have been conducted by unaffiliated parties.

Since most of these transactions have been structured as cash offers for less than all of the outstanding limited partnership units, these transactions generally have not been subject to the roll-up or going private rules, both of which require enhanced disclosure regarding the fairness of the transaction and any conflicts of interests presented by the party making the transaction. However, many of the same concerns that led to the development of a specialized regulatory scheme for roll-ups of limited partnerships are raised by these transactions -- notably the conflict of interest presented by the participation of affiliated entities in purchasing the limited partnership interests and the inability of these investors to realize fair market value for their interests through a trading market, as opposed to accepting what is perceived as an "inadequate offer."

In preparing disclosure documents for these transactions, bidders are advised to remember that the 1991 release adopting the roll-up provisions specifically addresses transactions which, although by definition not roll-ups, raise similar concerns. The release states that the disclosure required by the roll-up rules must be considered from an antifraud perspective (Securities Act Release No. 6922 (October 30, 1991)). Bidders are also advised to provide balanced disclosure as required by Securities Act Release No. 6900 (June 17, 1991), including describing risks of the transaction in bullet form on the cover page, providing a detailed table of contents and writing the document in "plain English."

The staff is closely reviewing the disclosure in these transactions and expects that bidders, whether or not affiliated with the general partner, will provide investors with sufficient disclosure to consider adequately the conflicts presented by any affiliation between the bidder and the general partner and disparities between the value of their interests and the consideration offered, including whether any reports or appraisals that are materially related to the transaction have been prepared by a third party. Financial information relating to the partnership also should be provided, such as selected financial data required by Item 301 of Regulation S-K. If the target partnership is a real estate limited partnership, disclosure comparable to that required by Items 14 (description of real estate) and 15 (operating data) of Form S-11 should be provided. An unaffiliated bidder is required to disclose only information that is otherwise publicly available unless it has received non-public information from the target, in which case the non-public information also would need to be disclosed. Soliciting dealer fees or any other payments to brokers, dealers or agents for soliciting tenders should be prominently disclosed in the offering documents.

2. Third-Party Credit Enhancements

Third-party credit enhancements differ slightly from guarantees. A guarantee running directly to the security holder is a security within Section 2(1) of the Securities Act and must be covered by a Securities Act registration statement filed by the guarantor, as issuer. A third party credit enhancement is an agreement between a third party and the issuer or a trustee that does not run directly to the security holders. A party providing credit enhancement generally is not a co-issuer. However, if an investor's return is materially dependent upon the third party credit enhancement, the staff requires additional disclosure about the credit provider. The disclosure must provide sufficient information on the third party to permit an investor to determine the ability of the third party to fund the credit enhancement. In most cases, the disclosure of the third party's audited financial statements presented in accordance with generally accepted accounting principles would be required. However, if such financial statements are not available, statements prepared under statutory standards may be acceptable (e.g., statutory financial statements of insurance companies serving as credit enhancers).

The staff considers the following factors in assessing the sufficiency of the disclosure in this area: (1) the amount of the credit enhancement in relation to the issuer's income and cash flows; (2) the duration of the credit enhancement; (3) conditions precedent to the application of the credit enhancement; and (4) other factors that indicate a material relationship between the credit enhancer and the purchaser's anticipated return.

3. Third-Party Derivative Securities

In Morgan Stanley & Co., Inc. (June 24, 1996), the Division addressed disclosure issues relating to Securities Act Section 5 registered offerings of securities that are exchangeable, on either an optional or a mandatory basis ("Exchangeable Securities"), for the equity securities (or the cash value thereof) of another issuer ("Underlying Securities").

The Division took the view that complete disclosure regarding the issuer of the Underlying Securities is material to investors at the time of both the initial sale of the Exchangeable Securities and on a continuous basis thereafter until the Underlying Securities (or the cash value thereof) have been exchanged for the Exchangeable Securities and other payment obligations on the Exchangeable Securities, if any, have been satisfied. The Division also took the view that this complete disclosure is not required to be set forth in the filings of the issuer of the Exchangeable Securities where there is sufficient market interest and publicly available information regarding the issuer of the Underlying Securities.

The Division stated that sufficient market interest and publicly available information exists where the issuer of the Underlying Securities (i) has a class of equity securities registered under Exchange Act Section 12; and (ii) is either (a) eligible to use Securities Act Form S-3 or F-3 for a primary offering of non-investment grade securities pursuant to General Instruction B.1 of such forms; or (b) meets the listing criteria that an issuer of the

Underlying Securities would have to meet if the class of Exchangeable Securities was to be listed on a national securities exchange as equity linked securities, such as American Stock Exchange Rule 107.B.

The Division also stated that where there is sufficient market interest and publicly available information, as described above, the issuer of the Exchangeable Securities may include abbreviated disclosure about the issuer of and terms of the Underlying Securities in its Securities Act registration statement and Exchange Act periodic reports.

Finally, the Division stated that the abbreviated disclosure would include at least: (i) a brief discussion of the business of the issuer of the Underlying Securities; (ii) disclosure about the availability of information with respect to the issuer of the Underlying Securities similar to that required by Regulation S-K Item 502(a); and (iii) information concerning the market price of the Underlying Securities similar to that called for Regulation S-K Item 201(a).

EITF Issues Nos. 86-28 and 96-12 address certain aspects of the accounting for third-party derivative securities.

4. Management's Disclosure Obligation Regarding Non-Management Nominees for Election of Directors

In connection with the preparation of proxy material for an annual meeting, an issues has arisen that concerns the obligation of a company to disclose information about non-management nominees of a shareholder who has provided adequate notice pursuant to a company by-law regarding his or her intention to nominate certain persons as candidates for the election of directors. An interpretive issue arises as to whether Item 7 of Schedule 14A and Items 401 and 404 of Regulation S-K, whose requirements are incorporated into the schedule through Item 7, obligate the company to furnish line-item disclosure about those shareholder nominees. Similarly, an issue arises as to whether the company is required to place the shareholder nominees on its form of proxy.

Under these circumstances, the staff has taken the position that Note B to Schedule 14A obligates the company to provide line-item disclosure only with respect to proposals made by or on behalf of the company, including the election of the company's nominees for directors. In addition, a soliciting party is required under Exchange Act Rule 14a-4 to include on its proxy card only the names of nominees for which the soliciting party is seeking proxy authority. In rendering this advice, the staff did not address the issue of the disclosure otherwise necessary in the proxy statement, pursuant to the proxy antifraud provisions of Exchange Act Rule 14a-9, with respect to the existence of opposition candidates for election to the board.

5. Debt or Preferred Stock Convertible at Fixed Discount to the Market

The staff has addressed issues involving the issuance of convertible preferred stock and convertible debt securities with a nondetachable conversion feature that is "in the money" at the date of issue (a "beneficial conversion feature"). These securities may be convertible into common stock at the lower of a conversion rate fixed at the date of issue or a fixed discount to the common stock's market price at the date of conversion.

In one recent example, the number of common shares into which a $1,000 par preferred stock would convert was equivalent to the greater of 200 shares (based on the initially fixed $5 conversion rate) or the par amount divided by 75% of the stock fair value at the date of conversion. Shares into which the preferred stock would convert had full registration rights. If the stock price declines below $5, the shares issuable on conversion at 75% of the market price can be resold by the investor at market price to recover the original investment and an additional yield on that investment.

The staff believes that a beneficial conversion feature should be recognized and measured by allocating a portion of the proceeds equal to the intrinsic value of that feature to additional paid-in capital. This amount should be calculated at the date of issue as the difference between the conversion price and the fair value of the common stock into which the security is convertible, multiplied by the number of shares into which the security is convertible. If the security provides more than one method of determining the conversion rate, this computation should be made using the conversion terms that are most beneficial to the investor. If the registrant's common stock is traded in a public market, the staff believes that the quoted market price is the best measure of the common stock's fair value and that the quoted market price should not be adjusted to reflect transferability restrictions, large block factors, avoided underwriters' fees, or time value discounts, because of the difficulty in measuring those factors objectively.

For convertible preferred securities, the staff believes that any discount resulting from an allocation of proceeds to the beneficial conversion feature is analogous to a dividend and should be recognized as a return to the preferred shareholders over the minimum period in which the preferred shareholders can realize that return. The staff believes that issuers of these securities should apply the guidance in Staff Accounting Bulletin Topic 5-Q, "Increasing Rate Preferred Stock," and amortize the resulting discount using the effective interest method from the date of issuance through the date the security is first convertible.

For convertible debt securities, the staff believes that any discount resulting from an allocation of proceeds to the beneficial conversion feature increases the effective interest rate of the security and should be reflected as a charge to interest expense. Because the security has been issued with beneficial conversion terms, the staff has presumed that the stated maturity date of the instrument is not substantive and, therefore, the amortization period should be from the date the security is issued to the date it first becomes convertible. If the issuer reasonably determines that a period other than the period to the first conversion date is substantive, the discount should be amortized over that period. In that circumstance, if the security is converted prior to full amortization of the discount, the staff believes the unamortized portion of the discount should be charged to interest expense in the period of conversion.

The staff has objected to accounting that fails to account for a beneficial conversion feature as discussed here and has concluded that the affected financial statements should be restated in those circumstances.

For more information, refer to EITF Announcement No. D-60.

6. Disclosure of Non-GAAP Measures Such as Earnings Before Interest, Taxes, Depreciation and Amortization ("EBITDA")

Some registrants choose to present a non-GAAP financial measure such as EBITDA or FFO (funds from operations) in their disclosure documents. Although such measures can be useful in some circumstances, an unbalanced presentation can be confusing and lead to undue reliance on the measure by investors. Problems associated with presentations of non-GAAP measures were highlighted by the Commission in Accounting Series Release No. 142. Some comments cited frequently by the staff include the following:

1. A non-GAAP measure should be presented in a manner that does not give it greater authority or prominence than conventionally computed earnings or cash flows as reported in the GAAP financial statements. For example, the staff recommends that EBITDA and similar measures be located within an "other data" section in selected financial data. Discussions in MD&A of results as measured in the GAAP financial statements should be no less complete than discussions of performance or liquidity as depicted by non-GAAP measures.

2. Wherever the non-GAAP measure is used, a footnote or other reference to a complete explanation of its calculation and components should be provided. Since all companies and analysts do not calculate these non-GAAP measures in the same fashion, the staff recommends that the footnote or other disclosure alert investors to the fact that the measure presented may not be comparable to similarly titled measures reported by other companies.

3. Management should consider how any non-GAAP measure is expected to be used by investors, identify significant factors that should be considered, and discuss significant trends or requirements not captured by the measure to ensure balance and avoid undue reliance on the measure. Notwithstanding disclosures by competitors or requests from financial analysts, the staff believes that most non-GAAP measures generally should be avoided unless management itself believes that the measure provides relevant and useful information.

4. Non-GAAP measures that measure cash or "funds" generated by operations (liquidity) should be balanced with equally prominent disclosure of amounts from the statement of cash flows (cash flows from operations, investing and financing activities) and, in some cases, the ratio or deficiency of earnings to fixed charges. Explanation may be necessary to the extent that funds depicted by the measure are not available for management's discretionary use (due to legal or functional requirements to conserve funds for capital replacement and expansion, debt service and balloon

maturities, deferred interest and dividend payments, and other commitments and uncertainties). Presentations of cash flow per share should be avoided in all circumstances, unless substantially all cash flow is distributed to investors annually.

5. A frequent disclosure issue is the use of a non-GAAP measure in a discussion of operating performance when the measure is primarily a measure of liquidity, capital resources, or debt service capacity. For example, calculations that depict an adjusted or normalized measure of working capital or funds generated by operations and available to meet capital and debt requirements often are presented inappropriately as if they should be used as alternative measures of earnings, return on investment or similar performance or efficiency factors. In that case, the staff will request the measure's presentation in an appropriate context with clarification of its expected use.

6. If management is presenting the non-GAAP calculation as an alternative or pro forma measure of performance, the staff discourages adjustments to eliminate or smooth items characterized as nonrecurring, infrequent or unusual. Different unusual items are likely to occur every period, and companies and investors may differ as to what types of events warrant adjustment. Trends may be distorted and disclosure unbalanced if only certain items are adjusted while the effects of other infrequent events or transactions (whether favorable or unfavorable) are not considered or highlighted. Of course, all such special items should be highlighted in the registrant's disclosures to permit analysis by investors. Where management intends the measure to be indicative of liquidity and communicates that use through the context of its presentation, the staff ordinarily will not object to adjustment for non-cash charges relating to special items if it is meaningful to investors in the circumstances.

7. Investment Banking Firm Disclaimers

Boards of directors of companies soliciting shareholder voting and/or investment decisions in connection with mergers and other extraordinary transactions often retain investment banking firms as financial advisors, in many cases to render an opinion on the financial fairness of the transaction. In connection with its review of proxy statements, Securities Act registration statements and other Commission filings made in this context, the staff increasingly has observed the appearance of disclaimers by or on behalf of the financial advisor regarding shareholders' right to rely on a fairness opinion that the advisor has furnished to the registrant's board, a special committee of the board, and/or the registrant. Examples of such disclaimers include the following:

- "No one other than the Board of Directors [or the Special Committee and/or the Company] has the right to rely on this opinion;"

- "This opinion is provided solely/only to the Board of Directors [or the Special Committee and/or the Company];"
- "This opinion is solely/only for the benefit of the Board of Directors [or the Special Committee and/or Company];"
- "No one may rely on this opinion without the prior consent of the Financial Advisor;" and
- "This opinion is addressed [solely/only] to the Board of Directors [Special Committee and/or the Company] and is not intended to be relied upon by any shareholder."

During the review and comment process, the staff has objected to such statements as inconsistent with the balance of the registrant's disclosure addressing the fairness to shareholders of the proposed transaction from a financial perspective. Specifically, the staff has requested that any such direct or indirect disclaimer of responsibility to shareholders, whether made by or on behalf of the financial advisor, be deleted from any portion of the disclosure document in which it appears (including exhibits thereto). Alternatively, the registrant may add an explanation that clarifies:

(a) the basis for the advisor's belief that shareholders cannot rely on its opinion, including (but not limited to) whether the advisor intends to assert the substance of the disclaimer as a defense to shareholder claims that might be brought against it under applicable state law;

(b) whether the governing state law has addressed the availability of such a defense to the advisor in connection with any such shareholder claim; if not, a statement must be added that the issue necessarily would have to be resolved by a court of competent jurisdiction; and

(c) that the availability or non-availability of such a defense will have no effect on the rights and responsibilities of the board of directors under governing state law, or the rights and responsibilities of the board or the advisor under the federal securities laws.

8. <u>Securities Act Registration Issues Arising in Connection With Mergers and Other Extraordinary Transactions</u>

In some cases involving a negotiated "friendly" merger or other business combination between a registrant and another entity (or person) that has been submitted to a shareholder vote, a third party may wish to present a competing proposal that would involve acceptance of the third party's securities as consideration (<u>e.g.</u>, through an exchange offer or merger). Before commencing its own, competing transaction, however, the third party may wish to solicit in opposition to the "friendly" transaction then pending before the target company's shareholders. In such a case, the third party should remain mindful that, depending on the facts and circumstances, communications regarding its "competing" bid may be deemed an "offer to sell" the third party's securities that triggers the application of the registration requirements of the Securities Act, particularly where such communications refer to the price and/or other material terms of the potential competing transaction. Generally speaking, however, the third party's disclosure of the following information in connection with its solicitation in opposition to the pending "friendly" merger, without more, would not raise Section 5 concerns:

> (a) the name of the third party or other person or entity that might be issuing securities in the potential competing transaction, as well as the names of any other parties to such transaction; a brief description of the potential competing transaction; and any legend or similar statement required by State or federal law or administrative authority; or
>
> (b) a communication that is subject to and meets the requirements of Exchange Act Rule 14a-12.

See, e.g., Securities Act Rules 145(b), 135 and 134.

In cases where the third party's solicitations trigger compliance with the registration and prospectus delivery provisions of the Securities Act, the third party should file promptly its registration statement to cover the securities offering to target shareholders.

In view of the number of communications the third party may disseminate in opposition to the "friendly" transaction during the "waiting period," the staff will not object if the "core" proxy statement/prospectus is not redelivered with each additional communication so long as:

- Prior to dissemination of additional communications, the preliminary proxy statement/prospectus (without a proxy card containing a proposal on the third party's competing package) is sent or given to all target company shareholders eligible to vote at the shareholder's annual or special meeting at which shareholders will consider and vote on the "friendly" proposal.
- Each additional communication is filed as a pre-effective amendment to the registration statement. In lieu of filing a pre-effective amendment, a registrant eligible to use Form S-3 or F-3 may file the additional communications under cover of Form 8-K that is incorporated by reference into the proxy statement/prospectus which is part of the registration statement.
- Each additional communication used after delivery of the preliminary prospectus includes a statement to the effect that the third party has filed a registration statement, that the preliminary prospectus has been sent or given to all shareholders eligible to vote at the meeting at which the "friendly" transaction will be considered, and that the proxy statement/prospectus is incorporated by reference into the communication.

The staff's procedures outlined above are limited solely to the dissemination of additional communications and are not applicable to the dissemination of revisions to the "core" document.

Securities Act registration issues also may arise in connection with the announcement of a negotiated, stock-for-stock merger by one or both of the parties to the prospective transaction. Such announcements, which typically are accompanied or followed by various other market communications regarding the planned transaction, frequently are made by the parties' senior management, their respective investment bankers and/or other representatives prior to the filing of the requisite Securities Act registration statement. While issuers in these circumstances may have obligations under federal securities antifraud and stock exchange rules to make timely disclosure of the impending transaction, they should remain mindful that such pre-filing communications may go beyond what arguably is necessary and appropriate for compliance with applicable antifraud and SRO provisions and, as such, could be deemed to be constitute market conditioning violative of Section 5. Whatever its content, moreover, the information conveyed in these pre-filing communications must be reflected in the offering documents subsequently filed with the Commission and delivered to shareholders.

B. Legal and Processing Issues

1. Coordination with Other Government Agencies

On occasion, the staff communicates with other government agencies when disclosure indicates that the rules and regulations enforced by that government entity may materially effect the issuer's operations. For example, the staff continues to have an informal understanding with the staff of the Environmental Protection Agency ("EPA") whereby the Commission staff receives from the EPA lists of companies identified as potentially responsible parties on hazardous waste sites; companies subject to cleanup requirements under Resource Conservation and Recovery Act; and companies named in criminal and civil proceedings under environmental laws. The staff uses this information in its review process.

2. Monitor of Form 12b-25 Notices

The staff has implemented procedures to strengthen its monitoring efforts of all Forms 12b-25 notices of late filing. Notices are being monitored, with appropriate action taken depending upon the issuer's reason for delay and whether the subject filing is subsequently filed during the extension period. Possible staff action includes referral to the Division of Enforcement and prioritization of the subject report for staff review.

3. Safe Harbor for Forward-Looking Statements

On December 22, 1995, the Private Securities Litigation Reform Act of 1995 (the "Act") was enacted. The Act provides over two dozen separate changes to the securities laws, including a statutory safe harbor for forward-looking statements.

The Division has been monitoring disclosure intended to comply with the statutory safe harbor protection. Disclosures generally indicate that the filing contains forward-looking statements within the meaning of the Act, and then a cross-reference to the various risk factors is provided. For the most part, there has not been a noticeable increase in the amount of forward-looking information being provided. Information that was provided in the past is now labeled as forward-looking information. Additionally, the cautionary language has been fairly generic and boilerplate. The staff is not expressing a view as to whether such disclosure qualifies for the safe harbor. In order to make this clear to registrants, a separate paragraph has been added to all comment letters indicating that the staff is not expressing a view as to whether the disclosure qualifies for the safe harbor under the Act. The staff, however, is commenting on such disclosures to the extent that changes are needed to make it clear, understandable, consistent and otherwise in compliance with other disclosure standards. In addition, the staff is conducting an overall review of disclosure practices to determine whether additional Commission action would be appropriate.

4. <u>Related Public and Private Offerings</u>

Some companies with pending registration statements have advised the staff that they intend to withdraw the registration statement and shortly thereafter complete the offering without registration in reliance upon the Section 4(2) private offering exemption. This appears to be proposed for both timing and disclosure reasons. In the staff's view, this procedure ordinarily would not be consistent with Section 5 of the Securities Act. The filing of a registration statement for a specific securities offering (as contrasted with a generic shelf registration) constitutes a general solicitation for that securities offering rendering Section 4(2) unavailable for the same offering. In addition, the procedure raises significant integration issues under the traditional five factor test and the staff's integration policy positions since the subsequent private offering does not appear to be a separate offering.

A related issue arises when a company files a registration statement to register issuances of securities to purchasers who committed to purchase securities from the issuer prior to the filing of the registration statement on the condition that the securities be registered prior to issuance. It appears that the purpose of this procedure is to provide the purchasers with registered (rather than restricted) securities. The staff does not believe that this procedure is consistent with the registration provisions of the Securities Act, which cover offers and sales of securities, not issuances. In this situation, it appears that the offers were made and the commitments obtained prior to filing in reliance upon the Section 4(2) private placement exemption. If so, the registration statement should cover resales by the purchasers, not issuances to the purchasers.

The use of "lock-up agreements" in business combination transactions is common. What is not common or consistent is the extent to which these agreements are now used to lock up target shareholders beyond key executives and "blocking" shareholders of the target. While the signing of a lock-up agreement constitutes the making of an investment decision, the staff, noting the realities of these transactions, traditionally has not raised issues with respect to these agreements in connection with acquisitions of public companies. Recently, however, acquisition registration statements have been filed where 100% of the target shares are locked up or the "lock-up" group is expanded to include non-traditional "members" such as middle management.

5. Equity Swap Arrangements

Equity swap arrangements (including the related equity security) and similar devices typically shift some or all of the economic interests and risks of an equity security. These arrangements raise a number of legal and regulatory issues under the federal securities laws. Application of Exchange Act Section 16 to these arrangements is addressed in Exchange Act Releases No. 34514 and 37260. Those releases stated that equity swaps and similar transactions are subject to Section 16, and discussed the manner in which they should be reported. The staff continues to consider the issues raised by equity swaps and other risk-shifting transactions in other areas, including disclosure of security holdings and executive compensation, Schedule 13D reporting and transactions subject to Rule 144, Rule 144A and Regulation S. The treatment of these transactions under Rule 144 is addressed in Securities Act Release No. 7391; see Section VIII.B. The treatment of these transactions under Regulation S is addressed in Securities Act Release No. 7392; see Section VII.B.

6. Use of Form S-8 in Capital Raising Transactions

It has come to the staff's attention that issuers have used Form S-8 to register securities in situations in which the securities will be offered and sold in capital raising transactions (rather than in connection with employee benefit plans), or to compensate persons who assist in capital raising transactions. Form S-8 is not available in that context. If the form is used in that context, serious disclosure issues are raised, since the disclosures called for by the form would not be appropriate for a capital raising transaction.

7. Non-Qualified Deferred Compensation Plans

A typical non-qualified deferred compensation plan permits an employee to defer compensation over a set dollar amount. Those monies are retained by the employer. The employee will then either receive a fixed rate of return on the deferred monies or the employer may permit the employee to index the return on those monies off of a number of investment return alternatives.

In a number of no-action positions, the Division has indicated that it would not recommend enforcement action if transactions in non-qualified deferred compensation plans were not registered. The requests in those instances set forth two bases for the determination that registration under the Securities Act was not required. First, those requests set forth the argument that the offer and sale of interests in the deferred compensation plan did not involve the offer or sale of a security because the decision to participate in those plans was based primarily on tax management, not investment, purposes. Second, the requests contained the argument that the employees participating in the plan were top-level executives who did not need the protections provided by registration under the Securities Act. In providing the no-action position requested, the Division's responses state that, while not agreeing with the analysis in the request, it would not recommend enforcement action if transactions under the plans were not registered. The Division has not taken such a no-action position since 1991.

Due to a number of market and regulatory factors, non-qualified deferred compensation plans have greatly proliferated, both with respect to the number of employers offering such plans and the number of employees participating. At this time, the Division is not prepared to disregard the argument that the debt owing to plan participants is analogous to investment notes, which typically are viewed as debt securities. Further, the staff is not persuaded that there is a meaningful distinction between those plans that offer returns tied to different investment alternatives and those that offer only a fixed rate. The Division, therefore, will not grant requests for no-action with respect to any non-qualified deferred compensation plan, including those that have an interest only return. The Division has not stated affirmatively, however, that all interest only deferred compensation plans involve securities. Instead, the Division currently is leaving that question for counsel's analysis of the facts and circumstances. To the extent that interests in a non-qualified deferred compensation plan are securities, registration would be required unless the offerings under the plan would qualify for an exemption, e.g., Section 4(2).

Form S-8 would be available when an employer registers the offer and sale of interests in the deferred compensation plan under the Securities Act. The filing fee should be based on the amount of compensation being deferred, not on the ultimate investment return. As the "deferred compensation obligations" to be registered are obligations of the issuer/employer, not interests in the plan, the registration of the "deferred compensation obligations" would not result in a requirement that a deferred compensation plan file a Form 11-K with respect to those securities. Further, based on the unique terms of the "deferred compensation obligations" (both with respect to interest and maturity), compliance with the Trust Indenture Act of 1939 has not been required.

8. Schedule 13E-3 Filing Obligations of Issuers or Affiliates Engaged in a Going-Private Transaction

Generally, Exchange Act Rule 13e-3 requires that each issuer and affiliate engaged, directly or indirectly, in a going-private transaction file a Schedule 13E-3 with the Commission and furnish the required disclosures (e.g., the statement of "reasonable belief" as to the fairness or unfairness of the proposed transaction) directly to the holders of the class of equity securities that is the subject of the transaction. A joint filing may be permissible in this situation, provided each filing person individually makes the required disclosures and signs the Schedule 13E-3.

Two separate but related issues may be raised with respect to the determination of "filing-person" status in situations where a third party proposes a transaction with an issuer that has at least one of the requisite "going-private" effects: first, what entities or persons are "affiliates" of the issuer within the scope of Rule 13e-3(a)(1) and, second, when should those affiliates be deemed to be engaged, either directly or indirectly, in the going-private transaction. Resolution of both issues necessarily turns on all relevant facts and circumstances of a particular transaction. The following considerations should be noted:

(a) The staff consistently has taken the position that members of senior management of the issuer that is going private are affiliates of that issuer. Depending on the particular facts and circumstances of the transaction, such management also might be deemed to be engaged in the transaction. As a result, such management-affiliates may incur a Schedule 13E-3 filing obligation separate from that of the issuer. For example, the staff has taken the position that members of senior management of an issuer that will be going private are required to file a Schedule 13E-3 where the transaction will be effected through merger of the issuer into the purchaser or that purchaser's acquisition subsidiary, even though:

(i) such management's involvement in the issuer's negotiations with the purchaser is limited to the terms of each manager's future employment with and/or equity participation in the surviving company; and

(ii) the issuer's board of directors appointed a special committee of outside directors to negotiate all other terms of the transaction except management's role in the surviving entity.

An important aspect of the staff's analysis was the fact that the issuer's management ultimately would hold a material amount of the surviving company's outstanding equity securities, occupy seats on the board of this company in addition to senior management positions, and otherwise be in a position to "control" the surviving company within the meaning of Exchange Act Rule 12b-2 (i.e., "possession, direct or indirect, of the power to direct or cause the direction of the management and policies of a person, whether through the ownership of voting securities, by contract, or otherwise.").

(b) Questions have arisen regarding the nature and scope of the Schedule 13E-3 filing obligation of an acquiring person, or "purchaser," in a merger or other going-private transaction. In the situation described in (a) above, where management of the issuer-seller that will be going private is essentially "on both sides" of the transaction, the purchaser also may be deemed to be an affiliate of the issuer engaged in the transaction and, as a consequence, required to file on Schedule 13E-3. See Exchange Act Release No. 16075 (August 2, 1979) (noting that "affiliates of the seller often become affiliates of the purchaser through means other than equity ownership, and thereby are in control of the seller's business both before and after the transaction. In such cases the sale, in substance and effect, is being made to an affiliate of the issuer ...."). Accordingly, the issuer-seller, its senior management and the purchaser may be deemed Schedule 13E-3 filing persons in connection with the going-private transaction. Where the purchaser has created a merger subsidiary or other acquisition vehicle to effect the transaction, moreover, the staff will "look through" the acquisition vehicle and treat as a separate, affiliated purchaser the intermediate or ultimate parent of that acquisition vehicle. Accordingly, both the acquisition vehicle and the entity or person who formed it to acquire the issuer would have separate filing obligations (although, as noted, a joint filing may be permitted by the staff).

9. **Reports of Accounting Firms and Other Advisers**

Companies are retaining the financial consulting arm of accounting firms and other advisers to participate in the preparation of "synergy studies" or other reports. These reports are used to solicit security holders or investors. The staff is considering several matters regarding the effect of these reports on (i) auditor independence and (ii) consents under Section 7 of the Securities Act.

10. **Elimination of Opinions Relating To "Poison Pills" Registered on Form 8-A**

As recently amended, Exchange Act Form 8-A becomes effective automatically without action by the Commission. Historically, the staff required an opinion of counsel as to the legality of "poison pill" rights registered on that Form before it would declare the registration statement effective. As these registration statements now become effective automatically, the staff will no longer require issuers to provide these opinions.

11. **Trust Indenture Act Issues Arising in Certain Transactions Exempt from Securities Act Registration**

Offerings exempt from registration under Sections 3(a)(9) and 3(a)(10) of the Securities Act and Section 1145(a) of the Bankruptcy Code are not exempt from qualification under the Trust Indenture Act. Like Section 5 of the Securities Act, Section 306 of the Trust Indenture Act works transactionally. Unless the indenture for a debt security is qualified under Section 305 of the Trust Indenture Act, which covers registered offerings, or exempt from qualification under Section 304, the sale of the debt security violates Section 306 of the statute. Section 306(c) forbids any offer of the debt security until an application for qualification of the related indenture has been filed with the Commission.

The Division has recently noted a number of offerings of debt securities for issuers in Chapter 11 proceedings where the applications for qualification on Form T-3 were not filed until after approval of the plans of reorganization by both creditors and other claimants and the bankruptcy courts. The Division's view is that the offering event in bankruptcy is the solicitation of plan approval from creditors and other claimants. Accordingly, the application for qualification in these cases should be filed before such approval is sought.

C. **Industry-Specific Issues**

1. **Real Estate**

a. **Review of Filings**

The Division has issued three releases regarding real estate disclosure in the last few years. On June 17, 1991, the Commission issued an interpretive release relating to partnership offerings and reorganizations (Securities Act Release No. 6900); on October 30, 1991, final rules concerning disclosure of roll-up transactions were issued (Securities Act Release No. 6922). On December 1, 1994, the Commission adopted amendments to its roll-up rules (Securities Act Release No. 7113). The staff considers the disclosure guidelines of each of these releases in connection with its reviews of registration statements and proxy statements filed by limited partnerships and real estate investment trusts.

Current real estate filings relate primarily to real estate investment trusts (REITs) and, to a lesser extent, limited partnerships and limited liability companies. Frequently, REIT filings contain an UPREIT structure which includes an Umbrella Operating Partnership formed by the sponsor and affiliated partnerships to contribute properties or partnership interests to the REIT. In connection with REIT initial public offerings, the staff considers the availability of any claimed exemption from Securities Act registration for the pre-formation roll-up transactions undertaken to form the operating partnership.

Primary offerings by Operating Partnerships must comply with appropriate form requirements. Operating Partnerships may use Form S-3 if the applicable requirements are met, specifically, Instruction I.C., but since the Operating Partnership is unlikely to be able to meet the requirements of Staff Accounting Bulletin 53, separate financial statements and related disclosure must be provided either in the registration statement or through incorporation by reference of a voluntary Form 10. Following the offering, applicable reports must be filed by the Operating Partnership.

Reviews of limited partnership offerings and proxy solicitation materials continue to focus on prior performance and on claims made by sponsors concerning investment obligations and future performance. These reviews also focus on changes to partnership objectives and structure. Finally, the staff continues to examine the practices and disclosure associated with the solicitation of proxies and registration statements related to roll-ups, pursuant to the revised rules. See also Section X.A.1 for a discussion of the disclosure required in tender offers for limited partnership units.

b. <u>Sales Literature Used in Connection with the Offering of Limited Partnerships</u>

Item 19 of Industry Guide 5 requires that sales literature used in the offering of limited partnership units, including material marked for "Broker Dealer Use Only," be submitted for staff review. These materials should provide a balanced presentation of the risks and rewards involved in the offering. All information must be consistent with the information and representations contained in the prospectus and the sales literature should not be presented in a manner which obscures the prospectus cover page. Registrants should contact the staff before using submitted sales materials.

c. <u>Low Income Housing, Rehabilitation, and Historic Tax Credit Real Estate Limited Partnerships</u>

Certain real estate limited partnership offerings indicate the sponsor's intention to invest in low income housing or other programs eligible for federal or state income tax credits. Most of these offerings highlight the percentage returns to the investor of the tax credits on a simple annualized basis. Since the tax credits are available for only 10 years and the enabling statutes require a 15-year holding period for the property, the rate of return disclosure should include the effects of the time value of money. Further, since it is possible that the property may have no or little residual value at the end of the 15-year holding period, the disclosure of the rate of return should assume a zero resale value of the property.

Further, prior performance disclosure of the results of earlier tax credit offerings by the sponsor should be included. Disclosure of the total amount of tax credits generated for each year should be included as should the amount of tax credits per $1000 invested.

2. Exemption from Registration for Bank and Thrift Holding Company Formations

Section 3(a)(12) of the Securities Act provides an exemption from registration for securities issued in connection with the formation of a bank or savings association holding company where shareholders maintain the same proportional interest in the holding company as they had in the bank or savings association; the rights and interests of the shareholders are substantially the same after the transaction as before it; and the holding company has substantially the same assets and liabilities, on a consolidated basis, as the bank or savings association had before the transaction. The staff has informally taken the position that the exemption would not be available if the new holding company's corporate charter contained antitakeover provisions that were not in the governing documents of the predecessor bank or thrift.

3. Structured Financings

In fall 1992, the Commission extended the benefits of Rule 415 "shelf" registration through the expansion of the availability of Form S-3 to investment grade asset-backed securities offerings (Securities Act Release No. 6964 (October 22, 1992)(the "Shelf Release")). Shortly thereafter, the Commission adopted Rule 3a-7 under the Investment Company Act of 1940 excluding from the definition of "investment company" structured financings that meet the rule's conditions (Investment Company Act Release No. 19105 (November 19, 1992)). These changes appear to have precipitated, or at least coincided with, a movement in the structured finance market toward securitization of assets in the public markets that previously were offered in the private markets. Significant disclosure and eligibility issues continue to come up as a result of market developments.

a. Asset Concentration

The Shelf Release expressly does not adopt a specific asset concentration test. Instead, asset concentration questions have been addressed through existing disclosure rules. While an asset concentration test was not included, the release indicates that the definition of asset-backed security does not encompass securities issued in structured financings for one obligor or group of related obligors.

(i) Multiple Core Prospectuses

Another issue involving asset concentration arises in the context of pooling several different types of underlying assets. The staff permits issuers to register on a single shelf registration statement asset-backed securities supported by more than one category of underlying assets without specifying the amount of each type to be offered. The registration statement must specifically identify the various asset categories and include a separate core prospectus for each such category. In considering whether a separate core prospectus is required, the staff will consider whether the assets described are intended to be pooled together or securitized separately. If the latter, separate core prospectuses ordinarily would be required.

(ii) Commercial Mortgages

For securitization of commercial mortgages and leases, where the mortgage loan is a non-recourse obligation of the mortgagor, disclosure related to the operating property(ies) will be required where concentration exists. The staff applies the standards described in Staff Accounting Bulletin 71/71A ("SAB 71/71A"). SAB 71/71A generally employs a 20% asset concentration test to determine whether audited property financial statements are required. At concentration levels between 10-20%, financial and other information regarding the underlying properties is required. In determining whether these concentration thresholds are crossed, loans to the same obligor, group of related obligors, or loans on related properties may be aggregated.

In addition, where a mortgage loan or loans of a single obligor, or group of related obligors, accounts for more than 45% of the pool assets, one or more co-issuers may exist. See FBC Conduit Trust I, First Boston Mortgage Securities Corporation (October 6, 1987).

b. Securitizing Outstanding Securities

(i) Corporate Debt Securities

The pooling and securitization of outstanding corporate debt securities of other issuers may be registered on Form S-3 if the requirements of the Form for asset-backed securities offerings are met, provided that the depositor would be free to publicly resell the securities without registration. Thus, a depositor generally cannot include restricted securities (i.e., privately-placed securities where the Rule 144(k) two-year holding period has not run) nor can it include registered securities if the securitization is part of the original distribution. To provide certainty in deciding what is part of the original distribution in resecuritizations by affiliates of underwriters involved in the original offering, the staff has used a bright line test (i.e., securities purchased in the secondary market and at least three months after the depositor had sold out any unsold allotment are not viewed as part of the original dispatch).

Where 20% or more of the pool consists of the securities of a single issuer, the staff requires audited financial statements of such issuer to be included in the prospectus. However, if the underlying issuer is eligible to use Form S-3 for a primary common stock offering, and the depositor's transaction in the securities is purely secondary (e.g., there is no tie to the issuer or the issuer's distribution), the staff would accept a reference in the prospectus to the issuer's periodic reports on file with the Commission. Of course, the prospectus must include a description of the material terms of the pooled securities.

In connection with Exchange Act reporting, reference to the S-3 eligible underlying issuer's periodic reports on file with the Commission will be accepted in lieu of direct disclosure of this information. In addition, the staff generally requires the depositor to undertake to provide financial and other information relating to such underlying issuer directly in its reports in the event such underlying issuer terminates reporting after the pooling transaction. No such undertaking is required, however, if, at the time of the pooling transaction, the underlying issuer has a class of common equity registered under the Exchange Act.

(ii) <u>Asset-Backed Securities</u>

Securitization of outstanding asset-backed securities is treated similarly if the underlying trust has outstanding securities held by non-affiliates in excess of $75 million and files periodic reports with the Commission. The securities of government-sponsored enterprises ("GSE") which have a comparable market float and which make information publicly available comparable to that of Exchange Act reporting entities are treated similarly.

(iii) <u>Municipal Securities</u>

The offering of asset-backed securities supported by pools of municipal bonds where asset concentration exists, in general, requires that financial statements and other information relating to the underlying municipal issuer be provided. This information must be included directly in the prospectus, must be current, and must otherwise satisfy fully the disclosure requirements under the federal securities regulations.

While there may be instances where financial statements of the municipal issuer are not material to the investor in the asset-backed security, such instances would appear to be rare and the staff will require appropriate legal opinions and other documentation necessary to support the conclusion that financial and other information relating to the municipal issuer is not material to investors.

c. <u>Structuring the Offering</u>

Often the payment terms of asset-backed securities are tailored to meet the particular investment needs of the investor. Prior to effectiveness of the registration statement, investors often ask the underwriter for various computational materials so as to analyze prepayment and other assumptions affecting yield. These computational materials are not permissible prospectuses under the Securities Act and the Commission's rules and regulations. However, recognizing the realities of the asset-backed market, the staff has issued three no-action letters that recognize the industry's practice of providing written information (other than the statutory prospectus) to prospective purchasers of asset-backed securities when negotiating and structuring the securities to meet purchasers' investment criteria. These letters generally permit the provision of limited information outside the preliminary prospectus to purchasers, provided that the final information is filed as part of the registration statement.

d. Delinquent Assets

The definition of "asset-backed security" in Form S-3 states that the assets must "by their terms convert into cash within a finite time period." The staff issued a no-action letter in which it acknowledged that an offering that includes a concentration of delinquent assets may be eligible to be offered on Form S-3 so long as the concentration is less than 20% of the assets. A concentration of 20% or more would not appear to be eligible to be offered on Form S-3 because foreclosure on an asset is not converting to cash by its terms. See The Bond Market Association (Oct. 16, 1997), described in section XII.H.

4. Disclosures by Electric Utilities

Electric utility companies are facing increasing competition. The regulatory framework in which they operate is undergoing significant change, although the path and pace of that change vary from jurisdiction to jurisdiction. Clear and balanced disclosure is necessary to inform investors about the specific risks and uncertainties that are reasonably likely to affect the reporting company. Consequences of the competitive and regulatory changes may include impairment of significant recorded assets, material reductions of profit margins, and increased costs of capital. Those risks, quantified to the extent practicable, should be discussed in Management's Discussion and Analysis ("MD&A").

Many regulated utilities account for costs differently from other public companies. Under SFAS No. 71, an electric utility may defer certain costs of providing services if the rates established by its regulators are designed to recover the utility's specific costs and the economic environment gives reasonable assurance that those rates can be charged and collected throughout the periods necessary to recover the costs. When a utility ceases to operate under those conditions, significant costs previously deferred under SFAS No. 71 as regulatory assets must be written off and methods of amortizing capital assets must be revised to conform with lives appropriate in a competitive environment. The resulting reduction in reported equity and operating margin, accompanied by the increased market risks, may create new requirements for equity capital and push borrowing costs higher. While some companies may be affected only marginally in the next several years, others may suffer serious financial consequences.

Disclosures responsive to Item 101 (Description of Business) of Regulation S-K include a description of the competitive conditions faced by the registrant and material features of its regulatory environment. Item 303 (Management's Discussion and Analysis) requires meaningful explanation of how changes in competition and rate setting practices have affected or are reasonably likely to affect operating results. If recovery of identifiable categories of capital assets, regulatory assets or other deferred costs is subject to material uncertainties, quantitative disclosure is warranted.

For example, if the registrant has submitted information to state and/or federal regulators in an effort to implement special rate and/or depreciation plans, the staff believes that a description of those plans, including the type and amount of potentially "stranded" costs identified in those plans, should be discussed in MD&A. Potentially stranded investments and costs commonly include differences between regulatory accumulated depreciation for plant and the accumulated depreciation which would have been recorded based on generally accepted accounting principles, and expected or estimated differences between the carrying amount of plant assets and the amount that would be recoverable in a deregulated environment.

Avoiding boilerplate or overly general disclosures, the registrant should identify specific segments or customer classes that are most likely to be affected by regulatory or competitive changes, and describe clearly how specific assets, revenues and operating margins may be affected. For example, registrants should disclose the relative proportion of operations affected by special non-traditional rate plans with specific groups of customers, including industrial customers, and quantify to the extent practicable the current and expected impact of those arrangements. Regulatory developments and uncertainties unique to individual significant jurisdictions should be highlighted, and any material effects that are reasonably likely to occur should be discussed and quantified. Required disclosures in financial statements about accounting policies governing cost deferral and depreciation may warrant additional explanation in MD&A if unique or unusual practices materially affect reported results or the loss of eligibility to use the accounting method is reasonably likely and would have a material effect.

5. Physician Practice Management Companies

The changing structure of the health services market and the diversity in arrangements between physicians and the providers of management and administrative services (PPMs) raise significant accounting and disclosure issues. The nature of these issues is continually evolving and the specific nature of the management agreements dictates the presentation of the information in any document. Issues relating to financial statement presentation are currently under consideration by the Emerging Issues Task Force.

The PPM may assist in the formation of the medical practice group or may contract with it after its formation. Generally, the PPM will acquire the non-medical practice assets and will contract with the medical practice group to be the exclusive provider of facilities, equipment and non-medical services and may procure managed care contracts. The physicians of the practice group typically enter into various employment, non-compete and operating agreements with the PPM or each other which govern the affairs of the physician group and its relationship with the PPM. State prohibitions on the corporate practice of medicine impact the type and amount of control, if any, that the PPM may have over the physician group. Some PPMs have entered into written agreements with stockholders of medical practices giving the PPM certain rights relating to the management of the medical practices.

Disclosure Issues

The PPM must clearly and accurately describe its business and contractual relationships. Issuers should address these questions:

What does the PPM do? What is the exact nature of its business?

- Describe the contractual relationship among the PPM and the medical practices. Describe the PPM's rights and limitations under the contracts.

- Disclose how the PPM's fees are determined. If the fees are based upon a percentage of certain items, what are those percentages, or what is the range of the percentages? What items affect the calculation?

- Even if the PPM combines the operations of the medical practice group for financial statement purposes or has consolidated subsidiaries that provide the medical services, the PPM must clearly distinguish the services it provides from the practice of medicine.

What is the PPM's relationship with managed care providers?

- Disclose whether the PPM (or an assignee) enters into direct contracts with managed care companies or whether the physician groups contract directly with the managed care companies.

- Identify the party who assumes the risk under managed care contracts (i.e. the PPM or the physician group). If the PPM assumes the contracts, are there any issues relating to medical licensing?

- Who assumes the risk associated with capitated payment contracts? If the PPM assumes the risk, does this subject it to regulation as an insurance company?

Is the PPM subject to any state or federal regulations?

- Describe any state prohibitions on the corporate practice of medicine and discuss the impact upon the PPM.

- Is the PPM subject to regulation as an insurer?

- What is the effect of federal anti-kickback and self-referral restrictions?

Financial Statement Issues

Although some PPMs present the revenues and expenses of the medical groups as their own revenues and expenses, the staff has challenged the appropriateness of this presentation in recent months. Issues relating to consolidation, acquisition, and reporting of PPMs are being addressed under the umbrella of EITF Issue No. 97-2.

The staff will not object, at the present time, to the display of the revenues and expenses of the medical practice in the statement of operations of a PPM if the terms of the management agreement provide the PPM with a net profits or equivalent interest in the preponderance of the medical services furnished by the medical group. A net profits interest arises when the management fee is derived from the profit of the medical practice.

If the revenues and expenses of the medical practice are displayed in the financial statement of the PPM, they must be disclosed separately on the face or in a note to the financial statements with a meaningful explanation of the basis for their inclusion. Management fee and lease income from the medical group and associated disclosure also should be provided. The actual aggregate management fee income and selling, general and administration expenses of the PPM must be clearly disclosed on the face of the income statement with footnote disclosure of the material contract terms bearing on their calculation. All material commitments and guarantees of the PPM to the medical group and material amounts paid under those arrangements must be disclosed.

Absent a preponderance of a net profits interest in the medical practice, inclusion of the revenues and expenses of the medical practice within the financial statements of the PPM would appear to mischaracterize the PPM's business and financial results.

Separate financial statements of a medical practice with which a PPM will consummate, or has recently consummated, a significant management agreement generally are not required if the PPM does not consolidate the practice, and does not guarantee any minimum practice income, extend unusual credit terms, or fund operating losses. However, if the PPM is expected to have a material dependence on the PC, separate financial information about the practice would be material to investors. For example, if the management fee from the practice is expected to generate more than 20% of the PPM's revenues in the next 12 months, the staff has requested audited financial statements of the practice. However, the staff has accepted only unaudited summary financial information about the practice for the three most recent fiscal years if audited financial statements are not readily available and its owners are not promoters of the offering being registered.

Historical information about the practice for any period before its ownership by the current owners would not be requested unless the PPM is of the view that a change in an owner does not fundamentally change the underlying business. If the owners of a practice generating 20% or more of the PPM's revenues own 10% or more of the PPM at the time of its initial public offering or are promoters of the offering, audited financial statements of that practice for at least its most recent fiscal year ordinarily would be required, unless effects of providing the management services to the practice have been included in the PPM's audited financial statements for at least nine months. If financial information of a managed practice is presented, care should be taken to avoid the impression that an investor is obtaining an interest in the practice or that the historical results are indicative of future results under the altered incentive structure and management affiliates established with the PPM.

The staff believes that pro forma operating results depicting the effects of consummating a management agreement with a practice cannot be reasonably presented if the PPM has not managed practices for at least a year, due to the lack of historical financial statements depicting the PPM's own overhead. In those start-up situations, management is encouraged to provide any forward-looking information that it believes is appropriate, but the data should not be characterized as "pro forma" financial information. If sufficient historical information is available, pro forma information may be presented based on the practice's historical expenses and the terms of the management agreements. Fee income based on revenues or operating results of the practice should not be included in the pro forma data unless management has reasonably concluded that the changes in the owner's incentive structure are unlikely to affect the conduct of the medical practice, and that assessment is disclosed.

Management's Discussion and Analysis

The financial terms of the management contracts, including disclosure of the rights and obligations of both parties, the basis for management fees and the ability of the PPM to manage profitability of medical practice should be discussed fully. If there are several types of contracts, the financial terms of each should be described.

Issuance of Securities and Grant of Options

Securities issued as compensation to physician employees of the medical groups before the filing of a registration statement for an IPO may be made in reliance on Rule 701 (Morgan Health Group, Inc. (December 18, 1996)).

After effectiveness of a registration statement, the grant and exercise of options to the medical groups is not appropriate using Form S-8 since the physicians are not employees of the Company. These offers and sales should be on Form S-1 or Form S-3, as applicable.

Promoter Disclosure

If assets acquired at the time of the IPO are accounted for at book value in reliance on Staff Accounting Bulletin 48 ("SAB 48"), the characterization of physicians as promoters for purposes of the SAB 48 analysis subjects the physicians to identification as promoters under Item 404 of Regulation S-K. In addition, SAB 48 is not applicable to any shares given to employees or consultants for future services.

XI. ACCOUNTING ISSUES

A. Staff Accounting Bulletin 98 - Earnings Per Share

Staff Accounting Bulletin 98 (SAB 98) was issued on February 3, 1998. SAB 98 makes technical revisions to various existing SABs to conform their guidance with the requirements of FASB Statement No. 128, "Earnings Per Share." The most significant revision relates to the calculation of earnings per share when there have been issuances of stock or options at prices below the IPO price in periods preceding an initial public offering (SAB Topic 4:D). Previously, Topic 4:D specified a retroactive computation method to reflect the dilutive nature of such issuances for all prior periods presented. SAB 98 requires registrants to follow Statement 128 (which generally requires issuances to be reflected in earnings per share from issuance date forward) but cautions registrants that the staff considers issuances for nominal consideration before an IPO to be in-substance stock splits that should be retroactively reflected under Statement 128. The revisions do not change existing requirements to recognize expense for stock or options issued in exchange for employee or non-employee services under APB Opinion 25 or FASB Statement 123. The revisions are expected to simplify the calculation and presentation of earnings per share by IPO registrants.

B. Issues Involving Recently Issued Accounting Standards

1. SFAS No. 123 (Stock-Based Compensation) Disclosures

With the adoption of SFAS No. 123, two methods of accounting for stock-based compensation are acceptable. Notes to the financial statements should explain which method of accounting for stock-based compensation has been applied. Companies that continue to follow APB Opinion No. 25 must include in notes to the financial statements certain pro forma data specified in paragraph 45 of SFAS No. 123 to disclose the effects had the new standard's provisions been applied. A registrant that is continuing to apply APB Opinion No. 25 need not include those pro forma disclosures in its condensed interim financial statements, although disclosure of that information on a quarterly basis is encouraged. Registrants also should note that SFAS No. 123 governs the accounting for all issuances of equity instruments for consideration other than employee services. See also EITF Issue Nos. 96-3 and 96-18.

The keen interest of investors in stock compensation, as demonstrated by continuing press coverage, and the related party nature of stock plans create a presumption that the disclosures ordinarily will be material to readers of the financial statements if stock compensation is a significant component of compensation arrangements. Preparers of financial statements recognized before the adoption of SFAS 123 that disclosure of the number of options granted to employees is typically material. The staff has challenged the view of some registrants that the estimated fair value of those options, revealed through the required pro forma earnings disclosure and related assumptions, is not material to investors.

2. Impact of FASB Statement No. 128, "Earnings Per Share"

In February 1997, the FASB issued Statement No. 128, "Earnings per Share." The Statement establishes standards for computing and presenting earnings per share (EPS). It simplifies and supersedes the existing EPS guidance found in APB Opinion 15 and its 102 interpretations. The Statement is effective for financial statements issued for periods ending after December 31, 1997. Since Statement No. 128 may impact the computation of EPS when it is adopted, registrants should consider disclosing the expected impact of this statement, in a manner similar to that specified in Staff Accounting Bulletin 74 (see below). For calendar year-end registrants, these disclosures should appear in the Form 10-Qs filed in 1997.

3. Disclosures about Segments (SFAS 131)

Companies should consider the requirements of SAB 74 (see below) in light of the recent issuance of SFAS 131. Companies that expect a material future change in their segment financial information are encouraged to apply the provisions of SAB 74, including: (1) a discussion of the standard and its requirements, and (2) the impact on their current segment groupings.

4. <u>General Guidance about New Accounting Standards (SAB 74)</u>

Staff Accounting Bulletin 74 (Topic 11:M) discusses disclosures that a registrant should provide in its financial statements and/or MD&A regarding the impact that recently issued accounting standards will have on its financial statements when the standard is adopted in a future period. Disclosures that should be considered include a brief description of the standard and its anticipated adoption date, the method by which the standard will be adopted, the impact that the standard will have on the financial statements to the extent reasonably estimable, and any other effects that are reasonably likely to occur (e.g., changes in business practices, changes in availability or cost of capital, violations of debt covenants, etc.). In this regard, registrants should consider the effects of not only standards recently issued by the FASB, but also Statements of Position and Practice Bulletins issued by the AICPA and consensus positions of the EITF.

C. <u>Applicability of SAB 48 to Purchase Business Combinations; Identification of an Accounting Acquiror</u>

On July 31, 1996, the staff issued Staff Accounting Bulletin 97 ("SAB 97") setting forth its views regarding two issues involving purchase business combinations: (a) the application of SAB 48, "Transfer of Nonmonetary Assets by Promoters or Shareholders," to purchase business combinations consummated and (b) the identification of an accounting acquiror in purchase business combinations.

SAB 97 states that SAB 48 was not intended to modify the requirements of Accounting Principles Board Opinion Number 16, *Business Combinations* ("APB Opinion 16"). If a business combination fails to meet the conditions specified by APB Opinion 16 for the pooling-of-interests method of accounting, it should be accounted for using the purchase method. Under the purchase method, the acquiring company allocates the cost of the acquired company to the individual assets acquired and liabilities assumed based on their fair values, rather than using their historical, or promoter's, cost as is prescribed by SAB 48 for certain exchanges of stock for nonmonetary assets. The clarification regarding the application of SAB 48 to business combinations is applicable to all merger agreements entered into after the issuance of SAB 97.

SAB 97 also expresses the staff's view that an acquiring entity must be identified in any business combination that does not meet the conditions specified in APB Opinion 16 for application of the pooling-of-interests method. If no single former shareholder group of the combining companies obtains more than 50% of the outstanding stock of the new combined entity, the staff believes that the shareholder group receiving the largest ownership interest in the new combined entity should be presumed to be the accounting acquiror unless objective and verifiable evidence rebuts that presumption and supports the identification of a different shareholder group as the acquiror for accounting purposes. SAB 97 also indicates that financial statements of the accounting acquiror should not be presented in filings on a basis combined with the pre- acquisition financial statements of the acquired companies, except to the extent prescribed by Article 11 of Regulation S-X ("Pro Forma Financial Statements").

D. Treasury Stock Acquisitions Following Consummation of a Business Combination Accounted for as a Pooling-of-Interests

On March 19, 1996, the staff issued Staff Accounting Bulletin 96 ("SAB 96") setting forth its views with respect to treasury stock acquisitions following a business combination accounted for using the pooling-of-interests method. SAB 96 is interpretive of paragraph 48 of Accounting Principles Board Opinion Number 16, *Business Combinations* ("APB Opinion 16") and earlier Commission interpretative guidance relating to that paragraph (Accounting Series Release ("ASR") Numbers 146 and 146-A). Paragraph 48 states, "Some transactions after a combination is consummated are inconsistent with the combining of entire existing interests of common stockholders. Including those transactions in the negotiations and terms of the combination, either explicitly or by intent, counteracts the effect of combining stockholder interests."

Stock acquisitions expected to occur after a combination that would be permitted prior to its consummation do not preclude the application of pooling-of- interests accounting to the combination. Accordingly, planned transactions involving reacquisitions of either untainted treasury stock (as discussed in ASR 146 and 146-A) or tainted treasury stock up to the limits permitted under paragraph 47 of APB Opinion 16 would not violate requirements for pooling-of-interests accounting. Other treasury stock acquisitions planned to occur after the combination would preclude application of the pooling-of-interests method.

In applying the 90% test of paragraph 47 of APB Opinion 16 at the consummation date, the staff believes that, unless the shares to be reacquired would be untainted, the maximum number of shares that may be reacquired within two years of consummation of the combination pursuant to any planned transaction should be aggregated (without reduction for planned reissuances) with other "paragraph 47 exceptions." If the total paragraph 47 exceptions exceed 10% of any combining company's outstanding shares, the staff believes that application of pooling-of-interests accounting to the combination would not be appropriate.

SAB 96 states the staff's presumption that a reacquisition of treasury stock within six months following consummation of a business combination is a planned transaction that is part of the combination plan, whether or not the shares are acquired in the open market or from shareholders of the combining companies. Other actions occurring within six months after a business combination also provide persuasive evidence of a prior intention to acquire treasury stock that was part of the combination plan. For example, the staff believes that the announcement of an intention to reacquire shares made within six months following consummation of a business combination provides persuasive evidence of an intention that was part of the combination plan.

SAB 96 states that an intention to resume reacquiring tainted treasury stock pursuant to a pre-existing plan cannot be distinguished from an intention formulated concurrently with development of the plan of combination. Unless treasury stock reacquired will be untainted treasury stock, the assertion that those shares were acquired for reasons other than the business combination is not sufficient to distinguish the intention to resume reacquiring treasury stock from other planned transactions to reacquire shares issued to effect the combination.

The staff generally has not questioned the use of pooling-of-interests accounting where treasury stock was acquired more than six months after the combination is consummated if there is no evidence that the reacquisitions were contemplated as part of the combination.

E. Financial Statements of Subsidiaries that Guarantee Securities Issued by Parent Company

If debt or preferred stock registered under the Securities Act may be guaranteed by one or more of the issuer's subsidiaries, each guarantee (as well as the guaranteed security) must be covered by an effective registration statement. Rule 3-10(a) of Regulation S-X requires financial statements of guarantors of registered securities to be included in the registration statement. Moreover, the guarantor subsidiary, like its parent, is required to file periodic reports pursuant to Section 15(d) of the Exchange Act at least for the fiscal year during which the Securities Act registration statement became effective.

The staff will accept in some circumstances a registrant's proposal to include other disclosures in lieu of full separate audited financial statements of the guarantor subsidiary, and will take no action with respect to a guarantor that does not file separate Exchange Act reports. Issuers seeking periodic reporting relief ordinarily should address their requests to the Office of the Chief Counsel of the Division of Corporation Finance.

Topic 1.G. of the Staff Accounting Bulletins (SAB 53) provides relief from the general requirement of full separate disclosure and reporting by subsidiary-issuers where investors rely upon the parent's guarantee for the repayment of principal and interest on the subsidiary-issuer's guaranteed securities. On the other hand, Topic 1.H. states as a general rule that separate financial statements for a subsidiary-guarantor and a parent-issuer would be material to investors. However, in certain circumstances where subsidiary-guarantors are present, the staff has provided additional relief.

If the registered security is guaranteed by all direct and indirect subsidiaries of the parent company and the parent has no operations or assets other than its investment in its subsidiaries, the staff generally would not require the registration statement to include any audited financial information of the guarantor subsidiaries, provided that the registrant indicates the basis for their omission. If the registered security is guaranteed by all direct and indirect consolidated subsidiaries of the parent but the parent does have other assets or operations, the staff generally will accept, in lieu of separate financial statements of the guarantor subsidiaries, either summarized parent-only financial information or summarized combined financial information of the guarantor subsidiaries provided in an audited note to the parent's financial statements. The alternative disclosures described in this paragraph also have been accepted where the nonguarantor subsidiaries are inconsequential (i.e., when each of the assets and pre-tax income of and parent's net investment in the nonguarantor subsidiaries on an individual and combined basis is less than 3%).

In other circumstances in which the security is guaranteed on a full, unconditional, and joint and several basis by one or more of the issuer's wholly owned subsidiaries, the financial information required in the note to the parent's financial statements ordinarily should be consolidating condensed financial statements which depict, in separate columns, the parent company, the guarantor subsidiaries (on a combined basis), and the nonguarantor subsidiaries (on a combined basis), with an additional column reflecting eliminating adjustments. Additional columns may be necessary if the enforceability of the guarantees may differ under the laws of the foreign or domestic jurisdictions in which they can be enforced.

If condensed financial statements are accepted in lieu of full financial statements, registrants should follow the general guidance in Rule 10-01 of Regulation S-X concerning their form and content. However, the information should be in sufficient detail to allow investors to determine the nature of the assets held by, and the operations and cash flows of, each of the consolidating groups and include a discussion of any significant restrictions on the parent's and the guarantors' ability to obtain funds from their subsidiaries by dividend or loan. Additional financial and narrative information about individual guarantors should be disclosed if the information would be material for an investor to evaluate the sufficiency of the guarantee.

If one or more of the guarantor subsidiaries is not wholly owned or if one or more of the guarantees is not full, unconditional, and joint and several, the staff will expect the issuer to furnish full audited financial statements of the guarantor subsidiaries pursuant to Rule 3-10.

Also, if historical operations of a guarantor subsidiary were not included in the audited consolidated financial statements of the issuer for at least one complete year because it was recently acquired or is a probable acquisition, the "substantial collateral" test defined in Rule 3-10 of Regulation S-X should be used to determine whether financial statements of the recently acquired guarantor subsidiary are required. If the book value, par value, or market value (purchase price), whichever is greater, of any recently acquired guarantor subsidiary equals 20% or more of the principal amount of the guaranteed debt securities, the financial statements required by Rule 3-01 and Rule 3-02 of Regulation S-X for the periods before their inclusion in the audited financial statements of the parent are required. These financial statements, when combined with the periods included in parent's audited consolidated financial statements, should equal the periods required by Rules 3-01 and Rule 3-02 of Regulation S-X.

Registrants should note that the guidance in SAB 53 explained above for application to guarantor subsidiaries does not apply to affiliates whose securities collateralize another registered security, even if that affiliate is a wholly owned subsidiary of the issuer of the registered security. Rule 3-10 of Regulation S-X provides that financial statements of each affiliate whose securities constitute a substantial portion of the collateral for any class of security must be furnished.

F. <u>Mandatorily Redeemable Securities of Subsidiaries Holding Debt of Registrant</u>

Registrants should consider the adequacy of disclosures about mandatorily redeemable securities issued by a finance subsidiary of a parent company when the financial subsidiary holds only debt instruments issued by the parent, particularly if the outstanding security of the finance subsidiary is guaranteed by the parent and mirrors the cash flows of the debt of the parent held by the finance subsidiary. The staff believes that disclosures in these situations often must be expanded to provide investors with a fair and balanced picture of the registrant's effective capitalization and leverage. Inclusion of the outstanding public security in minority interest with minimal disclosure of its characteristics is not adequate, particularly when Section 12(h) reporting relief is requested by registrants for the finance subsidiary. In those situations, the parent should disclose the subsidiary's outstanding securities as a separate line item in the parent's balance sheet captioned "Company-obligated mandatorily redeemable security of subsidiary holding solely parent debentures," "Guaranteed preferred beneficial interests in Company's debentures," or similar descriptive wording. Notes to the financial statements should describe fully the terms of the securities and explain that those terms parallel the terms of the company's debentures which comprise substantially all of the assets of the consolidated trust or subsidiary.

G. <u>Accountant's Refusals to Re-issue Audit Reports</u>

Some accounting firms have adopted risk management policies that lead them to refuse to re-issue their reports on the audits of financial statements that have been included previously in Commission filings. In some cases, accountants whose reports on acquired businesses were included in a registrant's Form 8-K have declined to permit that report to be included in a registrant's subsequent registration statement. In other cases, accountants have declined to reissue their reports on the registrant's financial statements after the registrant engaged a different auditor for subsequent periods. The Commission's staff is not in a position to evaluate the reasons for an accountant's refusal to re-issue its report and will not intervene in disputes between registrants and their auditors. Moreover, the staff will not waive the requirements for the audit report or the accountant's consent to be named as an expert in filings. If a registrant is unable to re-use the previously issued audit report in a current filing, the registrant must engage another accountant to re-audit those financial statements. A registrant that is unable to obtain either re-issuance of an audit report or a new audit by a different firm may be precluded from raising capital in a public offering.

When registrants engage an accountant to perform audit services, they should consider the need for the accountant to re-issue its audit report in future periods. It may be appropriate to address in the audit services contract the registrant's expectations regarding the use of the audit report in filings that it or its successors may make under either the Exchange Act or the Securities Act and the circumstances under which the accountant may decline to permit its re-use.

XII. SIGNIFICANT NO-ACTION AND INTERPRETIVE LETTERS THROUGH JANUARY 1998

A. Section 2(a)(10) of the Securities Act

Net Roadshow, Inc. - July 30, 1997

The Division took the position that it would not recommend enforcement action if Net Roadshow transmits roadshows via the Internet:

- for the purposes and according to the procedures described in the request; and
- in reliance on counsel's opinion that the transmissions are not prospectuses within the meaning of Securities Act Section 2(a)(10).

Some of the key procedures described in the request include:

(1) an entire "live" roadshow, including any questions and answers, will be transmitted on the Internet and editing (except in limited circumstances) and staging are not permitted;

(2) transmissions of the roadshow will not be available until a registration statement has been filed with the Commission for the subject offering;

(3) transmissions will not be made widely available; access is password-protected and limited only to those "qualified" investors who customarily are invited to attend a "live" roadshow (e.g., registered broker-dealers and investment advisers);

(4) the roadshow may be viewed for one day only by each person or entity given password access;

(5) viewers must agree not to copy, download or further distribute the transmissions (Net Roadshow has also installed technology to prevent copying, downloading or printing of transmissions other than the filed prospectus);

(6) each transmission will include visual statements or "crawls" emphasizing the prohibition on copying, downloading or further distributing;

(7) a copy of the filed prospectus will be available on-line before and during each roadshow transmission, and will be able to be downloaded by the viewer in its entirety; and

(8) issuers and underwriters will be required to take reasonable steps to ensure that information disclosed in the transmission is not inconsistent with the filed prospectus.

Private Financial Network ("PFN") - March 12, 1997

The Division took the position that it would not recommend enforcement action if PFN transmits by satellite, telephone or cable a video of an issuer's road show presentation to PFN's subscribers for the purposes and pursuant to the procedures described in reliance on counsel's opinion that the transmissions are not prospectuses within the meaning of Securities Act Section 2(a)(10).

The procedures described in the request include: (1) transmissions will be available only to PFN's subscribers who agree not to videotape, copy or further distribute the transmissions; (2) before a transmission, each of PFN's subscribers will receive a filed prospectus from the issuer or the underwriter; (3) issuers and underwriters will be required to take reasonable steps to ensure that information disclosed in the road show is not inconsistent with the filed prospectus; and (4) each transmission will include visual statements or "crawls" emphasizing the prohibition on videotaping, copying or further distributing.

Dissemination of Research Materials Relating to Asset-Backed Securities - February 7, 1997

The Division stated that, under the conditions specified, the publication or distribution by a broker or dealer (collectively, "Broker/Dealer") of information, an opinion or a recommendation as to investment grade asset-backed securities (as defined for Securities Act Form S-3 eligibility purposes) ("ABS") will not be deemed, for purposes of Securities Act Sections 2(a)(10) and 5(c), to be an offer of ABS registered or proposed to be registered under the Securities Act ("Registered Securities") whether or not the Broker/Dealer is or will be a participant in the distribution of the Registered Securities.

The conditions relate to (i) the Broker/Dealer's previous publication or distribution of opinions or recommendations on specified types of ABS collateral; (ii) the sufficiency of public information to provide a basis for the Broker/Dealer's expressed view; (iii) relationships between the Broker/Dealer and a participant in the offering; (iv) whether the Broker/Dealer makes a specific recommendation on a specific ABS of a specific issuer; and (v) whether the Broker/Dealer recommends ABS backed by collateral substantially similar to that backing the Registered Securities.

In addition, the Division stated that more conditions must be met if the Registered Securities have not yet been offered or are part of an unsold allotment or subscription. The Division also stated that, in the case of a multi-tranche offering of ABS, each tranche, as described, is treated as a different Registered Security. Finally, the Division stated that its position may be modified or withdrawn if the Commission or the Division determines that this is necessary or appropriate in the public interest or otherwise in furtherance of the federal securities laws.

B. **Section 3(a)(2) of the Securities Act**

State Street Bank and Trust Company ("State Street") - August 1, 1996

The Division (as well as the Divisions of Investment Management and Market Regulation) addressed State Street's proposal to offer units ("Units") in specified collective trust funds ("Funds") it maintains to plans ("457 Plans") meeting the definition of "eligible deferred compensation plan" in Section 457 of the Internal Revenue Code where specified restrictions are imposed on the ability of employers to withdraw assets from the 457 Plans. The Divisions also addressed past no-action letters as to 457 Plans.

The Division stated that it would not recommend enforcement action if State Street, in reliance on an opinion of counsel that the exemptions under Section 3(a)(2) of the Securities Act and Section 3(a)(12) of the Exchange Act are available, offers Units to 457 Plans without registration under these Acts. The Division of Market Regulation concurred with the Division as to the Exchange Act. The Division of Investment Management stated that it would not recommend enforcement action if State Street offers and sells Units to 457 Plans without registering the Funds as investment companies in reliance on Section 3(c)(11) of the Investment Company Act.

The Divisions noted that they previously had issued a number of no-action letters relating to 457 Plans based largely on the general representation that plan assets would not be used for any purpose other than the exclusive benefit of participants except to the extent that plan assets must remain subject to the claims of general creditors of the employer to preserve the plan's qualification under Section 457. The Divisions also noted, however, that they now believe that this general representation no longer provides an adequate basis for no-action relief without specific additional restrictions on the ability of an employer to withdraw assets similar to those specified by State Street.

An agreement ("Agreement") between State Street and a 457 Plan would, among other things, specifically prohibit an employer from withdrawing 457 Plan assets except for the following purposes: (1) to transfer 457 Plan assets to a trustee in bankruptcy in the event of the employer's insolvency or bankruptcy, or to any other agent independent of the employer authorized to act in such proceedings; (2) to satisfy the claims of the employer's general creditors in the event of the employer's insolvency or bankruptcy; (3) to pay benefits to an employee participating in a 457 Plan; (4) to transfer assets to a 457 Plan's custodian or other person designated by a sponsoring employer in case the Agreement is terminated or a withdrawal is made for the purpose of using another investment manager or investment arrangement; (5) to distribute 457 Plan assets to participating employees in the event a 457 Plan is terminated pursuant to a plan of liquidation; or (6) to reimburse an employer for any 457 Plan benefits that the employer may have paid out of its other assets, or to correct an excess deferral or other mistaken investment in a Fund.

The Divisions concluded that, consequently, the prior no-action letters no longer represent the Divisions' position on enforcement action in the 457 Plan area. The Divisions stated, however, that to facilitate an orderly transition to their current position, they will not recommend enforcement action for a period of 12 months from the date of the response if persons continue to rely on prior letters. Finally, the Divisions took the position that at the end of that period, however, banks and insurance companies wishing to continue including 457 Plans in their collective trust funds or separate accounts should, for new contracts, enter into an agreement similar to the Agreement with the sponsor of each such 457 Plan, and for existing contracts, use reasonable efforts to amend plan documents and/or supporting contracts to conform to the Agreement (or an agreement similar to the Agreement).

C. Section 5 of the Securities Act

Net Roadshow, Inc. ("Net Roadshow") - January 30, 1998

The Division stated that it would not recommend enforcement action if Net Roadshow transmits road shows over its Internet website solely to "qualified institutional buyers" ("QIBS") within the meaning of Securities Act Rule 144A(a)(1) on behalf of a QIB (or person acting on its behalf) that purchases securities from an issuer for resale to other QIBS under Rule 144A ("Seller").

The Division noted counsel's opinion that the activities described would be consistent with Rule 144A(d)(1) and conditioned its position on Net Roadshow's compliance with the following conditions in connection with each road show.

(1) Net Roadshow will deny access to its website for viewing a particular road show (including any notice of the road show posted on Net Roadshow's website) to all but

 (A) New Roadshow's or the Seller's employees or authorized agents for that road show; and

 (B) the institutions for which the Seller has confirmed its reasonable belief regarding their QIB status.

(2) The confidential password assigned to QIBS for a particular road show will be unique to that road show, and will expire no later than the date the related offering terminates.

(3) Each Seller's confirmation to Net Roadshow will include the following:

 (A) a representation that the Seller is a QIB;

 (B) an adequate basis for the Seller's representation of its "reasonable belief" that:

  (i) each entity to which the Seller has assigned a confidential password is a QIB; and

  (ii) the offering to which the particular road show relates is not subject to Securities Act registration.

(4) Net Roadshow otherwise has no actual knowledge or reason to believe, that:

(A) the Seller is not a QIB;

(B) any of the entities to which the Seller has assigned a confidential password is not a QIB; or

(C) the securities offering to which a particular road show relates is subject to Securities Act registration.

(5) Net Roadshow is not an affiliate of any Seller or issuer of a security that is the subject of a particular road show.

Finally, the Division stated that the Commission or staff may reevaluate this no-action position in the future because regulatory responses to legal issues raised by technological developments may evolve.

<u>Internet Capital Corporation. ("ICC") - December 24, 1997</u>

The Division (as well as the Division of Market Regulation) addressed ICC's electronic posting and delivery of prospectuses and other offering materials for unaffiliated issuers.

ICC will provide this service in connection with Securities Act registered offerings, Securities Act Regulation A offerings and SCOR offerings. ICC will not provide this service in connection with offerings under Securities Act Regulation D Rules 505 and 506. For example, as to registered offerings, ICC will post on its website notices that comply with Securities Act Rule 134 and related preliminary prospectuses that comply with Securities Act Rule 430 and final prospectuses.

The Division stated that it would not recommend enforcement action as a result of the electronic posting and delivery. The Division expressly disclaimed providing a view on whether

- ICC, in engaging in the activities described, would be an "underwriter" within the meaning of Securities Act Section 2(a)(11); and

- the prospectus delivery procedures described would satisfy the standards set forth in Securities Act Release Nos. 7233 (October 6, 1995) and/or 7288 (May 9, 1996).

The Division of Market Regulation took the position that it would not recommend enforcement action under Exchange Act Section 15(a) if ICC establishes and operates the described Internet web site without registering as a broker-dealer under Exchange Act Section 15(b).

The Divisions noted that their positions were based in part on the oral representation that no ICC affiliate will do business with an issuer or assist an issuer in connection with the issuer's offering of its securities on ICC's web site. Finally, the Divisions noted that their no-action positions may be reevaluated in the future because regulatory responses to ongoing technological developments may evolve.

The Securities Transfer Association, Inc. - October 24, 1997

The Division took the position that it would not recommend enforcement action if, in reliance on an opinion of counsel that registration under the Securities Act is not required, a bank or issuer uses its Internet Web site in connection with an open-market stock purchase plan ("Plan") as described in the request and without compliance with the Securities Act's registration provisions.

The uses described in the request include the following:

- an issuer places on its Web site a notice of Plan availability and a hypertext link to the bank Plan sponsor's Web site; and
- a bank Plan sponsor places on its Web site a list of issuers for which it sponsors Plans and the related Plan materials.

Brown & Wood LLP - February 7, 1997

The Division addressed the resale by specified holders ("Holders") of securities ("Exchange Capital Securities") acquired in a Securities Act registered exchange offer ("Exchange Offer") for substantially similar privately placed financing trust issued securities ("Capital Securities").

The Division concluded that a Holder may resell the Exchange Capital Securities without compliance with Securities Act registration and delivery requirements where the Holder acquires the Exchange Capital Securities in the ordinary course of its business and has no arrangement or understanding with any person to participate in the distribution of the Exchange Capital Securities.

In reaching this position, the Division particularly noted (1) the described characteristics of the Capital Securities; and (2) the described actions to be taken in connection with the Exchange Offer.

Dissemination of Research Materials Relating to Asset-Backed Securities - February 7, 1997

The Division addressed the publication or distribution by a broker or dealer of information, an opinion or a recommendation as to asset-backed securities. See Section XII.A for a discussion of this letter.

IPONET - July 26, 1996

With respect to public offerings, the Division addressed the application of Securities Act Rule 134 to an electronic coupon or card. The Division stated that the reference in Rule 134(d) to "an enclosed or attached coupon or card, or in some other manner" would be equally applicable to the acceptance of indications of interest via electronic coupon or card as well as paper coupon or card. In this regard, the Division noted the representation that Rule 134(d)'s other requirements will be satisfied in connection with the acceptance of such indications of interest.

The Division also addressed, in the electronic context, the definitions of "general solicitation" and "general advertising" under Securities Act Regulation D Rule 502(c). The Division took the position that the initial qualification of accredited or sophisticated investors by means of a generic questionnaire, followed by the subsequent posting of a notice of a private offering in a password-protected page of IPONET accessible only to IPONET members who previously qualified as accredited investors, would not involve any form of "general solicitation" or "general advertising" within the meaning of Rule 502(c).

In reaching this conclusion, the Division noted that (i) both the invitation to complete the questionnaire used to determine whether an investor is accredited or sophisticated and the questionnaire itself will be generic in nature and will not reference any specific transactions posted or to be posted on the password-protected page of IPONET; (ii) the password-protected page of IPONET will be available to a particular investor only after the supervisor of IPONET has made the determination that the particular potential investor is accredited or sophisticated; and (iii) a potential investor could purchase securities only in transactions that are posted on the password-protected page of IPONET after that investor's qualification with IPONET. In this regard, the Division stated that it took no position as to whether the information obtained by the supervisor is sufficient to form a reasonable basis for believing an investor to be accredited or sophisticated.

Real Goods Trading Corporation (the "Company") - June 24, 1996

The Division (as well as the Divisions of Investment Management and Market Regulation) addressed the Company's proposed trading system ("System") that would provide information about prospective buyers and sellers (the "Participants") of the Company's common stock ("Common Stock"). The Division took the position that the Company's activities in connection with the establishment and maintenance of the System would not require that offers or sales made through the System be registered under the Securities Act. The Division of Investment Management took the position that the Company may engage in the activities specified without registering under the Investment Advisers Act. The Division of Market Regulation took the position that it would not recommend enforcement action under Exchange Act Section 5, 6 or 15 if the Company operates the System in the manner specified without registration as a national securities exchange under Section 6 or as a broker-dealer under Section 15 of the Exchange Act.

In reaching these positions, the Divisions noted that (i) the Company will provide specified notices regarding operation of and participation on the System that will be set forth or contained on the screens and/or hard copy by which System information is provided; (ii) the Company is an Exchange Act Section 12 registrant and will retain that status or, if it should cease to be a Section 12 registrant, otherwise undertake to make publicly available the information required by Exchange Act Section 13(a) in the same manner that Participants will obtain access to the System (e.g., electronic mail, facsimile, mail, the Company's World-Wide Web site, etc.); (iii) the Company will keep records of all quotes entered into the System and make those records available to the Commission and the Pacific Stock Exchange (or any other regulated market on which Company securities are listed) upon reasonable request; (iv) the Company's advertising will comply with specified representations; (v) neither the Company nor any affiliate of the Company will use the System, directly or indirectly, to offer to buy or sell securities, except in compliance with the securities laws, including any applicable registration requirements (absent an available exemption therefrom); and (vi) neither the Company nor any affiliate of the Company will (a) receive any compensation for creating or maintaining the System; (b) receive any compensation for the use of the System; (c) be involved in any purchase or sale negotiations arising from the System; (d) provide information regarding the advisability of buying or selling Common Stock or any other securities; or (e) receive, transfer or hold funds or securities as an incident of operating the System.

D. Rules 144 and 145

Peapod, Inc. ("Peapod") - November 10, 1997

The Division took the position that limited partners of a partnership and the shareholders of its corporate general partner could "tack," under Securities Act Rule 144(d), their holding periods for their limited partnership interests and shares, respectively, onto their holding periods for the shares of Peapod received in a conversion (and, in the case of the general partner's shareholders, the general partner's subsequent liquidation).

In the conversion,

- all the equity interests in the partnership were exchanged for Peapod shares;
- the partnership was dissolved; and
- all of the partnership's assets and liabilities were transferred to Peapod.

In reaching this conclusion, the Division noted in particular specified agreements and their contemplation of the partnership's conversion to corporate form in advance of, and to facilitate, the new corporation's public offering.

Rite Aid Corporation - October 20, 1997

The Division expressed the view that, where securities originally issued in a Securities Act Rule 145(a) transaction are transferred as gifts to third parties by a person Rule 145(c) deems an underwriter, the donees in the transfers who are not the issuer's affiliates may make unregistered public resales of the securities in the same manner and to the same extent as the donor.

Nextel Communications, Inc. - August 19, 1997

The Division stated that, where securities originally issued in a Securities Act Rule 145(a) transaction are privately sold by a person deemed an underwriter by Rule 145(c) (other than an affiliate of the issuer), an unaffiliated purchaser of the securities may make unregistered public resales of the securities to the same extent and in the same manner as the private seller.

First Bank System, Inc. - July 30, 1997

The Division stated that when an affiliate pledgor defaults on a loan that is collateralized by securities that are not "restricted" in the hands of the pledgor, and the pledgee bank forecloses on the pledge, the pledgee bank may sell those securities without regard to the holding period requirement of Securities Act Rule 144.

E. **Regulation D**

Wolf, Block, Schorr and Solis-Cohen - December 11, 1996

The Division stated that a limited liability company, although not specified in the list of organizations in Securities Act Rule 501(a)(3), may be treated as an "accredited investor" as defined in Rule 501(a)(3) if it satisfies the other requirements of that definition.

Royce Exchange Fund ("Fund") - August 28, 1996

The Division stated that a "general solicitation" within the meaning of Rule 502(c) under the Securities Act would not be involved if investors are sought for the Fund in the manner specified from portfolio company related persons, investor advisor clients and placement agent/subplacement agent relationships.

In reaching this conclusion, the Division noted in particular (1) the nature and extent of the pre-existing relationship required between Quest Advisory Corp. ("Quest"), the Fund's manager and investment adviser, and any portfolio companies whose shareholders may be solicited to invest in the Fund, between Quest and its portfolio-company contacts and between the portfolio companies and the specified portfolio company-related persons; and (2) the nature and extent of the pre-existing relationship required between Quest and the registered investment advisers whose clients may be solicited to invest in the Fund and between the registered investment advisers and their clients.

F. **Rule 701**

Princeton Medical Management Resources, Inc. ("Company") - September 12, 1997

The Division stated that non-employee physicians who contract with the Company (a physician practice management service organization that organizes networks of primary care physicians and provides management services to the members of those networks) can be regarded as "consultants or advisors" under Securities Act Rule 701(b)(1). The Division also stated that, as is customary, it expressed no opinion on the exempt status of transactions to be effected under the rule.

G. **Section 18(b)(4)(A) of the Securities Act**

David M. Katz, Esq. - April 24, 1997

The Division addressed one of the definitions of "covered security" provided by Securities Act Section 18(b). Section 18(b)(4)(A) states that a security is a "covered security" as to a transaction that is exempt from Securities Act registration under Securities Act Section 4(1) or 4(3), provided that the issuer "files reports" with the Commission under Exchange Act Section 13 or 15(d). The Division stated that an issuer "files reports" for purposes of Section 18(b)(4)(A) if it has completed a registered initial public offering under the Securities Act, but has not yet been required to file any reports under Section 13 or 15(d).

H. Securities Act Forms

Ropes & Gray - October 30, 1997

The Division stated that post-effective amendments to deregister unsold shares are not required in fee transfers from Securities Act registration forms other than Form S-8 or in fee transfers from Form S-8 solely of fees paid pursuant to Rule 457(h)(3) with respect to additional securities offered for resale.

The Division also stated that the filing of the Securities Act registration statement to which the fee is transferred is deemed to deregister the unsold shares for which the transferred fee originally was paid.

Finally, the Division stated that registrants who wish to transfer Securities Act registration fees also should consult the Rule 429 interpretations in the latest version of the Division of Corporation Finance Manual of Publicly Available Telephone Interpretations, which is available on the Commission's Internet web site (http://www.sec.gov), and Securities Act Rel. 7168 (May 11, 1995).

The Bond Market Association - October 16, 1997

The Division provided its views on the availability of Securities Act Form S-3 to asset-backed securities.

The Division stated that an asset-backed security will not fail to meet the definition of "asset-backed security" in Form S-3, General Instruction I.B.5, solely because the security is supported by assets having total delinquencies (as described in the request) of up to 20% at the time of the proposed offering.

The Division also stated that, regardless of whether an asset-backed security meets the definition of "asset-backed security" in General Instruction I.B.5, the security may nevertheless be eligible for registration on Form S-3 as long as the issuer satisfies General Instruction I.A.'s registrant requirements and General Instruction I.B.2.'s transaction requirements.

Use of Form S-3 for Transferred Options - August 7, 1997

The Division addressed the use of Securities Act Form S-3 to register shares underlying options ("Transferred Options") issued in employee benefit plans that have been transferred by gift from employees to their immediate family members, trusts for the benefit of the employee's immediate family members, or partnerships and corporations whose sole equity owners are the employee's immediate family members. The shares underlying the Transferred Options would be eligible for registration on Form S-8 but for the transfer. Exchange Act Rule 16a-1(e) defines "immediate family," as used here, as any child, stepchild, grandchild, parent, stepparent, grandparent, spouse, sibling, mother-in-law, father-in-law, son-in-law, daughter-in-law, brother-in-law or sister-in-law, including adoptive relationships.

The Division took the view that:

(1) Transferred Options are "transferable warrants" for purposes of Form S-3 General Instruction I.B.4. (which makes Form S-3 available for the exercise of transferable warrants);

(2) Like shares registrable on Form S-8, shares underlying a Transferred Option may be registered on Form S-3 for sale to the persons described above at any time before the Transferred Option is exercised, without regard to when the Transferred Option becomes exercisable; and

(3) Securities Act Rule 429(b) may be used to transfer from Form S-8 to Form S-3 that portion of the Securities Act registration fee that relates to shares, previously registered on Form S-8, that underlie Transferred Options, provided that the Form S-8 subsequently is post-effectively amended to deregister shares for which the fee is transferred. See also Ropes & Gray, October 30, 1997, above.

Merrill Lynch & Co., Inc. (the "Company") - May 16, 1996

The Division stated that it would not object if the Company uses Form S-8 under the Securities Act in connection with exercises of transferable stock options ("Transferable Stock Options") subject to specified transfer restrictions by former employees and by executors, administrators and beneficiaries of estates of employees or former employees, provided that the Transferable Stock Options being exercised have never been transferred by the original grantees and are only exercisable by executors, administrators and beneficiaries of their estates due to such grantees' deaths.

In reaching this position, the Division noted in particular that a Transferable Stock Option is not transferable by any person other than the original grantee or the estate of the original grantee (which is permitted to transfer such Transferable Stock Option only to the beneficiaries of such estate).

I. Proxy Rules

Merrill Lynch, Pierce, Fenner & Smith Incorporated ("Company") - October 24, 1997

The Division took the position that it would not recommend enforcement action if the Company prepares and disseminates research reports in accordance with Securities Act Rule 138 or 139 in connection with registered securities transactions, without compliance with the filing, disclosure and dissemination requirements of the proxy rules under Exchange Act Section 14(a).

The Division stated that its position was conditioned on the research report referring, as required by law or applicable rules, to any relationship that may exist between the Company, as issuer of a particular research report, and any participant in a relevant proxy solicitation. The Division also stated that its position did not address the applicability of the federal securities laws' anti-fraud provisions to the activities described in the request.

Finally, the Division stated that it may re-evaluate its no-action position in the future because the request raises issues in an evolving area of the federal securities laws.

J. **Section 16 Rules**

Peter J. Kight - October 16, 1997

The Division addressed the application of Exchange Act Section 16 to transactions involving an irrevocable grantor retained annuity trust ("GRAT").

A grantor ("Grantor"), subject to Section 16 because an officer of a company ("Company") with common stock registered under Exchange Act Section 12, proposes to create a GRAT for estate planning purposes. Grantor proposes to transfer ("Transfer") to the GRAT shares of Company common stock Grantor now owns ("Shares") that constitute less than ten percent of the Company's outstanding common stock.

The GRAT will make a series of fixed annuity payments ("Annuity Payments") to Grantor, payable in either cash or Shares, over a specified time period ("Annuity Period"). During the Annuity Period, Grantor is the GRAT's trustee and beneficiary. After the Annuity Period, Grantor's minor children who share Grantor's household ("Children") are the GRAT's beneficiaries. The dollar amount of the Annuity Payments is established at the time of the Transfer. The present value of the Annuity Payments does not exceed the fair market value of the Shares at the time of the Transfer.

The Division took the position that Rule 16a-13 (exempting changes in form of ownership from Section 16) applies to the Transfer and any Annuity Payments paid in Shares. The Division stated that other transactions in the Shares by the GRAT during the Annuity Period are considered the Grantor's transactions. The Division also stated that the Annuity Period's termination effects a gift of Shares to the Children eligible both for exemption under Rule 16b-5 (exempting bona fide gifts from Section 16(b)) and deferred reporting on Form 5. Finally, the Division stated that after the Annuity Period ends, under Rule 16a-1(a)(2)(ii)(A) Grantor continues to report the Shares the Children hold as beneficially owned by Grantor as long as the Children share Grantor's household.

American Express Company ("Company") - February 26, 1997

The Division stated that persons ("Insiders") subject to Exchange Act Section 16 may report in Table II on Form 5 (or earlier on Form 4) on an aggregate basis Company phantom stock acquired from the Company where the Insiders had no control over the time or amount acquired.

American Bar Association - December 20, 1996

The Division expressed its views regarding: (1) timing standards for the determination of Non-Employee Director status under Rules 16b-3(b)(3)(i)(B), (C) and (D); (2) exclusion from the Rule 16b-3(b)(1) definition of Discretionary Transaction for cash settlement of certain derivative securities; (3) application to Internal Revenue Code Section 401(a)(9) transactions of the Rule 16b-3(b)(1)(iii) exclusion from the definition of Discretionary Transaction; (4) application of the Note 3 specific approval standards to subsequent transactions pursuant to cash settlement of derivative securities, single-fund deferral plans and multi-fund deferral plans; (5) reporting requirements applicable to transactions in phantom stock units; and (6) scope of the Rule 16a-12 exemption for transactions pursuant to domestic relations orders.

American Society of Corporate Secretaries - December 11, 1996

The Division expressed its views regarding: (1) use of a subcommittee to satisfy the Non-Employee Director approval conditions of Rules 16b-3(d) and (e); (2) application of Rule 16b-3(e) to exercise and tax withholding rights that were granted under former Rule 16b-3; (3) exemptive conditions applicable to repayment of a loan into an issuer equity securities fund; (4) plans within the scope of the Rule 16b-3(c) exemption for tax-conditioned plans; (5) application of the Regulation S-K Item 404(a) and (b) standards to the tests for Non-Employee Director status under Rules 16b-3(b)(3)(i)(C) and (D); (6) termination of the Rule 16b-3(d)(3) six-month holding period following death of the insider; (7) application to Internal Revenue Code Section 401(a)(28) transactions of the Rule 16b-3(b)(1)(iii) exclusion from the definition of Discretionary Transaction; and (8) application of the Note 3 specific approval standards to plans that allow directors' fees to be received in stock rather than in cash.

NOTES

4

NASAA INTERNET RELATED RESOLUTIONS

submitted by NASAA

NASAA RESOLUTION

WHEREAS, capital formation and the methods by which issuers seek to raise capital have evolved over time: and

WHEREAS, the Internet, or the World Wide Web. or similar proprietary or common carrier electronic systems (hereinafter collectively referred to as the "Internet") have facilitated greatly the ability to communicate with a large number of persons: and

WHEREAS, the North American Securities Administrators Association (NASAA) has recognized that offers of securities have been, and will continue to be made on the Internet, and has created a committee to address the issues raised thereby; and

WHEREAS, it is appropriate for state securities regulators to develop a uniform policy concerning offers of securities on the Internet that is consistent with the goals of investor protection and access to capital markets; and

WHEREAS, a communication made on the Internet is directed generally to anyone who has access to the Internet; and

WHEREAS, a communication designed to raise capital and that is placed on the Internet may be construed as an offer of securities (Internet Offer); and

NOW THEREFORE, be it resolved that:

1. NASAA will develop a pilot program to monitor Internet Offers and subsequent sales resulting from such offers.
2. NASAA encourages States to take appropriate steps to exempt Internet Offers from the registration provisions of their securities laws where the following conditions apply:
   - A. The Internet Offer indicates. directly or indirectly, that the securities are not being offered to the residents of a particular state; and
   - B. An offer is not otherwise specifically directed to any person in a state by, or on behalf of an the issuer of securities.
3. NASAA encourages States to take appropriate steps that would allow sales of securities that were the subject of an Internet Offer where the following conditions apply:
   - A. No sales of the securities shall be made in any state until the offering has been registered and declared effective and the final prospectus or Form U-7 has been delivered to the investor prior to such sale; or
   - B. The sales are exempt from registration.

Adopted January 7, 1996 in Hilton Head, South Carolina.

MODEL ACCREDITED INVESTOR EXEMPTION
Adopted 4/27/97

Any offer or sale of a security by an issuer in a transaction that meets the requirements of this rule is exempted from [Sections requiring registration and filing of advertising materials].

(A) Sales of securities shall be made only to persons who are or the issuer reasonably believes are accredited investors. "Accredited investor" is defined in 17 CFR 230.501(a) [amendment or successor rule][some states may elect to include the entire text of SEC Rule 501(a) in lieu of an incorporation by reference].

(B) The exemption is not available to an issuer that is in the development stage that either has no specific business plan or purpose or has indicated that its business plan is to engage in a merger or acquisition with an unidentified company or companies, or other entity or person.

(C) The issuer reasonably believes that all purchasers are purchasing for investment and not with the view to or for sale in connection with a distribution of the security. Any resale of a security sold in reliance on this exemption within 12 months of sale shall be presumed to be with a view to distribution and not for investment, except a resale pursuant to a registration statement effective under sections [insert registration sections] or to an accredited investor pursuant to an exemption available under [state securities act].

(D) (1) The exemption is not available to an issuer if the issuer, any of the issuer's predecessors, any affiliated issuer, any of the issuer's directors, officers, general partners, beneficial owners of 10% or more of any class of its equity securities, any of the issuer's promoters presently connected with the issuer in any capacity, any underwriter of the securities to be offered, or any partner, director or officer of such underwriter:

(a) within the last five years, has filed a registration statement which is the subject of a currently effective registration stop order entered by any state securities administrator or the United States Securities and Exchange Commission;

(b) within the last five years, has been convicted of any criminal offense in connection with the offer, purchase or sale of any security, or involving fraud or deceit;

(c) is currently subject to any state or federal administrative enforcement order or judgment, entered within the last five years, finding fraud or deceit in connection with the purchase or sale of any security; or

(d) is currently subject to any order, judgment or decree of any court of competent jurisdiction, entered within the last five years, temporarily, preliminary or permanently restraining or enjoining such party from engaging in or continuing to engage in any conduct or practice involving fraud or deceit in connection with the purchase or sale of any security.

(2) Subparagraph (D)(1) shall not apply if:

(a) the party subject to the disqualification is licensed or registered to conduct securities related business in the state in which the order, judgment or decree creating the disqualification was entered against such party;

(b) before the first offer under this exemption, the state securities administrator, or the court or regulatory authority that entered the order, judgment, or decree, waives the disqualification; or

(c) the issuer establishes that it did not know and in the exercise of reasonable care, based on a factual inquiry, could not have known that a disqualification existed under this paragraph.

(E) (1) A general announcement of the proposed offering may be made by any means.

(2) The general announcement shall include only the following information, unless additional information is specifically permitted by the [Administrator]:

(a) The name, address and telephone number of the issuer of the securities;

(b) The name, a brief description and price (if known) of any security to be issued;

(c) A brief description of the business of the issuer in 25 words or less;

(d) The type, number and aggregate amount of securities being offered;

(e) The name, address and telephone number of the person to contact for additional information; and

(f) A statement that:
(i) sales will only be made to accredited investors;

(ii) no money or other consideration is being solicited or will be accepted by way of this general announcement; and

(iii) the securities have not been registered with or approved by any state securities agency or the U.S. Securities and Exchange Commission and are being offered and sold pursuant to an exemption from registration.

(F) The issuer, in connection with an offer, may provide information in addition to the general announcement under paragraph (E), if such information:

(1) is delivered through an electronic database that is restricted to persons who have been pre-qualified as accredited investors; or

(2) is delivered after the issuer reasonably believes that the prospective purchaser is an accredited investor.

(G) No telephone solicitation shall be permitted unless prior to placing the call, the issuer reasonably believes that the prospective purchaser to be solicited is an accredited investor.

(H) Dissemination of the general announcement of the proposed offering to persons who are not accredited investors shall not disqualify the issuer from claiming the exemption under this rule.

(I) The issuer shall file with the [Commission/Division] a notice of transaction, a consent to service of process, a copy of the general announcement, and a [$fee/fee language] within 15 days after the first sale in this state.]

INTERPRETIVE ORDER
CONCERNING BROKER-DEALERS, INVESTMENT ADVISERS, BROKER-DEALER AGENTS AND INVESTMENT ADVISER REPRESENTATIVES USING THE INTERNET FOR GENERAL DISSEMINATION OF INFORMATION ON PRODUCTS AND SERVICES

Adopted April 27, 1997

WHEREAS the [Administrator] (the "Administrator") is charged with the administration of [name of state securities act], the (Jurisdiction's) Uniform Securities Act (the "Act") and Sections 000, et seq. of the Regulations of the Jurisdiction promulgated under the Act;

WHEREAS, at Section 412(a) of the Act, it is provided, in part, that "[t]he [Administrator] may from time to time make, amend and rescind such ... orders as necessary to carry out the provisions of this act ...;"

WHEREAS, at Section 201(a) of the Act, it is provided "[i]t is unlawful for any person to transact business in this state as a broker-dealer or agent unless he is registered under this act...;"

WHEREAS, at Section 201(c) of the Act, it is further provided "[i]t is unlawful for any person to transact business in this state as an investment adviser unless ... he is so registered under this act...;" [Note: may also insert similar provision governing investment adviser agents/representatives]

WHEREAS the [Administrator] acknowledges that the Internet, the World Wide Web, and similar proprietary or common carrier electronic systems (collectively, the "Internet") have facilitated greatly the ability of broker-dealers, investment advisers, broker-dealer agents and investment adviser agents/representatives to advertise and otherwise disseminate information on products and services to prospective customers and clients;

WHEREAS the [Administrator] also acknowledges that certain communications made on the Internet are directed generally to anyone having access to the Internet and may be transmitted through postings on Bulletin Boards, displays on "Home Pages" or similar methods (hereinafter, "Internet Communications");

WHEREAS the [Administrator] further acknowledges that in certain instances, by distributing information on available products and services through Internet Communications available to persons in this state, broker-dealers, investment advisers, their broker-dealer agents and their investment adviser agents/representatives could be construed as "transacting business" for purposes of Sections 201(a) and 201(c) of the Act so as to require registration in this state, since the Internet Communications would be received in this state regardless of the intent of the person originating such communication; and

WHEREAS the [Administrator] finds that the issuance of this Order is necessary and appropriate in the public interest and for the protection of investors and consistent with the purposes fairly intended by the policy and provisions of the Act;

NOW THEREFORE, IT IS HEREBY ORDERED as follows:

1. Broker-dealers, investment advisers, broker-dealer agents (hereinafter "BD agents") and investment adviser agents/representatives (hereinafter "IA reps") who use the Internet, the World Wide Web, and similar proprietary or common carrier electronic systems (collectively, hereinafter the "Internet") to distribute information on available products and services through certain communications made on the Internet directed generally to anyone having access to the Internet, and transmitted through postings on Bulletin Boards, displays on "Home Pages" or similar methods (hereinafter, "Internet Communications") shall not be deemed to be "transacting business" in this state for purposes of Sections 201(a) and 201(c) of the Act based solely on that fact if the following conditions are observed:

   A. The Internet Communication contains a legend in which it is clearly stated that

      (1) the broker-dealer, investment adviser, BD agent or IA rep in question may only transact business in this state if first registered, excluded or exempted from state broker-dealer, investment adviser, BD agent or IA rep registration requirements, as may be; and

      (2) follow-up, individualized responses to persons in this state by such broker-dealer, investment adviser, BD agent or IA rep that involve either the effecting or attempting to effect transactions in securities, or the rendering of personalized investment advice for compensation, as may be, will not be made absent compliance with state broker-dealer, investment adviser, BD agent or IA rep registration requirements, or an applicable exemption or exclusion;

   B. The Internet Communication contains a mechanism, including and without limitation, technical "firewalls" or other implemented policies and procedures, designed reasonably to ensure that prior to any subsequent, direct communication with prospective customers or clients in this state, said broker-dealer, investment adviser, BD agent or IA rep is first registered in this state or qualifies for an exemption or exclusion from such requirement. Nothing in this paragraph shall be construed to relieve a state registered broker-dealer, investment adviser, BD agent or IA rep from any applicable securities registration requirement in this state;

C. The Internet Communication does not involve either effecting or attempting to effect transactions in securities, or the rendering of personalized investment advice for compensation, as may be, in this state over the Internet, but is limited to the dissemination of general information on products and services; and

D. In the case of a BD agent or IA rep:

(1) the affiliation with the broker-dealer or investment adviser of the BD agent or IA rep is prominently disclosed within the Internet Communication;

(2) the broker-dealer or investment adviser with whom the BD agent or IA rep is associated retains responsibility for reviewing and approving the content of any Internet Communication by a BD agent or IA rep;

(3) the broker-dealer or investment adviser with whom the BD agent or IA rep is associated first authorizes the distribution of information on the particular products and services through the Internet Communication; and

(4) in disseminating information through the Internet Communication, the BD agent or IA rep acts within the scope of the authority granted by the broker-dealer or investment adviser;

2. The position expressed in this Interpretive Order extends to state broker-dealer, investment adviser, BD agent and IA rep registration requirements only, and does not excuse compliance with applicable securities registration, antifraud or related provisions;

3. Nothing in this Order shall be construed to affect the activities of any broker-dealer, investment adviser, BD agent and IA rep engaged in business in this state that is not subject to the jurisdiction of the Administrator as a result of the National Securities Markets Improvements Act of 1996, as amended; and

4. This Order shall remain in effect unless and until subsequently amended or rescinded.

So ordered at (city, state) this _____ day of
________________________________, 1997

____
(name)
(title)

NOTES

5

EXHIBIT A

CORPORATION FINANCE IN THE INFORMATION AGE,

Remarks by Arthur Levitt,
Chairman, U.S. Securities and
Exchange Commission

"CORPORATE FINANCE IN THE INFORMATION AGE"

REMARKS BY

ARTHUR LEVITT, CHAIRMAN
U.S. SECURITIES AND EXCHANGE COMMISSION

SECURITIES REGULATION INSTITUTE
SAN DIEGO, CALIFORNIA

JANUARY 23, 1997

U.S. SECURITIES AND EXCHANGE COMMISSION
450 Fifth Street, N.W.
Washington, D.C. 20549

Check against delivery

REMARKS BY CHAIRMAN ARTHUR LEVITT
UNITED STATES SECURITIES AND EXCHANGE COMMISSION
SECURITIES REGULATION INSTITUTE
SAN DIEGO, CALIFORNIA -- JANUARY 23, 1997

I want to talk to you today about the very heart of our system of securities regulation -- the offering process, and how we might improve it.

The Securities Act governs the way companies communicate with investors when they want to raise money. It was written in 1933.

The first transatlantic phone call had been placed just a few years before.

The first talking motion picture had been produced.

The radio and the telephone were the front line of communications technology.

The diesel locomotive had recently been introduced.

We live in a very different world today.

Jets can transport us virtually anywhere on the face of the earth within the span of a single day.

The amount of information available to the average investor is enormous -- television, radio, wire services, newspapers, magazines, personal computers, FAX machines, on-line services, and the Internet saturate our waking hours with information.

Our financial markets are now global -- capital and information flow across borders almost instantaneously.

In addition to stocks and bonds, new and complicated financial instruments have been developed, whose value can change many times faster than the market itself.

Each of these late-20th century developments has come up against, and clashed with, a communications framework that was conceived in 1933.

The `33 Act erected barriers to conveying information beyond that contained in the prospectus. In 1933, that was difficult; in 1997, it is impossible.

And so we live in a world in which some executives believe that corporate communications must come to a standstill during an offering -- even to the point where they cannot say a word in response to negative articles in the press.

A world in which offerings that are permitted offshore become part of a global communications network that could bring news of these offerings back onshore, where they are forbidden.

A world in which the rules are different for private offerings, but vast communications networks leave few things truly "private."

A world in which the primary source of offering information is the prospectus, which in many cases reaches investors only after they've parted with their money.

A world in which the SEC's EDGAR system puts prospectuses up on the Internet faster than they reach investors through the US mail.

As you know, these problems did not suddenly appear in the 1990s. Many intelligent people have anticipated them, understood them, and tried to solve them over the decades.

In 1939, SEC Chairman William O. Douglas wrote that it should be possible someday to consolidate the reporting requirements imposed by the various securities laws. In trying to explain why, almost a half-century later, that day had not quite arrived, Harvard University Professor Louis Loss resorted to an elliptical phrase by a German poet, that "the mills of God grind slowly."

While I am personally reluctant to lay the entire blame on God, it's true that the process has moved slowly. Professor Loss knew this from personal experience -- he served as Reporter of The American Law Institute during a decade-long effort to produce an integrated Federal Securities Code. Just two years earlier, in 1966, Milton Cohen had laid the groundwork for such a project in a seminal article in the *Harvard Law Review*.

Two years after the new code was assembled and approved by the ALI membership, the proposal received the SEC's endorsement . . . only to disappear in the corridors of Congress in early 1981.

Several of the ideals embodied in that legislative proposal lived on, however, giving rise to such developments as the integrated disclosure system of 1982, which also brought the advance of "shelf" registration.

I've followed these attempts to modernize the `33 Act with interest through much of my career, and I've discussed with many of you how best to weigh the advantages of change with the stability of tradition. Some counsel caution, prudence -- an almost monastic reverence for a law as sacred as the tablets handed down from Mt. Sinai Others have urged a top-to-bottom re-examination of legislation that is outmoded, and largely irrelevant to a world of exotic investment instruments, globalized markets, and a dazzling array of communications technologies. I've approached the issue not as a scholar or a lawyer, but as a businessman who has experienced SEC regulation and prospered -- sometimes because of it, and sometimes in spite of it. I know from that experience that we can do better.

I recognize that this is a complex area of the law. The key questions demand answers, but defy easy answers. Indeed, it is only after 3½ years of being an active participant in this dialogue that I find myself in a position to begin to address some of these issues.

In the course of those years, I have asked two panels to study different aspects of US capital formation in some detail. In 1995, I created a Task Force on Disclosure Simplification and asked it to examine every single SEC rule related to corporation finance, with a view toward simplifying the regulatory structure. Its March 1996 report recommended that we eliminate or modify fully a quarter of the rules and half the forms; we've already done away with 44 rules and 4 forms, and more will disappear shortly.

The Advisory Committee on Capital Formation and Regulatory Processes, ably chaired by Commissioner Steve Wallman, had a broader mandate: I charged it to study different models for the offering process. In the area of corporate finance, few Commissioners in recent history have been as creative and focused as Steve Wallman, who I believe will be long remembered for the scope of his intellect and his dedication to change. In July 1996, the Wallman Committee proposed a system that would register not transactions, but companies, and rely on periodic disclosure more than a prospectus. This scheme would apply to larger companies, to begin with. The Commission immediately asked for comments not only on that model, but also on other ways to modernize regulation of the offering process.

Several months later, however, the earth shifted under our feet: last October, President Clinton signed the National Securities Markets Improvement Act, far-reaching legislation designed to update the law in several important ways. Among other changes, Congress granted us broad exemptive authority under the Securities Act of 1933.

Taken together, these events offer an almost unique opportunity for change.

This is the first Commission in history to hold exemptive authority from the '33 Act in its hands. A new vista of possibilities has opened up.

Among the new models proposed is one from a committee of the American Bar Association. As I understand it, this system would eliminate all restrictions on offering communications -- whatever restrictions remained would apply only to sales, and would not mandate use of a prospectus for most offerings. The proposal would also eliminate much of the distinction between public and private offerings. And it would apply to large and small companies.

Other commenters think we're focused on the wrong thing completely -- they believe that most of the problems with the existing system can be solved by revisiting the liability provisions under the federal securities laws.

Still others have come to us with laundry lists of things they would revise or eliminate, as if the candy store has now been opened after 64 years of waiting. Although we're in no mind to give away the store, I am open to change -- so long as it does not compromise investor protection.

Our challenge is huge: it is to rethink the way we permit companies to communicate with investors.

I haven't pre-judged any of the proposals, and I'm not prepared to pass judgement on them today. But I will share with you my vision of the result we desire -- my notion of the end we wish to achieve, whatever the means we decide to use to get there.

American investors deserve a market in which the theory of the regulator matches the reality of the regulated; in which the media anticipated by the law are the same media used in real life; in which there is no gap between the way the SEC allows investors to receive information, and the way in which investors actually do receive information.

The offering model we end up with should be flexible enough that it does not need to be rewired with each new advance in communications -- such as Internet TV, for example, which is right around the corner.

This is really just common sense -- and, as I noted, we have no monopoly on wisdom -- people have been talking about these questions for many decades now. Technology changes, but the underlying issues remain the same. Commissioner Wallman is the latest in a series of thoughtful and insightful students of the offering process. While we may not all agree on every detail of what a new process would look like, I believe we do agree that there's never been a greater need, or a better opportunity, to make significant changes.

Whatever the eventual decision -- whether we keep the

current system, switch to a form of company registration, tune up the `33 Act, or some other solution as yet unseen -- we should not wait until we've found the Holy Grail to begin taking action. There are many steps we can take right now to better match the theory of investor communications with the reality of investor communications. It's never too early to apply common sense.

I see three main areas of improvement in the offering process that are within our grasp today: more timely and useful disclosure for investors; more rational regulation for companies; and greater use of developing technologies. Let me sketch out a few thoughts in each area:

<u>More timely and useful disclosure for investors</u>

The Wallman Committee advised that we should not blindly enact a series of deregulatory changes without closely considering what investor disclosure enhancements may be needed. I agree.

Much of the disclosure debate centers on the prospectus. Unfortunately, the statutory prospectus is typically delivered after investors part with their money, and is often written in a manner that makes it inaccessible to many.

In many cases, the problem is not a lack of information; quite the opposite. Too much information can be as much a problem as too little. <u>More</u> disclosure does not always mean <u>better</u> disclosure.

I believe investors would be better served by essential information that arrives <u>before</u> they are asked to commit to a purchase. Whether this would be a preliminary prospectus, a summary, or perhaps, for certain securities, merely a "term sheet" -- it would be easy to read and easy to deliver instantly and electronically, perhaps along with the company's latest periodic reports. Were we to make substantial progress in providing investors with essential information in advance of their purchase decisions, we might then be able to revisit the question of whether and when companies have to put a final prospectus into the hands of investors.

I am also intrigued by the notion, put forward by the Wallman Committee, of broadening the field of material events companies are required to report under Form 8-K. It's a safe bet that investors want to know about such events as the resignation or termination of top executives, or default by the company on its corporate debt.

Perhaps it is also time for the Commission to take a page from foreign regulators and think about replacing the 8-K list of events with a simple requirement that companies report significant changes when they occur.

In addition to communicating vital information more clearly and more quickly, we should also re-examine the **content of disclosure documents.** One area that is ripe for improvement is the forward-looking disclosure provided by companies. Analysts typically get this information in conference calls with senior management; other investors rarely have such an opportunity. When asked to explain this uneven disclosure, companies cite a fear of liability for so-called "soft" information.

Congress responded by enacting the Private Securities Litigation Reform Act of 1995. The SEC staff has since been reviewing the quality of forward-looking disclosures, to see if practices have improved. I am sorry to report that they have not. In fact, rather than taking advantage of the new safe harbor to communicate forecasts more clearly, companies are using even more boilerplate, in the form of cautionary language.

It appears that the legal requirements of the safe harbor are being "over-lawyered." There's been a call for greater guidance from the SEC. One of the most common questions has to do with the requirement for meaningful cautionary statements that identify important factors that might cause the actual results to vary. For the moment, let me just say that it is not "meaningful" to provide only a generic laundry list of possible risks. Good cautionary language should provide the reader with disclosure through the eyes of management, not litigation counsel. If you would tell the board of directors that you expect a new product to be available as of a certain date, what would you tell them at the same time to protect yourself if the target is not met? In meeting the target, what are you most worried about at the time? Your board wouldn't want a boilerplate list of risks; investors don't want it, either.

There's one other way to improve disclosure fairly quickly, and that is **in its presentation.** Impenetrable prospectuses undermine the purposes of the federal securities laws. Disclosure is not disclosure if it does not communicate.

The time has come to pierce the shroud of jargon and boilerplate surrounding the prospectus. We recently established a pilot program in the Division of Corporation Finance offering expedited review to companies that wrote their prospectuses in plain English. Already we have had dozens of volunteers, including household names like Bell Atlantic, NYNEX, ITT, and GE Capital. And less than two weeks ago, the Commission proposed new plain English requirements for prospectuses that derived from the Task Force report.

More rational regulation of companies

It turns out that investors are not the only ones who are confused today -- certain concepts of the federal securities laws have come to be known among practitioners as "Metaphysics," because of the complexities and fine distinctions that they involve. That doesn't strike me as a healthy state of affairs.

One way to improve this is for the SEC to provide more guidance. I commit to you today that the Commission will endeavor to write clearer and simpler rules, and provide better insight into our analysis of issues.

Two areas in particular cry out for common sense. The first involves **distinctions between public and private offerings**. For valid reasons the SEC has prevented companies from transferring from a private offering to a registered public offering, and vice versa. But our positions have sometimes impeded valid attempts to raise capital.

The time has come to consider removing some of these barriers. I believe we should be encouraging the public disclosure and investor protections that accompany a registered offering. Likewise, if market conditions should change and threaten a public offering, I think it would be unfortunate to send a company away empty-handed when there are sophisticated investors available who would purchase securities in a private transaction. We are developing proposals to allow this.

I alluded earlier to the **"quiet period"** as another area of uncertainty for companies. It should be made clear that the quiet period does not chill company communication in the ordinary course of business.

If I were to make changes, I would shorten the quiet period to a specified brief time before filing a registration statement. If something is said well in <u>advance</u> of a public offering, it's hard to argue that someone is conditioning the market. If it is said <u>after</u> a registration statement is filed, the investor has the prospectus, and perhaps a wealth of other public information available to put things in adequate context.

During the newly defined quiet period, a company would still be able to discuss a proposed offering, but in a limited way. Communications that do not mention an offering would be free of restrictions, other than the applicable state or federal anti-fraud rules.

In the course of the recent debate over ways to modernize the Securities Act, one thing has really surprised me: the few voices speaking up on behalf of **small business**. And yet, their cost of capital is high and they would reap the biggest benefits from regulatory relief.

Certainly we should adopt some of the small business suggestions of the Task Force on Disclosure Simplification, as well as a shorter holding period under Rule 144 -- which I expect to accomplish in the next few weeks. We should consider making it easier for small companies to advertise for qualified investors without triggering a registration requirement; we should permit some form of "testing the waters" in more offerings; and we should allow small businesses to have some of the timing advantages of shelf registration.

I don't want to make any of this sound too easy; as always, the devil is in the details. But I believe that we can and should make progress in these and other areas soon.

Greater use of technology

I'll close with a subject that has been much discussed in the past year: the opportunities raised by the advances in technology. I've already mentioned electronic delivery of information to investors either directly or indirectly, and the SEC has issued guidance about how such delivery complies with the federal securities laws. I have to say I'm surprised that Wall Street has not responded more quickly to electronic delivery opportunities.

Few sectors of our economy use technology in more sophisticated ways than the securities industry. But somehow, that technology hasn't yet been harnessed to delivering prospectuses to customers. I recognize the problems in drafting such documents on time, especially in a world of three-day settlement. But it seems to me that electronic delivery can only help. I call upon the industry to take better advantage of this opportunity.

At the same time, the SEC is getting its own virtual house in better order. Our EDGAR system is one of the more successful government computer projects. But in today's world where eight-month-old technology can become obsolete, it is no surprise that eight-year-old EDGAR needs to be modernized. The technology is now at hand to make EDGAR more user-friendly.

I envision a new EDGAR with enhanced graphics capabilities to accept charts and photos; an EDGAR that accommodates different word processors; an EDGAR that can accomplish tasks at the click of a mouse. The first round of bids on the new EDGAR contract is due soon, so it should not be long before we start work on a new system.

One of our key technology issues today, as you know, is the offering of securities on the Internet. A number of small US businesses have begun to do so. But some foreign companies are concerned about describing their securities on their Web page, because US investors might view the foreign home pages, possibly triggering the registration requirements of our securities laws.

If foreign companies are selling securities to US investors

publicly via the Internet, they need to register with the SEC. I've worked hard to encourage foreign companies to list here -- a record 870 companies now do so. But that's not enough. There is an urgent need to develop a set of high-quality international accounting standards, so that US investors know they are protected even when they invest overseas. We are working closely with the appropriate international bodies to attain this goal -- but, like our predecessors on the Commission, we will not compromise rigorous standards and an effective, independent standard-setter to protect US investors.

One other current area of confusion for foreign companies arises when they are selling offshore, but want to sell privately to a limited number of US institutional buyers. In those cases, we would look for a clear indication that the foreign company is not interested in attracting U.S. public investors -- such as a warning that the securities are not registered in the US and are not being offered to the general public here.

It's not my intention to answer every problem related to cross-border capital in this speech, but merely to signal an openness to new ideas about solutions. I have asked the staff to provide more definitive guidance or create a safe harbor, as needed, to help foreign issuers who are trying to do the right thing.

Conclusion

The events of the past year have given us a rare opportunity to improve the offering process for both investors and companies.

At times like these, the initial reaction is sometimes to scrap the old system. Yet even the most zealous revolutionary would have to agree that the capital formation system in the US is working fairly well -- we have the deepest, most liquid and transparent financial markets in the world.

In 1934, businesses raised $641 million in our capital markets; in 1984, $126.8 billion; and last year, that figure was well over a trillion dollars. The total turnover on our stock market in 1995 was $5.1 trillion; the next largest market, Japan, had $1.2 trillion.

It would be foolish to throw the system that produced those results out the window, in the name of modernization.

But it would be equally foolish to deny that there is room for improvement, or to resist change in the name of our current success.

We have the most productive system of capital formation in history, and the market has reached record heights. Change can be disruptive under those circumstances. But we became preeminent as a nation not by resisting change, but by embracing it.

Change has always been the hallmark of our markets, and the SEC has succeeded by recognizing that fact and responding to it. That's why we will keep this debate moving forward in the weeks and months ahead -- until the theory of disclosure matches the realities of the marketplace in the age of information.

# # #

EXHIBIT B

SEC NO-ACTION LETTER, PRIVATE FINANCIAL NETWORK (MARCH 1997)

, Private Financial Network

Company: Private Financial Network

Public Availability Date: March 12, 1997

WSB File No. 031097020

Fiche Locator No. 2729F6

WSB Subject Category: 032

Reference:
Securities Act of 1933, Section 2(10)

INQUIRY LETTER
WILMER, CUTLER & PICKERING
2445 M STREET N W
WASHINGTON, D C 20037-1420
TELEPHONE(202) 663-6000

March 12, 1997

Mr. Brian J. Lane
Director
Division of Corporation Finance
U.S. Securities and Exchange Commission
450 Fifth Street, N.W.
Washington, D.C. 20549

Re: *Private Financial Network*

Dear Mr. Lane:

Wilmer, Cutler & Pickering requests your advice concerning the applicability of Section 2(10) of the Securities Act of 1933 (the "1933 Act") to limited audience, video transmissions of "road show" meetings concerning public offerings of certain securities. The road shows will be transmitted on the Private Financial Network ("PFN"), which is a wholly-owned subsidiary of MSNBC Interactive LLC, a joint venture of the National Broadcasting Co., Inc. and Microsoft Corporation.

We seek your assurance that the Staff of the Division of Corporation Finance (the "Division") would not recommend enforcement action to the Commission if PFN transmitted road shows to its subscribers as described herein and operated on the basis that such transmissions were not prospectuses under Section 2(10) of the 1933 Act.

Current Operations of PFN

PFN was launched approximately three years ago as a companion to the "First Call" textual research service owned by Thompson Financial Services. Inc. First Call distributes textual research summaries from more than 55 brokerage firms to more than 1,400 investment firms; PFN provides a companion video component.

PFN currently has fewer than 100 subscribers, principally registered broker-dealers and investment advisers. Each PFN subscriber enters into a user contract, pursuant to which it acquires the right to receive and display this programming on their workplace computer screens and television monitors. Current PFN programming includes interviews, such as with chief executive officers; coverage of analysts' meetings; coverage of news conferences and product announcements by major companies; and coverage of brokerage conferences. PFN does not currently transmit road shows.

PFN is distributed to its subscribers by KU satellite, by T1 telephone circuits, and by fiber optic or other cable. Reception of satellite transmission requires a decoder made available only to PFN subscribers. Distribution by telephone lines or cable is also secure and directed to a particular personal computer or other receiver.

How Road Shows Are Conducted

A "road show" typically consists of a series of individual presentations by an issuer and its underwriters, intended to develop potential investors' interest in a public offering by showcasing the issuer, its management, and the securities being offered. Stephen J. Schulte, *IPO Road Shows: A Primer for the Practitioner* in 26th Ann. Ins. on Sec. Reg., ch. 20, at 529

(1994). These presentations are typically held in various cities during the "waiting period" before the registration statement is declared effective, which allows underwriters to help assess demand for the offering and price the securities. *Id.* at 531-32; 1 Louis Loss & Joel Seligman, *Securities Regulation* 337 (3d ed. 1989).

Each road show presentation generally lasts about two hours, usually over the course of a breakfast or lunch. Schulte, *supra*, at 534. Depending on the projected size of an offering, the issuer's industry, and the investors targeted, the road show may be held over a number of days, or stretch into weeks, and may be held on a regional, national, or international basis. *Id.* at 529. Attendees at road show presentations include potential investors, securities firms, securities trading and sales personnel, portfolio managers, and analysts. *Id.*; *see also* Larry W. Sonsini, Richard J. Char, Gail Clayton Husick, *The Regulation of the Registration and Distribution Process Under the Securities Act of 1933* in 26th Ann. Ins. on Sec. Reg., ch. 21, at 624 (1994); Gregory M. Priest, *Practical Aspects of the Initial Public Offering*, 861 PLI/Corp 617, 625 (1994). Each attendee is provided with a copy of the preliminary prospectus filed with the Commission. Schulte, *supra*, at 558.

During a road show meeting, the issuer's management and underwriters make presentations, generally lasting about 30 minutes, to explain the issuer's business and industry and review the basic terms of the offering. Schulte, *supra* at 553-34; Tom Pratt, *On the Road Again . . .*, Investment Dealers' Digest, Sept. 20, 1993. After these presentations, speakers may address matters that may be of particular interest or concern to an audience and will also respond to questions from attendees. Schulte, *supra*, at 534. Visual aids, such as slides, charts, and videotapes, are often used. *Id.* at 536-37. Closed-circuit television may also be used to accommodate large audiences. *See id.* at 554-55.

Proposed Video Transmissions of Road Shows

PFN proposes to transmit road shows for public offerings to its subscribers, either live as the shows occur or on a delayed basis. PFN will not transmit a single road show to any subscriber more than two times. As compensation, PFN will receive only its regular subscription fees and a flat fee for the product and transmission of the road shows.

In practice, PFN transmissions of road shows will help issuers channel timely and consistent information about themselves and their securities to potential investors who otherwise could attend the shows but might find it expensive or difficult to do so. And, as discussed more fully below, each PFN transmission of a road show will have three features that will help ensure compliance with the 1933 Act: (1) video transmissions will be available only to PFN subscribers, who will agree not to videotape, copy or further distribute the transmissions; (2) before a road show is transmitted, each PFN subscriber will receive a filed prospectus from the issuer or the underwriter; and (3) issuers and underwriters will be required to take reasonable steps to ensure that information disclosed in the road show is not inconsistent with the filed prospectus; and (4) each transmission will include visual statements or "crawls" emphasizing the importance of the filed prospectus and the prohibition against videotaping, copying or further distribution.

Restricted Audience. The audience for the video transmissions will be restricted to PFN subscribers. Transmissions will be available only to PFN subscribers.

Primacy of Filed Prospectus. The issuer and/or the underwriter will be contractually required to distribute prospectuses to all PFN subscribers before any road show airs. If road shows are transmitted during the waiting period, a Section 10(b) preliminary prospectus (the so-called "red herring") will be distributed to all subscribers in advance of the transmission. If road shows are transmitted after the effective date of the relevant registration statement, a Section 10(a) statutory prospectus will be distributed to all subscribers in advance. [1] PFN subscribers will be required to agree and acknowledge in their contracts that they must receive the relevant prospectus before viewing any road show that PFN transmits.

Content. The road shows themselves will not be edited for content. Subscribers generally will see the road shows in their entirety. [2] Although issuers and underwriters will have exclusive control over the content of the road show transmissions, they will be contractually required to take reasonable steps to ensure that information discussed in the road show is not inconsistent with the filed prospectus.

Transmissions of road shows will begin and end with the following visual statement emphasizing the primacy of the filed prospectus:

> A prospectus has been furnished to each subscriber, and subscribers should refer to the prospectus and/or the registration statement for more complete information about the offering.

If the registration statement is not effective when a road show is transmitted, the transmission also will include visual statements of the Rule 134(b) legend, to the effect that the securities may not be sold and offers to buy cannot be accepted before the effective date. [3] Additionally, the viewers will be reminded by crawls at least three times during a transmission that reception is restricted to PFN subscribers who have received a prospectus and that transmissions cannot be videotaped or copies or used in any manner to sell securities to the general public.

Legal Analysis

Section 2(10) of the 1933 Act defines prospectus, in pertinent part, to include "any . . . communication, written or by radio or television, which offers any security for sale or confirms the sale of any security. . . ." For the reasons discussed below, we believe that PFN's limited audience transmissions of road shows would not be prospectuses requiring compliance with Section 10.

Clearly, road shows and other such selling efforts during the waiting period are not *themselves* "prospectuses" because they are oral and visual -- not "written." Russell B. Stevenson, Jr., *The Waiting Period and SEC Processing*, C951 ALI-ABA 133 (July 28, 1994). [4] Video transmissions of essentially the *same* material would be prospectuses only if such transmissions constituted "radio" or "television" within the meaning of Section 2(10). We do not believe that they would.

The reference in Section 2(10) to "radio" or "television" is to *broadcasting*, not to the use of radio or television technology for closed-circuit or other controlled retransmission of non-prospectus materials. That Congress intended to reach only radio and television *broadcasts* in Section 2(10) is clear from Section 10(f) of the 1933 Act, which provides that "in any case where a prospectus consists of a radio or television *broadcast*, copies thereof shall be filed with the Commission under such rules and regulations as it shall prescribe." (Emphasis added). By limiting the reach of Section 10(f) to broadcasts, Congress made clear that it was concerned with mass communications to the public, and that the only sort of radio and television transmission that could be deemed a prospectus was a broadcast. [5]

In 1933, "radio" meant broadcasts scattered over a 360-degree radius, not person-to-person transmissions. When Congress added "television" to Section 2(10) in 1954, it sought only to "eliminate any possible doubt . . . that might arise through amendment of the act at this time without express recognition of technical advances in the radio industry." S. Rep. No. 1036 at 12; H.R. Rep. No. 1542 at 21, 83rd Cong., 2d Sess. (1954). Thus, Congress equated television as it existed in 1954 with radio as it existed in 1933. Importantly, television in 1954 -- like radio then and in 1933 -- was used only for broadcasts scattered over a 360-degree radius. As the word "broad"cast itself implies, anyone with a television set or radio in the viewing or listening area could pick up a broadcast signal. Once the signal was sent, there was no way to tell who received it. There was also no way to ensure that everyone who received it previously had received a prospectus meeting the requirements of Section 10.

The mere fact that video transmissions are associated with television technology does not make them "television" within the meaning of Section 2(10). Indeed, the Division has taken at least two no-action positions that appear to be based on this distinction. In *Exploration, Inc.*, SEC No-Action Letter, 1986 SEC No-Act. LEXIS 2891 (Nov. 10, 1986), the Division took a no-action position regarding videotapes shown on television monitors at road shows and distributed to prospective underwriters and selling group members. And in *Producers Funding Corp.*, SEC No-Action, 1982 WL 30515 (March 9, 1982), the Division took a no-action position regarding cable telecasts of "backers' auditions," or condensed versions, of Broadway plays, which would conclude with tombstone advertisements to encourage investment in the plays.

The United States Supreme Court recently recognized that "when the 1933 Act was drawn and adopted, the term 'prospectus' was well understood to refer to a document soliciting *the public* to acquire securities from the issuer." *Gustafson v. Alloyd Co., Inc.*, No. 93-404, slip op. at 13 (U.S. Feb. 28, 1995) (emphasis added). Thus the Court concluded that when Congress employed this "term of art" in Section 2(10), it intended to reach only those documents or communications that are widely disseminated to an undifferentiated public rather than to a discrete, "invited" audience.

> From the terms "prospectus, notice, circular, advertisement, or letter," it is apparent that the list in Section 2(10) refers to documents of wide dissemination. In a similar manner, the list includes communications 'by radio or television' but not face-to-face or telephonic communications. Inclusion of the term "communication" in that list suggests that it too refers to a public communication.

Id.; *see also id.* at 14 ("The term 'written communication' includes communications held out to the public at large . . . .")

In sum, references to radio and television in Section 2(10) were intended to prevent mass communications to the public unaccompanied by the sort of disclosure required by Section 10. In 1954, Congress simply did not consider the possibility that the distribution or reception of television could be restricted to recipients of a prospectus by mechanisms like secure person-to-person video transmissions. Video transmissions like those proposed by PFN are video teleconferences and to closed circuit television transmissions to overflow attendees at a road show. *See* Schulte, *supra*, at 554-55 (concluding closed circuit television should be permissible at road shows "because it is tantamount to a 'live' presentation where management is interacting face-to-face").

Moreover, PFN will take various steps to ensure that its video transmissions advance, rather than undermine, the goals of the 1933 Act. Issuers and underwriters will be required to take reasonable steps to ensure that information disclosed in a road show is not inconsistent with the prospectus on file with the Commission. They will have every incentive to do so, since the road shows will not be edited for content and the transmissions will create a record that could later be scrutinized. Perhaps most importantly, all PFN subscribers will receive a prospectus before a road show is transmitted. Such advance distribution is critical to the disclosure regime established by the 1933 Act. Indeed, the Division initially declined to take a no-action position in *Products Funding Corp.* when no such distribution was proposed in connection with cable telecasts of backers' auditions. *Producers Funding Corp.*, SEC No-Action, 1982 WL 30065 (Dec. 28, 1981). The Division reversed its position, however, after Producers Funding filed a supplemental request providing that the filed prospectus would be distributed electronically to every viewer. *Producers Funding Corp.*, SEC No-Action, 1982

WL 30515 (March 9, 1982). Similarly, in *Exploration, Inc.*, the Division took a no-action position based in part on the contemporaneous distribution of preliminary prospectuses. *Exploration, Inc.*, SEC No-Action Letter, 1986 SEC No-Act. LEXIS 2891 (Nov. 10, 1986).

Conclusion

Permitting video transmissions under the controlled conditions proposed above will help American companies and the financial industry benefit from technology not available (and certainly not of concern to Congress) in 1954 -- even as they comply with the disclosure and other requirements of the federal securities laws. As our discussion demonstrates, Congress did not consider video transmissions to a limited audience when it included "radio" and "television" in the term "prospectus." Under the circumstances presented here, PFN transmissions will be nothing more than electronic extensions of road shows and should not be deemed prospectuses.

In accordance with the foregoing, we request that you advise us that the Division would not recommend enforcement action to the Commission if PFN transmitted road shows for the purposes and pursuant to the procedures outlined above and operated on the basis that such transmissions were not prospectuses within the meaning of Section 2(10) of the 1933 Act.

In accordance with Release No. 33-6269, we are enclosing seven copies of this letter with the original. Should you have any questions regarding this request, please contact me at 202-663-6278.

Sincerely,

Stephen M. Cutler
for Wilmer, Cutler & Pickering

Enclosures

STAFF REPLY LETTER

March 12, 1997

RESPONSE OF THE OFFICE OF CHIEF COUNSEL
DIVISION OF CORPORATION FINANCE

Re: Private Financial Network ("PFN")
Incoming letter dated March 12, 1997

Based on the facts presented, the Division will not recommend any enforcement action to the Commission if PFN transmits a company's road show presentation to PFN's subscribers for the purposes and pursuant to the procedures described in your letter in reliance on your opinion as counsel that such transmissions are not prospectuses within the meaning of Section 2(10) of the Securities Act of 1933.

Because this position is based on the representations made to the Division in your letter, it should be noted that any different facts or conditions might require another conclusion. Further, this response represents the Division's position on enforcement action only and does not purport to express any legal conclusion on the questions presented.

Sincerely,

Martin P. Dunn
Chief Counsel

[1]Under these circumstances, the transmissions would be expressly excluded from the definition of prospectus under §2(10)(a), which exempts from the definition of a prospectus any "communication sent or given after the effective date of the registration statement if prior or at the time of such communication a written prospectus meeting the requirements of sub(a) of section 10 . . . was sent or given to the person to whom the communication was made." 15 U.S.C. §77b(10(a). *See* Morris Cheston and Alex Seldin, *Gun-Jumping and Free Writing: Communications Hazards to Avoid When Going Public*, in 8 Insights 11 (May 1994).

[2]PFN reserves the right, in connection with delayed transmissions, to edit out "dead time" arising from logistical or similar problems at the road shows and to give the issuer and/or underwriter the opportunity to edit out misstatements or mistakes.

[3]The Rule 134(b) legend in its entirety provides as follows:

A registration statement relating to these securities has been filed with the Securities and Exchange Commission but has not yet become effective. These securities may not be sold nor may offers to buy be accepted prior to the time the registration statement becomes effective. This transmission shall not constitute an offer to sell or the solicitation of an offer to buy nor shall there be any sale of these securities in any State in which such offer, solicitation or sale would be unlawful prior to registration or qualification under the securities laws of any such State.

[4]Of course, such oral communications, while not prospectuses, remain subject to the antifraud provisions of the 1933 Act and the Securities Exchange Act of 1934. Schulte, *supra*, at 547; Sonsini, et al., *supra*, at 625.

[5]Section 10(f) has remained essentially unchanged since 1933, other than the 1954 addition of "television." *See* Pub. L. No. 22, §10(d), 73rd Cong., 1st Sess. (May 27, 1933); *see also* S. Rep. No. 1036 at 18; H.R. Rep. No. 1542 at 26, 83rd Cong., 2d Sess. (1954) (noting technical amendments to then §10(d)).

EXHIBIT C

SEC NO-ACTION LETTER, NET ROADSHOW (SEPT. 1997)

, Net Roadshow, Inc.

Company: Net Roadshow, Inc.

Public Availability Date: September 08, 1997

WSB File No. 090897012

Fiche Locator No. 2789E10

WSB Subject Category: 032

Reference:
Securities Act of 1933, Section 2(10)

INQUIRY LETTER 1
TROUTMAN SANDERS LLP
NATIONSBANK PLAZA
800 PEACHTREE STREET, N.E. - SUITE 5200
ATLANTA, GEORGIA 30308-2216
TELEPHONE(404) 885-3000

July 23, 1997

Catherine T. Dixon, Chief Counsel
Division of Corporation Finance
U.S. Securities and Exchange Commission
Mail Stop 3-3
450 Fifth Street, N.W.
Washington, D.C. 20549

RE: Request for Confidential Treatment

Dear Ms. Dixon:

This firm serves as legal counsel to Brad Hammond and Net Roadshow, Inc. ("Company"). Accompanying this letter is a request ("No-Action Request") made by this firm on behalf of the Company seeking confirmation of our opinion as to a legal interpretation of Section 2(10) of the Securities Act of 1933, as amended ("Act") and requesting that on the basis of the facts stated in the No-Action Request, the Staff would not recommend that the Commission take enforcement action based on the proposal of the Company.

On behalf of the Company, we hereby request that the No-Action Request be afforded confidential treatment for a period of time not to exceed 120 days from the date the response has been sent or given by the Commission to the Company. Considerations for our request for confidential treatment of the No-Action Request are as follows:

(i) The information contained in the No-Action Request constitutes trade secrets and confidential information of a commercial or financial nature and is property of the Company;

(ii) The information contained in the No-Action Request is privileged and confidential and the dissemination of such material into the public domain would be detrimental to the Company and its business operations:

(iii) The disclosure of this information would affect adversely the Company's competitive position and, as a result, the Company should not be required to disclose such information to the public at the present time; and

(iv) The Company has, and will, take measures available to it to protect the confidential nature of the proposal including, but not limited to, requiring that potential customers enter into a confidentiality agreement with the Company prior to viewing a presentation of the proposal.

Sincerely,

Thomas M. Duffy, for
TROUTMAN SANDERS, LLP

TMD:llt

INQUIRY LETTER 2
TROUTMAN SANDERS LLP
NATIONSBANK PLAZA
800 PEACHTREE STREET, N.E. - SUITE 5200
ATLANTA, GEORGIA 30308-2216
TELEPHONE(404) 885-3000

July 23, 1997

Catherine T. Dixon, Chief Counsel
Division of Corporation Finance
U.S. Securities and Exchange Commission
Mail Stop 3-3
450 Fifth Street, N.W.
Washington, D.C. 20549

Re: No-Action Request/Section 2(10) of the Securities Act of 1933, as amended ("Act")

Dear Ms. Dixon:

This firm serves as legal counsel to Brad Hammond and Net Roadshow, Inc. ("Company"). The Company desires to provide road shows for public offerings to qualified investors over the Internet. We would appreciate confirmation in the form of a no-action response of our opinion that our client may provide road shows for public offerings for qualified investors over the Internet under the following facts and circumstances, and that such transmissions will not constitute a "prospectus" pursuant to Section 2(10) of the Act:

FACTUAL BACKGROUND

The format and flow of the requested Internet road show product is as follows:

1. First, a website for road shows regarding public offerings would be established. The website would provide an index of the road shows available for viewing by qualified investors and by the underwriting investment banks. The road shows would be indexed by the name of the offering company, the name of the underwriting investment bank, and by industry classification. The road shows will not be transmitted prior to the filing of a registration statement with the Securities and Exchange Commission ("Commission") as to each applicable offering.

2. To view a road show, the qualified investor would be required to contact an institutional salesman or the syndicate department at one of the underwriting investment banks. The qualified investors will be typical of the investors who would customarily be invited to attend a live road show, such as registered broker/dealers and investment advisers. (Institutional salesmen would also be permitted to call qualified institutional money managers to inform them that it is available for viewing.) An access code will be required to view the road show on the Internet. A log will be maintained of who specifically received the access code. The access code for each road show will be changed each day and each qualified investor will be allowed to view a road show one day only.

3. The Internet road show would be the *exact* same road show that qualified investors see live, as the live road show will be filmed in its entirety, including the filing of all questions and answers. The live road shows will not be edited for content and viewers will generally view the road shows in their entirety. [1] The Internet version of the road show will present the charts and oral presentation at a similar speed (like a slide show) as the live road show. In the event information changes between the time the road show is filmed and throughout the period the road show is available on the website, the display will include a periodic crawl providing a synopsis of such changes. The crawl will also provide that the viewer may contact the appropriate institutional salesman for further information about such changes.

4. A large and obvious button reading "PRELIMINARY PROSPECTUS" will be displayed at all times throughout the road show. A viewer would simply "click" on the "button" featuring the preliminary prospectus which is on file with the Commission to view it in its entirety.

5. Before viewing any road show, the potential view will be advised of, and must agree to, the following:

"The copying, downloading or distribution of any road show material is not permitted.

The Internet road show does not constitute a prospectus, in whole or in part. It is strongly recommended that each investor read the actual prospectus before making an investment decision."

The prospectus relating to this offering is available through this site for viewing before viewing the road show. The prospectus may be obtained by clicking on the button labeled "PRELIMINARY PROSPECTUS." Viewers should refer to the prospectus and/or the registration statement for more complete information about the offering.

A registration statement relating to these securities has been filed with the Securities and Exchange commission but has not yet become effective. These securities may not be sold nor offers to buy be accepted prior to the time the registration statement becomes effective. This transmission shall not constitute an offer to sell or the solicitation of an offer to buy nor shall there by any sale of these securities in any State in which such offer, solicitation or sale would be unlawful prior to registration or qualification under the securities laws of any State."

In the event the viewer does not agree to the above, the viewer will be denied access to the road show. The screen, throughout each road show, would also carry a disclaimer at all times stating that "the copying, downloading or distribution of any road show material is not permitted."

6. The viewer will be able to print the entire preliminary prospectus. The Company's transmissions include technology designed to prevent the copying, downloading or printing of any portion of the road show transmission other than the preliminary prospectus.

7. The viewer will be informed by a periodic crawl across the screen or by prominent text of the importance of viewing the filed prospectus.

8. The issuers and the underwriters of the road shows transmitted will be required to take such steps as are necessary in order to provide that the road show information as transmitted by the Internet is not inconsistent or contradictory with the information set forth in the filed prospectus or in the live road show.

9. The compensation to be received by the Company for the presentation of road shows over the Internet will not be contingent upon the degree of success of an underlying offering and will not be related to the size of an offering. The fees charged by the Company will be analogous to a production or printing cost in that the fees will be charged for the production of the material to be transmitted over the Internet. The Company's fees may vary depending upon whether the road show presentation is (i) produced but not transmitted, or (ii) produced and transmitted for any period of time.

10. We believe that the following benefits would be recognized in the marketplace if the Commission approves the request:

(i) No longer will some institutions and money managers be placed at an advantage over others on syndicate transactions. Our client believes that your approval of this process would "level the playing field" and provide each qualified investor the opportunity to view the road show.

(ii) Money managers located in geographic areas frequently missed by the live road show would be placed on more equal footing.

(iii) There would be wider availability of the road show and the preliminary prospectus to interested money managers.

(iv) The road show and the preliminary prospectus should be distributed faster giving qualified investors more time to make a fully informed investment decision.

(v) The participants in the road show would likely be more precise in the choice of words and graphs knowing the distribution channel and the viewing audience (including, potentially, the Commission).

In summary, we believe that this approach allows for "rapid dissemination of information to investors and financial markets in a more cost-efficient, widespread, and equitable manner," consistent with the recent position of the Commission as provided in Release No. 33-7233.

LEGAL ANALYSIS

Section 5(b) of the Act makes it unlawful to transmit any "prospectus" unless the prospectus meets the requirements of Section 2(10) of the Act. Section 2(10) of the Act defines "prospectus" to include any "prospectus, notice, circular, advertisement, letter, or communication, written or by radio or television, which offers any security for sale or confirms the sale of any security." We believe that the limited transmission by the Company of road shows, over an access code restricted Internet website, to the type of qualified investors who would customarily be invited to attend live road shows would not constitute "prospectuses" requiring compliance with Section 10 of the Act.

Road show presentations that occur after the filing and prior to the effectiveness of the registration statement ordinarily do not constitute "prospectuses" due to the fact that they are oral and visual and are not "written." [2] Thus, transmission of substantially the same communication by means of the Internet should not be deemed prospectuses unless the Internet transmissions constitute "radio" or "television" broadcasts within the meaning of Section 2(10) of the Act. We do not believe that such transmissions by means of the Internet would constitute "radio" or "television" broadcasts.

The use of the terms "radio" or "television" in Section 2(10) of the Act is for the purpose of regulating the "broadcasting" of materials relating to the offer of any security for sale. The intention of Congress as evidenced from the language of the statute was to prevent the broadcasting of a communication regarding the offer or sale of a security to an unlimited audience. [3] The references in Section 2(10) to "radio" or "television" are not intended to prohibit all uses of technology, such as radio or television or electronic media in the form of the Internet, but only to prohibit the transmission of materials which constitute a broadcast.

The Act specifically provides in Section 10(f) that where a prospectus does consist of a radio or television "broadcast," copies of the materials constituting the prospectus must be filed with the Commission. This provision of the Act indicates that communications which provide the widespread dissemination of information to the public regarding the offer of a security for sale are the types of communications fully within the scope of Section 10(f). The only type of radio or television transmission that could be deemed a prospectus would therefore be a broadcast to a mass audience. Accordingly, the only type of transmission by electronic media, such as the Internet, which could be deemed a prospectus would be a broadcast over the Internet which provided unlimited and widespread dissemination of the material being transmitted. The proposal of the Company will take such steps as are necessary in order to provide that access to the information will be limited so that such transmission will not constitute a broadcast.

While the use of media such as radio and television, and vehicles for electronic communication such as the Internet, have evolved since the adoption of the Act in 1933 and amended thereafter, it remains the intention of Congress for Section 2(10) to regulate broadcasts of information in a widely disseminated manner rather than to a limited audience. In *Gustafson v. Alloyd Co., Inc.*, No. 93-404 (U.S. Feb. 28, 1995) the United Supreme Court recognized this fact by holding, in part, that the term prospectus was intended to be a document which solicited the public to acquire securities. The term was not intended to refer to the dissemination of information to a limited viewing audience as contemplated by the Company.

In summary, references to the words "radio" and "television" in Section 2(10) are intended to prevent unlimited and wide spread dissemination or communication to the public of information regarding an offer for sale of a security without the type of disclosure required by Section 2(10) of the Act. By contrast, the Internet transmissions contemplated by the Company will be restricted in terms of the type of persons or entities to be provided with the access code required to view the transmission. The Company is also utilizing technology designed to prevent the person or entity viewing the presentation from copying, downloading, or otherwise reproducing the road show transmission. The only component of the road show transmitted by the Company over the Internet which may be copied or printed is the preliminary prospectus relating to each offering. The Company has taken these measures in order to provide that the transmission by the Company of road shows by means of the Internet will make the securities markets more efficient, furthering the goals of the Commission as evidence through the implementation of the EDGAR system and more recently, the adoption of Release No. 33-7233.

CONCLUSION

We believe that the proposal of our client would conform with the beliefs of the Commission that the use of electronic media within the securities industry will make the securities markets more efficient, as evidenced through the implementation of the EDGAR system and more recently, the adoption of Release No. 33-7233.

The presentation of a road show by means of the Internet as described in our client's proposal should be permissible because the information disseminated through the presentation will not constitute a prospectus or a broadcast. Our client's proposal specifically limits access to the transmissions through an access restricted website to the type of qualified investors who would customarily attend a road show, provides that prospective purchasers will not be provided with a paper version of the road show presentation made by means of the Internet, and includes technology designed to prevent the presentation from being copied, printed, or disseminated.

Based on the foregoing facts and analysis, we believe that providing road shows for public offerings to qualified investors over the Internet as described herein will not constitute the use of a "prospectus" under Section 2(10) of the Act. We respectfully request advice that you concur with this view or that the Division will not recommend that the Commission take enforcement action against our client if it engages in the transactions described above. If you wish additional information, or believe that additional representations or clarifications as to the proposed transaction are required before issuing a no-action response, we would appreciate your contacting us.

Thank you for your review of this no-action letter request.

Sincerely,

Thomas M. Duffy, for
TROUTMAN SANDERS LLP

TMD:llt

STAFF REPLY LETTER

July 30, 1997

RESPONSE OF THE OFFICE OF CHIEF COUNSEL
DIVISION OF CORPORATION FINANCE

Re: Net Roadshow, Inc. ("Net Roadshow")
Incoming letter dated July 23, 1997

Based on the facts presented, but without necessarily agreeing with your analysis, the Division will not recommend enforcement action to the Commission if Net Roadshow transmits an issuer's road show presentation over the Internet for the purposes and pursuant to the procedures described in your letter in reliance on your counsel's opinion that such transmissions are not prospectuses within the meaning of Section 2(a)(10) of the Securities Act of 1933. The Division notes that a roadshow transmission will not be conducted before the registration statement is filed with the Commission in connection with the particular public offering of securities.

The request for confidential treatment pursuant to Regulation 200.81 has been granted for the earlier of: (i) 120 days from the date of this response, or (ii) the date the information in your letter and this response is made publicly available by Net Roadshow, Inc.

This position is based on the representations and your counsel's opinion made to the Division in your letter. Any different facts or conditions might require different conclusions. Further, this response represents the Division's position on enforcement action only and does not express any legal conclusion on the question presented. Since regulatory responses to legal issues raised by technological developments may evolve, you should be aware that this no-action position may be reevaluated in the future.

Sincerely,

Mary J. Kosterlitz
Special Counsel

[1]The Company reserves the right to edit our "dead time" arising through logistical, organizational, or similar problems at live road shows and to give the issuer and/or underwriter the opportunity to edit our misstatements or mistakes.

[2]The communications, while not prospectuses, remain subject to the anti-fraud provisions of the Act and the Securities Exchange Act of 1934, as amended.

[3]Section 10(f) provides that "in any case where a prospectus consists of a radio or television broadcast, copies thereof shall be filed with the Commission under such rules and regulations as it shall prescribe."

EXHIBIT D

SEC NO-ACTION LETTER,
BLOOMBERG (DEC. 1997)

Bloomberg L.P.

Company: Bloomberg L.P.

Public Availability Date: December 01, 1997

WSB File No. 120197011

Fiche Locator No. 2815A3

WSB Subject Category: 032

Reference:
Securities Act of 1933, Section 2(a)(10)

--------------------Washington Service Bureau Summary--------------------

...The staff, while not necessarily agreeing with counsel's analysis, will not recommend Commission action if this limited partnership transmits, over its multi-media system, THE BLOOMBERG (the network), an issuer's road show presentation to network subscribers in reliance on counsel's legal opinion that such transmissions are not prospectuses within the meaning of 1933 Act section 2(a)(10). The staff particularly notes that a road show transmission will not be conducted before the registration statement is filed with the Commission in connection with the particular offering of securities. The company intends to transmit audio-visual recordings of live road shows. Access to the road shows by authorized viewers will be on a delayed basis only until it becomes technically possible to offer live transmission. The sponsoring underwriters will determine and have exclusive control over the content of the road shows and they will agree in writing with the company to ensure that the information disclosed is not inconsistent with the prospectus furnished to viewers. If the company transmits a road show to authorized subscribers during the actual course of the live road show, it will transmit on a real-time basis the same road show as the viewers at the road show are seeing. In circumstances where the road show presented on the network is presented after the conclusion of the live road show, the road show presented on the network will be exactly the same road show as institutional investors and others permitted to attend the live show saw live. If information changes between the time the road show is recorded and throughout the period the road show is available on the network, the display will include text providing a synopsis of such changes. The audience will be limited to subscribers of the network service that have been specifically enabled by a particular underwriting house to receive a transmission of the particular road show in question. In each case, the underwriter will agree in writing not to enable a viewer to receive the transmission unless the viewer is an institutional investor, investment adviser or other person of a type the underwriter would customarily invite to a road show and unless the underwriter has delivered to the viewer a copy of the most current prospectus before the scheduled transmission of the road show. If a road show is transmitted during the waiting period between filing and effectiveness of the registration statement, a 1933 Act section 10(b) preliminary prospectus will be distributed to the viewer. The company will receive as compensation the customary rental fees paid by the subscribers to the network service, which will not be increased by reason of the road show transmissions, and reimbursement by the issuer or sponsoring underwriter of any special expenses incurred in attending, recording and transmitting the road show, neither of which will be contingent on the size or successful conclusion of any offering.

INQUIRY LETTER
ORIGINAL TEXT ILLEGIBLE
ONE CITICORP CENTER
153 EAST 53RD STREET
NEW YORK, NY 10022-4677
TELEPHONE(212) 821-8000

October 22, 1997

1933 Act/2(10)
/5

CONFIDENTIAL TREATMENT REQUESTED

Mr. Brian J. Lane
Director, Division of
Corporation Finance
U.S. Securities and
Exchange Commission
Mail Stop 3-1
450 Fifth Street, N.W.

Washington, DC 20549

Dear Mr. Lane:

On behalf of our client, Bloomberg L.P. ("Bloomberg"), we request that you advise us that the Division of Corporation Finance (the "Division") would not recommend that the Commission commence enforcement action pursuant to the Securities Act of 1933, as amended (the "Securities Act"), if Bloomberg transmitted "road show" meetings concerning public offerings of certain securities over THE BLOOMBERG$_{sr}$ service to certain subscribers as described herein, on the basis that such transmissions are not prospectuses under Section 2(10) of the Securities Act.

Content of road shows. As you know, road shows are an oral means by which securities underwriters present information to their institutional customers that are considering making purchases in securities offerings underwritten by the investment banks. These meetings are designed to present salient points about the issuer, its industry and the offering. They often include oral presentation by senior officers of the issuer as well as by members of the underwriting team working on the offering and research analysts who are familiar with the company and the industry or industries in which it participates.

Typically, the road show presentation, which may last an hour or more, is given in several cities. The attendees include, in addition to representatives of institutional investors and investment advisers, sales and trading personnel from the securities firms participating in the offering and securities analysts. At or before the road show, prospective purchasers are given copies of the most current prospectus. In the course of the road show, the presenters may entertain questions from those in attendance. Visual aids, such as slides, charts and videotapes, often are displayed. Where appropriate, samples of the issuer's products are sometimes made available. See generally, *Private Financial Network* (incoming letter dated March 12, 1997, and authorities cited therein), 1997 SEC No-Act. LEXIS 406.

Transmission over THE BLOOMBERG. Bloomberg intends to transmit over its multi-media system audio-visual recordings of live road shows. Access to the road show by authorized viewers will be on a delayed basis only until it becomes technically possible to offer "live" transmission. Initially, the road show will be "audio on demand," which means that an authorized viewer can receive the road show by typing in a prescribed keystroke routine on the keyboard attached to THE BLOOMBERG service. The Bloomberg Multimedia presentation will include complete audio, illustrated with still photographs and graphics. At a later time, the presentation may include video transmissions. [1] It is anticipated that, generally, viewers will view road shows in their entirety, but they will be able to interrupt their viewing, and view less than the entire road show, if they wish. [2]

The sponsoring underwriters will determine and have exclusive control over the content of the road shows. They will agree in writing with Bloomberg to ensure that the information disclosed in the road show is not inconsistent with the prospectus furnished to viewers. The issuer will ensure that statements made by its representatives will not be inconsistent with the prospectus furnished to viewers.

If Bloomberg transmits a road show to authorized subscribers during the actual course of the "live" road show, it will transmit on a real-time basis the same road show as the viewers at the road show are seeing. In such cases, the sponsoring underwriter may permit the subscribers to submit questions via the Bloomberg e-mail system to a Bloomberg representative at the road show during the "live" road show. The sponsoring underwriter may answer such questions during the road show presentation if it deems the questions to be of general interest to the audience.

In circumstances where the road show presented on THE BLOOMBERG is presented after the conclusion of the "live" road show, the road show presented on Bloomberg will be exactly the same road show as institutional investors and others permitted to attend the live road show saw live, as the live road show will have been recorded in its entirety, including the recording of all questions and answers. The live road show will not be edited for content. [3]

The Bloomberg version of the road show will present the charts and oral presentations at a similar speed (like a slide show) as the live road show. Until such time as Bloomberg introduces a full video format, the still pictures accompanying the audio will consist of photographs of the presenters at the road show, photographs of the issuer's logo, slides and charts presented at the road show, other photographs from the preliminary prospectus or from documents incorporated therein by reference, or a clock showing the amount of time left in the road show. Each road show will be indexed on THE BLOOMBERG service by subject matter and a brief agenda will be shown to indicate to the viewer by time segment the presenters and subject matters to be covered.

If information changes between the time the road show is recorded and throughout the period the road show is available on THE BLOOMBERG, the display will include text providing a synopsis of such changes. The text also will provide that the viewer may contact the appropriate institutional salesperson at the underwriter for further information about such changes.

Limited audience; prospectus delivery. Transmission of a road show will be subject to certain limitations that are designed to ensure delivery of the prospectus. The audience will be limited to subscribers of THE BLOOMBERG service that have been specifically enabled by a particular underwriting house to receive a transmission of the particular road show in question. In each case, the underwriter will agree in writing with Bloomberg not to enable a viewer to receive the transmission unless the viewer is an institutional investor, investment adviser or other person of a type the underwriter would customarily invite to a road show and unless the underwriter has delivered to the viewer, by courier or other means, a copy of the most current prospectus before the scheduled transmission of the road show.

Currently, users of THE BLOOMBERG can access any document in the Commission's EDGAR system by entering the issuer's ticker symbol and a key or other prompt indicating the type of security (e.g., equity, corp, pfd, or mtge), choosing EDGAR Filings from the menu that is displayed in response and then selecting a particular filing from a displayed list. In some cases in connection with the electronic road shows described in this letter, the prospectus also may be displayed on THE BLOOMBERG service in a way that will allow subscribers to view it before, during and after they gain access to the road show. In all cases, however, either the issuer or the underwriters will deliver paper prospectuses as described above unless they receive advance written consent from an individual customer to electronic delivery. [4]

Road shows that are conducted by the underwriters with which Bloomberg will be dealing, in connection with offerings that are to be registered under the Securities Act, never are conducted before the filing of the registration statement because section 5(c) of the Securities Act prohibits the making of pre-filing offers, by oral means or otherwise. [5] If the road show is transmitted during the "waiting period" between filing and effectiveness of the registration statement, a Section 10(b) preliminary prospectus (the so-called "red herring") will be the one the underwriter will distribute to the viewer. If the road show is transmitted after the effectiveness of the registration statement, a Section 10(a) statutory prospectus will be distributed.

In the case of an offering as to which a registration statement has been filed but has not yet become effective, the road show will be specially coded so that viewers that have the capacity to copy, print out or down-load information from THE BLOOMBERG service will not be able to do so for the road show and so that a viewer will be able to view the program any number of times during a single 24-hour period (which will commence upon his or her first accessing the program) and not thereafter. [6]

Each road show presentation will be preceded and concluded with the following statement:

> A preliminary prospectus has been furnished to each person authorized to receive this transmission. You should refer to the prospectus, and to the registration statement of which it is a part, for more complete information about the offering. By electing to view this transmission, you represent, warrant and agree that you will not videotape, record or otherwise attempt to reproduce or re-transmit the contents of this transmission.

If the registration statement is not effective when a road show is transmitted, the transmission also will include visual statements complying in substance with Rule 134(b) under the Securities Act, to the effect that the securities may not be sold and offers to buy cannot be accepted before the effective date. [7]

Compensation to Bloomberg. Bloomberg will receive as compensation the customary rental fees paid by subscribers to THE BLOOMBERG service, which will not be increased by reason of the road show transmissions, and reimbursement by the issuer or sponsoring underwriter of any special expenses incurred in attending, recording and transmitting the road show, neither of which will be contingent on the size or successful conclusion of any offering. Bloomberg also may decide to collect fees for access to a road show on a subscription/pay-per-view basis for the viewers authorized by the underwriters, as described above. In all such cases, the subscribers would have been authorized by the underwriter to receive the electronic road show, as described above.

Analysis. In *Private Financial Network, supra,* the Division considered a similar factual pattern in which electronic road shows are to be made available to a limited audience under circumstances where the viewer will be given a prospectus in advance, the viewer will be prohibited from copying or redistributing the road show, and the viewer will be reminded that the principal source of information about the issuer and the offering is the documents filed with the Commission in the Securities Act registration. The limitations on the character of the audience in Bloomberg's case are essentially the same as in Private Financial Network. The road show transmission should be viewed as the equivalent of oral statements and not as the delivery of a document that would be a prospectus within the meaning of Section 2(10) of the Securities Act. [8]

In Net Roadshow, Inc. (July 30, 1997), the Division indicated that it would not recommend enforcement action to the Commission if Net Roadshow, Inc. transmits an issuer's road show presentation over the Internet for the purposes and pursuant to the procedures described in the in-coming letter. Those purposes and procedures are in all material respects identical to those discussed above. The rationale supporting the Division's position in that instance supports also the position we are asking the Division to express here.

Conclusion. In view of the foregoing, we are of the opinion that the transmission of road shows over the Bloomberg under the circumstances described above should not be deemed to involve the transmission of a prospectus within the meaning of Section 2(10) of the Securities Act and we respectfully request that the Division advise us that it would not recommend that the Commission commence enforcement action pursuant to the Securities Act if Bloomberg transmitted "road show" meetings concerning public offerings over THE BLOOMBERG service under the circumstances above.

* * *

In accordance with the procedures set forth in Securities Act Release Nos. 6269 (Dec. 5, 1980) and 5127 (Jan. 25, 1971), seven copies of this letter are submitted herewith, and the specific subsections of the particular statute to which this letter pertains are indicated in the upper right-hand corner of the first page of this letter and each copy. We respectfully request the opportunity to meet with the staff if the staff proposes to deny or withhold any part of the no-action relief requested herein. Pursuant to Rule 81(b) of the Commission's Regulation Concerning Information and Requests, 17 C.F.R. §200.81(b), we further request that the staff accord confidential treatment of this letter and the staff response thereto until the earlier of 120 days from the date of such response or Bloomberg's first public announcement of the information contained in this letter. The request for confidential treatment is being submitted because certain of the facts set forth above are not now public and premature disclosure of them could adversely affect Bloomberg. If you have any questions or seek any additional information regarding this request, please telephone me at (212) 821-8206.

Very truly yours,

Roger D. Blanc

STAFF REPLY LETTER

October 22, 1997

RESPONSE OF THE OFFICE OF CHIEF COUNSEL
DIVISION OF CORPORATION FINANCE

Re: Bloomberg L.P. ("Bloomberg")
Incoming letter dated October 22, 1997

Based on the facts presented, but without necessarily agreeing with your analysis, the Division will not recommend enforcement action to the Commission if Bloomberg transmits an issuer's road show presentation to Bloomberg subscribers for the purposes and pursuant to the procedures described in your letter, in reliance upon your counsel's opinion that such transmissions are not prospectuses within the meaning of Section 2(a)(10) of the Securities Act of 1933. The Division notes that a road show transmission will not be conducted before the registration statement is filed with the Commission in connection with the particular public offering of securities.

Your request for confidential treatment pursuant to Rule 81(b), of the Commission's Regulation Concerning Information and Requests 17 C.F.R. §200.81(b), has been granted until the earlier of: (a) 120 days from the date of this response; or (b) the date that any information contained in your letter or this response is made publicly available by Bloomberg.

This position is based on the representations made to the Division in your letter, as well as your counsel's opinion as described therein. Any different facts or conditions therefore might require different conclusions. Moreover, this response represents the Division's position on enforcement action only and does not express any legal conclusion on the question presented. Because regulatory responses to legal issues raised by technological developments may evolve, you should be aware that this no-action position may be reevaluated in the future.

Sincerely,

Broc Romanek
Special Counsel

[1]The technology currently used by Bloomberg involves a closed-circuit system to dedicated Bloomberg terminals as well as to individual computers that can receive "open" Bloomberg data feeds. In each case, the user has an individual, private pass word that is used to obtain access to Bloomberg data. In the future, if Bloomberg uses the Internet or other publicly available data transmission facilities, it will use pass words or other security measures to limit access to persons who have proper authorization.

[2]This corresponds to the ability of a member of the audience of a live road show to arrive late, leave the room at any time

and then reenter.

[3]Bloomberg will reserve the right to edit out dead time arising through logistical, organizational or similar problems at live road shows and to give the issuer and/or underwriter the opportunity to edit out misstatements or mistakes.

[4]*See* "Use of Electronic Media for Delivery Purposes," Securities Act Release Nos. 7233 (October 6, 1995), 1995 SEC LEXIS 2662, and 7289 (May 9, 1996), 1996 SEC LEXIS 1298.

[5]See, e.g., Loss & Seligman, FUNDAMENTALS OF SECURITIES REGULATION 80 (3d ed. 1995).

[6]This could be accomplished by assigning special passwords for this purpose and changing the passwords each day, or by other means.

[7]The legend, based on Rule 134(b) but modified to refer to the transmission over THE BLOOMBERG and to conform to the Commission's recently proposed "plain English" guidelines, will read as follows:

The issuer of the securities discussed in this transmission has filed a registration statement with the Securities and Exchange Commission covering the offer and sale of the securities. The registration statement has not yet become effective. These securities may not be sold nor may offers to buy them be accepted before the registration statement becomes effective. This transmission does not offer any securities to you or ask you to buy any securities. The securities will not be sold in any State in which the sale would be illegal before registration or qualification under the securities laws of that State.

[8]While such oral communications are not prospectuses, the issuer and the underwriters, respectively, will remain subject to the antifraud provisions of the Securities Act and the Securities Exchange Act of 1934 in connection with any statements they make.

EXHIBIT E

SEC NO-ACTION LETTER, NET ROADSHOW II (JAN. 1998)

1998 SEC No-Act. LEXIS 107

Securities Exchange Act of 1934 -- Rule 144A

January 30, 1998

[*1] Net Roadshow, Inc.

TOTAL NUMBER OF LETTERS: 2

SEC-REPLY-1: SECURITIES AND EXCHANGE COMMISSION
WASHINGTON, D.C. 20549

January 30, 1998

RESPONSE OF THE OFFICE OF CHIEF COUNSEL
DIVISION OF CORPORATION FINANCE

Re: Net Roadshow, Inc. (the "Company")
Incoming letter dated January 20, 1998

Based on the facts presented in your letter, and your counsel's opinion that the activities described in your letter are consistent with Rule 144A(d)(1) under the Securities Act of 1933 (the "Act"), the Division will not recommend enforcement action to the Commission if the Company transmits road shows over its Internet website, on behalf of a "Seller" (as that term defined in your letter), solely to qualified institutional buyers" ("QIBS") within the meaning of Rule 144A(a)(1) under the Act. Moreover, the staff's no-action position is predicated on the Company's compliance with the following conditions in connection with each "Rule 144A Road Show" (as defined in your letter):

(A) the Company will deny access to its website for viewing of a particular road show (which road show shall be deemed to include the posting of any notice thereof on the Company's web site) to all persons or entities (other than employees or authorized agents [*2] of the Company or Seller for that road show), except those institutions for which the Seller has confirmed its reasonable belief regarding their QIB status (see Rule 144A(d)(1)).

(B) the confidential password assigned to QIBs for a particular road show will be unique to that road show, and will expire no later than the date of termination of the related offering.

(C) each Seller's "confirmation" to the Company (as described in your letter) will include the following:

(1) a representation that such Seller is a QIB within the meaning of Rule 144A(a)(1); and

(2) an adequate basis for such Seller's representations of its "reasonable belief" that:

(i) each entity to which the Seller has assigned a confidential password is a QIB; and

(ii) the offering to which the particular road show relates is not subject to

C:\NETRS2

registration under the Securities Act.

(D) the Company otherwise has no actual knowledge, or reason to believe, that:

(1) the Seller is not a QIB;

(2) any of the entities to which the Seller has assigned a confidential password is not a QIB; or

(3) the securities offering to which a particular road show relates is subject to registration under Section 5 [*3] of the Securities Act.

(E) the Company is not an affiliate of any Seller or issuer of a security that is the subject of a particular road show.

This position is based on the facts and circumstances outlined in your letter, as well as your counsel's opinion as described therein. Accordingly, any different facts or conditions might require a different conclusion. In addition, this response expresses the Division's position on enforcement action only, and as such does not express any legal conclusion on the question presented. Finally, because regulatory responses to legal issues raised by technological developments may evolve, you should be aware that this no-action position may be reevaluated in the future by either the staff or the Commission.

Sincerely,

Catherine T. Dixon
Chief Counsel

INQUIRY-1: TROUTMAN SANDERS LLP

ATTORNEYS AT LAW

A LIMITED LIABILITY PARTNERSHIP

NATIONSBANK PLAZA

600 PEACHTREE STREET, N.E. - SUITE 5200

ATLANTA, GEORGIA 30308-2216

TELEPHONE: 404-885-3000

FACSIMILE: 404-885-3995

INTERNET: Tommy.Duffy@troutmansanders.com

404-885-3296
January 20, 1998

Catherine T. Dixon, Chief Counsel
Division of Corporation Finance
U.S. Securities and Exchange Commission

Mail Stop [*4] 3-3
450 Fifth Street, N.W.
Washington, D.C. 20549

Re: No Action Request Rule 144A of the Securities Act of 1933, as amended (the "Securities Act or the "Act")

Dear Ms. Dixon:

This firm serves as counsel to Net Roadshow, Inc. (the "Company"). The Company desires to transmit, over the Internet, road shows that relate to offerings of securities made solely to "qualified institutional buyers" (or "QIBs" as such term is defined in Rule 144A(a)(1)) pursuant to Rule 144A under the Securities Act of 1933 (the "Act"). We would appreciate confirmation, in the form of a no-action response from the staff, of our opinion that the Company's transmission of a "Rule 144A Road Show" on behalf of a "Seller" (as these terms are defined below) is consistent with Rule 144A(d)(1) of the Act.

FACTUAL BACKGROUND

The format and flow of the requested Internet road show product is as follows:

1. For the purposes of this letter, any road show that the Company will transmit over the Internet will relate to unregistered securities offered and/or sold exclusively to QIBs by a "Seller", which term, for purposes of this letter, refers to a QIB (or person acting on its behalf) that purchases such securities from [*5] the issuer for resale to other QIBs under Rule 144A ("Rule 144A Road Show").

2. The Company will obtain from each Seller confirmation that such Seller is a QIB, and that such Seller reasonably believes that:

(i) the offering to which the Rule 144A Road Show pertains is not subject to registration under the Securities Act; and

(ii) only entities satisfying the Rule 144A(a)(1) definition of "QIB" will be permitted password-restricted access to a Rule 144A Road Show.

3. The Company will maintain a website accessible only to entities that the Seller has identified as QIBs eligible to participate in a particular offering and the corresponding road show. The Seller first will provide to the Company the "confirmation" described in paragraph 2, above, for each Rule 144A Road Show that the Company is to transmit, whereupon the Company will provide to the Seller, and the Seller will assign to each QIB, a confidential password, or restricted access code, necessary to gain access to that Rule 144A Road Show. Each QIB's password will be valid only for that road show, and will expire no later than the date of termination of the related offering.

4. Each Rule 144A Road Show presented on the Company's [*6] website would be the same road show that representatives of the QIBs attending the actual road show see live, as the live road show will be filmed in its entirety, including the filming of all questions and answers. The Company's transmission of the live road show will not be edited for content, and QIBs that enter the Company's website via the assigned password will generally view the road show in its

entirety. n1 The Internet version of the road show will present the charts and oral presentation at a similar speed (like a slide show) as the live road show. In the event information changes between the time the road show is filmed and throughout the period that such road show is available on the web site, the display will include a periodic crawl providing a synopsis of such changes. The crawl will also provide that the viewer may contact the appropriate representative of the Seller for further information about such changes.

n1 The Company reserves the right to edit out "dead time" arising through logistical, organizational, or similar problems at live road shows and to give the Seller (and/or the issuer, as applicable) the opportunity to edit out misstatements or mistakes. [*7]

The Offering Memorandum regarding each offering will be displayed at all times throughout the related road show. A viewer would simply "click" on the "button" featuring the Offering Memorandum to view it in its entirety.

5. Before viewing any road show, each QIB will be advised of, and must agree to, the following:

The offeree has provided the Seller with such information as has been requested by the Seller to determine whether the offeree is a "qualified institutional buyer" as defined in Rule 144A(a)(1) of the Securities Act of 1933, as amended.

The confidential password assigned by the Seller has not been disclosed to any person or entity other than an employee or authorized agent of the offeree.

The distribution of any road show material to any person or entity other than an employee or authorized agent of the QIB is not permitted.

It is strongly recommended that each investor read the Offering Memorandum before making an Investment decision.

The Offering Memorandum relating to this offering is available through this site for viewing before viewing the road show. The Offering Memorandum may be obtained by clicking on the button labeled "OFFERING MEMORANDUM." Viewers [*8] should refer to the Offering Memorandum for more complete information about the offering.

In the event the viewer does not agree to the above, the viewer will be denied access to the road show. The screen, throughout each road show, would also carry a disclaimer at all times stating that "the distribution of any road show material is not permitted."

6. Each QIB will be able to view and print the entire Offering Memorandum, or any portion thereof. As discussed above, each QIB will be advised that the road show materials may not be distributed to any person or entity other than an employee or authorized agent of the QIB.

7. The viewer will be informed by a periodic crawl across the screen or by prominent text of the importance of viewing the entire Offering Memorandum.

8. The compensation to be received by the Company for the presentation of road shows over the Internet will not be contingent upon the degree of success of an underlying offering and will not be related to the size of an offering.

The fees charged by the Company will be analogous to a production or printing cost in that the fees will be charged for the production of the material to be transmitted over the Internet. [*9] The Company's fees may vary depending upon whether the road show presentation is (i) produced but not transmitted, or (ii) produced and transmitted for any period of time.

9. We believe that the following benefits would be recognized in the marketplace if the Commission approves the no-action request:

(i) The Company believes this process would "level the playing field" by providing all QIBs invited to review the road show with the opportunity to view the road show at a time which is convenient to them;

(ii) QIBs located in geographic areas frequently missed by the live road show would be placed on more equal footing with other QIBs;

(iii) There would be wider availability of the road show and the Offering Memorandum to interested QIBs; and

(iv) The road show and the Offering Memorandum should be available to QIBs on a more timely basis, providing the QIBs with more time to make a fully informed investment decision.

LEGAL ANALYSIS

In IPONET, Interpretive Letter dated July 26, 1996, the staff indicated that the private offering of securities on a password protected web site to accredited investors would not constitute a "general solicitation" or "general advertising" within the [*10] meaning of Rule 502(c) of Regulation D. There, the requestor indicated that it would post notices of private offerings of securities, and the offerings themselves, on a website which would be password-protected and therefore accessible only to those previously qualified as accredited investors.

The Company will operate with substantially the same procedures as those discussed in IPONET by limiting access to QIBs when transmitting Rule 144A Road Shows. This website, which will both identify and contain the road show presentations, will be password-protected. The only parties provided with a password, and therefore allowed access to the Company's website to view the road show transmissions, will be entities which a Seller has confirmed it reasonably believes to be QIBs. As noted, the Seller also must confirm to the Company that it is a QIB. Based upon the staff's position in IPONET, we believe that electronic transmission of Rule 144A Road Shows (see paragraph 1 above) pursuant to a website protected by an access code system should suffice to ensure that all offers pursuant to a road show will be made exclusively to QIBs. See Rule 144A(d)(1).

The staff also addressed issues relating [*11] to the offering of securities under Rule 144A by electronic means in The Institutional Real Estate Clearing House ("IREC"), No Action Letter dated May 28, 1996. n2 In IREC, the staff indicated that it would not take enforcement action against an entity facilitating the trading of unregistered securities in the Rule 144A secondary market through the operation of a closed, screen-based information system. The staff's response was conditioned in part on the requirement that the only parties allowed to offer and sell securities under Rule 144A through the system were entities qualified as QIBs under Rule 144A.

n2 The Company acknowledges that the staff did not specifically address issues relating to the Act in this letter and the letter is limited to the issues addressed therein.

The Company's proposal to transmit information related to Rule 144A Road Shows is also comparable to the IREC facts and circumstances. In both situations, Sellers that are QIBs would be offering Rule 144A securities through a password-protected system to prospective purchasers reasonably believed by the Seller to be QIBs. In contrast with both IREC and IPONET, however, the Company's proposal will [*12] not allow the viewer to purchase securities via the Company's website. Instead, any viewer that decides to purchase the securities that are the subject of a particular Rule 144A Road Show will be required to consummate the transaction with the Seller alone, independently of and without any involvement by the Company.

CONCLUSION

The Company's presentation of a Rule 144A Road Show by means of the Internet as described herein, should be permissible because access to each such presentation will be limited solely to QIBs. n3 We believe that the proposal of the Company would conform with the present practice in the securities industry of conducting road shows in connection with offerings made to entities which the Seller reasonably believes to be QIBs in accordance with Rule 144A of the Act, with the only difference being that the "live" road shows would be presented electronically.

n3 The Rule 144A Road Show presentations remain subject to the anti-fraud and the anti-manipulation provisions of the Act and the Securities Exchange Act of 1934, as amended.

Based on the foregoing facts and analysis, we believe that the Company's system limiting access to Rule 144A Road Shows transmitted [*13] over the Company's website to entities which a Seller reasonably believes to be QIBs as described herein is consistent with Rule 144A(d)(1). We respectfully request that the Division agree not to recommend that the Commission take enforcement action against the Company if it establishes and operates the system described above. If you wish additional information, or believe that additional representations or clarifications as to the proposed transaction are required before issuing the No Action Response, we would appreciate your contacting us.

Thank you for your review of this No-Action Letter Request.

Sincerely,

Thomas M. Duffy for
Troutman Sanders LLP

EXHIBIT F

SEC NO-ACTION LETTER, INTERNET CAPITAL CORP.
(DEC. 1997)

1997 SEC No-Act. LEXIS 1096

Securities Act of 1933 -- Section 5

December 24, 1997

[*1] Internet Capital Corporation

TOTAL NUMBER OF LETTERS: 2

SEC-REPLY-1: SECURITIES AND EXCHANGE COMMISSION
WASHINGTON, D.C. 20549

December 24, 1997

RESPONSE OF THE OFFICE OF CHIEF COUNSEL
DIVISION OF CORPORATION FINANCE
DIVISION OF MARKET REGULATION

Re: Internet Capital Corporation
Revision of Divisions' no-action response dated
December 18, 1997

Based on the facts presented, but without necessarily agreeing with your analysis, the Division of Corporate Finance will not recommend enforcement action to the Commission if ICC provides for the electronic posting and delivery of prospectuses and other offering materials for unaffiliated issuers as described in your letter. We specifically express no view on whether ICC, in engaging in the activities you have described, would be acting as an "underwriter" within the meaning of Section 2(a)(11) of the Securities Act of 1933 ("Securities Act"), inasmuch as such determinations are inherently fact-based and must be made on a case-by-case basis. Nor are we expressing any view on whether the prospectus delivery procedures described in your letter satisfy the standards articulated by the Commission in Securities Act Release Nos. 7233 (October 6, 1995) and/or 7288 (May 9, 1996). [*2]

The Division of Market Regulation has asked that we also advise you that it will not recommend enforcement action to the Commission under Section 15(a) of the Securities Exchange Act of 1934 ("Exchange Act") if ICC establishes and operates the Internet web site described in your letter without registering as a broker-dealer pursuant to Section 15(b) of the Exchange Act.

These positions are based on the representations made to the Divisions in your letter, and on your oral representation that no affiliate of ICC will engage in any business with any issuer, or assist any issuer in any respect, in connection with the offering of such issuer's securities on ICC's web site as described in your letter. Accordingly, any different facts or conditions might require one or both of the Divisions to reach a different conclusion. Moreover, this response expresses the Divisions' respective positions on enforcement action only, and does not express any legal conclusion. Finally, because regulatory responses to legal issues raised by ongoing technological developments may evolve, you should be aware that these no-action positions maybe re-evaluated in the future.

Sincerely,

Mary Kosterlitz
Special [*3] Counsel

INQUIRY-1: WORKLAND & WITHERSPOON, PLLC

ATTORNEYS AT LAW

714 WASHINGTON MUTUAL FINANCIAL CENTER

601 WEST MAIN AVENUE

SPOKANE, WASHINGTON 99201-0677

Telephone: (509) 455-9077

Facsimile: (509) 624-6441

E-mail: workwith@workwith.com

December 18, 1997

Ms. Catherine Dixon
Chief Counsel
Division of Corporation Finance
Securities and Exchange Commission
450 Fifth Street NW
Washington, D.C. 20549

Ms. Catherine McGuire
Chief Counsel
Division of Market Regulation
Securities and Exchange Commission
450 Fifth Street NW
Washington, D.C. 20549

RE: THE INTERNET CAPITAL CORP.

Dear Ladies and Gentleman:

I am submitting this request for a No-Action Letter pursuant to Release No. 33-6269. Accordingly, enclosed are the original and six copies of this letter.

SUMMARY OF REQUEST

The specific requests for no-action assurance are set forth in detail later in this letter. As an introduction, The Internet Capital Corp. ("ICC" or the "Company"), seeks assurance on the following issue:

In connection with an offering, ICC may provide for electronic delivery and presentation of offering materials for third-party issuers via electronic transmission provided the requirements of Rule 134(d) of the [*4] Securities Act of 1933, as amended (the "Act"), are otherwise met.

The Internet Capital Corp.

The Company's founder and president, Dave Lenartz, is a 1982 graduate of Michigan Technological University with a degree in electrical engineering. Mr. Lenartz is also the founder and president of Byte Dynamics, Inc., a private company that develops and implements software communication and database systems. Its primary customers are Nynex, Kaiser Aluminum, and Itron, Inc.

The Company was incorporated in April 1996, for the purpose of developing a bulletin board system for small companies ("Issuers") to conduct securities offerings on the Internet. The Company's target clients are those entities wishing to obtain access to the capital markets but whose financial requirements ($ 100,000 to $ 2,000,000) are too small to interest a conventional underwriter, or the associated costs of an underwriting are too great.

The Company has developed a proprietary, intuitive Web-trading environment, the "Internet Capital Financial Forum," and intends to offer its services to potential Issuers on a contractual basis as an internet service provider. ICC has established a home page and other linked [*5] pages (collectively, the "Web Site") on the World Wide Web at http://www.inetcapital.com. ICC's business is to provide a software platform for those Issuers who wish to offer their securities in an electronic medium. ICC will not engage in the business of generating any reports, analysis or investment advice for potential investors.

ELECTRONIC DELIVERY OF PROSPECTUS MATERIAL(S)

For a flat fee, not contingent upon the success of the offering, the Company will provide the Web-trading environment via the Internet Capital Financial Forum for facilitating an Issuer's on-line securities offering. The service will be provided for Issuers of registered offerings as well as Regulation A and SCOR offerings. The Company will not provide this service for securities to be issued pursuant to Rule 505 or 506 of the Act. The process will work as follows for registered offering. A similar process will be implemented for Regulation A and SCOR offerings.

A. The Web Site will provide a means for the delivery of prospectus material(s) as a service function to its clients. This Web Site function is designed to achieve compliance with all applicable state and federal securities laws and [*6] regulations.

B. The Web Site is oriented to support a grouping of individual corporate bulletin board areas or "corporate listings." An individual who has logged on the Web Site may elect to visit any corporate bulletin board area where a tombstone, preliminary offering document, or final offering document can be viewed regarding a specific company. ICC will not alter the content of any preliminary or final offering document. Each corporate bulletin board area remains autonomous and is operated in a separate manner from all of the other corporate areas. Only offerings and information pertaining to that specific corporation are displayed in its bulletin board area. ICC intends to post on its Web Site "tombstone" advertisements meeting the requirements of Rule 134, together with the red herring prospectus meeting the requirements of Rule 430. Such "tombstone" advertisements and the red herring prospectus will set forth the names of the applicable Issuers. The distribution of the "tombstone" advertisement and the red herring prospectus will be in accordance with Release No. 33-7233, dated October 6, 1995. There will be no "hot links" between the Web Site and any other corporate marketing [*7] information or a corporation's home page.

C. The order in which a company's offering information will be displayed within the Web Site is determined by objective criteria (either alphabetical by name of Issuer, or sequential by date of listing). A disclaimer will state that the order of listing has been objectively determined and that the order of presentation in no way constitutes any judgment by ICC as to the merits of a particular offering. ICC's Web Site will also link to any "tombstone" advertisements or red herring prospectus the following statements from Rule 134(b)(1) and (d), respectively:

A registration statement relating to these securities has been filed with the Securities and Exchange Commission but has not yet become effective. These securities may not be sold, nor may offers be accepted, prior to the time the registration statement becomes effective This (communications) shall not constitute an offer to sell or the solicitation of an offer to buy, nor shall there be any sale of these securities in any state in which such offer, solicitation, or sale would be unlawful prior to registration or qualification under the securities laws of any state.

No offer to [*8] buy the securities can be accepted and no part of the purchase price can be received until the registration statement has become effective: and any such offer may be withdrawn or revoked, without obligation or commitment of any kind, at any time prior to notice of its acceptance given after the effective date. An indication of interest in response to this advertisement will involve no obligation or commitment of any kind.

D. Upon an Issuer's receipt of a notice of an effective date, ICC will post the final offering document on its Web Site. Only the final offering document will contain the subscription documents necessary to purchase the offered securities. In addition, ICC's Web Site will contain a disclosure statement as follows:

The Internet Capital Corp., is not an underwriter of the securities or functioning as a broker-dealer or agent of [Name of Issuer]. Customer orders for the purchase of the securities should be sent directly to [Issuer or Escrow Agent].

E. In no instance will ICC function as an underwriter of a security or as a broker/dealer of a security. ICC will merely function as the delivery mechanism for a client.

F. ICC will not receive any commissions [*9] nor take compensation of any kind based on the sale of any securities. ICC will charge each Issuer a one-time, flat fee (the "Listing Fee"). The Listing Fee will cover such items as development of the software, use of the software platform, design and graphics work, and technical consulting regarding the listing and access to the ICC system. The Listing Fee will be independent of the number of hits to the Web Site after listing, or success of the offering. In all cases, ICC will be completely independent of the Issuer. Neither ICC nor its directors, officers, or employees will have an interest in any Issuer to be listed or any agent of such Issuer. ICC will not receive, transfer, or hold funds or securities as a function of operating the system.

G. ICC will not provide information of any nature regarding the advisability of buying or selling securities. Individuals accessing a particular company's offering will be given the opportunity to download the prospectus electronically or request that the Issuer deliver a printed copy of the prospectus. ICC will not contract with an Issuer for ICC to assume liability for improper prospectus delivery. Instructions for sending the proper funds [*10] and subscription information to the Issuer or its agent will be provided within the prospectus. Subscription agreements will be included in the file delivered with a prospectus. Files must be delivered in their entirety, therefore, each person requesting electronic delivery of a prospectus is assured of receiving a subscription agreement. Conversely, no subscription agreements can be accessed without delivery of a prospectus.

H. Each Issuer desiring to list an offering with ICC will covenant to issue its securities in compliance with all applicable federal and State laws and regulations. The obligation to assure compliance with such laws and regulations will rest upon the Issuer.

I. After electronic delivery of a prospectus, ICC will have no further involvement in the transaction, including negotiations regarding prospective purchases, record keeping of completed transactions, or any reporting requirements of the Issuer.

USING THE WEB SITE

Logging On

Each individual who wishes to access the corporate listing areas is first required to go through a registration process. This registration process involves the disclosure of key information such as the individual's name and [*11] address, the state of residence, and the individual's selected log-on name and password. Further access to the Web Site by this individual can only be accomplished by the use of the selected log-on name and password. Access to the Web Site and the activity within will be strictly controlled by this method of first determining who is logging on and if the individual should be allowed access to the Web Site.

Validation Process

To enhance Web Site security, ICC has implemented an additional user registration or validation process, which ensures the proper identity of any individual wishing to access the interactive Web Site. The registration process is designed to positively validate that the individual entering the Web Site is using a true E-mail address or identity that can be effectively traced within the World Wide Web.

Security within the interactive Web Site will be strictly maintained, requiring prior registration and password protection for each individual visiting the Web Site. The user registration process will encompass three controlled steps that the individual must walk through in order to receive a proper password for entrance into the registered or corporate listing [*12] area.

The first step for a new user registration will require that an online user registration form be filled out. Information entered will include the individual's name, address, state of residence, etc. The user will also enter its E-mail address, which will effectively become the user's log-on identification for entrance into the Web Site.

In the second step, after the new user submits the completed user registration form, the interactive Web Site will generate a unique password for that individual and then automatically E-mail that password to the user.

In the third and final step, the new user can gain access to the corporate listings by returning to the Web Site and entering the user's E-mail address and unique password in the log-on sequence.

If the user has misrepresented itself by giving an invalid or non-existent E-mail address during the registration process, the user will not be able to receive a password and will not be able to gain entrance to the registered area of the Web Site. Only users that received their unique password identification at their valid E-mail addresses can gain access.

ICC recognizes the need to police the identity of the individuals to [*13] its Web Site and will make every attempt to do so. The Web Site will also display disclaimers detailing the penalties for fraud and misrepresentation.

Blue Sky Issues

ICC's Web Site is able to preclude any solicitation or viewing of an offering document by persons in non-registered state jurisdictions. An individual will only be able to view offering documents, which have been approved for offering to residents of his or her state.

REGISTRATION ISSUES

In its communications to the public and its clients, ICC will not characterize itself as being a broker or dealer, but merely an Internet web site provider for companies wishing to offer their securities on the Internet.

Broker and Dealer

Subject to certain exceptions, Section 15(a) of the Securities Exchange Act of 1934, as amended (the "Exchange Act"), requires registration of any broker or dealer. Section 3(a)(5) of the Exchange Act defines a "dealer" as "any person engaged in the business of buying and selling securities for his own account." Section 3(a)(4) defines a "broker" as "any person engaged in the business of effecting transactions in securities for the account of others. . ." ICC will not engage in the business [*14] of effecting transactions in securities for the account of others, nor in the business of buying and selling securities for its own account.

No transactions or negotiations will occur by or through ICC. In addition, neither ICC nor any of its officers, directors, or employees will handle or have access to the funds, securities, or property of any user of the Internet Capital Financial Forum. ICC will not receive any commissions nor take compensation of any kind for the sale of any securities. ICC will charge each Issuer a Listing Fee. No other fees, commissions, or compensation will be paid by the investors or the listing companies. The Listing Fee will not be contingent upon the outcome or completion of any securities transaction resulting from a listing on the Internet Capital Financial Forum or the number of hits to the Web Site.

Requiring ICC to register as a broker-dealer would not provide the Issuers with any additional protection. Because ICC will not handle or have access to funds, securities, or any other property of any Issuer or any investor, a minimum capital requirement is unnecessary. Any financial failure of ICC would result only in the loss of the Issuer's and [*15] investors' access to the Web Site and not a loss of funds, securities, or property. Furthermore, the costs of compliance with the record keeping and periodic reporting requirements far outweigh any benefits. Additionally, all funds and securities will be handled either by the issuer or its agent.

CONCLUSION

For the foregoing reasons, ICC requests that the Office of Chief Counsel concur that ICC may: (1) provide for the electronic distribution and presentation of prospectus materials for third-party Issuers; and (2) establish and operate the Web Site without registering it or any of its personnel who will manage and operate the system as a "broker" or "dealer" under Section 15(b) of the Exchange Act.

In the event the Office of Chief Counsel does not concur with any of these views, ICC respectfully requests an opportunity to discuss the matter prior to any final decision thereon. If there are any questions or further information required, please contact me at (509) 455-9077.

Very truly yours,

WORKLAND & WITHERSPOON, PLLC

Gregory B. Lipsker,
Counsel for The Internet Capital Corp.

EXHIBIT G

SEC NO-ACTION LETTER, IPONET (JULY 1996)

, IPONET

Company: IPONET

Public Availability Date: July 26, 1996

WSB File No. 080596012

Fiche Locator No. 2632G12

WSB Subject Categories: 023, 025, 032

References:
Securities Act of 1933, Section 2(10), Rule 134
Securities Act of 1933, Reg. D, Rule 502

INQUIRY LETTER

RADCLIFF, FRANDSEN, TRICKER & DONGELL
FORTIETH FLOOR
777 SOUTH FIGUEROA STREET
LOS ANGELES, CALIFORNIA 90017
TELEPHONE(213) 614-1990

July 23, 1996

Securities Act of 1933, as amended, Sections: 2(10), Rule 230.134
4(2)
Regulation D, Section 502(c)

Office of Chief Counsel
Division of Corporation Finance
Securities and Exchange Commission
Washington, D.C. 20549

Re: IPONET

Ladies and Gentlemen:

I am submitting this request for a No Action Letter pursuant to Release No. 33-6269. Accordingly, please find enclosed seven copies of this letter, together with the original.

Summary of Request

The specific requests for no action assurance are set forth in detail later in this letter. As an introduction, IPONET seeks assurance on the following issues:

1. *Indications of Interest may be Accepted Electronically.* In connection with a public offering, W.J. Gallagher & Company, Inc., may accept indications of interest via electronic coupon or card as well as a paper coupon or card, if the requirements of Rule 134(d) are otherwise met.

2. *The Posting of a Notice of a Private Offering in a Password-protected Page of IPONET Accessible Only to IPONET Members Who Have Previously Qualified as Accredited Investors Does Not Involve Any Form of General Solicitation or General Advertising Within the Meaning of Regulation D Section 502(c).* W.J. Gallagher & Company, Inc., through the IPONET web site, will solicit individuals who meet the "accredited investor" or sophisticated investor standards of Regulation D to register as "Accredited Investors" as a means of building a customer base and data base of accredited and sophisticated investors for W.J. Gallagher & Company, Inc. *After* an individual has been determined to meet the requirements of an Accredited Investor, the Accredited Investor may review offers for private offerings of securities from companies that have posted private offerings with IPONET in accordance with the rules otherwise applying under Regulation D. The solicitation for Accredited Investors will be independent of and will not be linked to or made specifically with reference to any pending private offering. Accredited Investors may not invest in private offerings that were posted on IPONET before the Accredited Investor registered. Under these circumstances, an offer of securities otherwise satisfying the requirements of Regulation D to accredited or sophisticated investors who have been independently and previously solicited as customers of W.J. Gallagher & Company, Inc. will not constitute a general solicitation or general advertising within the meaning of Regulation D Section 502(c).

The Facts

1. IPONET is a sole proprietorship, wholly owned by Leo J. Feldman ("Feldman"), an individual. W.J. Gallagher & company has established and will maintain a system to supervise the activities of Feldman, including those pursued through IPONET, that is reasonably designed to achieve compliance with all applicable securities laws and regulations, and with the rules of the NASD and any other applicable self-regulatory organization.

2. Feldman is a registered principal of W.J. Gallagher & Company, Inc. W.J. Gallagher & Company, Inc., conducts a general securities business, including participation in public offerings as a "selected dealer".

3. IPONET has established a home page and other linked pages (collectively "Site") on the World Wide Web located at http://www.zanax.com/iponet IPONET intends to post on its Site "tombstone" advertisements meeting the requirements of Rule 134, together with the red herring prospectus meeting the requirements of Rule 430. Such "tombstone" advertisements and the red herring prospectuses will set forth the names of the underwriters. In cases where W.J. Gallagher & Co., Inc., will not act as an underwriter, the name of W.J. Gallagher & Company, Inc., will not appear on the "tombstone" or on the red herring prospectus. The distribution of the "tombstone" advertisement and the red herring prospectus by the issuer and its underwriters through the Site will be in accordance with Release No. 33-7233, dated October 6, 1995. The Site will also set forth a separate statement substantially as follows: "The securities offered by Name of Issuer pursuant to the Preliminary Prospectus dated insert date are available through W.J. Gallagher & Company, Inc." In addition, in the case where W.J. Gallagher & Company, Inc., will not act as an underwriter, the Site will contain a statement substantially as follows: "W.J. Gallagher & Company, Inc., is not an underwriter of the securities of Name of Issuer, but is authorized to accept customer orders for the purchase of the securities." In such cases, W.J. Gallagher & Company, Inc., will not purchase any of the securities from the Issuer for resale, will not participate in any such undertaking directly or indirectly, will not participate in the management of the distribution of the issue or any part of the issue, and will not perform any function normally performed by an underwriter or underwriting syndicate. IPONET is not asking for the Division's view on whether IPONET or W.J. Gallagher & Co., Inc., is acting as an underwriter, since such determinations are made on a case by case basis.

4. The IPONET Site will also link to any "tombstone" advertisements or red herring prospectus the following statements from Rule 134(b)(1) and (d), respectively:

"A registration statement relating to these securities has been filed with the Securities and Exchange Commission but has not yet become effective. These securities may not be sold nor may offers to buy be accepted prior to the time the registration statement becomes effective. This (communication) shall not constitute an offer to sell or the solicitation of an offer to buy nor shall there be any sale of these securities in any State in which such offer, solicitation or sale would be unlawful prior to registration or qualification under the securities laws of any such State."

"No offer to buy the securities can be accepted and no part of the purchase price can be received until the registration statement has become effective, and any such offer may be withdrawn or revoked, without obligation or commitment of any kind, at any time prior to notice of its acceptance given after the effective date. As indication of interest in response to this advertisement will involve no obligation or commitment of any kind."

5. The Site will also contain an electronic "coupon" or "card" linked to each red herring prospectus. A visitor to the Site will be invited to complete and send this electronic "coupon" or "card", via e-mail or communications link in the Site itself or by printing the coupon or card and sending it by regular carrier, indicating an interest in purchasing the security.

6. In cases where W.J. Gallagher & Company, Inc., will not act as an underwriter, but the securities will be sold through W.J. Gallagher & Company, Inc., as one of the "selected dealers", W.J. Gallagher & Company, Inc., will receive a commission which will not exceed the usual and customary distributors' or sellers' commission.

7. The Site contains a section entitled "Accredited Investors". Persons who have previously registered as a member of IPONET are invited to request registration with IPONET as an "Accredited Investor". These Accredited Investors will be added to W.J. Gallagher & Company, Inc.'s customer and data base. In order to register, the member must complete an on-line questionnaire substantially in the form of Exhibit A, which is designed to allow W.J. Gallagher Company, Inc., and any potential issuer to determine, or to have a basis for a reasonable belief, that a member is an "accredited investor" within the meaning of Regulation D, Rule 501(a) or a sophisticated investor under Rule 506. The questionnaire may be completed on-line in a secured manner or printed out and returned in hard copy. W.J. Gallagher & Company, Inc., will verify the information in the questionnaire to determine that the member is an Accredited Investor. Once a Member is qualified and registered as an "Accredited Investor", then the Accredited Investor will be given a password which will allow the Accredited Investor to access a password-protected page where private offerings will be posted and the Accredited Investor may access further information. However, the IPONET site will only allow an Accredited Investor access to those private offerings which are posted subsequent in time to the Accredited Investors qualification with IPONET. If the Accredited Investor has consented, then IPONET may contact the Accredited Investor in the future about new private offerings that are posted on IPONET.

8. The name of the Accredited Investor will be kept confidential by IPONET and W.J. Gallagher & Company, Inc., and will not be released to the issuers making the private offerings unless the Accredited Investor specifically consents to such release to a particular issuer. This consent may be given on-line.

9. Private issuers may post their private offerings in the password-protected section of IPONET. No mention or description of the issuer of any nature will be available on IPONET to any person, other than those who have previously qualified as Accredited Investors, who must use their password to enter the password-protected part of IPONET.

10. In cases where W.J. Gallagher & Company, Inc., is not acting as a broker-dealer, IPONET will charge a "listing fee" of a set amount. The listing fee will cover such items as design and graphics work, technical consulting regarding the listing, and historical popularity of the Site (analogous to the circulation history of newspapers). The listing fee will be independent of the size of the private offering, any investment made by Accredited Investors, and the number of hits to the Site after listing. (In such cases, W.J. Gallagher & Company, Inc., will be completely independent of the issuer and W.J. Gallagher & Company, Inc., will receive no compensation of any nature.) In cases where W.J. Gallagher & Company, Inc., is acting as a broker-dealer, IPONET will still receive only the listing fee and nothing more. Neither W.J. Gallagher & Company, Inc., nor IPONET will have an affiliation with or any interest of any kind in the issuer prior to or at the time of the offering of the private offering.

11. An Accredited Investor may invest only in private offerings which are posted on IPONET subsequent in time to the registration of the Accredited Investor with IPONET, and then only after a sufficient time has elapsed between the IPONET member's registration as an Accredited Investor and the inception of a private offering so that the registration as an Accredited Investor is not deemed to be a solicitation for a particular private offering.

12. Each issuer desiring to list a private offering with IPONET will covenant to issues securities in a private offering in strict accordance with Regulation D. The obligation to assure compliance with Regulation D will rest upon the issuer.

Legal Analysis

1. *W.J. Gallagher & Company, Inc. May Accept Indications of Interest Via E-Mail*

Rule 134(d) provides as follows:

(d) A communication sent or delivered to any person pursuant to this rule which is accompanied or preceded by a prospectus which meets the requirements of Section 10 of the Act at the date of such communication, may solicit from the recipient of the communication an offer to buy the security or request the recipient to indicate, *upon an enclosed or attached coupon or card, or in some other manner* (emphasis added), whether he might be interested in the security, if the communication contains substantially the following statement:

"No offer to buy the securities can be accepted and no part of the purchase price can be received until the registration statement has become effective, and any such offer may be withdrawn or revoked, without obligation or commitment of any kind, at any time prior to notice of its acceptance given after the effective date. An indication of interest in response to this advertisement will involve no obligation or commitment of any kind."

As described above in *Facts*, paragraphs 3 and 4, the Site will contain the notices required by Rule 134(b)(1) and (d) linked to any tombstone advertisement and red herring prospectus.

Rule 134(d) specifically contemplated that indications of interest may be accepted by a "coupon or card, or in some other manner". IPONET's electronic "coupon" or "card" may be sent directly from the Site or independently via e-mail, or printed in hard copy and sent via regular carrier. An electronic or e-mail indication of interest as described should qualify as a card or coupon in harmony with Release No. 33-7233, October 6, 1995, and certainly qualifies under the phrase "some other manner" and is entirely consistent with the 1933 Act and the Rules thereunder. *See* the excerpt from Release No. 33-7233 set forth below.

2. *The Posting of a Notice of a Private Offering in a Password-protected Page of IPONET Accessible Only to IPONET Members Who Have Previously Qualified as Accredited Investors Does Not Involve Any Form of General Solicitation or General Advertising Within the Meaning of Regulation D Section 502(c).*

In *H.B. Shaine & Co., Inc.*, No Action Letter dated May 1, 1987, the staff indicated that a distribution by Shaine of questionnaires to prospective accredited and sophisticated investors to determine their suitability to participate in private offerings would not be deemed a "general solicitation or general advertisement". This view was premised upon several factors, including the use of a generic questionnaire and upon the elapse of a sufficient period of time between the completion of the questionnaire and the contemplation or inception of any particular offering.

As described above in *Facts*, paragraphs 7-11, W.J. Gallagher & Company, Inc., will follow substantially the same procedure as Shaine. The primary distinction appears to be simply that the questionnaire will be distributed electronically through the IPONET Site and the questionnaire may be returned either electronically through a link in the Site, through e-mail, or by hard copy, and one assumes that Shaine sent and received the questionnaires through traditional means. Similarly, the documents relating to a private offering to the Accredited Investors would be distributed electronically through the IPONET Site password protected page available only to Accredited Investors. The No Action Letter did not address the means of communication.

In Release No. 33-7233, the Commission stated:

The Commission appreciates the promise of electronic distribution of information in enhancing investors' ability to access, research, and analyze information, and in facilitating the provision of information by issuers and others. The Commission believes that, given the numerous benefits of electronic distribution of information and the facts that in many respects it may be more useful to investors than paper, its use should not be disfavored.* * * Given the numerous benefits of electronic media, the Commission encourages further technological research, development and application. *The Commission believes that the use of electronic media should be at least an equal alternative to the use of paper-based media. Accordingly, issuer or third party information that can be delivered in paper under the federal securities laws may be delivered in electronic format.* (Emphasis added.)

Accordingly, since W.J. Gallagher & Company, Inc., will be soliciting questionnaires for Accredited Investors and will be distributing information on private offerings electronically that it could otherwise properly do by paper, the posting of private offerings in a password protected page of IPONET would not involve general solicitation or general advertisement within the meaning of Rule 502(c) under the circumstances discussed above.

Conclusion.

We request that you concur with the conclusions set forth above. If you have questions or comments, please contact me directly.

Very truly yours,

Russell M. Frandsen, of
RADCLIFF, FRANDSEN, TRICKER
& DONGELL

RMF:kn

STAFF REPLY LETTER

July 26, 1996

RESPONSE OF THE OFFICE OF CHIEF COUNSEL
DIVISION OF CORPORATION FINANCE

Re: IPONET
Incoming letter dated July 23, 1996

Based on the facts presented, the Division's views are as follow:

(1) The reference in Rule 134(d) to "an enclosed or attached coupon or card, or in some other manner" would be equally applicable to the acceptance of indications of interest via electronic coupon or card as well as paper coupon or card by W.J. Gallagher & Company, Inc. ("Gallagher"). In this regard, we note your representation that the other requirements of Rule 134(d) will be satisfied in connection with the acceptance of such indications of interest.

(2) The qualification of accredited or sophisticated investors in the manner described and the posting of a notice of a private offering in a password-protected page of IPONET accessible only to IPONET members who have qualified as accredited investors would not involve any form of "general solicitation" or "general advertising" within the meaning of Rule 502(c) of Securities Act Regulation D. In reaching this conclusion, we note that (a) both the invitation to complete the questionnaire used to determine whether an investor is accredited or sophisticated and the questionnaire itself will be generic in nature and will not reference any specific transactions posted or to be posted on the password-protected page of IPONET; (b) the password-protected page of IPONET will be available to a particular investor only after Gallagher has made the determination that the particular potential investor is accredited or sophisticated; and (c) a potential investor could purchase securities only in transactions that are posted on the password-protected page of IPONET after that investor's qualification with IPONET. In this regard, we take no position as to whether the information obtained by Gallagher is sufficient to form a reasonable basis for believing an investor to be accredited or sophisticated.

Because these positions are based on the representations made to the Division in your letter, it should be noted that any different facts might require a different result.

Sincerely,

Joseph Babits
Special Counsel

EXHIBIT H

LETTER TO SEC
IN RE: IPONET

RADCLIFF, FRANDSEN, TRICKER & DONGELL
LAWYERS

WASHINGTON, D.C.
SUITE 211
601 NORTH FAIRFAX STREET
ALEXANDRIA, VIRGINIA 22314
TELEPHONE (703) 510-9675

HONOLULU
FOURTH FLOOR
FIVE WATERFRONT PLAZA
500 ALA MOANA BOULEVARD
HONOLULU, HAWAII 96813
TELEPHONE (808) 529-7400

FORTIETH FLOOR
777 SOUTH FIGUEROA STREET
LOS ANGELES, CALIFORNIA 90017-5800
TELEPHONE (213) 614-1990

FACSIMILES:
LOS ANGELES: (213) 489-9263
WASHINGTON, D.C.: (703) 510-8604
SAN FRANCISCO: (415) 989-5465
HONOLULU: (808) 524-8293
ROME: (39) 06-324-3392

SAN FRANCISCO
SUITE 1475
88 KEARNY STREET
SAN FRANCISCO, CALIFORNIA 94108
TELEPHONE (415) 399-8303

ROME
OF COUNSEL
PETTINARI & RIDOLFI
VIA TACITO, 7
00193 ROMA, ITALY
TELEPHONE (39) 06-323-5588

RUSSELL M. FRANDSEN
73314.2250@COMPUSERVE.COM
RMFRANDSEN@AOL.COM
FRANDSEN@DELPHI.COM

Securities Act of 1933, as amended, Sections: 2(10), Rule 230.134
4(2)
Regulation D, Section 502(c)

July 23, 1996

Office of Chief Counsel
Division of Corporation Finance
Securities and Exchange Commission
Washington, D.C. 20549

96 JUL 25 PM 1:58
OFFICE OF CHIEF COUNSEL

Re: IPONET

Ladies and Gentlemen:

I am submitting this request for a No Action Letter pursuant to Release No. 33-6269. Accordingly, please find enclosed seven copies of this letter, together with the original.

Summary of Request

The specific requests for no action assurance are set forth in detail later in this letter. As an introduction, IPONET seeks assurance on the following issues:

1. Indications of Interest may be Accepted Electronically. In connection with a public offering, W.J. Gallagher & Company, Inc., may accept indications of interest via electronic coupon or card as well as a paper coupon or card, if the requirements of Rule 134(d) are otherwise met.

2. The Posting of a Notice of a Private Offering in a Password-protected Page of IPONET Accessible Only to IPONET Members Who Have Previously Qualified as Accredited Investors Does Not Involve Any Form of General Solicitation or General Advertising Within the Meaning of Regulation D Section 502(c). W.J. Gallagher & Company, Inc., through the IPONET

web site, will solicit individuals who meet the "accredited investor" or sophisticated investor standards of Regulation D to register as "Accredited Investors" as a means of building a customer base and data base of accredited and sophisticated investors for W.J. Gallagher & Company, Inc. After an individual has been determined to meet the requirements of an Accredited Investor, the Accredited Investor may review offers for private offerings of securities from companies that have posted private offerings with IPONET in accordance with the rules otherwise applying under Regulation D. The solicitation for Accredited Investors will be independent of and will not be linked to or made specifically with reference to any pending private offering. Accredited Investors may not invest in private offerings that were posted on IPONET before the Accredited Investor registered. Under these circumstances, an offer of securities otherwise satisfying the requirements of Regulation D to accredited or sophisticated investors who have been independently and previously solicited as customers of W.J. Gallagher & Company, Inc. will not constitute a general solicitation or general advertising within the meaning of Regulation D Section 502(c).

The Facts

1. IPONET is a sole proprietorship, wholly owned by Leo J. Feldman ("Feldman"), an individual. W.J. Gallagher & company has established and will maintain a system to supervise the activities of Feldman, including those pursued through IPONET, that is reasonably designed to achieve compliance with all applicable securities laws and regulations, and with the rules of the NASD and any other applicable self-regulatory organization.

2. Feldman is a registered principal of W.J. Gallagher & Company, Inc. W.J. Gallagher & Company, Inc., conducts a general securities business, including participation in public offerings as a "selected dealer".

3. IPONET has established a home page and other linked pages (collectively "Site") on the World Wide Web located at http://www.zanax.com/iponet. IPONET intends to post on its Site "tombstone" advertisements meeting the requirements of Rule 134, together with the red herring prospectus meeting the requirements of Rule 430. Such "tombstone" advertisements and the red herring prospectuses will set forth the names of the underwriters,. In cases where W. J. Gallagher & Co., Inc. will not act as an underwriter, the name of W.J. Gallagher & Company, Inc., will not appear on the "tombstone" or on the red herring prospectus. The distribution of the "tombstone" advertisement and the red herring prospectus by the issuer and its underwriters through the Site will be in accordance with Release No. 33-7233, dated October 6, 1995. The Site will also set forth a separate statement substantially as follows: "The securities offered by [Name of Issuer] pursuant to the Preliminary Prospectus dated [insert date] are available through W.J. Gallagher & Company, Inc." In addition, in the case where W.J. Gallagher & Company, Inc., will not act as an underwriter, the Site will contain a statement substantially as follows: "W.J. Gallagher & Company, Inc., is not an underwriter of the securities of [Name of Issuer], but is

authorized to accept customer orders for the purchase of the securities." In such cases, W.J. Gallagher & Company, Inc., will not purchase any of the securities from the Issuer for resale, will not participate in any such undertaking directly or indirectly, will not participate in the management of the distribution of the issue or any part of the issue, and will not perform any function normally performed by an underwriter or underwriting syndicate. IPONET is not asking for the Division's view on whether IPONET or W.J. Gallagher & Co., Inc., is acting as an underwriter, since such determinations are made on a case by case basis.

4. The IPONET Site will also link to any "tombstone" advertisements or red herring prospectus the following statements from Rule 134 (b)(1) and (d), respectively:

> "A registration statement relating to these securities has been filed with the Securities and Exchange Commission but has not yet become effective. These securities may not be sold nor may offers to buy be accepted prior to the time the registration statement becomes effective. This (communication) shall not constitute an offer to sell or the solicitation of an offer to buy nor shall there be any sale of these securities in any State in which such offer, solicitation or sale would be unlawful prior to registration or qualification under the securities laws of any such State."

> "No offer to buy the securities can be accepted and no part of the purchase price can be received until the registration statement has become effective, and any such offer may be withdrawn or revoked, without obligation or commitment of any kind, at any time prior to notice of its acceptance given after the effective date. An indication of interest in response to this advertisement will involve no obligation or commitment of any kind."

5. The Site will also contain an electronic "coupon" or "card" linked to each red herring prospectus. A visitor to the Site will be invited to complete and send this electronic "coupon" or "card", via e-mail or communications link in the Site itself or by printing the coupon or card and sending it by regular carrier, indicating an interest in purchasing the security.

6. In cases where W.J. Gallagher & Company, Inc., will not act as an underwriter, but the securities will be sold through W.J. Gallagher & Company, Inc., as one of the "selected dealers", W.J. Gallagher & Company, Inc., will receive a commission which will not exceed the usual and customary distributors' or sellers' commission.

7. The Site contains a section entitled "Accredited Investor". Persons who have previously registered as a member of IPONET are invited to request registration with IPONET as an "Accredited Investor". These Accredited Investors will be added to W.J. Gallagher & Company, Inc.'s customer and data base. In order to register, the member must complete an on-line questionnaire substantially in the form of Exhibit A, which is designed to allow W.J. Gallagher & Company, Inc., and any potential issuer to determine, or to have a basis for a

reasonable belief, that a member is an "accredited investor" within the meaning of Regulation D, Rule 501(a) or a sophisticated investor under Rule 506. The questionnaire may be completed on-line in a secured manner or printed out and returned in hard copy. W.J. Gallagher & Company, Inc., will verify the information in the questionnaire to determine that the member is an Accredited Investor. Once a Member is qualified and registered as an "Accredited Investor", then the Accredited Investor will be given a password which will allow the Accredited Investor to access a password-protected page where private offerings will be posted and the Accredited Investor may access further information. However, the IPONET site will only allow an Accredited Investor access to those private offerings which are posted subsequent in time to the Accredited Investors qualification with IPONET. If the Accredited Investor has consented, then IPONET may contact the Accredited Investor in the future about new private offerings that are posted on IPONET.

8. The name of the Accredited Investor will be kept confidential by IPONET and W.J. Gallagher & Company, Inc.; and will not be released to the issuers making the private offerings unless the Accredited Investor specifically consents to such release to a particular issuer. This consent may be given on-line.

9. Private issuers may post their private offerings in the password-protected section of IPONET. No mention or description of the issuer of any nature will be available on IPONET to any person, other than those who have previously qualified as Accredited Investors, who must use their password to enter the password-protected part of IPONET.

10. In cases where W.J. Gallagher & Company, Inc., is not acting as a broker-dealer, IPONET will charge a "listing fee" of a set amount. The listing fee will cover such items as design and graphics work, technical consulting regarding the listing, and historical popularity of the Site (analogous to the circulation history of newspapers). The listing fee will be independent of the size of the private offering, any investment made by Accredited Investors, and the number of hits to the Site after listing. (In such cases, W.J. Gallagher & Company, Inc., will be completely independent of the issuer and W.J. Gallagher & Company, Inc., will receive no compensation of any nature.) In cases where W.J. Gallagher & Company, Inc., is acting as a broker-dealer, IPONET will still receive only the listing fee and nothing more. Neither W.J. Gallagher & Company, Inc., nor IPONET will have an affiliation with or any interest of any kind in the issuer prior to or at the time of the offering of the private offering.

11. An Accredited Investor may invest only in private offerings which are posted on IPONET subsequent in time to the registration of the Accredited Investor with IPONET, and then only after a sufficient time has elapsed between the IPONET member's registration as an Accredited Investor and the inception of a private offering so that the registration as an Accredited Investor is not deemed to be a solicitation for a particular private offering.

12. Each issuer desiring to list a private offering with IPONET will covenant to

issues securities in a private offering in strict accordance with Regulation D. The obligation to assure compliance with Regulation D will rest upon the issuer.

Legal Analysis

1. W.J. Gallagher & Company, Inc. May Accept Indications of Interest Via E-Mail.

Rule 134 (d) provides as follows:

> (d) A communication sent or delivered to any person pursuant to this rule which is accompanied or preceded by a prospectus which meets the requirements of Section 10 of the Act at the date of such communication, may solicit from the recipient of the communication an offer to buy the security or request the recipient to indicate, upon an enclosed or attached coupon or card, or in some other manner (emphasis added), whether he might be interested in the security, if the communication contains substantially the following statement:
>
> "No offer to buy the securities can be accepted and no part of the purchase price can be received until the registration statement has become effective, and any such offer may be withdrawn or revoked, without obligation or commitment of any kind, at any time prior to notice of its acceptance given after the effective date. An indication of interest in response to this advertisement will involve no obligation or commitment of any kind."

As described above in Facts, paragraphs 3 and 4, the Site will contain the notices required by Rule 134(b)(1) and (d) linked to any tombstone advertisement and red herring prospectus.

Rule 134(d) specifically contemplates that indications of interest may be accepted by a "coupon or card, or in some other manner". IPONET's electronic "coupon" or "card" may be sent directly from the Site or independently via e-mail, or printed in hard copy and sent via regular carrier. An electronic or e-mail indication of interest as described should qualify as a card or coupon in harmony with Release No. 33-7233, October 6, 1995, and certainly qualifies under the phrase "some other manner" and is entirely consistent with the 1933 Act and the Rules thereunder. See the excerpt from Release No. 33-7233 set forth below.

2. The Posting of a Notice of a Private Offering in a Password-protected Page of IPONET Accessible Only to IPONET Members Who Have Previously Qualified as Accredited Investors Does Not Involve Any Form of General Solicitation or General Advertising Within the Meaning of Regulation D Section 502(c).

In H.B. Shaine & Co., Inc., No Action Letter dated May 1, 1987, the staff indicated that a distribution by Shaine of questionnaires to prospective accredited and sophisticated investors to determine their suitability to participate in private offerings would not be deemed a "general solicitation or general advertisement". This view was premised upon several factors, including the use of a generic questionnaire and upon the elapse of a sufficient period of time between the completion of the questionnaire and the contemplation or inception of any particular offering.

As described above in Facts, paragraphs 7-11, W.J. Gallagher & Company, Inc., will follow substantially the same procedure as Shaine. The primary distinction appears to be simply that the questionnaire will be distributed electronically through the IPONET Site and the questionnaire may be returned either electronically through a link in the Site, through e-mail, or by hard copy, and one assumes that Shaine sent and received the questionnaires through traditional means. Similarly, the documents relating to a private offering to the Accredited Investors would be distributed electronically through the IPONET Site password protected page available only to Accredited Investors. The No Action Letter did not address the means of communication.

In Release No. 33-7233, the Commission stated:

> The Commission appreciates the promise of electronic distribution of information in enhancing investors' ability to access, research, and analyze information, and in facilitating the provision of information by issuers and others. The Commission believes that, given the numerous benefits of electronic distribution of information and the fact that in many respects it may be more useful to investors than paper, its use should not be disfavored. * * * Given the numerous benefits of electronic media, the Commission encourages further technological research, development and application. The Commission believes that the use of electronic media should be at least an equal alternative to the use of paper-based media. Accordingly, issuer or third party information that can be delivered in paper under the federal securities laws may be delivered in electronic format. (Emphasis added.)

Accordingly, since W.J. Gallagher & Company, Inc., will be soliciting questionnaires for Accredited Investors and will be distributing information on private offerings electronically that it could otherwise properly do by paper, the posting of private offerings in a password protected page of IPONET would not involve general solicitation or general advertisement within the meaning of Rule 502(c) under the circumstances discussed above.

Conclusion.

We request that you concur with the conclusions set forth above. If you have questions or comments, please contact me directly.

Very truly yours,

Russell M. Frandsen

Russell M. Frandsen, of
RADCLIFF, FRANDSEN, TRICKER
& DONGELL

RMF:kn

July 26, 1996

RESPONSE OF THE OFFICE OF CHIEF COUNSEL
DIVISION OF CORPORATION FINANCE

Re: IPONET
Incoming letter dated July 23, 1996

Based on the facts presented, the Division's views are as follow:

(1) The reference in Rule 134(d) to "an enclosed or attached coupon or card, or in some other manner" would be equally applicable to the acceptance of indications of interest via electronic coupon or card as well as paper coupon or card by W.J. Gallagher & Company, Inc. ("Gallagher"). In this regard, we note your representation that the other requirements of Rule 134(d) will be satisfied in connection with the acceptance of such indications of interest.

(2) The qualification of accredited or sophisticated investors in the manner described and the posting of a notice of a private offering in a password-protected page of IPONET accessible only to IPONET members who have qualified as accredited investors would not involve any form of "general solicitation" or "general advertising" within the meaning of Rule 502(c) of Securities Act Regulation D. In reaching this conclusion, we note that (a) both the invitation to complete the questionnaire used to determine whether an investor is accredited or sophisticated and the questionnaire itself will be generic in nature and will not reference any specific transactions posted or to be posted on the password-protected page of IPONET; (b) the password-protected page of IPONET will be available to a particular investor only after Gallagher has made the determination that the particular potential investor is accredited or sophisticated; and (c) a potential investor could purchase securities only in transactions that are posted on the password-protected page of IPONET after that investor's qualification with IPONET. In this regard, we take no position as to whether the information obtained by Gallagher is sufficient to form a reasonable basis for believing an investor to be accredited or sophisticated.

Because these positions are based on the representations made to the Division in your letter, it should be noted that any different facts might require a different result.

Sincerely,

Joseph Babits
Special Counsel

NOTES

6

INTERNET PROSPECTUSES

EXHIBIT A

INTERNET PROSPECTUS - YAHOO! INC. OFFERING (APRIL 1996)

IPO HOME PAGE

YAHOO! INC. COMPLETES INITIAL PUBLIC OFFERING OF 2,600,000 SHARES OF COMMON STOCK AT $13.00 PER SHARE

SUNNYVALE, California – April 11, 1996 – Yahoo! Inc. announced today the pricing of its initial public offering of 2,600,000 shares of Common Stock (NASDAQ National Market: YHOO) at $13.00 per share. All of the shares were sold by the Company. The net proceeds to the Company will be used for general corporate purposes. The offering was managed by Goldman, Sachs & Co., Donaldson, Lufkin & Jenrette Securities Corporation and Montgomery Securities.

Yahoo! offers a branded Internet navigational service that is among the most widely used guides to information and discovery on the World Wide Web. Yahoo! provides a context-based directory structure for Web resources, as well as a Web-wide search engine that is seamlessly integrated with the Yahoo! directory service. The Company is developing a global family of Yahoo! branded media properties in targeted subject matter, demographic and geographic areas.

Copies of the prospectus relating to the offering may be obtained from Goldman Sachs & Co., Prospectus Department, 85 Broad Street, New York, NY, 10004, (212) 902-1000. The prospectus will also be available on April 12 at http://ipo.yahoo.com/

\# # #

View or Download Preliminary Prospectus

Contacts:

Media only:
NRH Public Relations
(415) 615-7905
skye@nrh.com

Investors only:
Gary Valenzuela
Chief Finanical Officer
(408) 328-3382
investor_relations@yahoo.com

Karen Edwards
Director of Brand Management

Yahoo! Inc.

Prospectus Dated April 12, 1996

IMPORTANT INFORMATION

The prospectus is provided solely for informational purposes. No other information contained in or accessed through the Yahoo! Web site shall be deemed to be part of this Prospectus.

These securities have not been approved or disapproved by the Securities and Exchange Commission or any State Securities Commission nor has the Securities and Exchange Commission or any State Securities Commission passed upon the accuracy or adequacy of this prospectus. Any representation to the contrary is a criminal offense.

No person has been authorized to give any information or to make any representations other than those contained in this Prospectus and, if given or made, such information or representations must not be relied upon as having been authorized. This Prospectus does not constitute an offer to sell or the solicitation of an offer to buy any securities other than the securities to which it relates or any offer to sell or the solicitation of an offer to buy such securities in any circumstances in which such offer or solicitation is unlawful. Neither the delivery of this Prospectus nor any sale made hereunder shall, under any circumstances, create any implication that there has been no change in the affairs of the Company since the date hereof or that the information contained herein is correct as of any time subsequent to its date.

View or Download Preliminary Prospectus

2,600,000 Shares

Yahoo! Inc.

Common Stock
(par value $0.001 per share)

Goldman, Sachs & Co.

Donaldson, Lufkin & Jenrette
Securities Corporation

Montgomery Securities

Representatives of the Underwriters

Download the entire prospectus as a PDF document (812K)

TABLE OF CONTENTS

No person has been authorized to give any information or to make any representations other than those contained in this Prospectus and, if given or made, such information or representations must not be relied upon as having been authorized. This Prospectus does not constitute an offer to sell or the solicitation of an offer to buy any securities other than the securities to which it relates or any offer to sell or the solicitation of an offer to buy such securities in any circumstances in which such offer or solicitation is unlawful. Neither the delivery of this Prospectus nor any sale made hereunder shall, under any circumstances, create any implication that there has been no change in the affairs of the Company since the date hereof or that the information contained herein is correct as of any time subsequent to its date.

Until May 7, 1996 (25 days after the date of this Prospectus), all dealers effecting transactions in the Common Stock, whether or not participating in this distribution, may be required to deliver a Prospectus. This delivery requirement is in addition to the obligation of dealers to deliver a Prospectus when acting as Underwriters and with respect to their unsold allotments or subscriptions.

[Next Section]

2,600,000 Shares

Yahoo! Inc.

Common Stock
(par value $0.001 per share)

YAHOO!

All of the shares of Common Stock offered hereby are being offered by Yahoo! Inc. Prior to this offering, there has been no public market for the Common Stock of the Company. For factors considered in determining the initial public offering price, see "Underwriting".

In connection with this offering, the Underwriters have reserved approximately 200,000 shares of Common Stock for sale at the initial public offering price to persons associated with the Company.

See "Risk Factors" commencing on page 6 for certain considerations relevant to an investment in the Common Stock.

The Common Stock has been approved for quotation on the Nasdaq National Market under the symbol "YHOO".

THESE SECURITIES HAVE NOT BEEN APPROVED OR DISAPPROVED BY THE SECURITIES AND EXCHANGE COMMISSION OR ANY STATE SECURITIES COMMISSION NOR HAS THE SECURITIES AND EXCHANGE COMMISSION OR ANY STATE SECURITIES COMMISSION PASSED UPON THE ACCURACY OR ADEQUACY OF THIS PROSPECTUS. ANY REPRESENTATION TO THE CONTRARY IS A CRIMINAL OFFENSE.

	INITIAL PUBLIC OFFERING PRICE	UNDERWRITING DISCOUNT (1)	PROCEEDS TO COMPANY (2)
Per Share	$13.00	$0.91	$12.09
Total (3)	$33,800,000	$2,366,000	$31,434,000

---

(1) The Company has agreed to indemnify the Underwriters against certain liabilities, including liabilities under the Securities Act of 1933. See "Underwriting".

(2) Before deducting estimated offering expenses of $700,000 payable by the Company.

04/30/96 11:

(3) The Company has granted the Underwriters an option for 30 days to purchase up to an additional 390,000 shares at the initial public offering price per share, less the underwriting discount, solely to cover over-allotments. If such option is exercised in full, the total initial public offering price, underwriting discount and proceeds to the Company will be $38,870,000, $2,720,900 and $36,149,100, respectively. See "Underwriting".

The shares offered hereby are offered severally by the Underwriters, as specified herein, subject to receipt and acceptance by them and subject to their right to reject any order in whole or in part. It is expected that certificates for the shares will be ready for delivery in New York, New York, on or about April 17, 1996, against payment therefor in immediately available funds.

Goldman, Sachs & Co.
Donaldson, Lufkin & Jenrette
Securities Corporation
Montgomery Securities

The date of this Prospectus is April 12, 1996.

Yahoo! offers a branded Internet navigational service that is among the most widely used guides to information and discovery on the World Wide Web.

Click here to view picture "Yahoo!" ← CLICK HERE SEE NEXT PAGE

"Yahoo!", "Yahooligans!", "Web Launch", "School Bell", "The Scoop" and the *Yahoo!* logo are trademarks of Yahoo! Inc. All rights reserved. All other tradenames and trademarks appearing in this Prospectus are the property of their respective holders.

Prior to the completion of this offering, Yahoo! Inc. was not required to file reports with the Securities and Exchange Commission pursuant to the Securities Exchange Act of 1934.

IN CONNECTION WITH THIS OFFERING, THE UNDERWRITERS MAY OVER-ALLOT OR EFFECT TRANSACTIONS WHICH STABILIZE OR MAINTAIN THE MARKET PRICE OF THE COMMON STOCK OF THE COMPANY AT A LEVEL ABOVE THAT WHICH MIGHT OTHERWISE PREVAIL IN THE OPEN MARKET. SUCH TRANSACTIONS MAY BE EFFECTED ON THE NASDAQ NATIONAL MARKET, IN THE OVER-THE-COUNTER MARKET OR OTHERWISE. SUCH STABILIZING, IF COMMENCED, MAY BE DISCONTINUED AT ANY TIME.

Advertising on *Yahoo!* currently consists primarily of banner advertisements that appear on the top of directory pages within the *Yahoo!* main site. Hypertext links are embedded in each banner advertisement to provide the user with instant access to the advertiser's Web site to obtain additional information or purchase products and services.

[Go Back]

YAHOO!

NEW — COOL — RANDOM — HEADLINES — YAHOO INFO — ADD URL

IPO HOME PAGE

NCAA Tournaments Click Here for Our Promotions! Web Launch

Hyperlinks From IPO Page Disabled

Options

- **Arts**
  Humanities, Photography, Architecture, ...
- **Business and Economy** [Xtra!]
  Directory, Investments, Classifieds, Taxes, ...
- **Computers and Internet** [Xtra!]
  Internet, WWW, Software, Multimedia, ...
- **Education**
  Universities, K-12, Courses, ...
- **Entertainment** [Xtra!]
  TV, Movies, Music, Magazines, ...
- **Government**
  Politics [Xtra!], Agencies, Law, Military, ...
- **Health**
  Medicine, Drugs, Diseases, Fitness, ...
- **News** [Xtra!]
  World [Xtra!], Daily, Current Events, ...
- **Recreation**
  Sports [Xtra!], Games, Travel, Autos, ...
- **Reference**
  Libraries, Dictionaries, Phone Numbers, ...
- **Regional**
  Countries, Regions, U.S. States, ...
- **Science**
  CS, Biology, Astronomy, Engineering, ...
- **Social Science**
  Anthropology, Sociology, Economics, ...
- **Society and Culture**
  People, Environment, Religion, ...

Text-Only Yahoo – Contributors

Picture of Yahoo home page appearing in the prospectus, as downloaded from the IPO home page.

YAHOO!

NEW — COOL — RANDOM — HEADLINES — YAHOO INFO — ADD URL

Actually Yahoo home page on the World Wide Web

Yahoo! Picks   Yahoo! Internet Life *the guide to the web*   Web Launch

options

- **Arts**
  Humanities, Photography, Architecture, ...
- **News [Xtra!]**
  World [Xtra!], Daily, Current Events, ...
- **Business and Economy [Xtra!]**
  Directory, Investments, Classifieds, Taxes, ...
- **Recreation and Sports [Xtra!]**
  Sports, Games, Travel, Autos, Fishing, ...
- **Computers and Internet [Xtra!]**
  Internet, WWW, Software, Multimedia, ...
- **Reference**
  Libraries, Dictionaries, Phone Numbers, ...
- **Education**
  Universities, K-12, Courses, ...
- **Regional**
  Countries, Regions, U.S. States, ...
- **Entertainment [Xtra!]**
  TV, Movies, Music, Magazines, ...
- **Science**
  CS, Biology, Astronomy, Engineering, ...
- **Government**
  Politics [Xtra!], Agencies, Law, Military, ...
- **Social Science**
  Anthropology, Sociology, Economics, ...
- **Health**
  Medicine, Drugs, Diseases, Fitness, ...
- **Society and Culture**
  People, Environment, Religion, ...

Meet the Rest of the Family...

Surf Shop   Yahooligans!   Yahoo! Japan   Yahoo! Internet Life

Hyperlinks work here

EXHIBIT B

INTERNET PROSPECTUS – BERKSHIRE HATHAWAY INC. OFFERING (MAY 1996)

Berkshire Hathaway Inc.

Class B Common Stock Offering

($.1667 par value per share)

The public offering price per share of Class B Common Stock is expected to be approximately one-thirtieth (1/30th) of the closing sale price per share of Berkshire's Common Stock, $5.00 par value per share, on the New York Stock Exchange on the date of pricing.

Expected Pricing Date: May 8, 1996

The broker-dealer members of our selling group can provide you with a prospectus and additional information. If information is not available from your broker-dealer, call:

1-800-251-2621

A prospectus and list of selling group members is available on the Internet at:

http://brk.salomon.com

Salomon Brothers Inc

The offering referred to above constitutes a new financing for the company and all proceeds will go directly to the company. A registration statement relating to these securities has been filed with the Securities and Exchange Commission but has not yet become effective. These securities may not be sold nor may offers to buy be accepted prior to the time the registration statement becomes effective. This communication shall not constitute an offer to sell or the solicitation of an offer to buy nor shall there be any sale of these securities in any jurisdiction in which such offers, solicitation or sale would be unlawful prior to registration or qualification under the securities laws of such jurisdiction.

BERKSHIRE HATHAWAY INC.

Berkshire Hathaway Inc. Class B Share Offering

A registration statement relating to these securities has been filed with the Securities and Exchange Commision but has not yet become effective. These securities may not be sold nor may offers to buy be accepted prior to the time the registration statement becomes effective. Information on this site shall not constitute an offer to sell or the solicitation of an offer to buy nor shall there be any sale of these securities in any jurisdiction in which such offer, solicitation or sale would be unlawful prior to registration or qualification under the securities laws of any such jurisdiction.

I have read and I ACCEPT this legally required statement.

Berkshire / Salomon home page created solely for the offering

Berkshire Hathaway Inc.Class B Stock Offering

Welcome to the Berkshire Hathaway Class B Share Offering home page. We have created this site to direct individual investors to a participating broker who can provide information, a preliminary prospectus, and take indications of interest in purchasing Class B shares. Much of the information included on this site is also available on the Information Hotline at 1-800-251-2621

Please select what you want to look at by clicking on an item in the left-hand column.

- Find out if your broker is on a list of Participating Brokerage Firms or locate another broker on the list and obtain its phone number
- Learn how to contact the Two Participating National Discount Brokerages
- Obtain General Information on the Class B Share Offering
- Obtain an electronic copy of the preliminary Prospectus
- Obtain copies of Related Documents Incorporated by Reference
- Feedback Form

http://brk.salomon.com/fdealers.html

List of Brokers for the Berkshire Hathaway Inc. Class B Stock Issue

SEARCH CRITERIA *(Company names alphabetically)*
[A, B, C, D, E, F, G, H, I, J, K, L, M, N, O, P, R, S, T, U, V, W, Y]

Search the list of Brokers:

- A.G. Edwards & Sons, Inc. – 1-800-278-5373
- Advest, Inc. – 1-860-509-2000
- Alex. Brown & Sons Incorporated – 1-410-727-1700
- Allen & Company of Florida, Inc. – 1-941-688-9000
- Allen C. Ewing & Co. – 1-904-354-5573
- AmeriTrade, Inc. – 1-402-331-2744
- Ameritas Investment Corp. – 1-402-466-4565
- Apex Securities, Inc. – 1-800-856-2739
- Arthurs, Lestrange & Company Incorporated – 1-412-566-6826
- Baird, Patrick & Co., Inc. – 1-212-493-6600
- Bear, Stearns & Co. Inc. – 1-212-272-5900
- Branch, Cabell and Company – 1-804-225-1400
- Broker Dealer Financial Services Corp. – 1-800-352-5634
- BROOKSTREET SECURITIES CORPORATION – 1-800-268-2578
- Burnham Securities Inc. – 1-212-603-7571
- Carolan & Co., Inc. – 1-401-331-1932
- Cazenove & Co. – 011-44-171-588-2828
- Charles Schwab & Co., Inc. – 1-888-476-3337
- City Securities Corporation – 1-800-800-2489
- Coburn & Meredith, Inc. – 1-203-522-7171
- COLEMAN AND COMPANY SECURITIES, INC. – 1-212-262-1414
- Corporate Securities Group, Inc – 1-407-332-2805
- Cowen + Co. – 1-212-495-6617
- Craigie Incorporated – 1-804-649-3900
- CROWELL, WEEDON & CO. – 1-213-244-9309
- CS First Boston – 1-212-909-2288
- D.A. Davidson & Co. – 1-406-791-7207
- D.E. Frey & Company, Inc. – 1-303-863-4050
- Dain Bosworth Incorporated – 1-612-371-7666
- DAKIN SECURITIES CORPORATION – 1-415-288-2216
- Davenport & Co. of Virginia, Inc. – 1-804-780-2041
- David A. Noyes & Company – 1-317-637-1717
- Dean Witter Reynolds Inc. – 1-212-392-3232
- Dickinson & Co. – 1-515-247-8191
- Doley Securities, Inc. – 1-504-561-1128
- Donaldson, Lufkin & Jenrette Securities Corporation – 1-212-892-4154
- DRESDNER BANK - KLEINWORT BENSON – 011-44-171-623-8000
- Edgar M. Norris & Co., Inc. – 1-864-233-3655
- Edward D. Jones & Co. – 1-314-515-3340
- Emmett A. Larkin Company, Inc. – 1-415-986-2332

[remainder of list omitted]

The Two participating National Discount Brokers are:

- Fidelity Brokerage Services, Inc.
  - (1-800-544-5631)
- Charles Schwab & Co., Inc.
  - (1-888-476-3337)
  - (1-888-IP-OFFER)

to the Berkshire Hathaway Class B Share offering page

General Information on the Berkshire Hathaway Inc. Class B Share Offering

Berkshire Hathaway Inc. has filed a registration statement for Class B shares with the Securities and Exchange Commission. A large group of participating brokerage firms will collect indications of investor interest from Monday, April 22, through Tuesday, May 7. Berkshire Hathaway and Salomon Brothers expect to price the Class B share offering after the market closes on Wednesday, May 8, and expect trading to begin in the Class B shares on the New York Stock Exchange on Thursday, May 9. Please note that indications of interest in purchasing Class B shares should be submitted by Tuesday, May 7.

All prospective investors are urged to obtain the preliminary prospectus from a participating broker and to read it carefully for information about Berkshire Hathaway's business, the reason for the offering, and specific issues that Warren Buffett, Berkshire's Chairman, and Charles Munger, its Vice-Chairman, want prospective investors to consider.

Berkshire's existing common stock, to be re-designated as "Class A Common stock" at the time of the offering, is currently listed for trading on the New York Stock Exchange under the symbol BRK.

The price of the Class B shares will be approximately one-thirtieth of the closing sale price of Berkshire's existing Class A common stock on the day of pricing, which we expect to be Wednesday, May 8.

Each Class B share will have economic rights equivalent to one-thirtieth of an existing Class A common share and one-two-hundredth of the voting power of an existing Class A share.

Berkshire Hathaway Inc. is a holding company owning subsidiaries engaged in a number of diverse business activities, the most important of which is the property and casualty insurance business. The investment portfolios of Berkshire's insurance subsidiaries include meaningful equity positions in a number of publicly traded companies. The non-insurance subsidiaries engage in a variety of manufacturing, publication, retail, and finance businesses.

[illegible] to the Berkshire Hathaway Class B Share Offering page.

A registration statement relating to the securities has been filed with the United States Securities and Exchange Commission but has not yet become effective. Neither the Prospectus nor the Class B Common Stock has been or will be filed, recorded or registered, as applicable, in any jurisdiction other than the United States of America and certain states thereof and, subject to specific exceptions in certain jurisdictions other than the United States of America, the Class B Common Stock may not be offered or sold within any other jurisdiction that requires that the Prospectus be filed or recorded or that the Class B Common Stock be registered therein.

Before proceeding to review the Prospectus, interested parties must satisfy themselves that doing so will not contravene any applicable securities laws or regulations of jurisdictions other than the United States, and must ensure that they are not, due to residence, citizenship or otherwise, subject to such securities laws or regulations.

The offering referred to above will only be made available in the UK to persons (not being private customers within the meaning of the rules of UK Securities and Futures Authority) whose ordinary activities involve them in acquiring, holding, managing or disposing of investments as principal or agent for the purpose of their business or otherwise in circumstances which do not constitute an offer to the public within the meaning of the Public Offers of Securities Regulations 1995. Accordingly, the offering will only be available in the UK to persons having professional experience in matters relating to investment. Before proceeding, interested parties in the UK must satisfy themselves that they fall within this category.

I have read this required disclaimer, and I confirm that I [illegible] to review the Prospectus

---

[illegible] to the Salomon Brothers' Berkshire Hathaway Inc. Class B Issue page

Prospectus of the Berkshire Hathaway Class B Common Stock Issue

---

This is a PDF Version of the Prospectus

(Please ensure that your downloaded file is 79512 bytes in size and/or 18 pages in length)

If you do not have a PDF viewer, [button]

[button] to the Salomon Brothers' Berkshire Hathaway Inc. Class B Issue Page

Subject to Completion
April 19, 1996

Information contained herein is subject to completion or amendment. A registration statement relating to these securities has been filed with the Securities and Exchange Commission. These securities may not be sold nor may offers to buy be accepted prior to the time the registration statement becomes effective. This prospectus shall not constitute an offer to sell or the solicitation of an offer to buy nor shall there be any sale of these securities in any State in which such offer, solicitation or sale would be unlawful prior to registration or qualification under the securities law of any such State.

Prospectus

250,000 Shares

Berkshire Hathaway Inc.

Class B Common Stock

($.1667 par value)

Berkshire Hathaway Inc. ("Berkshire" or the "Company") is offering shares of its Class B Common Stock, $.1667 par value per share (the "Class B Common Stock"). The Company will assess investor demand for shares of Class B Common Stock in this offering and intends to increase the size of the offering as necessary to satisfy demand. The final maximum size of the offering will be publicly announced after the close of business on the last day before the initial public offering price is determined.

The initial public offering price per share of Class B Common Stock is expected to be approximately one-thirtieth (1/30th) of the closing sale price per share of Berkshire's common stock, $5.00 par value per share (referred to herein as the "Class A Common Stock"), on the New York Stock Exchange on the date of pricing. The closing sale price for the Class A Common Stock was $33,000 per share on the New York Stock Exchange on April 18, 1996, the last trading day before the date of this Prospectus.

Warren Buffett, as Berkshire's Chairman, and Charles Munger, as Berkshire's Vice Chairman, want you to know the following (and urge you to ignore anyone telling you that these statements are "boilerplate" or unimportant):

1. Mr. Buffett and Mr. Munger believe that Berkshire's Class A Common Stock is not undervalued at the market price stated above. *Neither Mr. Buffett nor Mr. Munger would currently buy Berkshire shares at that price, nor would they recommend that their families or friends do so.*
2. Berkshire's historical rate of growth in per-share book value is NOT indicative of possible future growth. *Because of the large size of Berkshire's capital base (approximately $17 billion at December 31, 1995), Berkshire's book value per share cannot increase in the future at a rate even close to its past rate.*
3. In recent years the market price of Berkshire shares has increased at a rate exceeding the growth in per-share intrinsic value. *Market overperformance of that kind cannot persist indefinitely. Inevitably, there will also occur periods of underperformance, perhaps substantial in degree.*
4. Berkshire has attempted to assess the current demand for Class B shares and has tailored the size of this offering to fully satisfy that demand. *Therefore, buyers hoping to capture quick profits are almost certain to be disappointed. Shares should be purchased only by investors who expect to remain holders for many years.*

For certain other risk factors and investment considerations, see "Certain Risk Factors and Investment Considerations" on page 6.

(Continued on inside cover page)

THESE SECURITIES HAVE NOT BEEN APPROVED OR DISAPPROVED BY THE SECURITIES AND EXCHANGE COMMISSION OR ANY STATE SECURITIES COMMISSION NOR HAS THE COMMISSION OR ANY STATE SECURITIES COMMISSION PASSED UPON THE ACCURACY OR ADEQUACY OF THIS PROSPECTUS. ANY REPRESENTATION TO THE CONTRARY IS A CRIMINAL OFFENSE.

	Price to Public	Underwriting Discount	Proceeds to Company(1)
Per Class B Share	$	$	$
Total(2)	$	$	$

(1) Before deducting expenses payable by the Company, estimated to be $.

(2) Berkshire has granted to the Underwriter an option, exercisable within 30 days after the date of this Prospectus, to purchase up to an aggregate of 37,500 additional shares of Class B Common Stock at the Price to Public, less the Underwriting Discount, solely to cover over-allotments, if any. If the Underwriter exercises such option in full, the total Price to Public, Underwriting Discount, and Proceeds to Company will be $, $, and $, respectively. See "Plan of Distribution."

The shares of Class B Common Stock are offered subject to receipt and acceptance by the Underwriter, to prior sale and to the Underwriter's right to reject any order in whole or in part and to withdraw, cancel or modify the offer without notice. It is expected that delivery of the shares of Class B Common Stock will be made at the office of Salomon Brothers Inc, Seven World Trade Center, New York, New York, or through the facilities of The Depository Trust Company, on or about May , 1996.

Salomon Brothers Inc

The date of this Prospectus is May 1996.

(continued from cover page)

This offering is subject to the approval and effectiveness of an amendment (the "Amendment") to Berkshire's Restated Certificate of Incorporation creating the Class B Common Stock, to be considered by Berkshire's shareholders at its annual meeting on May 6, 1996.

Berkshire has not paid a cash dividend on its common stock since 1967, and has no present intention to pay a dividend on Class B Common Stock or Class A Common Stock in the future.

Berkshire has applied to list the Class B Common Stock on the New York Stock Exchange.

Salomon Brothers Inc does not currently intend to purchase or sell shares of the Class B Common Stock following the initial offering of the shares of Class B Common Stock offered hereby, but may do so if its intention changes. Salomon Brothers Inc, acting as principal or agent, may use this Prospectus in connection with offers and sales of shares of Class B Common Stock offered hereby and any other shares of Class B Common Stock outstanding from time to time in the course of its business as a broker-dealer. Such sales, if any, will be made at prevailing market prices at the time of sale.

(end of cover page)

IN CONNECTION WITH THIS OFFERING, THE UNDERWRITER MAY OVER-ALLOT OR EFFECT TRANSACTIONS WHICH STABILIZE OR MAINTAIN THE MARKET PRICE OF SHARES OF CLASS B COMMON STOCK AT LEVELS ABOVE THOSE THAT MIGHT OTHERWISE PREVAIL IN THE OPEN MARKET. SUCH TRANSACTIONS MAY BE EFFECTED ON THE NEW YORK STOCK EXCHANGE OR OTHERWISE. SUCH STABILIZING, IF COMMENCED, MAY BE DISCONTINUED AT ANY TIME.

THE COMMISSIONER OF INSURANCE FOR THE STATE OF NORTH CAROLINA HAS NEITHER APPROVED NOR DISAPPROVED OF THIS OFFERING, NOR HAS THE COMMISSIONER ACTED UPON THE ACCURACY OR ADEQUACY OF THE PROSPECTUS.

AVAILABLE INFORMATION

The Company is subject to the informational requirements of the Securities Exchange Act of 1934, as amended (the "Exchange Act"), and in accordance therewith files reports, proxy statements and other information with the Securities and Exchange Commission (the "Commission"). All such reports, proxy statements and other information filed with the Commission concerning the Company can be inspected and copied at the public reference facilities maintained by the Commission at Room 1024, 450 Fifth Street, N.W., Washington, D.C. 20549, and at the Commission's regional offices at Seven World Trade Center, 13th Floor, New York, New York 10048, and 500 West Madison Street, Suite 1400, Chicago, Illinois 60661. Copies of such material can be obtained upon written request addressed to the Commission, Public Reference Section, 450 Fifth Street, N.W., Washington, D.C. 20549, at prescribed rates. The Company's Class A Common Stock is listed on the New York Stock Exchange. Application has been made to list the Class B Common Stock on the New York Stock Exchange. Reports, proxy statements, information statements and other information concerning the Company can be inspected at the offices of the New York Stock Exchange, 20 Broad Street, New York, New York 10005.

The Company has filed with the Commission a registration statement on Form S-3 (herein together with all amendments and exhibits, referred to as the "Registration Statement") under the Securities Act of 1933 (the "Securities Act"). This Prospectus does not contain all of the information set forth in the Registration Statement, certain parts of which are omitted in accordance with the rules and regulations of the Commission. For further information, reference is hereby made to the Registration Statement, which may be obtained from the Commission at its principal office in Washington, D.C. upon payment of charges prescribed by the Commission.

[remainder of prospectus omitted]

List of Related SEC Documents Incorporated by Reference

Additional amendments and documents incorporated by reference will be added to this site after filing

- S-3/A (04/29/96) 96483 bytes
- S-3/A (04/19/96) 152724 bytes
- S-3 (04/02/96) 162959 bytes
- 10-K (03/27/96) 288709 bytes
- 8-K (01/17/96) 34493 bytes
- 8-K (02/15/96) 11344 bytes
- 8-K (03/27/96) 24205 bytes
- 8-A12B (04/02/96) 9638 bytes
- 8-A12B/A (04/02/96) 9941 bytes

Hyperlinks to the SEC's EDGAR home page

 to the Berkshire Hathaway Class B Share Offering page

NOTES

7

THE ROAD LESS TRAVELED: THE ADVENT OF ELECTRONIC ROADSHOWS

Linda C. Quinn
Ottilie L. Jarmel

Reprinted with permission of Aspen Law and Business / Panel Publishers, a division of Aspen Publishers, Inc.

SECURITIES REGISTRATION

The Road Less Traveled: The Advent of Electronic Roadshows

In a recent no-action letter, the SEC opened the door for electronic roadshows. The authors discuss the policies underlying the SEC's no-action position and provide an overview of the law governing roadshows.

By Linda C. Quinn and Ottilie L. Jarmel

Driven largely by the increasing use of electronic media in the securities industry in recent years, there have been a number of requests to the Securities and Exchange Commission (SEC or Commission) to allow for electronic broadcast or other similar electronic coverage of roadshows. These requests have had some appeal for the Commission because of its concerns that current roadshow practices may encourage selective disclosure, particularly with respect to forward-looking information.[1] Typically attended by institutional investors, portfolio managers, analysts, and securities sales persons, roadshows involve presentations by management, and question and answer sessions that in many cases focus on the company's business strategy and prospects. Until this past spring, however, roadshows were the one area of the offering process virtually untouched by the electronic communications revolution. Reference to communications by radio and television in the definition of prospectus contained in the Securities Act of 1933 (Securities Act), together with the Commission staff's broad interpretation of the definition of prospectus, have historically precluded the use of electronic communications to transmit roadshows.

In March, reflecting the Commission's policy of encouraging the use of electronic media to communicate with investors,[2] the SEC staff issued a no-action letter to Private Financial Network (PFN) to allow it to broadcast roadshows electronically to its subscribers.[3] While on its face a modest first step, the PFN no-action letter lays the groundwork for allowing the roadshow process to take full advantage of the electronic communications technology that is radically changing the capital markets. It also potentially opens roadshows to the investing public. To fully appreciate the significance of the staff's initiative, a brief summary of roadshow practices and their place in the statutory scheme of the Securities Act is appropriate.

Roadshows, in Short

Introduced in the 1970s, roadshows are today an integral part of a securities offering, whether a public offering registered under the Securities Act or an exempt Rule 144A quasi-public style distribution.[4] In addition to marketing the specific securities being offered, the roadshow helps the issuer develop strong and ongoing investor interest in the company. Depending on the size and nature of the offering, the roadshow can consist of a series of meetings in the United States and frequently abroad, lasting from several days to several weeks, at which management makes presentations to potential investors and provides them with the opportunity to ask questions. Driven by institutional demand and a desire on the part of issuers to develop long-term relationships with institutional investors, roadshows today commonly include one-on-one meetings between key management and major potential institutional investors. More interactive, and less scripted than the more traditional group sessions, these meetings enable investors to explore more fully, in a question and answer format, the prospects of an issuer and the merits of an offering. They also give management an opportunity to adapt its presentation accordingly and gauge investor interest more quickly. Those one-on-one meetings are subject to the same regulatory regime as the more traditional group roadshow presentations.

Roadshows and the Statutory Framework Under the Securities Act

The Securities Act imposes significant restrictions on the marketing of securities. Unless exempt, securities offers must be registered under the Securities Act. Under Section 5(c) of the Securities Act, no offers, written or oral, can be made before a registration statement relating to the securities is on file with the Commission.

Linda C. Quinn is a partner, and Ottilie L. Jarmel is an associate, at Shearman & Sterling in New York, N.Y. This article presents their own views and does not neccessarily reflect the views of others at their firm. The authors thank David Blass, a summer associate at Shearman & Sterling and JD candidate at Columbia University School of Law, for his substantial contribution to this article.

"Offer for sale" has been broadly interpreted by the Commission to include publicity that "conditions the market" for, or arouses public interest in, a proposed securities offering.[5] No roadshow can take place before the filing of the registration statement.

Once the registration statement is filed, there is no regulatory limitation on oral offers. Of course, issuers and distributors of the securities are exposed to liability for any materially misleading statements or omissions of material facts made orally or in writing in the offer or sale of the securities, including statements made at roadshow meetings.[6] There are, on the other hand, statutory limitations on the use of written materials or communications by radio or television in connection with the offering.

Under Section 5(b)(1), prior to effectiveness of the registration statement, no prospectus may be used to market the securities other than a prospectus conforming to the requirements of Section 10 of the Securities Act, even if such non-conforming prospectus is accompanied by a prospectus meeting such requirements. Once the registration statement is effective, written documents may be used to offer the securities provided a prospectus meeting the requirements of Section 10(a) has been previously or at the same time sent or given to the potential purchaser. The basic premise of the Securities Act is that unless the offering is exempt from registration, investment decisions should be based principally on a prospectus that meets the informational requirements of Section 10. The term "prospectus" is defined broadly under Section 2(10) as "any notice, advertisement, or communication, written or *by radio or television*, which offers a security for sale or confirms the sale of a security."[7] It is this reference to radio and television in Section 2(10)'s definition of prospectus that, until now, has largely foreclosed, as a legal matter, the use of electronic communications to conduct roadshows.

Because they are essentially oral communications, roadshows are permitted once the registration statement is filed. Moreover, there is no legal limitation on the number or nature of potential investors that may attend or participate in such meetings. A company, for example, could, consistent with the Securities Act, hold a roadshow at Yankee Stadium. The customarily restricted invitee list for such meetings is more a function of practicality and may reflect efforts to manage risk of liability for soft or forward-looking information that may be discussed at such meetings.

Roadshows also are frequently used in exempt Rule 144A offerings. In these offerings, the critical limitation is the need to assure that the roadshow is conducted in a manner consistent with the prohibition on general solicitation and general advertising. Thus, the principal focus will be on assuring that those invited to, and attending, the roadshow are sophisticated investors to whom the issuer may appropriately offer the securities under Section 4(2) of the Securities Act. Unlike the registered offering, there is no statutory restriction on the use and distribution of written materials at a Rule 144A roadshow. Steps should be taken to keep any such materials confidential and preclude their public distribution which could result in a general solicitation. Typically, because of concerns that such materials run the risk of being viewed as offering material for liability purposes, only the offering circular will be distributed at the Rule 144A roadshow. The discussion that follows focuses on registered public offerings.

Roadshow Practices

Today, roadshows frequently are multimedia presentations. Care needs to be taken to assure that written materials are not used at the roadshow in a manner that causes them to be viewed as nonconforming prospectuses. Equally important, the presentation itself should not be communicated in a fashion that would convert the oral presentation into a Section 2(10) prospectus, *i.e.*, a written communication or communication by ra-

INSIGHTS

THE CORPORATE & SECURITIES LAW ADVISOR

INSIGHTS (ISSN No. 0894-3524) is published monthly by ASPEN LAW & BUSINESS, 1185 Avenue of the Americas, New York, NY 10036, 212-597-0200. One year subscription (12 issues) costs $395; a single issue costs $40. Postmaster: Send address changes to **INSIGHTS**, 7201 McKinney Circle, Frederick, MD 21704. To subscribe, call 1-800-638-8437. For customer service, call 1-800-234-1660. Periodicals postage pending at Englewood Cliffs, NJ.

dio or television. Typical issues that raise these concerns include the following.

Use of slides, graphs, and other written visual aids as part of the oral presentation. Use of such materials is standard practice in roadshows. No copies of such materials should be distributed. If they are distributed, they are likely to be viewed as nonconforming prospectuses in violation of Section 5. In a one-on-one meeting, use of such visual aids may be impractical. In such case, use of a paper copy of such slides or graphs should not be troublesome provided that the copy is retrieved from the investor at the end of the meeting.

Distribution of corporate publications. While there is no legal requirement to distribute the prospectus at a roadshow, it is good practice to do so. Distributions of documents incorporated by reference into the prospectus, *e.g.*, Forms 10-K and 10-Q and 8-K reports, also is appropriate.

There is, however, some difference of views as to whether SEC mandated disclosure documents that are not incorporated by reference can or should be distributed at the roadshow. The SEC has not specifically addressed the issue. Given the Commission's own requirement that a registration statement specifically note the availability of Exchange Act reports and other information filed with the Commission, distribution of such materials should not be problematic under Section 5.[8] The staff's no-action position in Scott & Fetzer,[9] in which it permitted newspaper advertisement by a registrant containing extracts from the company's annual report prior to effectiveness, has been viewed by some as support for the proposition that distribution of the annual report during the pendency of an offering by a public company should not be viewed as inconsistent with Section 5. On the other hand, given the lack of specific Commission guidance on the issue, and concerns about potential liability for information in such non-incorporated documents, particularly the annual report, some practitioners, particularly when representing the underwriters, advise against distribution of such documents.

Attendance of journalists at the roadshow. Primarily because of the potential for news stories based on the roadshow presentation being viewed as prospectuses for Section 5 purposes, journalists generally are excluded from roadshows. In addition, there are liability concerns with respect to public dissemination through news stories of some of the softer, more forward-looking information that may be discussed at the meeting.

Use of closed circuit TV. Use of closed circuit TV to allow more institutions to attend a roadshow presentation generally has not been viewed as raising Section 5 concerns, notwithstanding Section 2(10)'s reference to television. Typically, the transmission was live and interactive to assure that the broadcast was essentially the equivalent of actual attendance at the meeting. PFN suggests this may not be necessary as discussed below.

Use or distribution of audio or video tapes. Prior to the PFN letter, the use or distribution of audio or videotapes outside the actual roadshow presentation appeared problematic based on several no-action requests. In response to a request by Transamerica,[10] the SEC staff refused to provide a no-action letter with respect to a tape-recorded message over the telephone for employees in connection with an employee stock savings plan. The staff expressed the view that the recording would be a prospectus under Section 2(10).

In Exploration, Inc.,[11] the staff took a no-action position with respect to video tapes of roadshows but only as to distribution to syndicate members and selling dealers. The incoming letter had indicated that the video tapes also would be distributed to certain investors. The failure of the staff to include distribution of the video tapes to investors in its response had generally been viewed as foreclosing such use.

There is little question that audio or video tapes may be used as part of the roadshow presentation itself. In the past, some practitioners have advised that if such technology is used, management should be present to answer questions to reduce the potential for the video or audio broadcast from being viewed as a separate standalone communication that the SEC could characterize as a prospectus.

The Advent of Electronic Roadshows

Over the last several years, members of the Commission and the SEC staff have indicated that the time had come for the Commission to revisit these issues. With the passage of The National Securities Markets Improvement Act of 1996, the Commission now has full exemptive authority under the Securities Act that would permit it to allow broad public access to roadshows through electronic transmission.[12] However, the Commission has chosen, at least initially, as evidenced by the PFN no-action letter, to continue its policy of incremental adaptation of its rules and policies to the electronic media.

PFN, a private network and wholly-owned subsidiary of MSNBC Interactive LLC, a joint venture of the National Broadcasting Co., Inc. and Microsoft Corporation, provides business and financial coverage in multimedia format and was established as a companion to a textual research service. PFN requested that the SEC staff issue a no-action letter that would permit it to broadcast roadshows electronically, either live or on a delayed basis over a private network, to its subscribers. PFN noted that it currently has fewer than 100 subscribers, principally broker-dealers and investment advisers. In its request for no-action relief, PFN undertook to: (1) limit the availability of the video transmission of the roadshow to PFN subscribers who agreed not to videotape, copy or distribute the broadcast; (2) ensure that each subscriber received a copy of the prospectus, as filed with the Commission, prior to any transmission of the roadshow; (3) require issuers and underwriters to take reasonable steps to ensure that information disclosed in the roadshow was not inconsistent with the filed prospectus; and (4) include in each transmission a text "crawl" referring viewers to the filed prospectus for more information about the offering and containing a prohibition on videotaping, copying, distributing, or use in the sale of securities to the general public; roadshows broadcast prior to effectiveness were required to include a visual presentation of the legend required by Rule 134(b) under the Securities Act.

In requesting relief, PFN posited that its proposed controlled transmissions by KU satellite, T1 telephone circuits and fiber optic and other cable was not within the scope of the reference to radio or television in Section 2(10) and therefore were not prospectuses. PFN contended that the statutory reference to radio and television is to broadcasting, not to the use of radio or television technology for closed circuit or other controlled retransmission of non-prospectus materials. Citing *Gustafson*, PFN reasoned that prospectus as used in Section 2(10) is "intended to reach only those documents or communications that are widely disseminated to an undifferentiated public rather than to a discreet, 'invited audience.' "

Without discussion, the Commission staff agreed that it would not recommend enforcement action to the Commission if PFN transmitted a company's roadshow to PFN's subscribers for the purposes and pursuant to the procedures, described in the letter and in reliance on company counsel's opinion that such transmissions are not prospectuses within the meaning of Section 2(10). While PFN's request cites a number of factors upon which the staff could have based its no-action response, the staff did not give any guidance in its response as to its analysis of the issue or the rationale for its no-action position. Based on the statutory framework and the facts presented by PFN, it would appear that there were two key factors underlying the staff's no-action position. First is PFN's assurance that all persons to whom the roadshow was broadcast would have a copy of the prospectus at the time of the broadcast. Second is PFN's undertaking to incorporate into the broadcast effective reminders to the investor of the availability of detailed information about the issuer and the offering in the prospectus.

As to the other factors cited by PFN, these items can be viewed both as providing procedures to assure the availability of the prospectus to viewers of the electronic roadshow and improving the "atmospherics" for staff's first foray into the electronic roadshow arena. While PFN's current subscribers were described as primarily investment advisers and broker dealers, numbering less than 100, it is notable that PFN did not undertake to limit the growth of its subscriber base or to assure that each subscriber was a professional or institutional investor. Nor is there any statutory basis for applying a limit on the number or nature of participants in a roadshow audience.

PFN's undertaking to prohibit subscribers from copying or distributing copies of the broadcast is consistent with the staff's seeking to assure that persons receiving the broadcast have the prospectus. Hard copy increases the potential for leakage to nonsubscribers who may not have the prospectus. The purpose of the limitation on the number of broadcasts, on the other hand is not clear, and seems unnecessary both as a matter of Commission policy or to effect the purposes of the Securities Act.

Prior to the issuance of the PFN letter, views were split as to whether a key element of a roadshow was its interactive nature, *i.e.*, the ability for the audience to ask questions. The PFN letter specifically provides for taped, delayed transmissions making clear that the SEC staff, at least, does not view the ability to actively participate in the discussion as critical to characterizing the electronic broadcast as a non-prospectus communication.

Some may read PFN narrowly to suggest that the staff is basing its no-action position on the theory that under *Gustafson* the roadshow is not a prospectus because of its limited distribution. To date, the Commission has not generally concurred in this reading of *Gustafson*. Given the Commission's interest in encouraging more open access to roadshows, it seems unlikely that the staff would premise its first electronic roadshow initiative on principles of restricted access. It is more likely that the Commission and staff will find that public investors' interests are better served by basing relief on the premise that the oral presentation at the roadshow is not converted into a prospectus for purposes of Section 2(10) simply because of the electronic transmission. As an oral communication, the roadshow could be universally available to public investors.

Conclusion

PFN is a welcome first step in extending the benefits of electronic communications to the roadshow process. Although somewhat narrowly drawn, the ruling paves the way for broader reform and the prospect for innovation is unbounded. Whether this innovation will be channeled to afford public investors greater access to these presentations is an open question. Concerns about liability for the soft or forward-looking information may continue to cause issuers and underwriters to limit access to roadshow presentations to institutional investors.[13] Moreover, concerns that enhanced public access to roadshow presentations may undermine the possibility of relying on *Gustafson* to take such communications outside the ambit of Section 12(a)(2) may also encourage issuers and underwriters to continue to restrict access.

For those issuers that choose to afford public investors the opportunity to attend the roadshow electronically, PFN holds great promise. Applying the oral communication-public access reading of the PFN letter, today there appears little basis to object to Internet transmissions or CD-ROM presentations of roadshows provided they are configured to assure that delivery of the prospectus is integral to the transmission directly or by hyperlink or as part of the presentation on the CD-ROM. In such cases, restrictions on number of broadcasts, hard copy or public distribution would not only appear unnecessary but also counter productive to the Commission's efforts to encourage use of electronic communications technology to assure investors enhanced access to information.

NOTES

1. *See e.g.*, "UP NEXT: Net Road Shows SEC Issues No-Action Letter to MSNBC Unit" Financial Net News (March 17, 1997) (article quotes Commissioner Hunt supporting the concept of electronic roadshows); "Virtual Road Shows May Become a Reality Thanks to the SEC," Corp. Fin. Week (Sept. 16, 1996) (quoting Commissioner Wallman, "The Internet provides a great opportunity to level the playing field between large institutional investors and small retail investors;" *see also* "SEC Eyes Selective Disclosure of Non-Public Information," Corp. Fin. Week (April 3, 1995).

2. *See* Chairman Arthur Levitt "Corporate Finance in the Information Age," Securities Regulation Institute, San Diego, Calif. (Jan. 23, 1997) SEC Web site *www.sec.gov/news/speeches/spch 135*; *see also* Release No. 33-7233 (Oct. 13, 1995) in which the Commission articulates its policy to encourage and facilitate the use of electronic distribution of information based on its potential to enhance investors' ability to access, research, and analyze information and to facilitate, expedite, and lower the costs of issuers informing the markets.

3. Private Financial Network, 1997 SEC No-Act., Lexis 406 (March 12, 1997) (PFN letter).

4. *See* "Road Shows on the Internet through MSNBC Desktop Video," The Georgeson Reporter 5 (May 1997) (an interview with Victoria Crane, former Georgeson Vice President, describing MSNBC's Internet roadshow service entitled, "Virtual Roadshow"). *See* "How Seat-of-the-Pants IPO's Turned Into Global Events: In Today's Huge Deals, There's No Room For Error," Investment Dealers Digest (May 22, 1995); "On The Road Again . . . : With Few Exceptions Wall Street Road Shows Are Larger and More Grueling Than Ever," Investment Dealers Digest (Sept. 20, 1993); Schulte, IPO Road Shows—A Primer for the Practitioner, 962 PLI/Corp 93 (1996).

5. *See, e.g.*, Release Nos. 33-5180 (August 16, 1971); 5009 (Oct. 7, 1969); 4697 (May 28, 1964) and 3844 (Oct. 8, 1957). *See also* Chiappinelli, "Gun Jumping: The Problem of Extraneous Offers of Securities," 50 U. Pitt. L. Rev. 457 (Winter 1989).

6. Statements made on a roadshow are subject to Rule 10b-5 under the Securities Exchange Act of 1934 (Exchange Act). They may also be subject to Securities Act Section 12(a)(2) liability, although some have argued that, given the restricted nature of the roadshow audience, Section 12(a)(2) may not apply under *Gustafson v. Alloyd Co. Inc.*, 513 U.S. 561 (1995) (*Gustafson*). *See e.g.* Strickland and Neier, "Regulation of Road Shows," 962 PLI/Corp. 93 (1996) *See also In re Hyperion Securities Litigation* [1995-1996 Transfer Binder] Fed. Sec. L. Rep. (CCH) &98,906 (S.D.N.Y. July 14, 1995) and *In re Valence Technology Securities Litigation*, 1995 U.S. Dist. Lexis 10379 (Dis. Ct. Northern Cal., May 8, 1995) for example of suits brought based, in part, on claims of misleading statements at a roadshow.

7. Section 2(10) of the Securities Act specifically provides that certain limited written communications will not be deemed a prospectus and authorizes the Commission to adopt rules under such provision. Rule 134 was adopted pursuant to this authorization. Section 2(10) also excludes from the definition of prospectus written material delivered subsequent to effectiveness of the registration statement, if the Section 10(a) prospectus has been sent or given to the person prior to or with the written communication. Historically, the definition of prospectus has been broadly applied by the Commission. However in *Gustafson*, the Supreme Court took a far more narrow view as to the scope of Section 2(10) opining that "from the terms 'prospectus, notice, circular, advertisement, or letter,' it is apparent that the list refers to documents of wide dissemination. In a similar manner, the list includes communications by 'radio or television,' but not face-to-face or telephonic conversations." *Id.*

8. *See* Item 502 of Regulation S-K.

9. The Scott & Fetzer Company (avail. April 24, 1972).

10. Transamerica Corporation/Employees Stock Savings Plan (avail. May 24, 1978).

11. Exploration, Inc. (avail. Nov. 10, 1986).

12. The National Securities Markets Improvement Act of 1996 added Section 28 to the Securities Act, which provides the Commission with general exemptive authority.

13. The safe harbor for forward-looking information contained in The Private Securities Litigation Reform Act of 1995 provides some protection for companies that are reporting issuers under the Exchange Act at the time of the offering; it does not apply to initial public offerings or offerings by non-reporting companies.

NOTES

8

THE INTERNET: IDENTIFYING AND RESPONDING TO INTERNATIONAL JURISDICTIONAL AND REGULATORY COMPLIANCE ISSUES

Michael D. Mann
Donna I. Dennis
Thao H.V. Do
Steve T. Kang

I. Regulation of Electronic Markets

The Internet is revolutionizing the way we conduct and view business paradigms. By harnessing and understanding the Internet's greatest feature--its availability to any and every person, from any and every point in the world, businesses and consumers are developing new methods of commercial interaction with each other.

By providing instant access to market information, without cost or obligation to a broker, the consumer views the Internet as a tool of empowerment. The investment-hungry consumer has at his fingertips a treasure trove of up-to-the-moment market information and seemingly endless investment options. Whereas the old question was where to look, the new question for consumers is what to choose.

The Internet is also a boon for businesses, no matter whether it is a start-up or a mammoth investment bank spanning different continents. By bypassing the costly by-gone era requiring vast mailings of paper documentation, the Internet is an efficient and inexpensive method of accessing a worldwide network of consumers. The Internet is truly globalizing regional and national markets--indeed, a world-wide web.

Governments and their respective regulators, however, are struggling to understand how the interplay of commerce and the Internet fits into their existing legal framework. Governments define the scope of their legal frameworks and legal jurisdictional reach according to principles of immediate physical boundaries and governed territories. But the Internet allows its users to transcend physical boundaries. The incongruous juxtaposition of the existing international legal environment and the Internet has resulted in an unpredictable legal environment governing international commercial transactions conducted on the Internet. The million dollar question is: if a company establishes a web site on the Internet's world-wide web, is that company exposed to the risk of being sued anywhere or everywhere an Internet user can gain access to the company's web site, and essentially, anywhere and everywhere in the world?

The objectives of this discussion are (i) to provide a familiarity with the jurisdictional issue in general and (ii) by focusing on the protectionist and nationalist qualities which currently characterize existing jurisdictional tests, to prompt the audience to consider that every foreign state is casting wide its jurisdictional net. Since there is yet no international treaty regarding jurisdiction and the Internet, markets remain governed by domestic laws. Therefore, commercial transactions which cross international borders may or may not implicate the legal jurisdiction of the country into which they cross. Material which is posted on one's web site may expose the creator of the web site to the jurisdiction and laws of multiple foreign states.

A. Treatment of Jurisdiction by U.S.

Although it is expected to act in the spring of 1998, if not earlier, the Securities and Exchange Commission ("SEC") has not taken a pro-active role in defining the scope of its legal jurisdiction over international commercial transactions conducted on the Internet. The SEC has been involved in a lengthy process of evaluating its approach to the regulation of cross-border securities transactions in light of technological advances and has yet to release any regulatory guidance. Given this dearth of regulatory guidance, jurisdictional issues created by cross-border transaction conducted on the Internet have been left to the courts. Rather than treating the Internet as a revolutionizing force which may necessitate a newly-created niche in the legal framework, U.S. courts are applying traditional jurisdictional tests in analyzing legal jurisdictional reach in domestic cases involving the Internet.

1. Traditional jurisdictional tests are territorially based.

    a. The historical tenets of legal jurisdiction are traditional notions of fair play and substantial justice, notions which manifest themselves in territorially-based analyses.

    b. In determining whether it has legal jurisdiction over a non-resident defendant (i.e., the defendant resides in State B), a court presiding in State A, and whose legal jurisdictional scope extends as far as State A's territories, must determine whether the defendant has established minimum contacts with State A to justify dragging him into the State A's courts and applying State A's laws.

    c. In other words, State A's court must decide whether the non-resident defendant has committed some act, whether direct or indirect, by which the defendant purposefully availed himself of the privileges of protection of State A's laws.

    d. In addition, these contacts must be of the nature such that the non-resident defendant reasonably anticipated being brought into court in State A. In determining whether the non-resident reasonably anticipated being brought into State A's courts and the level of legal jurisdictional which it may possess over the non-resident defendant, a court will analyze (1) whether the non-resident defendant's contacts with State A are continuous and substantial and (2) whether the non-resident defendant purposefully directed his activities at residents in State A.

Consequently, in analyzing a court's legal jurisdiction over an individual, courts generally determine the relationship between the individual and the forum state.

2. Applying traditional territorially-based jurisdictional tests to cross-border commercial transactions conducted over the Internet

Given the territorial blindness of the Internet, it is difficult to draw bright lines to determine whether an act conducted over the Internet was directed to occur within or outside the U.S. In all likelihood, U.S. courts will make a fact-specific determination within the grounds of reasonability.

a. U.S. courts will determine the locale of the individual who was harmed by the conduct. Even though the web site is created and maintained from a foreign country, the fact that the U.S. user is harmed by the information or investment offered by the foreign web site may implicate U.S. legal jurisdiction.

b. U.S. courts will determine how the relationship between the U.S. resident and the foreign individual was created. A foreign company which uses "push" technology to enable it to disseminate automatically its information over the Internet to viewers in the U.S., without the viewer having attempted to log on to a particular web site, is using the Internet to direct its conduct within the U.S. and implicates U.S. legal jurisdiction. If the U.S. user actively bypassed barriers intended to restrict access to the foreign web site which passively makes available information, U.S. legal jurisdiction is more questionable.

c. U.S. courts will determine from where the conduct emanated. Even if the foreign web site is created and maintained in a foreign country and the information available on the web site is not specific to U.S. residents, a court has determined that it has legal jurisdiction over the foreign web site where access to the web site requires affirmative application and the applications of U.S. residents were accepted. In the same case, the U.S. court stated that in order to avoid U.S. legal jurisdiction, the web site must establish a process enabling it to screen applicants and thereby enabling it to deny access to U.S. residents.

d. U.S. courts will determine whether there was any physical presence within the U.S. or preparatory acts that occurred within the U.S. Where there was neither physical presence within the U.S. nor preparatory acts that occurred within the U.S., the mere accidental or insubstantial contact over the Internet with the U.S. may not implicate U.S. legal jurisdiction.

3. Safe Harbors from U.S. Legal Jurisdiction

As yet, there are few guaranteed safe harbors, if any at all, from implicating U.S. legal jurisdiction where a foreign person conducts a cross-border transaction which somehow enters U.S. territory.

a. A majority of courts have held that a foreign entity could avoid the application of U.S. securities laws by requiring a U.S. person to subscribe in London to an offering, even though preparatory acts and physical presence occurred in the U.S. Applying the courts' ruling to cross-border transactions over the Internet, a cross-border transaction involving U.S. residents could be exempt from the application of U.S. securities laws given the following scenario: the foreign entity could (1) provide preliminary information to individuals in the U.S., (2) require the U.S. residents to establish the brokerage account "in person", rather than through the Internet, outside U.S. territory, (3) require the U.S. residents to enter into contractual agreements whereby the U.S. residents contractually agree to the exclusive application of the foreign country's laws and jurisdiction and thereby waiving the enforceability of U.S. securities laws and (4) thereafter operate and continue the brokerage relationship over the Internet.

b. The second section of this outline discusses ways to manage the risk that a foreign regulator will assert jurisdiction. It may be up to the individual to establish his own safe harbor by turning the traditional territorially-based jurisdictional test on its head. At the core of the U.S. traditional jurisdictional test is the question of whether the conduct of the foreign person "entered" U.S. territory. In reaching its conclusions, U.S. courts make a fact-specific analysis. Consequently, it is left to the individual who enters into the cross-border transaction over the Internet and who wishes to avoid U.S. jurisdiction to create the understanding that he or his conduct did not enter U.S. territory. The methods by which one may simultaneously conduct cross-border transaction by using a tool which has the power to touch any person and any point in the world and avoid U.S. legal jurisdiction will be discussed further on.

B. Treatment of Jurisdiction by the U.K.

Like the U.S., the U.K. has yet to establish bright-line standards in determining whether conduct which implicates U.K. territory has actually resulted in an entrance into U.K. territory and thereby falling within U.K. legal jurisdiction. Rather than adopting a case-specific analysis, however, the Financial Services Authority ("FSA") of the U.K. has opted to adopt a restrictive approach in determining the existence of U.K. legal jurisdiction. In recent interpretations of the Financial Services Act of 1986, the FSA has chosen to broadly define "entry", and thereby throwing wide its jurisdictional net to encompass most cross-border commercial conduct over the Internet. Upon concluding that an entry into U.K. territory has occurred, the FSA imposes protectionist regulations.

1. Under Section 57 of the Act, an unauthorized person is prohibited from "issuing" or "causing to be issued" an investment advertisement in the U.K. unless its contents have been approved by an authorized person.

   a. The FSA interprets "investment advertisement" to encompass material circulated on the Internet which contains an invitation or information likely to lead directly or indirectly to persons entering into or offering to enter into investment agreements (whether they be agreements for purchase or sale of investments or for providing investment services).

   b. The FSA has stated that it is its general view that if an advertisement, posted anywhere on the Internet, is made available to or can be obtained by someone in the U.K. then that advertisement may be viewed as having been issued in the U.K. Whether the advertisement is available to someone in the U.K., it is sufficient that the advertisement can be pulled up on a computer screen in the U.K.

   c. Given this restrictive approach of the FSA, it is almost an impossible task to conduct commerce over the Internet without falling within the U.K. jurisdictional reach. Even if one's only foray onto the Internet is the origination and maintenance, from the U.S., of a web site that not only is intended for U.S. users alone but also passively offers investment information, the mere fact that if a user in the U.K. can access the web site and the investment information, then the U.S. web site has entered U.K. territory and U.K. legal jurisdiction attaches.

2. Enforcement and safe harbors from U.K. legal jurisdiction

   a. Violation of this particular section of the Act is a criminal offense and, therefore, punishable by imprisonment or a fine or both and can be the basis of a civil proceeding by the FSA for injunction and restitution.

   b. The Act provides a safe harbor for advertisements which are issued overseas through the medium of a magazine or a periodical published overseas and circulating principally overseas. At the moment, the FSA does not include material circulated through the Internet as falling within this safe harbor.

   c. To date, the U.K. authorities have refused to provide a safe harbor for information posted on a web site which is intended to be directed only at U.S. investors. For example, the FSA has warned that it may be insufficient to merely place a legend on the web site stating that the investment material is directed at or intended to be directed at only U.S. investors or to merely control access to the web site by requiring all persons accessing the web site to register.

   d. The FSA, however, has indicated recently that it will issue a response letter to the ICI regarding the use of web sites by U.S. investment advisers and mutual funds, which web sites are directed at and intended to be directed at only U.S. investors.

C. <u>Primary Objective of Regulators is to Regulate Fraud</u>

Even though the Internet places us on the brink of a brave new world, the key to opening the door to such new discoveries is not the Internet itself. Rather, the key to realizing the full potential of the Internet and its impact on global markets and electronic commerce is the emergence of a predictable legal environment. Nowhere is this more true than in international cross-border transactions over the Internet, where concerns about legal jurisdiction, choice of law, enforcement of contracts, liability and other issues abound. Despite overwhelming requests for legislative and regulatory guidance from the business community at large, governments and regulators have, as yet, held their cards close to their chests. In those few situations where regulators have actually discussed the Internet and its commercial ramifications, regulators appear to be primarily focused on regulating fraud.

1. International Organization of Securities Commissions

On September 22, 1997, the Technical Committee of the International Organization of Securities Commissions ("IOSCO") released the Report on Enforcement Issues Raised by the Increasing Use of Electronic Networks in the Securities and Futures Field. The Report is extremely important because the primary objective underlying the Committee's discussion was the need not only to regulate fraudulent activities on the Internet but also to recognize the legitimate uses of the Internet in the securities and futures field and therefore the need for regulators themselves to use the Internet to regulate fraudsters.

a. In its Report, the Technical Committee first discusses the several methods that can be used to disseminate information electronically. These methods include the world-wide web, the bulletin board system or news groups or message boards, e-mail and personal broadcast network or push media.

b. The Technical Committee goes on to discuss the characteristics of the Internet that aid the perpetration of fraud.

1) The Internet makes information dissemination easier because it is international, rapid, reaches a broad audience and the information can be as detailed as the sender wishes.

2) The Internet provides a means to make Internet fraud appear legitimate. By establishing electronic links to well-regarded reports which offer legitimate information, the fraudster increases his credibility.

3) The Internet permits information to be sent anonymously. Such anonymity enables individuals previously enjoined from illegal activity to mask their identities on the Internet. In addition, one particular individual responsible for transmitting information on a certain matter can give the appearance that the information originates from multiple sources.

c. The Technical Committee acknowledges that the characteristics of the Internet makes it an ideal environment where traditional frauds can flourish.

1) Price manipulation is a traditional type of financial fraud for which the Internet is particularly suited. By enabling false and misleading statements about particular instruments to be sent electronically, the Internet allows the fraudster to influence the price of securities.

2) The Internet also provides a means for fraudulent offerings of securities. Unregistered persons may offer securities and futures for sale, or unregistered securities and illegal off-exchange futures can be sold to the public.

3) The Internet also provides a means for individuals to dispense fraudulent advice. The Internet enables broker-dealers to reach an unlimited number of investors over the Internet.

4) The Internet allows promoters and investment managers to hide conflicts of interest. A promoter may send information to investors about a company but the investors may have no way of knowing that the promoter sending the information is receiving a compensation from the target company.

d. While the Technical Committee urges that regulators band together in order to more effectively detect fraud on the Internet, the Technical Committee discusses such coordinated efforts along the lines of the sharing of information and detection techniques. The Technical Committee does not propose a legal jurisdictional framework for international commerce over the Internet.

e. Despite this lack of guidance, the Report remains helpful. With the knowledge that regulators view the Internet as a new medium for the perpetration of fraud, one may draw the conclusion that regulators are not so readily eager to overly restrict cross-border transactions over the Internet. It is insufficient, however, to stop at that mere realization. One must instead take the next step, which is to differentiate one's cross-border commercial activities over the Internet and Internet methods from those fraudulent activities of which the Technical Committee is concerned.

D. Compliance

These legal jurisdictional issues involving cross-border transactions conducted over the Internet are not exercises in legal-babble. They demand attention from both companies conducting international transactions and companies which currently conduct domestic transactions. By ignoring these issues, companies risk economic and enforcement costs.

1. Enforceability

If one's cross-border activity over the Internet falls within the legal jurisdiction of a foreign country, one's cross-border transaction is subject to the laws and regulations of such country. Even though the cross-border transaction may be valid and legal within the U.S., there are no guarantees that the foreign country's laws and regulations will deem the transaction valid and legal. Essentially, the foreign country may deem the transaction to be unenforceable. Without legal enforceability, one's rights and obligations will have no legal support, and vice versa with respect to one's counterparty. If the transaction is not valid in the eyes of the law, one cannot rely on the legal framework to enforce any payment obligations against one's counterparty.

2. Enforcement action

If a foreign legal jurisdiction attaches to a registered securities firm's cross-border activity over the Internet and the jurisdiction deems the activity to be unlawful, irrespective of whether the firm resides in that country, it may by subject to an enforcement proceeding. If the firm is a U.S. registered firm, the SEC has the ability to sanction or otherwise place limitations on the firm on the basis of the foreign legal proceeding (see Section 203(e) of The Investment Advisors Act of 1940 and Section 9(b) of The Investment Company Act of 1940). Accordingly, even a U.S. firm with only U.S. operations could be at risk if it is subject to a foreign enforcement action because of its use of the Internet.

3. Standards of fitness and properness

Many legal securities frameworks include standards of "fitness and properness" which must be met before an entity or individual can be authorized to engage in any securities business. Satisfaction of the standards of "fitness and properness" depends on not only present circumstances but also past performance. A past violation of the jurisdiction's laws is factored into the analysis of whether the individual or entity may be deemed sufficiently fit and proper to be authorized to engage in securities transactions within the particular jurisdiction. There is little question that a finding of a violation of a country's laws related to Internet use should be relevant to this analysis. Thus, while today a domestic firm may have chosen not to register to do business in a foreign jurisdiction, it should be recognized that as business plans grow and change, its past violations could impede its ability to receive the needed regulatory approvals.

II. Managing the Web Site to Minimize the Risk of Liability Abroad

While there are no established guidelines for determining when a web site may be subject to foreign jurisdiction, there are five key areas that the owner of the site should consider in managing this risk: (i) managing access to the web site, (ii) developing appropriate legends; (iii) using language to clarify the intended audience, (iv) developing internal procedures to ensure compliance and (v) establishing compliance procedures for overseeing the site. In general, the key to minimizing liability will be to manage the web site in such a way that the investor materials contained therein are directed primarily toward U.S. residents and not foreign investors. Effective web site management therefore involves assembling a spectrum of different elements -- including all the various means at the company's disposal for promoting and operating the site and enforcing policies regarding the site -- into a coherent program that directs the site as a whole towards qualified investors and away from foreign investors. No single measure discussed below should be regarded as the *sine qua non* of an effective web site management policy. Rather, each is a potential piece of a comprehensive scheme designed to minimize foreign regulatory liability.

A. Managing Access to the Web Site

Because the Internet has no borders, investors anywhere in the world have equal access to any given web site unless its owner takes proactive measures to manage such access. As discussed in Part I, foreign regulators will look specifically at the question whether a site it "directed at" their residents. Thus, an investment company operating a web site should carefully review all the means by which it makes its site available to the public, including advertising of the site, hyperlinks, promotion in interactive chat rooms, the design of the site itself, and on-line services.

1. Advertising the web site address

   a. Many companies promote their businesses by purchasing "banner" advertisements on other web sites thereby creating a link from those sites to the advertisers' own sites.

      Where banners are taken out on sites located in foreign countries, any such advertising that created a link to a U.S.-based web site would almost certainly be construed by a foreign regulator as an affirmative act directing the web site at foreign investors. Thus, such banner advertising would increase the chances of a foreign regulator asserting jurisdiction over the investment company in connection with the web site.

   b. Off-line advertising (e.g., in print publications or television) in publications intended primarily for foreign audiences that makes reference to the web site would similarly increase the likelihood of foreign regulatory liability. Thus, foreign affiliates of a U.S. investment company should not mention the U.S. web site in any of their advertisements.

2. Hyperlinks to the web site

   a. Corporations may often establish hyperlinks from related sites or even affiliated corporations to their sites. Where the hyperlink allows a foreign investor to move from a local site to a U.S. site, the foreign host that is likely to be registered to do business in its country may assume responsibility for the U.S. site. Indeed, a regulator in the foreign country may conclude that, by linking its site to the materials in the U.S.-based site, the foreign affiliate is itself advertising the investment materials in the U.S. web site. Thus, the foreign regulator could assert that the foreign affiliate is advertising securities that are not registered in the foreign country. Conversely, if the link was initiated by the U.S. company, a foreign regulator could conclude that the U.S. affiliate is soliciting foreign investor access to the U.S. web site through the hyperlink.

3. Chat room promotion of the site

   Chat rooms have become a popular forum for discussing and promoting securities. If a registered representative of a U.S.-based investment company participated in chat rooms maintained by a foreign on-line service and promotes U.S. securities, the investment company may be seen as soliciting transactions in a foreign country.

4. On-line services

a. An investment company may make information regarding its services available through on-line services such as America On-Line. By entering into such an arrangement, an investment company obtains direct access to the service's subscriber base.

b. In some instances, the on-line service may provide the investment company's materials through its own servers. Under this arrangement, the subscriber can view or download the investment company's materials without ever accessing the company's site itself.

c. Under this arrangement, any subscriber of the on-line service can obtain the materials without passing through the investment company's site itself. The investment company therefore has less control over access to its materials and must take additional precautionary measures to reduce the risk of foreign regulatory liability.

d. An investment company providing its own materials to the public through an on-line service should take steps to ensure that access to those materials is restricted to U.S. residents.

-- The investment company should consider discussing with the on-line service — and setting forth contractually — appropriate management of access to investor materials through the on-line service.

-- The investment company may wish to seek indemnity for liability arising from conduct by the on-line service relating to distribution of the investment company's materials.

-- The investment company's compliance officers or in-house counsel should monitor how the on-line service is making its materials available to the public.

e. The on-line service itself faces the risk of securities law liability in foreign jurisdictions by making investor material available to inappropriate persons. This is particularly true where the on-line service has some control over the information being placed on its service — as is the case with on-line services like America On-Line. The FSA has already warned that Internet access providers may incur liability under U.K. securities laws under certain circumstances.

5. Measures to control inappropriate access to the site

Depending upon the height of concern that foreign investors may inappropriately use the web site, companies should consider implementing more draconian measures that would limit the ability of a foreign investor to view investment materials even after his initial entry to the site.

a. The least invasive of the measures to restrict access is to screen and block access from foreign servers

-- Technology exists that can detect the country from which a particular visitor to a web site is accessing the Internet.

-- This technology provides a method to identify that a query is being made from abroad without interacting with the investor.

-- The web can be designed either to limit access totally or to provide visitors who access the site from a foreign server with a special legend, see discussion infra Part II.B, advising them that the web site is directed at U.S. residents.

b. Questionnaires

-- Upon entering the site or portions of the site containing investment materials, visitors can be asked to state their place of residence. Respondents who indicate that they reside in the U.S. would have unimpeded access to the site. Respondents indicating a foreign residence could be sent to a page warning them that the investments discussed in the site are intended for U.S. residents and thereafter the site could disconnect.

-- A foreign investor can always circumvent the questionnaire by misrepresenting his or her place of residence. However, the investment company can then argue that it had a reasonable expectation that the investor was a U.S. resident and qualified to view the materials on the web site.

c. Registration and passwords

-- First-time visitors can be asked to register with the web site and obtain a user name and password before entering restricted areas of the site. Registration would involve submitting an on-line form requiring certain information such as the investor's place of residence. No fee would need to be charged. Upon subsequent visits to the site, the investor would need only enter his or her user name and password before proceeding onwards.

-- Applicants indicated a foreign residence would not be allowed to register and would be denied access to restricted areas of the site and/or informed that not all the investment materials on the site are not directed at or appropriate for them.

-- The disadvantage of any user registration system is that the web site becomes less accessible to users who want to browse through the site without completing a registration form. This illustrates the inevitable tension between managing the web site both to reduce the risk of regulatory liability and to maximize "user friendliness" and accessibility to customers.

B. Restrictive Legends

1. Use of language advising web site visitors that information on the site is directed toward U.S. and not foreign investors constitutes an important and effective means for limiting foreign regulatory liability.

a. At a minimum, the web site's home page should display a legend advising visitors that the information on the site is directed toward U.S. investors. The legend should further advise that the products on the web site are generally not available to foreign investors.

b. Similar disclaimer language should also appear on any page containing investment materials.

c. An additional precaution could require the visitor to the web site to acknowledge that he or she has read the disclaimer language and to represent that he or she is a U.S. resident or otherwise qualified to invest in the products offered on the web site.

d. The key is that the legend be prominently placed on the first web page and that all significant warnings appear in the legend itself.

2. Such restrictive language places foreign investors on notice that the material on the site is not intended for them due to foreign regulations and the investment company's web site policies. A foreign investor who chooses to ignore these express warnings and to circumvent the site's screening devices will generally be less sympathetic to foreign regulators and courts.

3. At the same time, such language provides clarification to foreign investors who enter the U.S. web site in the mistaken belief that they can participate in the investments offered on that site.

-- If the investment company is registered to do business in other countries and also maintains web sites abroad, the U.S. web site can be designed so that foreign investors can be directed via hypertext link to the appropriate foreign web site.

C. Using U.S. English and Forms

1. Language and terminology in the web site should reinforce the notion that the web site is directly at U.S. residents.

2. U.S. English rather than British English should be used.

3. Foreign languages or currency conversions also should avoided so as not to create the impression that foreign investors are welcome to peruse the web site's offerings. This is particularly true given that the Internet is dominated by American web sites, and foreign language web sites

generally arise only in foreign countries.

4. On-line application forms to open accounts or receive mailings of investor materials should not contain foreign alternatives. Thus, if the site has a pull down menu listing American states, it should not include, for example, U.K. or France unless investor relationships can be established legally in those countries.

D. Conforming the Firm's Conduct to its Web Site Policy

1. Web site policies and procedures may not succeed in screening out all attempts by foreign investors to access U.S. investor materials, open an account or attempt to enter into a transaction through the web site.

2. To deal with the occasional foreign application or trading order made on the web site, the investment company's back office should develop and enforce procedures to ensure that applications from foreign investors are declined.

3. By maintaining and enforcing written such policies and procedures, the investment company can demonstrate to foreign regulators that it has taken reasonable measures to ensure that foreign investors do not make use of web sites intended for the U.S. markets.

E. Compliance with Web Site Policies and Procedures

1. The investment company should take steps to ensure that the policies and procedures it adopts for its web site are implemented and then enforced. Because both the information and the design of web sites are frequently changed, this review will necessarily be ongoing in nature.

2. To be comprehensive, any such ongoing review must extend not only to the company's site, but also to any advertising of the site, hyperlinks to the site, materials offered by the company through on-line services and the other subjects discussed earlier in this outline.

3. It is advisable to set forth the company's web site policies and procedures in a written compliance manual. The manual should detail the steps taken by the company to ensure compliance with both domestic and foreign securities laws.

4. The company should also appoint an official responsible for monitoring

and controlling material posted on the web site, for deciding how access to the site will be limited, and for staying current with the relevant domestic and foreign securities laws.

5. The appointed compliance official or his or her associates should consider meeting with employees responsible for designing and operating the web site and educate them as to the relevant legal issues.

6. The compliance official should also consider testing the effectiveness of the established web site management policies and procedures. Such testing will normally be a simple matter. And since regulators, too, can easily test the web site without being detected, the investment company should be vigilant to catch any chinks in its armor before the regulators do.

NOTES

9

FINANCIAL SERVICES ON THE INTERNET AND THE UK REGULATORY REGIME

Michelle C. Wallach
John B. Travis

Prepared with the assistance of Christopher J. Bates, a partner in the London office of Clifford Chance.

Morgan Stanley Dean Witter

Financial Services on the Internet and the UK Regulatory Regime

The development of the Internet is enabling financial institutions to promote their business and to provide financial services to customers and counterparties in new ways. However, the development of the medium is being restricted by the need for firms to comply with often conflicting and burdensome requirements worldwide. There is a risk that these requirements will prevent the full exploitation of the benefits of the new medium, to the detriment of end users of financial services.

1. EXECUTIVE SUMMARY

One of the principal legislative issues today is how each country's legal regime regulates foreign firms conducting business over the Internet. This paper sets out some examples of how the Internet is being used by foreign financial services firms, highlights some of the features of the existing UK regulatory regime affecting such foreign firms accessing the Internet's worldwide web and discusses some possible avenues for regulatory reform. Foreign firms are defined herein as non-UK based firms acting from offices outside the UK. Of course, UK based firms using the Internet face similar regulatory issues under the laws of other countries. Therefore, if the UK can develop a satisfactory framework for dealing with non-UK based firms using the Internet, this framework could also benefit UK based firms and would be an important first step towards an international framework that resolves the issue of competing and, potentially, conflicting regulations in an appropriate and commercially viable way. (This paper does not address the UK law issues for UK based firms).

The Internet's worldwide web is different from other media used to advertise or promote financial services. In particular, there is no practical means of preventing a website from being accessed by persons anywhere in the world. Restricting access through passwords given only to existing customers (as in an Extranet service) would eliminate much of the value of the web as an advertising medium. There is far greater control over who will receive material promoted through other media, even if, as with newspapers and other periodicals, it is not always possible to preclude the possibility of incidental circulation in other countries.

However, the regulatory framework needs to do more than address the issue of advertising that is not directed at persons in the UK, even though it is accessible by UK persons. In addition to the question of whether any advertising is available to UK persons, the rules need to take account of other factors, including: whether a foreign firm has existing UK customers, whether the specific product or service advertised is available to UK persons, whether the product or service is really intended for UK professional or institutional investors, whether there are warning legends and disclaimers, whether adequate home state regulation exists, as well as the nature of the particular medium used to carry the advertisement. All of these factors should influence the extent to which UK regulation applies in a particular circumstance.

Accordingly, we believe that UK regulation of the Internet should be based on the following premises:

- A foreign firm using the Internet to promote its business may have no existing UK customers or counterparties, have no intention of dealing with UK customers or counterparties and may not, in fact, deal with UK customers or counterparties. In such a case, the only contact with the UK is the fact that its website is accessible by UK persons. Therefore, it would be unnecessarily burdensome for the firm to be subject to UK regulation with respect to the contents of the website.

- A foreign firm using the Internet may have existing customers or counterparties in the UK and intend to deal with UK customers and counterparties in the future. However, the specific products or services promoted on the Internet may not be available to UK persons. Again, in these circumstances, it would be unnecessarily burdensome for the firm to be subject to UK regulation with respect to the contents of the website.

- In contrast, UK regulators do have a legitimate regulatory interest where a foreign firm using the Internet does intend to deal with UK persons with respect to particular products or services promoted on the Internet. However, the extent of regulation in this situation should still depend on a number of additional factors, among them, the sophistication of the investor and the inclusion of appropriate legends or risk warnings.

In summary, our specific suggestions are as follows:

- ***Flexibility:*** The new UK legislative regime currently contemplated by the proposed financial regulatory reform should be flexible in light of changing technologies. The Financial Services Authority ("FSA") should have the power to make rules that can limit the extent of the authorisation and advertising restrictions imposed by the legislation. The FSA should also have powers to give guidance on the interpretation of both the legislation and the rules made under it and industry participants should be able to rely on that guidance.

- *Advertising restrictions:* The advertising restrictions in the new legislation should recognise a gradation of circumstances which require different levels of control:

    - Advertising that is not directed at UK persons should be exempted, whether or not the advertising happens to be available to persons in the UK.
    - The FSA should have the power to create non-exclusive "safe harbours" for cases where there are no significant UK investor protection concerns such as where the specific product or service is not available to UK persons or is only available to professional or institutional investors in the UK.
    - There should, in any event, be exemptions applicable to all forms of regulated product for advertising directed at professional and institutional investors and these exemptions should be capable of being combined with other exemptions.
    - Legends and risk warnings should be prominently displayed on a website when certain products or services are not provided generally.
    - Additionally, even where advertising by foreign persons is partly directed at other UK persons, there should be no requirement to have the advertisement approved by a UK authorised person if the advertising contains such appropriate legends or risk warnings.
    - A similar approach should be adopted in relation to prospectus requirements, including the introduction of a new "combinable" exemption for overseas directed offerings.

- *Authorisation requirements:* Whatever the structure of the authorisation requirements in the new legislation, foreign entities should remain free to conduct cross-border business with wholesale and institutional customers and large corporations. Any attempt to determine when authorisation is required by reference to where services are provided is unlikely to be workable. However, UK authorisation requirements should not apply merely because a foreign party deals with a UK consumer. Rather, the new legislation should build on the "overseas persons" exemption in the existing financial services legislation so that foreign persons are not subject to UK authorisation requirements if they have complied with UK advertising restrictions. Additionally, there should be a regime under which the FSA can grant (conditional or unconditional) exemptions from the authorisation requirements in appropriate circumstances such as where a foreign firm is subject to adequate regulation in its home state.

Clearly, the development of electronic commerce on the Internet has created complicated global issues. Therefore, there is a need for international cooperation to resolve these issues and the UK should work with other countries and international organisations to achieve a global solution. Additionally, countries, such as the UK, that have traditionally supported open markets should assume a leadership role by devising solutions that adequately protect their investors and residents but also respect principles of international comity. A new, more flexible and differentiated approach is required.

2. EXAMPLES

The following examples illustrate some of the ways in which the Internet is being (or might be) used in connection with financial transactions.

Example 1: A US company is conducting an initial public offering of its securities. The offering is registered with the US Securities and Exchange Commission and is underwritten by a syndicate of US broker-dealers that purchase the securities from the company and resell them to their clients in a "book built" distribution. In addition to sales to domestic clients, members of the US syndicate place the securities with international institutional investors (including institutional investors in London) in reliance on local private placement exemptions. The US company, or members of the US syndicate, post an electronic copy of the US prospectus on its/their Internet website(s). The prospectus is accompanied by information on how investors can contact syndicate members if they wish to buy the shares as well as an automated facility for transmitting orders for the shares to a syndicate member.

Example 2: A Canadian bank creates a website accessible to existing and potential customers in order to provide basic information about the bank and its subsidiaries. The website contains details of the types of loan facilities, deposit and current accounts, and broker-dealer and asset management services offered by the bank and its subsidiaries, including details about publicly-available mutual funds sponsored by it. The person accessing the website can obtain live share prices, review relevant articles published by employees of the firm, use an interactive calculator which shows required levels of savings to achieve particular investment objectives (e.g. retirement planning) and compare the relative performance of particular investments or markets by accessing a database.

Example 3: A Japanese broker-dealer establishes a new, execution-only, dealing service that is available to customers over the Internet who wish to trade in Japanese shares. Potential customers can access the website, read information about the service, review customer agreements and receive details of current share prices provided by an automatic feed from the stock exchange. An investor who wishes to subscribe to the service completes the requisite forms and agreements online and also arranges for funds to be transferred to the broker-dealer's account. Once the broker-dealer has completed its checks on the potential customer, the customer is issued a password and is able to enter orders to buy or sell Japanese securities online through the Internet.

3. EXISTING LEGISLATIVE PROVISIONS

The restrictions discussed below are intended to illustrate the range of UK legislative and regulatory provisions that need to be addressed by foreign firms conducting activities such as those set out in the examples. The discussion is not intended to be exhaustive. In particular, the focus is on the impact of legislation affecting investment and banking business, although examples of some of the relevant insurance and consumer credit provisions are provided as well. In addition, this paper focuses on the regulatory rules affecting the use of the Internet, rather than general law provisions such as the data protection, misleading advertising, trade descriptions, unfair contract terms, etc. legislation.

Advertising restrictions

There are four main sources of advertising restrictions in the existing regulatory regime:

- *Investment business:* The Financial Services Act 1986 (the "1986 Act") prohibits the issue of an investment advertisement "in" the UK unless the advertisement is issued or approved by an authorised person (s. 57 1986 Act). Contravention of this restriction is a criminal offence and affects the enforceability of contracts. In addition, it may affect a foreign firm's ability to rely on the "overseas persons" exemption from the authorisation requirements of the 1986 Act (para. 27 Schedule 1 1986 Act - see below). Contravention of the authorisation requirements also has both criminal and civil consequences. The website materials in each of the examples given above would constitute "investment advertisements" which would be regulated by s. 57. Consequently, the enforceability of otherwise lawful contracts may be questioned because the sites are deemed to be advertisements issued "in" the UK.

  Contravention of s. 57 with respect to electronic versions of investment advertisements may also affect the legality of the distribution of the paper version of the advertisement where the latter would otherwise have been lawful in reliance on the exemptions for advertisements issued only to certain classes of persons. For example, the syndicate members in example 1 might otherwise have been able to rely on the exemption in Article 11 of the Financial Services Act 1986 (Investment Advertisements) (Exemptions) Order 1996 for advertisements "issued only" to UK persons who fall within the defined class of "expert" investors and "other persons to whom the advertisement may be lawfully issued". The availability of the prospectus on the Internet may mean that the prospectus would be treated as having been issued to some persons in the UK outside of this (or other) exemptions. Therefore, the Article 11 exemption would no longer be available.

While it may be possible to overcome these restrictions by having the website approved by an authorised person for the purposes of s. 57, this approval will in itself raise issues as to compliance with applicable conduct of business rules and s. 76 of the 1986 Act (as to which see below).

The 1986 Act also controls the promotion of insurance contracts which constitute "investments". S.130 of the 1986 Act prohibits anyone from issuing advertisements "in" the UK relating to such contracts, or advising or procuring persons in the UK to enter into such contracts, unless the contract is made with a UK authorised person, a passported European insurer or an insurer from a territory designated as offering sufficient protection. These provisions might be an issue in example 2 if the sponsor of the website were an insurance company rather than a bank (or if one of the members of the bank group were an insurance company) and if the products advertised included relevant insurance contracts.

- *Deposit-taking:* The Banking Act 1987 (the "Banking Act") governs the issue, form and content of "deposit advertisements" (s. 37 Banking Act). The regulations made under these provisions apply to controlled advertisements which are, broadly, advertisements that could lead to deposits being taken at an office outside the European Economic Area (Banking Act 1987 (Advertisement) Regulations 1988). There is no prohibition against the issue of controlled advertisements so long as they contain certain minimum prescribed information. Unlike the 1986 Act, the Banking Act restrictions rely solely on minimum disclosure requirements and do not require persons not holding a UK authorisation to have relevant advertising "approved" by a UK authorised institution.

The Credit Institutions (Protection of Depositors) Regulations 1995 also control the issue, form and content of deposit advertisements issued "in" the UK. Regulation 48 of those regulations prohibits certain representations in deposit advertisements with respect to applicable deposit protection schemes and requires certain disclosures to be made in such advertisements. Regulations 46 and 47 of those regulations impose certain additional requirements on banks (both UK incorporated and foreign) that are licensed in the UK as well as passported European banks, including those without a branch in the UK. The territorial ambit of these latter restrictions is unclear.

The provisions on deposit advertising are relevant in example 2 and raise practical concerns as to compliance with minimum disclosure requirements and possible conflicts between the UK prohibitions against the making of certain statements which may conflict with home country requirements. These provisions might also be relevant if, in example 1, the public offer was an offer inviting subscriptions for bonds, rather than shares, and not a resale of the bonds by the underwriters, as the issue of bonds can involve the taking of "deposits".

- *Insurance:* The Insurance Companies Act 1982 ("ICA") also provides for regulations that control the issue of "insurance advertisements" (s. 72 ICA). Like the regulations made under the Banking Act, these regulations impose minimum content requirements on advertisements issued by insurers whose head offices are outside Europe and who are not authorised to carry on insurance business in the UK (regulations 35-37 of the Insurance Companies Regulations 1994). Additional disclosure requirements apply to invitations by intermediaries connected with insurance companies that invite UK residents to enter into insurance arrangements.

  Subsidiary restrictions include, for example, the Restriction of Advertisements (War Risks Insurance) Act 1939 which contains a prohibition on causing or permitting advertisements to appear that contain information on war risks insurance for UK property.

  These provisions would be an issue if, in example 2, the sponsor of the website were an insurance company rather than a bank (or if one of the members of the bank group were an insurance company).

- *Consumer credit:* The Consumer Credit Act 1974 ("CCA") controls the issue of advertising relating to, among other things, consumer loans, credit cards, leasing and hire purchase business and credit brokerage services (see in particular s. 43 CCA and the Consumer Credit (Advertisements) Regulations 1989). Advertisements must comply with very detailed form and content requirements unless an exemption applies. These rules and regulations would be an issue for the Canadian bank in example 2 if, for example, details of loan products were provided on the website.

An advertisement issued "outside the UK" is nevertheless deemed to be issued "in" the UK for the purposes of the investment business and banking advertising restrictions if it is directed at persons in the UK or is made available to them. There are exceptions for advertising in foreign periodicals or sound or television broadcasts principally aimed at persons outside the UK. See s. 207(3) 1986 Act and s. 32(7) Banking Act (which also applies to the relevant provisions of the Credit Institutions (Protection of Depositors) Regulations 1995). To date, the FSA's view has been that advertisements that can be accessed by UK persons are issued in the UK for the purposes of the 1986 Act, whether or not in fact anyone does so and whether or not the advertiser deals with any UK customers or counterparties as a result of the advertisement.

Although this is not explicitly stated, the advertising restrictions of the ICA and the CCA should only apply to advertisements issued or published "in" the UK. Although those Acts do not contain provisions equivalent to s. 207(3) of the 1986 Act or s. 32(7) of the Banking Act, the contents of a website could be regarded as issued or published in the UK for the purposes of the ICA and the CCA if the website is accessed by a person in the UK. Again, this conclusion would be the case whether or not the advertiser deals with any UK customers or counterparties as a result of the advertisement.

The use of the Internet also makes it increasingly difficult to identify who is the "issuer" of a particular website when the website is used to promote the services of a group of companies.

Clearly, if the mere fact that an Internet website is accessible, or is accessed, by persons in the UK itself triggers the application of UK rules then all financially-related websites worldwide are potentially affected. This broad interpretation of the rules causes material compliance issues for financial institutions. Even if reliance could be placed on a UK regulator's publicly stated intention not to take enforcement action with respect to particular types of advertising, a contravention of UK rules could affect the enforceability of otherwise legitimate transactions (see e.g. the discussion below concerning the impact on the overseas persons exemption). Therefore, we discuss below possible methods of reducing the regulatory burden imposed by the advertising restrictions on foreign firms.

Prospectus and similar requirements

The Public Offers of Securities Regulations 1995 (the "POS Regulations") require the registration and publication of a prospectus where an offer to the public is made to persons "in the UK". The definition of an "offer to the public" is restricted to contractual offers and invitations of contractual offers. For an institutional placing in the UK of the kind contemplated in example 1, there are a number of exemptions to the POS Regulations, including those for offers to professional investors or to a limited number of persons. Nevertheless, the territorial ambit of the POS Regulations is not entirely clear, such as where a public offer is made in a particular jurisdiction that is open generally to the world at large even if not specifically directed at persons in the UK. For example, the POS Regulations might apply where, as in example 1, a website offers facilities to transmit orders to the syndicate members or where a public offer of securities in one market is advertised in local newspapers with an incidental circulation in the UK. Similar issues arise with respect to the public offer restrictions in Part IV of the 1986 Act with respect to offers to the public "in the UK" of London-listed securities where there are simultaneous foreign offerings.

There are also difficulties in determining how the POS Regulations apply to secondary market trading activity and, in particular, to screen based trading of the kind contemplated in example 3. If offers are displayed on screens that are accessible to non-professionals, it is difficult to see which exemption might be available to protect those offers from prospectus requirements. The POS Regulations have no clear exemption for ordinary secondary market activity in non-London listed securities.

A separate regime applies to the promotion of collective investment schemes (s. 76 1986 Act). Unless an exemption applies, authorised persons cannot issue investment advertisements "in" the UK relating to schemes that are not authorised or recognised for UK purposes or advise or procure persons in the UK to become a member of such schemes. In practice, this restriction would be problematic in the context of example 2 if the Canadian bank sought to legitimise its advertising by having its website issued, or approved for issue, in the UK by an authorised person for the purposes of s. 57 of the 1986 Act. Unless all the funds whose particulars are included on the website are authorised or recognised schemes, the UK authorised person might violate either the restrictions imposed by conduct of business rules on the approval of advertisements relating to unregulated schemes or, if it "issues" the advertisement, the restrictions imposed by s. 76 of the 1986 Act. In practice, it might be necessary to put the fund information on password protected areas of the website, even though sales to particular categories of UK persons would otherwise be permitted under s. 76 and the Financial Services (Promotion of Unregulated Schemes) Regulations 1991. Such a limited access scheme, essentially creating an Extranet service, would defeat one of the Canadian bank's objectives: to use the website to promote its services to Canadian residents who are not its existing customers.

Authorisation requirements

At present, there are separate authorisation requirements for particular regimes:

- *Investment business:* The 1986 Act imposes authorisation requirements for persons carrying on investment business in the UK (s. 3 1986 Act). Contravention of this restriction is an offence and affects the enforceability of contracts. However, a foreign person not carrying on investment business through a UK permanent place of business can conduct investment business with UK persons if it can demonstrate that its doing so does not constitute the carrying on of a business in the UK or if it can rely on the so-called overseas persons exemptions in paragraphs 26 and 27 of Schedule 1 to the 1986 Act.[1]

For example, absent the use of the Internet, the US broker-dealers in example 1 might rely on the overseas persons exemption to make sales directly to UK institutional accounts, as those accounts can be approached directly from overseas without violating the cold calling and investment advertising restrictions of the 1986 Act. However, if the use of the Internet contravenes the investment advertising rules, the overseas persons exemption may no longer be available e.g. if the institutional account in fact learned of the offering through the Internet. Example 2 also raises the issue of whether any of the materials on the website might be considered "advice" which the FSA has generally regarded as being provided in the UK if it is received in the UK.

- *Deposit-taking:* The Banking Act imposes authorisation requirements on persons who accept deposits "in" the UK in the course of a deposit-taking business (s. 3 Banking Act). There is no definition of when a deposit will be regarded as accepted in the UK but it is clear that the deposit-taking business does not have to be carried on in the UK. It is not easy to determine when a deposit will be regarded as accepted "in" the UK. For example, it may be unclear whether a foreign bank accepts a deposit "in" the UK from a UK resident if the funds are transferred to the foreign bank's correspondent in London (e.g. where payment is in sterling). This question might be of concern to the Canadian bank in example 2 if, say, its Jersey subsidiary was accepting sterling deposits in this way. A new approach is needed, particularly in the context of the possible entry by the UK into monetary union.

---

1 However, the current provisions of paragraph 27 Schedule 1 to the 1986 Act contain one particular anomaly which needs to be addressed in any new legislation if the legislation follows the same approach. The current provisions make it clear that an overseas person can, acting on behalf of another overseas person, arrange deals in investments with UK persons (within paragraph 13 of Schedule 1) without requiring authorisation, so long as such overseas person has complied with the solicitation restrictions contained in ss. 56 and 57 of the 1986 Act. However, an overseas person may not deal in investments with a UK person (within paragraph 12 of Schedule 1) in reliance on the exemption if, in executing the deal, it is acting on behalf of another overseas person even if: (i) it and its foreign principal have complied with the solicitation restrictions; and (ii) the foreign principal could itself have relied on the exemption in relation to that transaction. This exclusion has caused practical problems in the past (e.g. where a foreign investment bank is making a takeover offer on behalf of a foreign bidder for a foreign company and seeks to have the bid document approved for the purpose of s. 57 in order to allow its circulation to UK shareholders). There is no reason to limit the scope of the exemption in this way. After all, the existing exemption allows an overseas person to rely on the exemption (with appropriate safeguards) where it is acting as agent for a UK person in dealing with other UK persons.

The Banking Act also restricts the use of banking names and descriptions by any person "carrying on business in the UK" (ss. 67-69 Banking Act) unless that person is an authorised institution and, if it wishes to use the word "bank" as part of its name, meets certain additional criteria. Again, the use of the Internet complicates the application of these restrictions.

- *Insurance:* The ICA requires any person carrying on insurance business in the UK to obtain authorisation (s. 2 ICA). No definition is given to elucidate when a foreign insurance company is regarded as carrying on business in the UK and this ambiguity has also been the subject of some controversy over the years.

- *Consumer credit:* The CCA provides that no-one shall carry on a consumer credit business or a consumer hire business without a licence (s. 21 CCA). Separate licensing provisions apply to credit brokerage. There are no comprehensive provisions restricting the territorial scope of the CCA, although it seems probable that the licensing requirements apply only where the relevant business is carried on "in" the UK. On this basis, then, while it may be unlikely that the Canadian bank in example 2 would need a UK licence merely because its website is accessible to UK persons, the licensing requirements might apply if it then sought to deal with a UK customer who responded to its website advertisement.

Conduct of business rules

There are two main circumstances where the conduct of business rules of a self-regulating organisation ("SRO"), such as SFA, IMRO or PIA, under the 1986 Act may be relevant in the examples.

First, as discussed previously, a foreign entity may seek to have its website issued or approved for issue in the UK by an authorised person for the purposes of s. 57 1986 Act in order to avoid a contravention of the investment advertising restrictions. For example, the Canadian bank in example 2 might seek to have its website approved by its London affiliate which is regulated by SFA. However, in that event, there are questions as to how the approval requirement can be practically operated in relation to websites with rapidly changing contents (or where screens are generated by databases which may interact with information supplied by the person accessing the website). In addition, compliance with the conduct of business rules as to required legends, specific statements and record keeping is difficult and burdensome, particularly when the sections of the website implicated by the rules are not even directed at UK residents.

Secondly, the foreign person may be regulated by an SRO through a branch in the UK. For example, the Canadian bank in example 2 might have a branch in the UK through which it is a member of SFA. In that event, the entity as a whole is an authorised person so that the restrictions of ss. 3 and 57 1986 Act no longer apply to it or advertisements issued by it. However, the entity, as in the previous paragraph, will be subject to the conduct of business rules and will have to comply with the requirements referred to above. In addition, the use of the Internet may affect the application of other rules as well. For example, the Canadian bank might do some business from Canada directly with UK institutional investors or on an unsolicited basis with other UK accounts in reliance on the overseas persons carve out from the SFA's rules (SFA Rule 5-1(2)). This carve out enables a firm to do investment business with UK customers and counterparties from a foreign office without complying with all of the SFA's conduct of business rules if that overseas office could (if it had been a separate entity) lawfully have conducted that business without authorisation under the 1986 Act. However, as already noted, the ability of an overseas person to avoid the authorisation requirements of the 1986 Act may depend on the overseas person not contravening s. 57 of the 1986 Act. In example 2, it is unclear whether the availability of the website to UK persons would have the impact of depriving the Canadian bank of the benefit of the overseas person carve-out.

There are other rules which also fail to deal adequately with these territoriality issues and, in particular, the application of UK regulatory requirements to entities that conduct business with UK persons from both a local UK branch and a foreign office.

For example, similar issues also arise with respect to the Money Laundering Regulations 1993. Such regulations impose customer identification, record keeping, notification and other compliance requirements on persons carrying on relevant financial business "in" the UK The regulations do not clarify the territoriality issue except where the business constitutes "investment business" regulated by the 1986 Act, in which case the 1986 Act definitions apply. However, ambiguity still remains as to how the regulations would apply in example 2 if the Canadian bank had a branch office in the UK from which it conducted investment business but it also dealt with UK residents responding to the website from its Canadian head office. Thus, the Regulations may duplicate home state rules, which is of particular concern in the context of European passported firms conducting cross-border business with UK customers and counterparties.

In addition, special rules, similar to conduct of business rules, apply to contracts of insurance and consumer credit. These rules regulate, for example, pre-contractual disclosure, the form and content of agreements, cooling off periods and the like. In relation to consumer credit, there is considerable debate as to the territorial ambit of such restrictions. These restrictions may apply whether or not the creditor requires a licence and whether or not the agreement is governed by foreign law. In practice, foreign institutions may feel compelled to comply with these provisions when dealing with UK customers regardless of how the business is originated (e.g. if the Canadian bank in example 2 received an enquiry from a UK individual seeking credit for a transaction in Canada).

Passported institutions

European passported institutions face additional difficulties. Under the regulations implementing the Second Banking Directive and the Investment Services Directive, a European bank or investment firm may not provide services "in" the UK on a cross-border basis unless it has complied with the relevant notification requirements. (See regulations 6 and 7 of the Banking Coordination (Second Council Directive) Regulations 1992 and of the Investment Services Regulations 1995.) The European Commission has sought to elucidate when a firm will be regarded as providing services "in" a Member State for the purposes of the Second Banking Directive through its interpretative communication on the Second Banking Directive. In particular, it has stated that "distance banking services, for example, through the Internet, should not ... require prior notification." However, unless Member States specifically amend their own rules to conform to the Commission's view, institutions are at risk if this interpretation is found to be incorrect. The UK has not amended its own rules.

Therefore, banks and investment firms doing cross-border business with UK customers and counterparties may be advised to comply with the notification requirements with respect to the UK even if there is doubt as to whether they need to and even if they could have, absent the notification, relied on either the overseas persons exemption from the authorisation requirements of the 1986 Act or the argument that they are not accepting deposits "in" the UK for the purposes of the Banking Act. If, in example 2, the Canadian bank were a French bank, it might very well feel compelled to comply with the notification requirements even if it did not anticipate conducting any business with UK residents.

Compliance with the notification requirements is, however, even more critical for a European bank or investment firm conducting cross-border investment business with UK customers and counterparties who might not be able to rely on the overseas persons exemption to do that business. Failure to comply strictly with the notification requirements may lead to the invalidation of the European bank's/firm's transactions under s.5 of the 1986 Act. A "quasi-European institution" (i.e. a European firm entitled to use the passport but which has not yet complied with the notification requirements) does not appear to be protected from the authorisation requirements of the 1986 Act. Even though regulations 6 and 7 of the 1992 and 1995 Regulations indicate that a contravention of those regulations does not invalidate any transaction, the protection conferred by regulation 5 of those regulations is only available to incoming institutions that have complied with the notification requirements. The

European Commission has stated that in its view failure to comply with the notification requirement "should not ... be considered a procedural condition affecting the validity of a banking contract."

Nevertheless, European passported institutions seeking to use the Internet in the manner of the non-EU entities in the examples given above face obstacles in so doing. So long as the European passported firm could have relied on the overseas persons exemption it will not be conducting "home-regulated investment business in the UK" within the meaning of the regulations and is thus largely free from UK conduct of business regulation. However, once that fact ceases to be the case, the European firm may be subject to the full panoply of the FSA's conduct of business rules, including requirements to pay fees, to contribute to the investor protection scheme, etc. See the Financial Services (European Institutions) Instrument 1993 and the Financial Services (Investment Firms) Rules 1995. The use of the Internet has an impact on these rules because the overseas persons exemption critically depends upon the interaction with s. 57 of the 1986 Act.

4. SOME POSSIBLE AVENUES FOR REFORM

Flexibility

It will be difficult to define solutions that adequately address the changing issues and concerns presented by the new world of electronic commerce. Thus, any new legislation needs to be flexible and capable of change without new primary legislation. However, it is not enough to rely on the making of change through the normal procedures for delegated legislation. This process has not proved a successful way of addressing the problems that have arisen in the past and will be more difficult as technological changes raise new issues that need to be effectively addressed in a timely fashion. The FSA needs to be given a role as the body closest to the market with established procedures for industry consultation. Industry participants need legal certainty, particularly where contraventions of rules could result in contracts becoming unenforceable.

As under the Banking Act and the 1986 Act, the Treasury should clearly have the power, through statutory instruments, to modify the scope of the authorisation requirements set out in the primary legislation. However, even if there is a policy objection to the FSA being given a general role in defining the scope of authorisation requirements through rule making, there is no fundamental reason why the FSA should not be given the power to make rules that affect particular aspects of the scope of the advertising and authorisation requirements. For example, the FSA already has powers to make rules derogating from the criminal prohibitions on market manipulation in relation to stabilisation (s. 47 1986 Act) and the prohibitions on cold calling (s. 56 1986 Act).

The new legislation should provide the FSA with broad powers to grant authorisation and to set conditions under which authorised firms operate. For example, at present, the service company regime effectively amounts to the granting of authorisation without extensive capital, conduct of business or other requirements. These authorisation powers could be used to deal with some of the problems faced by foreign firms using the Internet.

However, because authorisation may imply a degree of supervision or approval that may be inappropriate, the FSA should also be given powers to make rules exempting firms from the authorisation and advertising restrictions imposed by the new legislation. There should be no objection, in principle, to the FSA being given rule making powers of this kind, at least if the following conditions are satisfied:

- The rules should only be able to restrict, and not extend, the scope of the criminal law. Clearly, there may be objections to the FSA being able to create criminal offences. The same objection does not apply to rules that restrict the scope of criminal offences created by Parliament or by delegated legislation.

- The FSA's rule making power should be exercisable for a defined purpose so that it is capable of judicial review. For example, in the context of the current law, Part IV of Schedule 1 to the 1986 Act could specify that paragraphs 12 to 16 of the Schedule (which define the activities subject to authorisation requirements) do not apply to activities of overseas person in conformity with rules made by the FSA. The FSA might then be given power to make rules that exempt from the authorisation requirements other activities of an overseas person which appear in the FSA's judgment to have insufficient connection with the UK to justify requiring the overseas person to be authorised. Indeed, there is a strong argument that the FSA should have wider power to grant exemptions from the authorisation requirements of the Act where it deems it consistent with its statutory objectives.[2] Similar exemptive powers might be given to the FSA in relation to the advertising restrictions as well.

- There should be adequate publicity and consultation in the rule making process.

Exclusive competence in this area does not need to be granted to the FSA. Subsequent statutory instruments modifying the scope of the legislation should be able to override rules made by the FSA

2 Compare, for example, s. 15(a)(2) of the US Securities Exchange Act of 1934 (attached as Appendix A) which empowers the SEC, by rule or order, "as it deems consistent with the public interest and the protection of investors", conditionally or unconditionally to exempt any person or class of persons from the broker-dealer registration requirements.

in this respect. There is also no need to restrict this approach to cases where the relevant prohibition is set out in the primary legislation. For example, regulations made under the proposed legislation by the Treasury might also provide the FSA with flexibility to make rules to mitigate possible adverse effects in particular areas, such as in relation to the territorial scope of any prohibition created by those regulations. However, to permit further delegation of rule making power to the FSA in a statutory instrument will probably require some form of specific statutory authority.

The rule making powers given to the FSA should also state that the FSA has the power to provide guidance on the interpretation of its own rules and that industry participants can rely on that guidance. This objective can be achieved by including a general provision in the legislation similar to regulation 18 of the Common Unsolicited Calls Regulations which reflects other provisions in the existing rules of the FSA and the SROs.

However, it will not be enough to give the FSA powers to provide guidance on the interpretation and application of its own rules. There should also be a formal, statutorily endorsed procedure and mechanism for the FSA to give guidance with respect to the interpretation of the scope of the legislation itself and firms should be able to rely on such guidance. For example, the statute should explicitly protect a person against prosecution, or enforcement action by the FSA, where that person acts in reliance upon, and in accordance with the standards set forth in, any applicable formal guidance issued by the FSA. In addition, to the extent that the new legislation provides for civil remedies for contraventions (comparable to the rescission or restitutionary remedies provided for in relation to contraventions of ss. 3, 56 or 57 of the 1986 Act) a person should be given a defence where that person acted in reliance upon, and in accordance with the standards set forth in, any applicable formal guidance issued by the FSA. Given the interrelationship between financial services legislation and other legislation, these powers to provide guidance should extend to other, related legislation as well, such as the legislation on prospectuses and insider dealing.

However, including provisions that enable market participants to rely on guidance issued by the FSA (whether with respect to the interpretation of FSA's own rules or as to the scope of the legislation itself) will be of no value if the FSA does not actually issue guidance or if the guidance issued is so unclear or hedged with qualifications that firms cannot in practice rely on it. Such provisions must be combined with a commitment on the part of the FSA to respond to the industry's requests for guidance.

Advertising restrictions

The UK's black and white advertising restrictions are clearly a major source of concern for foreign firms because they fail to take account of the range of different facts and circumstances that surround an advertisement. For example:

- A foreign firm may publish advertising that is available to persons in the UK but the firm may have no existing UK customers or counterparties, have no intention of dealing with UK customers or counterparties and may not in fact deal with UK customers or counterparties. In such a case, the only contact with the UK is the fact that the advertising is available to UK persons.

- A foreign firm may publish advertising that is available to persons in the UK and may have existing customers or counterparties in the UK and intend to deal with UK customers and counterparties in the future. However, the specific products or services promoted by the advertising may not be available to UK persons.

- A foreign firm may publish advertising that is available to persons in the UK and the specific products or services promoted by the advertising may be available to UK persons but only to UK persons to whom it would otherwise be lawful to sell the product or service under applicable private placement or other exemptions.

- A foreign firm may publish advertising that is available to persons in the UK and is willing to deal with UK persons in relation to the specific products and services promoted by the advertising. However, the advertising is not targeted at UK persons and the foreign firm may have no means of knowing whether a UK person that approaches it in relation to the specific product or service has seen the advertising.

The Internet exacerbates the situation and creates special problems for advertising restrictions. The Internet's worldwide web is different from other media used to advertise or promote financial services. In particular, there is no practical means of preventing a website from being accessed by persons anywhere in the world. Restricting access through passwords given only to existing customers (as in an Extranet service) eliminates much of the value of the web as an advertising medium. Far greater control over who will receive material promoted through other media exists, even if, with newspapers and other periodicals, it is not always possible to preclude the possibility of incidental circulation in other countries.

Advertising restrictions clearly need to differentiate between different methods of delivery. Advertising on billboards, in UK domestic newspapers, broadcasting media or by direct mail (whether physical or electronic) should be subject to different levels of control than advertising done over the Internet where the advertiser cannot control whether such advertisement is accessible in the UK or the type of UK persons who will be able to access the information. In the case of advertising in UK domestic newspapers, broadcasting media or direct mail, there is more clearly an intention to access the UK and it may be justifiable for UK regulators to impose certain requirements as to the form and content of that advertising. Even so, the UK rules need to provide greater clarity as to when newspapers and periodicals are to be regarded as "circulating principally outside" the UK for the purposes of s. 207(3) of the 1986 and s. 32(7) of the Banking Act.[3]

What is needed is a change from the current system that applies a uniform set of standards to advertising and a move to rules that recognise a gradation of circumstances which require different levels of control. To achieve this result, the new legislation (or regulations made under it) could adopt a number of approaches that would reduce the burdens created by advertising restrictions for foreign firms:

a) ***Overseas directed advertising***

There should be provisions that exempt advertisements from any restrictions where the advertisement is not directed at persons in the UK. None of the existing advertising rules have effective exemptions of this kind and, as previously noted, at present the major advertising restrictions may be triggered by the mere availability of material to UK persons.

- Advertising restrictions should not apply to advertising material that can reasonably be regarded as directed at informing or influencing only persons who are outside the UK, merely because it is incidentally available to persons in the UK (compare Article 8(1) of the Financial Services Act 1986 (Investment Advertisements) (Exemptions) (No. 2) Order 1995). This approach should be the case whether or not the advertisement is issued in the UK, particularly as the place of "issue" of an advertisement is increasingly difficult to locate. In any event, the

---

3 Similar exceptions should also apply with respect to the other advertising regimes such as those with respect to insurance and consumer credit advertising. Compare also rule 902(k) of Regulation S under the US Securities Act of 1933 (attached as Appendix B) which defines a "publication with a general circulation in the United States" as a publication that is printed primarily for distribution in the US or that has had, during the preceding twelve months, an average circulation in the US of 15,000 or more copies per issue (and which enables US and other editions of a periodical to be treated separately for these purposes).

use of computer equipment in the UK, such as a UK-based server, should not of itself result in an advertisement being regarded as issued in the UK.

- Additionally, the FSA should be given powers to make rules that contain a non-exhaustive "blacklist" and "whitelist" of factors indicating that an advertisement is or is not directed at persons outside the UK. Such factors should include: the language of the advertisement, whether a UK contact telephone number is provided, the existence of warning legends, etc. (compare Articles 9 and 10 of the 1995 Order mentioned above).

- However, while a blacklist and whitelist of relevant factors will be of assistance to foreign firms, firms need some degree of certainty as to the cases where the UK advertising rules will not apply, in particular where contraventions could affect the enforceability of contracts entered into in good faith. Accordingly, the FSA should also have the power to create non-exclusive "safe harbours" where it would be conclusively presumed that advertising is directed at persons outside the UK because the activities do not present any significant UK investor protection issues such as if a specific product or service is not in fact available to persons in the UK or is only available in the UK to professional or institutional investors.

- A person should not be regarded as "in" the UK for these purposes if he or she is only temporarily in the UK (e.g. US customers who visit the UK and may use their laptop PC to access Internet services). Most importantly, the fact that the issuer of an advertisement transacts business with someone in the UK should not in itself be treated as meaning that its advertisement is directed at persons in the UK.

Nevertheless, an exemption for "overseas-directed advertising" would not resolve all the issues. Material on the Internet is often directed at the world in general, including the UK, even if it is not targeted primarily at UK persons.

b) ***Advertising to professionals and expert investors***

The advertising rules should recognise that UK professional or institutional investors do not require the protection of detailed disclosure requirements or other restrictions and that advertising may be directed only at professional or institutional investors in the UK, even if it is directed at a wider class of recipients overseas.

- In particular, all advertising restrictions should include appropriate exemptions for advertisements which are issued to, *or directed at*, persons in the UK, such as professional and institutional investors, who have sufficient expertise to be able to understand the issues involved in responding to the advertisement. For example, there are currently no such exemptions in the Banking Act advertising regime. With respect to s. 57 of the 1986 Act, certain exemptions are available for advertisements where the circulation of the advertisement is restricted to a defined category of "expert" persons (see Article 11 of the 1996 Order with respect to s. 57 1986 Act) but these are not available unless it is possible actually to restrict the circulation in the UK to the defined category of recipient (and thus may be of little assistance in relation to Internet advertising). Other exemptions are available for advertisements that can reasonably be regarded as directed at professionals (see Article 8 of the 1995 Order with respect to s. 57 1986 Act) but these are restricted to advertisements aimed at a different class of professional investor.

- It should be possible to "combine" exemptions. The advertising restrictions should not apply to an advertisement that is partly directed at persons outside the UK and partly directed at persons in the UK to whom it is lawful to direct a particular solicitation. For example, in example 1, the Internet version of the prospectus may be primarily directed at persons outside the UK and, to the extent that it is directed at persons in the UK, directed only at the institutional investors who could otherwise be lawfully solicited.

c) ***Advertising which is partly directed at UK non-professionals***

Even where advertising by foreign persons may be regarded as directed, in part, at UK persons who are not professional or institutional investors, there should be no requirement to have the advertisement approved by a UK authorised person provided the advertising contains appropriate disclosures or risk warnings. The level or type of required disclosures or risk warnings should depend on:

- the medium used for the advertising, so that greater restrictions should be imposed on advertising using media such as UK domestic newspapers, broadcast media, billboards or direct mail, where access can be controlled to a greater or lesser degree, so that only minimal requirements should apply to media, such as the Internet, where it is not possible to control who may access the information;

- whether the advertising can reasonably be regarded as being directed at individual consumers in the UK, so that fewer restrictions should be imposed on advertising that can reasonably be regarded as directed at business users of financial services even if they do not qualify as professional or institutional investors;

- whether the advertising relates to specific identified financial products or services, so that only minimal restrictions should apply to general "image" or corporate advertising;

- whether the advertising takes the form of a "direct offer advertisement" such as a specific advertisement containing a general offer or invitation which if accepted, using a specified form, would result in a financial commitment on the part of the respondent, so that fewer controls should apply to advertising where the respondent has to request further information from the advertiser; and

- whether the person whose services or products are being advertised is clearly identified as being a person located outside the UK, on the basis that UK users of financial services are less likely to be attracted by the services of a non-UK person.

For example:

- Advertising might require a reasonably prominent warning that the person whose services are being advertised is not regulated in the UK and that those dealing with that person will not have the protection of the UK regulatory regime. This approach has been adopted in the banking and insurance legislation. However, at least for advertising on the Internet, the rules should not prescribe the exact form of required legends. It should be possible to meet the requirements without following the exact words of prescribed formal legends so long as the substance of any required information is provided, e.g. by making clear that the applicable regulatory regime is that of a foreign country not the UK.[4]

- Provided that appropriate warnings of this kind are given, other form and content requirements relating to advertisements by foreign institutions, such as requirements to state interest rate information in a particular way, should be relaxed or removed for Internet advertising, at least for advertising other than direct offer advertising targeted at UK individual consumers.

- At least in the case of foreign advertisers, the rules should generally refrain from absolute prohibitions on providing specified information. For example, the current prohibitions in the banking advertising rules on providing certain information regarding deposit protection

---

4 Any requirements for legends or specific disclosures need to address the issues regarding the placement of the legends or disclosures within a website. There should be no requirement for these to appear on each and every page so long as there are reasonably prominent links to pages containing the required information in appropriate places.

schemes could conflict with domestic rules in other jurisdictions that require such information to be given.

Of course, this approach would not be a bar to UK remedies where advertising available in the UK contains false or misleading information.

d) *Advertising by authorised persons*

The advertising restrictions under the new regime should not apply to advertising issued by persons who are authorised to provide financial services in the UK, including European passported firms, or that advertises the services of such persons. The form and content of such advertising should be regulated solely by conduct of business rules. However, the UK should not duplicate the conduct of business rules imposed by the home state regulator of European passported firms and should not impose its own, additional form and content requirements on advertising material.

Even though there should be no requirement for foreign firms to follow this route, there should also be a procedure whereby a UK authorised person can "approve" the issue of advertisements by non-authorised firms so that such advertisements can be dealt with under (more flexible) conduct of business rules instead of the general regime applicable to advertising by non-authorised firms. This might also facilitate the management of advertising which promotes the services of both UK authorised persons and foreign persons which are part of a group of companies. The legislation should also make clear that an authorised person can "approve" an advertisement for these purposes even though it may contain sections which have not been individually reviewed by that person, e.g. the live stock prices or the screens generated by databases in examples 2 and 3.

e) *Prospectus requirements*

A similar approach should be adopted with respect to the POS Regulations. In particular, the POS Regulations need to address "overseas directed offerings"[5] of the kind described in example 1. The Directive on public offers of securities should not constrain the UK's ability to define when a public offer should be regarded as made "in" in the UK. Regulation 7(2) of the POS Regulations could be amended to include a new exemption for securities offered in an "overseas directed offering" where the offer is made in the UK by means of: (i) an advertisement published in a newspaper, journal, magazine or other periodical publication whose principal circulation is outside the UK; (ii) by means

---

5 Compare the definition of "overseas directed offering" in Rule 902(j) of Regulation S under the US Securities Act of 1933 (attached as Appendix C).

of a sound or television broadcast transmitted principally for reception outside the UK; or (iii) by other means not principally directed at persons in the UK (such as the Internet). Possible definitions of an "overseas directed offering" might include an offer where:

- the securities have been admitted to dealing on an exchange outside the UK,[6] or application has been made for such admission in connection with the offer; and

- the offer in the UK is part of a larger offer that is also occurring outside the UK.

The exemption would be "combinable" with other exemptions. If, for example, other "parts" of the offer made in the UK meet the requirements of other exemptions, such as offers made in an institutional placing which could otherwise have relied on the "professionals" exemption, those other parts should continue to benefit from the other exemptions. Regulation 7(3) of the POS Regulations currently permits "combinable" exemptions.

Additionally, there should then be a corresponding exemption from the investment advertising restrictions for any advertisement issued in the UK to which the "overseas directed offering" exemption applies.

Authorisation requirements

Significant differences exist between the structure of the authorisation requirements under the various existing UK laws regulating financial business. The approach taken by the 1986 Act has proved reasonably successful, particularly because of its helpful approach to cross-border wholesale business, including business with institutional investors and large companies. This approach has been particularly important in the light of London's role as a leading financial centre. This feature needs to be preserved and, perhaps, extended explicitly to the other legislation. Whatever the structure of the authorisation requirements in the new legislation, foreign entities should remain free to conduct cross-border business with wholesale and institutional customers and large corporations.

Any approach that attempts to resolve the issue of when authorisation is required by reference to where services are provided is unlikely to prove successful in differentiating between cases where regulation, particularly UK regulation, should or should not be imposed. Unless the "location" of financial services is defined as something concrete, such as the location of the supplier, location will

---

6 The POS Regulations do not apply where the securities are listed, or an application for listing is pending, on the London Stock Exchange.

be too difficult to identify, especially when services are provided over the Internet. In any event, from a policy standpoint, it is unclear why one should use the "location" of the services as the way of drawing a line between activities that should or should not be subjected to authorisation. In addition, any test that rests solely on whether the foreign person is regarded as "carrying on business in the UK" is unlikely to provide the certainty that institutions need.

Furthermore, it is not enough simply to assert that the authorisation requirements are designed to protect investors and that, therefore, any foreign person who deals with a UK resident investor should have to be authorised. Generally, even with consumers, it is recognised that the residence of a customer or counterparty in a country is not of itself a sufficient ground for asserting the application of that country's laws. For example:

- The European Commission stated in its interpretative communication on the Second Banking Directive that "there may be situations in which the consumer has deliberately avoided the protection afforded by his national law, particularly where he requests a service from a non-established bank without first having been canvassed in any way by that bank." This statement suggests it would contravene the Treaty of Rome if a Member State were to apply its own consumer protection laws to a non-established bank solely on the grounds that a consumer is resident in its territory.

- A similar approach is reflected in the Rome and Brussels Conventions on choice of law, jurisdiction and judgments. These Conventions, broadly speaking, provide a consumer, in certain restricted circumstances, with the protection of its home country's consumer protection laws and the right to sue a supplier of services in the consumer's home state. Such circumstances include where the contract has been solicited by a specific invitation to the consumer "in" its country of residence or by advertising "in" that country if the consumer does not travel abroad to make the contract or, in relation to sales of goods, if the supplier receives the consumer's order "in" that country or arranged for the consumer to travel abroad to make his order.[7]

What is clear is that at a certain point the interest of protecting the investor or consumer has to give way to other concerns. For example, consumers will usually lose the protection of their home country's laws if they travel abroad to obtain goods and services. In these circumstances, it should be clear to consumers that they are not protected by their own laws in the same way as if they had

---

7 Special jurisdiction rules apply to consumer credit and instalment sales, and special choice of law and jurisdiction rules apply to insurance.

bought the goods or services from a domestic supplier. It would be unreasonable to impose the consumer's domestic law requirements on the foreign supplier. Similarly, accessing a foreign website on the Internet is in many ways a "virtual voyage" as it is the consumer that "pulls" the information from the Internet rather than the supplier who "pushes" it to the consumer. So long as it is clear to consumers from the information received that they are not protected in the same way as when they deal with a domestic supplier, there is no reason to apply the full panoply of the laws of the consumer's home country.

Clearly, it is necessary to develop an appropriate response to the complexities of cross-border business. Further, the need for this response is accentuated by the burgeoning of electronic commerce and, within Europe, by the need to develop a regime which promotes rather than hinders the creation of the single market in financial services. A number of strategies could be employed:

- An "overseas persons" exemption (similar to that currently contained in the 1986 Act) should apply to all the authorisation requirements. A person who is not carrying on regulated business from a permanent place of business in the UK[8] should not be subject to the authorisation requirements of the new legislation if it only deals with UK customers or counterparties on an unsolicited basis or if it only solicits UK customers or counterparties in compliance with the advertising restrictions (and any other applicable solicitation restrictions, such as cold calling rules).[9] The legislation should also continue to exempt overseas persons from the authorisation requirements where they deal with UK customers or counterparties who are themselves authorised or deal with UK persons through a UK authorised person.

- Additionally, as stated previously, there should be a regime under which the FSA can grant (conditional or unconditional) exemptions from the authorisation requirements of the UK financial services laws to foreign firms or classes of foreign firms. Consideration should also be given to whether FSA should have a more general power to grant exemptions from the authorisation and advertising requirements of the new legislation. This authority would allow the FSA to craft regimes that provide appropriate protection to UK investors without imposing undue burdens on foreign firms.

---

8 The new regulations should also make it clear that the use of a server or other computer equipment in the UK should not of itself be regarded as the maintenance of a permanent place of business in the UK.

9 For deposit-taking, a move to the structure of the 1986 Act with respect to territorial scope requires addressing the issue of whether a UK person who takes deposits from someone outside the UK should be required to be authorised. The current exemption in para. 26 Schedule 1 of the 1986 Act for business conducted with or through authorised persons should also be preserved, at least for investment business.

For example, only minimal additional UK protections would be required where a foreign firm is adequately regulated in its home state. In these cases it may be sufficient to ensure that UK residents are able to resort to the protection of the UK courts e.g. by requiring the foreign entity to submit to their jurisdiction in relation to disputes with customers. In other cases, more extensive UK protections may be necessary, perhaps depending on the type and nature of the business being conducted.

Even though the objective of the legislation should be to protect investors, this goal does not mean that the same rules must be applied in all circumstances. For example, as regards European passported firms conducting cross-border business with UK customers and counterparties it should be possible for the UK to defer to the home state conduct of business rules rather than seeking to impose its own conduct of business rules in a duplicative fashion.

However, the UK should also not make the availability of exemptions from authorisation requirements, or conduct of business rules, conditional upon reciprocity even if this approach were consistent with the GATS. UK users of financial services benefit from competition and there is no need to restrict that competition where investor protection is otherwise adequately assured.

5. CONCLUSION

The development of electronic commerce on the Internet creates complicated issues for all countries seeking to devise satisfactory regulatory regimes for financial services. If all countries seek to impose their own laws, indiscriminately, on all firms doing business on the Internet then such duplicative regulations will restrict the development of the medium to the detriment of consumers. An international agreed solution to the problem of how regulation should be applied to the Internet is probably some time away. What is required, then, is for countries, such as the UK, that have traditionally supported open markets to show that solutions can be devised which adequately protect their investors and residents, but also respect principles of international comity and encourage technological development. At the same time, the UK should work with other countries and international organisations towards finding a global solution.

What is clear is that the treatment of electronic commerce on the Internet is inextricably linked with the treatment of cross-border business generally. Although, in principle, the legislation should discriminate as little as possible between different technological modes of delivering or advertising a service, the regime must take into account the different degrees of nexus that a foreign supplier or advertiser has with the UK, as well as the differential impact of particular technologies, such as the

Internet. The need to avoid imposing unnecessarily burdensome requirements that go beyond what is really required in the interests of investor protection must remain paramount.

The structural framework for achieving this goal must be flexible to adapt to a dynamic environment. This flexibility means providing the FSA the power to deal with practical situations as they arise. The proposed new legislation cannot simply adopt the old methods of attempting to define the territorial reach of UK law. As we all appreciate, the Internet knows no geographical boundaries, Therefore, a new, more flexible and differentiated approach is required as electronic commerce propels us into the 21st century.

Appendix A

S. 15(a)(2) US Securities Exchange Act of 1934

The Commission, by rule or order, as it deems consistent with the public interest and the protection of investors, may conditionally or unconditionally exempt from paragraph (1) of this subsection [s. 15(a)(1) requires brokers and dealers to be registered with the Securities Exchange Commission] any broker or dealer or class of brokers or dealers specified in such rule or order.

Appendix B

Rule 902(k) of Regulation S under the US Securities Act of 1933

(k) Publication With a General Circulation in the United States.

(1) "Publication with a general circulation in the United States" means any publication that:

(i) Is printed primarily for distribution in the United States; or

(ii) Has had, during the preceding twelve months, an average circulation in the United States of 15,000 or more copies per issue.

(2) Notwithstanding paragraph (k)(1) of this section, only the U.S. edition of any publication printing a separate U.S. edition will be deemed a publication with a general circulation in the United States if:

(i) Such publication, without consideration of its U.S. edition, would not meet the requirements of paragraph (k)(1) (i) or (ii) of this section; and

(ii) The U.S. edition itself meets the requirements of paragraph (k)(1) of this section.

Appendix C

Rule 902(j) of Regulation S under the US Securities Act of 1933

(j) Overseas Directed Offering. "Overseas directed offering" means

(1) An offering of securities of a foreign issuer that is directed into a single country other than the United States to the residents thereof and that is made in accordance with the local laws and customary practices and documentation of such country; or

(2) An offering of non-convertible debt securities, or securities described in 230.903(c)(4) (i) or (ii), of a domestic issuer that is directed into a single country other than the United States to the residents thereof and that is made in accordance with the local laws and customary practices and documentation of such country, provided that the principal and interest of the securities (or par value, as applicable) are denominated in a currency other than U.S. dollars and such securities are neither convertible into U.S. dollar-denominated securities nor linked to U.S. dollars (other than through related currency or interest rate swap transactions that are commercial in nature) in a manner that in effect converts the securities to U.S. dollar-denominated securities.

NOTES

10

MONEY LAUNDERING AND SUSPICIOUS ACTIVITY REPORTING: WHAT'S A BROKER-DEALER TO DO?

Betty Santangelo
Marc E. Elovitz

Stephen P. Davidson of Schulte Roth & Zabel LLP assisted in the preparation of this article.

Money Laundering and Suspicious Activity Reporting: What's a Broker-Dealer To Do?

INTRODUCTION

It is no longer novel to see the words "broker-dealer" and "money laundering" in the same sentence. The pressure on securities firms to prevent and detect money laundering has been mounting as prosecutors and regulators increase their enforcement efforts in this area. Faced with this increasingly challenging new environment, what is a broker-dealer to do?

To start with, broker-dealers must master a maze of existing statutes and regulations to ensure compliance and protect their businesses and reputations. Navigating through the maze also requires broker-dealers to keep abreast of interpretations of the money laundering statutes by prosecutors, and developments under consideration by regulators.

At the center of the maze are the federal criminal money laundering statutes that impose significant penalties for any broker-dealer engaging in money laundering. Even without any additional regulations, the existence of these statutes imposes obligations on broker-dealers to know their clients and to be alert to suspicious activity that could constitute red flags, warning them of possible money laundering, and thereby subjecting them to serious penalties. There is more, however, beginning with the concept of "Know Your Customer," which regulators have created in order to better protect financial institutions from exposure to money laundering charges, and culminating with the upcoming Suspicious Activity Reporting requirements, which place additional burdens on broker-dealers to monitor and report on their customers' activities. These regulations and concepts, while designed to protect financial institutions from being inadvertently drawn into charges of assisting money laundering, create pitfalls and difficulties for broker-dealers trying to wend their way through the regulatory maze.

Further complicating the situation, the rules are initially being fashioned by two different sets of regulators, neither of whom has had significant experience in regulating securities firms. Specifically, the United States Department of Treasury (the "Treasury Department" or "Treasury") through the Financial Crimes Enforcement Network[1] ("FinCEN"), which has historically dealt with the banking community, is trying to adapt its recently promulgated suspicious activity rules designed for banks to apply to **all** broker-dealers. Concurrently, the Board of Governors of the Federal Reserve System (the "Board"), which regulates banks and their subsidiaries, is for the first time applying its regulations to broker-dealer subsidiaries, a group that has never before been subject to such regulations.

From the perspective of all broker-dealers, there is therefore justifiable concern that rules developed in the banking context are being and will be applied to securities firms without adequate adjustments to reflect the myriad of differences between the two industries. Moreover, on the banking side, the broker-dealer subsidiaries of bank holding companies, as well as the banks, are wrestling competitively with what they perceive to be a lack

---

1 FinCEN was created in 1990 by the Treasury Department to establish, oversee and implement policies to prevent and detect money laundering. It accomplishes these objectives in two ways. First, it acts as a central depository for reports by financial institutions, including those required under BSA. Second, FinCEN provides intelligence information to law enforcement groups, enabling them to track criminals and their assets and to develop new strategies against money laundering. See Introducing the FinCEN Advisory, 1 FinCEN Advisory, at 3 (Mar. 1996).

of a level playing field between rules that are applicable to broker-dealer subsidiaries and those applicable to all other broker-dealers. Indeed, private banks have already expressed the concern that any inconsistency between the regulations applied to private banks and broker-dealers could create an "uneven playing field" with regard to similar products and services offered by the two. See G.A.O. Private Banking: Information on Private Banking and Its Vulnerability to Money Laundering, Rep. No. 98-19R (Oct. 30, 1997). The net effect of the current situation is confusion and frustration for the broker-dealer industry. In the midst of this confusion, broker-dealers are struggling to effectively and efficiently integrate know your customer practices and suspicious activity reporting into their businesses.[2]

I. SECURITIES FIRMS AND MONEY LAUNDERING

The popular conception of money laundering involves a narcotics ring, suitcases full of cash and a bank teller accepting dirty deposits. While money launderers may still find it necessary to engage in a transaction this obvious, most have become more sophisticated, as have the applicable laws and regulations.

The prosecutors' primary weapons in their arsenal against money laundering are two discrete statutes, codified at 18 U.S.C. §§ 1956 and 1957, that were established by the Money Laundering Control Act of 1986 and amended by the Annunzio-Wylie Anti-Money Laundering Act of 1992. Section 1956, entitled "Laundering of monetary instruments," criminalizes virtually all dealings with the proceeds of a "specified unlawful activity." There are three ways to commit a money laundering offense under this section. First,

---

2 As part of their effort to make some sense of this confusion, the broker-dealer industry has formed an *Ad Hoc* Bank Secrecy Act Advisory Group to discuss these issues with the Treasury Department and other regulators.

in order to convict a defendant of money laundering the government must establish that the defendant (1) conducted or attempted to conduct a "financial transaction;" (2) with knowledge that the property involved in the transaction represents the proceeds of some form of unlawful activity; and (3) the property in the transaction involves the proceeds of a "specified unlawful activity" (as defined in §1956(c)(7)). The government must also prove that the defendant acted (1) with intent to promote the carrying on of "specified unlawful activity;" or (2) with intent to engage in tax fraud or evasion; or (3) with knowledge that the transaction is designed in whole or part to (a) conceal or disguise the nature, location, source, ownership, or control of the proceeds of the "specified unlawful activity;" or (b) to avoid a transaction reporting requirement under Federal or State law. 18 U.S.C. §1956(a)(1) (Supp. 1997).

Second, the government can also establish a violation of the statute if it proves that the defendant "transported . . . or attempted to transport . . . a monetary instrument or funds from a place in the United States to or through a place outside the United States or to a place in the United States from or through a place outside the United States" with (1) intent to promote the carrying on of a "specified unlawful activity;" or (2) knowledge that the funds involved in the transaction represented the proceeds of some form of unlawful activity; and that the transfer of funds was intended (a) to conceal the nature, location, source, ownership, or control of the proceeds of specified unlawful activity; or (b) to avoid a transaction reporting requirement under Federal or State law. 18 U.S.C. §1956(a)(2) (Supp. 1997).[3]

---

[3] There is also a provision in the statute that obviates the need for the Government to prove any specified unlawful activity where there is a "sting" operation being conducted by the Government. 18 U.S.C. §1956(a)(2).

Third, a defendant is guilty of money laundering under this offense if he "conducted or attempted to conduct a financial transaction involving property represented to be the proceeds of specified unlawful activity, or property used to conduct or facilitate specified unlawful activity," with the intent (1) to promote the carrying on of specified unlawful activity; or (2) to conceal the nature, location, source, ownership, or control of property believed to be the proceeds of specified unlawful activity; or (3) to avoid a transaction reporting requirement under Federal or State law. 18 U.S.C. §1956(a)(3) (Supp. 1997).

Section 1957, entitled "Engaging in monetary transactions in property derived from specified unlawful activity," prohibits (1) an individual from "knowingly" engaging in, or attempting to engage in, a "monetary transaction" in "criminally derived property;" when (2) the value of the property is greater than $10,000; and (3) the property is derived from "specified unlawful activity." 18 U.S.C. §1957(a) (Supp. 1997). In essence, the offense set forth in section 1957 proscribes the knowing disbursement or receipt of over $10,000 of criminally derived funds through a financial institution -- such as a broker-dealer. The statute neither requires that the funds be used for any additional criminal purpose nor that the defendant engaged in the transaction with any specific intent. The defendant need only know that the money involved is derived from some criminal activity, not that the funds were derived from any specified unlawful activity. 18 U.S.C. §1957(c) (Supp. 1997). See also United States v. Maher, 108 F.3d 1513, 1526 (2d Cir. 1997).

Thus, Section 1957 is analagous to an offense under 1956(a)(1) involving a financial transaction, except that in lieu of the specific intent requirement, the transaction must simply involve more than $10,000 conducted through a financial institution.

A. Underlying Crimes.

Money launderers are not all drug traffickers. The proceeds of a wide range of crimes can be illegally laundered. Some underlying offenses that may be especially relevant to broker-dealers include securities violations, RICO violations, mail fraud and wire fraud. The government regularly predicates money laundering prosecutions on non-drug-related offenses. Indeed, money laundering counts are now routinely added to insider trading and other securities fraud charges.

For example, in January, 1998, a broker pled guilty to money laundering in connection with a securities fraud scheme in which he accepted cash and stock to help run up a company's share value using a network of other brokers, brokerage firms and stock promoters who also took bribes. See Michael Schroeder, Broker Admits He Got $3.2 Million in Cash, Stock to Manipulate Issue, Wall Street Journal, Jan. 15, 1998, at B16. In another recent case, a partner at the Philadelphia office of an international law firm was convicted of money laundering in connection with a fraud scheme. He took the profits of his fraud on two insurance companies and laundered them through accounts at a large securities firm in the names of shell corporations. The proceeds were eventually used to purchase, among other things, real estate and antiques -- all of which are subject to forfeiture under the anti-money laundering statutes. See Lawyer at Big Firm Used Offshore Shell Companies in Laundering Scheme, Money Laundering Alert, Vol. 9, No. 4, Jan. 1998, at 11.

B. Means of Transferring Money.

Money laundering is not limited to cash transactions, but, rather, can involve all types of transactions, including cashiers checks, travelers checks, money orders, personal checks, third-party checks, wire transfers and foreign bank drafts. Many, if not all, securities firms have policies restricting the acceptance of cash, and limiting the receipt of cash-equivalents such as money orders and travelers checks to very rare circumstances. Because of these policies, broker-dealers are more likely to be confronted with suspicious activity in the form of wire transfers and other negotiable instruments, including cashiers checks and third-party checks.

C. Broker's State of Mind.

Many broker-dealers erroneously believe that unless they are actively involved in assisting a money laundering scheme, they are free from liability. To the contrary, a broker who has knowledge of the tainted source of funds but still effects a trade involving such funds may be charged with money laundering. Where there is no direct evidence of such knowledge, courts have relied on circumstantial evidence to show that individuals were "willfully blind" or "recklessly disregarded" such knowledge, and therefore culpable. See United States v. Jensen, 69 F.3d 906, 912 (8th Cir. 1995) (government can rely on "willful blindness" to prove culpability under money laundering statute); United States v. Rodriguez, 53 F.3d 1439, 1447 (7th Cir. 1995) ("willful blindness . . . is the legal equivalent of knowledge").

Similarly, in United States v. Giraldi, 86 F.3d 1368 (5th Cir. 1996), the Fifth Circuit Court of Appeals affirmed the conviction of an employee of American Express Bank International. While there was no direct evidence that the employee knew the funds were tainted, the court held that circumstantial evidence was sufficient. The evidence included the fact that the employee failed to follow the bank's know your customer policy, even falsifying records so as to appear to conform with the policy. Additionally, the court found that the employee had failed to properly investigate the customer or the source of the funds when he opened the account. The court observed that the types of activity in the accounts should also have raised suspicions: the customer formed companies to open bank accounts in bank secrecy havens such as Switzerland and the Cayman Islands, and transmitted and received large sums of money by wire transfer. Particularly troubling to broker-dealers is the latter inference by the court -- that activity in the bank secrecy haven accounts involving wire transfers is inherently suspicious -- because for international broker-dealers it is not unusual for a customer to have such accounts and engage in these types of transactions, and without other warning signs they would not trigger suspicion.

D. Structuring of Deposits.

A more traditional method of money laundering is the structuring of transactions to evade currency reporting requirements. Structuring involves currency transactions undertaken for the purpose of evading the Bank Secrecy Act ("BSA") reporting requirement for cash deposits of more than $10,000. See 31 U.S.C. §5316, *et seq.*; 31 C.F.R. §103.22. Money launderers often break large amounts of currency down into amounts under $10,000 and attempt to make individual deposits. The deposits can take place over one or more days, at one or more financial institutions. If unreported, these structured deposits are a simple yet effective means of laundering dirty currency.

Some broker-dealers erroneously believe they are immune to charges of structuring at their institutions either because they prohibit cash deposits, accept only small cash deposits, or require the approval of Legal or Compliance personnel before accepting any cash. In fact, while broker-dealers are less likely than banks to see attempts to structure a large cash deposit into smaller amounts, such structured deposits may occur at a broker-dealer after the cash has already been used to purchase a number of instruments, such as money orders, travelers checks, or cashiers checks, each in an amount less than $10,000.

For example, a structuring prosecution involving employees of a securities firm -- John Hancock Financial Services Company -- led to guilty pleas by two mutual fund salesman to money laundering and structuring charges. United States v. Diaz; United States v. Elkins, Nos. 93-CR-10030-01,02 (D. Kan. June 1995). In those cases, government officers disguised as drug dealers approached the defendants with cash that they claimed was drug money. Over a period of months, the salesmen converted $70,000 cash into cashiers checks and money orders, each in amounts below the $10,000 reporting requirement threshold. Then, the salesmen invested the laundered funds in John Hancock mutual funds, eventually returning the proceeds from the sale of the mutual funds to the undercover officers.

Similarly, Edilberto Miranda, an ex-Prudential Bache broker, was sentenced to ten years in prison for laundering money from Colombian drug traffickers. Tom Lowry, Brokers May Watch for Money Laundering, USA Today, September 11, 1997, at 1B. (A copy is attached hereto as Exhibit A.) Miranda had been indicted on 14 counts of structuring deposits to avoid currency transaction reporting requirements and on charges of money laundering but was ultimately convicted only of money laundering conspiracy and one laundering count for moving nearly $2 million in proceeds from cocaine sales through stock accounts at Prudential and various real estate transactions. Conviction of Stockbroker has Ominous Lessons for Many Others, Money Laundering Alert, Vol. 8 No. 9, June 1997, at 3.

E. Penalties.

1. Section 1956.

Penalties under section 1956 can include fines against companies up to $500,000 per violation, or twice the amount of the property involved in the financial transaction. 18 U.S.C §1956(a)(1), (2) & (3) (Supp. 1997). Property involved in the transaction may also be subject to seizure and forfeiture. See 18 U.S.C. §§981, 982, 984 (1997). Individual officers, board members and employees are subject to the same fines, as well as up to 20 years imprisonment. In a widely-reported case, two bank employees of American Express Bank International in Texas who were convicted of money laundering were sentenced to 10 years and 3 1/2 years in prison, respectively. See Giraldi, 86 F.3d at 1370. The bank itself was subject to substantial forfeiture claims, which it eventually settled at a cost of nearly $36,000,000, consisting of: a $7 million fine, which government officials claimed to be the largest ever imposed on an American financial institution; $7 million in forfeited funds; $3 million for employee training, including "policies, procedures, training and audit in order to assure compliance with government regulations and statutes;" and nearly $19 million in claims to assets seized by the government which had been used to secure a loan from the bank. Am Ex Bank Unit Pays $35 Million in Laundering Case, Money Laundering Alert, Vol. 6, No. 3, Dec. 1994, at 1.

2. Section 1957.

Penalties for violations of section 1957 can include fines up to $250,000 per violation or not more than twice the amount of the criminally derived property in the transaction. Property involved in the transaction may also be subject to seizure and forfeiture.

See 18 U.S.C. §§981, 982, 984 (1997). Additionally, individual officers, board members and employees are subject to the same fines, as well as up to 10 years imprisonment. 18 U.S.C. §1957(b) (Supp. 1997).

3. Bank Secrecy Act.

Penalties for violating the cash reporting requirements under the Bank Secrecy Act ("BSA") may also be stiff. An individual's willful failure to report the receipt of cash totaling more than $10,000 is punishable by criminal fines up to $250,000 or five years in prison or both. 31 U.S.C. §5322(a) (1997); 31 C.F.R. §103.49(b) (1997). A person who knowingly makes a false statement or representation on a BSA report is subject to fines up to $10,000 or five years in prison, or both. 31 C.F.R. §103.49(d) (1997). Moreover, a BSA violation that is part of a pattern of illegal activity involving more than $100,000 in a twelve month period can result in double the maximum fine, up to $500,000, or ten years in prison, or both. 31 U.S.C. §5322(b) (1997). Civil penalties may be assessed for each willful failure to file a report, up to the greater of $25,000 or the amount involved in the transaction, up to $100,000. 31 U.S.C. §5321(a)(1) (1997); 31 C.F.R. §103.47(f) (1997).[4]

4. Sentencing.

The Sentencing Guidelines set forth higher penalties for money laundering offenses than for other white collar crimes, causing sentences for money laundering to be excessively high in relation to sentences that defendants would receive if charged only with the

---

4 For banks, the penalties can be even more severe. If a bank is convicted of certain money laundering or Bank Secrecy Act offenses, under certain circumstances the statute provides a "death penalty" for the bank, revoking the bank's "rights, privileges and franchises." See 12 U.S.C. §93(d) (1997).

underlying criminal offense. See U.S. Sentencing Guidelines Manual §§2S1.1-3 (1997). Prosecutors often use the leverage created by the stiff money laundering statutes to induce defendants to plead guilty or to agree to forfeiture in order to avoid more significant prison time than would be applicable in prosecutions brought solely on the basis of the underlying crimes. Money Laundering and the Drug Trade: Hearings Before the Subcomm. on Crime of the U.S. House Committee on the Judiciary, (July 24, 1997) (Statement of Michael F. Zeldin, Principal, Price-Waterhouse).

The U.S. Sentencing Commission recently expressed concern about prosecutors' use of the money laundering statutes and the great disparity in sentencing that often results from this approach. Moreover, the Commission noted that money laundering sentences are being imposed for a far wider scope of offenses than originally anticipated. United States Sentencing Commission, Report to the Congress on Sentencing Policy for Money Laundering Offense, Including Comments on Department of Justice Report, (Sept. 18, 1997). The Commission has called for a more consistent, effective and fair sentencing policy for money laundering offenses, and has sought to tie money laundering sentences "more directly to the seriousness of the defendant's actual offense conduct." Id. at 9. However, attempts to change the guidelines through legislation have met with serious resistance from the Justice Department. Id. at 2.

F. Sentencing Guidelines for Corporations.

The Organizational Sentencing Guidelines, effective November 1, 1991, replace the former, mainly discretionary, sentencing system with specific formulas to determine the sentence of an organization convicted of a federal crime, including the amounts of any fines to be paid. U.S. Sentencing Guidelines Manual (1997). These guidelines provide for a significant reduction in the prescribed money laundering penalties, described above, if, among other things, an organization has in place an effective compliance program and reported the offense to the government or cooperated with the investigation. Id. at §8C2.5. As a result, even before any violation is alleged, an organization can take considerable action to reduce its exposure by establishing an "effective compliance program." After a violation is detected, an organization can still take steps to limit its liability by reporting the violation to the government and cooperating in any investigation.

II. KNOW YOUR CUSTOMER

A. Statutory and Regulatory Bases for KYC Programs.

The Annunzio-Wylie Act Anti-Money Laundering Act of 1992 (the "Annunzio-Wylie Act") provides FinCEN with the authority to require all financial institutions to implement an anti-money laundering program and to maintain appropriate procedures to guard against money laundering. 31 U.S.C. §5318 (h)(1)&(2). FinCEN has indicated that this authority enables it to develop mandatory "Know Your Customer" ("KYC") policies and procedures.[5] Despite being so-empowered by Congress, FinCEN has not yet implemented KYC regulations for either banks or broker-dealers. Nor has any Bank or Securities regulatory agency, although the Board is presently considering KYC policies to which broker-dealer subsidiaries of

5 The regulation is intended to respond to recommendations of the International Financial Action Task Force that all member nations require financial institutions put into place comprehensive anti-money laundering programs and "Know Your Customer" policies. The Financial Action Task Force (FATF) is an international organization, comprised of representatives of the financial, regulatory and law enforcement communities from over 26 nations around the world, which serves as the world leader in the development of effective anti-money laundering programs.

banks (including Section 20 subsidiaries) would be subject, and is expected to announce them in the near future. Nevertheless, the anti-money laundering statutes themselves militate in favor of a KYC program even prior to the formal implementation of such regulations.

In addition, to the extent that broker-dealer subsidiaries of bank-holding companies are already subject to Suspicious Activity Reporting, they have another reason for implementing a KYC program. A KYC standard is implicit in such regulations, since one cannot identify which of a customer's transactions are suspicious unless one understands the customer's normal activity patterns. See 61 Fed. Reg. 4326, 4329 (Feb. 5, 1996)(explaining that the institution must rely on its "knowledge of its customer" to determine if activity is suspicious, "based on all the facts and circumstances relating to the transaction and bank customer in question").

B. Elements of a KYC Program.

Neither FinCEN, the Board, nor any other regulator has yet provided clear guidance about what a financial institution must know about its customer. However, recognizing that it is drawn from its experience with the banking industry and that it may be inappropriate or require some modification with regard to broker-dealers, some preliminary guidance can be drawn from the Board's prior comments on KYC and private banking activities. Board of Governors of the Federal Reserve System, Bank Secrecy Act Examination Manual, §601.0 "Know Your Customer" (Sept. 1997) (the "KYC Guidance"); Board of Governors of the Federal Reserve System, Guidance On Sound Risk Management Practices Governing Private Banking

Activities (July 1997) (the "Private Banking Guidance").[6] Another source of reference for types of KYC information that may be required of broker-dealers in the U.S. comes from the United Kingdom's recently revised "Guidance Notes for the Financial Sector," which contains a comprehensive know your customer policy that applies to investment businesses. See Guidance Notes for the Financial Sector, Joint Money Laundering Steering Group (June 1997) (the "U.K. Guidelines").

The Board has stressed that the precise contours of any KYC policy depend on the specific institution, its customers and its business. Banks and their broker-dealer subsidiaries are expected to design and implement a program reasonably tailored to the parameters of their particular business. The Board's reliance on this standard is based upon the assumption that the banking institution will know its business best. See generally L. Troshinsky, Fed to Issue 'Flexible' Know Your Customer Reg., International Banking Regulator, Vol. 10, No. 5, Feb. 3, 1997 ("the proposal will be flexible in that it will let each bank decide the best methods for 'knowing their customer.'")

Drawing on these various sources of guidance and information, a reasonable KYC program is likely to include the following.

1. Reasonable efforts to determine the true identity of all customers and ownership of all accounts.

The traditional KYC rules for broker-dealers have roots in requirements of the industry's self-regulatory organizations. New York Stock Exchange ("NYSE") Rule 405

---

6 The Board's guidance on private banking activities may provide a particularly good indicator of the regulations that the Board views as appropriate, because broker-dealers and private banks are sometimes viewed similarly by virtue of the comparable investment services they often provide to their wealthy clients.

requires member organizations to "[u]se due diligence to learn the essential facts relative to every customer." The National Association of Securities Dealers' ("NASD") Rules require broker-dealers to obtain basic information about their customers, such as name, address and whether the customer is of legal age. See NASD Manual (CCH), Conduct Rules (Formerly, Rules of Fair Practice) §3110(c)(1). NASD members must also make reasonable efforts to obtain the customer's tax identification or Social Security number, occupation and name and address of employer and whether the customer is an associated person of another member. See NASD Manual (CCH), Conduct Rules (Formerly, Rules of Fair Practice) §3110(c)(2).

The minimal information requirements of the NYSE and NASD Rules are essentially a floor for most firms. For purposes of compliance and for marketing needs, brokerage firms often obtain a significant amount of information about customers on new account forms. Brokers also obtain and maintain information about their customers as part of their responsibility to make suitable investment recommendations to their customers, taking into account their customers' resources, risk tolerance and investment goals. Thus, while complying with the suitability standards, brokers enhance their knowledge of their customers.

Traditionally, identity at a brokerage firm is verified through a number of vehicles. After the initial account opening information is obtained, brokers generally contact customers periodically at their homes or places of business to review the customer's securities holdings and to make recommendations or suggest investment strategies. During this process the broker verifies the accuracy of the customer's identity, phone number, and often home address or place of business. Regular contact is also maintained -- and the continued accuracy of identifying information verified -- when customers contact the broker to enter trades and the broker calls and sends a letter to confirm execution of the trade.

The Board has suggested that for personal accounts, a U.S. passport or driver's license with photograph should be required, along with additional identification, such as a credit card or a current utility bill from the customer's residence. KYC Guidance at 2. The Board's Guidance on Private Banking cites with approval a KYC policy that requires identification, references and follow-up contact/visitation reports. Private Banking Guidance at 4-5. The U.K. Guidelines establish as the overriding requirement that a firm "be satisfied that it has established the true identity of the prospective customer as far as it is reasonably possible." U.K. Guidelines at Identification Procedures: Wholesale Institutional and Private Client Investment Business §4.04. In keeping with that goal, the Guidelines require that customers' identities be verified through acceptable means for verification of identity in face-to-face meetings, including name, address, date of birth, and passport (for non-U.K. residents). Id. at §4.65. Such identification is not traditionally required by broker-dealers, and, indeed, would oftentimes be impractical in that context, given that most of these accounts are opened over the telephone. Instead, most broker-dealers rely on the time-tested procedures described above to satisfy themselves of their client's identity. However, given the difficulty inherent in verifying information about them, obtaining foreign passport information from foreigners or nonresident aliens is a prudent course of conduct for broker-dealers as well as banks. In addition, the Board's suggestion that broker-dealers determine why a customer seeks to open an account at a location outside of its residence or place of business is also worth following.

For corporate customers, the identification information recommended by the Board is more akin to that obtained by broker-dealers. For example, for business accounts, the Board has specified that financial institutions should obtain a certificate of incorporation or a partnership agreement. The U.K. Guidelines stress that particular care must be exercised to ensure that the person purporting to act on behalf of the corporation is so authorized and to confirm that the corporation exists for a legitimate purpose and is not merely a "brass plate company" in which the controlling parties cannot be identified. U.K. Guidelines at Identification Procedures: Wholesale Institutional and Private Client Investment Business §4.83. The NASD already requires broker-dealers to maintain, for business customers, the names of any persons authorized to transact business on behalf of the entity. See NASD Manual (CCH), Conduct Rules (Formerly, Rules of Fair Practice) §3110(c)(1)(D). Virtually all broker-dealers obtain certificates of incorporation and information regarding the authorized signatories on the corporate account. The Board goes further and requests that the name of a commercial enterprise be checked with a reporting agency or with prior bank references -- something that is not routinely done by broker-dealers. For large commercial accounts, the Board also suggests obtaining (1) financial statements; (2) a description of the principal line of business; (3) a list of major suppliers and customers and their geographic locations; (4) a description of the business' primary trade area, and whether international transactions are expected to be routine; and (5) a description of the business operations and the anticipated volume of cash sales.[7] These latter items may be difficult and costly for a broker-dealer to obtain, particularly given the limited nature of transactions conducted with the client.

---

7 The Board also suggests that for very large accounts or customers in special situations, the broker-dealer check references and public information databases.

2. Identification of the Source of Funds Used by the Customer to Open the Account.

The Board has indicated that it would like financial institutions to know whether the assets invested through brokerage firms have been legitimately obtained. For example, if the customer is an individual, it suggests that the source of inheritance or of employment be determined, and if the customer is an institution, the source of the institution's assets. In the context of private banking, the Board has suggested that the client's source of wealth or funds should be identified and corroborated. Private Banking Guidance at 5.

These are concepts that are particularly novel for broker-dealers. And, while no legitimate broker-dealer would knowingly accept an account where the funds were illegitimate, they are understandably concerned about any obligation requiring them to determine the source of a client's funds other than its disclosed business or employment. However, the ramifications of not knowing the source of a customer's assets or dealing with a customer whose assets are revealed to be laundered -- even if inadvertent on the broker's behalf -- can be damaging to a broker-dealer's reputation. A recent example demonstrating this is the case of Asif Ali Zardari, the husband of former Pakistani Prime Minister Benazir Bhutto. Zardari opened an account at a financial institution in Geneva in the name of corporate entities that he controlled. On the account application, Zardari listed his address as the Prime Minister's personal residence in Karachi, Pakistan, where he was widely known as "Mr. Ten Percent" for his role as an intermediary in government contracts. The account was opened and more than $40 million passed through it. Pakistani investigators now say that those funds were amassed through payoffs from foreign governments doing business with Pakistan. By looking into the source of the customer's assets at the opening of the account, the financial institution might have been able to avoid the embarrassment of being involved in this matter. John F. Burns, A Background Check Far From Ordinary, N.Y. Times, Jan. 9, 1998, at 8.

The Salinas matter is yet another example of a situation in which a reputable institution can be tainted by dealing with a customer whose assets turn out to be laundered funds. That case involves Raul Salinas de Gortari, the brother of former Mexican President Carlos Salinas de Gortari. According to press reports, Raul Salinas was provided with private banking services, apparently allowing him to move tens of millions of dollars outside of Mexico. Stephen E. Frank, Citicorp's Reed Says Charges Possible But Not Likely, in Salinas Investigation, Wall Street Journal, April 10, 1997, at A4. The U.S. Department of Justice is investigating allegations relating to the source of the funds and the role of U.S. financial institutions in the affair.

3. Monitoring of activity for unusual transactions or transactions disproportionate to customer's known business.

The Board considers the "primary objective" of a KYC program to be to enable a financial institutions to predict the types of transaction a customer is likely to engage in, so that accounts can be monitored for transactions that are inconsistent with the "transaction profile." The U.K. Guidelines also stress that the financial institution must ascertain the nature of the business that the customer expects to conduct, in order to show what can be expected as "normal activity." U.K. Guidelines at Identification Procedures: Wholesale Institutional and Private Client Investment Business §4.05. In private banking situations, the Board recommends documenting the type and volume of the transactions expected to be passing through the account, following up with documentation of the actual amounts flowing through the account. Private Banking Guidance at 5. While these procedures are consistent with the broker-dealer's obligation to meet its suitability requirements, they go somewhat further in that they require the broker-dealer also to understand the nature of the deposits the client will be making. In the Board's view, an understanding of the customer's typical transactions is intended to serve as a baseline against which to measure future transactions and to permit the broker-dealer to comply with its suspicious activity reporting obligations; the Board believes that significant departures, or other unusual account activity, should be investigated promptly.

The Board recognizes that sound policies can define different types of acceptable KYC information for different types of clients, such as individuals, companies, and trusts, and provide for modifications over time to reflect changes in industry practices. The suggestions made by the Board will need to be adapted in order to be applied to the practicalities of the broker-dealer industry. Board representatives have indicated their awareness that broker-dealers have valid methods of identifying clients different than traditional forms of identification. However, broker-dealer subsidiaries of banks are still in the unenviable position of having to fashion compliance programs to a degree satisfactory to a banking authority by which it has never been previously regulated and which may be unfamiliar with different, yet perfectly proper, practices drawn from traditional methods of doing business in the securities industry. Broker-dealers that are not bank subsidiaries would be well advised to look to the experiences of those that are, because these broker-dealer subsidiaries are likely to be viewed by the regulators as test cases for the rest of the broker-dealer industry.

C. KYC Issues When Using the Internet for Transactions.

The recent proliferation of brokerage activity on the internet raises new dimensions to the task of knowing your customer, for which there is little or no guidance available. In these situations, the challenge of knowing your customer is even greater than in the traditional broker-customer relationship. The brokerage firm must try to obtain the necessary customer information when the customer opens an account and conducts all activity over the internet -- with the brokerage firm not only not meeting the customer, but often never even speaking with him or her.

Even in this instance, however, the brokerage firm is capable of obtaining information regarding the customer and has several means of gathering the necessary data. First, in any on-line application form, the brokerage firm should require the customer to fill in as much personal information as possible -- beginning with enough to meet the minimal NYSE and NASD requirements -- preferably including references and information sufficient to determine the source of the customer's assets and the nature of anticipated transactions. Second, the brokerage firm can use databases and other publicly available information, such as media reports and TRW, to confirm information received -- such as name, address, date of birth and social security number -- and to verify the customer's identity.

However, given the lack of contact between the brokerage firm and the client, monitoring systems are not only necessary -- they are essential. When exceptional transactions are noted, the firm can contact the customer to inquire about the transaction. Such a procedure will also serve to further verify the accuracy of the customer's identity and phone number.

All of these procedures can help to ensure that financial institutions conducting business on the internet are complying with their Know Your Customer and Suspicious Activity Reporting requirements.

D. OFAC.

A comprehensive KYC policy will also assist broker-dealers and other financial institutions to comply with the regulations promulgated by the Treasury Department's Office of Foreign Assets Control ("OFAC"). In fact, OFAC has specifically cautioned the securities industry to have an OFAC compliance program in place. See Department of the Treasury, Foreign Assets Control Regulations for the Securities Industry, (Dec. 15, 1997) <http://www..ustreas.gov/treasury/services/fac/fac.html>.

1. Purpose of OFAC.

In order to meet United States foreign policy and national security goals, OFAC administers a series of laws that impose economic and trade sanctions against: (a) certain foreign governments and their agents, (b) agencies and organizations that sponsor terrorism, and (c) international narcotics traffickers. See 31 U.S.C. §§500-596 (1997). All United States citizens and permanent resident aliens, wherever they are located, entities and organizations located in the United States, and overseas branches and subsidiaries of U.S. companies, come under OFAC's jurisdiction and must comply with the sanctions imposed against these targets by the U.S. government.

2. Targeted Countries and Specially Designated Nationals and Blocked Persons.

OFAC currently administers sanctions programs involving Iraq, Iran, Libya, Cuba, North Korea, Burma (Myanmar), Sudan, Syria, the National Union for the Total Independence of Angola (UNITA), terrorists who threaten to disrupt the Middle East Peace Process as set forth on a list of Specially Designated Terrorists ("SDTs") and narcotics traffickers associated with the Colombian Cali drug cartel as set forth on a list of Specially Designated Narcotics Traffickers ("SDNTs"). Also, while sanctions against the Federal Republic of Yugoslavia have been suspended for new transactions since 1996, certain U.S. property of Serbia, Montenegro, and Serb-controlled Bosnia remains blocked.

U.S. sanctions apply to more than just transactions with the aforementioned countries. Specially Designated Nationals ("SDNs") are persons or entities who, while often not nationals of a specified target country, are nevertheless treated as nationals of the blocked countries in applying sanctions to their transactions. For instance, although in looking at the name one would never suspect it, Atlas Air Conditioning Company Limited in London, England is a SDN because of its connection to Iraq. OFAC has named numerous foreign agents and front organizations with whom transactions are prohibited in a list of "Specially Designated Nationals and Blocked Persons." OFAC periodically updates all of the aforementioned programs, adding or deleting targets whenever necessary.

One way to ensure that a broker-dealer is not engaged in transactions involving a blocked country or entity is by integrating these procedures into a comprehensive KYC plan. At the time information is gathered as part of a KYC plan, especially with respect to the customer's identity, the broker-dealer can confirm that the customer is neither a national of a targeted country nor a SDT, SDNT or SDN. Afterwards, by monitoring transactions, it can determine whether the customer is performing transactions with a sanctioned country or entity, such as Atlas Air Conditioning.

3. Compliance with OFAC Regulations.

Under the laws administered by OFAC, U.S. financial institutions are obligated to block property and payment of any illegal transactions, establish a blocked account to hold the funds, and report all blockings to OFAC within ten days of the requested transaction. If a financial institution fails to block and report an illicit transaction, that institution is in violation of the law and subject to penalties even if another institution involved in the transfer, such as a correspondent bank, takes the required steps and blocks and reports the transaction. A KYC policy can be a first step towards avoiding such costly and embarrassing penalties.

4. Penalties for Non-Compliance.

OFAC has the authority to impose civil penalties ranging up to $275,000 per violation of the various sanctions programs. Over the past several years, OFAC has imposed millions of dollars in civil penalties on U.S. financial institutions for the failure to block illegal transfers when a targeted country, SDN, SDT or SDNT was involved in the transfer. Additionally, OFAC criminal penalties provide for fines as high as $1,000,000 for individuals or corporations and up to twelve years imprisonment.

In determining a penalty after becoming aware that a U.S. financial institution was involved in a transaction with a targeted country, SDN, SDT or SDNT, OFAC will allow the financial institution to make a presentation as to why a penalty should not be imposed, or if imposed, why it should be in a lesser amount than originally proposed by OFAC. Mitigating factors in determining civil penalties include self-disclosure, the use and sophistication of interdict software, and other compliance programs. Again, the existence of a broad KYC program can be viewed by OFAC as a mitigating factor in determining a penalty.

See Department of the Treasury, Foreign Assets Control Regulations for the Financial Community, § III, (Dec. 15, 1997) <http://www.ustreas.gov/treasury/services/fac/fac.html>.

III. SUSPICIOUS ACTIVITY REPORTING

The Annunzio-Wylie Act authorizes FinCEN to issue regulations requiring all financial institutions and their directors, officers and employees to report any suspicious transaction relevant to a possible violation of law or regulation. 31 U.S.C. §5318(g)(1). FinCEN has used this authority to implement such regulations for banks. 31 C.F.R. 103.21(a). Parallel requirements have also been imposed by all the Federal banking regulatory authorities. See 12 C.F.R. §353.3 (Federal Deposit Insurance Corporation regulation); 12 C.F.R. §563.180 (Office of Thrift Supervision regulation); 12 C.F.R. §21.11 (Office of the Comptroller of Currency regulation); and 12 C.F.R. §§748.1 & 748.2 (National Credit Union Administration regulations).

Suspicious activity reporting for broker-dealers is not as yet required by FinCEN. FinCEN representatives have indicated, however, that it will soon propose suspicious activity reporting for all broker-dealers and that, as part of that regulation, broker-dealers will be required to develop a system for identifying suspicious activity. See Tom Lowry, Brokers May Watch for Money Laundering, USA Today, Sept. 11, 1997, at 1B. The Board's suspicious activity reporting regulation does apply to broker-dealers that are subsidiaries of bank holding companies. Thus, suspicious activity for those broker-dealers is mandated presently by the Board although as yet not by FinCEN.

Presently, for purposes of suspicious activity reporting, the broker-dealer world can be divided into two categories. The first category includes broker-dealers already subject to the requirements of various federal regulatory agencies by virtue of being subsidiaries of bank-holding companies. The second group includes all of the other broker-dealers, not yet subject to these regulations, but preparing for the anticipated Treasury Department announcement regarding regulations that will apply to all broker-dealers.

A. Suspicious Activity Reporting Obligations of Broker-Dealers that are Bank-Holding Company Subsidiaries.

1. Reporting Requirements.

Since April 1, 1996, banks, other depository financial institutions, and subsidiaries of bank-holding companies -- including broker-dealer subsidiaries -- are required by regulations issued by FinCEN or by the Board to file a "Suspicious Activity Report" ("SAR") when criminal activity is suspected. 31 C.F.R. §103.21 (Treasury Department); 12 C.F.R. §208.20 (the Board). Previously, banks were required to report known or suspected illegal activity by filing a Criminal Referral Form, and, if applicable for cash transactions, by filing a Currency Transaction Report and checking the "Suspicious Transaction" box on the top of the form.[8]

Under the rules of the Board applicable to broker-dealer subsidiaries of banks, the SAR must be filed in the following circumstances.

---

[8] In 1995, the General Accounting Office studied the systems for reporting transactions that raised a suspicion of money laundering. See G.A.O., Money Laundering: Needed Improvements for Reporting Suspicious Transactions Are Planned, Rep. No. 95-156 (May 30, 1995). In general terms, the GAO concluded that the then-existing Criminal Referral Form procedures did not provide an efficient means of identifying and acting upon suspicious transactions. Id. at 2. Chief among the difficulties noted by the GAO was the problems associated with the use of more than one type of form for different activities to be submitted to different regulators. Id. at 16. In addition, the forms themselves were not conducive to communicating the important information to the government in an easily understood manner. Id.

1. *Insider Abuse involving any amount*, i.e., if the broker-dealer detects known or suspected Federal criminal violations against the institution or involving transactions through the institution, and an insider of the institution is involved. 12 C.F.R. §208.20(c)(1). The amount involved is irrelevant. A SAR must be filed whenever the financial institution has a "substantial basis" to identify one of its "directors, officers, employees, agents or other institution-affiliated parties" as having committed or aided in the criminal act.

2. *Violations aggregating $5,000 or more where a suspect can be identified*, i.e., if the broker-dealer detects known or suspected Federal criminal violations aggregating $5,000 or more against the institution or involving transactions through the institution, and a suspect can be identified. 12 C.F.R. §208.20(c)(2).

3. *Violations aggregating $25,000 or more regardless of a potential suspect,* i.e., if the broker-dealer detects known or suspected Federal criminal violations aggregating $25,000 or more against the institution or involving transactions through the institution, regardless of whether a potential suspect can be identified. 12 C.F.R. §208.20(c)(3).

4. *Transactions aggregating $5,000 or more that involve potential money laundering or violations of the Bank Secrecy Act ("BSA").* The regulation requires reporting for transactions aggregating $5,000 or more when the broker-dealer knows, suspects, or has reason to suspect that (a) the transaction involves funds derived from illegal activities, or transactions intended to hide or disguise funds derived from illegal activities (including, without limitation, the ownership, nature, source, location, or control of such funds or assets) as part of a plan to violate or evade any law or regulation or to avoid any transaction reporting requirement under federal law; (b) the transaction is designed to evade a Bank Secrecy Act regulation; or (c)

the transaction has no business or apparent lawful purpose or is atypical for that customer, and the institution, after examination, has no reasonable explanation for the transaction.[9] 12 C.F.R. § 208.20(c)(4). Of particular concern to broker-dealers and banks alike is the last provision of this section which imposes a new and difficult burden on financial institutions to determine the legitimacy of each customer transaction as well as each customer's normal activity.

5. *Attempts.* Under both sets of regulations, the detection of any known or suspected *attempt* to commit any of the above acts requires that a SAR be filed. 12 C.F.R. §208.20(c)(1)-(4); 31 C.F.R. §103.21(a)(2).

6. *Exceptions.* SARs need not be filed for robberies or burglaries that are reported to law enforcement authorities or for lost, missing, counterfeit or stolen securities if, pursuant to 17 C.F.R. § 240.17f-1, the appropriate report is filed. 12 C.F.R. §208.20(f); 31 C.F.R. §103.21(c).

7. *Mechanics of Reporting.* Although the SAR requirement for non-bank subsidiaries is imposed by the Board, SARs are filed with FinCEN at the Detroit Computing Center, P.O. Box 33980, Detroit, MI 48232. 12 C.F.R. §208.20(c). SARs must be filed within thirty calendar days after the date the institution first detected facts that may constitute a basis for filing a SAR. If no suspect has been identified by that time, filing can be delayed for an additional thirty days. However, under certain circumstances, the Board must also be notified directly. For example, for ongoing violations requiring immediate attention, the

---

9 This fourth circumstance is the only portion of the Board rule which is also part of FinCEN's regulation. 31 C.F.R. §103.21(a)(2).

financial institution must notify the Board and law enforcement authorities by telephone, in addition to filing a SAR with FinCEN. 12 C.F.R. §208.20(d).

8. *Disclosure.* By statute, as well as regulation, financial institutions may not inform customers or third parties that a transaction has been reported as suspicious. 31 U.S.C. §5318(g)(2); 12 C.F.R. §208.20(j); 31 C.F.R. §103.21(e). The Treasury and Board regulations also require the reporting institution to decline to produce SARs in response to subpoenas in civil litigation and to report to FinCEN and the Board the receipt of such request and its response thereto. 12 C.F.R. §208.20(j); 31 C.F.R. §103.21(e).

9. *Recordkeeping.* Copies of filed SARs must be maintained, along with the supporting documentation, for five years from the filing date. 12 C.F.R. §208.20(g); 31 C.F.R. §103.21(d). This supporting documentation must be made available to appropriate law enforcement agencies upon request. Id. The penalty for failing to file a SAR in compliance with this regulation may subject the institution, and individuals affiliated with it, to "supervisory action." 12 C.F.R. §208.20(i); 31 C.F.R. §103.21(f). Under the Board's regulation, the filing of every SAR must be promptly communicated to the institution's board of directors, or a committee of that board. 12 C.F.R. §208.20(h).

10. *Related Reports.* The Board also encourages the voluntary filing of SARs with state and local law enforcement agencies, where appropriate. 12 C.F.R. §208.20(e).[10] The requirement to report suspicious activities is in addition to, not in lieu of, the requirement to file a Currency Transaction Report, Form 4789, for any transaction involving

---

10 As more fully discussed, infra, some states have mandatory reporting requirements.

currency of more than $10,000. See 31 C.F.R. §103.22. Brokerage firms are required to file a wide range of reports, in addition to SARs, that address suspicious or illegal activity, such as Forms U-4, U-5 and RE-3s. All of the firm's reporting mechanisms should be coordinated so that all suspicious or illegal activity is identified and comprehensively and consistently reported.

B. Suspicious Activity Reporting Requirements for All Broker-Dealers.

1. FinCEN's Proposed Regulations.

In consultation with the SEC and the SRO's, FinCEN is developing a suspicious activity reporting proposal to apply to all broker-dealers, and anticipates issuing its proposed regulation within the first quarter of 1998.[11] In the interim, some broker-dealers have voluntarily reported suspicious activity either by filing SARs or by writing "suspicious" across the top of the revised CTR forms (despite the removal of the "Suspicious Transaction" box from the form). See IRS Form 4789, Currency Transaction Report (revised, effective Oct. 1, 1995). FinCEN has expressly approved this practice in a "Q. & A." publication. See OCC 95-55, FinCEN Guidance on New CTR Form, 4 Fed. Banking Law Rep. (CCH) ¶44-872, at 47,523-3 (Oct. 6, 1995) (Answer to Question 2).

At present, it is anticipated that Suspicious Transaction reports will closely conform to the requirements imposed by FinCEN on the banks with some adjustments. Currently, FinCEN's SAR requirements simply require banks to file for transactions conducted

---

11 It is unclear whether FinCEN's newly-proposed SAR regulation will be applied similarly to all broker-dealers regardless of whether or not they are subsidiaries of bank holding companies.

or attempted by, at or through the bank, aggregating $5,000 or more if the financial institution knows, suspects or has reason to suspect that:

i. The transaction involves funds derived from illegal activities or is intended or conducted in order to hide or disguise funds or assets derived from illegal activities (including, without limitation, the ownership, nature, source, location, or control of such funds or assets) as part of a plan to violate or evade any federal law or regulation or to avoid any transaction reporting requirement under federal law or regulation (31 C.F.R. §103.21(a)(2)(i));

ii. The transaction is designed to evade any regulations promulgated under the Bank Secrecy Act (31 C.F.R. §103.21(a)(2)(ii)); or

iii. The transaction has no business or apparent lawful purpose or is not the sort in which the particular customer would normally be expected to engage, and the bank knows of no reasonable explanation for the transaction after examining the available facts, including the background and possible purpose for the transaction. 31 C.F.R. §103.21(a)(2)(iii).

It is likely that the recordkeeping and mechanics of reporting suspicious activity will be the same for broker-dealers as they are for banks. In light of the differences between the businesses of broker-dealers and banks, it is unclear whether the same exemptions will apply. In addition, because of the multitude of transactions that take place daily at securities firms, it is unclear whether the reporting thresholds will be the same or whether they will be raised to a higher level for the securities firms.

2. Self Regulatory Organizations' Directives.

There is also a reporting obligation imposed by the securities industry's self-regulatory organizations. While its authority for issuing such a directive is unclear, the NYSE indicated in an Information memo that brokerage firms should have procedures for reporting suspicious transactions. See NYSE Information Memo 89-5, (January 20, 1989). In at least one instance, the NYSE has disciplined a member for failing to have procedures to detect and report suspicious activity. In re Adler Coleman Clearing Corp., 1994 Westlaw 741753 *4 (NYSE Dec. 19, 1994). In that case, the NYSE found that the firm violated SEC Regulation 240.17a-8 by failing to maintain "procedures to monitor the multiple/structured receipt and disbursement of suspicious cash and other monetary instruments such as money orders and wire transfers." Id. The NASD has also issued a notice, similar to the Stock Exchange's Information memo, warning its members to adopt suspicious activity monitoring and reporting procedures. NASD Notice to Members No. 89-12 (Feb. 1989). [12]

C. Detecting Suspicious Activity.

To comply with the SAR reporting requirement, broker-dealer subsidiaries of bank-holding companies must monitor their client's accounts. All broker-dealers, however, should consider doing so in order to avoid the stigma and penalties of a money laundering prosecution and to satisfy the directives of the NYSE and NASD. At a minimum, since it is very likely that these proposals will become mandatory in the near future, and since the process of

---

[12] A broker-dealer must also be sensitive to its obligation to report certain types of activity directly to its regulator. For example, in the Solomon matter, the SEC criticized the General Counsel of the firm for failing to take appropriate follow up action upon learning of misconduct, including, among other things, notifying regulatory authorities. See Matter of John H. Gutfreund, Thomas W. Strauss, and John W. Meriwether, Fed. Sec. L. Rep. ¶85,067 (Dec. 3, 1992).

implementing such procedures is time consuming, broker-dealers should start now to prepare to comply with them.

Suspicious activity can be divided into two categories: that relating to a customer's identity or the nature of the customer's account, and that relating to activity in the customer's account. Whether or not activity is suspicious is a highly fact-specific inquiry. Any determination of what constitutes suspicious activity will vary depending on the client and the nature of the particular transaction. The following scenarios are examples of some red flags which may be indicative of activities that are regarded as suspicious.[13]

1. Red Flags Relating To Clients.

- A client is unwilling to provide, or unnecessarily delays in providing, bank references or account opening documents.
- A client appears to be acting as the agent for another entity but declines, evades or is reluctant to provide information in response to questions about that entity.
- A client has no discernible reason for using the firm's services, or maintaining an account with the firm in a particular geographic region.
- A client exhibits unusual concern about secrecy or requests information regarding how to conceal transactions from government authorities.
- A client conducts its business under unusual circumstances, at irregular hours, or in unusual locations.
- A client is located in a country that is usually considered to be a money laundering jurisdiction, bank secrecy haven or a narcotics producing country.
- A client exhibits an unusual lack of concern regarding risks and commissions or other transaction costs.

---

13 See generally Board of Governors of the Federal Reserve System, Bank Secrecy Act Examination Manual, §601.0 "Know Your Customer" (Sept. 1997).

- A client is the subject of news reports or rumors indicating possible criminal, regulatory or civil fraud violations.
- A client is the subject of an inquiry by a regulatory or a criminal investigatory agency.

2. Red Flags Relating To Account Activity.

- A client attempts to make payments in cash or cash equivalent instruments (e.g., cashiers checks, travelers checks, money orders) and withdraws the request after learning of the reporting requirements or repeatedly asks for exceptions to the firm's policy against such transactions.
- A client attempts to deposit bearer securities, third-party checks or other instruments.
- A client requests a wire transfer through its account in a country which is usually considered to be a money laundering jurisdiction, a bank secrecy haven or a narcotics producing country.
- A client engages in transactions that appear to have no legitimate business purpose, are inconsistent with the client's known legitimate business, or are inconsistent with normal trading practice.
- A client seeks to invest or transfer funds of a third party with whom the client has no fiduciary relationship.
- A client offers gifts or gratuities in excess of the firm's gift policies after being informed of those policies.
- A client makes payment using multiple monetary instruments purchased the same day especially if instruments are sequentially numbered, or just below bank reporting thresholds.
- A client makes frequent deposits or withdrawals of large amounts of currency for no apparent business reason, or for a business which generally does not involve large amounts of cash.
- A client receives wire transfers or deposits into an account and immediately transfers the funds out of the account by wire or by purchasing monetary instruments payable to another party.
- A client makes increased use of wire transfers when previously there had been no regular wire activity.

- A client makes international wire transfers with no history of such transfers or where the stated business of the customer does not warrant such activity.

3. Recent Suspicious Schemes.

An example of a current money laundering scheme is the system used in the "Colombian Black Market Peso Exchange." See Colombian Black Market Peso Exchange, 9 FinCEN Advisory (Nov. 1997). In this scheme, U.S. dollars are collected in the U.S. from illegal drug sales by the Colombian drug cartels. The rights to these dollars are then sold by the cartel to peso exchangers, usually in Colombia, who introduce the dollars into U.S. financial institutions in a variety of structured transactions, such as depositing amounts considerably under $10,000 into U.S. bank accounts to avoid currency transaction reporting. The peso exchangers then enter into agreements with Colombian importers in which the importers pay the exchangers pesos in return for the right to the U.S. drug dollars, now laundered and sitting in the U.S. financial institutions. Once the Colombian importers have the right to these dollars, they use them to pay U.S. businesses for products to be delivered to them in Colombia. Thus, U.S. companies are paid for legitimate goods with the proceeds of drug deals.

Two additional money laundering techniques that financial institutions should be on the lookout for are the so-called "Mexican Bank Drafts" and "Factored Third Party Checks" schemes. See Mexican Bank Drafts and Factored Third Party Checks, 6 FinCEN Advisory (Sept. 1996). Both schemes are used to recycle funds -- originally derived from criminal activity in the United States and then smuggled into Mexico -- back into the United States from Mexico. In the former scheme, smuggled currency is used in Mexico to purchase a "Mexican Bank Draft," a dollar denominated draft drawn by the Mexican bank to the order of the bank draft's purchaser, on that own bank's dollar account with a correspondent bank in the United States. The draft is then brought into the United States, where, after being negotiated or even endorsed to a third party who negotiates the draft at the U.S. correspondent institution, it eventually finds its way to the U.S. bank on which it is drawn. Id. at 2.

The latter scheme involves the "factoring" by Mexican financial intermediaries of bank checks drawn on a single U.S. institution. Using smuggled currency, the Mexican financial intermediary purchases the checks from smaller Mexican banks, and then forwards the collection of "factored" checks to the U.S. bank for collection. The collected funds are then directed back to the money launderers. Id.

D. Enforcement.

The indictment against Daiwa Bank demonstrates the high cost of failing to notify regulators of suspicious or plainly illegal activity. Daiwa was originally indicted for, among other things, failing to file a CRF. As part of a plea, Daiwa admitted "misprision of felony" for failing to reveal illegal trading activity in its New York branch office. See United States v. The Daiwa Bank, Ltd., Case No. 95 Cr. 947 (KMW) (S.D.N.Y., Indictment filed Nov. 2, 1995). Daiwa paid a $340 million fine. See Business in Brief, Atlanta Journal and Constitution, Feb. 29, 1996, at 63. After the Daiwa incident, it is clear that the regulators and prosecutors place a premium on prompt reporting.[14]

---

14 There are other ramifications for failing to file a Suspicious Activity Report. In a recent case, a federal judge denied Lehman Brothers its interest in an account of a client charged by the SEC with insider trading, despite the fact that it had an outstanding margin loan, and chastised the firm for ignoring suspicious circumstances, including trading that was atypical for that client. See William M. Bulkeley, Judge Criticizes Lehman for Its Role In Centennial Case, Wall Street Journal, December 23, 1997, at B-5.

E. Safe Harbor from Civil Liability.

While cognizant of their obligations under federal reporting regulations, broker-dealers are nevertheless concerned about potential civil exposure for reports that they do file. The federal law's safe harbor provisions that protect financial institutions from civil liability for their reporting of suspicious activity are essential to the program of encouraging full cooperation from financial institutions in the challenge to stop money laundering. This safe harbor provides that:

> Any financial institution that makes a disclosure of any possible violation of law or regulation or a disclosure pursuant to this subsection or to any other authority, and any director, officer, employee, or agent of such institution, shall not be liable to any person under any law or regulation of the United States or any constitution, law, or regulation of any State or political subdivision thereof, for such disclosure or for any failure to notify the person involved in the transaction or any other person of such disclosure.

31 U.S.C. §5318(g)(3) (Supp. 1997). See also 31 C.F.R. §103.21(e) (1997)(providing safe harbor protection specifically for filing of SARs); cf. 12 U.S.C. §3403(c) (1997) (safe harbor provision under the Right to Financial Privacy Act).

Originally, courts interpreted the safe harbor provision to give financial institutions broad protection from civil liability for reporting suspicious transactions. For instance, in Merrill Lynch, Pierce, Fenner & Smith v. Green, 936 F. Supp. 942 (S.D. Fla. 1996), the plaintiff, a Merrill Lynch accountholder, was attempting to arbitrate a claim that the funds in his account were wrongfully seized by the federal government. He had engaged in transactions that provoked suspicions at the securities firm, which subsequently voluntarily reported the suspicious activity to the federal government. Merrill Lynch argued that the Bank Secrecy Act's safe harbor provision bestowed it with complete statutory immunity from civil liability. The court agreed, holding that the safe harbor provision "conferr[ed] broad protection upon financial institutions." Id. at 944.

Similarly, in Brush v. Merrill Lynch, Pierce, Fenner & Smith, No. 701061 (Cal. Super. Ct., S.D. Cty., Sept. 20, 1996), the plaintiff sued Merrill Lynch after Merrill Lynch reported a suspicious transaction to a state prosecutor. The plaintiff, an attorney, had been arrested in connection with an insurance fraud case, and immediately following his arrest contacted Merrill Lynch to discuss transferring funds from his accounts into foreign accounts and accounts held by his family. Merrill Lynch maintained, among other defenses, that the safe harbor provision granted it absolute protection against such claims. The court agreed and dismissed the complaint. See also Velasquez-Campuzano v. Marfa National Bank, 896 F. Supp. 1415, 1423 (W.D. Tex. 1995) (breach of confidentiality and defamation claims against bank for filing criminal referral form barred by the Right to Financial Privacy Act; court noted that if safe harbor provision applied retroactively, it would have afforded "blanket immunity").

Several recent decisions, however, have cast doubt as to the absolute nature of the safe harbor provision, and have worried financial institutions that, safe harbor notwithstanding, they could still face liability under certain circumstances for reporting suspicious activities. In Digby v. Texas Bank, 943 S.W.2d 914 (Tex. Ct. App. 1997), the plaintiff brought a claim for malicious-prosecution against the bank that had reported him for bank fraud. Texas Bank, in its motion for summary judgment, argued that the safe harbor provision prohibited such a claim, and the trial court agreed, granting summary judgment for the bank. The Texas court of appeals, however, found that the bank was not entitled to protection because the bank had withheld information about the nature of the loan agreement from the government, specifically that actions undertaken by the plaintiff allegedly in violation of his agreement with the bank had been agreed to by the same bank officer who reported the suspicious activity to the government. Id. at 926. The court held that the bank was not entitled to immunity when "crucial mitigating information" was deliberately withheld from government authorities. Id. at 927. The court did, however, add that it agreed that "the immunity afforded to financial institutions under [the safe harbor provision] was intended to be broad," only that it could not be extended in this instance. Id.

Likewise, in two cases consolidated for appeal by the Eleventh Circuit Court of Appeals, the breadth of the safe harbor protection was again called into question. In Lopez v. First Union National Bank of Florida, 129 F.3d 1186 (11th Cir. 1997), the plaintiff sued for violations of the Electronic Communications Privacy Act ("ECPA") and the Right to Financial Privacy Act ("RFPA") after the bank disclosed information concerning her accounts to the federal government upon "verbal instructions" of federal law enforcement officials. Id. at 1188. After the district court dismissed the suit because of the safe harbor, the Court of Appeals reversed, holding that the government's "verbal instructions" were insufficient for the bank to take advantage of the safe harbor. Id. at 1194. In Coronado v. BankAtlantic Bancorp Inc., 129 F.3d 1186 (11th Cir. 1997), the companion case, the plaintiff asserted claims against BankAtlantic under the ECPA, RFPA, and Florida law. BankAtlantic had notified federal agents concerning "unusual amounts" and "unusual movements" of money at the bank. Subsequently, BankAtlantic provided the agents with access to the contents of 1,100 accounts, including plaintiff's, all of which the agents thereafter seized "upon allegations of money laundering." Id. at 1195. The Eleventh Circuit refused to invoke the safe harbor on behalf of the bank and dismiss the case, instead allowing the case to proceed on the ground that it was unclear whether there was suspicion surrounding all 1,100 accounts. The court reasoned that for the "safe harbor to protect a financial institution's disclosures, there must be some good faith basis for believing there is a nexus between the suspicion of illegal activity and the account or accounts from which information is disclosed." Id. (emphasis added). Since the bank had not shown a good faith basis for disclosing information on all 1,100 accounts, the safe harbor provision would not protect it.

In an interesting safe harbor case that settled before the court had an opportunity to issue any dispositive rulings, a former employee of Chase Manhattan Bank sued it and Chemical Bank, its predecessor bank. Zegarelli v. Chase Manhattan Bank and Chemical Bank, 96 Civ. 9582 (S.D.N.Y., filed Dec. 20, 1996). Plaintiff contended, *inter alia*, that after firing him, the bank filed a Criminal Referral Form, sparking a criminal investigation into his activities, in retaliation for his complaint to the bank that it had terminated his employment on the basis of his religion, age and national origin. Defendants had filed a motion to dismiss, in part on grounds that the retaliatory action claim was barred by the safe harbor provision. The parties, however, agreed upon a settlement before the court issued a decision on the motion.

Thus, while only a short time ago it appeared that the issue had been settled and the safe harbor would offer complete protection against liability for suspicious activity reporting, today the cases are in flux. The recent cases indicate that courts may yet hold financial institutions to a "good faith" standard in reporting suspicious activities, and therefore while financial institutions must still report all suspicious activity, by the same token they should be careful to follow the statutory requirements carefully.

Moreover, there is also uncertainty regarding the civil exposure to a broker-dealer, particularly where a client is introduced from a foreign affiliate. In those instances the U.S. broker-dealer may have exposure to civil lawsuits brought under foreign law where there is no safe harbor. Therefore, broker-dealers should pay particular attention in those situations involving foreign clients.[15]

IV. BSA REPORTING REQUIREMENTS

Under the Bank Secrecy Act and its regulations, all financial institutions, including broker-dealers, have certain reporting requirements.

A. Transactions Involving Currency Over $10,000.

Broker-dealers must file a Currency Transaction Report ("CTR" or Form 4789) with the Internal Revenue Service to report transactions over $10,000 in currency, including multiple transactions occurring during the course of the same day. 31 C.F.R. §103.22(a)(1). By requiring reporting of the aggregate of the transactions per day, the requirement addresses attempts to structure transactions to avoid currency reporting requirements. See 31 C.F.R. §103.53. The CTR requirement is not in lieu of, but in addition to Suspicious Activity Reporting, and applies to all currency transactions in excess of $10,000. Transactions under $10,000 that for various reasons are suspicious must be reported on a SAR. The new CTR form no longer has a suspicious transaction check-off box, because the SARs are designed to be used for suspicious reporting, but, as discussed above, Treasury has noted with

---

15 There is also an issue as to whether arbitration -- the forum in which most broker-dealer claims are litigated -- is an appropriate form for litigating safe harbor claims. See generally Merrill Lynch, Pierce, Fenner & Smith v. Green, 936 F. Supp. 942 (S.D. Fla. 1996). This issue is unlikely to be resolved by the proposed regulation.

approval the practice of broker-dealers filing such forms with the word suspicious written across the top.

B. Transactions Involving Currency or Bearer-Instruments Over $10,000 Transported Into or Out of the United States.

Broker-dealers must file Form 4790 with the U.S. Customs Service to report transactions in currency and/or bearer instruments which alone or in combination exceed $10,000 and which are shipped or transported into or outside of the United States. 31 C.F.R. §103.23(a). A broker-dealer is not required to file a Form 4790 "in respect to currency or other monetary instruments mailed or shipped through the postal service or by common carrier." 31 C.F.R. §103.23 (c)(2). Structuring of deposits to avoid the Form 4790 reporting requirement is also prohibited.

C. Trade or Business Receipts of Currency Over $10,000.

Broker-dealers that have affiliates must be careful to ensure that they too comply with reporting requirements even though they are not a BSA financial institution. Entities that are not subject to the BSA must file Form 8300 reporting receipt of currency or cash equivalents exceeding $10,000 (in one or more related transactions) if received in a trade or business. 26 U.S.C. §6050I. For example, commodity firms are covered by this regulation and not the BSA.

V. STATE REPORTING REQUIREMENTS

There are also various state currency and suspicious activity reporting requirements about which broker-dealers must be cognizant. In fact, all states can receive duplicate copies of CTRs, CMIRs and other required reports directly from FinCEN by entering into a Memorandum of Understanding with the Government, and the vast majority of states do so. And while some states have also enacted their own reporting requirements, many of them permit these regulations to be satisfied by reporting to the federal government. Some states do, however, require that broker-dealers file the duplicate copies of certain federal forms directly with them and not just the federal government. Still other states maintain reporting requirements that are separate from the federal government. It is therefore imperative that whenever any type of transaction report under the Bank Secrecy Act must be filed, broker-dealers review relevant state law to determine whether a duplicate form must be filed with the applicable state government.

1. Florida, Nebraska and Utah.

At least three states currently require securities broker-dealers to file duplicate copies of CTRs with the state.

a. Florida obligates broker-dealers to keep records of currency transactions in excess of $10,000 and file copies of the federal CTRs with the state when such transactions occur in or from the state of Florida. Fla. Stat. Ann. §517.12(14) (1997).

b. Nebraska law mandates that broker-dealers maintain a record of any currency transaction over $10,000 and file with the state a complete report of any such transaction within fifteen days after the date of the transaction. Neb. Rev. Stat. §§8-1802 and 8-1803 (1997).

c. Utah law requires that securities broker-dealers file a duplicate copy of a CTR with the Utah Division of Investigations any time that they are required to file a CTR with FinCEN. Utah Code Ann. §§76-10-1902 and 76-10-1906 (1997).

2. Georgia.

Other states, such as Georgia, require duplicate reporting of CTRs or SARs for banks, but do not have similar requirements for broker-dealers. See, e.g., Ga. Code Ann. §7-1-912 (1997).

3. Arizona.

Arizona requires broker-dealers to file forms similar to an SAR with the state. Under Arizona Rev. Stat. § 6-1241, a report -- known in Arizona as a "Suspicious Transaction Report" -- must be filed with the Attorney General's office when a customer's activity raises suspicion of money laundering or another racketeering violation, as those crimes are defined under Arizona law in Ariz. Rev. Stat. §13-2317 and 13-2301.

4. Other States.

Most states have statutes or regulations requiring that broker-dealers file duplicate copies of CTRs, yet because of a Memorandum of Understanding with the U.S. Treasury Department the broker-dealers are relieved of the obligation. Thus, for example, while Texas law requires broker-dealers to file duplicate copies of CTRs, CMIRs and other BSA reports with the Texas Attorney General, the prompt filing of the necessary report with the correct federal agency is considered to constitute compliance with the statute unless the attorney general (1) notifies the broker-dealer that the required return is not one that is regularly transmitted by the federal government, and (2) requests that the broker-dealer provide a duplicate of the filing to the attorney general. Tex. Rev. Civ. Stat. Art. 351(2) (1997).

VI. INTRODUCING FIRMS AND CLEARING FIRMS

The issues regarding know your customer and suspicious activity reporting become even more difficult when viewed in terms of the responsibilities of introducing brokerage firms and the firms that clear securities transactions for them. Traditionally, BSA requirements have fallen on the introducing firm since it is subject to the statute and receives the cash deposit which must be reported. However, with respect to the issues of Know Your Customer and SAR reporting, regulators appear to be uncomfortable allowing this responsibility to fall solely on the introducing firm. The introducing firms have argued that they are not privy to all of the data and analyses of deposit activity which the clearing firm or carrying firm is, and that the responsibility should fall on the clearing firm. See Stock Markets: NYSE Board Votes to Increase Clearing Firm Scrutiny of Complaints, 29 Securities Reg. & Law Rep. vol. 36, Sept. 12, 1997, at 1244. The clearing firm, on the other hand, strongly argues that it is the introducing firm that has always been responsible under the securities laws for knowing its customer and not the clearing firm, and that shifting this responsibility at this stage of the development in the relationship will cause a seachange in the business. See Patrick McGeehan and Michael Siconolfi, New Rules Expected on Clearing; More Responsibility Seen for Big Firms, Wall Street Journal, June 4, 1997, at C1.

The issue of the division of responsibility between introducing and clearing firms has been brought to the fore by the development of proposed rules by self-regulatory organizations in the wake of several highly publicized investigations into alleged questionable sales practices and fraudulent activity at introducing brokerage firms. Proposed Rule Change by the New York Stock Exchange, Inc., to Amend its Rule 382 Relating to

Carrying Agreements, File No. SR-NYSE-97-25, 62 Fed. Reg. 53,369 (Oct. 3, 1997); Proposed Rule Change by the National Association of Securities Dealers, Inc., to Amend its Rule 3230 Relating to the Clearing/Introducing Agreements, File No. SR-NASD-97-76 (Oct. 14, 1997).

The proposed rules increase the responsibility of the clearing firm with respect to the activity of the introducing firm. Among other things, the rules require the clearing firm to furnish written customer complaints they receive about an introducing firm to that firm and to that firm's Designated Examining Authority ("DEA"). The proposed rules also require clearing firms to provide to introducing firms annual lists of all the reports that they offer, and if requested by the introducing firms the reports themselves, enabling the introducing firms to better monitor customer accounts. The clearing firm must also provide yearly notice to the introducing firms' chief executive and compliance officers, as well as to the firm's DEA, of the reports offered to the firm and the reports requested or supplied to the firm.

This development in the area of introducing firms and clearing firms is likely to have an effect on the suspicious activity reporting rules that FinCEN will propose for all broker-dealers. The rule changes proposed by the NYSE and NASD are still pending approval by the SEC and there is as yet no proposed rule by FinCEN. FinCEN representatives have indicated that they are likely to propose a general rule placing a reporting requirement on the entity or entities in possession of the relevant facts. Such a rule would likely be interpreted to impose a reporting requirement on clearing firms for the activity of customers at the introducing firms of which they are aware. While it is hard to predict with any certainty what any of the final rules will look like, it seems safe to say that clearing firms will face some degree of increased recordkeeping and reporting responsibilities.

VII. FINCEN'S PROPOSED "MONEY SERVICES BUSINESSES" REGULATION

FinCEN has proposed to amend the BSA regulations to create a category of institutions called "money services businesses" ("MSBs"). 62 Fed. Reg. 27,890, 62 Fed. Reg. 27,900 and 62 Fed. Reg. 27,909 (May 21, 1997). Included would be businesses that provide check cashing, currency exchange, or money transmitting services, or that issue or redeem money orders, traveler's checks, or other similar instruments. The regulation imposes three requirements on these money services businesses:

1. MSBs must register with the Department of the Treasury and maintain a current list of their agents;

2. Those MSBs that are "money transmitters" must report and retain records of transactions in currency or monetary instruments between $750 and $10,000 in connection with the transmission or other transfer of funds to any person outside the United States; and

3. MSBs must report suspicious transactions involving at least $500 in funds or other assets.

The proposed regulation includes broker-dealers in the definition of money services businesses, but exempts them from the registration and list requirement. Broker-dealers are also exempted from the suspicious activity reporting requirement, most likely to avoid duplicating the requirements to be imposed when FinCEN promulgates a suspicious activity reporting requirement for all broker-dealers.

As presently drafted, the reporting and record retention requirement that does apply to broker-dealers is problematic. The $750 threshold is very low, suggesting that a large number of reportable transactions will be included with only a very small number involving any real cause for concern about money laundering. In addition, it is not evident why this provision should apply to broker-dealers that generally deal directly with their clients, while exempting depository institutions that accept funds transmission business from third-parties.

In its comment letter to FinCEN about the proposed MSB regulations, the Securities Industry Association and the *Ad Hoc* BSA Advisory Group argued that broker-dealers should be deleted from the definition of money services businesses because the regulation was designed to focus on businesses that are largely unregulated and frequently used to launder money or to evade the requirements of the BSA, the Internal Revenue Code, and other U.S. laws. See Letter from Judith Poppalardo and Betty Santangelo to Peter Djinis, Re: Proposed Amendments to the Bank Secrecy Act Regulations, (Sept. 24, 1997). (A copy is attached hereto as Exhibit B.) The letter points out that broker-dealers have not been shown to be subject to similar abuses and are already highly regulated. In public hearings, FinCEN representatives have indicated that FinCEN intends to treat broker-dealers and depository institutions alike with regard to reporting and record retention. However, revised regulations have not yet been issued.[16]

---

16 Commodities firms are also presently included in the MSB regulation but are expected to be treated similarly to broker-dealers.

VIII. ELECTRONIC FUNDS TRANSFERS

In 1995, the Department of Treasury, the Federal Reserve Board and other regulators promulgated a "Joint Rule" requiring banks, broker-dealers and other non-bank financial institutions to collect certain information and maintain records for domestic and international funds transfers of $3,000 or more. 31 C.F.R. §§103.33 (e)&(f). Treasury also promulgated a companion regulation known as the "Travel Rule" requiring that most of the information required by the Joint Rule be included in the transmittal of the funds, thus "traveling" with the transmittal. 31 C.F.R. §103.33(g).

A. The Joint Rule.

1. Recordkeeping requirements.

The Joint Rule requires that certain information regarding domestic and international funds transfers be recorded and retained. 31 C.F.R. §§ 103.33(e) & (f). Transfers for amounts less than $3,000 are exempt. Id. Also exempt are transfers between transmittors and recipients that are both either: (a) a domestic bank; (b) a wholly-owned domestic subsidiary of a domestic bank; (c) a domestic broker or dealer in securities; (d) a wholly-owned domestic subsidiary of a domestic broker or dealer in securities; (e) the United States; (f) a state or local government; or (g) a federal, state or local government agency or instrumentality. 31 C.F.R. §§103.33(e)(6)(i) & (f)(6)(i). Finally, the regulation exempts transfers between a party's own accounts at the same bank, broker-dealer, or other financial institution. 31 C.F.R. §§103.33 (e)(b)(ii) & (f)(b)(ii).

The Joint Rule requires less information for transfers involving "established customers," such as clients who maintain accounts with securities broker-dealers.

For established customers, the transmittor's financial institution is required to retain the following information for each payment order that it accepts of $3,000 or more:

- transmittor's name and address;
- amount of transmittal;
- execution date of the payment order;
- payment instructions from transmittor received with payment order;
- identity of recipient's financial institution; and
- name, address, account number and any other specific identifier of the recipient, if received with payment order.

31 C.F.R. §§103.33 (e)(1)(i) & (f)(1)(i). For those customers, recipient's financial institutions are required to retain the payment order containing the information from the transmittor's financial institution. 31 C.F.R. §§103.33 (e)(1)(iii) & (f)(1)(iii).

Information about the wire transfer must be retrievable by the customer's name and account number. 31 C.F.R. §§103.33 (e)(4) & (f)(4). For transmittor's financial institutions, information regarding a transfer must be retrievable by the name of the transmittor and the transmittor's account number, if such an account exists. For recipient's financial institutions, information must be retrievable by the name of the recipient and account number, if such an account exists. The rule permits financial institutions to keep these records by electronic data storage methods, such as optical disk storage, in addition to traditional methods of record retention such as retaining the original or a microfilm or other copy of the information.

B. The Travel Rule.

Most of the information required by the Joint Rule must be included in, and "travel" with, the transmittal through the transmittal process. 31 C.F.R. §103.33(g). Under this Travel Rule, the transmittor's financial institution must include in the transmittal order all of the information that it is required to record under the Joint Rule, as well as the transmittor's name and account number, if payment is ordered from an account, and the name and address or numerical identifier of the transmittor's financial institution. 31 C.F.R. §103.33(g)(1).

All of the exemptions to the Joint Rule requirements are applicable to the Travel Rule. 31 C.F.R. §103.33(g)(4). A broker-dealer acting as an intermediary financial institution is required to retain a copy of the transmittal order, and must include in its corresponding transmittal order all of the information it received from the sender in compliance with the Travel Rule. 31 C.F.R. §103.33(g)(2). FinCEN and the NASD have both issued advisories regarding application of the Travel Rule. See Funds "Travel Regulations" Questions and Answers, FinCEN Advisory, Issue No. 7, reprinted in 2 Bank Compliance Guide (CCH), §85-211, at 16, 199-6 (Jan. 1997); NASD Notice to Members 97-13 (Mar. 1997).[17]

C. Conditional Exceptions.

On January 26, 1998, in response to concerns from the banking and broker-dealer communities, the Treasury Department published in the Federal Register a notice granting a limited exception to the Travel Rule for institutions using automated customer

---

17 The Board, in its Bank Secrecy Act Examination Manual, has also illustrated how wire transfer systems operate and how money launderers can use these systems to their advantage. See Board of Governors of the Federal Reserve System, Bank Secrecy Act Examination Manual, §701.0 Wire Transfers (Sept. 1997).

information files ("CIF's") that contain the customer's account number, but either a post-office box mailing address, rather than a street address as required by the Travel Rule, or a special or coded name, rather than the customer's actual name as required by the Travel Rule. 63 Fed. Reg. 3,640 (Jan. 26, 1998) (to be codified at 31 C.F.R. pt. 103) ("Conditional Exceptions to Bank Secrecy Act Regulations Relating to Orders for Transmittals of Funds by Financial Institutions.")

Under the exception, the name and street address of the customer need not be provided if that information is not indicated by the CIF-system already in place at the financial institution. However, CIFs cannot be altered for a specific fund transmittal or transmittals, and the institution must itself know and be able to associate the information used in the funds transmittal order -- i.e., the post office box and coded name -- with the actual name and street address of the order's transmittor. When anything other than a non-actual name and street address is used, the transmittal order must include a question mark symbol ("?") immediately following any designation of the transmitter. Finally, any SAR or CTR filed by the institution must contain the actual name and street address for the transmittor.

IX. ELEMENTS OF AN ANTI-MONEY LAUNDERING PROGRAM FOR A SECURITIES FIRM

As part of the Annunzio-Wylie Act, Congress authorized the Treasury Department to require financial institutions to carry out anti-money laundering programs. 31 U.S.C. §5318(h). As contemplated by Congress, such a program would include at a minimum:

- the development of internal anti-money laundering policies, procedures and controls;
- the designation of a compliance officer;
- an ongoing employee training program; and

- an independent audit function to test the program.

Despite the authority granted to it by Congress in 1994, Treasury has not yet promulgated regulations requiring the adoption of such anti-money laundering programs. However, it is expected that in conjunction with the new Suspicious Activity Reporting regulation, Treasury may also promulgate regulations requiring broker-dealers to implement certain procedural systems designed to ensure suspicious activity reporting. See Tom Lowry, Brokers May Watch for Money Laundering, USA Today (Sept. 11, 1997) at 1B.

Apart from Congress' own language, there is little regulatory guidance on what such a program should include. The Federal Deposit Insurance Corporation ("FDIC") has provided guidelines for complying with the four-part program outlined by Congress. See FIL-29-96, Guidelines for Monitoring Bank Secrecy Act Compliance, 4 Fed. Banking Law Rep. (CCH) ¶44-125, at 47,121 (May 14, 1996). While these guidelines are not binding, they can be looked to for general guidance for all financial institutions.

Taking these guidelines into consideration, as well as all of the issues arising from the anti-money laundering laws and the concerns of all of the regulators, a satisfactory anti-money laundering compliance program should include the following.

1. A System of Anti-Money Laundering Policies, Procedures and Controls.

The firm's policy should be set forth in, and implemented by, a comprehensive manual establishing the procedures for the firm with regard to anti-money laundering laws, know your customer guidelines, Bank Secrecy Act compliance and suspicious activity reporting. Compliance by the firm's foreign operations with local anti-money laundering laws should also be addressed. See SR-96-5 (SUP), Examination Procedures for Anti-Money Laundering Controls in Foreign Offices of U.S. Banks, 5 Fed. Banking Law Rep. (CCH) ¶52-441 at 58,642 (Apr. 10, 1996).

The firm should make clear, through the endorsement of the policy by high-level executives, the importance of the anti-money laundering policy and compliance with anti-money laundering laws and regulations.

In order for the policy and procedures to work, the broker-dealer must have in place systems designed to capture the relevant information. A broker-dealer that accepts deposits of cash, cash-equivalent bearer instruments (money orders, travelers checks, cashiers checks) or third-party checks should have a system to identify potentially structured deposits. A system that codes all deposits by account will allow computer-sorting to identify patterns of deposits that might indicate structuring.

The broker-dealers system of procedures and controls should serve the following purposes:

a. identification of all information required by BSA reporting forms;

b. ensuring the accuracy and proper filing of reports required by the BSA;[18]

c. supervision of employees who accept cash, or engage in any other activity covered by BSA regulations;[19] and

---

18 The FDIC manual also includes references to exemptions which are not applicable to broker-dealers.

d. providing an internal review function by dividing BSA responsibilities so that, for example, in a cash transaction the employee accepting the cash is not responsible for completing and filing the Currency Transaction Report.

2. Designated Compliance Officer.

A senior official should be designated as responsible for anti-money laundering and BSA compliance and given the authority to make and enforce policies. The FDIC has indicated that the compliance officer should have authority over the policies and procedures relating to anti-money laundering and BSA compliance. See FIL-58-96, Designation of Bank Secrecy Compliance Officers, 4 Fed. Banking Law Rep. (CCH) ¶44-127 at 47,158 (Aug. 1, 1996). However, the designated senior official does not have to be someone involved in the major policy making functions of the institution. Id. In addition, responsibility for day-to-day compliance in each department or office should be designated to individuals in those departments or offices. Id.

Most broker-dealers already have full time in-house compliance departments devoted to the regulatory and supervisory oversight required by the SEC and the SROs, along with auditing departments for other internal purposes. However, because most broker-dealers do not deal in volumes of cash, they do not usually have compliance officers devoted exclusively to currency reporting or BSA responsibilities. One senior person should be designated with that responsibility.

---

19 As a general matter, it is a good policy to expressly prohibit brokers from handling cash transactions since criminal charges may arise from isolated transactions of a broker attempting to assist a client by circumventing firm procedures.

3. Employee Training.

All employees should be given an overview of the BSA requirements, the anti-money laundering laws, the know your customer rules and Suspicious Activity Reporting. In addition, special training with regard to those requirements should be given to those employees whose duties require knowledge of them. At brokerage firms, it is essential that cashiers and all individuals who deal with the client, including brokers and sales assistants, receive training with regard to the reporting requirements of the BSA and compliance with the anti-money laundering laws, the know your customer rules and Suspicious Activity Reporting. Employees must be able to recognize suspicious deposits. For example, a cashier should be able to identify money orders, cashiers checks or travelers checks which were purchased at different banks so that no one bank has a transaction over $10,000. Brokers, their sales assistants and cashiers, as well as management personnel, should also be trained in the latest money laundering techniques, such as the use of wire transfers, the "Black Market Peso" scams and the use of foreign bank drafts and personal checks. Training may benefit from a videotaped or computerized course that can standardize the training and ensure its consistency.

4. Independent Audit Function.

Audits should be conducted on at least an annual basis by outside auditors, or by inside auditors with no other involvement with currency transaction reporting. To accomplish the audit, the branch inspections or compliance visits typically performed by broker-dealers can be modified to incorporate a review of the above items. In addition, compliance visits specifically focused on anti-money laundering should be considered for branches in high risk areas such as Florida, California, Texas, Arizona and New York. These audits should include, at a minimum:

a. testing of internal procedures, including BSA, KYC and SAR procedures;

b. testing of knowledge of procedures by employees including cashiers, brokers and sales assistants;

c. analysis of a sampling of reportable transactions, including comparison of those transactions with CTR filings;

d. review of deposits for possible structured transactions;

e. review of transactions for possible suspicious activity;

f. testing of the BSA, KYC and SAR recordkeeping procedures; and

g. documentation of the findings of the independent testing and, where applicable, as in the case of broker-dealer subsidiaries, prompt reports of violations to the board of directors.

Items that can be reviewed during audits include:

a. Cash receipts;

b. Multiple cash deposits to related accounts;

c. Deposits of cash equivalents;

d. Deposits of bearer securities;

e. Completed Forms 4789 and 4790 on file;

f. Comparison of completed Forms 4789 and 4790 on file at the branch and those on file in the firm's central filing area;

g. SAR reports;

h. New account opening documentation, particularly of accounts opened by foreign entities or individuals;

i. Recent wire transfers, particularly for accounts opened for less than 6 months;

j. Computer coding of transactions involving cash and cash equivalents such as travelers checks, cashiers checks, and money orders to insure that currency transactions are accurately reflected as such; and

k. Procedures relating to compliance with the funds transfer regulations.

EXHIBIT A

BROKERS MAY WATCH FOR MONEY LAUNDERING

1ST STORY of Level 1 printed in FULL format.

USA TODAY

September 11, 1997, Thursday, FINAL EDITION

SECTION: MONEY; Pg. 1B

LENGTH: 436 words

HEADLINE: Brokers may watch for money laundering

BYLINE: Tom Lowry

DATELINE: NEW YORK

BODY:

NEW YORK -- As money continues to pour into the stock market, government officials are increasingly concerned over how much dirty currency is passing through Wall Street.

Treasury officials are proposing that broker-dealers be required to screen for money launderers, an additional regulatory task that has met with some opposition at firms.

But officials fear more criminals are cloaking illegal proceeds from such activities as drug trafficking, arms sales and mail fraud through brokerage accounts. Officials want to make it mandatory for the more than 5,700 registered brokerages to file "suspicious activity reports" (SARs) when they encounter unusual activities. The SARs would then be used by investigators.

The activities might include consistent use of money orders and personal checks; third-party deposits or wire transfers; deposits and withdrawals in accounts without investment activity; and big transactions by unemployed investors.

Commercial banks, once primary targets for money launderers, have been required to file SARs for years. Starting next month, Nevada casinos will have to file them, too.

"With the blurring of services offered by banks and broker-dealers, there's a growing acceptance by Wall Street firms of their vulnerability (to launderers)," says Peter Djinis, of the Treasury's Financial Crimes Enforcement Network, which is proposing the Wall Street rules.

Djinis and lawyers for large Wall Street firms, some that voluntarily file SARs already, are among speakers at a conference on money laundering here this week. It's being held two weeks after Edilberto Miranda, an ex-Prudential Bache broker in Miami, was sentenced to 10 years in prison for laundering money from Colombian drug traffickers.

LEXIS·NEXIS A member of the Reed Elsevier plc group
LEXIS·NEXIS A member of the Reed Elsevier plc group

"A shift of laundering activities to Wall Street is expected. The climate is ripe, and traffickers are getting much closer to their brokers," says Jena King, the federal prosecutor in the Miami case.

The government says it's impossible to estimate how much in illegal proceeds is laundered on Wall Street. But Djinis says with the bull market, "Criminals have an interest in making money as well."

In 1996, the Internal Revenue Service, U.S. Customs and the Secret Service reportedly met with compliance officers from major Wall Street firms to discuss ongoing probes into possible laundered funds in brokerage accounts.

Still, some say concerns are overblown. "It's not a big problem, but there's potential for serious embarrassment for a firm," says Betty Santangelo, a former Merrill Lynch general counsel.

LANGUAGE: ENGLISH

LOAD-DATE: September 11, 1997

EXHIBIT B

SIA - PROPOSED AMENDMENTS
TO THE BANK SECRECY ACT
REGULATIONS---
MSB REGISTRATION

Securities Industry Association

1401 Eye Street, NW • Washington, DC 20005-2225 • (202) 296-9410 • Fax (202) 296-9775

September 24, 1997

Peter Djinis
Associate Director
Office of Legal Counsel
Financial Crimes Enforcement Network
Department of the Treasury
2070 Chain Bridge Road
Vienna, VA 22182

Re: Proposed Amendments to the Bank Secrecy Act Regulations—MSB Registration; Money Transmitters—Special CTR Rule; and Suspicious Transaction Reporting—Money Services Businesses

Dear Mr. Djinis:

The Securities Industry Association ("SIA")[1] and the *Ad Hoc* Bank Secrecy Act ("BSA") Advisory Group[2] are pleased to have this opportunity to comment on proposed amendments to the BSA regulations relating to non-bank financial institutions.[3] Specifically, the Department of the Treasury, Financial Crimes Enforcement Network ("FinCEN") is proposing to amend the BSA regulations to revise the definition of certain financial institutions, and group them together in a separate category called "money services businesses." Money services business is a new term that is generally defined to include businesses that provide check cashing, currency exchange, or money transmitting services, or that issue or redeem money orders, traveler's checks, or other similar instruments.

---

[1] The Securities Industry Association ("SIA") is the trade association representing the business interests of about 760 securities firms in North America. Its members include securities organizations of virtually all types—investment banks, brokers, dealers, and mutual fund companies, as well as other firms functioning on the floors of the exchanges. SIA members are active in all exchange markets, in the over-the-counter markets, and in all phases of corporate and public finance. Collectively, they provide investors with a full spectrum of securities and investment services and account for 90% of securities firm revenue in the United States. This and other recent SIA comment letters can be found on SIA's Internet home page, http://www.sia.com.

[2] The *Ad Hoc* BSA Advisory Group is comprised of approximately 40 broker-dealers that meet for the purpose of sharing industry views on current anti-money laundering regulations.

[3] *See* 62 Fed. Reg. 27890.

120 Broadway • New York, NY 10271-0080 • (212) 608-1500 • Fax (212) 608-1604

The proposed amendments would require certain money services businesses to register with the Department of the Treasury and to maintain a current list of their agents for examination, on request, by any appropriate law enforcement agency. Registered broker-dealers are included in the definition of money services business by virtue of being money transmitters, but are expressly excluded from the registration and list requirements. In addition, FinCEN is proposing rules that will require money transmitters, a class of money services businesses, to report and retain records of, and obtain identifying information for, transactions in currency or monetary instruments of at least $750 but not more than $10,000 in connection with the transmission or other transfer of funds to any person outside the United States. Finally, FinCEN is proposing to amend the BSA regulations to require money transmitters, and issuers, sellers, and redeemers of money orders and traveler's checks, to report suspicious transactions involving at least $500 in funds or other assets. Broker-dealers are expressly excluded from suspicious activity reporting, no doubt because FinCEN intends to propose separate suspicious activity reporting regulations for broker-dealers in the near future.

As you know, the securities industry has been supportive of Treasury's efforts to combat money laundering and many firms have been working with FinCEN to implement suspicious activity reporting. In fact, many firms currently file suspicious activity reports on a voluntary basis.

As proposed, the definition of money services business includes broker-dealers. The inclusion of broker-dealers in the definition is a disturbing development to the industry. Although the proposal exempts broker-dealers from the registration and suspicious activity reporting requirements, it includes broker-dealers for purposes of the requirement to report transactions of at least $750 up to $10,000 inclusive in connection with the transmission or other transfer of funds to any person outside the United States.

Many firms have expressed their concerns to Treasury about the application of this requirement to broker-dealers. At a public meeting conducted by FinCEN on July 28, 1997 in New York City, members of the securities industry stated that the need to focus on such small transactions at a time when the industry is focused on, and gearing up for, the implementation of suspicious activity reporting would be unfortunate. Moreover, it is our understanding that depository institutions have been exempted from this reporting requirement despite the fact that depository institutions accept fund transmission business from non-customers. Since broker-dealers deal virtually exclusively with clients, there is an even stronger argument in favor of providing this exemption to broker-dealers. In response to these comments, Stanley E. Morris, Director of FinCEN, has stated that his intent is to treat broker-dealers the same as depository institutions for purposes of this portion of the regulation. We appreciate his responsiveness and we applaud this approach.[4]

Ideally, we believe FinCEN should delete broker-dealers from the definition of money services businesses. As stated in the Release, these regulations were designed to focus on businesses that are largely unregulated and are frequently used in sophisticated schemes to transfer large amounts of money that are the proceeds of unlawful enterprises and to evade the requirements of Title II of the BSA, the Internal Revenue Code of 1986, and other laws of the United States.[5] We understand FinCEN's concern regarding the pattern of abuse demonstrated in the Geographic Targeting Order. However, there is no evidence that broker-dealers are being similarly abused. Because broker-dealers are highly regulated and currently subject to the BSA, we see no reason for inclusion in the definition at this time, given that there is no other application to the industry. We therefore strongly urge FinCEN to delete broker-dealers from the definition.

Thank you for the opportunity to comment on the proposal. If you would like further information on our comments, please feel free to contact us.

Sincerely,

Judith Poppalardo

Judith Poppalardo
Assistant General Counsel
Securities Industry Association

Betty Santangelo

Betty Santangelo
Ad Hoc BSA Advisory Group

cc: Kate McGuire. Securities and Exchange Commission

[4] We also understand from Director Morris's comments that he is considering limiting these transactions to ones originating in currency and not monetary instruments. We believe that this modification makes a great deal of sense and encourage FinCEN to adopt these limitations.

[5] 62 Fed. Reg. 27890.

NOTES

11

SEC ENFORCEMENT AND THE INTERNET: MEETING THE CHALLENGE OF THE NEXT MILLENNIUM

John Reed Stark
Joseph J. Cella, III

This article was previously published in *The Business Lawyer*, Volume 52, No. 3, May 1997.

Reprinted by permission from ABA Publishing.

THE BUSINESS LAWYER

Section of Business Law • American Bar Association
University of Maryland School of Law

ARTICLES

***Technicolor IV*: Appraisal Valuation in a Two-Step Merger**
Jesse A. Finkelstein and Russell C. Silberglied

SEC Enforcement and the Internet: Meeting the Challenge of the Next Millennium
A Program for the Eagle and the Internet
Joseph J. Cella III and John Reed Stark

The Meaning of Item Four of Schedule 13D of the Securities Exchange Act of 1934: A New Framework & Analysis
Albert J. Li

Securitization of Oil, Gas, and Other Natural Resource Assets: Emerging Financing Techniques
Charles E. Harrell, James L. Rice III and W. Robert Shearer

REPORTS

Business Courts: Towards a More Efficient Judiciary
Ad Hoc Committee on Business Courts

Report of the Task Force on Rule 102(e) Proceedings: Rule 102(e) Sanctions Against Accountants
Task Force on Rule 102(e) Proceedings

Changes in the Model Business Corporation Act—Amendments Pertaining to Electronic Filings
Committee on Corporate Laws

REVIEW

The Public REIT Legal Sourcebook
By the National Association of Real Estate Trusts
Reviewed by Charles M. Elson

SURVEY

Consumer Financial Services Law

May 1997 • Volume 52 • Number 3

SEC Enforcement and the Internet: Meeting the Challenge of the Next Millennium

A Program for the Eagle and the Internet

*By Joseph J. Cella III and John Reed Stark**

"WHAT WE'VE GOT HERE IS A FAILURE TO COMMUNICATE"[1]

That is, of course, for those who invest the old fashioned way. Since being hit by the tidal wave of information available through the Internet, investors can communicate as never before, reaching out and researching potential investments from the comfort of their own living rooms almost as easily and as comprehensively as the most astute, informed Wall Street insider. Instead of handing over their life savings for all of this information, they need only invest a small amount of capital.

Outfitted with a home computer, some software, a phone line, and an Internet access provider, the investor can visit the cyber-office of a potential investment and gather all sorts of important data and information. From detailed product designs and comprehensive financial statements to annual reports and earnings projections, the cyber-investor can review a wide range of known facts about a company, plus a whole lot more. On the Internet, the investor can even meet the owners of a company and learn about their vision first hand or, instead, choose to investigate a company by meeting its partners and employees, or even its competitors or customers. If an investor wants to find out what happened at a shareholders

*Mr. Cella serves as Chief of the Office of Market Surveillance in the Division of Enforcement of the U.S. Securities and Exchange Commission. Mr. Stark serves as Special Counsel for Internet Projects in the Division of Enforcement of the U.S. Securities and Exchange Commission and is in charge of the Division's Internet Program; he also is an adjunct professor of law at Georgetown University Law Center. The U.S. Securities and Exchange Commission, as a matter of policy, disclaims any responsibility for any private publication or speech by any of its members of staff. The views expressed herein are those of the authors and do not necessarily reflect the views of the Commission or the authors' colleagues on the staff of the Commission. *See* 17 C.F.R. § 200.735-4(e)(1996). The authors would like to thank David P. Gionfriddo for his assistance in the preparation of this Article.

1. All quotes cited in the section headings of this Article are from the film COOL HAND LUKE (Warner Bros. 1967), produced by Gordon Carroll, directed by Stuart Rosenberg, and starring Paul Newman.

meeting or simply how many cars are parked outside a company's headquarters on a Sunday afternoon, the Internet might have the answers to these and other questions.

As for trading data, investors are linked through the Internet to a growing number of services that provide current stock quotations, price/earnings ratios, historical price and volume information, and a host of other empirical and analytical breakdowns. With the click of a mouse, users can custom design their own personal information superhighway and gather automatically all the information they need. In addition, with the growing popularity of bulletin board systems[2] (BBSs), newsgroups, and other cyber-message areas, the investor can talk with existing shareholders (both happy and disgruntled), former shareholders, short-sellers, analysts, brokers, venture capitalists, and just about any other type of securities professional, amateur, or neophyte.

How much does it cost for the investor to arrange all these meetings and gather all this research? The information itself is almost always free. So, other than ever-decreasing start-up costs of buying the necessary hardware, software, and access (from one of the estimated 1100 access providers in the United States),[3] unlimited information comes free of charge. That is quite a bargain.

The investor, though, is not the only one cheering. The entrepreneur, the inventor, and the small business owner now have a cheap and efficient alternative means to reach millions of potential interested parties without the expense of a road show, without hiring the usual cadre of lawyers and financial advisers, without hiring a printing service, and, most of all, without leaving the house. Moreover, securities historically doomed to bathe in their own illiquidity and large bid and asked spreads, such as limited partnerships, thinly traded over-the-counter (OTC) "Pink Sheet" stocks, and other securities unavailable for purchase or sale in the traditional marketplace, now have unprecedented ways of increasing their trading volume. Whether through a pairing of a buyer and seller via a simple Internet BBS, or through a more complicated arrangement such as an online trading facility, promoters, buyers, and sellers can meet instantly and transact business at very little cost to one another.

In only a matter of years, the Internet will unquestionably serve as important a role as the telephone or fax machine does for today's investors. Unfortunately, however, as investors turn to the Internet as a source of

2. A BBS is a central system accessed using a computer, a modem, phone lines, or a network connection, where data is placed by users for dissemination to one or more other users. Technically, America Online is really just a gigantic BBS, although most BBSs are much smaller. DANIEL P. DERN, THE INTERNET GUIDE FOR NEW USERS 196-98 (1994).

3. There are over 100 competing Internet service providers in the Washington, D.C. area alone, some charging less than $20 a month for all a user would need for complete and unlimited Internet access. Rob Pegoraro, *The FFWD Directory of Internet Service*, WASH. POST, Sept. 25, 1996, at R2.

information and guidance, and as a place where they can discover that golden investment opportunity, they will undoubtedly also encounter the dark side of the Internet. Inhabitants of the dark side, the crooks and thieves who are always on the lookout for a fresh scheme or a neoteric hook, will take advantage of the Internet to lie, cheat, steal, and spoil the boom for the rest of us. With the establishment of a new playing field in cyberspace, so also arrives more opportunities to rip-off unsuspecting investors for ill-gotten gains.

This is where the U.S. Securities and Exchange Commission (SEC or Commission) and its Division of Enforcement (Division) come in. The Division has prepared itself to remain effective tomorrow and tackle head-on the problems the widespread use of the Internet will engender. Since its inception, the Division's program for the Internet has taken advantage of the Internet's growth and has approached new problems from all angles. Most importantly, however, the Division has sought no new enforcement statutes, regulations, or remedies to catch and prosecute securities violations committed over the Internet.

"I CAN EAT 50 EGGS"

The hype about the Internet is not all just hype, and we "ain't seen nothin' yet." The seemingly tall stories about the Internet's staggering growth and its increasing use as a tool for the investor (big and small) are true. Overall, Internet usage statistics continue to swell at a ferocious pace; depending on who you ask, the number of users reported from various sources range from thirty to sixty million (with ten to thirty million in the United States).[4] A recent survey conducted by Find/SVP and Jupiter Communications claims that the number of U.S. households with access to the Internet more than doubled to 14.7 million in 1996 and, as of September 1996, roughly nine million adult Americans logged onto the Internet *daily*, while nearly twenty million logged on weekly.[5] Predictions for the year 2000 run as high as 500 million, with some claiming that the number of users actually doubles every six to nine months.[6] Retail sales over the Internet are expected to skyrocket from $530 million in 1996 to $6.6 billion by the end of the decade.[7] Of course, as the numbers have expanded, the Internet itself has also grown in size, from a small network of computers born from a U.S. Department of Defense experimental network,[8] to a

4. Andrew Kantor & Michael Neubarth, *Off the Charts*, INTERNET WORLD, Dec. 1996 at 45, 46-47; *see also* Nua Ltd., *Internet Surveys* (last modified Jan. 10, 1997) <http://www.nua.ie/surveys/1996graphs/USpopulation.html>.

5. Jared Sandberg, *U.S. Households with Internet Access Doubled to 14.7 Million in Past Year*, WALL ST. J., Oct. 21, 1996, at B11.

6. KENT D. STUCKEY, INTERNET AND ONLINE LAW, at xx (1996).

7. Lisa Greim, *Navidec Targets Net Commerce*, ROCKY MTN. NEWS, Feb. 23, 1997, at 7F; Tim McCollum, *Making the Internet Work for You*, NATION'S BUS., Mar. 1997, at 6.

8. STUCKEY, *supra* note 6, at xvi.

boundless cooperative message forwarding system linking computer networks all over the world.

Online investing through brokerages has experienced corresponding dramatic growth. According to a study by Forrester Research Inc., a Cambridge, Massachusetts consulting firm, entitled "Brokers and the Web," Forrester predicts that the number of online accounts will grow from 1.5 million in 1996 to ten million by 2001.[9] According to the American Association of Individual Investors, thirty-three brokers now offer some form of online trading, up from twenty in 1996 and only twelve in 1995.[10] PC Financial had only 10,000 accounts in 1990.[11] After its hook-up with Prodigy, however, it has increased to over 275,000.[12] Charles Schwab & Co. has more than 170,000 online accounts and more than twenty-eight percent of its daily volume is attributable to online trades.[13] Online investors also tend to be more active, holding larger positions, making bigger trades, and enjoying better discounts trading through a computer than they could obtain by trading through a full-service broker.[14]

Trading is no longer limited to stocks and related securities; Internet users can now even trade U.S. Treasuries online. Recently, Daiwa Securities America, Inc., brought its electronic trading system, known as The Odd-Lot Machine, to the World Wide Web (Web), enabling institutions to trade U.S. Treasuries over the Internet.[15] The first trade, for $1 million in two-year government notes, took place between Daiwa and First Union Capital Markets Group on August 30, 1996.[16]

Currently, mutual fund families, including major players such as Fidelity Investments and Vanguard Group, use their home pages to educate consumers on specific types of funds, brokerage services, and the importance of savings.[17] In addition, investors are able to download prospectuses through these pages. Fidelity has even begun to roll out an Internet trading

9. Kimberly Weisul, *Report: New 'Mid-Tier' Brokers to Get 60% of On-Line Trades; From Zero to Sixty in Five Years*, INVESTMENT DEALERS' DIG., Sept. 30, 1996, at 11. Forrester predicts that " '17% of wired households will be participating in the markets, managing over $524 billion in on-line accounts—8.5% of total retail investment assets.' " *Id.*

10. Theresa W. Carey, *Surf's Up*, BARRON'S, Mar. 17, 1997, at 33.

11. Gary Weiss, *Online Investing*, BUS. WK., June 5, 1995, at 64.

12. PC Financial Network, *Why PC Financial Network is #1* (visited Feb. 20, 1997) <http://www.pcfn.com/pcfn/why1.htm>.

13. Gary Weiss, *supra* note 11, at 64; email from Tom Taggart, Charles Schwab & Co., to Christopher Clark, Staff Member, *The Business Lawyer* (Feb. 26, 1997) (on file with *The Business Lawyer*, University of Maryland School of Law).

14. Andrew Lackey, *On-line services broaden options*, FRESNO BEE, July 14, 1996, at C3; Martin Zimmerman, *Fishing with the Net*, DALLAS MORNING NEWS, July 2, 1996, at 13D.

15. Kimberly Weisul, *First U.S. Treasury Trade Takes Place on Internet*, INVESTMENT DEALERS' DIG., Sept. 16, 1996, at 15; Web Finance, *News Stories* (visited Feb. 20, 1997) <http://www.webfinance.net/brokerage/psaus47.html>.

16. Weisul, *supra* note 15, at 15.

17. Fidelity Investments, *Homepage* (visited Feb. 20, 1997) <http://www.fidelity.com>; The Vanguard Group, *Homepage* (visited Feb. 20, 1997) <http://www.vanguard.com>.

capability for its clients.[18] Recently, Twentieth Century Mutual Funds quietly began to allow customers to buy shares of its funds through the Web, even allowing customers to order electronic fund transfers from their bank into a mutual fund (and customers can use any bank they want).[19] Customers can also purchase mutual funds over the Internet through several discount brokers, including Charles Schwab & Co. and K. Aufhauser & Co.[20] In all, Forrester Research, Inc., predicts total assets handled through online mutual fund transactions will reach $173.5 billion in 2001; it was $41.9 billion in 1996.[21]

Although small investors often remain out of luck when it comes to getting in on the hottest initial public offerings (IPOs), the Internet has at least narrowed the gap in terms of access to information. For instance, IPO information, long considered unobtainable for the average investor, is now available on the Internet for anyone interested.[22] Moreover, a plethora of IPO-related sites, including the SEC's own EDGAR site,[23] provide basic and enumerated IPO information to users, all instantaneously and free of charge.[24]

Even insurers, such as Hartford Life Insurance Company and Massachusetts Mutual Life, have hopped aboard the "Cyber Express" with their own home pages. Their sites provide listings of financial products, interactive estate tax calculators, and a wealth of information incorporating financial and investment concepts.[25] Mutual fund and U.S. equities data is also now available through Morningstar's presence on services such as America Online (AOL) and Compuserve, both of which are Internet access

18. Bruce Rule, *Fidelity Quietly Rolls Out Internet Trading Capability*, INVESTMENT DEALERS' DIG., Jan. 27, 1997, at 14.

19. Kimberly Weisul, *Mutual Fund Co. Becomes First to Offer Web Sales*, INVESTMENT DEALERS' DIG., Sept. 30, 1996, at 10. The Twentieth Century Group is now American Century Investments. *See American Century Investments* (visited Feb. 22, 1997) <http.//www.americancentury.com/funds/twentieth_century.html>.

20. Charles Schwab & Co., *e.Schwab Online Investing* (visited Feb. 20, 1997) <http://www.schwab.com/SchwabNOW/SNLib003/SN003Bodyi.html>; K. Aufhauser & Co., *Home Page* (visited Feb. 20, 1997) <http://www.aufhauser.com>.

21. Kathryn Haines, *Fund Firms See Savings on Web Trades*, WALL ST. J., Jan. 2, 1997, at 35.

22. Although any investor usually can receive IPO information by contacting an underwriter or other participating entity, the investor must first know about the offering, before it becomes oversubscribed, and would likely have to wait in order to receive the most recent information.

23. U.S. Securities & Exchange Commission, *EDGAR Database of Corporate Information* (last updated Mar. 5, 1997) <http://www.sec.gov/edgarhp.htm>.

24. Deborah Lohse, *Want IPO Information? Try the Internet*, WALL ST. J., Oct. 21, 1996, at C1.

25. Hartford Life Insurance Co., *Welcome to The Hartford* (visited Feb. 22, 1997) <http://www.thehartford.com>; Mass Mutual, *Home Page* (visited Feb. 22, 1997) <http://www.massmutual.com>.

providers and worldwide, subscriber-based electronic communications services.[26]

Even more startling, though, along with the Internet's increase in popularity over the last several years, is that use of the Internet as a forum for discussion of investments has grown correspondingly. Prodigy, an Internet access provider, estimates that some fifty percent of its two million users access the financial forums and features, which puts investments in a tie with news as the service's second most popular feature.[27] Similar growth explosions have occurred on the Motley Fool Bulletin Boards of AOL and the Silicon Investor, as well as AOL's Investor's Network,[28] and the many popular and emerging publicly available Internet newsgroups, Web bulletin boards, and other online investment forums dedicated exclusively to investing, securities, and commerce.

Digital legal tender is also rapidly becoming a reality and, given its inherent ease and efficiency (open for business twenty-four hours a day, 365 days a year), will make commerce on the Internet not just an option, but a necessity. Recently, the nation's two largest credit card associations, Visa and Mastercard International, Inc., announced an agreement on industry-standard software which they claim will allow consumers to buy goods over the Internet without fear that their credit card numbers will be stolen.[29] This could eventually alleviate the public's hesitation to send personal financial information pulsing through the wires of the Internet. DigiCash of Amsterdam, CyberCash of Virginia, ECash, smart cards such as the Mondex[30] system being consumer-tested in England, and other forms of virtual greenbacks are already a reality on the Internet, and continue to grow by leaps and bounds.

"WELL SOMETIMES NOTHIN' IS A REAL COOL HAND"

Sometimes, however, investors get ripped off. Given the potential for scam artists to use the Internet to sell investors a "whole lot of nothin'," just what are the Division's concerns? At present, the Division can break its concerns down into six categories. Given the rapidly changing environ-

26. Subscription information can be obtained from Wall Street Directory, Inc., on the Internet. *See* Wall Street Directory, Inc., *Morningstar Mutual Funds—AOL* (last modified Feb. 22, 1997) <http://www.wsdinc.com/products/p1659.shtml>.

27. Weiss, *supra* note 11, at 64.

28. *See, e.g.*, The Motley Fool, *The Motley Fool* (visited Feb. 22, 1997) <http://fool.web.aol.com/index.htm>.

29. Judith Evans, *Who Was That Masked Cybershopper?*, WASH. POST, Feb. 2, 1996, at F1.

30. Mondex is a joint venture of NatWest Bank, Midland Bank, and British Telecom formed to join the electronic cash game. MasterCard International recently said it would buy 51% of Mondex and promised significant investments to create a global electronic cash system. Valerie Block, *MasterCard Will Buy 51% Of Smart Card Firm Mondex*, AM. BANKER, Nov. 19, 1996, at 1.

ment, however, no Internet worldview is set in stone. The Division, therefore, remains poised to shift its attention to any new problem area that arises.

THE OFFER AND SALE OF BOGUS INVESTMENTS

In light of the wide range of (largely unregistered) investment opportunities offered over the Internet, and, in particular, the opportunities peddled over the Web and newsgroups, the Division is well aware of the use of the Web as a convenient means for scam artists to steal from investors. Ranging from traditional securities like stocks and bonds, to more esoteric investment opportunities involving anything from eel farms, cattle breeding, and oil and gas drilling to cyber-casinos, multi-level marketing programs, and portable nuclear reactors, securities hawked over the Internet come in a huge variety of shapes and sizes. The SEC has brought a host of cases thus far involving offerings over the Internet (which will be discussed in more detail) and, given the popularity and ease of offering securities over the Web, combined with the sheer simplicity of using newsgroups, message areas, and other BBSs, the SEC will probably bring more of these cases in the future.

The Web is a hypertext based information and resource system for the Internet[31] and, as the fastest growing part of the Internet, it is most likely responsible for the amazing interest in the Internet itself. Each screenful of information includes menu choices and highlighted words through which the user can call up further information, either from the same computer or by linking automatically to another computer anywhere in the world.[32]

The popularity of the Web as a means of solicitation of investors is obvious: the cost and ease of producing and activating a sophisticated and impressive looking Web site[33] has changed dramatically, empowering the offeror. Not just for the plain vanilla home page of yesteryear, though; rather, investors are presented with sleekly designed, multipage Web sites that include all the latest bells and whistles such as search engines, interactive graphics, sounds, video, and futuristic looking formats and links.[34]

Finding space on a server is easy and cheap; promoters of servers have become ubiquitous on the Web and in the telephone yellow pages. Many

31. STUCKEY, *supra* note 6, at xvi.

32. *Id.*

33. A Web site is the space on a server occupied by the information maintained by a company or individual. The information often occupies multiple "pages," the first of which is usually referred to as a "home" or index page because it guides the user through the information available at the site. *See* CRICKET LIU ET AL., MANAGING INTERNET INFORMATION SERVICES 309-10 (1994).

34. A link is embedded in a Web page and enables a user to jump from one piece of information to a related item no matter where on the Internet the information may be stored. G. BURGESS ALLISON, THE LAWYERS GUIDE TO THE INTERNET 147-49 (1995).

access providers even allocate to users free space for their own Web sites, in exchange for merely signing an access agreement. Moreover, countless software packages offer users simple and easy to follow instructions that make constructing a good looking Web site as easy as typing a word processing document. So, building the Web site is a breeze, hooking it up on the Web is a snap, and you need not be a programmer or technophile to succeed.

This is nothing less than an outstanding opening for the crooked securities solicitation. At very little cost and from the privacy of a basement office or living room, the fraudster can produce a home page that looks better and more sophisticated than that of a Fortune 500 company. Thieves have many tools at their fingertips; even a link can serve as an aid for an investment ruse. Just like visiting a site, using a link is usually free, so the fraudster might even provide a link to the home page of the SEC next to a representation that a particular security has received "approval" from the SEC or a link to a phony investment newsletter page (also owned and operated by the fraudster) which touts the investment as a tremendous investment opportunity.

Newsgroups are popular message areas that form part of Usenet.[35] Usenet is a group of systems that exchange debate, chat, and discussion in the form of newsgroups across the Internet.[36] BBSs, however, serve as message boards, where users can post messages, typically to solicit a reply or to comment on a prior message.[37] Message boards, cheap, easy to use, and potentially reaching millions of users, provide a great tool for offering securities. Recent reports have identified as many as 23,000 newsgroups (although some Internet service providers only carry between 10,000 and 20,000 newsgroups).[38]

Although message areas provide a fantastic opportunity to match the small investor with the unknown small company located thousands of miles away, no doubt there are those who will exploit these message areas as a fast and easy way to find a credulous investor and divorce them from their savings. Message boards exist on the Web and throughout the Internet that are specifically designated for postings from promoters who seek investors in search of less traditional investments, such as those not traded on an exchange or thinly traded in the OTC markets or listings. Posting a message, such as a solicitation for investors in a new company, like everything else on the Internet, costs next to nothing. In fact, in most cases, it is as simple as sending an email message. Moreover, the Internet also

35. Usenet actually stands for Users Network, a collection of discussion groups on almost any subject of interest to people, including investment and business opportunities. One should note, however, that in Usenet participants can maintain anonymity or disclose as much personal information as they desire.

36. DERN, *supra* note 2, at 196-98.

37. *Id.* at 36.

38. Rob Pegoraro, *Input/Output*, WASH. POST, Oct. 30, 1996, at R2.

hosts hundreds of classified advertisement areas exclusively dedicated to investment opportunities.

So, when a scam artist seeks an investor who might be particularly vulnerable to promises for easy money, he or she need look no further than a message board specifically tailored for those who want to "Make Money Fast" or a classified advertisement area such as "Get Rich Quick." (These are actual titles, available to just about every Internet user.)

Whether a posting or Web page on the Internet would fall within the purview of the federal securities laws depends on a number of factors, including whether the instrument of capital formation qualifies as a "security" under applicable definitions, whether the particular electronic communication constitutes an "offering," or whether the offering falls under an applicable exemption from registration. Under the modified *Howey* test, among the "investment opportunities" that have qualified as securities have been orange groves, Ponzi and pyramid schemes, and ostrich and eel farms.[39] Internet offerings will no doubt force the courts continually to reapply the *Howey* test to novel situations.

Other issues would include whether the manner of an Internet solicitation's "public dissemination" satisfied legal requirements. Online communication links cut across geographical borders and could result in issuers violating securities laws by transmitting offering documents into states where the issuer had failed to satisfy blue sky requirements. Spring Street Brewing Co., a New York microbrewery and believed to be the first issuer to offer securities through a formal online prospectus, faced this problem when it won specific approval from the SEC to market its $5 million IPO over the Internet last March.[40] Its solution was to include on the electronic offering document a warning specifying the states in which the offer was valid.[41]

Although courts may consider viewing a document on the Web or Usenet as a *de facto* public offering or solicitation, offers made in a chat room by one user to another, offers made via private emailings, or offers conducted on a bulletin board for exclusive use may create questions about

39. *See* SEC v. W.J. Howey Co., 328 U.S. 296 (1946); SEC v. Koscot Interplanetary, Inc., 497 F.2d 473 (5th Cir. 1974) (pyramid scheme); SEC v. Goodman, Litigation Release No. 15,079, 62 S.E.C. Docket (CCH) 2668 (Sept. 27, 1996) (ostriches); SEC v. Odulo, Litigation Release No. 14,616, 60 S.E.C. Docket (CCH) 120 (Aug. 24, 1995) (eels).

40. Spring Street established a home page on the Web which allowed potential investors using the Internet to examine and download its offering documents. Spring Street Brewing Co., *Homepage* (visited Mar. 19, 1997) <http://plaza.interport.net/witbeer>. Spring Street's IPO qualified as a Regulation A offering (i.e., the total amount to be raised by the offering was under $5 million) and was therefore exempt from SEC registration. Regulation A, 17 C.F.R. § 230.251 (1996). Nonetheless, the offering was registered in 18 states and the District of Columbia.

41. Spring Street Brewing Co., *WIT BEER Public Stock Offering* (visited Feb. 20, 1997) <http://plaza.interport.net/witbeer/wit_5.html>; *see also* Spring Street Brewing Co., SEC No-Action Letter, 1996 SEC No-Act. LEXIS 435 (Apr. 17, 1996).

how "public" an offering is or raise issues about whether a user actually made an "offer" at all.[42] Email presents a particularly sticky situation as it can either be one-to-one or one-to-many (as is the case with "listservs" or mailing lists, which send messages to a finite subscriber group),[43] and still remain "private" as the information is not intended to go beyond the designated recipients. Sometimes, however, the sender wishes to send an email for the world to see, like a posting to a Web site, a file transfer protocol (FTP)[44] site, or a Usenet group.

The promoters of unregistered Internet securities offerings often show little concern for the mandates of federal securities law. A company called "Pocket Made Inc.," which planned to introduce a "revolutionary automated cleaning device for which it has patent rights," recently posted newsgroup messages seeking to raise capital online.[45] Was the offering registered with the SEC? According to a recent report, no, and the offering's promoter seemed strangely nonchalant:

> "In a sense it was not legal, but the SEC will never enforce it," says Bill McAninch [vice president of operations, secretary, and treasurer of Pocket Made]. "Basically . . . we were advised not to panic, that the government understands that it's not legal but never has prosecuted anybody. They deliberately ignore low-level violations."[46]

Mr. McAninch may indeed change his tune nowadays, however, given that the SEC has brought at least nine cases thus far involving offerings over the Internet.[47] Further, given the popularity and ease of offering securities over the Web, combined with the sheer simplicity of using newsgroups, message areas, and other BBSs, the SEC will probably bring more of these cases in the future. Past cases were brought under the antifraud provisions of the Securities Act of 1933 (Securities Act)[48] and the Securities Exchange Act of 1934 (Exchange Act),[49] specifically, section 17(a) of the Securities Act,[50] and section 10(b) and Rule 10b-5 of the Exchange Act.[51]

42. In some SEC investigations, promoters defend themselves by saying that the Web page announcing the offering of securities was merely a vehicle to demonstrate the promoters' online expertise. In such cases, SEC staff must use both online (newsgroup posts, listings on Internet search engines) and conventional communications to establish the promoters' scienter.

43. DERN, *supra* note 2, at 131.

44. FTP stands for File Transfer Protocol Service, which allows the transferring or copying of files from one computer to another. Users and organizations can make information available to the public over the FTP and remain anonymous.

45. Gary Weiss, *supra* note 11, at 70.

46. *Id.*

47. *See infra* text accompanying notes 97-122.

48. 15 U.S.C. §§ 77a-77aa (1994 & West Supp. 1997).

49. *Id.* §§ 78a-78*ll*.

50. *Id.* § 77q(a) (1994).

51. *Id.* § 78j(b); 17 C.F.R. § 240.10b-5 (1996).

In the area of disclosure issues, the SEC's Division of Corporation Finance addressed, in a no-action letter, certain practices by an entity called IPONET.[52] IPONET involved a registered "dealer," who, vis-à-vis the IPONET Web site, wanted to solicit investors and determine if the investor is an "accredited investor" within the meaning of the standards of Regulation D.[53] After such a determination, the dealer would then allow the accredited investor access to a list of Regulation D offerings set forth on the IPONET Web site.

The SEC granted IPONET's request, stating that indications of interest may be accepted by an electronic "coupon" or "card" that are sent directly from a home page or independently via email if the requirements of Rule 134(d) are otherwise met.[54] The no-action letter also required that, in accordance with Rule 502(c) of Regulation D, the posting of a notice of a private offering should only be accessible by IPONET members, who would have to qualify as accredited investors.[55]

MARKET MANIPULATION

In addition to the offer and sale of securities over BBSs, the posting of information pertaining to particular securities over BBSs has become a critical source of information for the entire range of market participants, from the small investor to the multi-billion dollar mutual fund manager. A user can easily find information and postings on individual securities using a Usenet search engine to navigate the Internet newsgroups and review all postings concerning an individual security. Even easier is searching the contents of access-provider BBSs and dedicated Web forums, where the user can find information and postings on a particular security by simply reviewing the contents of a folder exclusively dedicated to that security. Postings describe everything from first-hand reporting of the discussions at a public company's annual shareholders meeting to whether the steak the Chief Executive Officer (CEO) had for dinner the night before was done rare or medium-well.

The sheer volume of messages contained in BBSs pertaining to individual stocks (in particular the BBSs of access providers) has grown considerably over the last year or so, mandating that market participants such as brokers, analysts, and short sellers monitor carefully all relevant message areas for the latest news. The word is out on the street that stock information posted over a BBS can, within minutes of a posting, influence the price of a stock or group of related stocks.

Along with such a tremendous flow of important information comes again the opportunity for exploitation by the unsavory. Stockholders, both

52. IPONET, SEC NO-Action Letter, 1996 WL 431821 (S.E.C.) (July 26, 1996).
53. 17 C.F.R. §§ 230.501-508 (1996).
54. *IPONET*, 1996 WL 431821 (S.E.C.), at *5.
55. *Id.* at *6.

short and long, now can reach millions of people instantly (at very little cost) and use false information to attempt to manipulate the price of a stock. Two methods in particular can serve the crook as a means of fooling the legitimate investor.

The first method is the cloaking of an author's true identity by false pretense or anonymity. In the simplest case, a user merely disguises himself, for example, by falsely proclaiming to be an insider of a public company while actually being an investor having a short interest in that company's stock. In the more sophisticated instance, the user sends postings via a "remailer" or other "anonymizing" tool[56] which provides anonymous email addresses to users who wish to hide their true identities. Anonymizing tools strip the identifying information from the message "header" when sending a message, removing any possible audit trail of the message.[57] One can procure the services of an array of anonymity tools over the Internet, with little effort and at little expense.[58]

The second method, even more disturbing than the first, is altering or falsifying emails, commonly called "spoofing." Spoofing involves the use of the identity or user ID of a real person for the purposes of impersonation.[59] Contrary to popular belief, email is far from private; if someone wants to read your email or newsgroup posting, or if someone wants to alter it, "spoof," or "forge" it, there exist many ways to do so. For example, when a user sends a message across cyberspace, a spy program called a "packet sniffer" can monitor your keystrokes, allowing a cracker[60] to read what you type and use that information to create a bogus posting that appears to be from you.[61] A nefarious system administrator might read your mail as it sits in a spooler waiting for delivery or as its sits in the newsgroup waiting to be read. An unscrupulous user on any of the series of other mail-routing computers might intercept your mail, alter it, and send it on, or may simply steal user information for a future plot of impersonation.

These are just a few of the ways a swindler can get the information of a *bona fide* user, such as an official at a public company, and then create a posting from that *bona fide* insider to manipulate the stock. Thus, even if a user knows the identity of the named author of a particular posting, and

56. Andre Bacard, *Anonymous Remailer FAQ* (last modified Nov. 15, 1996) <http://www.well.com/user/abacard/remail.html>.

57. *Id.*

58. The Surfing Lawyer, *Email: Issues and Software* (visited Feb. 22, 1997) <http://www.netlegal.com/email.html>.

59. DERN, *supra* note 2, at 378.

60. Some confusion exists with respect to the terms "hacker" and "cracker." Hackers are those whose lives are completely immersed in computers and computing. Crackers, on the other hand, focus on illegal activity. *Id.* Though crackers often call themselves hackers, the genuine hacker considers crackers a lower form of technophile.

61. Computer Network Security, *Eavesdropping* (visited Feb. 22, 1997) <http://www.weru.ksu.edu/people/dudley/SECURITY/Security.html>.

trusts that person as a worthy and credible source of information, the author may not actually be that person; the writer may, in fact, be a crook who has used a packet sniffer to steal a legitimate user's identity. Like cat burglars who creep in without ever being seen, stock manipulators can steal an identity and make it their own, only the cyber-cat burglars need not climb up the drain pipe for a break-in or even don ski masks to hide their identities.

Overall, BBSs offer investors, particularly small investors in small towns, access to some of the same information as a Wall Street analyst. Given the potential lack of credibility and overriding lack of integrity of a posting, however, an investment decision based on a posting could lead to disaster.

What exacerbates this concern is the remarkably benevolent culture and trustworthy nature of Internet users. Do you have a medical problem? Post a message on a medical advice newsgroup and you will receive a range of responses from patients to nurses to doctors, all wanting to help you get better. Are you traveling to a foreign country? Post a message asking for suggestions and you will receive a range of responses from fellow travelers telling you everything from the best hotel (and its best room) to the best nearby restaurant (and its best dessert). In the realm of investments, this overwhelmingly helpful and endearing feature could turn into a nightmare for the trusting investor who gets hoodwinked into taking the advice of a perfidious short seller.

Several sections of the Exchange Act could directly prohibit the manipulation of securities prices through the dissemination of false or misleading information over BBSs and newsgroups, including section 9(a)(2),[62] section 9(a)(3),[63] section 9(a)(4)[64] and, of course, section

62. 15 U.S.C. § 78i(a)(2) (1994). Section 9(a)(2) provides a very broad prohibition on the manipulation of a market for a security, making it unlawful for any person

> to effect, alone or with one or more other persons, a series of transactions in any security registered on a national securities exchange creating actual or apparent active trading in such security or raising or depressing the price of such security, for the purpose of inducing the purchase or sale of such security by others.

Id.

63. *Id.* § 78i(a)(3). Section 9(a)(3) addresses indirect manipulation by third parties, such as agents paid by market participants, who manipulate the prices of securities by broadcasting false or misleading information, specifically making it unlawful for

> a dealer or broker, or other person selling or offering for sale or purchasing or offering to purchase the security, to induce the purchase or sale of any security registered on a national securities exchange by the circulation or dissemination in the ordinary course of business of information to the effect that the price of any such security will or is likely to rise or fall because of market operations of any one or more persons conducted for the purpose of raising or depressing the prices of such security.

Id.

64. *Id.* § 78i(a)(4). Section 9(a)(4) prohibits any broker, dealer, or other person, selling or offering for sale, or purchasing or offering to purchase, a security registered on a national

10(b)[65] and Rules 10b-5[66] and 10b-1.[67]

To date, the SEC has brought several cases in which the issuer involved experienced a lot of "Usenet hype," with the most definitive market manipulation case being *SEC v. Charles O. Huttoe*.[68]

ONLINE TRADING FACILITIES

To date, the most innovative mechanism that has developed on the Internet's entrepreneurial platform falls within the realm of Internet trading of securities, specifically in the form of Internet trading by a company of its own stock and Internet trading facilities. These areas represent a tremendous opportunity for businesses and investors alike. A business can use the Internet as a cost-effective forum to reach more and more investors hungry for something new and different, while an investor can find liquidity for an investment and even find relief from the traditionally large and seemingly random bid and asked spreads on thinly traded stocks.

Whether cyberspace will become a mere medium for capital formation, or a jurisdiction unto itself, remains unclear at this time. Whether investors need protection from knave operators of such novel instruments of the capital formation process, however, has never been clearer. Although innovation and creativity have made U.S. securities markets the most efficient capital formation system in the world, careful and thoughtful government intervention from entities such as the SEC has ensured that U.S. markets also have the highest level of integrity and safety.

Of course, the SEC and the Division should not discourage such modernization but rather ferret out the abuses while offering assistance and guidance to the pioneers of the securities markets. In that vein, companies involved in the offering and trading of securities over the Internet must provide the same customer protections and capital safeguards often taken

securities exchange from inducing the purchase or sale of a security by means of any statement that was, in light of the circumstances under which it was made, false or misleading with respect to any material fact, and which he knew or had reasonable ground to believe was false and misleading. *Id.*

65. *Id.* § 78j(b). Section 10(b) prohibits the

> use or employ, in connection with the purchase or sale of any security registered on a national securities exchange or any security not so registered, any manipulative or deceptive device or contrivance in contravention of such rules and regulations as the commission may prescribe as necessary or appropriate in the public interest or for the protection of investors.

Id.

66. 17 C.F.R. § 240.10b-5 (1996).

67. *Id.* § 240.10b-1. Rule 10b-1 prohibits the use of such manipulative or deceptive devices or contrivances with respect to certain securities exempt from registration. *Id.*

68. SEC v. Huttoe, Litigation Release No. 15,153, 63 S.E.C. Docket (CCH) 427 (D.D.C. Nov. 7, 1996). See *infra* notes 97-122 and accompanying text for a discussion summarizing all SEC Internet-related cases to date.

for granted in the context of the traditional trading of securities, such as with a registered U.S. exchange.

As with traditional exchanges, these protections should mandate that (i) investors' funds and securities be handled appropriately, (ii) investors understand the risks involved in purchasing the often illiquid and speculative securities that are traded over the Internet, (iii) buyers be made aware of the last sale prices on a particular stock, and (iv) companies provide ongoing and adequate disclosure. Overall, entities providing exchange-like services must carefully handle access to, and control of, investor funds to provide all users with adequate protections.

With respect to merely trading in the securities of one's own company or operating an online trading facility, an operator could trigger other registration requirements of the federal securities laws, such as those contained in section 19 of the Exchange Act.[69]

In addition, other related registration requirements may emerge when participating in the operation of an online trading facility. For example, when an issuer holds and maintains funds, securities, and accounts of investors, the issuer may be required to register as a broker-dealer under section 15 of the Exchange Act.[70] Even users of an Internet trading facility should understand that, if they choose to post quotations simultaneously on both its Buyer and Seller bulletin boards, the users could be considered "dealers," required to register and comply with broker-dealer requirements under section 15 of the Exchange Act.[71]

The SEC has issued four important no-action letters in this area, pertaining to PerfectData Corporation (PerfectData), Real Goods Trading Information (Real Goods), the Flamemaster Corporation (Flamemaster), and Angel Capital Electronic Network (Angel Capital).[72] PerfectData, Real Goods, and Flamemaster essentially sought to offer shareholders the opportunity to meet on a Web page and identify themselves as viable buyers or sellers of the issuer and potentially trade shares with each other. The crux of the SEC's position on this issue is that the issuer should have no proprietary, financial, or other interest in the operation of the Web page.[73] The Web site is simply a place where investors can meet, like a rented room at an annual meeting or an office inside a company's headquarters.

With respect to Angel Capital, the staff of the SEC's Division of Market

69. 15 U.S.C. § 78s.

70. *Id.* § 78o(a).

71. *Id.*

72. Flamemaster Corp., SEC No-Action Letter, 1996 WL 762990 (S.E.C.) (Oct. 29, 1996); Angel Capital Electronic Network, SEC No-Action Letter, 1996 WL 636094 (S.E.C.) (Oct. 25, 1996); PerfectData Corp., SEC No-Action Letter, 1996 WL 480429 (S.E.C.) (Aug. 5, 1996); Real Goods Trading Corp., SEC No-Action Letter, [1996-1997 Transfer Binder] Fed. Sec. L. Rep. (CCH) ¶ 77,226, at 77,131 (June 24, 1996).

73. *Real Goods Trading Corp.*, [1996-1997 Transfer Binder] Fed. Sec. L. Rep. (CCH) at 77,134.

Regulation responded to a request from the U.S. Small Business Administration, stating that it would not object to the operation of the Angel Capital network if the nonprofit operators of the network do not register as an exchange, a broker-dealer, or an investment advisor.[74] The network is an Internet Web site that will allow accredited investors to gain access to small businesses whose shares are exempt from registration under Regulations A or D.[75]

As with the early phases of any new trading facility, online Internet trading facilities will undoubtedly experience a rocky and uncharted genesis and the opportunity for manipulations, such as the popular "pump and dump" schemes of the 1980s and 1990s, will certainly arise. Online trading facilities raise critical issues regarding security, broker-dealer, exchange, and transfer agent registration, interdealer quotation system, and manipulation issues. The Commission must mandate that any operator of an Internet trading facility take prudent steps to address its regulatory concerns and also to deter manipulations by unprincipled promoters and broker-dealers.

SPAMMING

As investors begin transacting business over the Internet, inevitably, they will find it in their own self-interest to reveal more and more about themselves in order to allow the interactive systems to cater more effectively to their needs and preferences. Already users disclose a wide range of information on the Internet, from business requirements to leisure interests.

Sometimes, these disclosures are carried out intentionally by completing a survey or providing registration information, and sometimes such disclosures are done without the user even knowing it, like when sending a posting to a particular newsgroup. For example, using a practice called "mining," a user can collect all the email addresses from a particular newsgroup by operating a fairly simple automated software mining program.[76] The user can then publish such information on a directory site where anyone can retrieve it or keep the information for private application.

Mining is only the tip of the iceberg; the Internet is not like radio, cable television, or any other traditional medium: it is a two way hook-up. Communication's technology on the Internet is interactive, meaning that information is constantly flowing in *two* directions, and an extraordinary long and unknown arm reaches into the office and into the living room through the Internet. For example, consider "cookie" files: files that are written onto a user's hard drive during visits to cookie-compatible Web sites. These

74. *Angel Capital Electronic Network*, 1996 WL 636094 (S.E.C.), at *8-*9.

75. 17 C.F.R. § 230.251-263 (1996); *id.* §§ 230.201-508.

76. Leslie Miller, *Cashing in on Web Treasure: Personal Data*, USA TODAY, Dec. 12, 1996, at D10.

cookies are not the kind found on a dessert tray; these cookies allow a particular site to track the activities of a user by recording details of that user's previous visits to the site.[77] A cookie file is created at the behest of the Web server but maintained automatically by a user's personal computer.[78]

The details recorded by cookie files include the date and time that a user visited a site or the user's "click stream," which is a user's history of what the user has viewed on the Web.[79] The cookie could possibly collect even more personal information like a user's address and phone number.[80] Some even argue that a Web site operator could design a cookie file that would "snoop through a user's hard drive, looking for something that resembles a Social Security number or a bank balance."[81]

Despite the "Big Brother" inferences, the ability to collect such crucial research information can prove instrumental for a company when planning its future growth and development, and can bring the consumer and the business closer together for a mutually beneficial purpose: profit for the corporation and satisfaction for the customer.[82] Unfortunately, here is the bad news: the most critical piece of consumer information, the user's email address, now becomes part of the public domain, and that could lead to unforeseen intrusions and abuses. Moreover, other sites can look at one's cookie file, get information about a user's Internet provider and his or her Internet protocol address, and compile some surprising information about a user, ranging from what part of the country a user lives in to the resolution of the user's monitor.[83] The cookie file might even indicate the last site a user visited and which browser the user utilized at the time.[84]

This is how a company, albeit unknown to the user, knows all about the user's habits and, most importantly, how to reach the user. So, in addition to receiving junk mail claiming that the recipient has just won $1 million, and answering annoying phone calls peddling the latest get rich quick product or service or the knock on the door from the traveling salesman, the user can now expect the beep notification of an email from the friendly neighborhood Internet "spammer."

Spammers, who practice their art by transmitting a message to an email list, combine the skills of mass mailers with the hard-pressure sales tactics

77. *See* Kim Komondo, *C is for Cookie*, COMPUTER LIFE, Jan. 1, 1997, at 193.

78. Zina Moukheiber, *DoubleClick is Watching You*, FORBES, Nov. 4, 1996, at 343.

79. *Id.*

80. *Id.* at 344.

81. *Id.* at 342. Browser software may alert a user that a Web page has "dropped a cookie on them," but the user never learns the purpose or extent of the cookie file. *Id.* at 343.

82. For example, DoubleClick, Inc., an Internet advertising broker in New York, has amassed profiles on 10 million anonymous Web users simply by tracking people's Web behavior, Internet addresses, operating systems, browsers, and Internet-service providers. *Id.* at 342-43.

83. *Id.*

84. *Id.*

of "boiler-room cold-callers."[85] Perhaps the spammer pulls a list of users from newsgroups catering to investors and then hits them with the latest news about the hottest new investment, directing the recipient to a Web site or simply offering an 800 number. With very little effort of time or money, the scam artist can reach an unlimited number of potential victims, and contact them over and over again at little additional cost.

Of the complaints received by the Division relating to the Internet, complaints about spamming in connection with investments rank first. Until laws are on the books to deter spamming, Internet spammers have free rein to send information about bogus investment products to anyone with a modem, whether they like it or not.

UNREGISTERED INVESTMENT ADVISERS AND INVESTMENT NEWSLETTERS

With the proliferation of all sorts of goods and services offered over the Internet, investment advisers peddling their services have not lagged far behind; just about every type of investment adviser has sprouted in cyberspace. Although the original drafters of the Investment Advisers Act of 1940 (Investment Advisers Act)[86] probably never contemplated the cyberspace investment adviser, the provisions of the Investment Advisers Act appear flexible enough to ensure its safeguarding provisions (disclosure, record-keeping, and other customer protections) apply equally to Internet-related activities.

Under certain circumstances, a person or entity acting as an "investment adviser" could trigger certain registration requirements of the federal securities laws.[87] Section 203(a) of the Investment Advisers Act generally makes it unlawful for any "investment adviser," unless registered, to use

85. Internet lore has it that the term "spam" derives from a famous Monty Python skit which featured the word spam repeated over and over. The term may also have come from someone's derision of the eponymous generic processed meat product, which some perceive as lacking in substance or content. (Spam is a registered trademark of Hormel Corporation.)

86. 15 U.S.C. §§ 80b-1 to -21 (1994 & West Supp. 1997).

87. The Investment Advisers Act defines the term "investment adviser" to include

> any person who, for compensation, engages in the business of advising others, either directly or through publications or writings, as to the value of securities or as to the advisability of investing in, purchasing, or selling securities, or who, for compensation and as part of a regular business, issues or promulgates analyses or reports concerning securities.

Id. § 80b-2(a) (1994). Any person or entity that satisfies these criteria must register under the Investment Advisers Act, unless an exemption applies. *Id.* § 80b-3(b) (1994 & West Supp. 1997). The most significant of these exemptions relate to banks and holding companies, brokers or dealers, and publishers of *bona fide* newspapers, magazines, and other publications of general and regular circulation.

any means of interstate commerce in its advisory business.[88] The Investment Advisers Act also requires investment advisers to maintain certain books and records, which are subject to periodic SEC examinations,[89] and makes it unlawful for "any investment adviser" (whether or not registered) to engage in fraudulent activities.[90]

On a related note, the proliferation of investment newsletters over the Internet has also grown considerably in the last few years. Again, like other innovations, this creates a real windfall for investors as they can use the Internet to research the opinions of others who may have significant experience or better knowledge about a particular company. Moreover, investment newsletters serve an important role for many market participants and can significantly impact the price of a publicly traded company's stock with a glowing tribute or scathing condemnation..

Merely because the investment newsletter is circulated in cyberspace, however, does not create an automatic exemption from the federal securities laws for its authors. For example, section 17(b) of the Securities Act could prohibit a user from posting certain promotional information and opinions concerning a security in an investment newsletter without also disclosing the nature and substance of any consideration received from the issuer of the company underlying that security.[91]

In the SEC's case against Systems of Excellence (SOE),[92] one of the most serious allegations concerned violations of section 17(b) by SGA Goldstar (SGA), an investment newsletter with wide dissemination over the Internet. The SEC accused SGA of receiving bribes from certain defendants, including SOE, to tout SOE stock to SGA's subscribers.[93] The use of an online newsletter as a co-conspirator for a manipulation scheme can have serious ramifications, not only by duping trusting investors but also by jeopardizing the integrity of important financial markets.

88. *Id.* § 80b-3(a) (1994); 17 C.F.R. § 275.204-3 (1996). The written disclosure statement required may be either a copy of Part II of the Adviser's Form ADV or a written statement containing the information required in that part of the form. *Id.*

89. 15 U.S.C. § 80b-4; 17 C.F.R. § 275.204-2.

90. 15 U.S.C. § 80b-6.

91. *Id.* § 77q(b). Specifically, § 17(b) of the Securities Act states that

> [i]t shall be unlawful for any *person*, by the use of any means or instruments of transportation or communication in interstate commerce or by the use of the mails, to publish, give publicity to, or circulate any notice, circular, advertisement, newspaper, article, letter, investment service, or communication which, though not purporting to offer a security for sale, describes such security for a consideration received or to be received, directly or indirectly, from an issuer, underwriter, or dealer, without fully disclosing the receipt, whether past or prospective, of such consideration and amount thereof.

Id. (emphasis added).

92. SEC v. Huttoe, Litigation Release No. 15,185, 63 S.E.C. Docket (CCH) 1011 (D.D.C. Dec. 12, 1996).

93. *Id.* This case is discussed in more detail *infra* text accompanying notes 119-22.

OFF-SHORE BROKER-DEALERS AND OTHER FINANCIAL SERVICE ENTITIES

International financial service entities such as foreign brokers, dealers, and investment advisers continue to enter the cyberarena, offering Web sites along with some interactive services for potential clients and customers. From their home countries, they vend their services to U.S. investors without ever crossing the border. Although these entities may indeed be wholly legitimate in their own countries, their actions may still trigger U.S. registration requirements.

For instance, take the case of offshore broker-dealers; many have already settled onto the Web, providing glossy and sophisticated sites describing their operations and customer service record. Some have even succeeded in aligning themselves next to legitimate U.S. broker-dealers on Web sites that provide classified listings of all available brokers and dealers. Bearing in mind that these brokers and dealers may have never landed on U.S. soil and may not have even ever picked up a telephone to solicit U.S. customers, they still might be violating the federal securities laws. Overall, Exchange Act Rule 15a and its provisions carefully regulate the activities of foreign broker-dealers in the United States and provide a very thorough and demanding list of requirements that pertain to the conduct of business by foreign broker-dealers with U.S. persons.[94]

Specifically, the Exchange Act makes it unlawful for any broker or dealer (including any foreign broker or dealer) to make use of any jurisdictional means to effect any transactions in, or to induce or to attempt to induce the purchase or sale of, any security unless such broker or dealer is registered with the SEC.[95] The SEC interprets this registration provision broadly. In the SEC's view, this provision could require registration by a broker-dealer operating outside of the United States, using only U.S. mail or telephone lines to trade securities with or for U.S. persons located in the United States,[96] or possibly a foreign broker-dealer whose only U.S. contacts are the execution of unsolicited orders from U.S. customers.[97]

The same could also hold true in the case of foreign investment advisers. Depending on the services offered or rendered, the foreign entity may have to meet the requirements previously outlined and could violate these provisions even if wholly legitimate within its own borders.

With respect to the violations of the antifraud provisions of the federal securities laws by international entities, the entire area has become a massive can of worms. Given the many problems associated with investigating and prosecuting offshore entities, from serving subpoenas to locating assets

94. 17 C.F.R. §§ 240.15a-2 to -6 (1996).

95. 15 U.S.C. § 78*o*(a)(1) (1994).

96. Registration Requirements for Foreign Broker-Dealers, Exchange Act Release No. 27,017, 54 Fed. Reg. 30,013, 30,016 n.41 (July 11, 1989).

97. *Id.* at 30,017 n.52.

to extradition, international authorities must work together, using present treaties, memoranda of understanding, and other formal and informal international agreements.

"WELL, I AIN'T HEARD THAT MUCH WORTH LISTENIN' TO. . . . JUST A LOT OF GUYS LAYIN' DOWN A LOT OF RULES AND REGULATIONS"

Before examining what the Division is doing about the previously raised concerns, it is important to note what the Division is *not* doing: the SEC has sought no new statutes, regulations, or rules to help protect Internet investors. Moreover, congressional intervention appears unnecessary. The swindles over the Internet are no different from the confidence games of the past; the only difference is the medium. Thus, present antifraud weapons will more than suffice.

Historically, the SEC has responded quickly to evolving markets and changing industry practice, such as the foreign payments program, the insider trading program, the municipal securities program, and the recent posture on derivatives cases.[98] Each program shared a common theme: a commitment to protect the investor from illicit, unethical conduct within a developing legal area. Most importantly, none of the programs required any new law, rule, or regulation for successful implementation.

The same holds true for the investigation and civil prosecution of securities violations committed over the Internet; the laws need not change, only their application will need to evolve. The Division's traditional firearms, embodied in the current Securities Act and Exchange Act, will likely provide adequate legal bases for prosecuting Internet securities fraud. For instance, the antifraud provisions of the section 10(b) of the Exchange Act[99] and Rule 10b-5[100] thereunder obviously would apply to any fraudulent communication over the Internet, just as they apply to any information communicated on paper, or over the radio or television.

Now, having said all of the above, just what is the Division doing? Like all other prior Division programs, no single method of attack against Internet securities fraud will be sufficient; what is needed is a multifaceted approach.

SURVEILLANCE

With the many changes in technology and markets, surveillance at the Division has always remained in a constant state of flux and revision. Naturally, as the Internet has grown, the Division and other areas of the

98. *See generally* William R. McLucas et al., *Common Sense, Flexibility, and Enforcement of Federal Securities Laws*, 51 Bus. Law. 1221 (1996).
99. 15 U.S.C. § 78j.
100. 17 C.F.R. § 240.10b-5 (1996).

Commission have correspondingly beefed up surveillance activity, assigning staff members to monitor the Internet, especially the Web and message areas like the newsgroups and bulletin boards. The Division has all the necessary commercial online access accounts, employs the latest browsing software for viewing the Internet (such as Netscape and Microsoft Internet Explorer) together with the powerful hardware necessary to do the job right (such as Pentium processors). The Division even has certain designated T1 lines[101] for direct Internet access. The surveillance program has grown sophisticated and detailed, while technological advances allow some automation of surveillance.

It is never wise to tip off the scam artists about methods of surveillance; suffice it to say, the Division will find most of the fraud, wherever it may lie. Of course, given its infinite territory, no program can guarantee to cover every nook and cranny. Unlike traditional thieves, however, Internet grifters typically face a double-edged sword: they want the investor to find their materials with ease but they also want to keep the federal authorities from noticing their activities. They want investors to contact them, but they also want to hide their identities and location. When they surface, which they usually must do sooner or later, the Division's surveillance, or surveillance by others, will detect them.

The Web has also become more organized, as search engines have begun to catalog services, such as investment offerings and Internet exchanges. Even Web pages designed to organize other Web pages have cropped up. Moreover, navigation has also become far simpler and more comprehensive, and will continue to get better in the future.

As with all other securities-related fraud, staff attorneys in the Division are also encouraged to investigate anything they believe to be suspicious, whether during office hours or at home. Whenever confronted with a suspicious offering or other potential securities violation, the Division staff attorney (with the acquiescence of his or her supervisor) can initiate an informal investigation immediately. In fact, staff attorneys are encouraged to keep their eyes and ears open at all times, just like the cop on the beat, whose responsibilities do not disappear while off-duty. Staff attorneys who have no Internet familiarity can receive Internet training at work and patrol the Internet whenever they have the time. The only restriction is that the Division cannot participate in any undercover operations and, before communicating with any potential witness, staff persons must identify themselves, state their principal purpose for the communication, and conform with a range of other important due process requirements.[102] The SEC's staff recently formed the "Cyberforce," a corps of volunteers who

101. T1 lines grant access at 1500 bits per second (more than 50 times faster than the average high-speed modem which transfers only 28.8 bits per second).

102. *See, e.g.*, Privacy Act of 1974, Pub. L. No. 93-579, 88 Stat. 1897 (codified as amended at 5 U.S.C. § 552a (1994)).

"surf" the Web for a few hours each week in search of securities law violations.

AGGRESSIVE INVESTIGATION AND PROSECUTION

As with all Division programs of the past, the most deterring aspect of the Division's program for the Internet lies in the prosecutions the Commission initiates. The prosecution of cases gets the message out to potential transgressors while possibly stopping the fraud *before* victims fall prey and lose their money. In the last two years, the SEC has taken action in several of these cases.

Pleasure Time, Inc.[103]

A complaint filed by the SEC on March 15, 1995, alleged that John C. Hicks and a partner raised more than $3 million by selling securities to approximately 20,000 investors, contacted both on the Internet and over the telephone. Investors were told that they would reap astronomical profits from a worldwide telephone lottery and were encouraged to recruit other investors through the Internet. The complaint alleged that the sales pitch failed to disclose the legal and regulatory obstacles to starting a lottery. The Commission requested a temporary restraining order (TRO), injunctions, and civil penalties against various participants in the scam. On the day the complaint was filed, the court entered the TRO, which included a freezing of assets.[104] Without admitting or denying the allegations, Hicks agreed to repay investors, although the condition was waived due to his inability to pay.[105]

IVT Systems[106]

In July 1995, Chicago-based Donald Spencer began soliciting investors over the Internet for his company, IVT Systems, Inc. Spencer told potential investors that the firm was building an ethanol plant in the Dominican Republic, and promised potential returns of fifty percent or more even though "there was no reasonable basis for this prediction," according to an SEC complaint filed March 29, 1996.[107] Spencer and IVT raised at least $113,500 from twelve investors. The Commission alleged that Spencer's literature contained lies about contracts with well-known companies

103. SEC v. Pleasure Time, Inc., Litigation Release No. 1440, 1995 SEC LEXIS 611 (S.D. Ohio Mar. 15, 1995).

104. *Id.* at *2.

105. SEC v. Pleasure Time, Inc., Litigation Release No. 14,865, 61 S.E.C. Docket (CCH) 969 (S.D. Ohio Feb. 26, 1996).

106. SEC v. Spencer, Litigation Release No. 14,856, 61 S.E.C. Docket (CCH) 1679 (N.D. Ill. Mar. 29, 1996).

107. *Id.*

and omitted other important information from investors. After the SEC filed its complaint, Spencer and IVT consented to an injunction from violating the antifraud provisions of the securities laws.[108]

Scott Frye[109]

In the spring of 1995, Scott Frye posted a notice over the Internet soliciting investors by promising "riskless profits and above-average returns" from investments in two Costa Rican enterprises that produced coconut chips: ICP and the Jupiter Agro Development Project. According to the SEC complaint, Frye misled potential investors by telling them a bank would guarantee their principal and a fifteen percent return in one year, and that one of the companies was a major distributor for A&P Supermarkets.

Gene Block and Renate Haag[110]

Starting in 1994, Renate Haag, of Langen, Germany and Malibu, California, offered investors what seemed like a good deal, through a business she called Haag and Partner. Soon, Gene Block of Durham, North Carolina, operating through Block Consulting Services, and Robert T. Riley, Jr., of St. Louis, Missouri, operating through the Roberts Group, were pitching Haag and Partner investments on the Web as well. They raised over $1 million by promising returns in some cases of 200% to 420% annually, and the promoters told investors their initial investments would be guaranteed against loss because they would be backed by "Prime Bank Guarantees." According to the Commission, however, Prime Bank Guarantees did not, in fact, exist. The court granted a TRO against Block and froze his assets; similar penalties were issued against the other defendants.[111]

Daniel Odulo[112]

In August 1995, the SEC filed a complaint against Daniel Odulo who solicited investors over several newsgroups of the Internet, including

108. SEC v. Spencer, Litigation Release No. 15,042, 62 S.E.C. Docket (CCH) 2271 (N.D. Ill. Sept. 12, 1996).

109. SEC v. Frye, Litigation Release No. 14,720, 60 S.E.C. Docket (CCH) 1787 (S.D.N.Y. Nov. 15, 1995).

110. SEC v. Block, Litigation Release No. 14,828, 61 S.E.C. Docket (CCH) 971 (D. Mass. Feb. 27, 1996); SEC v. Block, Litigation Release No. 14,804, 61 S.E.C. Docket (CCH) 579 (D. Mass. Jan. 30, 1996); SEC v. Block, Litigation Release No. 14,711, 60 S.E.C. Docket (CCH) 1608 (D. Mass. Nov. 2, 1995); SEC v. Block, Litigation Release No. 14,598, 59 S.E.C. Docket (CCH) 2543 (D. Mass. Aug. 10, 1995).

111. *Block*, 61 S.E.C. Docket (CCH) at 971.

112. SEC v. Odulo, Litigation Release No. 14,616, 1995 WL 505138 (S.E.C.) (D.R.I. Aug. 24, 1995); SEC v. Odulo, Litigation Release No. 14,591, 59 S.E.C. Docket (CCH) 2538 (D.R.I. Aug. 7, 1995).

"misc.invest" and "alt.make.money.fast." Odulo offered for sale bonds meant to raise money for a company called Golden Waters which he claimed would yield a "whopping 20% rate of return" for a very low risk.[113] Odulo also assured potential investors that they would be insured against potential losses, even though there was no such insurance, and made up the names of investment advisers who vouched for the bonds. According to the SEC complaint, Odulo failed to disclose that Golden Waters was a proposed new venture involving the acquisition and raising of eels and that he had no expertise in the culturing of eels. Moreover, the solicitation included several glowing endorsements from fabricated persons and entities. Odulo consented to an injunction from further violations of the securities laws but a monetary penalty was waived because of Odulo's financial condition.[114]

Octagon Technology Group, Inc., Michael J. Tidd, and Jeffrey L. Punzel[115]

In June 1996, the SEC sued Octagon Technology Group, Inc. (Octagon), a Schaumburg, Illinois, computer software company and two of its former officers for their roles in creating an elaborate sham offering of offshore debt securities on the Web. The Web site, established for the Agency for Interamerican Finance (AIF), a Panamanian shell subsidiary of Octagon, advertised AIF "Interamerican hard currency bonds" for sale to investors. The Commission alleged that this offering was essentially a fraud because no bonds ever existed, and AIF had no business operations or assets. AIF's Web pages, however, promised prospective investors a risk-free investment with guaranteed returns of 11.75% annually and portrayed AIF as a successful provider of investment capital to Latin American businesses. With the filing of the complaint, Octagon and its officers consented to an injunction against future violations of the antifraud provisions of the securities laws, and one officer paid a $5000 penalty.[116]

Octagon represents a good example of how small-time scam artists can paint a picture of a sophisticated and professional company and investment package by using a glittery Web page with the right bells and whistles. The AIF Web pages claimed that an entity known as Group American Pacific Financial, Ltd., S.A. (APF), a purported independent trust company, guaranteed principal and interest payments on the bonds up to $250,000 per investor. In fact, APF was another Panamanian shell subsidiary of Octagon which lacked assets or business operations. The AIF Web pages also included a facsimile reproduction of a *World Financial Report* magazine article

113. *Odulo*, 59 S.E.C. Docket (CCH) at 2538.
114. *Id.*
115. SEC v. Octagon Tech. Group, Inc., Litigation Release No. 14,942, 62 S.E.C. Docket (CCH) 380 (D.D.C. June 11, 1996).
116. *Id.*

touting the investment quality of the AIF bonds, the operations of AIF, and the quality of management. In fact, *World Financial Report* was nothing more than a fabrication of Octagon and its officers.

Obviously done to bolster their legitimacy, the AIF Web pages even mixed in legitimate publications with their investment puffery, such as a link to a *Business Week* article concerning online investing. The Web pages also incorporated resplendent graphic and multilingual voice components, and gave potential investors the ability to download directly to their computers, in one of multiple computer formats, all forms (in one of four languages) necessary to make an investment in AIF bonds. Octagon officers also used some of the more popular Internet newsgroups, such as "misc.invest," "misc.invest.stocks," and "misc.invest.funds," to advertise the brummagem and link potential investors to the Web pages.

There is no doubt that, as the interactive technology of the Web has increased, as access to newsgroups and links becomes faster and cheaper (it already costs nothing to add a link to a site or publish a posting in a newsgroup), and as software continues to eliminate the need for programming skills, lawbreakers like the Octagon Group can create the façade of a Fortune 500 company at little cost and with surprisingly very little effort.

William B. Sellin, Zaitech Holdings, Inc., and Baccaratt Holdings, Inc.[117]

Since October 1995, according to the SEC, William B. Sellin, a convicted felon and repeat securities law violator, had been conducting an ongoing, fraudulent offering of securities through newsgroup and bulletin board postings on the Internet, and through advertisements placed on CompuServe. Sellin solicited investments through at least forty-three advertisements in at least twenty-one Internet newsgroups. Sellin, through Zaitech and Baccaratt, offered promissory notes which he claimed were secured and collateralized by U.S. government securities and other assets. Sellin represented that he could deliver "guaranteed" annual returns ranging from twelve percent to twenty-two percent and announced that an investor could earn "$150,000 annually, tax free."[118] The Commission believed that these representations were false and misleading because (i) the investment, in fact, was not secured or collateralized by U.S. government securities; (ii) Sellin failed to disclose his long criminal record of regulatory sanctions and criminal convictions, including a Florida felony conviction for grand larceny; and (iii) Sellin failed to disclose the material risks associated with the investment. Given that the Internet provided Sellin "with direct access to millions of prospective investors worldwide with great speed and ease, minimal expense, and virtual anonymity," on July

117. SEC v. Sellin, Litigation Release No. 15,012, 62 S.E.C. Docket (CCH) 1603 (S.D. Fla. Aug. 12, 1996).

118. *Id.*

25, 1996, the U.S. District Court for the Southern District of Florida granted a TRO prohibiting the defendants from violating the antifraud provisions of the federal securities laws, froze the defendants' assets, and ordered the defendants to preserve records and account for proceeds received from their fraudulent scheme.[119] On August 12, 1996, the defendants consented to a permanent injunction from violating the antifraud provisions of the securities laws.[120]

Wye Resources, Inc. and Rehan Malik[121]

On September 26, 1996, the SEC filed a complaint against Wye Resources, Inc. (Wye) and Malik alleging that, during 1993 and early 1994, Wye and Malik engaged in a fraudulent promotional campaign targeted towards U.S. investors and improperly distributed Wye stock to those investors. Wye, a Canadian corporation headquartered in Toronto, Ontario, claimed to own interests in various gold and diamond mining properties. Malik, a resident of Labrador City, Newfoundland, served as Wye's president from June 24, 1993 through March 25, 1994. The SEC's complaint alleged that Wye and Malik engaged in a scheme to distribute approximately 5.3 million shares of Wye stock that were not properly issued under Canadian law nor properly registered with the Commission. According to the complaint, Wye directly distributed approximately 2.5 million of these improperly issued shares to U.S. investors. As of February 1, 1994, approximately four million shares, representing 28.9% of the Wye stock then outstanding, were held by U.S. investors. The complaint alleged that Wye and Malik specifically targeted U.S. investors by advertising in U.S. publications and posting Internet messages through "Emerging Growth Stock BBS," a New Orleans-based BBS. The Commission also alleged that certain of these advertisements and messages were false and misleading because they misrepresented, among other things, the status of Wye's ongoing exploitation of certain Zairian mining properties. For example, beginning in March 1993, prior to the time that Malik became Wye's president, Wye falsely claimed that it had successfully completed a sampling program during which it recovered ten gem-quality diamonds from its Zairian concessions. In reality, Wye's contractors had not set foot on the concessions themselves and purchased the diamonds from Zairian vendors located elsewhere. The SEC's complaint sought a permanent injunction against Wye and Malik for violations of section 5 of the Securities Act, and section 10(b) and Rule 10b-5 of the Exchange Act. The complaint also sought civil penalties against Malik. Simultaneously, the SEC announced the institution of administrative proceedings against two U.S. residents, Murray

119. *Id.*
120. *Id.*
121. SEC v. Wye Resources, Inc., Litigation Release No. 15,073, 62 S.E.C. Docket (CCH) 2533 (D.D.C. Sept. 26, 1996).

Aaron Huberfeld and Broad Capital Associates, Inc. (Broad Capital), in connection with the unregistered distribution of Wye securities. Both defendants consented to the issuance of an order finding they had violated section 5 of the Securities Act. Additionally, the order required them to disgorge their Wye stock profits totalling $426,790.05, and prejudgment interest thereon. [122]

Western Executive Group, Cash Systems USA, Inc., Charles R. Rietz, Robert R. Parrish, Robert J. Struth, and R. Stephen Edgel[123]

On October 7, 1996, the U.S. District Court for the Central District of California entered a TRO halting an alleged Ponzi scheme involving investment contracts for the sale and leaseback of automated teller machines (ATMs).[124] The defendants solicited investments in the ATM program over the Internet and raised over $3.49 million from at least 132 investors nationwide. This was the first SEC lawsuit involving ATMs and the largest lawsuit involving Internet investment fraud brought by the Commission to date. The SEC alleged that the defendants operated the Ponzi scheme from at least September 1995, when they began offering and selling investments in the ATM program. Investors simultaneously executed agreements with Western Executive Group (WEG) and Cash Systems USA, Inc. (Cash Systems) to purchase ATMs from WEG and immediately lease them back to Cash Systems. Investors were guaranteed monthly lease payments for five years, representing a 100% return of the investors' principal and an annual yield of 17.4%. As of July 1996, however, forty-two of the total 195 ATMs sold were operational and only two of the forty-two ATMs were profitable. Consequently, the defendants were using new investor funds to meet the monthly lease obligations to existing investors. The complaint also alleged that the defendants solicited investors nationwide over the Internet and through private investment seminars, mass mailings, and cold calling, and that the defendants provided investors with offering materials that misrepresented the number of ATMs operating and the financial returns the ATMs could produce.

Charles S. Huttoe[125]

Although the SEC has brought several cases in which the issuer involved experienced a lot of "Usenet hype," the most definitive case to date is *SEC*

122. *In re* Broad Capital Assocs., Inc., Securities Act Release No. 7338, 62 S.E.C. Docket (CCH) 2430 (Sept. 26, 1996).

123. SEC v. Western Executive Group, Inc., Litigation Release No. 15,106, 62 S.E.C. Docket (CCH) 2636 (C.D. Cal. Oct. 3, 1996); *see also* SEC v. Western Executive Group, Inc., Litigation Release No. 15,139, 63 S.E.C. Docket (CCH) 191 (C.D. Cal. Oct. 23, 1996); SEC v. Western Executive Group, Inc., Litigation Release No. 15,121, 63 S.E.C. Docket (CCH) 89 (C.D. Cal. Oct. 15, 1996).

124. *Western Executive Group, Inc.*, 63 S.E.C. Docket (CCH) at 89.

125. SEC v. Huttoe, Litigation Release No. 15,153, 63 S.E.C. Docket (CCH) 427 (D.D.C. Nov. 7, 1996).

v. Charles O. Huttoe. On November 7, 1996, the U.S. District Court for the District of Columbia entered a TRO and other emergency relief to stop, according to the Commission, a massive and ongoing market manipulation of SOE stock. SOE was a manufacturer and distributor of video teleconferencing equipment with offices in Virginia and Florida.[126]

The Commission alleged that Huttoe, SOE's Chairman of the Board and CEO, secretly distributed millions of SOE shares to family members and corporations, manipulated the market by issuing false information concerning SOE and its business, and then sold his own shares into the inflated market. As the first part of that scheme, Huttoe executed an unregistered distribution of tens of millions of shares of SOE stock by causing false Form S-8 registration statements to be submitted to SOE's transfer agent. The Commission further alleged that Huttoe secretly issued millions of those unregistered, but unrestricted and free trading, SOE shares to various Huttoe family members and entities that served as Huttoe's nominees, including Word Corporation and NTSI, and his wife, mother, and niece.

As the second step in the scheme, the Commission alleged that Huttoe artificially inflated the price of SOE shares by issuing a series of materially false and misleading press releases. Among other things, the releases announced nonexistent multimillion dollar sales of SOE products, an acquisition that had not occurred, and false revenue projections for SOE. The Commission further alleged that Huttoe caused SOE to fail to file required periodic reports, filed false periodic reports, and bribed SGA with stock to recommend SOE to subscribers of SGA's electronically disseminated tout sheet.[127] Additionally, the Commission alleged that Huttoe caused unregistered but free trading shares to be issued to Melcher and Terry, the principals of SGA.[128]

As the third step in the scheme, Huttoe, Melcher, and Terry took advantage of the inflated market for SOE stock, which they had created, by dumping their own SOE stock on unwitting investors. The Commission alleged that those sales were timed to take advantage of the false press releases concerning SOE. Indeed, such sales were heaviest when the price of SOE stock reached its peak in June 1996. As a result of this scheme, the defendants allegedly obtained illegal proceeds of more than $10 million. Throughout all the steps of the schemes, the Commission alleged that the defendants used the Internet as a means of manipulation; during the alleged scam, postings concerning SOE in Internet message areas totaled higher than 10,000.[129]

126. *Id.*
127. *Id.*
128. *Id.*
129. On January 31, 1997, Huttoe was sentenced to a federal prison term of forty-six months, followed by two years supervised release and a $10,000 fine, for one count of securities fraud and one count of money laundering in connection with the scheme. Huttoe

George Chelekis, KGC, Inc., and Hot Stocks Review, Inc.[130]

On February 25, 1997, the Commission filed a complaint in the U.S. District Court for the District of Columbia against George Chelekis (Chelekis), KGC, Inc., and Hot Stocks Review, Inc. The complaint alleged that from at least January 1995 through August 1995, Chelekis, a publisher who distributes various investment newsletters, known as the "Hot Stocks" publications, over the Internet and in print format, knowingly or recklessly made materially false and misleading statements concerning six publicly traded companies. The complaint further alleged that from April 1994 through September 1995, Chelekis failed to disclose in the Hot Stocks publications that he, and entities under his control, defendants KGC, Inc. and Hot Stocks Review, Inc., received at least $1.1 million from more than 150 issuers and 275,000 shares of stock from ten issuers, as payment for recommending securities of such issuers in the Hot Stocks publications. Without admitting or denying the allegations in the complaint, Chelekis, KGC, Inc., and Hot Stocks Review, Inc., consented to the entry of a final judgment permanently enjoining them from violating section 10(b) of the Exchange Act and Rule 10b-5 thereunder, and section 17(b) of the Securities Act.[131] The final judgment ordered the defendants to pay a total of $162,727, representing $75,050 in disgorgement, $12,627 in prejudgment interest and a $75,050 civil penalty.[132]

SELF-POLICING

Historically, self-policing has always served as an important part of every Division program, not merely because it encourages responsibility and ethical behavior amongst Wall Street participants, but also because it serves as yet another useful tool for patrolling an increasingly large and complicated marketplace. In line with these traditions, self-policing in the context of Internet-related securities fraud has proven a valuable resource for help in discovering miscreant securities-related conduct over the Internet.

There exists a remarkable Internet culture of self-policing by individual users who resent the intrusion of the crooks and thieves trying to exploit the Internet. The Division hopes to tap into this culture, encouraging users to report dubious offerings on the Web or suspicious postings on the many Usenet groups and BBSs via the "Enforcement Complaint Center." The Enforcement Complaint Center, which opened on June 14, 1996, now

had entered into a sealed plea agreement with the federal government on November 13, 1996. SEC v. Huttoe, Litigation Release No. 15,237, 63 S.E.C. Docket (CCH) 2061 (D.D.C. Jan. 31, 1997).

130. SEC v. Chelekis, Litigation Release No. 15,264, 63 S.E.C. Docket (CCH) 2489 (D.D.C. Feb. 25, 1997).

131. *Id.*

132. *Id.*

allows users to contact the Division directly through the Internet. The center, located as a link on the SEC home page,[133] allows users to communicate with the Division either by email or by submitting an "Enforcement Complaint Form." The center also offers other means of communications, including snailmail,[134] fax, an Internet fraud hotline, and a toll-free number.

The Enforcement Complaint Center has thus far resulted in a vast supply of leads for investigations and referrals, while also keeping the Division apprised of the latest trends and modus operandi of online riffraff. The center typically receives between thirty and forty messages per day (including weekends). More than seventy-five percent of these complaints are useful for investigations or referrals. Moreover, the content and quality of the complaints continues to demonstrate the sophistication of users, and their burning desire to protect and maintain the integrity of the Internet.

Not only do users typically include the relevant names, addresses, phone numbers, and other pertinent information concerning the persons and entities involved, the complainants usually have undertaken some cybersleuthing of their own (using all the latest available Internet tools). Typically, the center receives complaints concerning Internet fraud, although it invites reports of all types of securities fraud. Most complaints contain descriptions of the relevant Web sites, attachments of related materials, and even include the most important and otherwise unknown details, such as a deciphering of the header of a suspicious posting or email. Some complaints even provide a full legal analysis of potential securities violations, including cites to legal authority.

EDUCATION

A critical aspect of every Division program has always been education. The best defense to any securities scam is an informed and wary investing public. This means more than merely harping on the old adage that if an offer sounds too good to be true it probably is. The Division must work with the investing community and alert potential victims to the types of investment fraud occurring over the Internet.

In this regard, the Office of Investor Education and Assistance, with input from the Division, has published an extremely useful Investor Alert which contains an analysis and discussion of the types of online investment fraud and abuse together with suggestions for investors on how to avoid becoming the next victim. The alert even provides a checklist of steps to follow before making an investment over the Internet, as well as a list of

133. U.S. Securities & Exchange Commission, *SEC Division of Enforcement Complaint Center* (last modified Oct. 25, 1996) <http://www.sec.gov/enforce/comctr.htm>.

134. "Snailmail" refers to the U.S. Postal Service mail delivery system and is meant to imply the greater speed and convenience of email over postal mail. DERN, *supra* note 2, at 196-98.

questions to ask about any investment opportunity, particularly an opportunity offered in cyberspace.

A variety of other useful publications and information remain available on the SEC Web site, while the Division's litigation releases (as well as a search engine dedicated to the site) are contained on the Division's Web page. The Division will also consider publishing various alerts and litigation releases on various BBSs, including the more popular investment related newsgroups and message boards.[135]

The SEC also recently began posting relevant SEC information on Internet forums (such as commercial online providers, Internet forum areas, and newsgroups) where such information might help investors of a specific security. For instance, in the recent trading suspension of Omnigene Diagnostics, Inc., the SEC posted the press release concerning the trading suspensions and a copy of the actual suspension order in a stock forum on AOL dedicated to discussions concerning Omnigene.[136]

LIAISON WORK

Given the breadth of illicit activities on the Internet, jurisdictional crossover happens at every turn. Securities violations, in particular, are often also federal and state criminal fraud violations, Federal Trade Commission (FTC) violations, and Federal Communications Commission (FCC) violations, as well as violations of a host of local, state, and federal criminal and civil statutes, rules, and regulations.

Historically, the Division has succeeded in coordinating its efforts with nearly every existing law enforcement authority. The Division's policing of the Internet will follow a similar path of cooperation, joint action, and teamwork. In the context of its Internet program, the Division's informal and formal liaison work includes operations with the FTC, the U.S. Department of Justice and the Federal Bureau of Investigation, the FCC, and a range of other civil and criminal law enforcement authorities. In December 1996, the SEC teamed up with three other federal agencies and seventy state and local law enforcement officials from twenty-four states on "Surf Day," which resulted in the identification of more than 500 possible Internet scams.

The Division also works especially close with self-regulatory organizations, such as the New York Stock Exchange and the National Association

135. Such postings may not be necessary, however, given the persistent self-policing carried out by Internet users. For example, without asking users to do so, some have taken it upon themselves actually to attach a copy of the Cyberfraud Investor Alert to the bottom of postings that they deem suspicious. Thus, anyone reading the debatable posting will also read the SEC's investor alert.

136. *See* Omnigene Diagnostics, Inc., Exchange Act Release No. 37966, 63 S.E.C. Docket (CCH) 565 (Nov. 20, 1996); *see also* U.S. Sec. & Exch. Comm'n, *SEC Notice from AOL: OmniGene* (visited Jan. 27, 1997) <www.sec.gov/news/extra/omnigaol.htm>.

of Securities Dealers, Inc., as well as state regulatory authorities such as the North American Securities Administrators Association. The Enforcement Complaint Center also facilitates cooperative efforts with some of the more attenuated law enforcement entities that might not have developed any prior relationship with the SEC and simply want to forward certain information to the Division without having to create any new bureaucratic communications lines. The SEC will continue such liaison work and concentrate on working jointly to counter unlawful Internet activity, whether in the form of securities fraud or otherwise.

"IT'S BEGINNING TO LOOK LIKE YOU GOT THINGS FIXED SO I CAN'T NEVER WIN OUT. INSIDE, OUTSIDE, ALL THEM RULES AND REGULATIONS AND BOSSES . . . JUST WHERE AM I SUPPOSED TO FIT IN . . . WHAT DO I DO NOW . . . I GUESS I GOTTA FIND MY OWN WAY."

As the SEC addresses the excitement and challenge of the Internet, so moves the Division to find its own way as it undertakes to reconcile its mission with this exciting and futuristic medium of communication. The constant state of flux of Internet communications will continue to create fantastic opportunities for individual investors while also creating a formidable task for the Division to police this newly sprung turf. The synergy created by the joining of the Internet with global capital markets creates an ever-changing and developing investment emporium which has not only changed the way the players think but also the way the scofflaws think. Above all, the Division must position itself to respond quickly to the concerns of the investing public while also considering the mores of the Internet community.

Part of the difficulty that the Division (and other law enforcement officials) will have with policing securities violations on the Internet is the expansive interpretation of "free speech" principles applied to online communications by the leaders of the virtual community. Not only do users expect anonymity but they also expect to control whatever they transmit. The Internet's informal, uncensored, decentralized regulation, and often presumed-anonymous environment, encourages casual interaction among users, and something like a Wild West mentality among the critics and philosophers who give the medium its ideological direction.[137]

Coupled with an almost libertarian strain of antigovernmental sentiment that accompanies many of the major writings on the Internet, it is not hard to imagine that assertions of regulatory authority by the SEC and other agencies may face vigorous public opposition similar to what

137. ALLISON, *supra* note 34, at ix.

congressional supporters of the Exon-Coats bill[138] (regulating Internet communications) recently observed when they were flooded with email from online free speech advocates. Some users on the Internet's radical fringe even believe cyberspace to be 100% free-terrain, immune from all laws of geographically-bounded countries.

Hence, although neither the First Amendment, nor any other law on the books, confers the right to commit fraud,[139] the free speech concerns of Internet users will require the Division to be as active in informing and molding public opinion as it will be in winning favorable judicial precedent. The Division, through its Internet program, must show its support for, and even facilitate the functioning of, Internet self-regulation by augmenting the flow of investor information. Internet financial newsgroup users pride themselves on the ability to discern and publicly debunk, or "flame,"[140] phony securities offerings or illicit hype, and, until the freedom issues inherent in Internet speech are definitively worked out, the Division can aid the dialogue of online investors by publicizing the availability of its own online information sources and offering advice on how to discern Internet frauds.

Resource allocation for policing the Internet will also unquestionably increase in the future. In deploying its resources, the Division must consider the number of people who are potential targets of frauds over the Internet. Perhaps the staff could ignore a scam in the past when the offeror had only solicited a few people at a seminar or by mail; perhaps the staff would not view the offer as enough of a potential threat to the public to warrant a specific allocation of resources. Could the staff, however, ignore the very same offering if it was made at a seminar for 100 million?

The Division now has a strategy and an operation in place to address Internet securities fraud and remains armed and ready for the coming of the next millennium. Rather than simply reiterating the common themes among law enforcement agencies, the magnitude of Internet fraud and the financial restraints that prevent federal agencies from effectively policing the Internet, the Division is acting now and is using currently available

138. Communications Decency Act of 1996, Pub. L. No. 104-104, §§ 501-561, 110 Stat. 56 (to be codified in scattered sections of 47 U.S.C.).

139. "Liberty, declared Tom Paine, should never be mistaken for license. It is too precious a prize to be degraded by those who accept no obligation to others in the exercise of their freedoms." *The Pedlars of Child Abuse: We Know Who They Are; Yet No One Is Stopping Them*, GUARDIAN, Aug. 25, 1996, at 1.

140. The *ILC Glossary of Internet Terms* describes the evolution of the meaning of "flame":

> Originally, flame meant to carry forth in a passionate manner in the spirit of honorable debate. Flames most often involved the use of flowery language and flaming well was an art form. More recently flame has come to refer to any kind of derogatory comment no matter how witless or crude.

Internet Literacy Consultants, *ILC Glossary of Internet Terms*, at 6-7 (last modified Mar. 18, 1997) <http://workshop.matisse.net/files/glossary.html>.

resources. Rather than reacting to a future crisis, the Division has proactively initiated its program.

The Commission as a whole owes a duty to the public to use existing enforcement weapons to frustrate and deter any new developments in securities fraud. In the Commission's favor, the statutory tools are already in place and the SEC has an eager and vigorous staff, many of whom welcome the opportunity to incorporate the world of the Internet into their professional and not just their personal lives. The SEC now need only adapt the existing laws to meet the growing number of violations in the continually evolving Internet medium.

The realities of a static agency budget, a laissez-faire Congress, and an electorate exhibiting a rising antigovernment sentiment dictate that the Division's approach, while calculated and intelligent, should be cost-effective, education-oriented, and expansive in its appeal to the computer industry. The present Internet program, given its inherent flexibility, together with its multifaceted approach of emphasizing surveillance, prosecution, education, and coalition-building, provides a sound basis to battle securities crimes committed over the Internet. Most of all, the Division's Internet program is not a foray into a new regulatory area and does not damage the basic core of the enforcement program; rather, the program remains consistent with the Commission's overall commitment to fair markets for all investors.

Despite its great potential to benefit the public, especially the investor, the Internet will prove an irresistible target for con artists. By initiating a program for the Internet with fairness, vigilance, and agility, the Division will discourage perpetrators of Internet fraud before they find their niche and insure that the eagle remains on the street, even when that street is in cyberspace.

NOTES

12

TOMBSTONES: THE INTERNET'S IMPACT UPON SEC RULES OF ENGAGEMENT (INSIGHTS, FEBRUARY 1998)

John Reed Stark

This article previously appeared in INSIGHTS, Volume 12, Number 2, February 1998.

INSIGHTS

THE CORPORATE & SECURITIES LAW ADVISOR

Volume 12, Number 2, February 1998 Copyright © 1998 Aspen Law & Business

Year 2000: Disclosing the Risks to Markets and Firms

Page 4

VIVIAN A. MAESE of Salomon Smith Barney Holdings, Inc. and **MICHAEL D. MANN** and **DONNA I. DENNIS** of Richards Spears Kibbe & Orbe discuss the Year 2000 problem and offer suggestions to assist corporate counsel and other concerned parties in identifying and reducing the substantial business, regulatory, and litigation risks that it poses.

The Internet's Impact upon SEC Rules Of Engagement

Page 10

JOHN REED STARK of the SEC Division of Enforcement explores how the Internet has transformed the SEC enforcement program, not only changing what it enforces, but also how it does so.

Executive Compensation Practices May Limit Change of Control Severance Benefits

Page 15

MICHAEL KATZKE of Wachtell, Lipton, Rosen & Katz examines the impact that executive compensation arrangements may have on the ability of employees to receive full severance benefits following a change in control.

DEPARTMENTS

A Tribute

STATE CORNER

Earnings $ Share

Client Memos

SECURITIES ENFORCEMENT

Tombstones: The Internet's Impact Upon SEC Rules of Engagement

The SEC enforcement program has always evolved to address the ever-changing dynamics of domestic and global financial markets, and leaving a few tombstones behind is really nothing new. Yet, the enforcement division has never before experienced such a rapid and extreme transformation as the one initiated by the Internet. This article discusses five illustrations of how the Internet has transfigured SEC enforcement's rules of engagement, not only changing what to enforce but also changing how to enforce.

By John Reed Stark

Here Lies Lester Moore, Shot 4 Times With a 44, No Les, No More.

Interment is never an easy subject to discuss and does not typically fall within the jurisdiction of the Division of Enforcement of the United States Securities and Exchange Commission (SEC). But with the onslaught of the Internet, old concepts and notions of the traditional SEC enforcement paradigm continue to sound their own death knell, leaving only tombstones to mark their passage. As the Internet chisels the epitaphs on these tombstones, newborn principles and postulates infuse themselves into the SEC enforcement program.

The five illustrations that follow demonstrate that the Internet continues to change the playing field, requiring the SEC enforcement division to modify its *modus operandi* and flex its regulatory muscle, to combat this nascent and potentially dangerous threat to investors.[1]

I'm your Huckleberry and that's just my game.

The New Cyber Boiler-Rooms

Consider the fictional owner of an imaginary company called PhenomX, a manufacturer of a purported cure for cancer. To date, PhenomX has not sold any products, has not hired any employees, has not generated any income from operations, has only nominal assets, and has just begun to be quoted on the OTC Bulletin Board. PhenomX has just submitted its application for FDA approval of its sole drug, which PhenomX's president knows the FDA will reject; he knows this because the drug is merely coffee grinds in tablet form.

PhenomX's president, his family members and a few friends own all the ten million shares outstanding. The president, a recidivist scam artist, wants to pump up the price of PhenomX fraudulently, and sell his shares at the artificially inflated price. The president has only limited resources to set up a boiler room or to fund any other network of fraudsters; all he has is a little capital, a home computer, some Internet-related software, and Internet access. Unfortunately, that is all he needs. At almost no cost, the president can conduct an international and sophisticated market manipulation over the Internet from his own living room. All PhenomX's president must do is to take the four following steps:

Step 1: The Phony Web Page

The first step for PhenomX's president is to set up a central location on the Internet where potential investors can find out about PhenomX's miracle drug, in an interactive and user-friendly environment. On the World Wide Web space allocated to him for free by his Internet access provider, the president builds a flashy and elaborate PhenomX Home page.

The page presents a wide range of bogus enthusiastic reports about PhenomX, including a phony set of

John Reed Stark is special counsel for Internet Projects in the Division of Enforcement of the United States Securities and Exchange Commission (SEC) and is in charge of the Division's Internet Program. He is also an adjunct professor of law at Georgetown University Law Center where he teaches a course on the Internet and the Securities Laws. The SEC as a matter of policy disclaims any responsibility for any private publication or speech by any of its members or staff. The views expressed herein are those of the author and do not necessarily reflect the views of the SEC or the author's colleagues on the staff of the SEC. All quotes in the section headings of this article, including the Epitaph (found at Boot Hill Graveyard in Tombstone, Ariz.), are from the film *Tombstone* (Hollywood Pictures Corporation, 1993), produced by James Jacks, Sean Daniel and Bob Misiorowski, directed by George Cosmatos and starring Val Kilmer and Kurt Russell as the famed Doc Holiday and Wyatt Earp.

financial statements inflating the value of the potential PhenomX drug's patent and documents bearing the FDA seal with the actual names of FDA staff members asserting imminent FDA approval for the PhenomX drug. Despite the president's lack of experience with computer programming, he easily constructs the page with a simple Web page development software package downloaded free of charge from the Internet.

The page incorporates graphics, sound and video, all obtained for free from the Internet. The page even features a direct "video stream" that allows users to watch live action of PhenomX scientists hard at work (the video is a phony though users cannot tell the difference). In addition, the page contains all the information necessary for the purchase of PhenomX shares, a chat area for "real-time" talk about PhenomX, and a bulletin board allowing users to post messages.

Step 2: Spam, Spam, and Spam

The second step is to use email, via a bulk-email or a spamming[2] program, to contact as many potential investors as possible, about the fantastic investment opportunity that PhenomX represents. The PhenomX president employs a "mining" or "extractor" program that automatically collects email addresses from all over the Internet. He also spends some time personally gathering email addresses from the investment-related bulletin board systems, cyber message areas, newsgroups and the various Web discussion forums dedicated to speculative investing and unlisted securities. The president is relentless in developing an extensive email list of potential victims.

The president even collects a list of over 50,000 email addresses from sites dedicated to discussing Comparator Systems Corp. and Systems of Excellence, two of the most notorious stock manipulations involving the Internet—both companies the subjects of tens of thousands of Internet postings feverishly hyping their respective stocks.[3] The president reasons that if these people bought shares of Comparator and Systems of Excellence, they might purchase shares of PhenomX.

The president drafts a personalized note to explain that PhenomX represents an exceptional buying opportunity and is poised to skyrocket in price. On the note is a hyper-link to the PhenomX Web Site and a hyper-link to the page with all the necessary purchasing information. Next, with the click of a mouse, the president beams his personalized note to his private list of hundreds of thousands (even millions) of potential victims.

For still greater distribution, the president hires a bulk emailer, an entity that contracts to do mass mailings for a fee (typically about $100 per month) to send the email to several million more potential victims. Cybermailers boast that for every hundred emails sent out, seven responses result. This massive global solicitation is no longer a matter of opening up the white pages of the phone book and dialing every number— this is a customized mailing list of potential victims never before available to the average con artist.

Step 3: Begin the Buzz

Now PhenomX's president needs to create a "buzz" on the Internet about PhenomX. The president utilizes several means to accomplish this goal. The president smothers Internet forums with his spam (or some other marketing materials), by posting it to newsgroups and Web discussion areas dedicated to investing.

The president also creates discussion forums dedicated to talking about PhenomX while also posting his spam to discussion forums pertaining to other speculative securities, the whole time hoping to snare a few victims into purchasing PhenomX stock. The president responds to his own postings under various user names to create the illusion that people are having a discussion, when in reality it is just the president posting back and forth to himself, spreading more false information about "PhenomX."

Step 4: Tout or Bribe a Touter

The fourth and final step makes the buzz more sophisticated by employing an Internet investment newsletter. There are two options: the PhenomX president may personally construct his own Internet investment newsletter to recommend PhenomX, or, instead, bribe an unscrupulous online investment newsletter to feature PhenomX as the "pick of the month" or some other sham promotion.

To build a personal online investment newsletter, he simply chooses a catchy name, uses the same Web page building software employed for the PhenomX Web site, and beams the newsletter out (or a spam with a link to the newsletter) to the same list used for the PhenomX spam. The president posts the Internet address of the investment newsletter in various investment newsgroups and other online discussion forums that relate to investing. The newsletter, provided free of charge, even picks a few recent winners in the market and boasts that these stocks were prior newsletter picks.[4]

There it is–four easy steps to a successful "pump and dump" scheme, courtesy of the Internet. Don't doubt this four-step scenario. Record numbers of individuals now own securities, and expect to receive double (and sometimes triple) digit returns on stock investments. Hordes of neophyte investors have jumped head first into the stock market, experienced the boom of the past few years, and are hungry for more. This phenomenon exacerbates susceptibility to online fraud schemes like the one promulgated by the fictional PhenomX company, and marks this new crop of investors as potential targets for investment fraud.

Are you gonna do something or just stand there and bleed?

The New Offshore Cyber Fraud

There was a time when the offshore orchestration of a fraud upon U.S. investors, unless targeted towards the wealthy, was almost cost-prohibitive. Consider the operation of an offshore boiler-room selling a fraudulent investment opportunity. A boiler-room depends on two important elements for its success: first, the ability to contact a large number of potential investors and, second, the wherewithal to make the sale to the potential victim before the victim has time to deliberate about the investment. Conflicting time zones, differing currencies and most of all, the sheer costs of long distance telephone calls, overnight mailings and other communication–related expenses all contribute to hindering offshore fraudsters from preying on U.S. individual investors.

The Internet has, of course, changed all this. With the rapidly diminishing costs of Internet access, computer hardware and Internet-related software, a fraud emanating from the most remote emerging capital market costs about the same as one that emanates from the house next door, perhaps even less. International con artists can use Web pages, email, newsgroups, discussion forums and chatrooms just as easily as anyone within the United States. The obstacles created by differing time zones and other traditional notions of borders disappear when it comes to the Internet, and soon, universal digital legal tender may even reduce the problems caused by different currencies.

Internet offshore fraud may become the single greatest threat to U.S. investors. It raises a myriad of complex issues and forces U.S. law enforcement to rethink traditional notions of jurisdiction and sovereignty. When considering an Internet fraud that involves a foreign jurisdiction, the enforcement division must address issues associated with investigating and prosecuting foreign entities and individuals, from serving subpoenas and criminal duality to locating assets and extradition.

What an ugly thing to say.

The New Cyber-Defamation (of Character and Corporation)

Spurious rumor-mongering has always pervaded Wall Street, whether done for the purposes of market manipulation or just for spite. Historically though, the rumor mongers were usually limited in the numbers of individuals they could reach. Now, with the availability of the Internet, spreading negative publicity about a company or an individual has never been easier. Instantaneously, efficiently, and at very little cost, individuals can use the Internet to cast dispersions upon the most reputable of companies and individuals, reaching millions.

The Internet has become saturated with negative deceptive information about companies and their employees. The nefarious short-seller uses the Internet to spread false information pertaining to a publicly traded company and the treacherous promoter uses the Internet to advance false scuttlebutt about competitors. Of course, many of these rumors and ramblings published on the Internet strain credulity, and are simply ignored by users, but the accuracy of some information is more difficult to discern, even when employing the highest level of skepticism.

No subject is sacred, even SEC activities. In some Internet discussion forums, for example, users gossip about an SEC investigation when no such investigation exists. Hopefully, most individuals do not believe a false rumor about an SEC investigation in such instances, particularly when the company or individual loudly and flatly denies the existence of the investigation.

But what if the company or individual cannot make such a representation – because, in fact, an investigation does exist. While pending, members of the public inevitably learn some information pertaining to an SEC investigation, typically from witnesses asked (or subpoenaed) to testify or produce documents pursuant to that investigation.[5] Although an SEC investigation is not meant to be an indication by the Commission or its staff that any violations of law have occurred, or a reflection upon any person, entity or security, public dissemination about an SEC investigation can still damage the reputation of an individual and a company (even impacting the company's stock price). This is one of the many reasons why the enforcement division maintains a long-standing policy of confidentiality and deems nonpublic even the mere existence of an investigation.

Before the Internet, witnesses seeking to propagate information about an existing investigation were limited in the means used for dissemination—they could meet by the water-cooler, telephone, or use the mail to inform colleagues and friends. Now, with the increasing ease of Internet use, individuals can publish SEC correspondence and subpoenas, transcripts of testimonial proceedings, even information about SEC staff, such as the staff's background or possibly a home phone number. This could lead to even greater dangers. For example, a corrupt short-seller might learn of an actual SEC investigation from an Internet user, and then exploit the information, spreading a lie across the Internet that SEC is about to file a civil enforcement action, when the SEC staff are actually about to close the investigation.

You look like somebody just walked over your grave.

The New Cyber-Sleuths

Complaints and tips from members of the public have historically provided the largest single source of investigative leads for the enforcement division. Thus, it was only natural for the SEC to open its Enforcement Complaint Center (ECC) *(www.sec.gov/enforce/comctr.htm)* and expand the ways members of the public can contact the enforcement division to report potential securities violations over the Internet (or any other potential violation of the federal securities laws).

There is a genuine culture of vigilance and self-policing among Internet users, and the enforcement division hoped to tap into that culture and further its mission of protecting investors with the online construction of the ECC. The ECC, which began operation on June 14, 1996, provides a variety of means to contact the enforcement division, including an email box, toll-free number, fax number, and mailing address. The ECC also provides a user-friendly form to ensure that the complainant sends a complete report of the suspicious activity.

Thus far, returns from complaints made to the ECC have exceeded expectations. From its inception, the ECC began receiving about 100 complaints a week, and now receives more than 100 complaints each day. Not only does the ECC generate leads about specific entities and persons, but the ECC also permits the enforcement division to remain apprised of the latest trends and tactics of online riffraff.

Most startling is that complaints from Internet users are of a novel variety never encountered before. Hence, the genesis of the "Cybersleuth." The Cybersleuth reports more than just the fraudulent Web page or other potential Internet securities violation. Cybersleuths meticulously trace the headers of suspicious spams, relentlessly seeking to pierce any cloak of anonymity. Cybersleuths take time to provide painstaking details of potential violations, usually offering identifying information about themselves in case the SEC needs to contact them. Cybersleuths even list the potential securities violations of fraudsters by statute, rule and regulation, sometimes by precise citation. Cybersleuths receive no reward or bounty for their benevolence, just the satisfaction of helping to keep the Internet clean and safe for all investors, and their numbers continue to swell.

I am afraid we must redefine the nature of our association.

The New Cyber-Investigation of the Internet 'Killer Application'

A "killer application" is generally defined as any product that overwhelms the competition, significantly transforming a business - the first word processing package was a killer application as was Lotus 1-2-3. Not a day passes without business headlines announcing another company's progress in the hunt for the Internet's next killer application. The word is out—no arena is riper for the next killer application than securities, investments and finance. The enforcement division faces challenges on two fronts in this regard.

First, there are fraudsters who try to capitalize on the hype surrounding technology, feigning discovery of the next killer application and then operating a "pump and dump" scheme for their company's publicly traded stock.[6] Second, there are those who will implement new technologies like online trading facilities and Internet bulletin boards and unlawfully circumvent critical customer protection provisions embedded into the federal securities laws.

No matter what the fate of these futuristic market appliances, the bottom-line is that the enforcement division can no longer rely solely on its traditional investigative methods and tools of yesteryear to police the next killer application. The enforcement division now, more than ever, continuously updates its own computer and Internet resources while also engaging in proactive measures to take advantage of the Internet (and Internet killer applications) for its own benefit.

The enforcement division, for example, in the Internet's discussion forums, not only routinely announces SEC proceedings, such as trading suspensions,[7] but also collects information from members of the public.[8] On the Web, the Enforcement Complaint Center discussed above provides an interactive area for investors to communicate with the enforcement division directly.

The enforcement division also is constantly beefing up its technological arsenal, maintaining all the necessary online commercial provider accounts, T1 lines[9] for direct Internet access, and also employing the latest browsing software for viewing the Internet together with the powerful hardware necessary to do the job right.

So run you cur, and tell all the other curs the law's coming . . . you tell 'em I'm coming and Hell's coming with me you hear, Hell's coming with me.

Conclusion

As the rapid pace of technology continues to impact the SEC enforcement division, the newly fashioned cyber transgressions of today could very well shape the epitaphs on the tombstones of the next millennium. Yet, one group of judicial precepts will always remain notably absent from the list of tombstones—the powerful antifraud provisions of the federal securities laws that have served the SEC so well since their inception. Historically, the flexibility of the antifraud provisions has provided a statutory basis for the enforcement division to prosecute offenses ranging from unlawful insider trading to fraud in the sale of derivatives to pay-to-play municipal bond schemes. Internet related securities violations do not require any new enforcement statutes, rules or regulations; the present range of antifraud provisions embodied in the federal securities laws more than suffice.

The Internet has created fantastic opportunities for companies, entrepreneurs, brokers, dealers, exchanges, and every other participant in the financial markets, and, in many respects, the investor has emerged as the biggest winner of them all. Investors now have instantaneous financial information of almost every variety at their fingertips—all at little cost, at any time and from the comfort and privacy of their own homes. Advanced concepts of electronic disintermediation and cyber-commerce will undoubtedly lead to better access, cheaper costs and fairer markets for all participants. The investor of today, with the help of the Internet, has become more informed than ever before.

Unfortunately, the Internet has also spawned a new generation of scam artist—a generation that aims to spoil the information superhighway, and contaminate the exciting new financial emporium the Internet has created. These miscreants believe that the Internet's uncharted territory provides the ultimate opportunity to modify the investment playing field in their favor. These folks are dead wrong.

Over the past 65 years, no matter where the arena, cyberspace or otherwise, the SEC and its enforcement program has remained committed to stamping out fraud and maintaining fair markets for all investors. In carrying out its mission, the enforcement program has left a graveyard of tombstones behind, continually adapting and modifying its own rules of engagement whenever necessary. The Internet merely accelerates the changes, because the tombstones no longer creep up casually, they shoot up, right under your feet.

NOTES

1. For a thorough discussion of the SEC's response to Internet fraud and other Internet-related threats to investors, and an overview of the SEC enforcement division's Internet Program *see*, Joseph J. Cella III and John Reed Stark, SEC Enforcement and the Internet: Meeting the Challenge of the Next Millennium A Program for the Eagle and the Internet, 52 Bus. Law. 815 (May, 1997).

2. Spammers, who practice their art by transmitting an email message to email lists (much like the junk mailer sends brochures, offerings and other information via U.S. mail), combines the skills of a mass mailer with the hard core pressure sales tactics of "boiler-room" cold-callers. Internet lore has it that the term "spam" derives from a famous Monty Python skit, which featured the word spam repeated over and over. The term may also have come from someone's derision of the eponymous generic processed meat product, which some perceive as lacking in substance or content. (Spam is a registered trademark of Hormel Corporation.)

3. *See*, *SEC v. Charles O. Huttoe, et al.*, Civil Action No. 96-CV-02543 (GK) (D.D.C.); SEC Litigation Rel. 15153 (November 7, 1996) and *SEC v. Comparator Systems, et al.*, Civil Action No. 96-3856 (JGx) (C.D. Cal.); SEC Litigation Rel. No. 15056, 1996 SEC LEXIS 2478 (September 19, 1996). 96-3856 (LGB)

4. Section 17(b) of the Securities Act of 1933, often referred to as an anti-touting statute, clearly prohibits an Internet user from posting certain promotional information and opinions concerning a security in an investment newsletter without also disclosing the nature and substance of any consideration received from the issuer of the company underlying that security.

5. When SEC enforcement staff contact a witness during an investigation, enforcement staff must provide certain limited information to the witness, such as the staff's principal purpose in requesting information from the witness, the name of the investigation and, of course, the identity of the investigating SEC enforcement staff. *See* The Privacy Act of 1974, 5 U.S.C. §552a (providing certain notice and protections to persons from whom the government solicits information).

6. *See* note 4, *supra*.

7. *See e.g.*, SEC postings on America online and on the Silicon Investor announcing the trading suspension of Rocky Mountain International at *http://www.techstocks.com/~wsapi/investor/reply?s=suspension+rocky+mountain&sreply=3021750.*

8. *See e.g.*, SEC postings on *The Silicon Investor* at *http://www.techstocks.com* seeking information concerning SGA GoldStar prior publications.

9. T1 lines grant access at 1500 bits per second (more than 50 times faster than the average high speed modem which only transfers 28.8 bits per second).

EXHIBIT A

INTERNET RELATED SEC LITIGATION ANNOUNCEMENTS

==START OF PAGE 1======

UNITED STATES SECURITIES AND EXCHANGE COMMISSION

Litigation Release No. 15178 / December 6, 1996

SECURITIES AND EXCHANGE COMMISSION v. PLEASURE TIME, INC. D\B\A TELEPHONE INFORMATION SYSTEMS, ET AL. (S.D. OHIO, CIVIL ACTION NO. C-1-95-178, FILED NOVEMBER 26, 1996)

The Securities and Exchange Commission announced that on November 26, 1996, a Final Judgment Granting Permanent Injunction and Other Equitable Relief By Default (Final Judgment) was entered against Pleasure Time, Inc., d/b/a Telephone Information Systems (Pleasure Time), Minette Acra Kelly, d/b/a Group Dynamics Downline (GDD), Minette Acra Kelly (Acra), and Richard A. Welch (Welch), by the United States District Court for the Southern District of Ohio, Western Division, in Cincinnati, Ohio. The Final Judgment enjoins GDD and Acra from violating Sections 5(a), 5(c) and 17(a) of the Securities Act of 1933 (Securities Act) and Sections 10(b), 15(a)(1) and 15(c)(1) of the Securities Exchange Act of 1934 (Exchange Act) and Rules 10b-5 and 15cl-2 thereunder; and Pleasure Time and Welch are enjoined from violating Sections 5(a), 5(c) and 17(a) of the Securities Act and Section 10(b) of the Exchange Act and Rule 10b-5 thereunder. Further, Pleasure Time, GDD, Acra and Welch, jointly and severally, are ordered to disgorge the sum of $663,831, which represents the ill-gotten gains that they received from investors, and pre-judgment interest thereon in the amount of $46,567.

The Commission filed its complaint on March 13, 1995, seeking injunctive and other relief against Pleasure Time, GDD, Acra and Welch, entities and persons located in Florida and Ohio. The Commission's complaint alleges that the defendants participated in a fraudulent sales scheme involving unregistered securities that were offered and sold to approximately 20,000 investors raising over $3 million. Investors were recruited through a "multi-level marketing" system in which investors were encouraged to recruit other investors. Investors were recruited by telephone, facsimile delivery, and the Internet and other computer networks. They were allegedly told that they could reap enormous profits from a world wide telephone lottery. The lottery program was purportedly going to employ a 900 number to attract players with projected receipts of $300 million. According to the complaint, defendants understated and failed to disclose legal, regulatory and technical obstacles to starting a lottery. The complaint further alleges, among other things, that defendants variously violated the antifraud and registration provisions of the federal securities laws. For further information, see Lit. Release No. 14440, March 15, 1995. □

PLEASE NOTE THAT THIS POSTING IS BEING MADE BY THE UNITED STATES SECURITIES AND EXCHANGE COMMISSION.

SECURITIES AND EXCHANGE COMMISSION
Washington, D.C.

SECURITIES EXCHANGE ACT OF 1934
RELEASE NO. 34-38014 / December 4, 1996

The Securities and Exchange Commission announced the temporary suspension, pursuant to Section 12(k) of the Securities Exchange Act of 1934 (the "Exchange Act"), of over-the-counter trading of the securities of Interactive Multimedia Publishers, Inc. ("IMP") (trading symbol DROM), of Akron, Ohio, for a ten day period commencing at 9:30 a.m. (E.S.T.) on December 4, 1996 and terminating at 11:59 p.m. (E.S.T.) on December 17, 1996.

The Commission temporarily suspended trading in the securities of IMP because of questions that have been raised regarding the accuracy of disclosures concerning IMP's corporate history and the tradability of its shares.

The Commission cautions broker-dealers, shareholders, and prospective purchasers that they should carefully consider the foregoing information and any information subsequently issued by the company.

Further, brokers and dealers should be alert to the fact that, pursuant to Rule 15c2-11 under the Exchange Act, at the termination of trading suspension, no quotation may be entered unless and until they have strictly complied with all provisions of the rule. If any broker or dealer has any questions as to whether or not he or she has complied with the rule, he or she should not enter any quotation but immediately contact the staff of the Securities and Exchange Commission in Washington, D.C. If any broker or dealer is uncertain as to what is required by Rule 15c2-11, he or she should refrain from entering quotations relating to IMP's securities until such time as he or she has familiarized himself or herself with the rule and is certain that all of its provisions have been satisfied. If any broker or dealer enters any quotation in violation of Rule 15c2-11, the Commission will consider the need for prompt enforcement action.

If any broker-dealer or other person has any information relating to this matter, the Washington D.C. office of the Securities and Exchange Commission should be telephoned at (202) 942-4643.

The Commission acknowledges the assistance of the National Association of Securities Dealers, Inc. in connection with this matter.

BELOW IS AN UNOFFICIAL COPY OF THE COMMISSION ORDER SUSPENDING TRADING.

UNITED STATES OF AMERICA
Before The
SECURITIES AND EXCHANGE COMMISSION
December 4, 1996

In the Matter of INTERACTIVE MULTIMEDIA PUBLISHERS, INC. File No. 500-1	ORDER DIRECTING SUSPENSION OF TRADING

It appears to the Securities and Exchange Commission that there is a lack of current and accurate information concerning the securities of Interactive Multimedia Publishers, Inc. ("IMP") (trading symbol DROM) because of questions that have been raised regarding the accuracy of disclosures concerning IMP's corporate history and the tradability of its shares.

The Commission is of the opinion that the public interest and the protection of investors require a suspension of trading in the securities of the above listed company.

Therefore, it is ORDERED, pursuant to Section 12(k) of the Securities Exchange Act of 1934, that trading in the securities of Interactive Multimedia Publishers, Inc. (trading symbol DROM), over-the-counter, on the National Association of Securities Dealers, Inc.'s OTC Bulletin Board Service or otherwise, is suspended for the period from 9:30 a.m. E.S.T. December 4, 1996 through 11:59 p.m. E.S.T. on December 17, 1996.

By the Commission.

Jonathan G. Katz
Secretary

SECURITIES AND EXCHANGE COMMISSION
Washington, D.C.

SECURITIES EXCHANGE ACT OF 1934
RELEASE NO. 37984 / November 25, 1996

The Securities and Exchange Commission announced the temporary suspension, pursuant to Section 12(k) of the Securities Exchange Act of 1934 ("Exchange Act"), of the securities of Alliance Industries, Inc. ("Alliance") of Bakersfield, California for a ten-day period commencing at 9:30 a.m. (EDT) on November 26, 1996 and terminating at 12:00 midnight (EDT) on December 10, 1996.

The Commission temporarily suspended trading in the securities of Alliance because of questions that have been raised about the adequacy and accuracy of information available to the public on Alliance's internet home page and distributed to potential investors concerning, among other things, Alliance's projected sales, revenue and earnings as well as the valuation of its assets and its business prospects.

The Commission cautions broker-dealers, shareholders, and prospective purchasers that they should carefully consider the foregoing information along with other currently available information and any information subsequently issued by the company.

Furthermore, brokers and dealers should be alert to the fact that, pursuant to Rule 15c2-11 under the Exchange Act, as of the trading suspension, no quotation may be entered unless and until they have strictly complied with all of the provisions of this rule. If any broker or dealer has any questions as to whether or not he has complied with this rule, he should not enter any quotation but immediately contact the Staff of the Securities and Exchange Commission in Washington, D.C. If any broker or dealer is uncertain as to what is required by Rule 15c2-11, he or she should refrain from entering quotations relating to the securities in question until such time as he or she is familiar with the rule and is certain that tall of its provisions have been met. If any broker or dealer enters a quotation which is in violation of this rule, the Commission will consider the need for prompt enforcement action.

If any broker-dealer or other person has information that may relate to this matter, please contact Kevin J. O'Connor at the Washington, D.C. office of the Securities and Exhange Commission (202-942-4686).

Commission Posts OmniGene Notice on America OnLine

For Immediate Release *96-133*

Washington, D.C., November 20, 1996 -- At 9:30 this morning (EST), in response to serious questions raised about OmniGene Diagnostics, Inc., of West Palm Beach, Florida, the Securities and Exchange Commission suspended trading in the company's stock.

The SEC also took the additional step of posting information about the suspension, including its Order Suspending Trading, on an America OnLine message board that discussed OmniGene stock.

"While the Commission has thus far used the Internet through its Web site (www.sec.gov) to solicit information about possible fraudulent activities, we will now be using the Internet to alert investors to potential problems with specific securities when circumstances warrant. This is the first time we've done so, but it will not be the last," said William McLucas, Director of the Division of Enforcement.

http://www.sec.gov/news/omnigene.htm
Last update: 11/21/96

Return to SEC Home Page

SEC Notice Re OmniGene, as Posted on America OnLine

PLEASE NOTE THAT THIS POSTING IS BEING MADE BY THE UNITED STATES SECURITIES AND EXCHANGE COMMISSION.

SECURITIES AND EXCHANGE COMMISSION
Washington, D.C.

SECURITIES EXCHANGE ACT OF 1934
RELEASE NO. 34-37966

The Securities and Exchange Commission announced the temporary suspension, pursuant to Section 12(k) of the Securities Exchange Act of 1934 (the "Exchange Act"), of over-the-counter trading of the securities of OmniGene Diagnostics, Inc. ("ODI"), of West Palm Beach, Florida at 9:30 a.m. EST, on November 20, 1996, and terminating at 11:59 p.m. on December 4, 1996.

The Commission temporarily suspended trading in the securities of ODI because of questions that have been raised about the accuracy and adequacy of publicly disseminated information concerning, among other things, ODI's alleged ownership and other rights as to certain patents and trademarks, ODI's sales, past and projected, ODI's operations and facilities, and the number of freely traded shares of ODI common stock.

The Commission cautions broker-dealers, shareholders, and prospective purchasers that they should carefully consider the foregoing information along with all other currently available information and any information subsequently issued by the company.

Further, brokers and dealers should be alert to the fact that, pursuant to Rule 15c2-11 under the Exchange Act, at the termination of the trading suspension, no quotation may be entered unless and until they have strictly complied with all of the provisions of the rule. If any broker of dealer has any questions as to whether or not he has complied with the rule, he should not enter any quotation but immediately contact the staff of the Securities and Exchange Commission in Washington, D.C. If any broker or dealer is uncertain as to what is required by Rule 15c2-11, he should refrain from entering quotations relating to ODI's securities until such time as he has familiarized himself with the rule and is certain that all of its provisions have been met. If any broker or dealer enters any quotation which is in violation of the rule, the Commission will consider the need for prompt enforcement action.

If any broker-dealer or other person has any information which may relate to this matter, please contact Terence Tennant at the Miami, Florida office of the Securities and Exchange Commission should be telephoned at (305) 982-6346.

Here is an unofficial copy of the Commission order suspending trading.

UNITED STATES OF AMERICA
Before the
SECURITIES AND EXCHANGE COMMISSION

OMNIGENE DIAGNOSTICS, INC.

File No. 500-1

ORDER OF SUSPENSION OF TRADING

It appears to the Securities and Exchange Commission that there is a lack of current and accurate information concerning the securities of OmniGene Diagnostics, Inc. ("ODI"), because of questions regarding the accuracy of assertions by ODI, and by others, in documents sent to, and statements made to, market-makers of the stock of ODI, other broker-dealers, and to investors concerning, among other things, ODI's alleged ownership and other rights as to certain patents and trademarks, ODI's sales, past and projected, ODI's operations and facilities, and the number of freely traded shares of ODI common stock.

The Commission is of the opinion that the public interest and the protection of investors require a suspension of trading in the securities of the above-listed company.

Therefore, it is ordered, pursuant to Section 12(k) of the Securities Exchange Act of 1934, that trading in the above-listed company is suspended for the period from 9:30 a.m. EST, November 20, 1996 through 11:59 p.m. EST, on December 4, 1996.

By the Commission.

Jonathan G. Katz
Secretary

http://www.sec.gov/news/extra/omnigaol.htm
Last update: 11/21/96

Return to SEC Home Page

SECURITIES AND EXCHANGE COMMISSION
Washington, D.C.

LITIGATION RELEASE NO. 15153 /November 7, 1996

SECURITIES AND EXCHANGE COMMISSION v. CHARLES O. HUTTOE, ET AL., Civil Action No. 96-CV-02543 (GK)(D.D.C.)

The Securities and Exchange Commission ("Commission") announced the filing today of a Complaint and Applications for a Temporary Restraining Order, Preliminary Injunction and other emergency relief against Charles O. Huttoe ("Huttoe"), Huttoe & Associates, Inc., Word Corporation, National Trading Services, Inc. ("NTSI"), Karen Purvis, also known as Karen Purvis Huttoe ("Purvis"), Tammy Jo Perkins ("Perkins"), Josephine Brooks ("Brooks"), SGA Goldstar Research Inc. ("SGA"), Theodore R. Melcher, Jr. ("Melcher"), Shannon B. Terry ("Terry"), Systems of Excellence, Inc. ("SOE"), Alpha Securities Ltd. ("Alpha"), and Dunbar Holdings Ltd. ("Dunbar") in the United States District Court for the District of Columbia. The Complaint alleges a massive and ongoing market manipulation orchestrated by Huttoe, Chairman of the Board and Chief Executive Officer of SOE, a manufacturer and distributor of video teleconferencing equipment with offices in McLean, Virginia and Coral Gables, Florida. The Commission alleges that Huttoe secretly distributed millions of SOE shares to his family members and corporations, manipulated the market by issuing false favorable information concerning SOE and its business, and then sold his shares into the inflated market.

In particular, according to the Commission, as the first part of that scheme Huttoe executed an unregistered distribution of tens of millions of shares of SOE stock by causing a series of false purported Form S-8 registration statements to be submitted to SOE's transfer agent begining in March, 1995. Huttoe secretly issued millions of those unregistered but unrestricted and free trading SOE shares to various Huttoe family members and entities that served as Huttoe's nominees, including defendants Word Corporation, NTSI, Purvis (his wife), Brooks (his mother) and Perkins (his niece). According to the Commission, as the second step in the scheme, Huttoe artificially inflated the price of SOE shares by issuing a series of materially false and misleading press releases that, among other things, announced nonexistent multimillion dollar sales of SOE products, an acquisition that had not occurred, and revenue projections for SOE that were without any basis. The Complaint also alleges that as further efforts to inflate the price of SOE securities, Huttoe caused SOE to fail to file required periodic reports and to file false periodic reports with the Commission, and bribed SGA with stock to recommend SOE to subscribers to SGA's electronically disseminated tout sheet. The Commission alleges that Huttoe caused unregistered but free trading shares to be issued to Melcher and Terry, SGA's principals, some of which were issued in the names of Alpha and Dunbar, entities they control. The Complaint further alleges that as the third step in the scheme, Huttoe, Melcher, and Terry then took advantage of the inflated market for SOE stock that they had created by dumping their own SOE stock on unwitting investors. The Commission alleges that those sales were timed to take advantage of the false news concerning SOE, and were heaviest when SOE stock reached its highs in June, 1996. The Commission alleges that as a result of this scheme, the defendants obtained illegal proceeds of more than $10 million.

The complaint further alleges that Huttoe engaged in a massive coverup after SOE's auditors discovered evidence of his unregistered distribution of securities, and raised questions concerning it in mid-September, 1996. The Complaint alleges that over the course of the weekend of September 21-22, 1996, Huttoe orchestrated the fabrication and forgery of fraudulent "consulting agreements" that purported to be the consideration for nearly 40 million shares that had been issued pursuant to purported Form S-8 registration statements. The Complaint alleges that Huttoe retained a new auditor for SOE that Saturday, and that on the same day the new auditor rendered a clean opinion on SOE's financial statements. The Complaint alleges that on Monday, September 23 SOE filed a materially false Form 10-K that included the false accountant's report, and a materially false Form 10-Q. The Complaint alleges that the following day SOE filed sixteen materially false registration statements on Form S-8 that purported to cover the shares distributed months before, and that included as attachments the forged "consulting agreements."

As a result, the Complaint alleges that Huttoe violated Sections 5 and 17(a) of the Securities Act of 1933 ("Securities Act"), Sections 10(b), 13(b)(5), and 16(a) of the Securities Exchange Act of 1934 ("Exchange Act"), and Rules 10b-5, 13b2-1, 13b2-2, 16a-2, and 16a-3 thereunder; Huttoe & Associates, Inc., Word Corporation, and NTSI violated Sections 5 and 17(a) of the Securities Act and Section 10(b) of the Exchange Act, and Rule 10b-5 thereunder; Purvis, Perkins, and Brooks violated Section 5 of the Securities Act; SGA, Melcher, Terry, Dunbar, and Alpha violated Sections 5, 17(a) and 17(b) of the Securities Act and Section 10(b) and Rule 10b-5 of the Exchange Act; and SOE violated Sections 5 and 17(a) of the Securities Act and Sections 10(b), 13(a), and 13(b)(2)(A) and 13(b)(2)(B) of the Exchange Act, and Rules 10b-5, 12b-20, 13a-1, 13a-11, and 13a-13 thereunder. The Commission applied to the Court for orders that would, among other things, temporarily restrain defendants from violating the federal securities laws; temporarily freeze assets and accounts of defendants other than SOE; require Huttoe to temporarily surrender his passport and refrain from foreign travel; and direct defendants, other than SOE, to file an accounting. The Complaint seeks permanent injunctions against violations of the relevant provisions of the securities laws by defendants and disgorgement by defendants of illegal gains, together with prejudgment interest.

On October 7, 1996, the Commission issued an Order suspending trading in SOE securities for ten days. See Securities Exchange Act Rel. No. 37791 (October 7, 1996). The Commission's investigation in this matter is continuing.

UNITED STATES SECURITIES AND EXCHANGE COMMISSION

Litigation Release No. 15139 / October 29, 1996

SECURITIES AND EXCHANGE COMMISSION v. SCOTT A. FRYE, 95 Civ. 9205, U.S.D.C., S.D.N.Y. (JSM)

The Securities and Exchange Commission ("Commission") announced that, on August 17, 1996, the Honorable Barbara S. Jones, United States District Court Judge for the Southern District of New York, entered a Final Judgment of Permanent Injunction and Other Equitable Relief By Consent ("Final Judgment") against defendant Scott A. Frye ("Frye"). The Final Judgment enjoins Frye from future violations of Section 17(a) of the Securities Act of 1933 and Section 10(b) of the Securities Exchange Act of 1934 and Rule 10b-5 thereunder and does not impose civil penalties against him based on his demonstrated inability to pay.

As detailed in the Complaint, beginning in or about May 1995 through the filing of the Commission's action on October 27, 1995, Frye posted numerous messages on the InterNet, a decentralized web of computers, accessible to millions of potential investors across the country and world-wide, in which Frye solicited funds from investors. The Complaint alleges that Frye used messages posted on the InterNet, and other written materials which he distributed, in an attempt to lure investors with promises of riskless profits and above average returns from investments in two Costa Rican enterprises, ICP and the Jupiter Agro Development Project. However, as alleged in the Complaint, in connection with his solicitations, Frye made material misrepresentations of fact by, for example, falsely representing that one of his companies had a major distribution contract for its product with A&P Supermarkets ("A&P"), when, in fact, it had no distribution contracts with A&P.

For further information, see lit. rel. nos. 14702 and 14720.□

==START OF PAGE 1======

U.S. SECURITIES AND EXCHANGE COMMISSION

Litigation Release No. 15134 /October 23, 1996

SECURITIES AND EXCHANGE COMMISSION v. WESTERN EXECUTIVE GROUP, INC., CASH SYSTEMS USA, INC., CHARLES R. RIETZ, ROBERT R. PARRISH, ROBERT J. STRUTH and R. STEPHEN EDGEL, Civil Action No. 96-6938 GHK (JGx) (C.D. Cal.)

The Securities and Exchange Commission ("Commission") announced that on October 22, 1996, the Honorable George H. King, United States District Court Judge for the Central District of California, signed a Preliminary Injunction ("Order") halting a Ponzi scheme involving investment contracts for the sale and leaseback of automated teller machines ("ATMs"). The defendants offered the ATM investment program over the Internet to the public and raised over $3.49 million from at least 132 investors nationwide. This is the first lawsuit involving ATMs and the largest lawsuit involving Internet investment fraud brought by the Commission to date.

In its Complaint, the Commission alleges that the defendants have operated a Ponzi scheme from at least September 1995, when they began offering and selling investments involving the sale and leaseback of privately owned ATMs (ATMs not affiliated with banks). Through simultaneously executed agreements with both WEG and Cash Systems, investors purchased ATMs from WEG for $23,950 and immediately leased them back to Cash Systems. Investors were guaranteed monthly lease payments for five years which payments would allegedly return all of the investors' principal and a yield of 17.4% per year. However, as of July 1996, only 42 ATMs were operational even though the defendants had sold 195 ATMs, and only 2 of the 42 ATMs made enough money to cover their associated monthly lease payments and expenses. Consequently, the defendants were using new investor funds to pay existing investors their monthly lease payments.

The Commission obtained an order enjoining the following entities and individuals from future violations of the antifraud and registration provisions of the federal securities laws: Western Executive Group, Inc. ("WEG") headquartered in Reno, Nevada; Cash Systems USA, Inc. ("Cash Systems") headquartered in Reno, Nevada; Charles R. Rietz ("Rietz") of Mesa, Arizona; Robert R. Parrish ("Parrish") of Gilmer, Texas; Robert J. Struth ("Struth") of Southern California; and R. Stephen Edgel ("Edgel") of Carmichael, California. The Order also imposes an asset freeze against WEG and Cash Systems and appoints a receiver over WEG and Cash Systems.

The Complaint also alleges that the defendants solicited investors nationwide through private investment seminars, mass mailings, cold calling and over the Internet. Defendants
==START OF PAGE 2======

provided investors with offering materials which misrepresented the number of ATMs operating and the amount of money the ATMs made. Additionally, the offering materials failed to disclose that Rietz and Struth had previous orders entered against them for violating certain securities laws. The Complaint seeks a permanent injunction, and other relief, including disgorgement and civil penalties, against the defendants.

The Complaint alleges that the defendants violated Sections 5(a) and 5(c) of the Securities Act of 1933, as amended (the "Securities Act"), the registration provisions, and Section 17(a) of the Securities Act and Section 10(b) of the Securities Exchange Act of 1934, as amended (the "Exchange Act"), and Rule 10b-5 thereunder, the antifraud provisions. The Complaint also charges Parrish, Struth and Edgel with violations of Section 15(a) of the Exchange Act, the broker-dealer registration provisions.□

U.S. SECURITIES AND EXCHANGE COMMISSION

Litigation Release No. 15121 / October 15, 1996

SECURITIES AND EXCHANGE COMMISSION v. WESTERN EXECUTIVE GROUP, INC., CASH SYSTEMS USA, INC., CHARLES R. RIETZ, ROBERT R. PARRISH, ROBERT J. STRUTH and R. STEPHEN EDGEL, Civil Action No. 96-6938 GHK (JGx) (C.D. Cal.)

The Securities and Exchange Commission ("Commission") announced that on October 7, 1996, the Honorable George H. King, United States District Court Judge for the Central District of California, signed a Temporary Restraining Order ("Order") halting a Ponzi scheme involving investment contracts for the sale and leaseback of automated teller machines ("ATMs"). The defendants offered the ATM investment program over the Internet to the public and raised over $3.49 million from at least 132 investors nationwide. This is the first lawsuit involving ATMs and the largest lawsuit involving Internet investment fraud brought by the Commission to date.

In its Complaint, the Commission alleges that the defendants have operated a Ponzi scheme from at least September 1995, when they began offering and selling investments involving the sale and leaseback of privately owned ATMs (ATMs not affiliated with banks). Through simultaneously executed agreements with both WEG and Cash Systems, investors purchased ATMs from WEG for $23,950 and immediately leased them back to Cash Systems. Investors were guaranteed monthly lease payments for five years which payments would allegedly return all of the investors' principal and a yield of 17.4% per year. However, as of July 1996, only 42 ATMs were operational even though the defendants had sold 195 ATMs, and only 2 of the 42 ATMs made enough money to cover their associated monthly lease payments and expenses. Consequently, the defendants were using new investor funds to pay existing investors their monthly lease payments.

The Commission obtained an order temporarily enjoining the following entities and individuals from future violations of the antifraud and registration provisions of the federal securities laws: Western Executive Group, Inc. ("WEG") headquartered in Reno, Nevada; Cash Systems USA, Inc. ("Cash Systems") headquartered in Reno, Nevada; Charles R. Rietz ("Rietz") of Mesa, Arizona; Robert R. Parrish ("Parrish") of Gilmer, Texas; Robert J. Struth ("Struth") of Southern California; and R. Stephen Edgel ("Edgel") of Carmichael, California. The order also imposes an asset freeze against WEG and Cash Systems and appoints a temporary receiver over WEG and Cash Systems. A hearing to show cause why a preliminary injunction should not be granted will be held on October 21, 1996.

The Complaint also alleges that the defendants solicited investors nationwide through private investment seminars, mass mailings, cold calling and over the Internet. Defendants provided investors with offering materials which misrepresented the number of ATMs operating and the amount of money the ATMs made. Additionally, the offering materials failed to disclose that Rietz and Struth had previous orders entered against them for violating certain securities laws. The Complaint seeks preliminary and permanent injunctions, and other relief, including disgorgement and civil penalties, against the defendants.

The Complaint alleges that the defendants violated Sections 5(a) and 5(c) of the Securities Act of 1933, as amended (the "Securities Act"), the registration provisions, and Section 17(a) of the Securities Act and Section 10(b) of the Securities Exchange Act of 1934, as amended (the "Exchange Act"), and Rule 10b-5 thereunder, the antifraud provisions. The Complaint also charges Parrish, Struth and Edgel with violations of Section 15(a) of the Exchange Act, the broker-dealer registration provisions.

U.S. SECURITIES AND EXCHANGE COMMISSION
PACIFIC REGIONAL OFFICE
LOS ANGELES, CALIFORNIA

For Immediate Release

NEWS DIGEST

TEMPORARY RESTRAINING ORDER GRANTED IN SEC v. WESTERN EXECUTIVE GROUP, INC., ET AL.

On October 7, 1996, the Honorable George H. King, United States District Court Judge for the Central District of California, entered a Temporary Restraining Order (Order) prohibiting the offer and sale of investment contracts for the sale and leaseback of automated teller machines (ATMs) by Western Executive Group, Inc. (WEG), Cash Systems USA, Inc. (Cash Systems), Charles R. Rietz (Rietz), Robert R. Parrish (Parrish), Robert J. Struth (Struth) and R. Stephen Edgel (Edgel). The Order also appoints a temporary receiver over WEG and Cash Systems and freezes their assets.

The Complaint alleges that the defendants violated Sections 5(a), 5(c) and 17(a) of the Securities Act of 1933 and Section 10(b) of the Securities Exchange Act of 1934 (Exchange Act), and Rule 10b-5 thereunder, by engaging in the fraudulent offer and sale of interests in the ATM investment program. The defendants misrepresented the number of ATMs actually operating, the fact that the ATMs were not generating sufficient funds to pay investor returns and that the program was a Ponzi scheme. Rietz and Struth also failed to disclose their previous disciplinary history. The Complaint also charges Parrish, Struth and Edgel with acting as unregistered broker-dealers in violation of Section 15(a) of the Exchange Act.

SECURITIES AND EXCHANGE COMMISSION v. WESTERN EXECUTIVE GROUP, INC., CASH SYSTEMS USA, INC., CHARLES R. RIETZ, ROBERT R. PARRISH, ROBERT J. STRUTH and R. STEPHEN EDGEL, Civil Action No. 96-6938 GHK (JGx) (C.D. Cal.)

Lisa A. Gok
Assistant Regional Director
Office of Enforcement
Pacific Regional Office/Los Angeles
(213) 965-3835
□

SECURITIES AND EXCHANGE COMMISSION
Washington, D.C.

LITIGATION RELEASE No. 15073 / September 26, 1996

SECURITIES AND EXCHANGE COMMISSION v. WYE RESOURCES, INC. AND REHAN MALIK, Civil Action No. 96CV02223 (D.D.C., filed September 26, 1996).

The Securities and Exchange Commission ("Commission") today announced the filing of a complaint in the United States District Court for the District of Columbia against Wye Resources, Inc. ("Wye") and Rehan Malik. Wye is a Canadian corporation headquartered in Toronto, Ontario and claims to own interests in various gold and diamond mining properties. Rehan Malik ("Malik"), a resident of Labrador City, Newfoundland, served as Wye's President from June 24, 1993 through March 25, 1994. The complaint alleges that during 1993 and early 1994, Wye and Malik engaged in a fraudulent promotional campaign targeted towards U.S. investors and improperly distributed Wye stock to those investors.

The Commission's complaint specifically alleges that Wye and Malik engaged in a scheme to distribute approximately 5.3 million shares of Wye stock that were not properly issued under Canadian law nor properly registered with the Commission. According to the complaint, Wye directly distributed approximately 2.5 million of these improperly issued shares to U.S. investors. As of February 1, 1994, approximately 4 million shares, or 28.9 percent of the Wye stock then outstanding, was held by U.S. investors.

The complaint alleges that Wye and Malik specifically targeted U.S. investors by placing advertisements in U.S. publications and placing messages over the Internet through a New Orleans-based computer bulletin board service ("BBS") called the "Emerging Growth Stock" BBS. The complaint alleges that certain of these advertisements and messages were false and misleading in that they misrepresented, among other things, the status of Wye's ongoing exploitation of certain Zairian mining properties. For example, starting in March 1993, prior to the time that Malik became Wye's President, Wye falsely claimed that it had successfully completed a sampling program during which it recovered 10 gem-quality diamonds from its Zairian concessions. In reality, Wye's contractors had not set foot on the concessions themselves and purchased the diamonds from Zairian vendors located elsewhere.

The Commission's complaint seeks a permanent injunction against Wye and Malik for violations of Section 5 of the Securities Act of 1933 and Section 10(b) of the Securities Exchange Act of 1934 and Rule 10b-5 thereunder. The complaint also seeks civil penalties against Malik.

The Commission also today announced the institution of administrative proceedings against two U.S. residents, Murray Aaron Huberfeld and Broad Capital Associates, Inc., in connection with the unregistered distribution of Wye securities. Without admitting or denying the Commission's findings, both Broad Capital and Huberfeld consented to the issuance of an order finding that they violated Section 5 of the Securities Act. In addition, they agreed to the entry of an order requiring them to disgorge a total of $426,790.05, representing profits made as a result of transactions in Wye stock and prejudgment interest thereon. See In the Matter of Broad Capital Associates, Inc. and Murray Aaron Huberfeld, Administrative Proceeding File No. 3-9101 (Securities Act Release No. 7338).

The Commission wishes to acknowledge the assistance of the Ontario Securities Commission.

UNITED STATES SECURITIES AND EXCHANGE COMMISSION

LITIGATION RELEASE NO. 15012 / August 12, 1996

SECURITIES AND EXCHANGE COMMISSION V. WILLIAM B. SELLIN, II, ZAITECH HOLDINGS, INC. AND BACCARATT HOLDINGS, INC., Case No. 96-6825-CIV-Ungaro (S.D. Fla.)

The Securities and Exchange Commission ("Commission") announced that on August 1, 1996, a Final Judgment of Permanent Injunction was entered against William B. Sellin, II ("Sellin"), and two corporations he controls, Zaitech Holdings, Inc. and Baccaratt Holdings, Inc. (collectively, "Defendants") by the United States District Court for the Southern District of Florida. The Defendants consented to the entry of the permanent injunction without admitting or denying the Commission's allegations.

The Commission's Complaint and other papers filed with the Court on July 24, 1996, alleged that Sellin, a convicted felon and repeat securities law violator, conducted an ongoing, fraudulent offering of securities through newsgroup bulletin board postings on the Internet, and through advertisements placed on CompuServe, an Internet access provider and a world-wide, subscriber-based electronic communications service. Since October 1995, Sellin solicited investments through at least 43 advertisements in at least 21 newsgroups on the Internet. The Internet provides promoters, such as Sellin, with direct access to millions of prospective investors worldwide with great speed and ease, minimal expense and virtual anonymity. No allegation of any wrongdoing has been made in this case against CompuServe or any other Internet access provider.

According to the Commission's papers, Sellin, through Zaitech and Baccaratt, offered promissory notes which he claimed were secured and collateralized by U.S. Government securities and other assets. Sellin represented that he could deliver "guaranteed" returns of anywhere from 12% to 22% annually. Sellin also offered an investment opportunity to make "$150,000 annually, tax free." The Commission's papers alleged that these representations were false and misleading in that the investment was not secured or collateralized by U.S. Government securities; that Sellin failed to disclose his long record of regulatory sanctions and criminal convictions, including a Florida felony conviction for grand larceny; and that Sellin failed to disclose the material risks associated with the investment.

The Final Judgment permanently enjoins the Defendants from future violations of the antifraud provisions of the federal securities laws -- Section 17(a) of the Securities Act of 1933 and Section 10(b) of the Securities Exchange Act of 1934 and Rule 10b-5.

==START OF PAGE 2======

On July 25, 1996, the Court entered an order temporarily

restraining the Defendants from further violations of the antifraud provisions of the federal securities laws. The order also froze the Defendants' assets and ordered that Defendants preserve records and account for proceeds they received from their fraudulent scheme.□

SECURITIES AND EXCHANGE COMMISSION
Washington, D.C.

LITIGATION RELEASE NO. 14942 / June 11, 1996

SECURITIES AND EXCHANGE COMMISSION V. OCTAGON TECHNOLOGY GROUP, INC., MICHAEL J. TIDD, AND JEFFREY L. PUNZEL, Civil Action No. 96-1299, (D.D.C. June 11, 1996) (JR)

The Securities and Exchange Commission today sued a Schaumburg, IL computer software company and two of its former officers for their roles in creating an elaborate sham offering of offshore debt securities on the World Wide Web component of the Internet.

The suit, filed in federal district court for the District of Columbia, alleges the following:

Michael J. Tidd and Jeffrey L. Punzel, the former CEO and Vice President-Technology, respectively, of Octagon Technology Group, Inc., designed, drafted and linked to the Internet a World Wide Web homepage and related pages for the Agency For Interamerican Finance, a Panamanian shell subsidiary of Octagon, advertising AIF "Interamerican hard currency bonds" for sale to investors. The offering was essentially a sham. Although no bonds ever existed and AIF had no business operations or assets, the Web pages falsely promised prospective investors a risk-free investment with guaranteed returns of 11.75% annually and portrayed AIF as a successful provider of investment capital to Latin American businesses. Octagon has removed the Web pages from the Internet.

In or about late May 1995, Octagon and its officers linked the AIF Web pages to the Internet through a Zurich, Switzerland-based computer center. The AIF Web pages asked prospective investors to send checks for the purchase of AIF bonds to AIF's "investor satisfaction center," which was actually a rented mail drop in St. John, Antigua. Employees at the Antigua office were instructed to tell inquiring investors that AIF's fictitious director of "investor satisfaction" listed on the Web was simply "off island" and could not be reached by telephone, and to forward all mail received for AIF to Octagon in Schaumburg.

The AIF Web pages contained many false statements concerning AIF and the putative bonds it offered. The pages claimed that the Interamerican bonds had a guaranteed annual rate of return of 11.75%, would double an investor's money in six years and were risk free. Further, the pages went on to claim that Group American Pacific Financial, Ltd., S.A. ("APF"), a purported independent trust company, guaranteed principal and interest payments on the bonds up to 250,000 US$ per investor. In fact, APF was another Panamanian shell subsidiary of Octagon which lacked assets or business operations.

The AIF Web Pages also included a facsimile reproduction of a *World Financial Report* magazine article touting the investment quality of the AIF bonds, the operations of AIF, and the quality of its management. In fact, *World Financial Report* was nothing more than a fabrication of Tidd, Punzel and Octagon.

Between late May and late August 1995, Tidd, Punzel and Octagon publicized the AIF bond offering on the Internet and elsewhere. The AIF Web Pages were listed on numerous investment-related indices of World Wide Web pages, including the popular Yahoo! index. Punzel posted messages on three investment-related Internet newsgroups, giving the Web address of the AIF offering and describing it as what appeared to be "a pretty good opportunity" for investors, without disclosing his position with Octagon, or that the AIF bond offering was not a legitimate offering. At Tidd's direction, Octagon engaged a Cleveland, Ohio-based news bureau to internationally disseminate a press release announcing the AIF offering and guiding investors to the fraudulent AIF Web pages. No sales were made by the Defendants.

With the filing of the Complaint, Octagon, Tidd and Punzel, without admitting or denying the allegations contained in the Complaint, consented to the entry of Final Judgments enjoining them from future violations of the antifraud provision of the Securities Act of 1933, Section 17(a). In addition, Tidd has consented to pay a $5,000 penalty.

The Commission acknowledges the assistance of the Pennsylvania Securities Commission and the Illinois Securities Department in investigating this matter.

******

SEC Warns Investors on How to Avoid and Report Internet Fraud

The SEC's Office of Investor Education and Assistance is issuing a flyer for investors with practical tips on how they can spot, avoid, and report fraud on the Internet. Investors can get a copy of the flyer by calling the SEC's toll-free information line at 1-800-SEC-0330 or visiting the SEC's Web site at http://www.sec.gov. Copies of the flyer may also be obtained by calling the Office of Investor Education and Assistance or writing to the Office of Investor Education and Assistance, U.S. Securities and Exchange Commission, 450 Fifth Street, N.W., Mail Stop 11-2, Washington, DC 20549.

SECURITIES AND EXCHANGE COMMISSION

LITIGATION RELEASE NO. 14828 / February 28, 1996

SECURITIES AND EXCHANGE COMMISSION v. GENE BLOCK, INDIVIDUALLY AND D/B/A BLOCK CONSULTING SERVICES, RENATE HAAG, INDIVIDUALLY AND D/B/A HAAG + PARTNER, AND ROBERT T. RILEY, JR., INDIVIDUALLY AND D/B/A THE ROBERTS GROUP (United States District Court for the District of Massachusetts, Civil Action No. 95-11748RCL).

The Commission announced that on February 26, 1996, the Honorable Reginald C. Lindsay of the U.S. District Court for the District of Massachusetts entered a civil contempt order against Renate Haag ("Haag") of Langen, Germany and Malibu, California, doing business as Haag + Partner. The Court found Haag in contempt for failing to comply with the temporary restraining order entered against her on October 26, 1995. Specifically, Haag failed a) to file a sworn accounting with the Court and the Commission identifying investors in her investment scheme and the monies received from the investors, and b) to repatriate investor funds. If Haag fails to comply with the order by March 12, 1996, she was ordered to pay $5,000 per day until she fully complies with the order.

The relief was entered in connection with an enforcement action alleging that Haag was engaging in an ongoing, fraudulent securities offering of so-called "prime bank instruments" in violation of the antifraud and registration provisions of the federal securities laws. Specifically, the Commission alleges that since at least October 1994, Haag has been the central figure in a fraudulent scheme that has induced members of the public to invest over $1 million in her programs by promising, in some cases, returns as high as 200%-420% annually. In addition to Haag, Gene Block of Durham, North Carolina ("Block"), doing business as Block Consulting Services, and Robert T. Riley, Jr. of St. Louis, Missouri ("Riley"), doing business as The Roberts Group, were offering and selling the unregistered and fraudulent Haag + Partner programs through various methods, including advertisements on the Internet. Previously, on August 8, 1995, the Court entered a temporary restraining order and asset freeze on the Commission's ex parte motion against Block. On September 14, 1995, Block consented to the entry of a preliminary injunction. On January 30, 1996, the Court entered a preliminary injunction against Haag.

The Commission further alleges that as an inducement to potential investors, the Defendants have represented that investors' funds would be invested in risk-free, high-yield investment programs. The Defendants have falsely represented

that the initial investment is guaranteed against loss because a "Prime Bank Guarantee" will be used as security for the transaction. In fact, there are no legitimate financial

SECURITIES AND EXCHANGE COMMISSION
WASHINGTON D.C.

Litigation Release No. 14856 / March 29, 1996

SECURITIES AND EXCHANGE COMMISSION v. DONALD B. SPENCER AND IVT SYSTEMS, INC., Civ. Action No. 96 CIV-1800 (DHC) U.S.D.C., N.D.ILL.

The Securities and Exchange Commission today charged the founder and president of a Chicago-based Illinois corporation and his company with violations of the antifraud provisions of the federal securities laws for falsely promising enormous returns on investments, as well as for making other material misrepresentations and omissions to investors, by means of the InterNet, and for misappropriating investors' funds.

Named in the Complaint filed today in the United States District Court for the Northern District of Illinois is:

Donald B. Spencer ("Spencer"), a resident of Chicago, Illinois.

IVT Systems, Inc. ("IVT"), an Illinois corporation based in Chicago, Illinois. Spencer is the founder, president and majority shareholder of IVT.

The Complaint alleges that Spencer and IVT have used the InterNet, as well as other means of communication and publication, to engage in fraudulent securities offerings involving IVT. Since at least July 1995, Spencer and IVT have solicited investments on the InterNet and represented that the investments would be utilized to finance the construction by IVT of a proposed ethanol plant in the Dominican Republic. The defendants' InterNet solicitations promised a potential 50% and greater return on investment when there was no reasonable basis for this prediction. Spencer and IVT also disseminated information packets to interested potential investors which contained additional misrepresentations and omissions, such as that IVT had entered into contracts with well-known companies and consultants in the energy field for purposes of facilitating IVT's ethanol plant project. In fact, no such contracts existed.

Since 1990, Spencer and IVT have also sought to obtain investments from the public through other means, e.g., advertisements in newspapers and in person solicitations. All of the defendants' solicitation materials contained material misrepresentations and omissions. Spencer and IVT have raised at least $113,500 from twelve investors.

The Complaint seeks to permanently enjoin Spencer and IVT from violating the antifraud provisions of the federal securities laws. In addition, the Complaint seeks disgorgement of all funds that were misappropriated by Spencer and IVT and ancillary relief in the form of civil penalties. □

==START OF PAGE 1======

UNITED STATES SECURITIES AND EXCHANGE COMMISSION

Litigation Release No. 14825 / February 26, 1996

SECURITIES AND EXCHANGE COMMISSION v. PLEASURE TIME, INC. d\b\a TELEPHONE INFORMATION SYSTEMS, et al. (S.D. Ohio, Civil Action No. C-1-95-178)

The Securities and Exchange Commission announced that on August 1, 1995, an Order of Permanent Injunction and Other Relief was entered against John C. Hicks (Hicks) by the United States District Court for the Southern District of Ohio, Western Division, in Cincinnati, Ohio. Without admitting or denying the allegations in the Commission's complaint, except as to subject matter jurisdiction, Hicks consented to the entry of an order permanently enjoining him from violating Sections 5(a), 5(c) and 17(a) of the Securities Act of 1933 and Section 10(b) of the Exchange Act and Rule 10b-5 thereunder; and ordering disgorgement, plus prejudgment interest, payment of which was waived based on Hicks' demonstrated inability to pay.

The Commission filed its complaint on March 13, 1995, seeking injunctive and other relief against Hicks, Pleasure Time, Minette Acra-Kelly, d\b\a Group Dynamics Downline (GDD), Richard A. Welch (Welch), and Minette Acra-Kelly (Acra), entities and persons located in Florida, Ohio and Indiana. The Commission's complaint alleges that the defendants participated in a fraudulent sales scheme involving unregistered securities that were offered and sold to approximately 20,000 investors raising over $3 million. Investors were recruited through a "multi-level marketing" system in which investors were encouraged to recruit other investors. Investors were recruited by telephone, facsimile delivery, and the Internet and other computer networks.

They were allegedly told that they could reap enormous profits from a world wide telephone lottery. The lottery program was purportedly going to employ a 900 number to attract players with projected receipts of $300 million. According to the complaint, defendants understated and failed to disclose legal, regulatory and technical obstacles to starting a lottery. The complaint further alleges, among other things, that defendants variously violated the antifraud and registration provisions of the federal securities laws. On March 24, 1995, the United States District Court for the Southern District of Ohio entered a preliminary injunction order, including a freeze of assets, against Pleasure Time, GDD, Acra and Welch.

For further information, see Lit. Release No. 14440, March 15, 1995. □

instruments known as "Prime Bank Guarantees." The Defendants have also fraudulently represented that investors' funds are doubled by buying and selling "Bank Instruments." However, the Defendants have failed to disclose the nature of the "Bank Instruments," how the trading will generate such unrealistic returns, or the risk that the returns will not be achieved. None of the Defendants or their businesses are registered with the Commission as a broker-dealer, nor are they associated with any broker-dealer registered with the Commission.

The Commission alleges that the Defendants have violated the antifraud and registration provisions of the federal securities laws. The Commission seeks the following relief: (i) a permanent injunction prohibiting the Defendants from further violations of the antifraud and broker-dealer registration provisions of the federal securities laws; (ii) disgorgement of the Defendants' ill-gotten gains plus prejudgment interest thereon; and (iii) civil monetary penalties in an amount to be determined by the Court.

For further information, see Litigation Release Nos. 14598, 14711 and 14804.

1ST CASE of Level 1 printed in FULL format.

SECURITIES AND EXCHANGE COMMISSION v. DANIEL ODULO, INDIVIDUALLY AND D/B/A GOLDEN WATERS PRODUCTIONS (United States District Court for the District of Rhode Island, Civil Action No. 95-424P).

SECURITIES AND EXCHANGE COMMISSION

LITIGATION, RELEASE NO. 14616

1995 SEC LEXIS 2186

AUGUST 24, 1995

XT: [*1]

The Commission announced today, that on August 15, 1995 the Honorable Raymond Pettine of the U.S. District Court for the District of Rhode Island issued a -nal Judgment of Permanent Injunction against Daniel Odulo ("Odulo"), .dividually and d/b/a Golden Waters Productions ("Golden Waters"). Odulo, who nsented to this order without admitting or denying the Commission's legations, was enjoined from further violations of the antifraud provisions of :e federal securities laws. Based on Odulo's representations concerning his .nancial condition no monetary penalty was imposed.

The Commission's Complaint, filed on August 7, 1995, alleged that on or about y 9, 1995, Odulo posted a false and misleading solicitation on the Internet, .ich is accessible to hundreds of thousands of individuals across the country .d world-wide. The solicitation sought investors for a $ 500,000 offering of $ 000 denomination bonds, and contained material misrepresentations and issions. Odulo stated in the solicitation that the bonds would yield a hopping 20% rate of return" and were a "very low risk" investment. Odulo, wever, failed to disclose that Golden Waters was a proposed new venture 2] involving the acquisition and raising of eels, and that he had no pertise in the culturing of eels. Odulo also falsely stated in the licitation that Golden Waters "insures all of its product against any possible ss." Moreover, in order to lend credibility to his offering, Odulo made up lse endorsements of the bonds by fictitious investment advisers. Although iulo solicited investors to send their checks to a post office box in Rhode land, no one invested in this offering.

==START OF PAGE 1======

SECURITIES AND EXCHANGE COMMISSION
BOSTON, MASSACHUSETTS

LITIGATION RELEASE NO. 14804 / January 30, 1996

SECURITIES AND EXCHANGE COMMISSION v. GENE BLOCK, INDIVIDUALLY AND D/B/A BLOCK CONSULTING SERVICES, RENATE HAAG, INDIVIDUALLY AND D/B/A HAAG + PARTNER, AND ROBERT T. RILEY, JR., INDIVIDUALLY AND D/B/A THE ROBERTS GROUP (United States District Court for the District of Massachusetts, Civil Action No. 95-11748RCL).

The Commission announced that on January 30, 1996, the Honorable Reginald C. Lindsay of the U.S. District Court for the District of Massachusetts granted the Commission's application for a preliminary injunction against Renate Haag ("Haag") of Langen, Germany and Malibu, California, doing business as Haag + Partner. The Court also scheduled a contempt hearing against Haag on February 26, 1996 for failing to comply with a temporary restraining order that was entered against her on October 26, 1995.
Specifically, she has failed to file a sworn accounting, repatriate investor funds and identify all investors.

Under the terms of the preliminary injunction, Haag is preliminarily enjoined from continuing her fraudulent offering of securities. The Court's order also continues a freeze on Haag's assets, requires Haag to file a sworn accounting, orders the repatriation of investor funds and grants other relief. The relief was entered in connection with an enforcement action alleging that Haag was engaging in an ongoing, fraudulent securities offering of so-called "prime bank instruments" in violation of the antifraud and registration provisions of the federal securities laws.

Specifically, the Commission alleges that since at least October 1994, Haag has been the central figure in a fraudulent scheme that has induced members of the public to invest over $1 million in her programs by promising, in some cases, returns as high as 200%-420% annually. In addition to Haag, Gene Block of Durham, North Carolina ("Block"), doing business as Block Consulting Services, and Robert T. Riley, Jr. of St. Louis, Missouri ("Riley"), doing business as The Roberts Group, were offering and selling the unregistered and fraudulent Haag + Partner programs through various methods, including advertisements on the Internet. Previously, on August 8, 1995, the Court entered a temporary restraining order and asset freeze on the Commission's ex parte motion against Block. On September 14, 1995, Block consented to the entry of a preliminary injunction.

The Commission further alleges that as an inducement to potential investors, the Defendants have represented that

investors' funds would be invested in risk-free, high-yield investment programs. The Defendants have falsely represented that the initial investment is guaranteed against loss because a

"Prime Bank Guarantee" will be used as security for the transaction. In fact, there are no legitimate financial instruments known as "Prime Bank Guarantees." The Defendants have also fraudulently represented that investors' funds are doubled by buying and selling "Bank Instruments." However, the Defendants have failed to disclose the nature of the "Bank Instruments," how the trading will generate such unrealistic returns, or the risk that the returns will not be achieved. None of the Defendants or their businesses are registered with the Commission as a broker-dealer, nor are they associated with any broker-dealer registered with the Commission.

The Commission alleges that the Defendants have violated the antifraud and registration provisions of the federal securities laws. The Commission seeks the following relief: (i) a permanent injunction prohibiting the Defendants from further violations of the antifraud and broker-dealer registration provisions of the federal securities laws; (ii) disgorgement of the Defendants' ill-gotten gains plus prejudgment interest thereon; and (iii) civil monetary penalties in an amount to be determined by the Court.

For further information, see Litigation Release Nos. 14598 and 14711.

SECURITIES AND EXCHANGE COMMISSION
Washington, D.C.

LITIGATION RELEASE NO. 15264 / February 25, 1997

SECURITIES AND EXCHANGE COMMISSION v. GEORGE CHELEKIS, KGC, INC., AND HOT STOCKS REVIEW, INC., Civil Action No. 97CV-00374 (D.D.C.) (filed February 25, 1997)

On February 25, 1997, the Commission filed a complaint in the United States District Court for the District of Columbia against George Chelekis ("Chelekis"), KGC, Inc. and Hot Stocks Review, Inc. The complaint alleges that from at least January 1995 through August 1995, Chelekis, a publisher who distributes various investment newsletters, known as the "Hot Stocks" publications, over the Internet and in print format, knowingly or recklessly made materially false and misleading statements concerning six publicly-traded companies. The complaint further alleges that from April 1994 through September 1995, Chelekis failed to disclose in the Hot Stocks publications that he and entities that he controls, defendants KGC, Inc. and Hot Stocks Review, Inc., received at least $1.1 million from more than 150 issuers, and 275,500 shares of stock from 10 issuers, as payment for recommending securities of such issuers in the Hot Stocks publications.

Without admitting or denying the allegations in the complaint, Chelekis, KGC, Inc. and Hot Stocks Review, Inc. consented to the entry of a final judgment permanently enjoining them from violating Section 10(b) of the Securities Exchange Act of 1934, and Rule 10b-5 thereunder, and Section 17(b) of the Securities Act of 1933. The final judgment orders the defendants to pay a total of $162,727, representing $75,050 in disgorgement, $12,627 in prejudgment interest and a $75,050 civil penalty. □

SECURITIES AND EXCHANGE COMMISSION

Litigation Release No. 15634 / February 3, 1998

Securities and Exchange Commission v. First Zurich National U.S.A., LLC and Compunomics 139, Inc. Civil Action No. 98-CV-29D (USDC Wy.)

On February 2, 1998, the U.S. Securities and Exchange Commission (the "Commission") filed an emergency action seeking to halt an affinity fraud being promoted over the internet and targeting African Americans. On February 3, 1998, the Commission obtained a temporary restraining order, including an asset freeze, from the United States District Court for the District of Wyoming against First Zurich National U.S.A., LLC ("First Zurich"), a Wyoming limited liability company ("LLC") and Compunomics 139, Inc. ("Compunomics"), a Belizean corporation based in southern California and the corporate parent of First Zurich. The Commission has received substantial assistance in this case from the California Department of Corporations, the Wyoming State Securities Division and the Cheyenne, Wyoming office of the United States Postal Inspection Service.

Compunomics has been offering and selling First Zurich stock since at least April 1997, which Compunomics claims has been operating as a "global internet bank" since November 1997. The Commission alleges that First Zurich and Compunomics have failed to disclose to prospective and current investors that First Zurich cannot legally operate as a bank. The Office of the Comptroller of the Currency has not granted a national bank charter to First Zurich nor has the Wyoming State Banking Board authorized First Zurich to conduct banking operations. Moreover, First Zurich, as a Wyoming LLC, is not permitted under Wyoming corporate law to conduct banking operations.

The Commission further alleges that Compunomics has been offering and selling First Zurich stock to its current shareholders and has made a sales presentation to a national church conference attended by approximately 30,000 individuals. Compunomics is promoting First Zurich on the internet, as well as through written materials and promotional meetings. The Commission alleges that the defendants are seeking to raise $60 million from 5,000 investors over a ten-year period and are currently receiving a minimum of between $50,000 and $75,000 per month from at least 500 and possibly as many as 750 investors nationwide. Investors have signed option agreements obligating them to purchase a fixed amount of First Zurich's stock for $1.25 per share by making an initial $98 payment and then monthly minimum payments of $99 for ten years, representing a total investment of $11,978 per investor.

The Commission's complaint charges that the defendants have violated the antifraud provisions of the federal securities laws -- Section 17(a) of the Securities Act of 1933 and Section 10(b) of the Securities Exchange Act of 1934 and Rule 10b-5 thereunder.

Investors are again advised to read the SEC's "Cyberspace" Alert before purchasing any investment promoted on the internet. The free

======END OF PAGE 1======

publication, which alerts investors to the telltale signs of online investment fraud, is available on the Investor Assistance and Complaints link of the SEC's Home page on the World Wide Web <www.sec.gov>. It can also be obtained by calling 800-SEC-0330.

Investors are encouraged to report suspicious internet offerings (or other suspicious offerings) via e-mail to <enforcement@sec.gov>. A user-friendly form to assist you in making a report is available at the Enforcement Complaint Center on the Enforcement Division link of the SEC Home Page. Investors can also mail a report to the SEC's Enforcement Complaint Center, Mail Stop 8-4, 450 Fifth Street, N.W., Washington, D.C. 20549.

UNITED STATES SECURITIES AND EXCHANGE COMMISSION

LITIGATION RELEASE NO. 15609 / January 6, 1998

SECURITIES AND EXCHANGE COMMISSION V. STEVEN SAMBLIS, ET AL. Case No. 98-001-CIV-ORL-22-C.

The Securities and Exchange Commission ("SEC") announced that it filed a complaint today in the U.S. District Court for the Middle District of Florida in Orlando against Steven Samblis and his corporation New Stock, Inc. ("NSI"). According to the SEC's Complaint, Defendant Samblis is a resident of the Orlando, Florida area and self-professed stock picker. The SEC alleges that Samblis, together with co-defendant NSI, is passing himself off as an independent and impartial stock picker when, in fact, he is nothing more than a paid pitch man for the companies he hypes.

In its Complaint, the SEC alleges that in October 1997 Samblis published a magazine, New Stock, in which he enthusiastically recommended the securities of certain publicly-traded companies without disclosing that he had been paid at least $20,000 to make these recommendations. The SEC also alleges that Samblis was paid to issue thousands of E-mails over the Internet regarding these same securities. The SEC learned of Samblis' activities when detected by the Enforcement Division's Internet Surveillance program.

The SEC is seeking an expedited hearing and preliminary injunction against Samblis and NSI for violating Section 17(b) of the Securities Act of 1933. Section 17(b) makes it illegal for any person to distribute any publication recommending a security while being paid to do so without fully disclosing that he has been or will be paid for recommending the stock and the amount he has been or will be paid. In addition to a preliminary injunction, the SEC seeks a permanent injunction against Samblis and NSI, disgorgement of ill-gotten profits, and civil money penalties.

Investors are advised to read the SEC's "Cyberspace" Alert before purchasing any investment promoted on the Internet. The free publication, which alerts investors to the telltale signs of online investment fraud, is available on the Investor Assistance and Complaints link of the SEC's Home page on the World Wide Web <www.sec.gov>. It can also be obtained by calling 800-SEC-0330. Investors are encouraged to report suspicious Internet offerings (or other suspicious offerings) via e-mail to <enforcement@sec.gov>. A user-friendly form to assist you in making a report is available at the Enforcement Complaint Center on the Enforcement Division link of the SEC Home Page <www.sec.gov>. Investors can also mail a report to the SEC's Enforcement Complaint Center, Mail Stop 8-4, 450 Fifth Street, Washington, D.C. 20549.

SECURITIES AND EXCHANGE COMMISSION

Litigation Release No. 15601 / December 23, 1997

Securities and Exchange Commission v. Capital Acquisitions, Inc., The Somerset Group, Inc., Wayne Notwell and Clealon Mann Civil Action No. 2:97CV-0977S (USDC UT.)

On December 23, 1997, the U.S. Securities and Exchange Commission (the "Commission") obtained a temporary restraining order, including an asset freeze, from the United States District Court for the District of Utah to halt a $20 million Ponzi scheme. Named as defendants in the Commission's complaint, filed December 19, are Capital Acquisitions, Inc. ("Capital"), The Somerset Group, Inc. ("Somerset"), Wayne Notwell ("Notwell") and Clealon Mann ("Mann"), all of Salt Lake City, Utah.

Capital, headed by Notwell, has raised funds from investors since 1996 with the avowed purpose of conducting oil and gas drilling operations in Kansas and California. Capital has raised approximately $20 million from at least 600 investors nationwide through sales of three-year notes offering an annual "guaranteed" return of 20%. Investors were solicited through a network of sales agents directed by Mann and Somerset. At least one of those agents posted the offering on the Internet which led to its detection by the Commission's Internet Surveillance Program.

The Commission alleges that the defendants have defrauded investors by conducting a Ponzi scheme, with the source of the promised interest payments being funds received from the ongoing sale of Capital's notes. While Capital claims to be operating numerous oil wells in Kansas and California, it has failed to disclose that the income from the wells is insufficient to pay the promised returns, which instead are being paid from monies received from new investors.

The Commission further alleges that the offering materials used in the sales of Capital's notes fail to disclose other important information. For example, nothing is said about the excessive commissions, approximately 46% of the amount raised, being paid to the sales agents. Nor is there any disclosure that New England International Surety, Inc., a Panamanian company which is the purported guarantor on the notes, is to receive 20% of the amount raised. Further, the materials fail to mention that Capital, the issuer of the notes, has no control over investor funds. Instead, the funds are being pooled in a single account controlled by Mann, who disburses monthly interest payments to investors and commission payments to sales agents, and pays expenses associated with Capital's business operations. Finally, the materials fail to disclose that Capital, Mann and Somerset were previously ordered by the State of Kansas to cease and desist from offering investments in oil and gas ventures.

The Commission's complaint charges that the defendants have violated the antifraud provisions of the federal securities laws -- Section 17(a) of the Securities Act of 1933 and Section 10(b) of the Securities Exchange Act of 1934 and Rule 10b-5 thereunder -- as well as the registration provisions of the same laws -- Sections 5(a) and 5(c) of the Securities Act.

Investors are advised to read the SEC's "Cyberspace" Alert before purchasing any investment promoted on the Internet. The free publication, which alerts investors to the telltale signs of online investment fraud, is available on the Investor Assistance and Complaints link of the SEC's Home page on the World Wide Web <www.sec.gov>. It can also be obtained by calling 800-SEC-0330.

Investors are encouraged to report suspicious Internet offerings (or other suspicious offerings) via e-mail to <enforcement@sec.gov>. A user-friendly form to assist you in making a report is available at the Enforcement Complaint Center on the Enforcement Division link of the SEC Home Page. Investors can also mail a report to the SEC's Enforcement Complaint Center, Mail Stop 8-4, 450 Fifth Street, Washington, D.C. 20549.

U.S. SECURITIES AND EXCHANGE COMMISSION

LITIGATION RELEASE NO. 15237 / January 31, 1997

SECURITIES AND EXCHANGE COMMISSION v. CHARLES O. HUTTOE, ET AL., Civil Action No. 96-02543 (GK)(D.D.C.)

UNITED STATES v. CHARLES O. HUTTOE, Cr. 96-429-A (JC)(E.D.Va.)

The Securities and Exchange Commission announced that the Honorable James C. Catheris, United States District Judge for the Eastern District of Virginia, today sentenced Charles O. Huttoe ("Huttoe"), formerly the Chairman and Chief Executive Officer of Systems of Excellence, Inc. ("SOE") to a federal prison term of 46 months followed by 2 years supervised release and a $10,000 fine. Huttoe was sentenced pursuant to a criminal information charging him with one count of securities fraud in violation of Section 10(b) of the Exchange Act and Rule 10b-5 thereunder, and one count of money laundering in violation of 18 U.S.C. □ 1957. Huttoe entered into a plea agreement with the government on November 13, 1996. Both the criminal information and the plea agreement were filed under seal and remained sealed until late yesterday.

On November 7, 1996, the Commission obtained a Temporary Restraining Order ("TRO") against Huttoe and others based on a complaint alleging a massive securities fraud at SOE. The TRO among other things prohibited ongoing violations of the securities laws, froze Huttoe's assets and prohibited him from traveling outside the United States. The criminal case against Huttoe was the result of a coordinated investigative effort by the Commission, the U.S. Attorney's Office for the Eastern District of Virginia and the Internal Revenue Service - Criminal Investigation Division from Northern Virginia and Las Vegas, Nevada. Huttoe's plea agreement requires that he cooperate in ongoing investigations conducted by the U.S. Attorney's Office and the Securities and Exchange Commission.

The criminal information alleged that, in connection with the securities fraud count, from March 1995 through September 1996, Huttoe, in his capacity as Chairman and CEO of SOE, directed and controlled a massive distribution of the company's stock. In particular, the criminal information alleges that Huttoe distributed approximately 11 million shares of unregistered SOE stock to certain nominees, including three of his relatives, under his control. Although fraudulently created documents indicated that the shares had been issued to Huttoe's nominees in exchange for services rendered to the company, in fact these nominees did not provide such services to SOE. The criminal information further states that, pursuant to a scheme to manipulate the market price of SOE stock, after the issuance of a number of false press releases which caused an increase in the price of the stock, Huttoe directed the sale of the shares issued
==START OF PAGE 2======

to his nominees. According to the information Huttoe realized millions of dollars of trading profits as a result of the sale of the nominee shares. In connection with the money laundering count, the criminal information further alleged that Huttoe subsequently transferred approximately $7.55 million of the trading profits from brokerage accounts opened in the names of the nominees to at least four different bank accounts opened in the names of the nominees. Thereafter, Huttoe transferred approximately $7.3 million from these accounts to an account at Patriot National Bank in Virginia. Finally, Huttoe transferred approximately $7.2 million out of this account by wire or check to various individuals or entities.

The Commission also announced that on January 21, 1997, at a hearing in the Commission's case against Huttoe and others in United States District Court for the District of Columbia, the Honorable Gladys Kessler granted in part the Commission's motion to amend its Complaint. The amended Complaint names eleven individuals and entities as relief defendants for the purpose of securing the disgorgement of more than $12 million in illegal profits that the Commission previously alleged were obtained from the sale of SOE securities by Huttoe, members of his family and entities he controls (collectively the "Huttoe defendants"). The Court also granted the Commission's motion to amend the Complaint to add additional claims against defendants SGA Goldstar Research, Inc., Theodore Melcher, Shannon B. Terry, Alpha Securities Ltd. and Dunbar Holdings, Ltd. (collectively the "Goldstar defendants"). As amended, the Complaint alleges that the Goldstar defendants engaged in a systematic practice of publishing highly promotional investment recommendations for numerous issuers in exchange for compensation. The amended Complaint alleges that the Goldstar defendants failed to disclose either their compensation or whether they were selling their shares in the companies they were touting while they were recommending that subscribers to their newsletter purchase shares in those companies.

Previously the Court issued orders freezing the assets of the Huttoe defendants and the Goldstar defendants. The Court continued that emergency relief, which includes freezes on the funds transferred by the Huttoe defendants to the relief defendants, until the next hearing in this matter, which is set for March 7, 1997 at 9:30 a.m. See SEC v. Huttoe, et al., Lit. Rel. 15153 (November 7, 1996), Lit. Rel. 15185 (December 12, 1996). On October 7, 1996, the Commission issued an Order suspending trading in SOE securities for ten days. See Securities Exchange Act Rel. No. 37791 (October 7, 1996).

The Commission is cooperating with separate investigations in this matter carried on by the United States Attorney's Office for the Eastern District of Virginia and the Criminal Investigation Division of the Internal Revenue Service.
==START OF PAGE 3======

The Commission's investigation in this matter is continuing.□

Securities and Exchange Commission v. Capital Acquisitions, Inc., The Somerset Group, Inc., Wayne Notwell and Clealon Mann **Civil Action No. 2:97CV-0977S (USDC UT.)**

LITIGATION Release No. 15601; December 23, 1997.

Securities and Exchange Commission v. Capital Acquisitions, Inc., The Somerset Group, Inc., Wayne Notwell and Clealon Mann Civil Action No. 2:97CV-0977S (USDC UT.)

On December 23, 1997, the U.S. Securities and Exchange Commission (the "Commission") obtained a temporary restraining order, including an asset freeze, from the United States District Court for the District of Utah to halt a $20 million Ponzi scheme. Named as defendants in the Commission's complaint, filed December 19, are Capital Acquisitions, Inc. ("Capital"), The Somerset Group, Inc. ("Somerset"), Wayne Notwell ("Notwell") and Clealon Mann ("Mann"), all of Salt Lake City, Utah.

Capital, headed by Notwell, has raised funds from investors since 1996 with the avowed purpose of conducting oil and gas drilling operations in Kansas and California. Capital has raised approximately $20 million from at least 600 investors nationwide through sales of three-year notes offering an annual "guaranteed" return of 20%. Investors were solicited through a network of sales agents directed by Mann and Somerset. At least one of those agents posted the offering on the Internet which led to its detection by the Commission's Internet Surveillance Program.

The Commission alleges that the defendants have defrauded investors by conducting a Ponzi scheme, with the source of the promised interest payments being funds received from the ongoing sale of Capital's notes. While Capital claims to be operating numerous oil wells in Kansas and California, it has failed to disclose that the income from the wells is insufficient to pay the promised returns, which instead are being paid from monies received from new investors.

The Commission further alleges that the offering materials used in the sales of Capital's notes fail to disclose other important information. For example, nothing is said about the excessive commissions, approximately 46% of the amount raised, being paid to the sales agents. Nor is there any disclosure that New England International Surety, Inc., a Panamanian company which is the purported guarantor on the notes, is to receive 20% of the amount raised. Further, the materials fail to mention that Capital, the issuer of the notes, has no control over investor funds. Instead, the funds are being pooled in a single account controlled by Mann, who disburses monthly interest payments to investors and commission payments to sales agents, and pays expenses associated with Capital's business operations. Finally, the materials fail to disclose that Capital, Mann and Somerset were previously ordered by the State of Kansas to cease and desist from offering investments in oil and gas ventures.

The Commission's complaint charges that the defendants have violated the antifraud provisions of the federal securities laws--Section 17(a) of the Securities Act of 1933 and Section 10(b) of the Securities Exchange Act of 1934 and Rule 10b-5 thereunder--as well as the registration provisions of the same laws--Sections 5(a) and 5(c) of the Securities Act.

Investors are advised to read the SEC's "Cyberspace" Alert before purchasing any investment promoted on the Internet. The free publication, which alerts investors to the telltale signs of online investment fraud, is available on the Investor Assistance and Complaints link of the SEC's Home page on the World Wide Web __www.sec.gov_. It can also be obtained by calling 800-SEC-0330.

Investors are encouraged to report suspicious Internet offerings (or other suspicious offerings) via e-mail to __enforcement@sec.gov_. A user-friendly form to assist you in making a report is available at the Enforcement Complaint Center on the Enforcement Division link of the SEC Home Page. Investors can also mail a report to the SEC's Enforcement Complaint Center, Mail Stop 8-4, 450 Fifth Street, Washington, D.C. 20549.

SECURITIES AND EXCHANGE COMMISSION V. Steven Samblis, et al. **Case No. 98-001-CIV-ORL-22-C.**

Litigation Release No. 15609; January 6, 1998.

SECURITIES AND EXCHANGE COMMISSION V. Steven Samblis, et al. Case No. 98-001-CIV-ORL-22-C.

The Securities and Exchange Commission ("SEC") announced that it filed a complaint today in the U.S. District Court for the Middle District of Florida in Orlando against Steven Samblis and his corporation New Stock, Inc. ("NSI"). According to the SEC's Complaint, Defendant Samblis is a resident of the Orlando, Florida area and self-professed stock picker. The SEC alleges that Samblis, together with co-defendant NSI, is passing himself off as an independent and impartial stock picker when, in fact, he is nothing more than a paid pitch man for the companies he hypes.

In its Complaint, the SEC alleges that in October 1997 Samblis published a magazine, *New Stock,* in which he enthusiastically recommended the securities of certain publicly-traded companies without disclosing that he had been paid at least $20,000 to make these recommendations. The SEC also alleges that Samblis was paid to issue thousands of E-mails over the Internet regarding these same securities. The SEC learned of Samblis' activities when detected by the Enforcement Division's Internet Surveillance program.

Investors are advised to read the SEC's "Cyberspace" Alert before purchasing any investment promoted on the Internet. The free publication, which alerts investors to the telltale signs of online investment fraud, is available on the Investor Assistance and Complaints link of the SEC's Home page on the World Wide Web __www.sec.gov_. It can also be obtained by calling 800-SEC-0330. Investors are encouraged to report suspicious Internet offerings (or other suspicious offerings) via e-mail to __enforcement@sec.gov_. A user-friendly form to assist you in making a report is available at the Enforcement Complaint Center on the Enforcement Division link of the SEC Home Page __www.sec.gov_. Investors can also mail a report to the SEC's Enforcement Complaint Center, Mail Stop 8-4, 450 Fifth Street, Washington, D.C. 20549.

SECURITIES AND EXCHANGE COMMISSION v. SHELDON KRAFT, **Civil Action No. 98-CV-00095 (GK) (D.D.C.)** ***UNITED STATES v. SHELDON KRAFT***, **Cr. 98-18-A (E.D. VA.)**

Litigation Release No. 15617; January 14, 1998.

SECURITIES AND EXCHANGE COMMISSION v. SHELDON KRAFT, Civil Action No. 98-CV-00095 (GK) (D.D.C.) *UNITED STATES v. SHELDON KRAFT*, Cr. 98-18-A (E.D. VA.)

The Securities and Exchange Commission ("Commission") today filed a Complaint against Sheldon Kraft ("Kraft"), 46, a New York City stock broker, in the United States District Court for the District of Columbia. This case is another in a line of significant Commission enforcement actions and/or criminal prosecutions arising from this wide-ranging investigation of microcap fraud involving Systems of Excellence, Inc. ("SOE") and other issuers. The Complaint alleges that Kraft acted as the principal facilitator for Charles O. Huttoe ("Huttoe"), formerly the Chairman and CEO of SOE, in manipulating the market for the securities of that company. Simultaneously with the filing of the Complaint, Kraft consented, without admitting or denying the Commission's allegations, to an order enjoining him from violations of the securities registration and antifraud provisions of the federal securities laws, and requiring him to disgorge his illegal gains of $3,193,337 from the manipulation of SOE securities, together with prejudgment interest. In satisfaction of the disgorgement judgment, Kraft will disgorge all of his assets except his residence and household items. The disgorged assets include $1,107,000 in cash, plus certain real estate and claims that he has against his former employer. Any remainder of the disgorgement amount will be waived in light of Kraft's demonstrated inability to pay based on his sworn representations in his statement of financial condition. Kraft also agreed to a Commission order barring him from the securities industry and from participating in an offering of penny stock. The Commission's Complaint alleges the following:

Kraft met Huttoe in early 1995, and thereafter guided Huttoe throughout the manipulation of SOE. When SOE's original software business collapsed, Kraft found a high-tech video teleconferencing business to put into the SOE shell so as to make it attractive to investors. Thereafter, Kraft introduced Huttoe to his "total world"--Kraft's network of brokers, market makers, and stock touters--who Huttoe then bribed with SOE stock to manipulate the price of SOE. As a result of Kraft's introductions, Huttoe entered into such arrangements with five stock promoters who were to push sales of SOE stock to retail brokerage customers, three stock touters who would disseminate recommendations to purchase SOE via mass media and other means, and two traders at market making broker-dealer firms who agreed to support the price of SOE. As a result of these and other manipulative activities, SOE's stock price rose from pennies to $4 9/16 per share in just a few months. In addition, Kraft directed Huttoe in establishing nominee accounts through which Kraft secretly sold more than 6.3 million shares of SOE stock for Huttoe into the inflated market, on which Huttoe realized proceeds of approximately $9.62 million of his more than $12.5 million of illegal profits derived from the SOE manipulation.

For his part in the SOE fraud, Kraft demanded compensation in the form of direct cash payments from Huttoe and free trading shares of SOE stock that he had Huttoe issue in the names of his nominees. Kraft also obtained kickbacks from the persons he introduced to Huttoe in the form of cash or a portion of the SOE stock Huttoe supplied them in exchange for carrying out their roles in the manipulation. Kraft then sold his free SOE stock--a total of approximately 1.66 million shares--into the inflated market through nominee accounts in the United States and Canada. In addition, in exchange for directing the illegal sales of SOE stock in Huttoe's nominee accounts, Kraft received his ordinary commissions, and a percentage of the proceeds from the sale of stock through Huttoe's nominee accounts. In total, Kraft made illegal profits of $3,193,337 from his role in the SOE scheme.

The Commission's Complaint alleges that as a result of that conduct Kraft violated Sections 5 and 17(a) of the Securities Act of 1933, and Section 10(b) of the Securities Exchange Act of 1934 and Rule 10b-5 thereunder. The court order to which Kraft consented enjoins him from future violations of those provisions. Kraft also consented to the entry of a Commission order pursuant to Sections 15(b) and 19(h) of the Exchange Act barring him from association with any broker, dealer, municipal securities dealer, investment adviser or investment company, or participation in any offering of penny stock, based on the entry of the above injunction.

Also today in the United States District Court for the Eastern District of Virginia, Kraft pleaded guilty to a two-count criminal information charging him with one count of conspiracy to commit securities fraud and money laundering and one count of failure to file tax returns. Kraft's plea was in connection with, among other things, the fraud involving SOE.

Background

The Commission Prosecutions

The Criminal Prosecutions

In terms of criminal actions, Kraft is the fifth individual to plead guilty to felony charges stemming from these matters. On January 31, 1997, Huttoe, who presently is incarcerated, was sentenced to a federal prison term of 46 months, followed by two years supervised release, and a $10,000 fine, pursuant to a criminal information charging him with one count of securities fraud and one count of money laundering. On March 12, 1997, Finkel pleaded guilty to a criminal information charging him with one count of conspiracy to commit securities fraud and bank fraud, and is awaiting sentencing. On September 12, 1997, Melcher, who presently is incarcerated, was sentenced to a prison term of 12 months, followed by two years supervised release, and a $20,000 fine, pursuant to a criminal information charging him with conspiracy to commit securities fraud. On December 22, 1997, Davis, who is awaiting sentencing, pleaded guilty to one count of conspiracy to commit securities fraud and bank fraud, and one count of money laundering.

***

The Commission is cooperating with separate investigations in this matter carried on by the United States Attorney's Offices for the District of Nevada and the Eastern District of Virginia, and the Criminal Investigation Division of the Internal Revenue Service.

The Commission's investigation in this matter is continuing.

EXHIBIT B

SYSTEMS OF EXCELLENCE,
RELEASE NO. 34-37791 (OCT. 1996)

The Securities and Exchange Commission today ordered the temporary suspension, pursuant to Section 12(k) of the Securities Exchange Act of 1934 ('Exchange Act'), of trading in the securities of Systems of Excellence, Inc. ('SOE'), beginning at 9:00 a.m. EDT on October 7, 1996 and concluding at 11:59 p.m. EDT on October 21, 1996. SOE is located in Coral Gables, Florida and McLean, Virginia.

62 SEC-DOCKET 2742

Release No. 34-37791

October 7, 1996

The Securities and Exchange Commission today ordered the temporary suspension, pursuant to Section 12(k) of the Securities Exchange Act of 1934 ('Exchange Act'), of trading in the securities of Systems of Excellence, Inc. ('SOE'), beginning at 9:00 a.m. EDT on October 7, 1996 and concluding at 11:59 p.m. EDT on October 21, 1996. SOE is located in Coral Gables, Florida and McLean, Virginia.

The Commission ordered this trading suspension because of questions raised as to the adequacy and accuracy of publicly-disseminated information concerning, among other things: (1) SOE's reported financial condition; (2) the existence and value of services rendered to SOE in exchange for stock issued by SOE; (3) whether stock was issued by SOE to consultants without registration; (4) the reasons for changes in SOE's independent accountants; and (5) SOE's sales of its video teleconferencing products. The Commission determined that the public interest and the protection of investors requires a suspension of trading in SOE securities.

The Commission cautions broker-dealers, shareholders, and prospective purchasers that they should carefully consider the foregoing information along with all other currently available information and any information subsequently issued by the company.

Further, brokers and dealers should be alert to the fact that, pursuant to Rule 15c2-11 under the Exchange Act, at the termination of the trading suspension, no quotation may be entered unless and until they have strictly complied with all of the provisions of the rule. If any broker or dealer has any questions as to whether or not he has complied with the rule, he should not enter any quotation but immediately contact the staff of the Securities and Exchange Commission in Washington, D.C. If any broker or dealer is uncertain as to what is required by Rule 15c2-11, he should refrain from entering quotations relating to SOE's securities until such time as he has familiarized himself with the rule and is certain that all of its provisions have been met. If any broker or dealer enters any quotation which is in violation of the rule, the Commission will consider the need for prompt enforcement action.

EXHIBIT C

VARIOUS INTERNET RELATED SEC NO-ACTION LETTERS PERTAINING TO ONLINE TRADING FACILITIES

1ST LETTER of Level 1 printed in FULL format.

1996 SEC No-Act. LEXIS 435

Securities Exchange Act of 1933

April 17, 1996

[*1] Spring Street Brewing Company

TOTAL NUMBER OF LETTERS: 1

SEC-REPLY-1: SECURITIES AND EXCHANGE COMMISSION
WASHINGTON, D.C. 20549

March 22, 1996

Mr. Andrew D. Klein
President & Chief Executive Officer
Spring Street Brewing Company
113 University Place, Suite 11-B
New York, New York 10003

Dear Mr. Klein:

This letter follows up on the issues we discussed in our most recent telephone conversation concerning Spring Street Brewing Company's bulletin board-based stock trading mechanism, Wit-Trade. We thought it was important to communicate our concerns quickly following your suspension of activity earlier this week. Based on your experience as a securities lawyer, you will understand that we have a number of concerns about the Company's operation of Wit-Trade.

Innovation and creativity are the hallmark of our nation's securities markets, contributing enormously to the most efficient capital formation system in the world. We try to encourage such modernization, but it is our job, first and foremost, to insure protections for public investors. We recognize that Wit-Trade is an innovative mechanism that has the potential to provide Company shareholders with greater liquidity in their investments. We appreciate that the Company [*2] is providing this service at its own expense, and we understand that the Company is not involved in negotiating, crossing or otherwise facilitating the execution of the bids and offers posted on Wit-Trade. Nevertheless, we believe that, without certain modifications, investors using your system may not be adequately protected. In particular, we are concerned that investors' funds and securities be handled appropriately, that investors understand the risks involved in purchasing illiquid and speculative securities, that buyers are aware of last sale prices and that investors are provided with ongoing disclosure about the Company.

Access to and control of investor funds must be handled carefully to provide investors using your system with adequate protections. As you are not a registered broker-dealer, we suggest you modify your system to eliminate the Company's control over these funds. At a minimum, the Company should use an independent agent, such as a bank or escrow agent, to receive checks from buyers payable to the seller of the security or the bank (rather than payable to

Spring Street Brewing Company). Investors should send their checks directly to this independent agent, rather [*3] than to Spring Street.

To prevent customer confusion about the role of your system, you should supplement the information currently provided by adding information that is particularly relevant to first time investors, informing them of the risks inherent in investing in illiquid securities. For example, consistent with investor protection the Company should disclose that its shares are not traded on any registered securities exchange or through Nasdaq. Investors should be informed that the market for the Company's shares may be highly illiquid and that there is no guarantee that they will be able to sell the Company's shares at the price they paid for them, or at any particular published indication of interest.

Users of the system should be informed that if they choose to post quotations simultaneously on both the Buyer and Seller Bulletin Boards they may be considered a "dealer" that is required to register and comply with broker-dealer requirements under the federal securities laws. All transactions facilitated through Wit-Trade are, of course, subject to the antifraud provisions of the federal securities laws, including the anti-manipulation provisions.

We also believe that a transaction [*4] history would allow investors to make more informed investment decisions. We believe that the price and number of shares for recent transactions should be disclosed through the system; we understand that you are planning to provide certain price and volume information. To deter manipulation, it would be helpful if you kept records of all quotations posted on Wit-Trade and of all securities transactions effected through use of the system and make them available to us upon reasonable request.

In addition, the sale of securities through Wit-Trade appears to involve an offer or sale by Spring Street for purposes of the Securities Act of 1933. In this regard, please note that the Division of Corporation Finance's views regarding the application of the registration requirements of the Securities Act to services such as Wit-Trade are set forth in the no-action response to King & Spalding (November 17, 1992).

Absent an available exemption, Spring Street would be required to register under the Securities Act and undertake to keep the registration statement "evergreen" during the existence of Wit-Trade It is our view that the Regulation A exemption may be used in connection with a service [*5] such as Wit-Trade. In this regard, the offering circular used in connection with the Regulation A exemption should be delivered and updated in accordance with Regulation A. We note that the Company employed electronic delivery mechanisms in its original Regulation A offering. This approach would continue to be acceptable, although you should consider the Commission's interpretive guidance regarding electronic delivery released last October.

We are available to answer any questions. Because of the innovative nature of your system and the issues raised, we believe that interpretive relief is appropriate for your situation, and we look forward to working with you in anticipation of providing this relief.

Sincerely,

Abigail Arms

Associate Director - Legal
Division of Corporation Finance
202-942-2890

Catherine McGuire
Associate Director
Division of Market Regulation
202-942-0061

1ST LETTER of Level 1 printed in FULL format.

1996 SEC No-Act. LEXIS 972

Securities Exchange Act of 1934 -- Sections 5, 6, 15; Securities Act of 1933 -- Section 5

October 29, 1996

[*1] The Flamemaster Corporation

TOTAL NUMBER OF LETTERS: 2

SEC-REPLY-1: SECURITIES AND EXCHANGE COMMISSION
WASHINGTON, D.C. 20549

October 29, 1996

Bruce D. Stuart, Esq.
Law Offices of Bruce D. Stuart
8501 Wilshire Blvd. - Suite 215
Beverly Hills, CA 90211

Re: The Flamemaster Corporation

Dear Mr. Stuart:

On the basis of the facts presented in your letter dated October 23, 1996 ("Letter"), the Division of Market Regulation will not recommend an enforcement action to the Commission under Sections 5, 6, or 15 of the Securities Exchange Act of 1934 ("Exchange Act") if The Flamemaster Corporation ("FAME") operates its trading system (the "System") in the manner described in that letter without registration as a national securities exchange under Section 6 or as a broker-dealer under Section 15 of the Exchange Act. This is a position of the Division of Market Regulation regarding enforcement action under Sections 5, 6, and 15 of the Exchange Act only, and does not express any legal conclusions regarding the applicability of Sections 5, 6, or 15 of the Exchange Act or other statutory or regulatory provisions of the federal securities laws. This no-action position is subject to changes in current law, regulation, and interpretations [*2] governing issuer-based bulletin boards; any change may require the Division of Market Regulation to reevaluate and revoke or modify this no-action position.

In reaching this position, the Division of Market Regulation notes the following: (1) FAME will provide the described notices regarding operation of and participation on the System that will be set forth or contained on the screens and/or hard copy by which System information is provided; (2) FAME is a Section 12 registrant that will retain that status or, if it should cease to be a Section 12 registrant, otherwise undertake to make publicly available the information required by Section 13(a) of the Exchange Act in the same manner that participants will obtain access to the System (e.g., electronic mail, facsimile, mail, FAME's World-Wide Web site, etc.); (3) FAME will keep records of all quotes entered into the System and make those records available to the Commission and the National Association of Securities Dealers, Inc. (or any regulated market on which FAME securities are listed); (4) FAME's advertising will comply with the representations set forth in your Letter; (5) neither FAME nor any affiliate of FAME will use the [*3] System, directly or indirectly, to offer to buy or sell securities, except in compliance with the securities laws, including any applicable registration requirements (absent an available exemption therefrom); and (6) neither FAME nor any affiliate of FAME will (i) receive any compensation for creating or maintaining the System; (ii) receive any compensation for the use of the System; (iii) be involved in any purchase or sale negotiations arising from the System; (iv) provide information regarding the advisability of buying or selling FAME common stock or any other securities; or (v) receive, transfer, or hold funds or securities as an incident of operating the System.

The Division of Market Regulation notes that the facts presented with respect to the establishment and maintenance of the System are substantially identical to those presented in the no-action requests from Real Goods Trading Corp. (available June 24, 1996) and PerfectData Corp. (available August 5, 1996). Having stated its views on the application of the registration requirements of the Exchange Act to such systems, the Division of Market Regulation no longer will respond to requests for no-action assurance with [*4] respect to systems that are established and maintained in a substantially similar manner, unless they present novel or unusual issues.

The Division of Corporation Finance has asked us to inform you that, based on the facts presented, the activities of FAME in connection with the establishment and maintenance of the System would not require that offers and sales made through the System be registered under the Securities Act of 1933 (the "Securities Act"). Further, the Division of Corporation Finance notes that the facts presented with respect to the establishment and maintenance of the System are substantially identical to those presented in the no-action requests from Real Good Trading Corp. (available June 24, 1996) and PerfectData Corp. (available August 5, 1996). Having stated its views on the application of the registration requirements of the Securities Act to such systems, the Division of Corporation Finance no longer will respond to requests for no-action assurance with respect to systems that are established and maintained in a substantially similar manner, unless they present novel or unusual issues.

Because these positions are based on the representations made to [*5] the Divisions, any different facts or conditions might require different conclusions.

Sincerely,

Catherine McGuire
Chief Counsel

INQUIRY-1:
LAW OFFICES OF
BRUCE D. STUART

8501 WILSHIRE BOULEVARD
SUITE 215
BEVERLY HILLS
CALIFORNIA

LAW OFFICES OF
BRUCE D. STUART

SECURITIES AND EXCHANGE COMMISSION
RECEIVED
AUG 9 1996
DIVISION OF MARKET REGULATION

August 5, 1996

VIA FAX & U.S. MAIL

Catherine McGuire
Associate Director/Chief Counsel
Division of Market Regulation
Securities and Exchange Commission
450 Fifth Street, NW, Mail Stop 5-10
Washington, D.C. 20549

VIA FAX & U.S. MAIL

Martin P. Dunn
Chief Counsel
Division of Corporate Finance
Securities and Exchange Commission
450 Fifth Street NW, Mail Stop 3-3
Washington, D.C. 20549

VIA FAX & U.S. MAIL

Jack W. Murphy
Associate Director/Chief Counsel
Division of Investment Management
Securities and Exchange Commission
450 Fifth Street, NW, Mail Stop 10-6
Washington, D.C. 20549

Re: PerfectData Corporation
Securities Act of 1934 (Sections 5, 6 and 15);
Investment Advisers Act of 1940 (Section 204(a);
Securities Act of 1933 (Section 5)

Dear Ms. McGuire, Mr. Murphy and Mr. Dunn:

I am counsel to PerfectData Corporation ("PERF"), a California Corporation. Its stock is traded on NASDAQ Small Cap and is registered under Section 12 of the Securities Exchange Act of 1934, as Amended (the "Exchange Act"). PERF sells computer cleaning products and accessories.

8501
WILSHIRE BOULEVARD
SUITE 215
BEVERLY HILLS
CALIFORNIA
90211
310-358-2330
F 310-358-2344

I. BACKGROUND

On July 12, 1983, PERF went public through an S-1 offering under the Securities Act of 1933. The offering was fully subscribed. It's shares have been traded on NASDAQ Small Cap since that time. The shares of PERF Common Stock became registered under Section 12 of the Exchange Act at that time. Wells Fargo Bank is the transfer agent of the Common Stock.

Trading in the Common Stock was approximately 2,000 - 5,000 shares per day until May, 1996. Since that time, the volume has increased significantly, to approximately 10,000 to 600,000 shares per day.

PERF now proposes to establish an "off the grid" trading system (the "System") for the Common Stock. The System would function as a passive "bulletin board" providing information to prospective sellers and buyers of Common Stock ("Participants"). The information to be listed on the System would include: (i) the names, address and telephone numbers (or other contact mechanisms, such as electronic mail addresses) of interested buyers and sellers; (ii) the number of shares of Common Stock that are offered for sale or desired to be purchased; (iii) the price at which the Common Stock is offered for sale or desire to be purchased; and (iv) the date on which the information was entered into the System. Participants would transmit the above information either (i) by direct interface using PERF's World Wide Web site or (ii) by telephone, facsimile, mail or electronic mail directed to PERF, which would enter the data into the System. The information would remain in the System until such time as a Participant indicates that a transaction was completed or the Participant no longer is interested in buying or selling, although PERF also may put a time limit on how long the information will be posted. PERF anticipates that Participants will obtain access to the System primarily by electronic mail, although information may also be relayed by telephone, facsimile, mail or any other method, including via PERF's World Wide Web site.

No transactions would be effected by the System itself, and PERF will have no role in effecting transactions between Participants; rather all transactions would be effected only by direct contact between the Participants. Although PERF would have no transactions records, it will retain records of the quotations listed for not less than three years and make them available to the staff of the Securities and Exchange Commission (the "Commission") and to the NASDAQ Stock Exchange (or any other regulated market on which the shares are listed) on reasonable request thereof. Each Participant would be required to rely on its own exemption under the Securities Act including, without limitation, Section 4(1) thereof. PERF proposes to advertise to shareholders and other members of the public the availability and possible benefits of the System. The System may be free standing or may be integrated into PERF's World Wide Web site or both.

Neither PERF nor any affiliate of PERF will (i) receive any compensation for creating or maintaining the System; (ii) receive any compensation for the use of the System; (ii) be involved in any purchase or sale negotiations arising from the System; (iv) give advice regarding the merits or shortcomings of any particular trade; (v) use the System, directly or indirectly, to offer to buy or sell securities, except in compliance with the securities laws, including any applicable registration requirements (absent an available exemption therefrom) [1]; or (vi) receive, transfer or hold funds or securities as an incident of operating the System.

The screens and hard copy by which the System data is provided to Participants will include the following information:

- Identification of the national securities exchange or other regulated securities market that lists PERF Common Stock;
- PERF is not a registered national securities exchange, securities information processor, broker, dealer or investment adviser;
- The information set forth on the System does not consist of firm quotes, but rather is merely a list of the names, addresses and telephone numbers of interested sellers and buyers, the number of shares of Common Stock offered or

[1] Offers and sales of nonrestricted securities by persons other than PERF or affiliates of PERF could be made in reliance upon the exemptions from registration provided by Sections 4(l), 4(3), or 4(4), as appropriate. Offers and sales of controlled or restricted securities may be made through a registered offering or in reliance upon an exemption from registration, such as the Section 4(l) exemption, if the requirements of Rule 144 are satisfied. In this regard, it is recognized that the "manner of sale" requirements of Rule 144 would be applicable to such transactions. Offers or sales of securities by PERF may be made either in registered transactions or in accordance with an available exemption, such as Regulation A or Rule 504 of Regulation D under the Securities Act.

desired to be purchased, and the price at which the proposed transaction would occur. PERF does not assure that any particular transaction will occur as to any particular number of shares or at any particular price. All transactions between Participants must be executed by the Participants independent of PERF or any of its affiliates;

- All applicable state and federal securities laws (including the anti-fraud and anti-manipulation provisions) apply to any offer made or transaction consummated using the System;

- The name, address and telephone number of PERF's transfer agent;

- Any person that is a broker-dealer, an associated person of a broker-dealer, or who has a state securities license is responsible for identifying that fact;

- "Two sided quotes" in which a person indicates a bid to buy at one price and an offer to sell at a higher price are prohibited. [2]

- The registration requirements of the federal securities laws apply to all offers and sales through the System, absent an available exemption. Offers and sales of controlled or restricted securities may be made in reliance upon the Section 4(1) exemption if the requirements of Rule 144, including the "manner of sale" requirements, are salified. Please note that the public information, volume, manner of sale and notification requirements of Rule 144 do not apply to transactions that satisfy the requirements of Rule 144(k).

PERF may make announcements relating to, and advertise or otherwise publicize, the existence and availability of the System and provide information about the use and benefits of the System.

---

[2] PERF may in the future permit two-sided quotes. If PERF chooses to permit two-sided quotes, the screens and hard copy by which the System data is provided to Participants will include a statement that: Any person providing "two-sided-quotes" in which a person indicates a bid to buy at one price and an offer to sell at a higher price, may in certain circumstances, be considered a dealer who is required to register with the SEC and comply with applicable provisions of the federal securities laws.

PERF may use any mechanism for providing information about the System. In its communications with the public PERF will not characterize itself or the System as being a "broker", a "dealer", or an "exchange." To the same extent as required of any company whose securities are traded on a national securities exchange or NASDAQ, PERF will be mindful of the statutory provisions relating to solicitations of any offer to buy. If PERF provides information about PERF or the System during an offering of its securities that is registered with the Commission, PERF also will be sensitive to and abide by the general limitations of the federal securities laws regarding publicity by a company that is "in registration." Of course, all information provided by PERF regarding either the System or PERF will be consistent with the antifraud and antimanipulation requirements of the federal securities laws.

We respectfully request that the staff (the "Staff") of the Commission concur with our view that PERF may establish and operate the System as described herein without (i) PERF registering as an "investment adviser" under Section 203(a) of the Investment Advisers Act of 1940, as amended (the "Advisers Act"); (ii) PERF, or any of its personnel who will manage and operate the System, registering as a "broker" and/or "dealer" under Section 15(a) of the Exchange Act; (iii) the registration of the System as a "national securities exchange" under Section 6 of the Exchange Act; or (iv) the registration of offers and sales made through the System under the Securities Act.

II. REGISTRATION ISSUES

Broker and Dealer

Subject to certain exceptions, Section 15(a) of the Exchange Act requires registration of any broker or dealer. Section 3(a)(5) of the Exchange Act defines a "dealer" as "any person engaged in the business of buying and selling securities for his own account." Section (3)(a)(4) defines a "broker" "any person engaged in the business of effecting transactions in securities for the accounts of others . . ." PERF will not be engaging in any activities requiring it to register as a broker or dealer under Section 15(a). This conclusion is consistent with the Staff's determination regarding a system similar to the System in *Farmland Industries, Inc.* (August 26, 1991).

Requiring PERF to register as a broker-dealer would not provide the Participants with any additional protection. Because

PERF will not handle or hold funds or shares of Common Stock of any Participant, a minimum capital requirement is unnecessary. Any financial failure of PERf would result only in the loss of the Participants' access to the System, and not a loss of their funds. Furthermore, the costs of compliance with the record keeping and periodic reporting requirements would far outweigh any benefits.

National Securities Exchange

Section 5 of the Exchange Act provides that it is unlawful for an exchange to effect any transaction in a security unless such exchange is registered as a national securities exchange under Section 6 of the Exchange Act or is exempted from such a registration upon application to the Commission.

Section 3(a)(1) of the Exchange Act defines "exchange" as:

> any organization, association or group of persons, whether incorporated or unincorporated, which constitutes, maintains, or provides a market place or facilities for bringing together purchasers and sellers of securities or for otherwise performing with respect to securities the functions commonly performed by a stock exchange as that term is generally understood, and includes the market place and the market facilities maintained by such exchange.

Based on the law and the foregoing facts, we are of the opinion that the System would not be an "exchange" within the meaning of the Exchange Act. In addition, PERF notes that it is a Section 12 registrant and will retain that status or, if it should cease to be a Section 12 registrant, otherwise undertake to make publicly available the information required by Section 13(a) of the Exchange Act in the same manner that Participants will obtain access to the System (e.g. electronic mail, facsimile, mail, PERF's World Wide Web site, etc). Consequently, there are no issues raised regarding the necessity of providing information to System Participants.

Investment Adviser

Subject to certain exceptions, Section 203(a) of the Advisers Act requires the registration of an investment adviser. Section 202(a)(11) of the Adverse Act defines an "investment adviser" as:

> any person who, for compensation, engages in the business of advising others, either directly or through publications or writings, as to the value of securities or as to the advisability of investing in, purchasing, or selling securities, or who, for compensation and as a part of a regular business, issues or promulgates analyses or reports concerning securities . . .

As indicated above, neither PERF nor the System will provide information regarding the advisability of buying or selling Common Stock or any other securities. Similarly, PERF will not receive any compensation for operating the System. The System will merely provide a passive medium for Participants to obtain information regarding other Participants who are interested in buying or selling Common Stock. Thus, PERF will not be engaging in any activities requiring registration as an investment adviser under the Advisers Act. This conclusion is consistent with the Staff's determination regarding a system similar to the System in *Farmland Industries, Inc., supra*.

Securities Act of 1933

Section 5 of the Securities Act makes it unlawful for any person to offer, sell, or solicit an offer to purchase any security unless a registration statement has been filed with respect to that security, absent an available exemption. In view of the manner in which the System will be established and operated, PERF believes that the operation of the System does not constitute an offer to sell or the solicitation of an offer to buy PERF Common Stock on the part of PERF. As such, PERF activities in connection with the establishment and maintenance of the System would not require Securities Act registration of offers or sales made through the System.

III. CONCLUSION

For the foregoing reasons, we request that the Staff concur with our view that PERF may establish and operate the System without (i) PERF registering as an "investment adviser" under Section 203(a) of the Advisers Act, (ii) PERF, or any of its personnel who will manage and operate the System, registering as a "broker" and/or "dealer" under Section 15(a) of the Exchange Act; (iii) the registration of the System as a "national securities exchange" under Section 6 of the Exchange Act; or (iv) registering offers and sales made through the System under the Securities Act.

In the event that the Staff does not concur with any of our views, we kindly request an opportunity to discuss the matter prior to any final decision thereon. If you have any questions or wish to receive any further information, please contact me at 310-358-2330.

Very truly yours,

Bruce D. Stuart

BDS:lw

UNITED STATES
SECURITIES AND EXCHANGE COMMISSION
WASHINGTON, D.C. 20549

DIVISION OF
MARKET REGULATION

August 5, 1996

Bruce D. Stuart, Esq.
Law Offices of Bruce D. Stuart
8501 Wilshire Blvd. - Suite 215
Beverly Hills, CA 90211

Re: PerfectData Corporation

Dear Mr. Stuart:

On the basis of the facts presented in your letter dated August 5, 1996 ("Letter"), the Division of Market Regulation will not recommend an enforcement action to the Commission under Sections 5, 6, or 15 of the Securities Exchange Act of 1934 ("Exchange Act") if PerfectData Corporation ("PERF") operates its trading system (the "System") in the manner described in that Letter without registration as a national securities exchange under Section 6 or as a broker-dealer under Section 15 of the Exchange Act. This is a position of the Division of Market Regulation regarding enforcement action under Sections 5, 6, and 15 of the Exchange Act only, and does not express any legal conclusions regarding the applicability of Sections 5, 6, or 15 of the Exchange Act or other statutory or regulatory provisions of the federal securities laws. This no-action position is subject to changes in current law, regulation, and interpretations governing issuer-based bulletin boards; any change may require the Division of Market Regulation to reevaluate and revoke or modify this no-action position.

In reaching this position, the Division of Market Regulation notes the following: (1) PERF will provide the described notices regarding operation of and participation on the System that will be set forth or contained on the screens and/or hard copy by which System information is provided; (2) PERF is a Section 12 registrant that will retain that status or, if it should cease to be a Section 12 registrant, otherwise undertake to make publicly available the information required by Section 13(a) of the Exchange Act in the same manner that Participants will obtain access to the System (e.g., electronic mail, facsimile, mail, PERF's World-Wide Web site, etc.); (3) PERF will keep records of all quotes entered into the System and make those records available to the Commission and the National Association of Securities Dealers, Inc. (or any other regulated market on which PERF securities are listed); (4) PERF's advertising will comply with the representations set forth in your Letter; (5) neither PERF nor any affiliate of PERF will use the System, directly or indirectly, to offer to buy or sell securities, except in compliance with the securities laws, including any applicable registration requirements (absent an available exemption therefrom); and (6) neither PERF nor any affiliate of PERF will (i) receive any compensation for creating or maintaining the System; (ii) receive any compensation for the use of the System; (iii) be involved in any purchase or sale negotiations arising from the System; (iv) provide information regarding the advisability of buying or selling PERF common stock or any other securities; or (v) receive, transfer, or hold funds or securities as an incident of operating the System.

The Division of Corporation Finance has asked us to inform you of its view that, based on the facts presented in your Letter, the activities of PERF in connection with the establishment and maintenance of the System would not require that offers or sales made through the System be registered under the Securities Act of 1933.

The Division of Investment Management has asked us to inform you that PERF may engage in the activities described in your Letter without becoming an investment adviser as defined in the Investment Advisers Act of 1940 ("Advisers Act"). The position of the Division of Investment Management is particularly based upon your representations that neither PERF nor any affiliate will: (1) receive compensation for creating or maintaining the System or for the use of the System; (2) be involved in any purchase or sale negotiations arising from the System; or (3) give advice regarding the merits or shortcomings of any particular trade. Having stated their views with respect to the status under the Advisers Act of an issuer that creates an electronic bulletin board to facilitate trading of its securities,[1] the staff of the Division of Investment Management will no longer respond to letters raising this question unless a novel or unique issue is presented.

Because these positions are based on the representations made to the Divisions, any different facts or conditions might require different conclusions.

Sincerely,

Catherine McGuire
Chief Counsel

---

[1] See Real Goods Trading Corp. (pub. avail. June 24, 1996); see also Farmland Industries, Inc. (pub. avail. Aug. 26, 1991).

United States

Securities and Exchange Commission

Washington, D.C. 20549

October 25, 1996

Jere W. Glover
Chief Counsel for Advocacy
U.S. Small Business Administration
409 3rd Street, S.W.
Washington, D.C. 20416

Gregory J. Dean, Jr.
Assistant Chief Counsel for Banking and Finance
U.S. Small Business Administration
409 3rd Street, S.W.
Washington,. D.C. 20416

Re: Angel Capital Electronic Network

Dear Mr. Glover and Mr. Dean

On the basis of your representation and the facts set forth in your letter of October 23, 1996, the Division of Market Regulation will not recommend enforcement action to the Commission under Section 15(a) of the Securities Exchange Act of 1934 ("Exchange Act") against the Angel Capital Electronic Network (the "Network"), or the various universities and non-profit entities (and/or their non-profit subsidies) that will participate in operating the Network ("Network Operators"), if the Network and Network Operators engage in the activities described in your letter without registering with the Commission as broker-dealers pursuant to Section 15(b) of the Exchange Act. In taking this position, the Division particularly notes that the Network and the Network Operators will not: (1) provide advice about the merits of particular opportunities or ventures; (2) receive compensation from Network users other than nominal, flat fees to cover administrative costs and that such fees will not be made contingent upon the outcome or completion of any securities transaction resulting from a listing on the Network; (3) participate in any negotiations between investors and listing companies; (4) directly assist investors or listing companies with the completion of any transaction, for example, through the provision of closing documentation or paid referrals to attorneys or other professionals; (5) handle funds or securities involved in completing a transaction; or (6) hold themselves out as providing any securities-related services other than a listing or matching service. The Division also notes that you have represented that Network officials, participants, and employees with direct or indirect operating or supervisory control over Network Operators will not participate as entrepreneurs or investors in any company listed on the Network, except in compliance with federal securities laws and unless such participation is disclosed to users of the Network, and that such persons will not discuss any matters with listing companies, investors or other persons that might require familiarity with securities or the exercise of judgment concerning securities activities. In addition, you have represented that no transactions or negotiations will occur by or through the Network.

Also, on the basis of your representations and the facts set forth in your letter, the Division will not recommend enforcement action under Section 5 or Section 6 of the Exchange Act if the Network and the Network Operators engage in the activities described in your letter without the registration of the Network as a national securities exchange under Section 6 of the Exchange Act.

The Division of Investment Management has asked us to inform you that, with respect to the listing service created and maintained by the Network and the Network Operators, the staff has taken the position that information relating to securities does not constitute an "analysis" or "report" within the meaning of Section 202(a)(11) of the Investment Advisers Act of 1940 ("Advisers Act") if: (1) the information is readily available in its raw state; (2) the categories of information presented are not highly selective; and (3) the information is not organized or presented in a manner that suggests the purchase, holding, or sale of any security. See Missouri Innovation Center, Inc. (pub. avail. Oct 17, 1995)("Missouri Innovation")(and cases cited therein).

In this regard, we note your representations that: (1) the information concerning the listed companies will be readily available in documents from the issuer or its agents and, where applicable, will be filed with the appropriate state or federal authority; (2) the listed companies will be assigned a number sequentially in the order that the information is entered into the Network's database and information about the companies will be presented on the Network in that order; (3) the search feature included in the Network will be based on objective criteria that the investor must enter into the system. You also represent that any company that meets specified objective criteria may be listed.

Further, you represent that neither the Network nor the Network Operators will: (1) be involved in any purchase or sale negotiations arising from the Network; or (2) give advice regarding the merits or shortcomings of any particular company or transaction. E.g., Missouri Innovation. Under these circumstances, the Division of Investment Management will not recommend enforcement action if the Network or Network Operators engage in the activities described in your letter without registering under the Advisers Act.

Because this response is based on the representations made to the Divisions in your letter and telephone conversations with the staff, any different facts or conditions might require a different conclusion. Further, this response expresses the Divisions' positions on enforcement action only and does not express any legal conclusions with respect to the applicability of the statutory or regulatory provisions of the federal securities laws. The position of the Division of Market Regulation with respect to registration under Section 6 of the Exchange Act is further subject to changes in current law, regulation and interpretations governing exchange registration and related matters; any change may require the Division to reevaluate and revoke or modify this no-action position.

Sincerely,

Catherine McGuire
Chief Counsel

CM\GJJ\dn

Oct. 25 1996

Catherine McGuire, Associate Director
and Chief Counsel
Division of Market Regulation
U.S. Securities and Exchange Commission
450 Fifth Street, N.W.

Washington, D.C. 20549

Jack W. Murphy, Associate Director
and Chief Counsel
Division of Investment Management
U.S. Securities and Exchange Commission
450 Fifth Street, N.W.
Washington, D.C. 20549

Dear Ms. McGuire and Mr. Murphy:

On behalf of the Angel Capital Electronic Network (ACE-Net)(the "Network"), we request confirmation from the Division of Investment Management that the staff would not recommend enforcement action against the Network and the various universities and non-profit entities (and/or their non-profit subsidiaries) that will participate in operating the Network ("Network Operators") if the Network and the Network Operators do not register as "investment advisers" under Section 203(a) of the Investment Advisers Act of 1940, as amended ("Investment Advisers Act").

In addition, we also request confirmation from the staff of the Division of Market Regulation that it would not recommend enforcement action against the Network and the Network Operators if the Network and the Network Operators do not register as "brokers" or "dealers" under Section 15(b) of the Securities Exchange Act of 1934, as amended ("Exchange Act"), and if the Network and Network Operators do not register as "exchanges" under Section 6 of the same Act.

BACKGROUND

The Office of Advocacy of the U. S. Small Business Administration has the statutory responsibility to represent the interests of small businesses within the federal government. Related to this, the Office is working to implement the recommendations from the 1995 White House Conference on Small Business.

Access to capital was one of the top issues at the 1995 White House Conference on Small Business. Fifteen of the top 60 recommendations were related to capital formation. These recommendations received 24% of the total votes, more than any other issue topic. At the conference, many small business owners voiced their frustrations with seeking capital through the equity markets. Access to the equity markets appeared to be even more troublesome for owners of small innovation- and high technology-based businesses.

In the past year, the Office of Advocacy held nine focus groups across the country with small business owners, venture capitalists, angel investors, attorneys, accountants, capital formation leaders, academicians, state securities regulators and state economic development agencies to discover the problems small businesses confront when seeking to issue securities.

In addition to the focus groups, the Office of Advocacy contracted with the Center for Venture Research, University of New Hampshire, to study the contributions of accredited investors, or "angels," to the capitalization of small firms.

We found that the greatest obstacles a small corporation confronts are: 1) limited exposure to experienced, accredited investors and 2) high transaction costs of soliciting and/or obtaining equity capital.

Based upon the recommendations of the 1995 White House Conference on Small Business, the issues raised by the focus group meetings, and the findings from our completed research, we believe that the creation of an electronic listing service available over the Internet indexing small corporate stock offerings will facilitate small companies' access to accredited investors.

PROPOSAL

It is our intention to create the Network, an Internet World Wide Web site that will list small corporate offerings. The Network will be run by entities referred to herein as Network Operators, specifically universities and/or non-profit entities (and/or their non-profit subsidiaries) specializing in entrepreneurism. The Network's World Wide Web homepage will allow accredited investors to access a password-controlled listing of small corporate stock offerings and to download offering circulars.

We are currently in discussion with the following universities and non-profit entities as potential Network Operators:

Center for Venture Research
Whittemore School of Business and Economics
University of New Hampshire
Durham, New Hampshire

Accelerate Technology Small Business Development Center
Graduate School of Management
University of California, Irvine
Irvine, California

UCSD-CONNECT
Extended Studies and Public Service
University of California, San Diego
San Diego, California

Business and Technology Development
North Carolina Biotechnology Center
Research Triangle Park, North Carolina

Ben Franklin Technology Center
of Southeastern Pennsylvania
Philadelphia, Pennsylvania

Technology Capital Network at MIT
Cambridge, Massachusetts

KTEC-Kansas Technology Enterprise Corporation
Topeka, Kansas

Economic Development Institute
Advanced Technology Development Center
Georgia Institute of Technology

Office of Advocacy PRESS RELEASE
U.S. Small Business Administration
Release Number 96-08 ADVO
Contact: Sarah Fleming (202) 205-6941

SBA'S Office of Advocacy Announces Angel Capital Electronic Network – ACE-Net

WASHINGTON - The U.S. Small Business Administration's (SBA) Office of Advocacy today announced a dramatic initiative--a nationwide Internet network that will give new options to small companies looking for investors and investors looking for promising opportunities.

The SBA's Office of Advocacy developed the Angel Capital Electronic Network (ACE-*Net*) in consultation with the Securities and Exchange Commission (SEC), state securities regulators and their organization, the North American Securities Administrators' Association (NASAA).

"I applaud the development and implementation of ACE-*Net*," said Vice President Al Gore. "This is a prime example of how the Clinton Administation is reinventing government to better serve the needs of small business entrepreneurs across America. ACE-*Net* is an exciting and innovative way to use technology, benefiting both small businesses and investors."

The network will allow accredited "angel" investors--wealthy individual investors with business savvy--to identify participating entrepreneurs. Until ACE-*Net*, small businesses have been severely limited in their ability to link with angels on a national basis.

"Small business' exposure to the angel investor has been problematic and the ability of angels to look at small companies from across the country has been limited. We appreciate the guidance of the SEC, as well as the state securities regulators and NASAA, in assisting us to develop ACE-*Net*, which will permit listing this information on the Internet in accordance with federal and state securities laws," said Office of Advocacy Chief Counsel Jere W. Glover. "ACE-*Net* will truly expand opportunities for both angels and small innovative companies."

According to SBA Administrator Philip Lader, "President Clinton directed the SBA to increase access to capital for all small businesses and we have developed a number of exciting financing programs for small companies. For example, the Small Business Investment Company (SBIC) program has been revamped, attracting more private capital in the last 24 months than in the preceding 15 years combined. However, there is still a need for

access to seed and startup capital for small businesses in the $250,000 to $5 million range, and ACE-*Net* is designed to bridge that gap."

ACE-*Net* was designed with recommendations from organizations experienced in the matching of angels and entrepreneurs, including the Center for Venture Research, University of New Hampshire, and the ACE-*Net* network operators (state- or university-based and/or other non-profit organizations).

Participating angels and entrepreneurs gain access to the password-controlled ACE-*Net* by contacting one of the regional network operators. The operators are experienced in mentoring entrepreneurs and in outreach to angels and companies. The two network operators open for business today are:

Technology Capital Network at MIT, and
The Capital Network, Inc., Austin, TX.

Other network operators opening access to ACE-*Net* soon are:

The Accelerate Technology Small Business Development Center at the University of California-Irvine;
UCSD-CONNECT in San Diego;
The North Carolina Biotechnology Center in Research Triangle Park;
The Ben Franklin Partnership in Philadelphia;
The Kansas Technology Enterprise Corporation in Topeka; and The Advanced Technology Development Center at the Georgia Institute of Technology in Atlanta.

The Internet home page for ACE-*Net* and the central computer system will be operated by the Center for Venture Research at the University of New Hampshire and will be connected to each of the network members via the Internet.

Bard Salmon, chairman of the Technology Capital Network at MIT, says that ACE-*Net* "will rapidly become the most visited

meeting place for accredited investors and entrepreneurs seeking funding. The initiative takes advantage of recent changes in federal regulations that greatly reduce the dollar and time expense of registering small corporate offerings, for example, permitting exemptions from full registration with the SEC for certain offerings under $5 million."

ACE-*Net* has received a "no-action" letter from the SEC, which means that the staff of the SEC will not recommend any enforcement action against ACE-*Net* as long as its participants are complying with the terms set forth in the no-action letter.

All offering listings will be searchable by an on-line search engine that will permit the angels to quickly find the type of company, technology/market, investment size, geographic location and minority-/women-owned status of the company. ACE-*Net* will also permit the angels to place specific search criteria on the network, and it will e-mail them back whenever a company is listed that meets their interests.

The idea to create ACE-*Net* had its beginning at the 1995 White House Conference on Small Business. During the conference, many small business owners, especially owners of high-technology-based businesses, voiced their frustrations about seeking capital through the equity markets. "A recommendation to improve these opportunities ranked 13th in the conference's 60 final recommendations," said Administrator Lader. "ACE-*Net* is the response small businesses wanted."

White House Conference Delegate and elected Regional Implementation Chair Marianne Hamm, chief operating officer of AccSys Technology, Inc., Pleasanton, Calif., said, "ACE-*Net* answers the critical need for technology companies, particularly those owned by women and minorities, to improve their access to angels. With ACE-*Net* we will have a level playing field for presenting our plans to angels across the country."

Robin Risser, CEO of Picometrix, Ann Arbor, Mich., also a delegate and elected regional implementation chair for the White House Conference, as well as a member of Michigan's Governor's Committee on

Capital Formation, said, "ACE-*Net* will be especially beneficial to small companies in the states that do not have existing strong venture capital funds. Our companies will now have the same access to angels as those in the historically strong venture and angel markets."

Funding for the inauguration of ACE-*Net* has been provided by the SBA and the Office of Advocacy. The Small Business Innovation Research (SBIR) Office of the Department of Defense also provided seed funding to prepay the listing of 200 DoD SBIR awardees interested in raising equity capital. It is the intent of the Office of Advocacy that ACE-*Net* be fully self-supporting from subscription fees in the near future.

Angel investors or entrepreneurs interested in ACE-*Net* subscriptions can contact network members via the Internet. The listing of potential business investments will be available for examination only by accredited angel investors via password. Details are provided on the Internet at <http://www.sbaonline.sba.gov> and at <http://ace-net.unh.edu>.

For more information, contact Jere Glover, Chief Counsel, Office of Advocacy, U.S. Small Business Administration, at 202-205-6533, or fax 202-205-6928.

Return to the ACE-*Net* Home Page

Atlanta, Georgia

The Capital Network, Inc.
Austin, Texas

The primary mission of these university-based and non-profit entities is to help start and sustain new enterprises through capital, technology, technical and training assistance. These entities provide assistance and offer courses on managerial training, financial planning, and federal and state tax and securities laws.

The Network will have one central computer system, initially operated by the Center for Venture Research, University of New Hampshire, which will be electronically connected to each of the Network Operators. Each of the Network Operators may operate an electronic matching service and/or listing service independent of the Network.

Listings on the Network's homepage will consist of small corporate offerings exempt from federal registration under Regulation A or Regulation D, Rule 504. Accredited investors registered with the Network Operators will be able to access through the Network's homepage a small corporation's "tombstone" advertisement, and an offering circular in the form of the Small Corporate Offering Registration Form (SCOR Form or Registration Form U-7). In addition, "solicitation of interest documents" ("testing the waters" documents) pursuant to Regulation A may be listed on the Network. These documents will be prepared by the small corporation. It will be the responsibility of the small corporation to be in full compliance with the appropriate filing and registration requirements of federal and state securities laws and regulations.

Upon subscribing to the Network, the small company will receive an entrepreneur number (sequentially generated) when the information is entered into the Network's data base. Any and all tables generated by the data base will display the Network's listings in the chronological order in which the information was entered into the data base.

Access to information regarding the small corporate securities listed on the Network will be available only to "accredited investors" through a password system. Before being given a password, each investor will be required to certify that the investor is an "accredited investor" within the meaning of Rule 501 of Regulation D under the Securities Act of 1933. Investors will be required to provide this certification on an annual basis as part of an investor's subscription renewal. It will be the responsibility of the small company to determine independently, before completion of any sale, whether the investor satisfies the criteria for an "accredited investor" within the appropriate jurisdiction.

The Network Operators will be the initial contact for small companies that want to list their stock on the Network and for accredited investors who want to subscribe to the Network. To be listed on the Network, small companies will be required to have a qualified or registered offering pursuant to federal and/or state securities laws and regulations or be qualified for an exemption from registration. Small companies must present a completed offering circular utilizing the SCOR form for listing under Regulation A or Regulation D, Rule 504. For testing the waters document listings or for listings in states with "accredited investor exemptions," small companies must submit documents as specified by the Network.

In addition, each company must certify as part of the entrepreneur subscription form that it does not fall under the "Disqualifications" provisions as adopted by the North American Securities Administrators Association (NASAA) in its "Statement of Policy Regarding Small Company Registrations," on April 28,

1996. The small company will send the completed documents, the completed entrepreneur subscription form and the subscription fee to the local Network Operator. The Network Operator will forward the documents to the Center for Venture Research which will add the documents to the Network's data base.

Accredited investors will be required to fill out a form which will require the investor to self-certify as to accredited investor status. The form and subscription fee will be mailed to the local Network Operator. After the form has been received, the local Network Operator will direct that the pass-word be sent electronically from the Center for Venture Research to the investor subscriber. In addition, the investor may send the subscription form electronically; however, a pass-word will not be released until the local Network Operator has received the paper copy. After the investor has received the pass-word, he or she may log on at either the local Network Operator's homepage or directly to the Network's main homepage.

It is anticipated that many investors will subscribe to both the Network and the local Network Operator's listing or matching service. Each Network Operator, however, will clearly inform potential subscribers that the listings available on the Network are separate from those available through any other listing or matching service, and that investors will be required to subscribe separately to the Network.

Subscribers to the listing and/or matching services operated by each of the Network Operators who have not subscribed separately to the Network and have not provided the required certification regarding their status as "accredited investors" will not be given access to Network's small corporate listings. Such persons will, however, be able to view the Network's homepage which will provide general information to the public about the Network as well as information regarding qualifications for becoming a Network subscriber.

Investors who have registered with their local Network Operator will be able to access the Network's homepage and review the lists of companies. The investor may then either review or download the publicly filed SCOR forms of the listed companies. If an investor wishes to purchase stock from a small company listed on the Network, the investor must contact the small company directly.

No trading will take place on the Network and no Network Operator will participate in any sales transaction.

To help accredited investors review the listings on the Network a search engine may be utilized at their discretion. The subscriber must choose criteria and enter it into the system or the system will default to show all listings of a particular state. The search engine will enable an accredited investor to set basic search criteria to engage a search. The search criteria will include, but not be limited to the state in which to invest, the type of business/industry of the company, the amount the company is seeking to raise, the amount the investor wishes to invest, and the identification of minority- and/or women-owned businesses. These basic search criteria will permit the accredited investor to narrow the list of companies to only those within the investor's areas of interest.

In addition, the search engine will be able to notify the accredited investor via the Internet when a company that lists on the Network has characteristics that correlate to the investor's specified basic search criteria (e.g., "all registered offerings for a particular state"). The search engine will be based upon the following: (i) the engine will operate only for the investor and not for companies listed on the Network, (ii) the notices will be sent to all investors interested in the same basic criteria, (iii) the notices will not send the name of the company or specific securities information but will require the investor to log on the Network to receive the names and securities information concerning the small companies listed on the

Network, and (iv) the notices will consist only of indexed, fact-based data. The search engine and notification system are only to be used as a means to raise and continue interest in the Network and to facilitate review of the Network's listings.

The Network Operators will establish an Advisory Board for the Network. The Advisory Board will establish the Network homepage's specifications, Internet access specifications, and overall Network operating procedures. In addition, the Advisory Board will be responsible for approving the designation of additional universities and/or other non-profit entities as Network Operators.

As the Network will contain a data base of investors and small corporations, the Center for Venture Research, University of New Hampshire, will have all proprietary rights to the data base that is created from the Network system. Precautions, however, will be taken to ensure the confidentiality of the investors and small companies. The Center for Venture Research will be permitted to use aggregated statistical data generated from the data base for teaching and research purposes relating primarily to entrepreneurship.

The Network will be funded, in part, by nominal, flat fees that will be charged to the participating small companies and accredited investors. It is expected that such fees will cover part of the administrative expenses associated with operating the Network. These fees will not be made contingent upon the outcome or completion of any securities transaction resulting from a listing on the Network. (During the initial "trial period" of the Network, fees may be waived for small companies and accredited investors.) Additional Network funding may be sought from federal and state governmental agencies, foundations, corporate and individual sponsors.

Network sponsors will be allowed a box located on the screen of the Network's homepage and the Network Operators' homepage. This box will contain either advertising information furnished by the sponsor and/or will connect the viewer to the sponsor's homepage (very much like what is currently available on the World Wide Web portion of the Internet). Sponsorship of the Network will not grant a sponsor either special access to the Network's listings or decision-making authority over the Network. Small corporations that are listed on the Network will be ineligible to become Network sponsors.

DISCUSSION

The Investment Advisers Act of 1940

The Network and the Network Operators do not believe that they are required to register as "investment advisers" as set forth under Section 203(a) of the Investment Advisers Act of 1940.

The Network and Network Operators will not be engaged in the business of advising others concerning the advisability of investing in the small companies listed on the Internet World Wide Web homepage nor will they be in the regular business of issuing or promulgating analyses or reports concerning securities.

Neither the Network nor the Network Operators will make any recommendations concerning any offering of securities listed on the Network. The Network and Network Operators will not (i) advise any listing companies or investors on the merits of any investment opportunity, (ii) participate in negotiating the terms of any investment, (iii) hold themselves out as providing any securities-related services other than a listing or matching service, (iv) directly assist investors or listing companies with the completion of any transaction, for example, through the provision of closing documentation or paid referrals to attorneys or other professionals, or (v) handle funds or securities involved in completing the transaction. In addition, no fees, other than the nominal fees to cover administrative costs, will be assessed and no fee will be made contingent upon the completion of any securities transaction resulting from a listing on the Network.

Network officials, participants, and employees and participating university officers, directors and employees with direct or indirect operating or supervisory control over Network Operators will not participate as entrepreneurs or investors in any company listed on the Network, except in compliance with the federal securities laws and unless such participation is disclosed to users of the Network.

The Securities Exchange Act of 1934

The Network and the Network Operators do not believe that they are required to register as "brokers" or "dealers" under Section 15(b) of the Exchange Act of 1934. In addition, it is believed that the Network and Network Operators are not required to register as "exchanges" under Section 6 of the same Act.

While a "broker" is defined in Section 3(a)(4) of the Exchange Act as a person engaged "in the business of effecting transactions in securities for the account of others," and a "dealer" is defined in Section 3(a)(5) of the Exchange Act as a person engaged "in the business of buying and selling securities for his own account," the Network and Network Operators neither effect the transactions in securities listed on the Network nor are in the business of buying and selling securities listed on the Network.

Specifically, the Network and the Network Operators will not: (i) provide advice about the merits of particular opportunities or ventures, (ii) receive compensation from Network users other than the nominal, flat fees to cover administrative costs, (iii) participate in any negotiations between investors and listing companies, (iv) directly assist investors or listing companies with the completion of any transaction, for example, through the provision of closing documentation or paid referrals to attorneys or other professionals, (v) handle funds or securities involved in completing a transaction, or (vi) hold themselves out as providing any securities-related services other than a listing or matching service.

Network officials, participants, and employees and participating university officers, directors and employees with direct or indirect operating or supervisory control over Network Operators will not participate as entrepreneurs or investors in any company listed on the Network, except in compliance with the federal securities laws and unless such participation is disclosed to users of the Network. Also, such persons will not discuss any matters with listing companies, investors, or other persons that might require familiarity with securities or the exercise of judgment concerning securities activities.

No transactions or negotiations will occur by or through the Network. In addition, the Network and the Network Operators will not maintain possession of the funds, securities, or property of any user of the Network.

The Network and the Network Operators will not receive compensation other than the nominal, flat fees to cover administrative expenses. No other fees, commissions or compensation will be due from the investors or the listing companies. The fees will not be made contingent upon the outcome or completion of any securities transaction resulting from a listing on the Network.

With regard to the registration of the Network and the Network Operators as "exchanges" under Section 6 of the Exchange Act, the Network and the Network Operators do not believe that they are required to register. The Network will not perform the functions commonly performed by a stock exchange. The Network will only be a listing service for small corporate stock offerings and will not effect any transaction in a security nor report any such transaction for companies listed on the Network. Once an accredited investor decides to invest in a company listed on the Network, the investor must contact the small company directly.

In particular, we believe that operation of the Network, as proposed, will not entail operation of an "exchange" for the purposes of Section 3(a)(1) of the Exchange Act. See Delta Government Options Exchange, Securities Exchange Act Release No. 17611 (January 12, 1990) (the "Delta Order"). We believe that the proposed operation of the Network will not involve an "exchange" within the Commission's articulated reasoning because it merely facilitates access to information about the listed companies to accredited investors, and neither centralizes trading nor provides buy and sell quotations about particular securities.

The Commission further stated that the term "exchange" was not intended to encompass markets that "serve as bulletin boards for the episodic display, by broker-dealers and institutions, of buying and selling interest." *Id.* The Network, in bringing together potential investors and small companies in need of venture capital, will neither offer participants the opportunity to display orders in securities they are interested in trading nor allow them to match with countervailing interests.

CONCLUSION

1) The Network and the Network Operators should not be required to register under Section 203 of the Investment Advisers Act since the Network will not be engaged in the business of dispensing advice to investors on the worthiness of small corporate stocks listed on the Network.

2) The Network and the Network Operators should not be required to register under Section 15(b) of the Exchange Act. The Network and the Network Operators will not be engaged in the business of effecting securities transactions nor will they be engaged in the business of buying and selling securities.

3) The Network and the Network Operators should not be required to register as exchanges under Section 6 of the Exchange Act. The Network is solely a listing service and does not effect any transactions in securities or report any such transactions to third parties.

ACTION REQUESTED

We respectfully request that the staff of the Commission confirm that it will not recommend enforcement action against the Network and/or the Network Operators.

Thank you for your consideration of this matter. If you need clarification or have any questions concerning the establishment of the Network, please contact us at (202) 205-6533.

Sincerely,

Jere W. Glover
Chief Counsel for Advocacy

Gregory J. Dean, Jr.
Assistant Chief Counsel
for Banking and Finance

EXHIBIT D

USE OF ELECTRONIC MEDIA FOR DELIVERY PURPOSES RELEASE NO. 33-7233; 34-36345

[Use of Electronic Media for Delivery Purposes Release No. 33-7233; 34-36345; IC-21399. October 6, 1995. 60 F. R. 53458.]

17 CFR 231.7233 (§§241.36345; 271.21399)

ACTION: Interpretation; Solicitation of comment.

SUMMARY: The Securities and Exchange Commission (the "Commission") is publishing its views with respect to the use of electronic media for information delivery under the Securities Act of 1933, the Securities Exchange Act of 1934, and the Investment Company Act of 1940. This interpretive guidance is intended to assist market participants in using electronic media to provide information under the federal securities laws and to encourage continued research and development and use of such media. The Commission is seeking comment on issues discussed in this release. In a companion release, the Commission is proposing technical amendments to Commission rules that are currently premised on the distribution of paper documents. DATES: This Interpretation is effective on October 6, 1995. Comments should be received on or before [insert date 45 days after Federal Register publication].

ADDRESSES: Comments should be submitted in triplicate to Jonathan G. Katz, Secretary, Securities and Exchange Commission, 450 Fifth Street, NW, Stop 6-9, Washington, D.C. 20549. Comment letters should refer to File No. S7-31-95. All comments received will be available for public inspection and copying at the Commission's Public Reference Room, 450 Fifth Street, NW, Washington, D.C. 20549.

FOR FURTHER INFORMATION CONTACT: Joseph Babits or James Budge (202) 942-2910, Division of Corporation Finance; and, with regard to questions concerning investment companies or investment advisers, Robert G. Bagnall or Emanuel D. Strauss (202) 942-0660, Division of Investment Management, U.S. Securities and Exchange Commission, 450 Fifth Street, NW, Washington, D.C. 20549.

SUPPLEMENTARY INFORMATION:

I. INTRODUCTION

The Commission today is publishing its views with respect to using electronic media as a means of delivering information required under the Securities Act of 1933 ("Securities Act"), [1] the Securities Exchange Act of 1934 ("Exchange Act"), [2] and the Investment Company Act of 1940 ("Investment Company Act"). [3] Advances in computers and electronic media technology are enabling companies to disseminate information to more people at a faster and more cost-effective rate than traditional distribution methods, which have been largely paper-based. The Commission appreciates the promise of electronic distribution of information in enhancing investors' ability to access, research, and analyze information, and in facilitating the provision of information by issuers and others. The Commission believes that, given the numerous benefits of electronic distribution of information and the fact that in many respects it may be more useful to investors than paper, its use should not be disfavored.

Until recently, on-line use of corporate information was generally limited to large corporations and institutional investors. The dramatic growth in personal computer ownership, [4] however, is enabling many small investors to access on-line corporate information just as readily as institutions. Access to information through electronic means permits small investors to communicate quickly and efficiently with companies as well as with each other. [5]

Use of electronic media also enhances the efficiency of the securities markets by allowing for the rapid dissemination of information to investors and financial markets in a more cost-efficient, widespread, and equitable manner than traditional paper-based methods. Recognizing the multiple benefits of electronic technology, the Commission initiated its Electronic Data Gathering, Analysis, and Retrieval ("EDGAR") system in 1984 to automate the receipt, processing and dissemination of disclosure documents filed with the Commission under the Securities Act, Exchange Act and Investment Company Act. [6] As a result of this automation, filings made with the Commission through EDGAR are available promptly to the public and financial markets. Today, more than 70% of all domestic public companies file electronically through EDGAR, and by May 1996, all domestic registrants will be required to file electronically through EDGAR. [7]

The EDGAR rules apply only to filings made with the Commission; the rules do not affect the obligation of filers to deliver to security holders or potential investors documents such as prospectuses, tender offer materials and proxy or information statements. [8] As the ability to send and receive information in electronic form has become more prevalent, issuers and other market participants have begun requesting interpretive guidance regarding the electronic delivery of these documents. [9] Moreover, hundreds of issuers are providing information through electronic means, primarily through computer networks.

In February 1995, the Commission's Division of Corporation Finance issued an interpretive letter intending to address certain legal issues relating to electronic delivery of prospectuses ("Brown & Wood letter"). [10] The Brown & Wood letter established a number of conditions in order for a prospectus to be considered "delivered" electronically. The intention at the time of the release of the Brown & Wood letter was that the Commission would review this area in greater detail after the issuance of the letter with a view toward, through an appropriate release, providing further interpretive advice or proposed rulemaking. Because of these developments, along with the fact that none of the federal securities statutes exclusively require paper delivery of information, the Commission believes that interpretive guidance on the use of electronic media is appropriate. While the Commission anticipates that issuers and others will rely upon the guidance of this release, continued reliance on the generally more stringent requirements of the Brown & Wood letter is no longer required, but would be permissible.

This interpretive release addresses only the procedural aspects under the federal securities laws of electronic delivery, and does not affect the rights and responsibilities of any party under the federal securities laws. [11] This release addresses the delivery of information by or on behalf of issuers, as well as by or on behalf of third parties (such as persons making tender offers or soliciting proxies) with respect to issuers. [12]

Additionally, to facilitate further electronic delivery, the Commission proposes in a companion release to codify certain interpretations regarding Commission rules that are premised on the distribution of paper documents. [13] The rules would be revised to make it clear that paper-based requirements relating to font size, bold-face type, red ink, graphics, and mailing may be modified as appropriate for documents delivered in electronic format. [14] The proposals are not intended to affect any substantive requirement.

Given the numerous benefits of electronic media, the Commission encourages further technological research, development and application. The Commission believes that the use of electronic media should be at least an equal alternative to the use of paper-based media. Accordingly, issuer or third party information that can be delivered in paper under the federal securities laws may be delivered in electronic format. [15] The Commission also expects that paper delivery of information will continue to be made available by issuers and others until such time as electronic media become more universally accessible and accepted, although the Commission recognizes that, for example, various offerings may now be made exclusively through electronic means. [16]

In connection with the June 1995 proposals on permitting the use of abbreviated financial statements in documents delivered to investors, [17] comment was solicited on whether the increasing availability of disclosure through electronic media warrants reassessment of the current overall regulatory framework. [18] Any comments received on the June 1995 proposals will be evaluated and appropriate action will be considered. By issuing this release in the interim, however, the Commission intends to assist issuers and other market participants in using electronic media to comply with the current regulatory scheme.

II. USE OF ELECTRONIC MEDIA

A. General

The federal securities statutes do not prescribe the medium to be used for providing information by or on behalf of issuers, or by or on behalf of third parties with respect to issuers. [19] The Commission believes that delivery of information through an electronic medium generally could satisfy delivery or transmission obligations under the federal securities laws.

The federal securities laws, among other purposes, seek to promote fair and orderly markets by requiring the disclosure of material information that enables investors to make informed investment and voting decisions. The extent to which required disclosure is made, as opposed to the medium for providing it, should be most important to the analysis of whether sufficient disclosure has occurred under the securities laws. An electronic medium would not provide an adequate means for the delivery of required disclosure, and thus not serve the statutory purposes, if the medium does not permit effective communication to investors or is practically unavailable. [20]

The Commission believes that the question of whether delivery through electronic media has been achieved is most easily examined by analogy to paper delivery procedures. The Commission would view information distributed through electronic means as satisfying the delivery or transmission requirements of the federal securities laws if such distribution results in the delivery [21] to the intended recipients of substantially equivalent information as these recipients would have had if the information were delivered to them in paper form. [22] As is the case with paper delivery, there should be an opportunity to retain a permanent record of the information.

B. Guidance Regarding Electronic Delivery

The Commission believes that the analysis of whether an electronic communication is delivered or transmitted for purposes of the federal securities laws should be determined in accordance with the preceding discussion. In making such determination with respect to information communicated, in particular, over the Internet, through on-line services, or through analogous computer networks, the Commission believes that the following concepts discussed in this section reflect issues that should be considered in determining whether applicable statutory requirements have been satisfied.

This release is intended to provide guidance and a degree of certainty regarding the manner in which electronic delivery can be achieved. An issuer or other party that structures its delivery in accordance with the principles and examples set forth below can be assured that it is satisfying its delivery obligations under the federal securities laws. The Commission wishes to emphasize, however, that the factors discussed below are not the only factors relevant to determining whether the legal requirements pertaining to delivery or transmission of documents have been satisfied. If an issuer or third party develops a method of electronic delivery that differs from those discussed below, but provides assurance comparable to paper delivery that the required information will be delivered, that method may satisfy delivery or transmission obligations. The ultimate responsibility for satisfying the applicable statutory requirements remains with the issuer or other party to whom the law assigns the responsibility.

Notice. When an issuer delivers a paper document through the postal mail, the investor will most likely be made aware that new information exists and that the investor might have to take some action within a certain period of time. The Commission believes that those providing electronic information should consider the extent to which the electronic communication provides timely and adequate notice to investors that information for them is available and, if necessary, consider supplementing the electronic communication with another communication that would provide notice similar to that provided by delivery in paper. If an electronic document itself is provided--for example, on computer disk, CD-ROM, audio tape, videotape, or e-mail--that communication itself should generally be sufficient notice. If the document is provided on an Internet Web site, however, separate notice would be necessary to satisfy the delivery requirements unless the issuer can otherwise evidence that delivery to the investor has been satisfied or the document is not required to be delivered under the federal securities laws. [23]

Access. When a document is delivered through the postal mail, a recipient generally is provided with access to the required disclosure. The Commission believes that recipients who are provided information through electronic delivery should have comparable access; consequently, the use of a particular medium should not be so burdensome that intended recipients cannot effectively access the information provided. [24] Moreover, as is the case with a paper document, a recipient should have the opportunity to retain the information or have ongoing access equivalent to personal retention. [25]

If disclosure is made available by posting it on the Internet, making it available through on-line services, or making it available by similar means, the document should be accessible for as long as the delivery requirement applies. [26]

Finally, because of possible system failures, computer incompatibilities, and those cases, for example, where consents are used in connection with the delivery of information electronically and the person providing the consent revokes it, a necessary precaution given the current state and use of communications technology is that issuers must be able to make available paper versions of documents delivered in an electronic medium. Specifically, the Commission believes that, as a matter of policy, where a person has a right to receive a document under the federal securities laws and chooses to receive it electronically, that person should be provided with a paper version of the document if any consent to receive documents electronically were revoked or the person specifically requests a paper copy (regardless of whether any previously provided consent was revoked). [27]

C. Evidence to Show Delivery

Providing information through postal mail provides reasonable assurance that the delivery requirement is satisfied. The Commission believes that issuers and others [28] providing electronic delivery of information should similarly have reason to believe that any electronic means so selected will result in the satisfaction of the delivery requirements. Examples of procedures evidencing satisfaction of the delivery requirements include: (1) obtaining an informed consent from an investor to receive the information through a particular electronic medium [29] coupled with assuring appropriate notice and access, as discussed above; (2) obtaining evidence that an investor actually received the information, for example, by electronic mail returnreceipt or confirmation of accessing, downloading, or printing (see example 36); (3) disseminating information through certain facsimile methods (see example 32); (4) an investor's accessing a document with hyperlinking to a required document (see examples 15 and 35); and (5) using forms or other material available only by accessing the information (see examples 31 and 33).

The Commission requests comment on these concepts and on whether additional or alternative concepts would be more useful.

D. Examples

A series of examples is provided below to illustrate various applications of the above concepts and to provide guidance in applying them to specific facts and circumstances. The analysis required to determine compliance with the delivery requirements is fact-specific, and any different or additional facts might require a different conclusion. Although this interpretation is effective immediately, the Commission requests comment on whether other examples might be appropriate for publication in a subsequent release.

Securities Act

(1) Company XYZ places its final prospectus on its Internet Web site. Company XYZ then confirms by mail the sale of securities to investors with a note stating that the final prospectus is available on its Web site and giving the Internet location of the Web site.

Unlike paper delivery of a final prospectus where access to the document can be presumed with delivery, not all investors purchasing securities could be presumed to have the ability to access the final prospectus via an Internet Web site. Therefore, absent other factors such as express consent from the investor or an investor's actually accessing the document on the Web site, the procedures described above by themselves would not satisfy the delivery requirements under the Securities Act.

(2) Company XYZ places its final prospectus on its Internet Web site. Company XYZ then confirms by mail the sale of securities to those investors who have consented to electronic delivery via the Company's Internet Web site. A note on the bottom of the confirmation [30] states that the final prospectus is available on its Web site and the Internet location of the Web site.

This would satisfy delivery obligations, as it is reasonable to presume that investors who have consented to delivery of the final prospectus via an Internet Web site have the ability to access the final prospectus once such investors are supplied with notice of the Internet location of the Web site.

(3) While reviewing Company XYZ's preliminary prospectus on its Internet Web site, Investor John Doe consented to delivery of all future documents only through electronic mail, not by Web site access. Company XYZ subsequently places its final prospectus on its Internet Web site. Company XYZ then confirms by mail the sale of securities to John Doe. A note on the bottom of the confirmation states that the final prospectus is available on its Internet Web site and the location of that Web site.

Again, absent other factors such as John Doe's actually accessing the final prospectus on the Web site, the above-stated procedure of Company XYZ would not by itself satisfy the obligations to deliver the final prospectus to John Doe, as John Doe consented to delivery only by electronic mail, not via an Internet Web site. If consent is to be relied upon, the consent should indicate the specific electronic medium or media that may be used for delivery.

(4) While reviewing Company XYZ's preliminary prospectus on its Internet Web site, Investor John Doe consented to delivery of all future Company documents by 3 " floppy disk. Company XYZ places its final prospectus on its Internet Web site. Company XYZ then confirms by mail the sale of securities to John Doe. A 3 " floppy disk containing the final prospectus is included with the confirmation.

This would satisfy the obligation to deliver the final prospectus to John Doe, since the Company included with the confirmation the final prospectus on a 3 " floppy disk.

(5) Investor John Doe consents to delivery of all documents electronically via Company XYZ's Web site. Two days after consenting, John Doe realizes that the online service he subscribes to does not allow Internet access. John Doe notifies Company XYZ that he is revoking his consent for any electronic delivery as he is not able to access the Company's Internet Web site. Three weeks later, John Doe receives in the mail a confirmation of his purchase of Company XYZ's securities stating the Internet location of the Company's Web site where the final prospectus can be obtained.

Since John Doe revoked his consent for electronic delivery, the Company's notice to John Doe is insufficient because the Company knows that its attempted delivery through the Internet will not satisfy the statutory requirements for John Doe. A final paper prospectus would have to be delivered to John Doe instead. Although a consent is revocable at any time, revocation would have to be given to the company or its agent a reasonable time before electronic delivery has commenced for the company to be on notice that electronic delivery will not satisfy the statutory requirements.

(6) Company LMN, a non-reporting issuer, commences an initial public offering. Company LMN agrees with its underwriter, Brokerage Firm DFG, to place its preliminary prospectus on the Company's Internet Web site at least 48 hours prior to confirmations being sent. Investors John and Jane Doe are both expected to purchase securities in the Company's initial public offering. Both John and Jane Doe previously provided Company LMN with consents for electronic delivery through the Company's Internet Web site. Brokerage Firm DFG, pursuant to its prospectus delivery obligation under Exchange Act Rule 15c2-8(b), [31] provides notice to John and Jane Doe at least 48 hours prior to sending them confirmations.

The underwriter may satisfy its obligation under Rule 15c28(b) to John and Jane Doe by this means since both have consented to electronic delivery through the Company's Internet Web site. Although consent was not provided directly to the underwriter, the underwriter can rely on the consent supplied to the Company. Similarly, had the consent been provided to the underwriter, the Company could rely on it as well.

(7) Company ABC contracts with Company QRS, a computer technology company, to place its preliminary and final prospectuses on Company QRS's Internet Web site. Investor John Doe requests a copy of Company ABC's preliminary prospectus via electronic mail from Company ABC's underwriter, Brokerage Firm DFG. The underwriter sends a return electronic mail to John Doe asking if he would like the electronic or paper version of the preliminary prospectus. John Doe replies that the electronic version via the Internet Web site would be preferable. The underwriter then informs John Doe of the Internet location of Company QRS's Web site where the preliminary prospectus for Company ABC is available.

This would satisfy Brokerage Firm DFG's obligation to take reasonable steps to furnish to any person making a written request for a prospectus a copy of such prospectus. [32] John Doe's request for the electronic version via the Internet indicates that such electronic delivery would be effective. [33]

(8) Company XYZ sends the final prospectus via electronic mail to those investors that previously had requested delivery by electronic mail.

The Company would meet its delivery obligation with this procedure.

(9) Company XYZ places a preliminary prospectus on its Internet Web site. After a material amendment to the registration statement, it is determined that recirculation of an updated prospectus will be required prior to effectiveness. Company XYZ updates the preliminary prospectus on its Web site.

The Company need only send notice of the update to those investors who are expected to purchase securities in the offering (or takes other measures to deliver the information to those investors). There is no need to send notice to individuals who are not expected to purchase securities in the offering.

(10) Company XYZ places its final prospectus on its Internet Web site. Its underwriters mail confirmations of sales to all purchasers. At the same time the confirmations are mailed, the underwriters send via electronic mail notice of the location of the Internet Web site where the final prospectus is available. Notice is sent to all investors who had consented to electronic delivery via an Internet Web site and who provided their electronic mail addresses for purposes of being notified. To those investors that did not provide an electronic mail address but did consent to electronic delivery of the final prospectus, the underwriters mailed the notice of the location of the Internet Web site with the confirmation.

As the notice made investors aware of the availability and location of the electronic document, the delivery requirement would be satisfied.

(11) Company XYZ posts its final prospectus for sale of its common stock on its Internet Web site. Company XYZ's stock is traded on the New York Stock Exchange (NYSE). The NYSE requests 300 paper copies of Company XYZ's final prospectus pursuant to Securities Act Rule 153. [34] Rather than sending 300 copies of its final prospectus to the NYSE, Company XYZ provides the NYSE with notice of its Internet Web site, where the final prospectus can be accessed and downloaded.

This would be insufficient delivery under Securities Act Rule 153. Company XYZ must supply the 300 paper copies to the NYSE. The NYSE must be in the position to provide paper copies of Company XYZ's final prospectus because there is no reasonable expectation that delivery would otherwise be satisfied with regard to investors who do not use any electronic means to receive information. The NYSE would, however, satisfy its delivery obligations with respect to any investor who received delivery of the information through electronic means.

(12) Company XYZ places its preliminary prospectus on its Internet Web site. Upon effectiveness of its registration statement, the Company decides to deliver a term sheet pursuant to Securities Act Rule 434. The term sheet, however, will not be placed on the Company's Web site, but will be delivered in paper format with confirmation of the sale to all investors.

Delivery of a mixed medium final prospectus would satisfy delivery obligations. Generally, if investors received the preliminary prospectus electronically, issuers are encouraged to deliver all documents that constitute the final prospectus in electronic format. However, confirmations cannot be furnished electronically unless the Commission has specifically approved

such delivery. [35]

(13) Company XYZ wants to deliver to investors a CD-ROM version of its prospectus. The CD-ROM version includes within the prospectus a movie illustrating the Company's operations. Investors viewing the CD-ROM prospectus would not have to exit the prospectus in order to view the movie, as the movie is actually a part of the prospectus.

While Company XYZ may include the movie as part of the prospectus, it would need to file with the Commission as an appendix to the prospectus the script of the movie and a fair and accurate narrative description of the graphic or image material just as it would have to supplementally provide to the Commission scripts and descriptions of such material in sales material.

(14) Company XYZ places a copy of its final prospectus on its Internet Web site. The electronic final prospectus will remain there throughout the period for which delivery is required. Company XYZ also places supplemental sales literature on its Internet Web site. Both the sales literature and the prospectus can be accessed from the same menu, are clearly identified on, and appear in close proximity to each other; [36] the supplemental sales literature may be accessed before viewing or downloading the prospectus.

Sales literature, whether in paper or electronic form, is required to be preceded or accompanied by a final prospectus. [37] In this example, the prospectus would accompany the sales literature since investors can access both the prospectus and sales literature from the same menu. The sales literature and final prospectus should appear in close proximity to each other on the menu. For example, the sales literature should not be presented on the first page of a menu while the final prospectus is buried within the menu.

(15) Company XYZ places its sales literature in a discussion forum located on the Internet World Wide Web. The sales literature contains a hyperlink to the Company's final prospectus. While viewing the literature the individual can click on a box marked "final prospectus," and almost instantly the person will be linked directly to the Company's Web site and the final prospectus will appear on the person's computer screen.

Sales literature, whether in paper or electronic form, is required to be preceded or accompanied by a final prospectus. The hyperlink function enables the final prospectus to be viewed directly as if it were packaged in the same envelope as the sales literature. Therefore, the final prospectus would be considered to have accompanied the sales literature. Consequently, the placing of sales literature in a discussion forum on a Web site would satisfy delivery obligations provided that a hyperlink that provides direct access to the final prospectus is included.

(16) Company XYZ places a preliminary prospectus on its Internet Web site and provides direct access via a hyperlink to a research report on the Company written by ABC Corporation, a registered brokerage firm. The investor reviewing the preliminary prospectus can click on a box marked "ABC's research report" and the investor will be linked to the brokerage firm's Web site where the research report is available.

The hyperlink function provides the ability to access information located on another Web site almost instantaneously. This direct and quick access to ABC's research report would be similar to the Company including the paper version of the research report in the same envelope that it is using to mail the paper version of the preliminary prospectus to potential investors. During the waiting period, the Company may make offers only through the use of a preliminary prospectus, [38] whether in paper or electronic format; therefore, its use of the research report under these circumstances would not be permissible.

(17) Company XYZ places its final prospectus on its Internet Web site. The Company then mails sales literature to individuals for whom delivery through the Internet Web site was effective (regardless of whether the individuals consented to delivery). Similarly, Brokerage Firm ABC mails Company XYZ sales literature to its customers for whom delivery through the Internet Web site was effective (regardless of whether the individuals consented to delivery). In the forepart of Company XYZ's sales literature is notice of the availability and Internet Web site location of its final prospectus.

The mailing of sales literature to these individuals is permissible, provided that notice of the availability of the final prospectus and its Internet Web site location accompanies or precedes the sales literature. When notice is included within sales literature, it should be in the forepart of the literature and clearly highlighted to make investors aware of the availability and location of the final prospectus.

(18) Company XYZ places a tombstone advertisement complying with Securities Act Rule 134 [39] on its Internet Web site.

This would be permissible, provided that the advertisement otherwise complies with Rule 134.

(19) Company XYZ files a registration statement with the Commission. The Company then places a "tombstone" advertisement in accordance with Securities Act Rule 134 in the Wall Street Journal. In the advertisement the Company includes the name and address of the underwriter from whom a paper prospectus can be obtained as well as the location of its Internet Web site where an electronic prospectus can be obtained.

This inclusion of an electronic address for obtaining the materials in this "tombstone" advertisement would be permissible under Rule 134. (Similarly, an advertisement made pursuant to Rule 14a-2(a)(6) [40] indicating the availability of proxy soliciting materials and the location of an Internet Web site where electronic proxy soliciting materials could be obtained would be permissible.)

(20) Company XYZ wants to raise $5 million by selling its common stock in a private placement pursuant to Securities

Act Rule 506 of Regulation D. The Company places its offering materials on its Internet Web site, which requires various information from a person attempting to access the materials to be provided to the Company prior to displaying the offering materials.

The placing of the offering materials on the Internet would not be consistent with the prohibition against general solicitation or advertising in Rule 502(c) of Regulation D. [41] Where prospective purchasers have been otherwise located without a general solicitation, a proprietary computer service could be used to deliver required disclosure documents.

(21) Company XYZ wants to raise $5 million by selling its common stock in a private placement pursuant to Rule 506 of Regulation D to certain individuals who have been located without a general solicitation. The Company transmits the offering materials via electronic mail addresses provided by these persons.

This would not be inconsistent with the offering restrictions in the rule.

(22) Company XYZ pays John Doe $10,000 to write a report about the Company and post the report on the Internet. John Doe writes the report and places it on the Growth Companies Investment Bulletin Board located on the Internet. The report does not disclose the $10,000 that the Company paid John Doe.

The Securities Act requires that the $10,000 compensation paid by Company XYZ to John Doe be disclosed in the report, regardless of whether it is in electronic or paper form. [42]

Exchange Act

(23) Company XYZ places its annual report and proxy soliciting materials on its Internet Web site. The Company then sends notice to all its record holders that its annual report and proxy soliciting materials are available on its Internet Web site along with the Internet location of the Web site and a telephone number that shareholders may call to request a paper copy.

Similar to Example (1), a company should not presume that all record holders have the ability to access the annual report and proxy soliciting materials via an Internet Web site. Therefore, absent other factors such as a consent from, or actual access by, a Company shareholder, posting of the annual report and proxy soliciting materials via the Company's Internet Web site would be insufficient to constitute delivery to all record holders. The Company, however, may place the materials on its Web site, but in this instance, it also would need to furnish paper copies of the materials to its record holders.

(24) In January 1995, Company XYZ places a copy of its final prospectus on its Internet Web site. The prospectus will remain there throughout the period for which delivery is required. Prior to viewing the final prospectus, Investor John Doe provides an express consent to the delivery of the prospectus and all future documents related to the offering via Company XYZ's Web site. Investor John Doe subsequently purchases the securities. In connection with its May 1995 annual meeting, Company XYZ places proxy soliciting materials on its Web site and places an advertisement in the Wall Street Journal indicating that its proxy materials are now available on its Web site.

This advertisement by itself, even coupled with the express consent that related to the offering documents, is insufficient for the company to assume that it has delivered its proxy statement to Investor John Doe. Although John Doe had provided consent to receiving documents electronically, there is no reason to believe that notice provided in the Wall Street Journal would make John aware of the availability of the proxy materials. Company XYZ must provide more direct delivery or notice to John Doe of the proxy materials. Notice by publication in a newspaper or on a Web site or bulletin board is insufficient.

(25) In September 1994, John Doe, a shareholder in Company XYZ, requests all future corporate communications including proxy statements and annual reports to shareholders ("annual report") to be delivered electronically through the Company's Internet Web site. The consent form states that Company XYZ expects that its annual report and proxy materials for its annual meeting will be available on its Web site on April 1, 1995. On April 1, 1995, the Company places its annual report and proxy soliciting materials on its Web site.

Unlike the delivery of paper annual reports and proxy soliciting materials, where the mere appearance in the mail of such materials places the shareholder on notice within close proximity to the time when shareholder action is requested, the advance request in this example, without more, may not be close enough in time to the requested action to be effective. However, if the Company reasonably expects for other specific reasons, such as a history of communications with that shareholder, that the shareholder would have effective delivery of the information through the Web site, then the procedure could be acceptable.

(26) Record holder Jane Doe consents to delivery of all documents via Company XYZ's Web site. On April 1, 1995, Company XYZ provides notice to Jane Doe that its annual report and proxy materials are available on its Web site for its annual meeting scheduled to be held on May 5, 1995. On April 5, 1995, Jane Doe notifies the Company that her computer is broken and requests a paper copy of the annual report and proxy materials.

Because Jane Doe's notice to the Company indicates that electronic delivery will be ineffective, the Company should provide Jane Doe with paper copies of the annual report and proxy materials within a reasonable time of her request. She does not need to withdraw her consent in order to receive the paper copies.

(27) Company XYZ places its quarterly report to shareholders and Forms 8-K on its Internet Web site and advertises the location of its Web site in the Wall Street Journal. The Company takes no other action to deliver these materials to shareholders.

This would be permissible, since there generally is no requirement to deliver such materials to shareholders at all.

(28) Company XYZ places its annual report and proxy soliciting materials for the election of directors on its Internet Web site and provides notice to all record holders that previously had consented to electronic delivery via the Company's Web site. The record holders are instructed to print the proxy card, execute the proxy and then mail it back to the Company.

This would be consistent with the proxy rules.

(29) Brokerage Firm ABC solicits its customers who are beneficial owners of Company XYZ to determine whether they would like to receive Company XYZ's annual report and proxy soliciting materials electronically via the Internet rather than in paper. The Brokerage Firm then informs the Company that 100 beneficial holders would like to receive the materials electronically and 200 beneficial holders would prefer paper materials.

The Company provides the Brokerage Firm with the location of its Internet Web site where the materials are posted and copies of its paper documents for the 200 beneficial owners who do not wish to receive the electronic delivery. The Brokerage Firm then forwards the notice of the location of the electronic materials to those beneficial holders who consented to receive electronic delivery and forwards the paper materials to those who did not. [43]

This would be consistent with the proxy rules.

(30) Company XYZ wishes to produce its annual report on videotape and CD-ROM. The videotape and CD-ROM will contain all the material information disclosed in the glossy annual report. Before distributing the Company's annual report, the Company sends a letter asking its shareholders whether they would be interested in receiving the Company's annual report on videotape or CD-ROM instead of paper. The Company then sends the videotape version of its annual report to its shareholders who wish to receive the videotape and the CD-ROM version to those shareholders who wish to receive the CD-ROM. The paper glossy annual report is sent to those shareholders who do not wish to receive either electronic format.

The federal securities laws do not preclude the delivery of a document through different media.

Mutual Funds

The Commission is aware that investment companies, particularly open-end investment companies ("mutual funds" or "funds") have been active in using electronic means to communicate with their shareholders and prospective investors. [44] Given the extent to which funds have embraced the new technologies, the Commission believes that it is appropriate to include the following additional examples, which are tailored to the fund industry. Unless otherwise noted, however, investment companies other than mutual funds and other corporate issuers or third parties may use these examples for guidance as well.

Examples

(31) A fund sends an e-mail to a recipient with a prospectus attached. The prospectus file includes an application form. The recipient fills out the form and mails it with a check to the fund.

Delivery of the prospectus may be inferred from the recipient's use of the form (provided the fund can identify it as coming from the electronically transmitted prospectus).

(306) A current prospectus is faxed to a potential investor who has requested the prospectus and provided the phone number of the fax machine.

This transmission satisfies the prospectus delivery requirements.

(33) A current prospectus and an application are faxed to a potential investor. The investor did not request the fax, but the sender knows the investor's fax machine phone number.

If the investor completes and mails in the application form included in the faxed prospectus, delivery of the electronic prospectus may be inferred.

(34) A fund sends an unsolicited e-mail with a prospectus attached in one file, and supplemental sales literature in a separate file. The investor can access the sales literature and the prospectus with equal ease.

The fund may send the supplemental sales literature in this fashion. [45] Electronic delivery of the prospectus may be inferred even if the prospectus is not accessed. This would be analogous to an investor receiving by mail a prospectus and supplemental sales literature in the same envelope and electing to review the sales literature, but not the prospectus.

(35) A fund posts its supplemental sales literature and prospectus on a file server for open access over the Internet. The supplemental sales literature contains hyperlinks to the fund's electronic prospectus and includes a caption referring the investor to the prospectus. The investor would not need any additional software or need to take burdensome steps to access the prospectus and thus has reasonably comparable access to both documents. This system also provides for the downloading or printing of prospectuses and sales literature. An investor would not be required to retrieve, download, or print a prospectus before viewing the sales literature. The system does not require any consent by its users.

When a user accesses the supplemental sales literature, electronic delivery of the prospectus can be inferred. This scenario is analogous to an investor's selecting an envelope containing a paper prospectus and supplemental sales literature from a display at an office of a broker-dealer. This electronic delivery of the prospectus would be sufficient for other purposes if the fund could reasonably establish that the investor has actually accessed the sales literature or the prospectus.

(36) A prospectus is made available through an on-line system that allows users to access, download or print the entire prospectus and has the capacity to track which users accessed, printed or downloaded which documents.

A fund may rely upon a user's having accessed, printed or downloaded a prospectus for the fund in order to deliver supplemental sales literature or an order form for the fund or to establish delivery of the prospectus in connection with a sale of fund shares.

(37) A fund's prospectus is available through an on-line service that does not have the capacity for downloading or printing or to track retrieval by a user. Investors do not provide any consent. The fund mails or e-mails supplemental sales literature, or an application to all of the service's subscribers, without including a prospectus.

Absent other factors that would indicate delivery of the prospectus, the fund may not send the supplemental sales literature or an application in this fashion, because it is not preceded or accompanied by the prospectus for purposes of Section 2(10)(a) of the Securities Act. [46] This would be true even if the general subscription agreement for the service contained a provision consenting to receipt of documents, because such consent would not be sufficient to give the fund reason to believe that delivery requirements relating to the prospectus will actually be satisfied.

(38) A server available through the Internet contains a fund's prospectus and application form in separate files. Users can download or print the application form without first accessing, downloading or printing the prospectus; the form includes a statement that by signing the form, the investor certifies that he or she has received the prospectus. Logistically it is significantly more burdensome to access the prospectus than the application form (e.g., the investor needs to download special software before accessing the prospectus).

The statement in the form about receipt of the prospectus would not by itself constitute electronic delivery of the prospectus. and the application form is not evidence of delivery of the prospectus, given the need to download special software before the prospectus can be viewed.

(39) A server available through the Internet contains a fund's prospectus. Users must download the prospectus to view or print it. When a user downloads the prospectus, the user receives the prospectus and an application form in separate files. It is not significantly more burdensome to access the prospectus than the application form (e.g., no additional software is necessary to read either document, although the documents may be in different formats).

If the fund can identify the application form as coming from the electronic system, electronic delivery of the prospectus can be inferred. The application form is evidence of delivery of the prospectus.

(40) A fund's prospectus and application form are available through an electronic system like that described in the preceding example, except that the investor needs to download special software before the prospectus and application form can be downloaded.

If the fund can identify the application form as coming from the electronic system, electronic delivery of the prospectus can be inferred. The application form is evidence of access to the prospectus.

(41) A fund sends an e-mail with an attached file containing an advertisement satisfying the requirements of Securities Act Rule 482. [47]

There is no prospectus delivery requirement in this context; a Rule 482 advertisement need not be preceded or accompanied by a prospectus.

(42) A fund transmits prospectuses over an electronic bulletin board. Investors provide specific consent to receipt of the prospectus through that system. The consent states that the current version of the prospectus will be made continuously available and notice of material amendments will be given by mail, e-mail, or some other manner specifically directed to investors.

The prospectus delivery requirements will be satisfied with respect to subsequent additional purchases by those investors.

(43) A fund places its prospectus on its Internet Web site and revises the electronic version whenever the prospectus is modified. The fund materially amends the prospectus and decides to send a postcard or e-mail to persons to whom the prospectus has been delivered through electronic means or who have consented to electronic delivery notifying them of the availability of the amended prospectus.

This procedure provides for delivery of the prospectus to those who have consented and to those to whom the prospectus has been previously delivered (if the fund expects those persons to be able to receive the amended prospectus). Alternatively, the fund could choose to satisfy its prospectus delivery requirements by sending a paper copy of the amended prospectus to investors in the fund, including investors who consented to receive documents electronically.

(44) A fund places its prospectus on its Internet Web site. Potential investor John Doe obtains access to the prospectus. John Doe does not purchase shares in the fund. Subsequently, the prospectus is amended.

The fund does not need to provide John Doe with notice of the amendment.

(45) A fund puts proxy solicitation materials on the fund's server on the World Wide Web. At the same time, the fund sends out postcards or e-mail messages (with investors having consented to receive notification by e-mail) giving notification that the proxy materials are available. Investors have signed up to receive documents through the server.

This would be consistent with the proxy rules.

(46) A fund transmits annual and semi-annual reports over an electronic bulletin board system. The fund makes the current versions of these materials available and informs investors who have consented to electronic delivery of this fact. The fund provides separate notification each time a shareholder report is posted by including the notification in the preceding quarterly account statement or shareholder newsletter. The notice informs investors of a date by which the report will be available.

Notification to shareholders in a statement or newsletter delivered within the preceding quarter would be considered sufficient notice under Section 30(d) of the Investment Company Act [48] and the rules thereunder to constitute delivery.

(47) A fund sends investors upon request a CD-ROM containing its current prospectus and registration statement materials for the fund's offering.

This would provide delivery to investors. [49]

(48) Prospectuses and other materials are available through a computer server that requires users to obtain a user ID and password before they can access documents on the system. The process for obtaining the ID and password requires significant information from the user and involves a delay of one day or even several days before the user can access the system. After a user accesses a prospectus, a fund sends him or her supplemental sales literature.

The process provides for delivery of the prospectus. Although the system imposes burdens in the process for obtaining access to the prospectus, these burdens are part of the process of providing access to all the information, including the supplemental sales literature, and not burdens upon access to the prospectus that is delivered.

(49) A prospectus is made available through an on-line system that allows users to download the entire prospectus. The system does not permit on- line viewing. An investor downloads the prospectus.

Assuming downloading, this method would satisfy the delivery requirements because on-line viewing is not a prerequisite to electronic delivery.

(50) A fund provides its prospectus, annual and semi-annual reports through an Internet Web site. After one year, the fund decides to terminate the Web site.

The fund may cease making its prospectus available through the Web site as soon as the fund no longer plans to rely on electronic delivery for satisfying its prospectus delivery requirements. [50] Generally, an annual or semi-annual report should be available until superseded by a later report. The fund in this example could terminate the posting of the most recent report when it is superseded by a new one, or earlier if it provides a replacement paper copy to shareholders who received the report electronically.

(51) The text of a fund's prospectus transmitted electronically on a CD-ROM or an Internet Web site follows the sequence requirements of Form N-1A. [51] The prospectus includes a summary, which contains hyperlinks that allow the investor to move to later sections of the prospectus or to other documents (e.g., the fund's statement of additional information or annual report). The summary is part of the prospectus text that is subject to the form's sequence requirements.

Even though the hyperlinks allow an investor to choose to view information out of sequence, the prospectus satisfies the requirements of Form N-1A, because the main text does comply with the sequence requirement.

(52) A fund places its prospectus (information required by Part A of Form N-1A) on its Internet Web site. The fund does not put its Statement of Additional Information ("SAI") (information required by Part B of Form N-1A) on its Web site; instead, it provides a paper copy of its SAI free of charge to any person that requests it.

Delivery of a paper copy of an SAI does not prevent a fund from satisfying its prospectus delivery requirements electronically.

III. PROPOSED AMENDMENTS

This release is intended to address practices involving electronic delivery that are acceptable under current rules; no substantive changes to filing or delivery requirements are contemplated here. However, in order to make it clear that current rules should be read to encompass electronic as well as paper dissemination, the Commission is proposing in a companion release a number of technical amendments to its rules. [52]

IV. ELECTRONIC FILING ISSUES

As emphasized previously, this release addresses only issues relating to electronic delivery of required disclosure documents and does not affect the Commission's electronic filing requirements. However, the Commission recognizes that the same rapid development of electronic communications in recent years that has led to the issuance of this release also has implications for how the Commission should receive, process and make publicly available the documents filed with it pursuant to the federal securities laws. Currently, filings are accepted by the Commission only in the electronic formats prescribed by the EDGAR system, or in paper, where the filer has not yet become subject to mandated electronic filing requirements or where there is an exemption pursuant to the electronic filing rules. While EDGAR may be modified in the future to accept and process a broader array of electronic formats, there may be ways to allow the filing of documents prepared and delivered in other electronic media on a more expedited timetable. As the Commission continues with its review of this area, it intends to issue additional releases. Comment on the costs and benefits to filers and the federal government with respect to these issues should be provided by persons submitting comment on these issues.

V. SOLICITATION OF COMMENT

Any interested persons wishing to submit written comments relating to the views expressed in this release, or with respect to the rule proposals in the companion release, are invited to do so by submitting them in triplicate to Jonathan G. Katz, Secretary, U.S. Securities and Exchange Commission, 450 Fifth Street, N.W., Washington, D.C., 20549. Commenters should refer to File Number S7-31-95. Comment is requested not only on the specific issues discussed on the release, but on any other approaches or issues that should be considered in connection with facilitating the use of electronic media to further the disclosure purposes of the federal securities laws. Comment is sought from the point of view of both parties providing the disclosure, such as issuers and those acting on behalf of issuers, and parties receiving and using the disclosure, such as investors and shareholders. The Commission further requests comment on any competitive burdens that might result from the adoption of the proposals. Comments on this inquiry will be considered by the Commission in complying with its responsibilities under Section 23(a) of the Exchange Act. [53]

AMENDMENT OF THE CODE OF FEDERAL REGULATIONS

For the reasons set out in the preamble, Title 17 Chapter II of the Code of Federal Regulations is amended as set forth below:

PART 231--INTERPRETIVE RELEASES RELATING TO THE SECURITIES ACT OF 1933 AND GENERAL RULES AND REGULATIONS THEREUNDER

1. Part 231 is amended by adding Release No. 33-7233 and the release date of October 6, 1995, to the list of interpretive releases.

PART 241--INTERPRETIVE RELEASES RELATING TO THE SECURITIES EXCHANGE ACT OF 1934 AND GENERAL RULES AND REGULATIONS THEREUNDER

2. Part 241 is amended by adding Release No. 34-36345 and the release date of October 6, 1995, to the list of interpretive releases.

PART 271--INTERPRETIVE RELEASES RELATING TO THE INVESTMENT COMPANY ACT OF 1940 AND GENERAL RULES AND REGULATIONS THEREUNDER

3. Part 271 is amended by adding Release No. IC-21399 and the release date of October 6, 1995, to the list of interpretive releases.

By the Commission.

[1] 15 U.S.C. 77a et seq.

[2] 15 U.S.C. 78a et seq.

[3] 15 U.S.C. 80a-1 et seq.

[4] While estimates of computer ownership vary from survey to survey, it is anticipated that computer ownership will grow dramatically in the next few years. One recent survey suggests that nearly half of all American households own at least one computer and about 16% of those households that own a computer subscribe to online services. See B. L. McLaughlan, "Wired Nations: Half of U.S. Homes Now Have a Computer," The Detroit News, July 21, 1995, Meet News section. Another survey, however, found that only 31% of American households own a personal computer. See J. Morrison, "Hot Modems, Cold Lives: Refugees From Cyberspace," The New York Times, April 30, 1995, Section 1, col. 2, p. 45.

[5] See, G. Weiss, "Online Investing--At Your Fingertips Is A Powerful New Financial Tool," Business Week, June 5, 1995, at 64.

[6] Access to EDGAR filings is generally available through information resellers that have purchased the data from the EDGAR dissemination subsystem and created a variety of on-line and CD-ROM versions. At the present time, 20 firms purchase data and create value-added products for analysts and the investor community. In addition, there is strong interest in ensuring that EDGAR documents are available, especially to individual investors, at the lowest possible cost. In January 1993, the New York University School of Business and the Internet Multicasting Service, a non-profit organization, received a grant from the National Science Foundation to make most EDGAR material available on the Internet. This grant expired on October 1, 1995. The Commission recently announced that it would package EDGAR filings with its own separate Internet service. This service, which began September 28, 1995, makes EDGAR filings as well as certain Commission releases and announcements available on the Internet. The Internet World Wide Web site address is http://www.sec.gov.

[7] In order to encourage the rapid dissemination of additional information considered valuable by many members of the investment community, the Commission today is announcing its intention to expand the capacity of the EDGAR system to accommodate the electronic filing of ownership and transaction reports filed pursuant to Section 16 of the Exchange Act [15 U.S.C. 78p] and Rule 144 [17 CFR 230.144] under the Securities Act. See Release No. 33-7231. The necessary programming already has been initiated and filers should be able to file these documents electronically on a voluntary basis by late 1995 or early 1996. A further announcement will be made when the effective date is determined.

[8] See Release No. 33-6977 at Section V.F (February 23, 1993) [58 FR 14628].

[9] For purposes of this release, the term "electronic" refers to media such as audiotapes, videotapes, facsimiles, CD-ROM, electronic mail, bulletin boards, Internet Web sites and computer networks (e.g., local area networks and commercial on-line services) to provide documents required by the federal securities laws to investors, security holders, and offerees. Such documents include: prospectuses required to be delivered in connection with offerings under the Securities Act; annual reports to security holders and proxy or information statements required to be furnished pursuant to Section 14 of the Exchange Act [15 U.S.C. 78n]; annual and semi-annual reports required by Section 30(d) of the Investment Company Act [15 U.S.C. 80a-29(d)]; documents furnished to investors in connection with tender offers or going private transactions; offering circulars delivered in connection with Regulation A [17 CFR 230.251-263] offerings; and disclosure required to be furnished in connection with Regulation D [17 CFR 230.505, 506] offerings (issuers should be mindful of the current prohibition in Rules 505 and 506 regarding general solicitation, see Examples 20 and 21). Other documents may include annual reports on Form 10-K [17 CFR 249.310] and other reports required to be furnished upon request to a security holder or the recipient of a prospectus using incorporation by reference. Additionally, this release addresses the electronic delivery of elective information, such as quarterly reports to security holders and sales literature. But see n. 12,

below.

[10] See Brown & Wood (February 17, 1995).

[11] The liability provisions of the federal securities laws apply equally to electronic and paper-based media. For instance, the antifraud provisions of the federal securities laws as set forth in Section 10(b) of the Exchange Act [15 U.S.C. 78j(b)] and Rule 10b-5 [17 CFR 240.10b-5] thereunder would apply to any information delivered electronically, as it does to information delivered in paper. As another example, Section 17(b) of the Securities Act [15 U.S.C. 77q(b)] would apply to any report circulated on the Internet just as if the report were provided in paper.

In addition, this release does not affect any applicable state laws or self-regulatory organization rules. Consequently, issuers and others need to consider the potential application of state law (e.g., state securities laws and business corporation laws) and other rules. At least one state has addressed issues relating to the use of electronic media in securities offerings. Recently, the Pennsylvania Securities Commission issued an order, effective for a period of one year beginning September 1, 1995, exempting from state qualification requirements securities offers made on the Internet where: 1) the offer indicates directly or indirectly that the securities are not being offered to persons in Pennsylvania; 2) an offer is not being made to any person in Pennsylvania by other means; and 3) no sales of the issuer's securities are made in Pennsylvania as a result of the Internet offer. See Order of the Pennsylvania Securities Commission In Re Offers Effected Through Internet That Do Not Result In Sales In Pennsylvania, dated August 31, 1995. In addition, the North American Securities Administrators Association, Inc., an association of securities commissioners from each of the 50 states, the District of Columbia, Puerto Rico, Mexico, and several Canadian provinces, has a committee that is addressing various issues, including jurisdictional authority, surrounding the use of electronic media in the offering of securities across state lines.

The National Association of Securities Dealers, Inc. recently reminded its members of the applicability of its Rules for Fair Practice to electronic communications. See Special Notice to Members, 95-80, September 26, 1995.

[12] Although Section 2(10) of the Securities Act [15 U.S.C. 77b(10)] defines "prospectus" to include a writing that "confirms the sale of any security," this release does not authorize transmission of confirmations, as required by Rule 10b-10 under the Exchange Act [17 CFR 240.10b-10] through electronic means. Consequently, while this release anticipates the electronic delivery of Section 10(a) prospectuses [15 U.S.C. 77j(a)], confirmations that are used to satisfy the delivery of a Section 10(a) prospectus, as permitted by Securities Act Rule 434 [17 CFR 230.434], cannot be delivered electronically at this time, unless specifically permitted as discussed below.

Under current interpretations of Rule 10b-10, confirmations may not be delivered electronically unless the Commission has specifically permitted such delivery. The Commission has recognized the use of a facsimile machine to send customer confirmations. Thus, if a customer has a facsimile machine, a broker-dealer would fulfill its confirmation delivery obligation if it sent the confirmation via facsimile transmission. Release No. 34-34962 (November 9, 1994), 60 FR 59612, 59614 n.28. The Commission, acting by delegated authority, also has allowed, under specified conditions, confirmations to be sent by electronic means. See, e.g., Thomson Financial Services (October 8, 1993). Applications for exemption from the requirements under Rule 10b-10 for delivery by paper or facsimile, pursuant to paragraph (e) of the Rule, may be sent to Catherine McGuire, Chief Counsel, Division of Market Regulation, U.S. Securities and Exchange Commission, 450 Fifth Street, N.W., Mail Stop 5-10, Washington, D.C. 20549.

The Commission has directed the Division of Market Regulation to review this and other rules to determine if and under what conditions electronic delivery of information required by those rules is feasible. The Commission expects that this review will result in the issuance of additional releases relating to these rules.

[13] See Release No. 33-7234.

[14] See Section III, below.

[15] See n. 9 and 12, above.

[16] See n. 27, below.

[17] Release No. 33-7183 (June 27, 1995) [60 FR 35604].

[18] See Section II.B to Release No. 33-7183.

[19] But see n. 12, above.

[20] Electronically delivered documents must be prepared, updated, and delivered consistent with the provisions of the federal securities laws in the same manner as paper documents. Regardless of whether information is delivered through paper or electronic means, it should, of course, convey all material and required information. If a paper document is

required to present information in a certain order, then the electronic document should convey the information in substantially the same order. For example, in an audio or video prospectus, the information required to be on the cover page of a paper prospectus pursuant to Item 501(c) of Regulation S-K [17 CFR 229.501(c)] (e.g., red herring language) must be among the first information presented through the audio or video media.

Information need not be provided solely through one medium. For example, the Commission anticipates that, for practical reasons, many proxy solicitations would continue to be delivered only in paper by an issuer, while that issuer may choose to deliver other documents, such as an annual report to shareholders ("annual reports") through electronic means.

[21] Under the various federal securities statutes and rules, there are differing delivery obligations depending upon the context of the requirements. This release does not alter these requirements.

[22] Issuers and other persons required to satisfy delivery requirements should consider establishing record-keeping or other procedures to evidence satisfaction of applicable requirements through electronic means. Presumably, such procedures would be analogous to comparable procedures followed when a paper document is delivered.

Those providing information also should take reasonable precautions to ensure the integrity and security of that information, regardless of whether it is to be delivered through electronic means or paper, so as to ensure that it is the information intended to be delivered.

[23] For example, in an offering, notice of an updated or final prospectus and/or the updated or final prospectus itself need not be sent at all, through any means, to persons who have received an electronic preliminary prospectus, but to whom securities are not expected to be sold. Of course, the final prospectus would have to be delivered, through electronic means or otherwise, to those investors to whom securities are sold.

[24] For example, if an investor must proceed through a confusing series of ever-changing menus to access a required document so that it is not reasonable to expect that access would generally occur, this procedure would likely be viewed as unduly burdensome. In that case, delivery would be deemed not to have occurred unless delivery otherwise could be shown.

There are some circumstances where burdensome procedures may be appropriate. See Example 48.

[25] In many cases, the investor will be able to download the document from the electronic medium, which is sufficient to satisfy this need.

[26] For example, after a paper preliminary prospectus has been provided, issuers make the most recent version of the prospectus available to all persons to whom they expect to sell. If an issuer posts electronically a preliminary prospectus on its Web site, the prospectus should be updated to the same degree as paper and be available to all persons to whom the issuer expects to sell securities in reliance on the electronic delivery of the prospectus. It likely would not be sufficient to show effective delivery if the information was merely posted for a brief period of time and then taken off the Web site, absent some other showing that delivery of the updated prospectus actually had occurred. In the case of a continuous offering, the prospectus should remain available for as long as the issuer will rely on its delivery through the electronic system. Annual reports should be available electronically for a sufficient length of time for delivery to be satisfied. In the case of proxy soliciting materials regarding the election of directors, investors might reasonably expect the proxy soliciting materials and annual report to be available on the Web site until their votes have been cast and the meeting adjourned.

[27] This policy would not preclude an issuer from structuring its offering as one that will be made only through electronic documents. However, companies conducting initial public offerings must consider prospectus delivery requirements for secondary market trading under Securities Act Rule 174 [17 CFR 230.174].

Further, if a potential investor makes it known that the receipt of information through electronic means by that person is no longer to be relied upon by the issuer (for example, due to the revocation of a consent previously given), then the issuer would not be able to rely on the electronic delivery of information subsequently to provide information to such person. If such subsequent information is required to be provided under the federal securities laws to such person because, for example, the person is now a shareholder and is entitled to receive a proxy statement then, absent some alternative, the issuer would be required to deliver the information through paper.

[28] For example, broker-dealers, banks, associations and other fiduciary entities may have delivery obligations to forward proxy soliciting materials and annual reports to shareholders under Exchange Act Rules 14b-1 and 14b-2 [17 CFR 240.14b-1 and 240.14b-2]. See Example 29.

[29] If a consent is used, the consent should be an informed consent. Recipients generally should be apprised: that information provided would be available through a specific electronic medium or source (e.g., via a limited proprietary system, or at a World Wide Web site); of the potential that investors may incur costs (e.g., on-line time); and of the period

during, and the documents for, which the consent will be effective. For instance, investors should be made aware of whether the consent extends to more than one type of document. If an investor revokes a consent that extends to more than one document, and consent is being relied upon by the provider of the information to ensure effective delivery or transmission, future documents should be delivered in paper unless the provider of the information has an alternative mechanism for ensuring effective electronic delivery. If not, it would appear likely that continued electronic delivery, after revocation of the consent, would not be considered to result in the investor's having access to the information and, therefore, the delivery requirement would not be satisfied.

Moreover, an issuer could rely on consents provided to an underwriter, a brokerage firm or other service provider. Similarly, an underwriter or brokerage firm could rely on a consent that its customer provided to the issuer, and deliver that issuer's documents through the same electronic medium.

Information may be provided through more than one medium; for example, proxy statements and proxy cards might continue to be delivered in paper while prospectuses might be delivered electronically. If the recipient of information provides a general consent to receive all documents electronically, it would be permissible for a provider of information to attempt to accommodate that request if the provider so desired.

[30] A separate document accompanying the confirmation also may be used.

[31] 17 CFR 240.15c2-8(b).

[32] Exchange Act Rule 15c2-8(c), (d) [17 CFR 240.15c28(c), (d)].

[33] In Release No. 34-35705 (May 11, 1995) [60 FR 26604], the Commission stated that a managing underwriter may discharge its obligations pursuant to Rule 15c2-8(g) or (h) by delivering a prospectus (or any portion thereof) electronically to a participating broker-dealer, if the recipient broker-dealer expressly consents to delivery in such form, consistent with the Brown & Wood letter. As reflected in that release and as further discussed in this release and Examples 6 and 7 above, it is the Commission's view that broker-dealers may use a variety of means to satisfy the prospectus delivery obligations of Rule 15c2-8, including electronic delivery.

[34] 17 CFR 230.153.

[35] See n. 12, above.

[36] In this example, the prospectus is accessible on the same menu as the supplemental sales literature; consequently, the existence of the prospectus and its location are readily ascertainable by the investor viewing the sales literature.

[37] Section 5(b) of the Securities Act.

[38] Section 5(b) of the Securities Act.

[39] 17 CFR 230.134.

[40] 17 CFR 240.14a-2(a)(6).

[41] 17 CFR 230.502(c). In Release 33-7185 (June 27, 1995), the Commission solicited comment on the question of whether the prohibition against general solicitation in Regulation D offerings should be reconsidered.

[42] Section 17(b) of the Securities Act.

[43] Exchange Act Rule 14b-1. This example also is applicable to delivery by banks and other entities pursuant to Rule 14b-2.

[44] See E. Savitz, "Let A Thousand Web Site Bloom," Barron's, June 26, 1995, at 50.

[45] Sections 2(10)(a) and 5(b) of the Securities Act.

[46] This is analogous to printing a fund prospectus in a magazine of general circulation and subsequently mailing supplemental sales literature to the magazine's subscribers, which would not comply with Sections 2(10) and 5(b) of the Securities Act. See William C. Lloyd (State of Wisconsin), June 7, 1990.

[47] Rule 482 [17 CFR 230.482] permits a registered investment company or business development company to use an "omitting prospectus" advertisement that contains only information the substance of which is included in the company's

Section 10(a) prospectus.

[48] 15 U.S.C. 80a-29(d).

[49] The analysis would be the same if an investor requests and receives information on a diskette.

[50] Continued sales of fund shares or delivery of sales literature or application forms to investors who had received the prospectus electronically would require delivery of paper prospectus to those investors. Funds should consider whether paper prospectuses should also be sent to other investors (e.g., recent purchasers).

[51] 17 CFR 274.11A.

[52] See Release No. 33-7234 for the text of those amendments. Rule changes are proposed to be made to the following rules and forms: Rule 253 of Regulation A [17 CFR 230.253]; Rule 420 of Regulation C [17 CFR 230.420]; Rules 481 and 482 of Regulation C [17 CFR 230.481, 230.482]; Rule 605 of Regulation E [17 CFR 230.605]; Rule 304 of Regulation S-T [17 CFR 232.304]; Forms F-7 [17 CFR 239.37], F-8 [17 CFR 239.38], F-9 [17 CFR 239.39]; F-10 [17 CFR 239.40] and F-80 [17 CFR 239.41]; Rule 12b-12 [17 CFR 240.12b-12]; Rule 13e-3 [17 CFR 240.13e-3]; Rule 13e-4 [17 CFR 240.13e-4]; Schedule 13E-4F [17 CFR 240.13e-102]; Rule 14a-3 [17 CFR 240.14a-3]; Rule 14a-5 [17 CFR 240.14a-5]; Rule 14a-7 [17 CFR 240.14a-7]; Rule 14c-4 [17 CFR 240.14c-4]; Rule 14c-7 [17 CFR 240.14c-7]; Rule 14d-5 [17 CFR 240.14d-5]; Schedule 14D-1F [17 CFR 240.14d-102]; Schedule 14D-9F [17 CFR 240.14d-103]; and Rule 8b-12 [17 CFR 270.8b-12]; Rule 30d-1 [17 CFR 270.30d-1] and Rule 30d-2 [17 CFR 270.30d-2].

[53] 15 U.S.C. 78w(a).

EXHIBIT E

USE OF ELECTRONIC MEDIA FOR DELIVERY PURPOSES RELEASE NO. 33-7289; 34-37183

SECURITIES AND EXCHANGE COMMISSION

17 CFR Parts 200, 228, 229, 230, 232, 239, 240, 270 and 274

[Release No. 33-7289, 34-37183, IC-21946; File No. S7-31-95]

RIN 3235-AG67

Use of Electronic Media for Delivery Purposes

AGENCY: Securities and Exchange Commission.

ACTION: Final rules.

SUMMARY: The Securities and Exchange Commission ("Commission") today is adopting technical amendments to its rules that are premised on the distribution of paper documents. These amendments are intended to clarify certain rules in light of the interpretations set forth in the Commission's October 6, 1995 release (Release No. 33-7233 [60 FR 53458]) regarding the use of electronic media for the dissemination of issuer-related information under the federal securities laws ("October Interpretive Release") and the availability of electronic filings on the Commission's World Wide Web site.

EFFECTIVE DATE: The amendments will become effective [30 days after publication in the Federal Register].

FOR FURTHER INFORMATION CONTACT: Joseph P. Babits or James R. Budge, (202) 942-2910, Division of Corporation Finance; and, with regard to questions concerning investment companies and investment advisers, Kathleen K. Clarke, (202) 942-0721, Division of Investment Management, U.S. Securities and Exchange Commission, 450 Fifth Street, N.W., Washington, D.C. 20549.

SUPPLEMENTARY INFORMATION: To clarify certain rules in light of the interpretations relating to electronic distribution of securities-related information as set forth in the October Interpretive Release, the Commission is adopting technical amendments to the following rules and forms: Rule 200.80, 1/ Item 502 of Regulation S-B; 2/ Item 502 of Regulation S-K; 3/ Rule 120 4/ of the Securities Act of 1933 ("Securities Act"); 5/ Rule 253 of Regulation A; 6/ Rule 420 of Regulation C; 7/ Rules 481 and 482 of Regulation C; 8/ Rule 605 of Regulation E; 9/ Rule 304 of Regulation S-T; 10/ Forms F-7, 11/ F-8, 12/ F-9, 13/ F-10 14/ and F-80; 15/ Rule 12b-12; 16/ Rule 13e-3; 17/ Rule 13e-4; 18/ Schedule

---

1/ 17 CFR 200.80.

2/ 17 CFR 228.502.

3/ 17 CFR 229.502. Two unrelated technical corrections to Item 601(c) of Regulations S-B and S-K [17 CFR 228.601(c) and 229.601(c), respectively] also are included in this release.

4/ 17 CFR 230.120.

5/ 15 U.S.C. 77a et seq.

6/ 17 CFR 230.253.

7/ 17 CFR 230.420.

8/ 17 CFR 230.481 and 230.482.

9/ 17 CFR 230.605.

10/ 17 CFR 232.304.

11/ 17 CFR 239.37.

12/ 17 CFR 239.38.

13/ 17 CFR 239.39.

14/ 17 CFR 239.40.

15/ 17 CFR 239.41.

16/ 17 CFR 240.12b-12.

17/ 17 CFR 240.13e-3.

18/ 17 CFR 240.13e-4.

13E-4F; 19/ Rule 14a-3; 20/ Rule 14a-5; 21/ Rule 14a-7; 22/ Rule 14c-4; 23/ Rule 14c-7; 24/ Rule 14d-5; 25/ Schedule 14D-1F; 26/ Schedule 14D-9F; 27/ under the Securities Exchange Act of 1934 ("Exchange Act"); 28/ and Rule 8b-12; 29/ Rule 30d-1; 30/ Rule 30d-2; 31/ Form N-1A; 32/ Form N-2; 33/ Form N-3; 34/ and Form N-4 35/ under the Investment Company Act of 1940 ("Investment Company Act"). 36/

19/ 17 CFR 240.13e-102.

20/ 17 CFR 240.14a-3.

21/ 17 CFR 240.14a-5.

22/ 17 CFR 240.14a-7.

23/ 17 CFR 240.14c-4.

24/ 17 CFR 240.14c-7.

25/ 17 CFR 240.14d-5.

26/ 17 CFR 240.14d-102.

27/ 17 CFR 240.14d-103.

28/ 15 U.S.C. 78a *et seq*.

29/ 17 CFR 270.8b-12.

30/ 17 CFR 270.30d-1.

31/ 17 CFR 270.30d-2.

32/ 17 CFR 274.11A.

33/ 17 CFR 274.11a-1.

34/ 17 CFR 274.11b.

35/ 17 CFR 274.11c.

36/ 15 U.S.C. 80a-1 *et seq*.

I. INTRODUCTION

In its October Interpretive Release, the Commission recognized the promise of electronic distribution of information in enhancing investors' ability to access, research, and analyze information, and in facilitating the provision of information by issuers and others. 37/ Acknowledging the wide spectrum of media available to issuers and others who distribute securities-related information, as well as the fact that strict compliance with requirements applicable to printed material may not be possible in all electronic media, in a companion release, the Commission proposed for comment technical amendments to rules that were premised on the distribution of paper documents ("Proposing Release"). 38/

The Commission received 12 letters of comment on various issues raised in its October Interpretive Release and Proposing Release; the majority of commenters focused on the October Interpretive Release rather than the Proposing Release. 39/ Except as noted, the Commission is adopting the amendments as proposed, 40/ and certain other technical rule changes are being made that did not require proposal. 41/ The amendments are designed to

---

37/ The Commission has issued a second interpretive release dealing with electronic communication issues relating to broker-dealers, transfer agents, and investment advisers. Several additional examples also were included. See Release No. 33-7288 (May 9, 1996).

38/ Release No. 33-7234 (October 6, 1995) [60 FR 53468].

39/ These letters are available for inspection and copying in the Commission's public reference room located at 450 Fifth Street, N.W., Washington, D.C. (File No. S7-31-95).

40/ Certain clarifying modifications have been made to the proposed language of Rule 304(c) of Regulation S-T and the note to Rule 14d-5.

41/ See technical changes to Rule 200.80 of the Commission's rules relating to organization, conduct and ethics and information and requests, Securities Act Rule 120, Item 502 of Regulations S-K and S-B, and Item 601(c) of Regulations S-K and S-B, and to the following Investment Company Act (continued...)

maintain the intent of the original requirements while allowing flexibility to issuers and others in the choice of distribution medium.

A. General Formatting Requirements

As proposed, Commission rules that prescribe the physical appearance of a paper document, such as type size and font requirements, are being amended to provide that the issuer, when delivering an electronic version of a document, may comply with the requirements by presenting the information in a format readily communicated to investors. Where legends are required to be printed in red ink or bold-face type, or in a different font size, the amended rules will allow issuers to satisfy such requirements by presenting the legends in any manner reasonably calculated to draw attention to them.

B. Graphic, Image and Audio Information

1. Documents delivered to investors

With respect to documents delivered to investors, the proposed rules provided that if material graphic, image and audio information is included in one version of a disclosure document, but not in other versions, the issuer must include in the other versions a fair and accurate description or transcript of the omitted information. The Commission has determined that this language is not

41/(...continued)
registration statement forms: Form N-1A for open-end investment companies; Form N-2 for closed-end companies; Form N-3 for separate accounts offering variable annuity contracts that are registered under the Investment Company Act as management investment companies; and Form N-4 for separate accounts offering variable annuity contracts that are registered under the Investment Company Act as unit investment trusts. The amendments to Rules 200.80 and 120 relate to agency organization, procedure or practice; therefore, publication for notice and comment is not required under the Administrative Procedure Act. 5 U.S.C. 553(b). With respect to the amendments to Regulations S-K and S-B, and to the Investment Company Act registration statement forms, the Commission for good cause finds that publication of these amendments for notice and comment is unnecessary because they are minor, technical changes. 5 U.S.C. 553(b).

necessary to ensure compliance with the federal securities laws; consequently, the adopted rules do not include it. Where more than one version of a document is delivered to investors, each version must contain all information required by, and otherwise comply with, the requirements of the applicable form and other provisions of the federal securities laws. 42/ The issuer (or other party to whom the law assigns the responsibility) remains responsible for ensuring that each version satisfies applicable statutory and regulatory requirements. 43/

2. **Documents filed with the Commission**

Documents containing video, audio and graphic presentations currently cannot be filed on the EDGAR system. Where these presentations are used in documents delivered to investors, Rule 304 of Regulation S-T has always required electronic filers to provide fair and accurate descriptions of omitted materials in their EDGAR filings. Rule 304 initially was phrased in terms of graphic and image material included in "the paper format version" of an EDGAR filing. To reflect the possibility of the delivery of an electronic version that differs from the EDGAR filing, the Commission is amending Rule 304 to provide that wherever the "document delivered to investors or others" includes graphic, image or audio information that cannot be reproduced in an electronic filing on EDGAR, the

---

42/ See Release No. 33-7288 (May 9, 1996), Part IV, example (7).

43/ Differing versions of a document may need to be filed with the Commission. For example, differing prospectuses should be filed with the Commission pursuant to Rule 424 [17 CFR 230.424] or Rule 497 [17 CFR 230.497]. Alternatively, the company may file with the Commission as an appendix to the prospectus a fair and accurate description of any omitted material. As discussed below, graphic, image and audio material should be described in EDGAR filings pursuant to Rule 304 of Regulation S-T.

EDGAR filing must include a fair and accurate narrative description, tabular presentation or transcript of the omitted material. 44/

C. **Rules Where Mailing Is Identified as a Delivery Method**

Certain Commission rules provide that information may be distributed to investors by mail. While some indicate that reasonably prompt alternative delivery methods may be used, 45/ others specifically require "mailing." These rules should be read consistently to allow the use of alternative methods of distribution that are reasonably prompt. These rules are being amended where necessary to reflect this view. 46/

D. **Identification of Where Filings Are Available for Inspection**

Rule 200.80 identifies the public reference rooms located in Washington, D.C. and other designated Regional Offices as the primary locations where documents filed with the Commission may be inspected and copied; in addition, Securities Act Rule 120 states that registration statements are available for public inspection during business hours at Commission headquarters. Other rules require

---

44/ Of course, immaterial differences would not need to be described. The rule retains the provisions that all such omitted material is deemed filed as part of the electronic filing and that copies of the document as distributed should be retained by the issuer for a period of five years.

One commenter suggested that rather than require descriptions, the Commission should allow the filing of documents in formats that currently are not compatible with EDGAR. This suggestion fundamentally relates to the design of the EDGAR system, which currently is being reevaluated by the staff; any necessary rulemaking related to electronic filing will be undertaken as modifications to the EDGAR system are developed and implemented in the future.

45/ See e.g., Rule 14d-4(a)(2)(ii) [17 CFR 240.14d-4(a)(2)(ii)].

46/ Where the costs of distribution are to be calculated under the rules, the amendments provide that methods analogous to those applicable to mailing should be used where alternative delivery methods are chosen. In that regard, the proposed change to Rule 14d-5 has been modified to provide greater guidance with respect to cost calculation under that rule.

a registrant that is a reporting company to include on the inside front cover of a prospectus a statement to the effect that reports and other information filed by the registrant may be inspected and copied at the Commission's public reference rooms. 47/ The Commission now also makes electronic filings publicly available on the Internet within 24 hours of acceptance. 48/ Consequently, the Commission believes it is appropriate, as a reflection of this agency's current dissemination procedures and practices, to amend Rules 200.80(c) and 120 to include a statement that electronic filings are publicly available on the Commission's Web site. 49/ The prospectus requirements also have been amended to provide for the inclusion of a statement that the Commission maintains a Web site that contains reports, proxy and information statements and other information regarding registrants that file electronically with the Commission. 50/

The Commission also is amending certain investment company registration statement forms to provide for inclusion of a statement on the cover page of prospectuses that the Commission maintains a Web site that contains the Statement of Additional Information, material incorporated by reference, and other information regarding registrants that file electronically with the Commission. 51/

47/ Item 502(a) of Regulations S-K and S-B [17 CFR 229.502(a) and 228.502(a), respectively].

48/ See Commission News Release No. 95-195 (September 28, 1995).

49/ A correction to the cross reference to confidential treatment rules in Rule 120 also is being adopted.

50/ Item 502(a) of Regulations S-K and S-B. The Commission's Internet address is http://www.sec.gov.

51/ See amendments to Item 1(a)(iii)(C) of Form N-1A; Item 1.1.d(C) of Form N-2; Item 1(a)(vi)(C) of Form N-3; and Item 1(a)(v)(C) of Form N-4. This new requirement would apply to any prospectus that is disseminated (continued...)

This new requirement is limited to prospectuses disseminated electronically by investment companies that are electronic filers because it should not impose any significant additional burden on such registrants to include the disclosure in those prospectuses. The Commission intends to propose expanding this requirement to apply to all investment company prospectuses as part of future amendments to investment company registration forms.

II. COST-BENEFIT ANALYSIS

Quick and broad access to material information was one of the fundamental premises upon which the federal securities laws were adopted, and electronic distribution no doubt will benefit issuers and investors through cheaper and faster communication of information. While the Commission expects the increased use of electronic media to benefit securities markets and investors by making disclosure available faster and more cheaply, it does not anticipate that the amendments will, in and of themselves, result in substantial economic costs or benefits. Those benefits will be derived from advances in technology, and not from the minor technical amendments that are the subject of this rulemaking.

III. REGULATORY FLEXIBILITY ACT CERTIFICATION

Pursuant to Section 605(b) of the Regulatory Flexibility Act, 5 U.S.C. 605(b), the Chairman of the Commission has certified that the amendments will not have a significant economic impact on a substantial number of small entities.

51/(...continued)
electronically by an investment company that is an electronic filer after the effective date of these rules, but the new disclosure would not necessitate filing a prospectus supplement or "stickering" the prospectus.

This certification, including the reasons therefor, was attached to the Proposing Release as Appendix A.

IV. STATUTORY BASES

The amendments to the Commission's rules under the Securities Act and amendments to the Commission's rules under the Exchange Act are being made pursuant to Sections 6, 7, 8, 10 and 19(a) of the Securities Act and Sections 3, 4, 10, 12, 13, 14, 15, 16 and 23 of the Exchange Act. The amendments to the Commission's rules under the Investment Company Act are being made pursuant to Sections 8(b) and 38(a) under the Investment Company Act, as amended.

List of Subjects

17 CFR Parts 200, 228, 229, 230, 232, 239, 240, 270 and 274

Reporting and recordkeeping requirements, Securities, and Investment companies.

TEXT OF THE AMENDMENTS

In accordance with the foregoing, Title 17, chapter II of the Code of Federal Regulations is amended as follows:

PART 200 --ORGANIZATION; CONDUCT AND ETHICS; AND INFORMATION AND REQUESTS

1. The authority citation for Part 200 continues to read in part as follows:

Authority: 15 U.S.C. 77s, 78d-1, 78d-2, 78w, 78ll(d), 79t, 77sss, 80a-37, 80b-11, unless otherwise noted.

* * * * *

2. By amending §200.80 by adding paragraph (c)(3), to read as follows:

§200.80 Commission records and information.

* * * * *

(c)(1) * * *

(3) Electronic filings made through the Electronic Data Gathering, Analysis, and Retrieval system are publicly available through the Commission's Web site (http://www.sec.gov).

* * * * *

PART 228 --INTEGRATED DISCLOSURE SYSTEM FOR SMALL BUSINESS ISSUERS

3. The authority citation for Part 228 continues to read as follows:

Authority: 15 U.S.C. 77e, 77f, 77g, 77h, 77j, 77k, 77s, 77aa(25), 77aa(26), 77ddd, 77eee, 77ggg, 77hhh, 77jjj, 77nnn, 77sss, 78l, 78m, 78n, 78o, 78w, 78ll, 80a-8, 80a-29, 80a-30, 80a-37, 80b-11, unless otherwise noted.

4. By amending §228.502 by revising paragraph (a)(2) to read as follows:

§228.502 (Item 502) Inside Front and Outside Back Cover Pages of Prospectus.

* * * * *

(a)(1) * * *

(2) If the small business issuer is a reporting company, state that the reports and other information filed by the small business issuer may be inspected and copied at the public reference facilities of the Commission in Washington D.C., and at some of its Regional Offices (include addresses), and that copies of such material can be obtained from the Public Reference Section of the Commission, 450 Fifth Street, N.W., Washington D.C., 20549, at prescribed rates. If the small business issuer is an electronic filer, state that the Commission maintains a Web site that contains reports, proxy and information statements and other information regarding issuers that file electronically with the Commission and state the address of such site (http://www.sec.gov); and

* * * * *

5. By amending §228.601(c) by revising the headings "Note 1 to paragraph (c)(1)(vi)" to read "Note 1 to paragraph (c)(1)" and "Note 2 to paragraph (c)(1)(vi)" to read "Note 2 to paragraph (c)(1)".

PART 229 -- STANDARD INSTRUCTIONS FOR FILING FORMS UNDER SECURITIES ACT OF 1933, SECURITIES EXCHANGE ACT OF 1934 AND ENERGY POLICY AND CONSERVATION ACT OF 1975 – REGULATION S-K

6. The authority citation for Part 229 continues to read in part as follows:

Authority: 15 U.S.C. 77e, 77f, 77g, 77h, 77j, 77k, 77s, 77aa(25), 77aa(26), 77ddd, 77eee, 77ggg, 77hhh, 77iii, 77jjj, 77nnn, 77sss, 78c, 78i, 78j, 78l, 78m, 78n, 78o, 78w, 78ll(d), 79e, 79n, 79t, 80a-8, 80a-29, 80a-30, 80a-37, 80b-11, unless otherwise noted.

* * * * *

7. By amending §229.502 by revising paragraph (a)(2) to read as follows:

§229.502 (Item 502) Inside front and outside back cover pages of prospectus.

* * * * *

(a) * * *

(2) State that reports (and where the registrant is subject to sections 14(a) and 14(c) of the Exchange Act, proxy and information statements) and other information filed by the registrant can be inspected and copied at the public reference facilities maintained by the Commission in Washington, D.C., and at certain of its Regional Offices, and state the current address of each such facility (see §§200.11(b) and 200.80(c) of this chapter), and that copies of such material can be obtained from the Public Reference Section of the Commission, 450 Fifth Street, N.W., Washington, D.C. 20549 at prescribed rates. If the registrant is an electronic filer, state that the Commission maintains a Web site that contains

12

reports, proxy and information statements and other information regarding registrants that file electronically with the Commission and state the address of such site (http://www.sec.gov); and

* * * * *

8. By amending §229.601(c) by revising the heading "Note 1 to paragraph (c)(1)(vi)" to read "Note 1 to paragraph (c)(1)" and "Note 2 to paragraph (c)(1)(vi)" to read "Note 2 to paragraph (c)(1)".

PART 230 - GENERAL RULES AND REGULATIONS, SECURITIES ACT OF 1933

9. The authority citation for Part 230 continues to read in part as follows:

AUTHORITY: 15 U.S.C. 77b, 77f, 77g, 77h, 77j, 77s, 77sss, 78c, 78d, 78l, 78m, 78n, 78o, 78w, 78ll(d), 79t, 80a-8, 80a-29, 80a-30, and 80a-37, unless otherwise noted.

* * * * *

10. By revising §230.120 to read as follows:

§230.120 Inspection of registration statements.

Except for material contracts or portions thereof accorded confidential treatment pursuant to §230.406, all registration statements are available for public inspection, during business hours, at the principal office of the Commission in Washington, D.C. Electronic registration statements made through the Electronic Data Gathering, Analysis, and Retrieval system are publicly available through the Commission's Web site (http://www.sec.gov).

11. By amending §230.253 by designating the text of paragraph (b) after the heading as paragraph (b)(1) and by adding paragraph (b)(2), to read as follows:

§230.253 Offering circular.

* * * * *

(b) Presentation of information. (1) * * *

(2) Where an offering circular is distributed through an electronic medium, issuers may satisfy legibility requirements applicable to printed documents by presenting all required information in a format readily communicated to investors.

* * * * *

12. By amending §230.420 by designating the text as paragraph (a) and by adding paragraph (b), to read as follows:

§230.420 Legibility of prospectus.

(a) * * *

(b) Where a prospectus is distributed through an electronic medium, issuers may satisfy legibility requirements applicable to printed documents, such as paper size, type size and font, bold-face type, italics and red ink, by presenting all required information in a format readily communicated to investors, and where indicated, in a manner reasonably calculated to draw investor attention to specific information.

13. By amending §230.481 to add paragraph (h) to read as follows:

§230.481 Information required in prospectus.

* * * * *

(h) Where a prospectus is distributed through an electronic medium, issuers may satisfy legibility requirements applicable to printed documents, such as paper size, type size and font, bold-face type, italics and red ink, by presenting all required information in a format readily communicated to investors, and where indicated, in a manner reasonably calculated to draw investor attention to specific information.

14. By amending §230.482 by removing the note following paragraph (a)(7) and adding a note to paragraph (a)(6), to read as follows:

§230.482 **Advertising by an investment company as satisfying requirements of section 10.**

(a) * * *

(6) * * *

Note to paragraph (a)(6). All advertisements made pursuant to this rule are subject to Rule 420 [17 CFR 230.420].

* * * * *

15. By amending §230.605 by designating the text of paragraph (c) as paragraph (c)(1) and by adding paragraph (c)(2) to read as follows:

§230.605 **Filing and use of the offering circular.**

* * * * *

(c)(1) * * *

(2) Where an offering circular is distributed through an electronic medium, issuers may satisfy legibility requirements applicable to printed documents by presenting all required information in a format readily communicated to investors.

* * * * *

PART 232 --REGULATION S-T -- GENERAL RULES AND REGULATIONS FOR ELECTRONIC FILINGS

16. The authority citation for Part 232 continues to read as follows:

AUTHORITY: 15 U.S.C. 77f, 77g, 77h, 77j, 77s(a), 77sss(a), 78c(b), 78l, 78m, 78n, 78o(d), 78w(a), 78ll(d), 79t(a), 80a-8, 80a-29, 80a-30 and 80a-37.

17. By amending §232.304 by revising the section heading, paragraphs (a), (b)(1), and (c) to read as follows:

§232.304 Graphic, image and audio material.

(a) If a filer includes graphic, image or audio material in a document delivered to investors and others that cannot be reproduced in an electronic filing, the electronically filed version of that document shall include a fair and accurate narrative description, tabular representation or transcript of the omitted material. Such descriptions, representations or transcripts may be included in the text of the electronic filing at the point where the graphic, image or audio material is presented in the delivered version, or they may be listed in an appendix to the electronic filing. Immaterial differences between the delivered and electronically filed versions, such as pagination, color, type size or style, or corporate logo need not be described.

(b)(1) The graphic, image and audio material in the version of a document delivered to investors and others shall be deemed part of the electronic filing and subject to the liability and anti-fraud provisions of the federal securities laws.

(2) * * *

(c) An electronic filer shall retain for a period of five years a copy of each publicly distributed document, in the format used, that contains graphic, image or audio material where such material is not included in the version filed with the Commission. The five-year period shall commence as of the filing date, or the date that appears on the document, whichever is later. Upon request, an electronic filer shall furnish to the Commission or its staff a copy of any or all of the documents contained in the file.

* * * * *

PART 239 -- FORMS PRESCRIBED UNDER THE SECURITIES ACT OF 1933

18. The authority citation for Part 239 continues to read in part as follows:

AUTHORITY: 15 U.S.C. 77f, 77g, 77h, 77j, 77s, 77sss, 78c, 78l, 78m, 78n, 78o(d), 78w(a), 78ll(d), 79e, 79f, 79g, 79j, 79l, 79m, 79n, 79q, 79t, 80a-8, 80a-29, 80a-30 and 80a-37, unless otherwise noted.

* * * * *

19. By amending Form F-7 (referenced in §239.37) by adding a note to Part I, Item 2, to read as follows:

Note -- The text of Form F-7 does not, and this amendment will not, appear in the Code of Federal Regulations.

Form F-7

REGISTRATION STATEMENT UNDER THE SECURITIES ACT OF 1933

* * * * *

PART I

INFORMATION REQUIRED TO BE SENT TO SHAREHOLDERS

* * * * *

Item 2. Information Legends

* * * * *

Note to Item 2. If the home-jurisdiction document(s) are delivered through an electronic medium, the issuer may satisfy the legibility requirements for the required legends relating to type size and font by presenting the legends in any manner reasonably calculated to draw investor attention to it.

* * * * *

20. By amending Form F-8 (referenced in §239.38) by adding a note to Part I, Item 2, to read as follows:

Note -- The text of Form F-8 does not, and this amendment will not, appear in the Code of Federal Regulations.

Form F-8

REGISTRATION STATEMENT UNDER THE SECURITIES ACT OF 1933

* * * * *

PART I

INFORMATION REQUIRED TO BE DELIVERED TO OFFEREES OR PURCHASERS

* * * * *

Item 2. **Informational Legends**

* * * * *

Note to Item 2. If the home-jurisdiction document(s) are delivered through an electronic medium, the issuer may satisfy the legibility requirements for the required legends relating to type size and font by presenting the legends in any manner reasonably calculated to draw investor attention to it.

* * * * *

21. By amending Form F-9 (referenced in §239.39) by adding a note to Part I, Item 2, to read as follows:

Note -- The text of Form F-9 does not, and this amendment will not, appear in the Code of Federal Regulations.

Form F-9

REGISTRATION STATEMENT UNDER THE SECURITIES ACT OF 1933

* * * * *

PART I

INFORMATION REQUIRED TO BE DELIVERED TO OFFEREES OR PURCHASERS

* * * * *

Item 2. **Informational Legends**

* * * * *

Note to Item 2. If the home-jurisdiction document(s) are delivered through an electronic medium, the issuer may satisfy the legibility requirements for the required legends relating to type size and font by presenting the legends in any manner reasonably calculated to draw investor attention to it.

* * * * *

22. By amending Form F-10 (referenced in §239.40) by adding a note to Part I, Item 3, to read as follows:

Note -- The text of Form F-10 does not, and this amendment will not, appear in the Code of Federal Regulations.

Form F-10

REGISTRATION STATEMENT UNDER THE SECURITIES ACT OF 1933

* * * * *

PART I

INFORMATION REQUIRED TO BE DELIVERED TO OFFEREES OR PURCHASERS

* * * * *

Item 3. Informational Legends

* * * * *

Note to Item 3. If the home-jurisdiction document(s) are delivered through an electronic medium, the issuer may satisfy the legibility requirements for the required legends relating to type size and font by presenting the legends in any manner reasonably calculated to draw investor attention to it.

* * * * *

23. By amending Form F-80 (referenced in §239.41) by adding a note to Part I, Item 2, to read as follows:

Note -- The text of Form F-80 does not, and this amendment will not, appear in the Code of Federal Regulations.

Form F-80

REGISTRATION STATEMENT UNDER THE SECURITIES ACT OF 1933

* * * * *

PART I

INFORMATION REQUIRED TO BE DELIVERED TO OFFEREES OR PURCHASERS

* * * * *

Item 2. Informational Legends

* * * * *

Note to Item 2. If the home-jurisdiction document(s) are delivered through an electronic medium, the issuer may satisfy the legibility requirements for the required legends relating to type size and font by presenting the legends in any manner reasonably calculated to draw investor attention to it.

* * * * *

PART 240 - GENERAL RULES AND REGULATIONS, SECURITIES EXCHANGE ACT OF 1934

24. The authority citation for Part 240 continues to read in part as follows:

AUTHORITY: 15 U.S.C. 77c, 77d, 77g, 77j, 77s, 77eee, 77ggg, 77nnn, 77sss, 77ttt, 78c, 78d, 78i, 78j, 78l, 78m, 78n, 78o, 78p, 78q, 78s, 78w, 78x, 78ll(d), 79q, 79t, 80a-20, 80a-23, 80a-29, 80a-37, 80b-3, 80b-4 and 80b-11, unless otherwise noted.

* * * * *

25. The authority citation following §240.14d-5 is removed.

26. By amending §240.12b-12 by adding paragraph (e) to read as follows:

§240.12b-12 Requirements as to paper, printing and language.

* * * * *

(e) Where a statement or report is distributed to investors through an electronic medium, issuers may satisfy legibility requirements applicable to printed

20

documents, such as paper size and type size and font, by presenting all required information in a format readily communicated to investors.

27. By amending §240.13e-3 by designating the instructions to paragraph (e)(3) immediately following paragraph (e)(3)(ii)(B) as "Instructions to paragraph (e)(3)" and by adding instruction 3 thereto, to read as follows:

§240.13e-3 Going private transactions by certain issuers or their affiliates.

* * * * *

(e)(3) * * *

Instructions to paragraph (e)(3).

1. * * *

2. * * *

3. If the information delivered to security holders is distributed through an electronic medium and the legend required by paragraph (e)(3)(ii) is included, issuers may satisfy the legibility requirement relating to type size and font by presenting the legend in any manner reasonably calculated to draw security holder attention to it.

* * * * *

28. By amending §240.13e-4 by revising paragraph (e)(1)(ii)(A), to read as follows:

§240.13e-4 Tender offers by issuers.

* * * * *

(e) * * *

(1) * * *

(ii) * * *

(A) By mailing or otherwise furnishing promptly the statement required by paragraph (d)(1) of this section to each security holder whose name appears on the most recent shareholder list of the issuer;

* * * * *

29. By amending Schedule 13E-4F (§240.13e-102) by adding a note to Item 2 of Part I, to read as follows:

§240.13e-102 Schedule 13E-4F. Tender offer statement pursuant to section 13(e)(1) of the Securities Exchange Act of 1934 and §240.13e-4 thereunder.

* * * * *

Part I – Information Required to Be Sent to Shareholders

* * * * *

Item 2. * * *

<u>Note to Item 2.</u>

If the home jurisdiction document(s) are delivered through an electronic medium, the issuer may satisfy the legibility requirements for the required legends relating to type size and fonts by presenting the legend in any manner reasonably calculated to draw security holder attention to it.

* * * * *

30. By amending §240.14a-3 by designating the text of paragraph (b)(2) as (b)(2)(i) and by adding paragraph (b)(2)(ii), to read as follows:

§240.14a-3 Information to be furnished to security holders.

* * * * *

(b) * * *

(2)(i) * * *

(ii) Where the annual report to security holders is delivered through an electronic medium, issuers may satisfy legibility requirements applicable to printed documents, such as type size and font, by presenting all required information in a format readily communicated to investors.

* * * * *

31. By amending §240.14a-5 by designating the text of paragraph (d) as paragraph (d)(1) and by adding paragraph (d)(2), to read as follows:

§240.14a-5 **Presentation of information in proxy statement.**

* * * * *

(d)(1) * * *

(2) Where a proxy statement is delivered through an electronic medium, issuers may satisfy legibility requirements applicable to printed documents, such as type size and font, by presenting all required information in a format readily communicated to investors.

* * * * *

32. By amending §240.14a-7 by adding a note at the end of the section, to read as follows:

§240.14a-7 **Obligations of registrants to provide a list of, or mail soliciting material to, security holders.**

* * * * *

Note to §240.14a-7. Reasonably prompt methods of distribution to security holders may be used instead of mailing. If an alternative distribution method is chosen, the costs of that method should be considered where necessary rather than the costs of mailing.

33. By amending §240.14c-4 by adding paragraph (d), to read as follows:

§240.14c-4 **Presentation of information in information statement.**

* * * * *

(d) Where an information statement is delivered through an electronic medium, issuers may satisfy legibility requirements applicable to printed documents, such as type size and font, by presenting all required information in a format readily communicated to investors.

34. By amending §240.14c-7 by revising paragraph (c), to read as follows:

§240.14c-7 Providing copies of material for certain beneficial owners.

* * * * *

(c) A registrant, at its option, may send by mail or other equally prompt means, its annual report to security holders to the beneficial owners whose identifying information is provided by record holders and respondent banks, pursuant to §240.14b-1(b)(3) and §240.14b-2(b)(4)(ii) and (iii), provided that such registrant notifies the record holders and respondent banks at the time it makes the inquiry required by paragraph (a) of this section that the registrant will send the annual report to security holders to the beneficial owners so identified.

* * * * *

35. By amending §240.14d-5 by adding a note at the end of the section, to read as follows:

§240.14d-5 Dissemination of certain tender offers by the use of stockholder lists and security position listings.

* * * * *

Note to §240.14d-5. Reasonably prompt methods of distribution to security holders may be used instead of mailing. If alternative methods are chosen, the approximate direct costs of distribution shall be computed by adding the estimated direct costs of preparing the document for distribution through the chosen medium (including updating of shareholder lists) plus the estimated reasonable cost of distribution through that medium. Direct costs incidental to the distribution of tender offer materials and amendments thereto may include all reasonable charges paid by the subject company to third parties for supplies or services, including costs attendant to preparing shareholder lists, handling the bidder's materials, and contacting participants named on security position listings, but shall not include indirect costs, such as employee time which is devoted to either contesting or supporting the tender offer on behalf of the subject company.

36. By amending Schedule 14D-1F (§240.14d-102) by adding a note to Item 2 of Part I, to read as follows:

§240.14d-102 **Schedule 14D-1F. Tender offer statement pursuant to rule 14d-1(b) under the Securities Exchange Act of 1934.**

* * * * *

PART I -- INFORMATION REQUIRED TO BE SENT TO SHAREHOLDERS

* * * * *

Item 2. Informational Legends

* * * * *

Note to Item 2.

If the home-jurisdiction document(s) are delivered through an electronic medium, the issuer may satisfy the legibility requirements for the required legends relating to type size and font by presenting the legend in any manner reasonably calculated to draw security holder attention to it.

* * * * *

37. By amending Schedule 14D-9F (§240.14d-103) by adding a note to Item 2 of Part I, to read as follows:

§240.14d-103 **Schedule 14D-9F. Solicitation/recommendation statement pursuant to section 14(d)(4) of the Securities Exchange Act of 1934 and rules 14d-1(b) and 14e-2(c) thereunder.**

* * * * *

Part I -- Information Required to Be Sent to Shareholders

* * * * *

Item 2. Informational Legends

* * * * *

Note to Item 2.

If the home jurisdiction document(s) are delivered through an electronic medium, the issuer may satisfy the legibility requirements for the required legends relating to type size and font by presenting the legend in any manner reasonably calculated to draw security holder attention to it.

* * * * *

PART 270 --GENERAL RULES AND REGULATIONS, INVESTMENT COMPANY ACT OF 1940

38. The authority citation for Part 270 continues to read, in part, as follows:

AUTHORITY: 15 U.S.C. 80a-1 et seq., 80a-37, 80a-39, unless other otherwise noted;

* * * * *

39. The authority citations following §270.8b-12 are removed.

40. By amending §270.8b-12 by adding paragraph (f) to read as follows:

§270.8b-12 Requirements as to paper, printing and language.

* * * * *

(f) Where a registration statement or report is distributed through an electronic medium, issuers may satisfy legibility requirements applicable to printed documents, such as paper size, type size and font, bold-face type, italics and red ink, by presenting all required information in a format readily communicated to investors, and where indicated, in a manner reasonably calculated to draw investor attention to specific information.

41. By amending §270.30d-1 by revising the word "mailed" in paragraph (c) to read "transmitted", revising the word "mailed" in the last sentence of

paragraph (d)(2) to read "transmitted", and revising the word "mailed" in paragraph (e) to read "transmitted".

42. By amending §270.30d-2 by removing from the first sentence the phrase "by mail, postage prepaid,"; and in the second sentence, by revising the word "mailed" to read "transmitted" and by revising the word "mailing" to read "transmitting".

PART 239 --FORMS PRESCRIBED UNDER THE SECURITIES ACT OF 1933

PART 274 --FORMS PRESCRIBED UNDER THE INVESTMENT COMPANY ACT OF 1940

43. The authority citation for Part 274 continues to read as follows:

AUTHORITY: 15 U.S.C. 77f, 77g, 77h, 77j, 77s, 78c(b), 78l, 78m, 78n, 78o(d), 80a-8, 80a-24, and 80a-29, unless otherwise noted.

44. By amending Part A, Information Required in a Prospectus, Item 1(a)(iii) of Form N-1A (referenced in §§239.15A and 274.11A) by adding a sentence to the end of the parenthetical following paragraph (C) to read as follows:

[Note: The text of Form N-1A does not and these amendments will not appear in the Code of Federal Regulations.]

Form N-1A

* * * * *

PART A

INFORMATION REQUIRED IN A PROSPECTUS

Item 1. Cover Page

(a) * * *

(iii) * * *

(C) * * * (* * * If the Registrant intends to disseminate its prospectus electronically and is an electronic filer, also include the information that the Commission maintains a Web site (http://www.sec.gov) that contains the Statement of Additional Information, material incorporated by reference, and other information regarding registrants that file electronically with the Commission.);

* * * * *

45. By amending Part A, Information Required in a Prospectus, Item 1.1.d of Form N-2 (referenced in §§239.14 and 274.11a-1) by adding a sentence at the end of the parenthetical following paragraph (C) to read as follows:

[Note: The text of Form N-2 does not and these amendments will not appear in the Code of Federal Regulations.]

Form N-2

* * * * *

Part A-INFORMATION REQUIRED IN A PROSPECTUS

Item 1. Outside Front Cover

1. * * *

d. * * *

(C) * * * (* * * If the Registrant intends to disseminate its prospectus electronically and is an electronic filer, also include the information that the Commission maintains a Web site (http://www.sec.gov) that contains the Statement of Additional Information, material incorporated by reference, and other information regarding registrants that file electronically with the Commission.);

* * * * *

46. By amending Part A, Information Required in a Prospectus, Item 1(a)(vi) of Form N-3 (referenced in §§239.17a and 274.11b) by adding a sentence at the end of the parenthetical following paragraph (C) to read as follows:

[Note: The text of Form N-3 does not and these amendments will not appear in the Code of Federal Regulations.]

Form N-3

* * * * *

Part A

INFORMATION REQUIRED IN A PROSPECTUS

Item 1. Cover Page

(a) * * *

(vi) * * *

(C) * * * (* * * If the Registrant intends to disseminate its prospectus electronically and is an electronic filer, also include the information that the Commission maintains a Web site (http://www.sec.gov) that contains the Statement of Additional Information, material incorporated by reference, and other information regarding registrants that file electronically with the Commission.);

* * * * *

47. By amending Part A, Information Required in a Prospectus, Item 1(a)(v) of Form N-4 (referenced in §§239.17b and 274.11c) by adding a sentence at the end of the parenthetical following paragraph (C) to read as follows:

[Note: The text of Form N-4 does not and these amendments will not appear in the Code of Federal Regulations.]

Form N-4

* * * * *

Part A

INFORMATION REQUIRED IN A PROSPECTUS

Item 1. Cover Page

(a) * * *

(v) * * *

(C) * * * (* * * If the Registrant intends to disseminate its prospectus electronically and is an electronic filer, also include the information that the Commission maintains a Web site (http://www.sec.gov) that contains the Statement of Additional Information, material incorporated by reference, and other information regarding registrants that file electronically with the Commission.);

* * * * *

By the Commission.

Jonathan G. Katz
Secretary

Dated: May 9, 1996

EXHIBIT F

USE OF ELECTRONIC MEDIA BY
BROKER-DEALERS,
TRANSFER AGENTS, AND
INVESTMENT ADVISERS
FOR DELIVERY INFORMATION
RELEASE NO. 33-7288; 34-37182

===START OF PAGE 1======

SECURITIES AND EXCHANGE COMMISSION

17 CFR Parts 231, 241, 271, and 276

Release No. 33-7288; 34-37182; IC-21945; IA-1562 File No. S7-13-96

USE OF ELECTRONIC MEDIA BY BROKER-DEALERS, TRANSFER AGENTS, AND INVESTMENT ADVISERS FOR DELIVERY OF INFORMATION; ADDITIONAL EXAMPLES UNDER THE SECURITIES ACT OF 1933, SECURITIES EXCHANGE ACT OF 1934, AND INVESTMENT COMPANY ACT OF 1940

AGENCY: Securities and Exchange Commission.

ACTION: Interpretation; Solicitation of Comments.

SUMMARY: The Securities and Exchange Commission ("Commission") is publishing its views with respect to the use of electronic media by broker-dealers, transfer agents, and investment advisers to deliver information as required under the Securities Exchange Act of 1934 and the Investment Advisers Act of 1940. This interpretation is intended to provide guidance in using electronic media to fulfill broker-dealers' obligations to deliver information to customers, transfer agents' obligations to deliver information upon written request, and investment advisers' disclosure delivery obligations. The Commission also is supplementing its interpretive release published on October 6, 1995, with seven additional examples illustrating the application of that earlier release to information delivery under the Securities Act of 1933, the Securities Exchange Act of 1934, and the Investment Company Act of 1940. Finally, the Commission is seeking comment on the issues discussed in this release.

DATES: This interpretation is effective on [insert date of publication in the Federal Register].

Comments must be received on or before [insert date 45 days after date of publication in the Federal Register].

ADDRESSES: Comments should be submitted in triplicate to Jonathan G. Katz, Secretary, Securities and Exchange Commission, 450 Fifth Street, N.W., Mail Stop 6-9, Washington, D.C. 20549. Comments also may be submitted electronically at the following electronic mail address: rule-comments@sec.gov. All comment letters should refer to File Number S7-13-96. This file number should be included on the subject line if comments are submitted using electronic mail. Comment letters will be available for public inspection and copying at the Commission's Public Reference Room, 450 Fifth Street, N.W., Washington, D.C. 20549. Electronically submitted comment letters will be posted on the Commission's Internet web site (http://www.sec.gov).
===START OF PAGE 2======

FOR FURTHER INFORMATION CONTACT: Catherine McGuire, Chief Counsel, or Elizabeth King, Special Counsel, or Jack Drogin, Special Counsel (concerning Rules 10b-10, 10b-16, 15c1-5, 15c1-6, 15c2-12, and 15g-2 through 15g-9 under the Securities Exchange Act of 1934, and the release generally), 202/942-0073, Office of Chief Counsel, Mail Stop 5-10; Sheila Slevin, Assistant Director (concerning information about technology generally), 202/942-

0796, Mail Stop 5-1; Michael Walinskas, Special Counsel (concerning Rule 9b-1 under the Securities Exchange Act of 1934), 202/942-0188, Mail Stop 5-1; Elizabeth MacGregor, Special Counsel (concerning Rule 11Ac1-3 under the Securities Exchange Act of 1934), 202/942-0158, Mail Stop 5-1; Alan Reed, Attorney (concerning Rules 15c2-8 and 15c2-11 under the Securities Exchange Act of 1934), 202/942-0772, Mail Stop 5-1; Michael A. Macchiaroli, Associate Director (concerning Exchange Act Rules 8c-1, 15c2-5, 15c3-2, 15c3-3, and 17a-5), 202/942-0132, Mail Stop 5-1; Jerry Carpenter, Assistant Director (concerning Exchange Act Rule 17Ad-5), 202/942-4187, Mail Stop 5-1, Division of Market Regulation; Jack W. Murphy, Chief Counsel or Amy Doberman, Assistant Chief Counsel (concerning the Investment Advisers Act of 1940 and the examples illustrating application of electronic delivery to mutual funds), 202/942-0660, Mail Stop 10-6, Division of Investment Management; Joseph Babits, Special Counsel (concerning the examples regarding application of electronic delivery to issuers other than mutual funds), 202/942-2910, Mail Stop 3-7, Division of Corporation Finance, Securities and Exchange Commission, 450 Fifth Street, N.W., Washington, D.C. 20549.

SUPPLEMENTARY INFORMATION:

I. Introduction

On October 6, 1995, the Commission published an interpretive release expressing its views on the electronic delivery of documents, such as prospectuses, annual reports to shareholders, and proxy solicitation materials under the Securities Act of 1933 ("Securities Act"), the Securities Exchange Act of 1934 ("Exchange Act"), and the Investment Company Act of 1940 ("October Interpretive Release").-[1]- In the October

---------FOOTNOTES----------

-[1]- Securities Act Release No. 7233 (Oct. 6, 1995), 60 FR 53458 (Oct. 13, 1995) (hereinafter "October Interpretive Release"). In a companion release, the Commission proposed technical amendments to certain of its rules that currently are premised on the distribution of paper documents. Securities Act Release No. 7234 (Oct. 6, 1995), 60 FR 53467 (Oct. 13, 1995). Today the Commission is adopting these technical amendments substantially (continued...)

===START OF PAGE 3======

Interpretive Release, the Commission directed the Division of Market Regulation ("Division") to review Rule 10b-10 and other rules it administers under the Exchange Act to determine if and under what conditions electronic delivery of information required by those rules is feasible.-[2]- Accordingly, the Division conducted a review of the rules it administers under the Exchange Act. Based on that review, the Commission is issuing this release, which expresses its views with respect to the delivery of information through electronic media in satisfaction of broker-dealer and transfer agent requirements to deliver information under the Exchange Act and the rules thereunder. In conjunction with the results of that review, the Commission is publishing its views on the use of electronic media with respect to the disclosure delivery obligations of investment advisers and persons acting on their behalf-[3]- under the Investment Advisers Act of 1940 ("Advisers Act").

This release addresses only the procedural aspects under the federal securities laws of the delivery of information by broker-dealers, transfer agents, and investment advisers. It does not affect the rights and responsibilities of any party under the federal securities laws.-[4]- This release also does not

---------FOOTNOTES----------

-[1]-(...continued)
as proposed. Securities Act Release No. 7289 (May 9, 1996).

-[2]- October Interpretive Release, supra note 1, at 53459, n.12.

-[3]- The term investment adviser is used in the rest of this release to refer to both investment advisers and persons acting on their behalf (including any solicitor receiving cash compensation from an adviser in accordance with Advisers Act Rule 206(4)-3, 17 CFR 275.206(4)-3).

-[4]- The substantive requirements and liability provisions of the federal securities laws apply equally to electronic and paper-based media. For example, the antifraud provisions of the Exchange Act and Rule 10b-5 thereunder, as well as section 206 of the Advisers Act and the rules thereunder, apply to information delivered and communications transmitted electronically, to the same extent as they apply to information delivered in paper form. See October Interpretive Release, supra note 1, at 53459, n.11. In addition, broker-dealers, transfer agents, and investment advisers continue to be subject to their respective recordkeeping (continued...)

---------FOOTNOTES----------

-[4]-(...continued)
requirements under Exchange Act Rules 17a-3 and 17a-4, 17 CFR 240.17a-3 and 240.17a-4, Exchange Act Rules 17Ad-6 and 16Ad-7, 17 CFR 240.17Ad-6 and 240.17Ad-7, and Advisers Act Rule 204-2, 17 CFR 275.204-2.

The Commission proposed for comment amendments to the broker-dealer record preservation rule, which would permit broker-dealers to employ, under certain conditions, optical storage technology to maintain required records. See Exchange Act Release No. 32609 (July 9, 1993), 58 FR 38092 (July 15, 1993) ("Proposing Release"). At the time these amendments were proposed, concerns were expressed that optical disk images would make it difficult, from an examination and discovery perspective, to detect alterations made to handwritten records and to records containing handwritten text. To address these concerns, the Proposing Release solicited comments on the adequacy of optical disk technology to preserve handwritten records or records that contain handwritten text.

Simultaneous with the issuance of the Proposing Release, the Division of Market Regulation, with the Commission's concurrence, issued a no-action letter permitting broker-dealers to use optical disk technology immediately. See Letter from Michael A. Macchiaroli, Associate Director, Division of Market Regulation, SEC to Mr. Michael D. Udoff, Chairman, Ad Hoc Record Retention Committee, Securities Industry Association, Inc., (June 18, 1993). The no-action letter permits the optical storage of all paper records, including handwritten records, except those records required to be made under paragraphs (a)(6) and (a)(7) of Rule 17a-3 (proprietary and customer order tickets).

The Commission's request for comment in the Proposing Release regarding handwritten records was in no way intended to limit reliance on the no-action letter. In addition, the Commission notes that paperless order tickets (i.e., those generated by computers) may, under the no-action letter, be stored on optical disks. The Commission understands that most of the large firms generate paperless order tickets rather than handwritten order tickets.

Finally, the Commission is aware that questions have (continued...)

===START OF PAGE 5======

address or affect the applicability of any self-regulatory organization ("SRO") rules,-[5]- or of any state laws.

---------FOOTNOTES----------

-[4]-(...continued) been raised regarding the application of the optical storage no-action letter. The staff of the Division of Market Regulation is prepared to discuss with interested persons any issues in connection with this letter, as well as with the Proposing Release.

-[5]- See, e.g., National Association of Securities Dealers, Inc. ("NASD") Notice to Members 95-80 (Sept. 26, 1995), NASD Rules of Fair Practice □ 35, and New York Stock Exchange, Inc. ("NYSE") Rule 472, which govern member firm responsibilities relating to communications with the public, including electronic communications.

In order to determine whether new guidelines are needed for the use of electronic communications, on January 12, 1996, the NYSE sent a survey to its members and member organizations regarding the use of electronic systems to communicate with customers. The NYSE asked its members to return the survey by February 15, 1996. NYSE Information Memorandum (Jan. 12, 1996). The Commission understands that the NASD intends to send a similar survey to its members.

The Commission strongly encourages the SROs to continue to work with broker-dealers to adapt SRO supervisory review requirements governing communications with customers to accommodate the use of electronic communications by broker-dealers. Because electronic delivery systems allow broker-dealers and their associated persons to freely contact the general public, as well as their clients, firms should maintain effective supervision and records of associated persons' communications to avoid potential sales practice problems. The Commission believes, however, that the SROs' rules concerning the supervisory requirements for electronic communications should be based on the content and audience of the message, and not merely the electronic form of the communication. For example, the SROs should consider whether electronic mail communications, that, as a practical matter, replace or substitute for telephone conversations, in many cases would not require advance authorization or prior supervisory review.

The Commission also recognizes that broker-dealers are concerned about the costs of maintaining electronic communications as records on a long term basis, and it intends to discuss these concerns further with the securities industry.

==START OF PAGE 6======

Broker-dealers, transfer agents, and investment advisers, therefore, are reminded to consider the applicability of SRO rules and state laws in connection with delivering information electronically.-[6]- The release further does not affect any rules promulgated under the Exchange Act by agencies other than the Commission.-[7]-

Finally, this interpretation does not address the existing paper filing requirements with the Commission,-[8]- other

---------FOOTNOTES----------

-[6]- Article 8 of the UCC was revised substantially in 1994, and the revisions were endorsed by both the American Law Institute and the National Conference of Commissioners on Uniform State Laws. This revised version has been adopted by 13 states. Under Revised Article 8 Section 8-102(6), parties to a transaction may "transmit information by any mechanism agreed upon by the persons transmitting and receiving the information." Revised Article 8 eliminates the current Section 8-319 requirement for a signed writing evidencing the terms of a securities transaction.

In states that have not yet codified the 1994 amendments, a confirmation bearing the broker-dealer's letterhead or some other identifying marking, generally, fulfills that requirement. See e.g., Kohlmeyer and Co. v. Bowen, 192 S.E.2d 400, 126 Ga. App. 700 (Ga. Ct. App. 1972); See also Bains v. Piper, Jaffray & Hopwood, 497 N.W.2d 263 (Minn. Ct. App. 1993) (computer generated confirmation held to satisfy the UCC requirement for a writing).

-[7]- See, e.g., Treas. Reg. □□ 404.4(e) and 403.5(d) (rules regarding hold in custody repurchase agreements applicable to government securities brokers and dealers that are financial institutions).

-[8]- For example, this interpretation does not apply to any requirements to file information with the Commission in connection with registering under sections 15, 15A, 15B, or 15C of the Exchange Act as a broker-dealer, national securities association, municipal securities dealer, or government securities broker-dealer. Broker-dealers currently register with the Commission, the SROs, and the states through the Central Registration Depository ("CRD") system operated by the NASD. A redesign of the CRD system will allow broker-dealers to file uniform registration forms (continued...)

===START OF PAGE 7======

regulatory authorities,-[9]- and other third parties.-[10]-

II. Use of Electronic Media

In the October Interpretive Release, the Commission noted that the electronic distribution of information provides numerous benefits and that the use of this type of medium is growing among all participants in the securities industry. The Commission concluded that issuers, third parties (such as persons making tender offers or soliciting proxies), and persons acting on behalf of such third parties may use electronic media, in

---------FOOTNOTES----------

-[8]-(...continued) electronically. In connection with the CRD redesign the Commission intends to adopt amendments to Form BD, the uniform application for broker-dealer registration under the Exchange Act. See Exchange Act Release No. 35224 (Jan. 12, 1995), 60 FR 4040 (Jan. 19, 1995) (proposing amendments to Form BD).

Because, at the present time, the Commission does not have the technological capacity to receive electronic transmissions of information from broker-dealers, transfer agents, or investment advisers, this interpretation also does not apply to other requirements to file information with the Commission under the Exchange and Advisers Acts. See, e.g., Exchange Act Rule 9b-1, 17 CFR 240.9b-1 (options markets' obligation to file with the Commission any revisions to an options disclosure document); Advisers Act Form ADV, 17 CFR 279.1 (application for registration of investment advisers). The Commission, nevertheless, recognizes the desirability of electronic filing and is examining the feasibility of establishing systems capable of receiving information electronically.

-[9]- For example, the notice requirements to the National Association of Securities Dealers, Inc. under Exchange Act Rule 10b-17, also are not within the scope of this interpretation. 17 CFR 240.10b-17.

-[10]- For example, Rule 15a-6 requires U.S. registered broker-dealers, under certain circumstances, to obtain certain foreign persons' consent to service of process. 17 CFR 240.15a-6(a)(3)(iii)(D). The Commission has never taken a position as to the specific means by which the U.S. broker-dealer may meet this obligation, but believes that a consent to service of process may be obtained through the use of a facsimile.

===START OF PAGE 8======

accordance with the guidance provided in the October Interpretive Release, to deliver information. In addition, the Commission believes that broker-dealers, transfer agents, and investment advisers may satisfy their delivery obligations under the Exchange Act and the Advisers Act by using electronic media as an alternative to paper-based media.-[11]-

This interpretation is intended to provide broker-dealers, transfer agents, and investment advisers with guidance in using electronic media to satisfy delivery requirements under the federal securities laws. This release generally covers those requirements that obligate broker-dealers to deliver information to customers, obligate transfer agents to deliver information upon written request, and obligate investment advisers to deliver information to their clients or prospective clients. Broker-dealers and investment advisers also may rely on this interpretation in obtaining customers' and clients' consents as required under certain provisions of the Exchange and Advisers Acts and the rules thereunder.-[12]- A discussion of the information delivery requirements covered by this interpretation is provided in section III of this release ("Covered Delivery Requirements"). Unless the Commission indicates otherwise, this interpretive release also is intended to apply to all rules promulgated under the Exchange and Advisers Acts, including rules promulgated subsequent to the issuance of this release, requiring broker-dealers or investment advisers to deliver information to customers or clients, and to rules requiring transfer agents to deliver information in response to written requests.

---------FOOTNOTES----------

-[11]- The exact nature of the broker-dealer's, transfer agent's, and investment adviser's delivery obligations is defined broadly and includes such terms as "give," "furnish," "send," and "deliver." The Commission believes that, in general, these terms are sufficiently broad to accommodate the contemplated electronic transmission of documents by or on behalf of the broker-dealer, transfer agent, or investment adviser and, when called for, from a customer to a broker-dealer, transfer agent, or investment adviser. But see infra notes 12 and 50.

-[12]- In connection with transactions in penny stocks, however, the Commission believes that in order to fulfill the purposes of the Securities Enforcement Remedies and Penny Stock Reform Act of 1990, broker-dealers should continue to have customers manually sign and return in paper form any documents that require a customer's signature or written agreement. See infra note 50.

===START OF PAGE 9======

A. General

This discussion is intended to complement the discussion in the October Interpretive Release and to provide general guidance concerning issues under the Exchange and Advisers Acts. The Commission believes that broker-dealers, transfer agents, and investment advisers should be able to satisfy their obligations under the federal securities laws to deliver information required under the Covered Delivery Requirements by electronic distribution. The framework set forth in the October Interpretive Release is applicable to such electronic distribution.

In the October Interpretive Release, the Commission stated that it would view information distributed through electronic means as satisfying the delivery or transmission requirements of the federal securities laws if such distribution results in the delivery to the intended recipients of substantially equivalent information as such recipients would have if the required information were delivered to them in paper form.-[13]- The Commission is not specifying the electronic medium or source that broker-dealers, transfer agents, and investment advisers may use.

Like paper documents, electronically delivered documents must be prepared and delivered in a manner consistent with the federal securities laws. Regardless of whether information is delivered in paper form or by electronic means, it should convey all material and required information. If a paper document is required to present information in a certain order, for instance, then the information delivered electronically should be in substantially the same order.-[14]-

Moreover, regardless of whether information is delivered in paper or electronic form, broker-dealers and investment advisers must reasonably supervise firm personnel with a view to preventing violations.-[15]- Thus, broker-dealers and investment advisers should consider the need for systems and procedures to deter or detect misconduct by firm personnel in connection with the delivery of information, whether by

---------FOOTNOTES----------

-[13]- October Interpretive Release, supra note 1, at 53460. See also supra example 7.

-[14]- For a discussion of how requirements to present information in a certain order may be applied to documents containing hyperlinks, see example 51 in the October Interpretive Release. Id. at 53466.

-[15]- See Exchange Act □ 15(b)(4)(E); Advisers Act □ 203(e)(5). See also NASD Rules of Fair Practice □ 27; NYSE Rule 342.

==START OF PAGE 10======

electronic or paper means.-[16]-

The Commission believes that, as a matter of policy, a person who has a right to receive a document under the federal securities laws and chooses to receive it electronically, should be provided with the information in paper form whenever specifically requesting paper.-[17]-

In the October Interpretive Release, the Commission discussed issues of notice and access that should be considered in determining whether the legal requirements pertaining to

---------FOOTNOTES----------

-[16]- See, e.g., In re: Bryant, Securities Exchange Act

Release No. 32357 (May 24, 1993), (Commission upheld a finding of the National Association of Securities Dealers, Inc. that, among other things, the failure to develop procedures to supervise a registered representative, who sent a false confirmation statement on behalf of the broker-dealer, and to enforce existing procedures constituted a failure to supervise on the part of the president of the firm).

-[17]- For example if a person revokes consent to receiving information electronically, even following delivery of the information, a paper copy should be delivered upon request. Revocation, however, is not a prerequisite to requesting a paper copy.

The Commission understands that it can be very costly for broker-dealers to maintain records for long periods of time. This is particularly true with respect to information that is specific to a customer's account or to a transaction, such as the type of information defined below as Personal Financial Information. See infra section II.B. For this reason, the Commission has limited the time period that broker-dealers must preserve records required to be made under Exchange Act Rules 17a-3. 17 CFR 240.17a-3. Specifically, Exchange Act Rule 17a-4 requires broker-dealers to preserve records for a period of six years (3 years in the case of certain types of information), the first two years in an easily accessible place. 17 CFR 240.17a-4. For these same reasons, the Commission believes it is reasonable to expect that broker-dealers would provide customers with information in paper form upon request for a period of two years. Transfer agents and investment advisers are subject to similar recordkeeping requirements. 17 CFR 250.17Ad-6 and 240.17Ad-7; 17 CFR 275.204-2.

===START OF PAGE 11======

delivery or transmission of documents have been satisfied,-[18]- and stated that persons using electronic delivery of information should have reason to believe that any electronic means so selected will result in the satisfaction of the delivery requirements.-[19]- The Commission believes that broker-dealers, transfer agents, and investment advisers should apply the same considerations in using electronic media to satisfy their delivery obligations under the Covered Delivery Requirements.

1. Notice

Broker-dealers, transfer agents, and investment advisers providing information electronically should consider the extent to which electronic communication provides timely and adequate notice that such information is available electronically.-[20]- When information is delivered on paper through the postal mail, recipients most likely will be made aware that they have received information that they may wish to review and, therefore, separate notice is not necessary. Information transmitted through electronic media, however, may not always provide a similar likelihood of notice that information has been sent that the recipient may wish to review.-[21]- Broker-dealers, transfer agents, and investment advisers, therefore, should consider whether it is necessary to supplement the electronic communication with another communication that would provide notice similar to that provided

---------FOOTNOTES----------

-[18]- October Interpretive Release, supra note 1, at 53460-61.

-[19]- Id. at 53461.

-[20]- See id. at 53460. See also infra section II.B.2. regarding additional requirements when broker-dealers, transfer agents, and investment advisers send certain types of information (defined as Personal Financial Information) to customers.

-[21]- For example, if information is provided by physically delivered material (such as a computer diskette or CD-ROM) or by electronic mail, that communication itself generally should be sufficient notice. If information is made available electronically through a passive delivery system, such as an Internet Web Site, however, separate notice would be necessary to satisfy the delivery requirements unless the broker-dealer, transfer agent, or investment adviser can otherwise evidence that delivery to the customer or client has been satisfied.

===START OF PAGE 12======

by delivery in paper through the postal mail.

2. Access

The Commission believes that customers, securities holders, and clients who are provided information through electronic delivery from broker-dealers, transfer agents, and investment advisers should have access to that information comparable to that which would be provided if the information were delivered in paper form. Thus, the use of a particular medium should not be so burdensome that intended recipients cannot effectively access the information provided. Also, persons to whom information is sent electronically should have an opportunity to retain the information through the selected medium or have ongoing access equivalent to personal retention.-[22]-

3. Evidence to Show Delivery

Providing information through postal mail provides reasonable assurance that the delivery requirements of the federal securities laws have been satisfied. The Commission believes that broker-dealers, transfer agents, and investment advisers similarly should have reason to believe that electronically delivered information will result in the satisfaction of the delivery requirements under the federal securities laws. Thus, whether using paper or electronic media, broker-dealers, transfer agents, and investment advisers should consider the need to establish procedures to ensure that applicable delivery obligations are met.

Broker-dealers, transfer agents, and investment advisers may be able to evidence satisfaction of delivery obligations, for example, by: (1) obtaining the intended recipient's informed consent-[23]- to delivery through a specified electronic

---------FOOTNOTES----------

-[22]- For example, the intended recipient's ability to download or print information delivered electronically would enable a recipient to retain a permanent record. See October Interpretive Release, supra note 1, at 53460.

-[23]- See id. at 53460. If a consent is used, the consent should be an informed consent. An informed consent should specify the electronic medium or source through which the information will be delivered and the period during which the consent will be effective, and should describe the information that will be delivered using such means. The broker-dealer, transfer agent, or investment adviser also should inform the customer (continued...)

===START OF PAGE 13======

medium, and ensuring that the recipient has appropriate notice and access, as discussed above; (2) obtaining evidence that the intended recipient actually received the information, such as by an electronic mail return-receipt or by confirmation that the information was accessed, downloaded, or printed;-[24]- or (3) disseminatin, information through certain facsimile methods. In order to ensure that information is delivered as intended, broker-dealers, transfer agents, and investment advisers delivering information using either electronic or paper-media should take reasonable precautions to ensure the integrity and security of that information.-[25]-

B. Personal Financial Information

Certain information that broker-dealers, transfer agents, and investment advisers deliver is specific to a particular person's personal financial matters ("Personal Financial Information"). For example, the information reported to customers under Exchange Act Rule 10b-10 relates to specific securities transactions and includes the identity and number of shares bought or sold and the net dollar price for the shares. Under Exchange Act Rule 10b-16, a broker-dealer that imposes finance charges on a customer's account during a quarterly period must deliver a quarterly statement disclosing, among other

---------FOOTNOTES----------

-[23]-(...continued)
that there may be potential costs associated with electronic delivery, such as on-line charges. Except where a manual signature is required under the penny stock rules, see infra note 50, broker-dealers may obtain consents either manually or electronically. In most cases in which a request for information is made through an electronic medium, consent to receive the requested information by means of electronic delivery may be presumed.

In addition, if the broker-dealer, transfer agent, or investment adviser is relying on the consent to ensure effective delivery and the intended recipient revokes the consent, future documents should be delivered in paper.

-[24]- For example, depending on the circumstances and the procedures used, customers' and clients' written consent or acknowledgement, as required under certain Exchange and Advisers Acts rules and discussed infra notes 28-29 and accompanying text, may serve as sufficient evidence to show delivery.

-[25]- October Interpretive Release, supra note 1, at 53460, n.22.

==START OF PAGE 14======

things, the account's beginning and closing balances, debits and credits entered during the period, the interest charged, and the rate or rates of interest. Similarly, under Advisers Act Rule 206(3)-2, investment advisers engaging in agency cross transactions involving clients are required to send the clients disclosure about those transactions.-[26]-

1. Confidentiality and Security

Broker-dealers, transfer agents, and investment advisers sending Personal Financial Information should take reasonable precautions to ensure the integrity, confidentiality, and security of that information, regardless of whether it is delivered through electronic means or in paper form. The Commission believes that broker-dealers, transfer agents, and investment advisers transmitting Personal Financial Information electronically must tailor those precautions to the medium used in order to ensure that the information is reasonably secure from tampering or alteration.

2. Consent

Because of the need to maintain the confidentiality and security of Personal Financial Information, it is important that the intended recipient is willing to accept the delivery of such information through electronic media and has actual notice that the Personal Financial Information will be delivered electronically. Therefore, in order to ensure that Personal Financial Information can be delivered in a manner that maintains the information's confidentiality, unless a broker-dealer, transfer agent, or investment adviser is responding to a request for information that is made through electronic media or the person making the request specifies delivery through a particular electronic medium, the broker-dealer, transfer agent, or investment adviser should obtain the intended recipient's informed consent prior to delivering Personal Financial Information electronically.-[27]- This consent will ensure that the intended recipient is willing to accept the delivery of

---------FOOTNOTES----------

-[26]- 17 CFR 275.206(3)-2(a)(2) (written confirmation of each transaction "at or before the completion of each such transaction"); 17 CFR 275.206(3)-2(a)(3) (annual written disclosure statement identifying transactions). In addition, investment advisers having custody of client assets are required to send an itemized statement to each client at least quarterly showing assets in custody of the adviser. 17 CFR 275.206(4)-2(a)(4).

-[27]- See discussion supra note 23 regarding informed consent.

==START OF PAGE 15======

Personal Financial Information through electronic media and has actual notice that the Personal Financial Information will be delivered electronically. The Commission believes that such consent by the customer or client to the delivery of Personal Financial Information may be made either by a manual signature or by electronic means.

C. Communications From Broker-Dealers' Customers and Investment Advisers' Clients

In addition to requirements to deliver information, the Exchange Act and the Advisers Act provide for broker-dealers and investment advisers to "receive" or "obtain" responses from their customers or clients. For example, Exchange Act Rules 8c-1 and 15c2-1 require, under certain circumstances, broker-dealers to obtain a customer's written consent in order to hypothecate securities. Similarly, under the Advisers Act, certain provisions call for clients to consent to a transaction or acknowledge receipt of certain disclosures.-[28]- The Commission generally views an electronic communication from a customer to a broker-dealer or from a client to an investment adviser as satisfying the requirements for such written consent or acknowledgement.-[29]-

D. Electronic Transmission of Non-Required Disclosure

The guidance provided above is intended to permit broker-dealers, transfer agents, and investment advisers to comply with their delivery obligations under the federal securities laws when using electronic media. This interpretation does not apply to the electronic delivery of non-required information that in some cases is being provided voluntarily to customers, securities

---------FOOTNOTES----------

-[28]- See, e.g. Advisers Act □□ 205(a)(2) and 206(3); 17 CFR 275.206(3)-2(a)(1); 17 CFR 275.206(4)-3(a)(2)(iii).

-[29]- Of course, broker-dealers and investment advisers should be cognizant of their responsibilities to prevent, and the potential liability associated with, unauthorized transactions. See, e.g., supra note 16. In this regard, the Commission believes that broker-dealers and investment advisers should have reasonable assurance that the response received from a customer or client is authentic.

In addition, for policy reason discussed infra note 50, the Commission will continue to require broker-dealers to obtain the manual signature of customers on certain disclosure documents required under Exchange Act Rules 15g-2 and 15g-9.

==START OF PAGE 16======

holders, and clients-[30]- in that it is not necessary (although it is, of course, permitted) to conform the electronic delivery of such information to the guidance in this release. Nevertheless, the Commission urges broker-dealers, transfer agents, and investment advisers to take into consideration the need to implement security measures when using electronic media to provide personal financial information.

The staff also has received inquiries about the permissibility of using various electronic media to disseminate advertisements for an investment adviser's services or other information that is not subject to a delivery requirement. Such communications are permissible, subject to the same requirements and restrictions that apply to such communications in paper. For example, electronically disseminated advertisements are subject to the same prohibitions against misleading disclosure as advertisements in paper.-[31]- Materials concerning an adviser that are potentially available to ten or more persons through an electronic system would be considered subject to the recordkeeping requirements applicable to such communications.-[32]- Similarly, if an adviser uses a publicly available electronic medium such as a World Wide Web site to provide information about its services, the adviser would not qualify for the exemption from registration in section 203(b)(3) of the Advisers Act. That exemption is available only if, among other things, an adviser does not hold itself out generally to the public as an investment adviser.

III. Covered Delivery Requirements

For clarity, below is a list of current rules under the

---------FOOTNOTES----------

-[30]- See, e.g., Kimberly Weisul, Calvert Becomes First Fund to Offer Info On-Line; Mutual Fund Company Dodges the Security Issue, Investment Dealers' Digest, Jan. 22, 1996, at 9; Jon Birger, Prudential Web Site to Let Clients Track Their Accounts Daily, Bond Buyer, Oct. 18, 1995, at 10.

-[31]- See 17 CFR 275.206(4)-1. Broker-dealers' advertisements and sales literature are subject to NASD rules, which have been recently been amended specifically to include electronic communications. NASD, Notice to Members 95-74 (Sept. 1995); NASD, Notice to Members 95-80 (Sept. 26, 1995).

-[32]- 17 CFR 275.204-2(a)(11). Broker-dealers also are subject to recordkeeping requirements that would be applicable to all electronic communications received and sent by the firm relating to its business. 17 CFR 17a-4(a)(4).

==START OF PAGE 17======

Exchange Act and requirements under the Advisers Act to which broker-dealers, transfer agents, and investment advisers may apply the guidance provided in this interpretation. The Commission believes that the list sets forth all of the rules that require or permit communications between broker-dealers, transfer agents, investment advisers and customers, securities holders, and clients under the Exchange and Advisers Acts.-[33]- The interpretation in this release is intended to cover all optional and required communications under the Exchange and Advisers Acts between broker-dealers, transfer agents, and investment advisers, and customers, securities holders, and clients.-[34]-

A. Exchange Act

Subject to the guidelines in this release, broker-dealers

and transfer agents may fulfill their requirements to deliver information to customers and securities holders under the following Exchange Act rules:-[35]-

ù Rule 8c-1, which requires broker-dealers to obtain customers' written consent in order to hypothecate securities under circumstances that would permit the commingling of customers' securities and to give

---------FOOTNOTES----------

-[33]- The summary provided of the delivery obligations under the Covered Delivery Requirements is intended for ease of reference only. It is not intended to be a statement of all the requirements under the rules and provisions listed, and has no legal force or effect. Reference should be made to the full text of the rules, which is published in the Code of Federal Regulations, as well as to relevant releases, interpretations, and no-action letters, and to the full text of the Exchange and Advisers Acts, 15 U.S.C. □□ 77 and 78, et seq.

-[34]- But see supra notes 4-10 and accompanying text. See also infra notes 35 and 50.

-[35]- This release does not address the prospectus delivery requirements under Exchange Act Rule 15c2-8. 17 CFR 240.15c2-8. Broker-dealer requirements to deliver a preliminary prospectus in connection with the issuance of securities by an issuer that has not previously been required to file reports pursuant to Exchange Act Section 13(a), 15 U.S.C. 78m(a), or 15(d), 15 U.S.C. 78o(d), were addressed in the October Interpretive Release. See October Interpretive Release, supra note 1, at 53462, n. 31.

==START OF PAGE 18======

written notice to a pledgee that, among other things, a security pledged is carried for the account of a customer.-[36]-

ù Rule 9b-1, which, among other things, requires a broker-dealer to furnish to each customer, and keep current, an options disclosure document, prior to accepting an order to purchase or sell an option on behalf of that customer.-[37]-

ù Rule 10b-10, which requires a broker-dealer to give or send confirmation information to customers.-[38]- In addition, broker-dealers must furnish to customers upon written request information such as the factors that affect the yield calculation related to asset-based securities.-[39]-

ù Rule 10b-16, which requires both initial and periodic written disclosure of the credit terms of margin

---------FOOTNOTES----------

-[36]- 17 CFR 240.8c-1(a)(1) and (f).

-[37]- 17 CFR 240.9b-1(d).

-[38]- 17 CFR 240.10b-10. This release, therefore, resolves the issues in the October Interpretive Release with respect to Exchange Act Rule 10b-10, which requires broker-dealers to send confirmations at or before completion of the transaction by permitting electronic delivery of the confirmation. 17 CFR 240.10b-10. See October Interpretive Release, supra note 1, at 53459, n.12.

In a release adopting certain amendments to Rule 10b-10, the Commission recognized the use of a facsimile machine to send customer confirmation statements. At that time, however, the Commission believed that the use of other electronic means to send confirmations should be viewed on a case-by-case basis. See Exchange Act Release No. 34962 (Nov. 10, 1994); 59 FR 59612 (Nov. 17, 1994). This interpretation supersedes the view expressed in the 1994 release.

Broker-dealers are reminded that, when a prospectus is required to be delivered, it should be delivered prior to, or concurrent with, delivery of the confirmation. Thus, if a confirmation is sent by facsimile, the prospectus also should be sent by facsimile or equally prompt means.

-[39]- 17 CFR 240.10b-10(a)(7).

==START OF PAGE 19======

loans.-[40]-

ù Rule 11Ac1-3, which requires a broker-dealer to deliver to each customer, upon opening a new account and on an annual basis thereafter, an account statement disclosing the broker-dealer's policies relating to payment for order flow and its order routing policies.-[41]-

ù Rule 15c1-5, which requires, under specified circumstances, written disclosure of control if a broker-dealer or municipal securities dealer is controlled by, controlling, or under common control with the issuer of a security.-[42]-

ù Rule 15c1-6, which requires a broker-dealer or municipal securities dealer receiving advisory fees to disclose any participation or financial interest in the distribution of a security at or before the completion of a transaction in such security for the account of a customer.-[43]-

ù Rule 15c2-1, which requires broker-dealers to obtain customers' written consent in order to hypothecate securities under circumstances that would permit the commingling of customers' securities.-[44]-

ù Rule 15c2-5, which requires a written statement making disclosures prior to effecting transactions in special insurance premium funding accounts that would involve an extension or arrangement of credit, as well as retaining for its files, a written statement setting forth the basis for making a determination that the arrangement is suitable for the customer.-[45]-

ù Rule 15c2-11, with regard to the requirement that broker-dealers make certain information enumerated in

---------FOOTNOTES----------

-[40]- 17 CFR 240.10b-16.

-[41]- 17 CFR 240.11Ac1-3.

-[42]- 17 CFR 240.15c1-5.

-[43]- 17 CFR 240.15c1-6.

-[44]- 17 CFR 240.15c2-1(a)(1).

-[45]- 17 CFR 240.15c2-5.

==START OF PAGE 20======

the rule reasonably available upon request.-[46]-

ù Rule 15c2-12, with regard to the requirements that municipal securities underwriters provide, upon request, a preliminary official statement (if one exists) and a final official statement.-[47]-

ù Rule 15c3-2, which requires a broker-dealer to give or send to its customers a written notification of a free credit balance, that the broker-dealer may use that free credit balance in its business operations, and that the funds are payable upon demand of the customer.-[48]-

ù Rule 15c3-3, which requires that broker-dealers obtain repurchase agreements in writing and confirm in writing the specific securities that are the subject of hold in custody repurchase agreements.-[49]-

ù Rules 15g-3 through 15g-8, which require a broker-dealer, among other things, to disclose to its customers, both prior to effecting a transaction in a penny stock and on the written confirmation, bid and ask quotations and broker-dealer and associated person compensation.-[50]-

---------FOOTNOTES----------

-[46]- 17 CFR 240.15c2-11(a)(4) and (a)(5).

-[47]- 17 CFR 240.15c2-12.

-[48]- 17 CFR 240.15c3-2.

-[49]- 17 CFR 240.15c3-3(b)(4).

-[50]- 17 CFR 240.15g-3 through 15g-8.

The Commission believes that the requirements under Exchange Act Rules 15g-2 and 15g-9, which require broker-dealers to obtain from a customer prior to effecting transactions in penny stocks (1) a manually signed acknowledgement of the receipt of a risk disclosure document, (2) a written agreement to transactions involving penny stocks, and (3) a manually signed and dated copy of a written suitability statement, should not be met by means of electronic media. In adopting these provisions pursuant to the Securities Enforcement Remedies and Penny Stock Reform Act of 1990, the Commission intended to provide customers with an opportunity to make an informed, deliberate decision without the high pressure sales practices that sometimes are characteristic of transactions in these securities. For similar reasons, a facsimile copy of a customer's signature has not been sufficient to satisfy the requirements under Rules 15g-2 and (continued...)

==START OF PAGE 21======

ù Rule 17a-5, which requires a broker-dealer to send to its customers audited and unaudited financial statements.-[51]-

ù Rule 17Ad-5, which requires a transfer agent to respond within certain time frames to written requests for the status of items presented for transfer, for acknowledgement of transfer instructions, for confirmation of a transfer agent's possession of a certificate, for a transcript of a person's account, or for dividend and interest payments.-[52]-

B. Advisers Act

ù Section 205(a)(2) of the Advisers Act, which requires an investment adviser to obtain its client's consent to the assignment of an advisory contract.-[53]-

---------FOOTNOTES----------

-[50]-(...continued)
15g-9 that certain documents be manually signed and dated. See Exchange Act Release No. 32576 (July 2, 1993); NASD Notice to Members 90-65 (Oct. 1990); NASD Notice to Members 90-18 (Mar. 1990).

While broker-dealers may not meet the signature requirement under Rule 15g-9 by electronic means, the Commission believes that, consistent with the guidance set forth in this interpretation, they may meet their delivery obligations to their customers under this rule by electronic means. The "risk disclosure document" that broker-dealers are required to furnish to their customers under Rule 15g-2 is subject to strict formatting and typefacing restrictions. In order to comply with the requirements set forth in the instructions to Schedule 15G, a risk disclosure document delivered electronically, when printed, would have to result in a document that meets the requirements and contains the exact text of Schedule 15G.

When the Commission next reviews the penny stock rules, it may be willing to consider a "cooling-off" period as an alternative to the requirement of a manual signature under Rules 15g-2 and 15g-9. The Commission requests comment on this approach.

-[51]- 17 CFR 240.17a-5(c).

-[52]- 17 CFR 17Ad-5. Under certain circumstances, transfer agents currently are permitted to respond to requests by telephone.

-[53]- 15 U.S.C. 80b-5(a)(2).

==START OF PAGE 22======

ù Section 205(a)(3) of the Advisers Act, which requires an investment adviser to notify its clients, if the adviser is organized as a partnership and there is a change in members of partnership.-[54]-

ù Section 206(3) of the Advisers Act, which prohibits certain principal and agency transactions with a client without prior written disclosure about the transaction and consent of the client.-[55]-

ù Rule 204-3, which requires investment advisers to deliver a written disclosure statement, or "brochure," to clients at least 48 hours before entering into an advisory contract, unless the client has the right to terminate the contract without penalty within five business days.-[56]- In addition, investment advisers are required, except in certain cases, to make available "without charge" updates to its brochure.-[57]-

---------FOOTNOTES----------

-[54]- 15 U.S.C. 80b-5(a)(3).

-[55]- 15 U.S.C. 80b-6(3).

-[56]- 17 CFR 275.204-3(b). To the extent an adviser relies on 48-hour advance delivery rather than the five-day cancellation period, the 48-hour period would be measured from the time at which notice is given to the client that the statement is available through a specified electronic medium or source. Investment advisers should have reason to believe that the nature of the system or any limitations on the client's access to that system will not result in any material delay in the client's access to the information following receipt of the notice.

-[57]- 17 CFR 275.204-3(c). If a client has elected to receive the disclosure statement electronically, and neither the adviser nor any system used by the adviser to disseminate updates electronically imposes a charge upon the client specifically for the receipt of this information, the Commission would consider this requirement satisfied, even though a system selected by a client to gain access to the adviser's system may impose charges for access, printing or downloading. Alternatively, the Commission would consider the requirement satisfied so long as a paper version of the update is available without charge,

(continued...)

==START OF PAGE 23======

ù Rule 205-3(d), which requires disclosure regarding advisory arrangements involving performance fees.-[58]-

ù Rule 206(3)-2, which permits agency cross transactions, provided that the investment adviser provides general written disclosure about its role in the transactions, receives from clients consent to agency cross transactions, and sends both written confirmation of each transaction and an annual written disclosure statement.-[59]-

ù Rule 206(4)-2, which requires certain disclosure relating to adviser custody of client assets.-[60]-

ù Rule 206(4)-3, which requires certain disclosures to be made by solicitors who receive cash solicitation fees from advisers and a signed and dated acknowledgement from clients of the receipt of the investment advisers and solicitors written disclosure statements.-[61]-

IV. Additional Securities Act, Exchange Act, and Investment Company Act Examples

The October Interpretive Release included a series of examples illustrating the general concepts set forth earlier in that release in order to provide guidance in applying those concepts to specific facts and circumstances. The Commission is publishing here the following, additional examples to provide

---------FOOTNOTES----------

-[57]-(...continued) notwithstanding any charges that may be imposed upon a client for access, printing or downloading by the system used by an adviser to disseminate updates electronically.

-[58]- 17 CFR 275.205-3(d).

-[59]- 17 CFR 275.206(3)-2.

-[60]- 17 CFR 275.206(4)-2.

-[61]- 17 CFR 275.206(4)-3. Cf. Investment Company Act Release No. 21260 at n. 38 (July 27, 1995), 60 FR 39574 (contemplating that notification required under proposed Investment Company Act Rule 3a-4 could be provided electronically by investment advisers and other sponsors of investment advisory programs).

further guidance and illustration. These examples are based on questions that have been raised with the staff by industry representatives since the publication of the October Interpretive Release. Any party (whether or not a registered investment company) may look to these examples for guidance.

(1) Company XYZ places a prospectus for any securities offering on its electronic mail system. Company XYZ also uses its electronic mail system to disseminate documents required under the Exchange Act. Employees use the company's electronic mail in the ordinary course of performing their duties as employees and ordinarily are expected to log-on to electronic mail routinely to receive mail and communications. Those employees who do not log-on have alternative means of receiving electronic mail messages, such as having them sent to secretaries

or co-workers who then deliver them to the employee. The electronic mail either includes the actual document or announces the availability of the document and provides information as to how to access the document through the local area network. The electronic mail also prominently states that a paper version of the document is available upon request.

This would satisfy delivery obligations with respect to employees who use the company's electronic mail system in the course of performing their duties or who are expected to have alternative means made available to receive electronic mail messages.

(2) Company XYZ places a notice announcing its unregistered Dividend Reinvestment Plan-[62]- on its Internet Web site under a menu heading "Dividend Reinvestment Plan." The announcement also contains the phone number of the Company's agent (which is independent from the Company) from whom additional information regarding the operation of the Dividend Reinvestment Plan can be obtained. Additionally, the Company's Internet Web site contains a hypertext link to the independent agent's Internet Web site where a brochure describing the operation of the Dividend Reinvestment Plan and an enrollment card can be obtained.

---------FOOTNOTES----------

-[62]- A company need not register its dividend reinvestment plan under the Securities Act where its involvement in the plan is limited to administrative or ministerial functions. For additional information, including a listing of permitted functions, see Securities Act Release No. 4790 (July 13, 1965), 30 FR 9059 (July 20, 1965); Securities Act Release No. 5515 (July 22, 1974), 39 FR 28520 (August 8, 1974); Securities Act Release No. 6188 (February 1, 1980), 45 FR 8960 (February 11, 1980).

==START OF PAGE 25======

This would be permissible, so long as the information on the Company's Internet Web site is limited to the announcement of the unregistered Dividend Reinvestment Plan and the name and address of the independent agent from whom additional information can be obtained. (This would be analogous to the communications that an issuer of an unregistered plan could make in paper format.) As with communications in paper format, the Company may not use its Internet Web site to advertise the Dividend Reinvestment Plan or its benefits. Further, the use of a hypertext link to the home page of the independent agent would be permitted; however, the Company could not provide a hypertext link directly to the Dividend Reinvestment Plan materials.

(3) Brokerage firm ABC, a recordholder of Company XYZ's common stock, received consents from beneficial holders of Company XYZ's common stock for electronic delivery of Company XYZ's annual report and proxy materials and for electronic processing of voting instructions. These customers are provided with the Internet Web site address where Company XYZ's annual report and proxy materials are located and the Internet Web site address where they can provide their voting instructions electronically to the brokerage firm.

The electronic processing of voting instructions from

beneficial holders and the electronic voting of proxies would be consistent with the proxy rules. Issuers and others are reminded to consider any applicable state laws or self-regulatory organization rules.

(4) A fund makes supplemental sales literature and its prospectus available through a commercial on-line service. Under section 5(b) of the Securities Act, sales literature, whether in paper or electronic form is required to be preceded or accompanied by a final prospectus meeting the requirements of section 10(a) of the Securities Act. By contrast, an advertisement satisfying the requirements of Securities Act Rule 134 or 482 need not be preceded or accompanied by a prospectus. Users could click on a box in the supplemental sales literature to have the prospectus downloaded or to request that a prospectus be mailed. While the system permits the sales literature to be viewed on-line, it does not allow users to view the prospectus. Unlike the system in example 36 in the October Interpretive Release, this system would not require that a user have downloaded or printed the prospectus before viewing the supplemental sales literature. Users accessing the supplemental sales literature would give specific consent to electronic delivery of the prospectus.

This would not satisfy the prospectus delivery requirement because there would not be sufficient access to the prospectus. Because the system does not give users the opportunity to view the prospectus, it would lack the sort of reasonably comparable
===START OF PAGE 26======

access to the prospectus and the sales literature present in examples 14, 15, and 35 in the October Interpretive Release. The opportunity to request that a prospectus be mailed or downloaded would not, under current technology, be considered to give investors sufficient access to the prospectus. Instead, it would be analogous to giving investors sales literature in paper with a toll-free telephone number for requesting the prospectus: under those circumstances the prospectus would be received later and would not be considered to have preceded or accompanied the sales literature.-[63]-

(5) A fund places its prospectus on its site on the World Wide Web or some other electronic system. Shareholders provide a written, revocable consent to receive prospectuses electronically through the system. The consent informs shareholders that the current version of each prospectus will be available continuously on the system and that the fund will use the quarterly account statement or quarterly newsletter as the means of notification of prospectus amendments. It also states that another means of notification may be used, but only after shareholders have been notified of the change by the then current means of notification.-[64]- The fund replaces its prospectus with an annual amendment updating the fund's financial information and making other changes.-[65]- The fund has provided notification that the prospectus will be updated by including notification in the preceding account statement or shareholder newsletter; the notification provides the approximate date on which the amendment will be available. A subsequent amendment to the fund's prospectus reflects the addition of a redemption fee.

---------FOOTNOTES----------

-[63]- As technology develops, some users may have the capacity to download and view a prospectus in no more time than it takes to jump via hyperlink from the sales literature to the prospectus. Under those circumstances, the capacity to download would be considered to give those users reasonably comparable access to the prospectus that would provide sufficient access.

-[64]- A change in means of notification under such circumstances would also be effective in the case of notification of the availability of shareholder reports discussed in example 46 in the October Interpretive Release. October Interpretive Release, supra note 1.

-[65]- Under section 10(a)(3) of the Securities Act, a fund that continuously offers its shares would have to amend its prospectus no less frequently than every 16 months in order to include updated financial statements.

==START OF PAGE 27======

Notification of the prospectus amendment has been included in the preceding statement or newsletter.-[66]-

Just as the use of a newsletter or statement in example 46 in the October Interpretive Release constituted sufficient notice for effective delivery of the semi-annual reports required under the Investment Company Act of 1940, the use of a newsletter or statement here would constitute sufficient notice for effective delivery with respect to the scheduled prospectus update.

(6) A fund's on-line prospectus has the same text as the paper version, but the text appears in a different format. For example, text that appears as a block in the margin of a page in the paper prospectus appears in a box in the flow of the text in the electronic version. The fund does not make a separate filing under Securities Act Rule 497 with respect to the electronic version.

The mere difference in format without any difference in text would not qualify the electronic version as a different "form of prospectus" for which filing is required.

(7) An investment company produces both an electronic version (such as a CD-ROM) and a paper version of its prospectus. Each version contains all information required by, and otherwise complies with, the applicable form and all other applicable provisions of the federal securities laws. The electronic version contains a movie that does not appear in the paper version. Each version of the prospectus indicates that there may be other versions of the prospectus and, if the issuer determines to make such other versions available, provides information on how to obtain such other versions.-[67]- The paper version does not include a summary or transcript of the movie in the electronic version. Both versions of the prospectus are filed with the Commission as part of the company's registration

---------FOOTNOTES----------

-[66]- With unscheduled material prospectus amendments

for which such advance notice would not be feasible, the fund would need to use other forms of notification such as a postcard or e-mail message. See October Interpretive Release, supra note 1, example 43.

-[67]- The facts of this example should not be read as imposing any obligation on the issuer to make such other versions of its prospectus available to any person.

==START OF PAGE 28======

statement, or separately pursuant to Rule 497.-[68]-

The use of either version of the prospectus to satisfy delivery requirements would be permissible.-[69]- The issuer (or other party to whom the law assigns the responsibility) remains responsible for ensuring that each version satisfies applicable statutory requirements.-[70]-

V. Solicitation of Comments

Any interested person wishing to submit written comments relating to the views expressed in this release are invited to do so by submitting them in triplicate to Jonathan G. Katz, Secretary, Securities and Exchange Commission, 450 Fifth Street, N.W., Mail Stop 6-9, Washington, D.C. 20549. Comments also may be submitted electronically at the following electronic mail address: rule-comments@sec.gov. All comment letters should refer to File Number S7-13-96. This file number should be included on the subject line if comments are submitted using electronic mail. Comment is requested not only on the specific issues discussed in detail in the release, but on any other issues that should be considered in connection with facilitating the use of electronic media by broker-dealers, transfer agents, and investment advisers. Comment is sought from both the point of view of the sender and the intended recipient. The Commission further requests comment on any competitive burdens that may result from this interpretation. Comments must be received on or before [insert date 45 days after date of publication in the Federal Register]. Comments received will be available for public inspection and copying in the Commission's public reading room, 450 Fifth Street, N.W., Washington, D.C. 20549. Electronically submitted comment letters will be posted on the Commission's Internet web site (http://www.sec.gov).

List of Subjects

17 CFR Parts 231 and 241

---------FOOTNOTES----------

-[68]- Alternatively, the company may file with the Commission as an appendix to the prospectus the script of the movie and a fair and accurate narrative description of the graphic or image material. See October Interpretive Release, supra note 1, example 13.

-[69]- Of course, the general principles concerning electronic delivery, as described in the October Interpretive Release, supra note 1, would apply.

-[70]- See id. at 53460.

==START OF PAGE 29======

Securities.

17 CFR Parts 271 and 276

Investment companies, Securities.

Amendment to the Code of Federal Regulations

The Commission is amending Title 17, Chapter II of the Code of Federal Regulations in the manner set forth below:

PART 231 - INTERPRETATIVE RELEASES RELATING TO THE SECURITIES ACT OF 1933 AND GENERAL RULES AND REGULATIONS THEREUNDER

Part 231 is amended by adding Release No. 33-7288 and the release date of May 9, 1996 to the list of interpretive releases.

PART 241 - INTERPRETATIVE RELEASES RELATING TO THE SECURITIES EXCHANGE ACT OF 1934 AND GENERAL RULES AND REGULATIONS THEREUNDER

Part 241 is amended by adding Release No. 34-37182 and the release date of May 9, 1996 to the list of interpretive releases.

PART 271 - INTERPRETATIVE RELEASES RELATING TO THE INVESTMENT COMPANY ACT OF 1940 AND GENERAL RULES AND REGULATIONS THEREUNDER

Part 271 is amended by adding Release No. IC-21945 and the release date of May 9, 1996 to the list of interpretive releases.

PART 276 - INTERPRETATIVE RELEASES RELATING TO THE INVESTMENT ADVISERS ACT OF 1940 AND GENERAL RULES AND REGULATIONS THEREUNDER

Part 276 is amended by adding Release No. IA-1562 and the release date of May 9, 1996 to the list of interpretive releases.

By the Commission.

Jonathan G. Katz
Secretary

Dated: May 9, 1996

------------------- BEGINNING OF PAGE #1 -------------------
SECURITIES AND EXCHANGE COMMISSION

17 CFR PARTS 231, 241 and 271

RELEASE NO. 33-7233; 34-36345; IC-21399

FILE NO. S7-31-95

RIN 3235-AG67

USE OF ELECTRONIC MEDIA FOR DELIVERY PURPOSES

AGENCY: Securities and Exchange Commission.

ACTION: Interpretation; Solicitation of comment.

SUMMARY: The Securities and Exchange Commission (the "Commission") is publishing its views with respect to the use of electronic media for information delivery under the Securities Act of 1933, the Securities Exchange Act of 1934, and the Investment Company Act of 1940. This interpretive guidance is intended to assist market participants in using electronic media to provide information under the federal securities laws and to encourage continued research and development and use of such media. The Commission is seeking comment on issues discussed in this release. In a companion release, the Commission is proposing technical amendments to Commission rules that are currently premised on the distribution of paper documents.
DATES: This Interpretation is effective on October 6, 1995. Comments should be received on or before [insert date 45 days after Federal Register publication].

ADDRESSES: Comments should be submitted in triplicate to Jonathan G. Katz, Secretary, Securities and Exchange Commission, 450 Fifth Street, NW, Stop 6-9, Washington, D.C. 20549. Comment letters should refer to File No. S7-31-95. All comments received will be available for public inspection and copying at the Commission's Public Reference Room, 450 Fifth Street, NW, Washington, D.C. 20549.

FOR FURTHER INFORMATION CONTACT: Joseph Babits or James Budge (202) 942-2910, Division of Corporation Finance; and, with regard to questions concerning investment companies or investment advisers, Robert G. Bagnall or Emanuel D. Strauss (202) 942-0660, Division of Investment Management, U.S. Securities and Exchange Commission, 450 Fifth Street, NW, Washington, D.C. 20549.

SUPPLEMENTARY INFORMATION:

I. INTRODUCTION

The Commission today is publishing its views with respect to using electronic media as a means of delivering information required under the Securities Act of 1933 ("Securities Act"), -[1]- the Securities Exchange Act of 1934 ("Exchange Act"), -[2]-
and the Investment Company Act of 1940 ("Investment Company Act"). -[3]- Advances in computers and electronic media technology are enabling companies to disseminate information to more people at a faster and more cost-effective rate than traditional distribution methods, which have been largely

--------- FOOTNOTES ---------

-[1]- 15 U.S.C. 77a et seq.

-[2]- 15 U.S.C. 78a et seq.

-[3]- 15 U.S.C. 80a-1 et seq.

-------------------- BEGINNING OF PAGE #2 -------------------

paper-based. The Commission appreciates the promise of electronic distribution of information in enhancing investors' ability to access, research, and analyze information, and in facilitating the provision of information by issuers and others. The Commission believes that, given the numerous benefits of electronic distribution of information and the fact that in many respects it may be more useful to investors than paper, its use should not be disfavored.

Until recently, on-line use of corporate information was generally limited to large corporations and institutional investors. The dramatic growth in personal computer ownership, -[4]- however, is enabling many small investors to access on-line corporate information just as readily as institutions. Access to information through electronic means permits small investors to communicate quickly and efficiently with companies as well as with each other. -[5]-

Use of electronic media also enhances the efficiency of the securities markets by allowing for the rapid dissemination of information to investors and financial markets in a more cost-efficient, widespread, and equitable manner than traditional paper-based methods. Recognizing the multiple benefits of electronic technology, the Commission initiated its Electronic Data Gathering, Analysis, and Retrieval ("EDGAR") system in 1984 to automate the receipt, processing and dissemination of disclosure documents filed with the Commission under the Securities Act, Exchange Act and Investment Company Act. -[6]-

--------- FOOTNOTES ---------

-[4]- While estimates of computer ownership vary from survey to survey, it is anticipated that computer ownership will grow dramatically in the next few years. One recent survey suggests that nearly half of all American households own at least one computer and about 16% of those households that own a computer subscribe to on-line services. See B. L. McLaughlan, "Wired Nations: Half of U.S. Homes Now Have a Computer," The Detroit News, July 21, 1995, Meet News section. Another survey, however, found that only 31% of American households own a personal computer. See J. Morrison, "Hot Modems, Cold Lives: Refugees From Cyberspace," The New York Times, April 30, 1995, Section 1, col. 2, p. 45.

-[5]- See, G. Weiss, "Online Investing -- At Your Fingertips Is A Powerful New Financial Tool," Business Week, June 5, 1995, at 64.

-[6]- Access to EDGAR filings is generally available through information resellers that have purchased the data from the EDGAR dissemination subsystem and created a variety of on-line and CD-ROM versions. At the present time, 20 firms purchase data and create value-added products for analysts and the investor community. In addition, there is strong interest in ensuring that EDGAR documents are available, especially to individual investors, at the lowest possible cost. In January 1993, the New York University School of Business and the Internet Multicasting Service, a non-profit organization, received a grant from the National Science Foundation to make most EDGAR material available on the Internet. This grant expired on October 1, 1995. The Commission recently announced that it would package EDGAR filings with its own (continued...)

-------------------- BEGINNING OF PAGE #3 ------------------

As a result of this automation, filings made with the Commission through EDGAR are available promptly to the public and financial markets. Today, more than 70% of all domestic public companies file electronically through EDGAR, and by May 1996, all domestic registrants will be required to file electronically through EDGAR. -[7]-

The EDGAR rules apply only to filings made with the Commission; the rules do not affect the obligation of filers to deliver to security holders or potential investors documents such as prospectuses, tender offer materials and proxy or information statements. -[8]- As the ability to send and receive information in electronic form has become more prevalent, issuers and other market participants have begun requesting interpretive guidance regarding the electronic delivery of these documents. -[9]-

--------- FOOTNOTES ---------

-[6]-(...continued) separate Internet service. This service, which began September 28, 1995, makes EDGAR filings as well as certain Commission releases and announcements available on the Internet. The Internet World Wide Web site address is http://www.sec.gov.

-[7]- In order to encourage the rapid dissemination of additional information considered valuable by many members of the investment community, the Commission today is announcing its intention to expand the capacity of the EDGAR system to accommodate the electronic filing of ownership and transaction reports filed pursuant to Section 16 of the Exchange Act [15 U.S.C. 78p] and Rule 144 [17 CFR 230.144] under the Securities Act. See Release No. 33-7231. The necessary programming already has been initiated and filers should be able to file these documents electronically on a voluntary basis by late 1995 or early 1996. A further announcement will be made when the effective date is determined.

-[8]- See Release No. 33-6977 at Section V.F (February 23, 1993) [58 FR 14628].

-[9]- For purposes of this release, the term "electronic" refers to media such as audiotapes, videotapes, facsimiles, CD-ROM, electronic mail, bulletin boards, Internet Web sites and computer networks (e.g., local area networks and commercial on-line services) to provide documents required by the federal securities laws to investors, security holders, and offerees. Such documents include: prospectuses required to be delivered in connection with offerings under the Securities Act; annual reports to security holders and proxy or information statements required to be furnished pursuant to Section 14 of the Exchange Act [15 U.S.C. 78n]; annual and semi-annual reports required by Section 30(d) of the Investment Company Act [15 U.S.C. 80a-29(d)]; documents furnished to investors in connection with tender offers or going private transactions; offering circulars delivered in connection with Regulation A [17 CFR 230.251-263] offerings; and disclosure required to be furnished in connection with Regulation D [17 CFR 230.505, 506] offerings (issuers should be mindful of the current prohibition in Rules 505 and 506 regarding general

(continued...)

-------------------- BEGINNING OF PAGE #4 -------------------

Moreover, hundreds of issuers are providing information through electronic means, primarily through computer networks.

In February 1995, the Commission's Division of Corporation Finance issued an interpretive letter intending to address certain legal issues relating to electronic delivery of prospectuses ("Brown & Wood letter"). -[10]- The Brown & Wood letter established a number of conditions in order for a prospectus to be considered "delivered" electronically. The intention at the time of the release of the Brown & Wood letter was that the Commission would review this area in greater detail after the issuance of the letter with a view toward, through an appropriate release, providing further interpretive advice or proposed rulemaking. Because of these developments, along with the fact that none of the federal securities statutes exclusively require paper delivery of information, the Commission believes that interpretive guidance on the use of electronic media is appropriate. While the Commission anticipates that issuers and others will rely upon the guidance of this release, continued reliance on the generally more stringent requirements of the Brown & Wood letter is no longer required, but would be permissible.

This interpretive release addresses only the procedural aspects under the federal securities laws of electronic delivery, and does not affect the rights and responsibilities of any party under the federal securities laws. -[11]- This release addresses

--------- FOOTNOTES ---------

-[9]-(...continued)

solicitation, see Examples 20 and 21). Other documents may include annual reports on Form 10-K [17 CFR 249.310] and other reports required to be furnished upon request to a security holder or the recipient of a prospectus using incorporation by reference. Additionally, this release addresses the electronic delivery of elective information, such as quarterly reports to security holders and sales literature. But see n. 12, below.

-[10]- See Brown & Wood (February 17, 1995).

-[11]- The liability provisions of the federal securities laws apply equally to electronic and paper-based media. For instance, the antifraud provisions of the federal securities laws as set forth in Section 10(b) of the Exchange Act [15 U.S.C. 78j(b)] and Rule 10b-5 [17 CFR 240.10b-5] thereunder would apply to any information delivered electronically, as it does to information delivered in paper. As another example, Section 17(b) of the Securities Act [15 U.S.C. 77q(b)] would apply to any report circulated on the Internet just as if the report were provided in paper.

In addition, this release does not affect any applicable state laws or self-regulatory organization rules. Consequently, issuers and others need to consider the potential application of state law (e.g., state securities laws and business corporation laws) and other rules. At least one state has addressed issues relating to the use of electronic media in securities offerings. Recently, the Pennsylvania Securities Commission issued an order, effective for a period of one year beginning September 1, 1995, exempting from state qualification requirements securities offers made on the Internet where: 1) the offer (continued...)

-------------------- BEGINNING OF PAGE #5 -------------------

the delivery of information by or on behalf of issuers, as well as by or on behalf of third parties (such as persons making tender offers or soliciting proxies) with respect to issuers. -[12]-

--------- FOOTNOTES ---------

-[11]-(...continued)
indicates directly or indirectly that the securities are not being offered to persons in Pennsylvania; 2) an offer is not being made to any person in Pennsylvania by other means; and 3) no sales of the issuer's securities are made in Pennsylvania as a result of the Internet offer. See Order of the Pennsylvania Securities Commission In Re Offers Effected Through Internet That Do Not Result In Sales In Pennsylvania, dated August 31, 1995. In addition, the North American Securities Administrators Association, Inc., an association of securities commissioners from each of the 50 states, the District of Columbia, Puerto Rico, Mexico, and several Canadian provinces, has a committee that is addressing various issues, including jurisdictional authority, surrounding the use of electronic media in the offering of securities across state lines.

The National Association of Securities Dealers, Inc. recently reminded its members of the applicability of its Rules for Fair Practice to electronic communications. See Special Notice to Members, 95-80, September 26, 1995.

-[12]- Although Section 2(10) of the Securities Act [15 U.S.C. 77b(10)] defines "prospectus" to include a writing that "confirms the sale of any security," this release does not authorize transmission of confirmations, as required by Rule 10b-10 under the Exchange Act [17 CFR 240.10b-10] through electronic means. Consequently, while this release anticipates the electronic delivery of Section 10(a) prospectuses [15 U.S.C. 77j(a)], confirmations that are used to satisfy the delivery of a Section 10(a) prospectus, as permitted by Securities Act Rule 434 [17 CFR 230.434], cannot be delivered electronically at this time, unless specifically permitted as discussed below.

Under current interpretations of Rule 10b-10, confirmations may not be delivered electronically unless the Commission has specifically permitted such delivery. The Commission has recognized the use of a facsimile machine to send customer confirmations. Thus, if a customer has a facsimile machine, a broker-dealer would fulfill its confirmation delivery obligation if it sent the confirmation via facsimile transmission. Release No. 34-34962 (November 9, 1994), 60 FR 59612, 59614 n.28. The Commission, acting by delegated authority, also has allowed, under specified conditions, confirmations to be sent by electronic means. See, e.g., Thomson Financial Services (October 8, 1993). Applications for exemption from the requirements under Rule 10b-10 for delivery by paper or facsimile, pursuant to paragraph (e) of the Rule, may be sent to Catherine McGuire, Chief Counsel, Division of Market Regulation, U.S. Securities and Exchange Commission, 450 Fifth Street, N.W., Mail Stop 5-10, Washington, D.C. 20549.

The Commission has directed the Division of Market Regulation to review this and other rules to determine if (continued...)

-------------------- BEGINNING OF PAGE #6 -------------------

Additionally, to facilitate further electronic delivery, the Commission proposes in a companion release to codify certain interpretations regarding Commission rules that are premised on the distribution of paper documents. -[13]- The rules would be revised to make it clear that paper-based requirements relating to font size, bold-face type, red ink, graphics, and mailing may be modified as appropriate for documents delivered in electronic format. -[14]- The proposals are not intended to affect any substantive requirement.

Given the numerous benefits of electronic media, the Commission encourages further technological research, development and application. The Commission believes that the use of electronic media should be at least an equal alternative to the use of paper-based media. Accordingly, issuer or third party information that can be delivered in paper under the federal securities laws may be delivered in electronic format. -[15]- The Commission also expects that paper delivery of information will continue to be made available by issuers and others until such time as electronic media become more universally accessible and accepted, although the Commission recognizes that, for example, various offerings may now be made exclusively through electronic means. -[16]-

In connection with the June 1995 proposals on permitting the use of abbreviated financial statements in documents delivered to investors, -[17]- comment was solicited on whether the increasing availability of disclosure through electronic media warrants reassessment of the current overall regulatory framework. -[18]-

Any comments received on the June 1995 proposals will be evaluated and appropriate action will be considered. By issuing this release in the interim, however, the Commission intends to assist issuers and other market participants in using electronic media to comply with the current regulatory scheme.

II. USE OF ELECTRONIC MEDIA

A. General

The federal securities statutes do not prescribe the medium to be used for providing information by or on behalf of issuers, or by or on behalf of third parties with respect to issuers. -[19]- The Commission believes that delivery of information through an electronic medium generally could satisfy delivery or transmission obligations under the federal securities laws.

The federal securities laws, among other purposes, seek to promote fair and orderly markets by requiring the disclosure of

--------- FOOTNOTES ---------

-[12]-(...continued)
and under what conditions electronic delivery of information required by those rules is feasible. The Commission expects that this review will result in the issuance of additional releases relating to these rules.

-[13]- See Release No. 33-7234.

-[14]- See Section III, below.

-[15]- See n. 9 and 12, above.

-[16]- See n. 27, below.

-[17]- Release No. 33-7183 (June 27, 1995) [60 FR 35604].

-[18]- See Section II.B to Release No. 33-7183.

-[19]- But see n. 12, above.

-------------------- BEGINNING OF PAGE #7 -------------------

material information that enables investors to make informed investment and voting decisions. The extent to which required disclosure is made, as opposed to the medium for providing it, should be most important to the analysis of whether sufficient disclosure has occurred under the securities laws. An electronic medium would not provide an adequate means for the delivery of required disclosure, and thus not serve the statutory purposes, if the medium does not permit effective communication to investors or is practically unavailable. -[20]-

The Commission believes that the question of whether delivery through electronic media has been achieved is most easily examined by analogy to paper delivery procedures. The Commission would view information distributed through electronic means as satisfying the delivery or transmission requirements of the federal securities laws if such distribution results in the delivery -[21]- to the intended recipients of substantially equivalent information as these recipients would have had if the information were delivered to them in paper form. -[22]- As is the case with paper delivery, there should be an opportunity to retain a permanent record of the information.

--------- FOOTNOTES ---------

-[20]- Electronically delivered documents must be prepared, updated, and delivered consistent with the provisions of the federal securities laws in the same manner as paper documents. Regardless of whether information is delivered through paper or electronic means, it should, of course, convey all material and required information. If a paper document is required to present information in a certain order, then the electronic document should convey the information in substantially the same order. For example, in an audio or video prospectus, the information required to be on the cover page of a paper prospectus pursuant to Item 501(c) of Regulation S-K [17 CFR 229.501(c)] (e.g., red herring language) must be among the first information presented through the audio or video media.

Information need not be provided solely through one medium. For example, the Commission anticipates that, for practical reasons, many proxy solicitations would continue to be delivered only in paper by an issuer, while that issuer may choose to deliver other documents, such as an annual report to shareholders ("annual reports") through electronic means.

-[21]- Under the various federal securities statutes and rules, there are differing delivery obligations depending upon the context of the requirements. This release does not alter these requirements.

-[22]- Issuers and other persons required to satisfy delivery requirements should consider establishing record-keeping or other procedures to evidence satisfaction of applicable requirements through electronic means. Presumably, such procedures would be analogous to comparable procedures followed when a paper document is delivered.

Those providing information also should take reasonable precautions to ensure the integrity and security of that information, regardless of whether it is to be delivered through electronic means or paper, so as to ensure that it is the information intended to be delivered.

-------------------- BEGINNING OF PAGE #8 -------------------

B. Guidance Regarding Electronic Delivery

The Commission believes that the analysis of whether an electronic communication is delivered or transmitted for purposes of the federal securities laws should be determined in accordance with the preceding discussion. In making such determination with respect to information communicated, in particular, over the Internet, through on-line services, or through analogous computer networks, the Commission believes that the following concepts discussed in this section reflect issues that should be considered in determining whether applicable statutory requirements have been satisfied.

This release is intended to provide guidance and a degree of certainty regarding the manner in which electronic delivery can be achieved. An issuer or other party that structures its delivery in accordance with the principles and examples set forth below can be assured that it is satisfying its delivery obligations under the federal securities laws. The Commission wishes to emphasize, however, that the factors discussed below are not the only factors relevant to determining whether the legal requirements pertaining to delivery or transmission of documents have been satisfied. If an issuer or third party develops a method of electronic delivery that differs from those discussed below, but provides assurance comparable to paper delivery that the required information will be delivered, that method may satisfy delivery or transmission obligations. The ultimate responsibility for satisfying the applicable statutory requirements remains with the issuer or other party to whom the law assigns the responsibility.

Notice. When an issuer delivers a paper document through the postal mail, the investor will most likely be made aware that new information exists and that the investor might have to take some action within a certain period of time. The Commission believes that those providing electronic information should consider the extent to which the electronic communication provides timely and adequate notice to investors that information for them is available and, if necessary, consider supplementing the electronic communication with another communication that would provide notice similar to that provided by delivery in paper. If an electronic document itself is provided -- for example, on computer disk, CD-ROM, audio tape, videotape, or e-mail -- that communication itself should generally be sufficient notice. If the document is provided on an Internet Web site, however, separate notice would be necessary to satisfy the delivery requirements unless the issuer can otherwise evidence that delivery to the investor has been satisfied or the document is not required to be delivered under the federal securities laws. -[23]-

Access. When a document is delivered through the postal mail, a recipient generally is provided with access to the required disclosure. The Commission believes that recipients who are provided information through electronic delivery should have comparable access; consequently, the use of a particular medium should not be so burdensome that intended recipients cannot

--------- FOOTNOTES ---------

-[23]- For example, in an offering, notice of an updated or final prospectus and/or the updated or final prospectus itself need not be sent at all, through any means, to persons who have received an electronic preliminary prospectus, but to whom securities are not expected to be sold. Of course, the final prospectus would have to be delivered, through electronic means or otherwise, to those investors to whom securities are sold.

------------------- BEGINNING OF PAGE #9 -------------------

effectively access the information provided. -[24]- Moreover, as is the case with a paper document, a recipient should have the opportunity to retain the information or have ongoing access equivalent to personal retention. -[25]-

If disclosure is made available by posting it on the Internet, making it available through on-line services, or making it available by similar means, the document should be accessible for as long as the delivery requirement applies. -[26]-

Finally, because of possible system failures, computer incompatibilities, and those cases, for example, where consents are used in connection with the delivery of information electronically and the person providing the consent revokes it, a necessary precaution given the current state and use of communications technology is that issuers must be able to make available paper versions of documents delivered in an electronic medium. Specifically, the Commission believes that, as a matter of policy, where a person has a right to receive a document under the federal securities laws and chooses to receive it electronically, that person should be provided with a paper version of the document if any consent to receive documents electronically were revoked or the person specifically requests a paper copy (regardless of whether any previously provided consent

--------- FOOTNOTES ---------

-[24]- For example, if an investor must proceed through a confusing series of ever-changing menus to access a required document so that it is not reasonable to expect that access would generally occur, this procedure would likely be viewed as unduly burdensome. In that case, delivery would be deemed not to have occurred unless delivery otherwise could be shown.

There are some circumstances where burdensome procedures may be appropriate. See Example 48.

-[25]- In many cases, the investor will be able to download the document from the electronic medium, which is sufficient to satisfy this need.

-[26]- For example, after a paper preliminary prospectus has been provided, issuers make the most recent version of the prospectus available to all persons to whom they expect to sell. If an issuer posts electronically a preliminary prospectus on its Web site, the prospectus should be updated to the same degree as paper and be available to all persons to whom the issuer expects to sell securities in reliance on the electronic delivery of the prospectus. It likely would not be sufficient to show effective delivery if the information was merely posted for a brief period of time and then taken off the Web site, absent some other showing that delivery of the updated prospectus actually had occurred. In the case of a continuous offering, the prospectus should remain available for as long as the issuer will rely on its delivery through the electronic system. Annual reports should be available electronically for a sufficient length of time for delivery to be satisfied. In the case of proxy soliciting materials regarding the election of directors, investors might reasonably expect the proxy soliciting materials and annual report to be available on the Web site until their votes have been cast and the meeting adjourned.

-------------------- BEGINNING OF PAGE #10 ------------------

was revoked). -[27]-

C. Evidence to Show Delivery

Providing information through postal mail provides reasonable assurance that the delivery requirement is satisfied. The Commission believes that issuers and others -[28]- providing electronic delivery of information should similarly have reason to believe that any electronic means so selected will result in the satisfaction of the delivery requirements. Examples of procedures evidencing satisfaction of the delivery requirements include: (1) obtaining an informed consent from an investor to receive the information through a particular electronic medium -[29]- coupled with assuring appropriate notice and access, as

--------- FOOTNOTES ---------

-[27]- This policy would not preclude an issuer from structuring its offering as one that will be made only through electronic documents. However, companies conducting initial public offerings must consider prospectus delivery requirements for secondary market trading under Securities Act Rule 174 [17 CFR 230.174].

Further, if a potential investor makes it known that the receipt of information through electronic means by that person is no longer to be relied upon by the issuer (for example, due to the revocation of a consent previously given), then the issuer would not be able to rely on the electronic delivery of information subsequently to provide information to such person. If such subsequent information is required to be provided under the federal securities laws to such person because, for example, the person is now a shareholder and is entitled to receive a proxy statement then, absent some alternative, the issuer would be required to deliver the information through paper.

-[28]- For example, broker-dealers, banks, associations and other fiduciary entities may have delivery obligations to forward proxy soliciting materials and annual reports to shareholders under Exchange Act Rules 14b-1 and 14b-2 [17 CFR 240.14b-1 and 240.14b-2]. See Example 29.

-[29]- If a consent is used, the consent should be an informed consent. Recipients generally should be apprised: that information provided would be available through a specific electronic medium or source (e.g., via a limited proprietary system, or at a World Wide Web site); of the potential that investors may incur costs (e.g., on-line time); and of the period during, and the documents for, which the consent will be effective. For instance, investors should be made aware of whether the consent extends to more than one type of document. If an investor revokes a consent that extends to more than one document, and consent is being relied upon by the provider of the information to ensure effective delivery or transmission, future documents should be delivered in paper unless the provider of the information has an alternative mechanism for ensuring effective electronic delivery. If not, it would appear likely that continued electronic delivery, after revocation of the consent, would not be considered to result in the investor's having access to the information and, therefore, the delivery requirement would not be satisfied.

(continued...)

-------------------- BEGINNING OF PAGE #11 -------------------

discussed above; (2) obtaining evidence that an investor actually received the information, for example, by electronic mail return-receipt or confirmation of accessing, downloading, or printing (see example 36); (3) disseminating information through certain facsimile methods (see example 32); (4) an investor's accessing a document with hyperlinking to a required document (see examples 15 and 35); and (5) using forms or other material available only by accessing the information (see examples 31 and 33).

The Commission requests comment on these concepts and on whether additional or alternative concepts would be more useful.

D. Examples

A series of examples is provided below to illustrate various applications of the above concepts and to provide guidance in applying them to specific facts and circumstances. The analysis required to determine compliance with the delivery requirements is fact-specific, and any different or additional facts might require a different conclusion. Although this interpretation is effective immediately, the Commission requests comment on whether other examples might be appropriate for publication in a subsequent release.

Securities Act

(1) Company XYZ places its final prospectus on its Internet Web site. Company XYZ then confirms by mail the sale of securities to investors with a note stating that the final prospectus is available on its Web site and giving the Internet location of the Web site.

Unlike paper delivery of a final prospectus where access to the document can be presumed with delivery, not all investors purchasing securities could be presumed to have the ability to access the final prospectus via an Internet Web site. Therefore, absent other factors such as express consent from the investor or an investor's actually accessing the document on the Web site, the procedures described above by themselves would not satisfy the delivery requirements under the Securities Act.

(2) Company XYZ places its final prospectus on its Internet Web site. Company XYZ then confirms by mail the sale of securities to those investors who have consented to electronic delivery via the Company's Internet Web site. A note on the bottom of the confirmation -[30]- states that the final

--------- FOOTNOTES ---------

-[29]-(...continued)

Moreover, an issuer could rely on consents provided to an underwriter, a brokerage firm or other service provider. Similarly, an underwriter or brokerage firm could rely on a consent that its customer provided to the issuer, and deliver that issuer's documents through the same electronic medium.

Information may be provided through more than one medium; for example, proxy statements and proxy cards might continue to be delivered in paper while prospectuses might be delivered electronically. If the recipient of information provides a general consent to receive all documents electronically, it would be permissible for a provider of information to attempt to accommodate that request if the provider so desired.

-[30]- A separate document accompanying the confirmation also may be used.

-------------------- BEGINNING OF PAGE #12 -------------------

prospectus is available on its Web site and the Internet location of the Web site.

This would satisfy delivery obligations, as it is reasonable to presume that investors who have consented to delivery of the final prospectus via an Internet Web site have the ability to access the final prospectus once such investors are supplied with notice of the Internet location of the Web site.

(3) While reviewing Company XYZ's preliminary prospectus on its Internet Web site, Investor John Doe consented to delivery of all future documents only through electronic mail, not by Web site access. Company XYZ subsequently places its final prospectus on its Internet Web site. Company XYZ then confirms by mail the sale of securities to John Doe. A note on the bottom of the confirmation states that the final prospectus is available on its Internet Web site and the location of that Web site.

Again, absent other factors such as John Doe's actually accessing the final prospectus on the Web site, the above-stated procedure of Company XYZ would not by itself satisfy the obligations to deliver the final prospectus to John Doe, as John Doe consented to delivery only by electronic mail, not via an Internet Web site. If consent is to be relied upon, the consent should indicate the specific electronic medium or media that may be used for delivery.

(4) While reviewing Company XYZ's preliminary prospectus on its Internet Web site, Investor John Doe consented to delivery of all future Company documents by 3 " floppy disk. Company XYZ places its final prospectus on its Internet Web site. Company XYZ then confirms by mail the sale of securities to John Doe. A 3 " floppy disk containing the final prospectus is included with the confirmation.

This would satisfy the obligation to deliver the final prospectus to John Doe, since the Company included with the confirmation the final prospectus on a 3 " floppy disk.

(5) Investor John Doe consents to delivery of all documents electronically via Company XYZ's Web site. Two days after consenting, John Doe realizes that the online service he

subscribes to does not allow Internet access. John Doe notifies Company XYZ that he is revoking his consent for any electronic delivery as he is not able to access the Company's Internet Web site. Three weeks later, John Doe receives in the mail a confirmation of his purchase of Company XYZ's securities stating the Internet location of the Company's Web site where the final prospectus can be obtained.

Since John Doe revoked his consent for electronic delivery, the Company's notice to John Doe is insufficient because the Company knows that its attempted delivery through the Internet will not satisfy the statutory requirements for John Doe. A final paper prospectus would have to be delivered to John Doe instead. Although a consent is revocable at any time, revocation would have to be given to the company or its agent a reasonable time before electronic delivery has commenced for the company to be on notice that electronic delivery will not satisfy the statutory requirements.

(6) Company LMN, a non-reporting issuer, commences an initial public offering. Company LMN agrees with its underwriter, Brokerage Firm DFG, to place its preliminary

-------------------- BEGINNING OF PAGE #13 -------------------

prospectus on the Company's Internet Web site at least 48 hours prior to confirmations being sent. Investors John and Jane Doe are both expected to purchase securities in the Company's initial public offering. Both John and Jane Doe previously provided Company LMN with consents for electronic delivery through the Company's Internet Web site. Brokerage Firm DFG, pursuant to its prospectus delivery obligation under Exchange Act Rule 15c2-8(b), -[31]-
provides notice to John and Jane Doe at least 48 hours prior to sending them confirmations.

The underwriter may satisfy its obligation under Rule 15c2-8(b) to John and Jane Doe by this means since both have consented to electronic delivery through the Company's Internet Web site. Although consent was not provided directly to the underwriter, the underwriter can rely on the consent supplied to the Company. Similarly, had the consent been provided to the underwriter, the Company could rely on it as well.

(7) Company ABC contracts with Company QRS, a computer technology company, to place its preliminary and final prospectuses on Company QRS's Internet Web site. Investor John Doe requests a copy of Company ABC's preliminary prospectus via electronic mail from Company ABC's underwriter, Brokerage Firm DFG. The underwriter sends a return electronic mail to John Doe asking if he would like the electronic or paper version of the preliminary prospectus. John Doe replies that the electronic version via the Internet Web site would be preferable. The underwriter then informs John Doe of the Internet location of Company QRS's Web site where the preliminary prospectus for Company ABC is available.

This would satisfy Brokerage Firm DFG's obligation to take reasonable steps to furnish to any person making a written request for a prospectus a copy of such prospectus. -[32]- John Doe's request for the electronic version via the Internet indicates that such electronic delivery would be effective. -[33]-

(8) Company XYZ sends the final prospectus via electronic mail to those investors that previously had requested delivery by electronic mail.

The Company would meet its delivery obligation with this procedure.

--------- FOOTNOTES ---------

-[31]- 17 CFR 240.15c2-8(b).

-[32]- Exchange Act Rule 15c2-8(c), (d) [17 CFR 240.15c2-8(c), (d)].

-[33]- In Release No. 34-35705 (May 11, 1995) [60 FR 26604], the Commission stated that a managing underwriter may discharge its obligations pursuant to Rule 15c2-8(g) or (h) by delivering a prospectus (or any portion thereof) electronically to a participating broker-dealer, if the recipient broker-dealer expressly consents to delivery in such form, consistent with the Brown & Wood letter. As reflected in that release and as further discussed in this release and Examples 6 and 7 above, it is the Commission's view that broker-dealers may use a variety of means to satisfy the prospectus delivery obligations of Rule 15c2-8, including electronic delivery.

-------------------- BEGINNING OF PAGE #14 -------------------

(9) Company XYZ places a preliminary prospectus on its Internet Web site. After a material amendment to the registration statement, it is determined that recirculation of an updated prospectus will be required prior to effectiveness. Company XYZ updates the preliminary prospectus on its Web site.

The Company need only send notice of the update to those investors who are expected to purchase securities in the offering (or takes other measures to deliver the information to those investors). There is no need to send notice to individuals who are not expected to purchase securities in the offering.

(10) Company XYZ places its final prospectus on its Internet Web site. Its underwriters mail confirmations of sales to all purchasers. At the same time the confirmations are mailed, the underwriters send via electronic mail notice of the location of the Internet Web site where the final prospectus is available. Notice is sent to all investors who had consented to electronic delivery via an Internet Web site and who provided their electronic mail addresses for purposes of being notified. To those investors that did not provide an electronic mail address but did consent to electronic delivery of the final prospectus, the underwriters mailed the notice of the location of the Internet Web site with the confirmation.

As the notice made investors aware of the availability and location of the electronic document, the delivery requirement would be satisfied.

(11) Company XYZ posts its final prospectus for sale of its common stock on its Internet Web site. Company XYZ's stock is traded on the New York Stock Exchange (NYSE). The NYSE requests

300 paper copies of Company XYZ's final prospectus pursuant to Securities Act Rule 153. -[34]- Rather than sending 300 copies of its final prospectus to the NYSE, Company XYZ provides the NYSE with notice of its Internet Web site, where the final prospectus can be accessed and downloaded.

This would be insufficient delivery under Securities Act Rule 153. Company XYZ must supply the 300 paper copies to the NYSE. The NYSE must be in the position to provide paper copies of Company XYZ's final prospectus because there is no reasonable expectation that delivery would otherwise be satisfied with regard to investors who do not use any electronic means to receive information. The NYSE would, however, satisfy its delivery obligations with respect to any investor who received delivery of the information through electronic means.

(12) Company XYZ places its preliminary prospectus on its Internet Web site. Upon effectiveness of its registration statement, the Company decides to deliver a term sheet pursuant to Securities Act Rule 434. The term sheet, however, will not be placed on the Company's Web site, but will be delivered in paper format with confirmation of the sale to all investors.

Delivery of a mixed medium final prospectus would satisfy delivery obligations. Generally, if investors received the preliminary prospectus electronically, issuers are encouraged to deliver all documents that constitute the final prospectus in electronic format. However, confirmations cannot be furnished electronically unless the Commission has specifically approved

--------- FOOTNOTES ---------

-[34]- 17 CFR 230.153.

-------------------- BEGINNING OF PAGE #15 -------------------

such delivery. -[35]-

(13) Company XYZ wants to deliver to investors a CD-ROM version of its prospectus. The CD-ROM version includes within the prospectus a movie illustrating the Company's operations. Investors viewing the CD-ROM prospectus would not have to exit the prospectus in order to view the movie, as the movie is actually a part of the prospectus.

While Company XYZ may include the movie as part of the prospectus, it would need to file with the Commission as an appendix to the prospectus the script of the movie and a fair and accurate narrative description of the graphic or image material just as it would have to supplementally provide to the Commission scripts and descriptions of such material in sales material.

(14) Company XYZ places a copy of its final prospectus on its Internet Web site. The electronic final prospectus will remain there throughout the period for which delivery is required. Company XYZ also places supplemental sales literature on its Internet Web site. Both the sales literature and the prospectus can be accessed from the same menu, are clearly identified on, and appear in close proximity to each other; -[36]- the supplemental sales literature may be accessed before viewing or downloading the prospectus.

Sales literature, whether in paper or electronic form, is

required to be preceded or accompanied by a final prospectus. -[37]- In this example, the prospectus would accompany the sales literature since investors can access both the prospectus and sales literature from the same menu. The sales literature and final prospectus should appear in close proximity to each other on the menu. For example, the sales literature should not be presented on the first page of a menu while the final prospectus is buried within the menu.

(15) Company XYZ places its sales literature in a discussion forum located on the Internet World Wide Web. The sales literature contains a hyperlink to the Company's final prospectus. While viewing the literature the individual can click on a box marked "final prospectus," and almost instantly the person will be linked directly to the Company's Web site and the final prospectus will appear on the person's computer screen.

Sales literature, whether in paper or electronic form, is required to be preceded or accompanied by a final prospectus. The hyperlink function enables the final prospectus to be viewed directly as if it were packaged in the same envelope as the sales literature. Therefore, the final prospectus would be considered to have accompanied the sales literature. Consequently, the placing of sales literature in a discussion forum on a Web site would satisfy delivery obligations provided that a hyperlink that

--------- FOOTNOTES ---------

-[35]- See n. 12, above.

-[36]- In this example, the prospectus is accessible on the same menu as the supplemental sales literature; consequently, the existence of the prospectus and its location are readily ascertainable by the investor viewing the sales literature.

-[37]- Section 5(b) of the Securities Act.

-------------------- BEGINNING OF PAGE #16 -------------------

provides direct access to the final prospectus is included.

(16) Company XYZ places a preliminary prospectus on its Internet Web site and provides direct access via a hyperlink to a research report on the Company written by ABC Corporation, a registered brokerage firm. The investor reviewing the preliminary prospectus can click on a box marked "ABC's research report" and the investor will be linked to the brokerage firm's Web site where the research report is available.

The hyperlink function provides the ability to access information located on another Web site almost instantaneously. This direct and quick access to ABC's research report would be similar to the Company including the paper version of the research report in the same envelope that it is using to mail the paper version of the preliminary prospectus to potential investors. During the waiting period, the Company may make offers only through the use of a preliminary prospectus, -[38]- whether in paper or electronic format; therefore, its use of the research report under these circumstances would not be permissible.

(17) Company XYZ places its final prospectus on its Internet Web site. The Company then mails sales literature to individuals for whom delivery through the Internet Web site was effective (regardless of whether the individuals consented to delivery). Similarly, Brokerage Firm ABC mails Company XYZ sales literature to its customers for whom delivery through the Internet Web site was effective (regardless of whether the individuals consented to delivery). In the forepart of Company XYZ's sales literature is notice of the availability and Internet Web site location of its final prospectus.

The mailing of sales literature to these individuals is permissible, provided that notice of the availability of the final prospectus and its Internet Web site location accompanies or precedes the sales literature. When notice is included within sales literature, it should be in the forepart of the literature and clearly highlighted to make investors aware of the availability and location of the final prospectus.

(18) Company XYZ places a tombstone advertisement complying with Securities Act Rule 134 -[39]- on its Internet Web site.

This would be permissible, provided that the advertisement otherwise complies with Rule 134.

(19) Company XYZ files a registration statement with the Commission. The Company then places a "tombstone" advertisement in accordance with Securities Act Rule 134 in the Wall Street Journal. In the advertisement the Company includes the name and address of the underwriter from whom a paper prospectus can be obtained as well as the location of its Internet Web site where an electronic prospectus can be obtained.

This inclusion of an electronic address for obtaining the materials in this "tombstone" advertisement would be permissible under Rule 134. (Similarly, an advertisement made pursuant to

--------- FOOTNOTES ---------

-[38]- Section 5(b) of the Securities Act.

-[39]- 17 CFR 230.134.

-------------------- BEGINNING OF PAGE #17 --------------------

Rule 14a-2(a)(6) -[40]- indicating the availability of proxy soliciting materials and the location of an Internet Web site where electronic proxy soliciting materials could be obtained would be permissible.)

(20) Company XYZ wants to raise $5 million by selling its common stock in a private placement pursuant to Securities Act Rule 506 of Regulation D. The Company places its offering materials on its Internet Web site, which requires various information from a person attempting to access the materials to be provided to the Company prior to displaying the offering materials.

The placing of the offering materials on the Internet would not be consistent with the prohibition against general solicitation or advertising in Rule 502(c) of Regulation D.

-[41]- Where prospective purchasers have been otherwise located without a general solicitation, a proprietary computer service could be used to deliver required disclosure documents.

(21) Company XYZ wants to raise $5 million by selling its common stock in a private placement pursuant to Rule 506 of Regulation D to certain individuals who have been located without a general solicitation. The Company transmits the offering materials via electronic mail addresses provided by these persons.

This would not be inconsistent with the offering restrictions in the rule.

(22) Company XYZ pays John Doe $10,000 to write a report about the Company and post the report on the Internet. John Doe writes the report and places it on the Growth Companies Investment Bulletin Board located on the Internet. The report does not disclose the $10,000 that the Company paid John Doe.

The Securities Act requires that the $10,000 compensation paid by Company XYZ to John Doe be disclosed in the report, regardless of whether it is in electronic or paper form. -[42]-

Exchange Act

(23) Company XYZ places its annual report and proxy soliciting materials on its Internet Web site. The Company then sends notice to all its record holders that its annual report and proxy soliciting materials are available on its Internet Web site along with the Internet location of the Web site and a telephone number that shareholders may call to request a paper copy.

Similar to Example (1), a company should not presume that all record holders have the ability to access the annual report and proxy soliciting materials via an Internet Web site. Therefore, absent other factors such as a consent from, or actual access by, a Company shareholder, posting of the annual report

--------- FOOTNOTES ---------

-[40]- 17 CFR 240.14a-2(a)(6).

-[41]- 17 CFR 230.502(c). In Release 33-7185 (June 27, 1995), the Commission solicited comment on the question of whether the prohibition against general solicitation in Regulation D offerings should be reconsidered.

-[42]- Section 17(b) of the Securities Act.

-------------------- BEGINNING OF PAGE #18 -------------------

and proxy soliciting materials via the Company's Internet Web site would be insufficient to constitute delivery to all record holders. The Company, however, may place the materials on its Web site, but in this instance, it also would need to furnish paper copies of the materials to its record holders.

(24) In January 1995, Company XYZ places a copy of its final prospectus on its Internet Web site. The prospectus will remain there throughout the period for which delivery is required. Prior to viewing the final prospectus, Investor John Doe provides an express consent to the delivery of the prospectus and all

future documents related to the offering via Company XYZ's Web site. Investor John Doe subsequently purchases the securities. In connection with its May 1995 annual meeting, Company XYZ places proxy soliciting materials on its Web site and places an advertisement in the Wall Street Journal indicating that its proxy materials are now available on its Web site.

This advertisement by itself, even coupled with the express consent that related to the offering documents, is insufficient for the company to assume that it has delivered its proxy statement to Investor John Doe. Although John Doe had provided consent to receiving documents electronically, there is no reason to believe that notice provided in the Wall Street Journal would make John aware of the availability of the proxy materials. Company XYZ must provide more direct delivery or notice to John Doe of the proxy materials. Notice by publication in a newspaper or on a Web site or bulletin board is insufficient.

(25) In September 1994, John Doe, a shareholder in Company XYZ, requests all future corporate communications including proxy statements and annual reports to shareholders ("annual report") to be delivered electronically through the Company's Internet Web site. The consent form states that Company XYZ expects that its annual report and proxy materials for its annual meeting will be available on its Web site on April 1, 1995. On April 1, 1995, the Company places its annual report and proxy soliciting materials on its Web site.

Unlike the delivery of paper annual reports and proxy soliciting materials, where the mere appearance in the mail of such materials places the shareholder on notice within close proximity to the time when shareholder action is requested, the advance request in this example, without more, may not be close enough in time to the requested action to be effective. However, if the Company reasonably expects for other specific reasons, such as a history of communications with that shareholder, that the shareholder would have effective delivery of the information through the Web site, then the procedure could be acceptable.

(26) Record holder Jane Doe consents to delivery of all documents via Company XYZ's Web site. On April 1, 1995, Company XYZ provides notice to Jane Doe that its annual report and proxy materials are available on its Web site for its annual meeting scheduled to be held on May 5, 1995. On April 5, 1995, Jane Doe notifies the Company that her computer is broken and requests a paper copy of the annual report and proxy materials.

Because Jane Doe's notice to the Company indicates that electronic delivery will be ineffective, the Company should provide Jane Doe with paper copies of the annual report and proxy materials within a reasonable time of her request. She does not need to withdraw her consent in order to receive the paper copies.

-------------------- BEGINNING OF PAGE #19 -------------------

(27) Company XYZ places its quarterly report to shareholders and Forms 8-K on its Internet Web site and advertises the location of its Web site in the Wall Street Journal. The Company takes no other action to deliver these materials to shareholders.

This would be permissible, since there generally is no

requirement to deliver such materials to shareholders at all.

(28) Company XYZ places its annual report and proxy soliciting materials for the election of directors on its Internet Web site and provides notice to all record holders that previously had consented to electronic delivery via the Company's Web site. The record holders are instructed to print the proxy card, execute the proxy and then mail it back to the Company.

This would be consistent with the proxy rules.

(29) Brokerage Firm ABC solicits its customers who are beneficial owners of Company XYZ to determine whether they would like to receive Company XYZ's annual report and proxy soliciting materials electronically via the Internet rather than in paper. The Brokerage Firm then informs the Company that 100 beneficial holders would like to receive the materials electronically and 200 beneficial holders would prefer paper materials.

The Company provides the Brokerage Firm with the location of its Internet Web site where the materials are posted and copies of its paper documents for the 200 beneficial owners who do not wish to receive the electronic delivery. The Brokerage Firm then forwards the notice of the location of the electronic materials to those benefi ial holders who consented to receive electronic delivery and forwards the paper materials to those who did not. -[43]-

This would be consistent with the proxy rules.

(30) Company XYZ wishes to produce its annual report on videotape and CD-ROM. The videotape and CD-ROM will contain all the material information disclosed in the glossy annual report. Before distributing the Company's annual report, the Company sends a letter asking its shareholders whether they would be interested in receiving the Company's annual report on videotape or CD-ROM instead of paper. The Company then sends the videotape version of its annual report to its shareholders who wish to receive the videotape and the CD-ROM version to those shareholders who wish to receive the CD-ROM. The paper glossy annual report is sent to those shareholders who do not wish to receive either electronic format.

The federal securities laws do not preclude the delivery of a document through different media.

Mutual Funds

The Commission is aware that investment companies, particularly open-end investment companies ("mutual funds" or "funds") have been active in using electronic means to

--------- FOOTNOTES ---------

-[43]- Exchange Act Rule 14b-1. This example also is applicable to delivery by banks and other entities pursuant to Rule 14b-2.

-------------------- BEGINNING OF PAGE #20 -------------------

communicate with their shareholders and prospective investors. -[44]- Given the extent to which funds have embraced the new technologies, the Commission believes that it is appropriate to include the following additional examples, which are tailored to the fund industry. Unless otherwise noted, however, investment companies other than mutual funds and other corporate issuers or third parties may use these examples for guidance as well.

Examples

(31) A fund sends an e-mail to a recipient with a prospectus attached. The prospectus file includes an application form. The recipient fills out the form and mails it with a check to the fund.

Delivery of the prospectus may be inferred from the recipient's use of the form (provided the fund can identify it as coming from the electronically transmitted prospectus).

(32) A current prospectus is faxed to a potential investor who has requested the prospectus and provided the phone number of the fax machine.

This transmission satisfies the prospectus delivery requirements.

(33) A current prospectus and an application are faxed to a potential investor. The investor did not request the fax, but the sender knows the investor's fax machine phone number.

If the investor completes and mails in the application form included in the faxed prospectus, delivery of the electronic prospectus may be inferred.

(34) A fund sends an unsolicited e-mail with a prospectus attached in one file, and supplemental sales literature in a separate file. The investor can access the sales literature and the prospectus with equal ease.

The fund may send the supplemental sales literature in this fashion. -[45]- Electronic delivery of the prospectus may be inferred even if the prospectus is not accessed. This would be analogous to an investor receiving by mail a prospectus and supplemental sales literature in the same envelope and electing to review the sales literature, but not the prospectus.

(35) A fund posts its supplemental sales literature and prospectus on a file server for open access over the Internet. The supplemental sales literature contains hyperlinks to the fund's electronic prospectus and includes a caption referring the investor to the prospectus. The investor would not need any additional software or need to take burdensome steps to access the prospectus and thus has reasonably comparable access to both documents. This system also provides for the downloading or printing of prospectuses and sales literature. An investor would not be required to retrieve, download, or print a prospectus before viewing the sales literature. The system does not require any consent by its users.

--------- FOOTNOTES ---------

-[44]- See E. Savitz, "Let A Thousand Web Site Bloom," Barron's, June 26, 1995, at 50.

-[45]- Sections 2(10)(a) and 5(b) of the Securities Act.

When a user accesses the supplemental sales literature, electronic delivery of the prospectus can be inferred. This scenario is analogous to an investor's selecting an envelope containing a paper prospectus and supplemental sales literature from a display at an office of a broker-dealer. This electronic delivery of the prospectus would be sufficient for other purposes if the fund could reasonably establish that the investor has actually accessed the sales literature or the prospectus.

(36) A prospectus is made available through an on-line system that allows users to access, download or print the entire prospectus and has the capacity to track which users accessed, printed or downloaded which documents.

A fund may rely upon a user's having accessed, printed or downloaded a prospectus for the fund in order to deliver supplemental sales literature or an order form for the fund or to establish delivery of the prospectus in connection with a sale of fund shares.

(37) A fund's prospectus is available through an on-line service that does not have the capacity for downloading or printing or to track retrieval by a user. Investors do not provide any consent. The fund mails or e-mails supplemental sales literature, or an application to all of the service's subscribers, without including a prospectus.

Absent other factors that would indicate delivery of the prospectus, the fund may not send the supplemental sales literature or an application in this fashion, because it is not preceded or accompanied by the prospectus for purposes of Section 2(10)(a) of the Securities Act. -[46]- This would be true even if the general subscription agreement for the service contained a provision consenting to receipt of documents, because such consent would not be sufficient to give the fund reason to believe that delivery requirements relating to the prospectus will actually be satisfied.

(38) A server available through the Internet contains a fund's prospectus and application form in separate files. Users can download or print the application form without first accessing, downloading or printing the prospectus; the form includes a statement that by signing the form, the investor certifies that he or she has received the prospectus. Logistically it is significantly more burdensome to access the prospectus than the application form (e.g., the investor needs to download special software before accessing the prospectus).

The statement in the form about receipt of the prospectus would not by itself constitute electronic delivery of the prospectus, and the application form is not evidence of delivery of the prospectus, given the need to download special software before the prospectus can be viewed.

(39) A server available through the Internet contains a

--------- FOOTNOTES ---------

-[46]- This is analogous to printing a fund prospectus in a

magazine of general circulation and subsequently mailing supplemental sales literature to the magazine's subscribers, which would not comply with Sections 2(10) and 5(b) of the Securities Act. See William C. Lloyd (State of Wisconsin), June 7, 1990.

-------------------- BEGINNING OF PAGE #22 ------------------

fund's prospectus. Users must download the prospectus to view or print it. When a user downloads the prospectus, the user receives the prospectus and an application form in separate files. It is not significantly more burdensome to access the prospectus than the application form (e.g., no additional software is necessary to read either document, although the documents may be in different formats).

If the fund can identify the application form as coming from the electronic system, electronic delivery of the prospectus can be inferred. The application form is evidence of delivery of the prospectus.

(40) A fund's prospectus and application form are available through an electronic system like that described in the preceding example, except that the investor needs to download special software before the prospectus and application form can be downloaded.

If the fund can identify the application form as coming from the electronic system, electronic delivery of the prospectus can be inferred. The application form is evidence of access to the prospectus.

(41) A fund sends an e-mail with an attached file containing an advertisement satisfying the requirements of Securities Act Rule 482. -[47]-

There is no prospectus delivery requirement in this context; a Rule 482 advertisement need not be preceded or accompanied by a prospectus.

(42) A fund transmits prospectuses over an electronic bulletin board. Investors provide specific consent to receipt of the prospectus through that system. The consent states that the current version of the prospectus will be made continuously available and notice of material amendments will be given by mail, e-mail, or some other manner specifically directed to investors.

The prospectus delivery requirements will be satisfied with respect to subsequent additional purchases by those investors.

(43) A fund places its prospectus on its Internet Web site and revises the electronic version whenever the prospectus is modified. The fund materially amends the prospectus and decides to send a postcard or e-mail to persons to whom the prospectus has been delivered through electronic means or who have consented to electronic delivery notifying them of the availability of the amended prospectus.

This procedure provides for delivery of the prospectus to those who have consented and to those to whom the prospectus has been previously delivered (if the fund expects those persons to be able to receive the amended prospectus). Alternatively, the fund could choose to satisfy its prospectus delivery requirements by sending a paper copy of the amended prospectus to investors in

--------- FOOTNOTES ---------

-[47]- Rule 482 [17 CFR 230.482] permits a registered investment company or business development company to use an "omitting prospectus" advertisement that contains only information the substance of which is included in the company's Section 10(a) prospectus.

-------------------- BEGINNING OF PAGE #23 --------------------

the fund, including investors who consented to receive documents electronically.

(44) A fund places its prospectus on its Internet Web site. Potential investor John Doe obtains access to the prospectus. John Doe does not purchase shares in the fund. Subsequently, the prospectus is amended.

The fund does not need to provide John Doe with notice of the amendment.

(45) A fund puts proxy solicitation materials on the fund's server on the World Wide Web. At the same time, the fund sends out postcards or e-mail messages (with investors having consented to receive notification by e-mail) giving notification that the proxy materials are available. Investors have signed up to receive documents through the server.

This would be consistent with the proxy rules.

(46) A fund transmits annual and semi-annual reports over an electronic bulletin board system. The fund makes the current versions of these materials available and informs investors who have consented to electronic delivery of this fact. The fund provides separate notification each time a shareholder report is posted by including the notification in the precedin~ ~.arterly account statement or shareholder newsletter. T' ..otice informs investors of a date by which the report will be available.

Notification to shareholders in a statement or newsletter delivered within the preceding quarter would be considered sufficient notice under Section 30(d) of the Investment Company Act -[48]-and the rules thereunder to constitute delivery.

(47) A fund sends investors upon request a CD-ROM containing its current prospectus and registration statement materials for the fund's offering.

This would provide delivery to investors. -[49]-

(48) Prospectuses and other materials are available through a computer server that requires users to obtain a user ID and password before they can access documents on the system. The process for obtaining the ID and password requires significant information from the user and involves a delay of one day or even several days before the user can access the system. After a user accesses a prospectus, a fund sends him or her supplemental sales literature.

The process provides for delivery of the prospectus.

Although the system imposes burdens in the process for obtaining access to the prospectus, these burdens are part of the process of providing access to all the information, including the supplemental sales literature, and not burdens upon access to the prospectus that is delivered.

(49) A prospectus is made available through an on-line system that allows users to download the entire prospectus. The

--------- FOOTNOTES ---------

-[48]- 15 U.S.C. 80a-29(d).

-[49]- The analysis would be the same if an investor requests and receives information on a diskette.

-------------------- BEGINNING OF PAGE #24 -------------------

system does not permit on-line viewing. An investor downloads the prospectus.

Assuming downloading, this method would satisfy the delivery requirements because on-line viewing is not a prerequisite to electronic delivery.

(50) A fund provides its prospectus, annual and semi-annual reports through an Internet Web site. After one year, the fund decides to terminate the Web site.

The fund may cease making its prospectus available through the Web site as soon as the fund no longer plans to rely on electronic delivery for satisfying its prospectus delivery requirements. -[50]- Generally, an annual or semi-annual report should be available until superseded by a later report. The fund in this example could terminate the posting of the most recent report when it is superseded by a new one, or earlier if it provides a replacement paper copy to shareholders who received the report electronically.

(51) The text of a fund's prospectus transmitted electronically on a CD-ROM or an Internet Web site follows the sequence requirements of Form N-1A. -[51]- The prospectus includes a summary, which contains hyperlinks that allow the investor to move to later sections of the prospectus or to other documents (e.g., the fund's statement of additional information or annual report). The summary is part of the prospectus text that is subject to the form's sequence requirements.

Even though the hyperlinks allow an investor to choose to view information out of sequence, the prospectus satisfies the requirements of Form N-1A, because the main text does comply with the sequence requirement.

(52) A fund places its prospectus (information required by Part A of Form N-1A) on its Internet Web site. The fund does not put its Statement of Additional Information ("SAI") (information required by Part B of Form N-1A) on its Web site; instead, it provides a paper copy of its SAI free of charge to any person that requests it.

Delivery of a paper copy of an SAI does not prevent a fund from satisfying its prospectus delivery requirements

Jonathan G. Katz
Secretary

Dated: October 6, 1995

--------- FOOTNOTES ---------

-[53]- 15 U.S.C. 78w(a).

electronically.

III. PROPOSED AMENDMENTS

This release is intended to address practices involving electronic delivery that are acceptable under current rules; no substantive changes to filing or delivery requirements are contemplated here. However, in order to make it clear that current rules should be read to encompass electronic as well as paper dissemination, the Commission is proposing in a companion

--------- FOOTNOTES ---------

-[50]- Continued sales of fund shares or delivery of sales literature or application forms to investors who had received the prospectus electronically would require delivery of paper prospectus to those investors. Funds should consider whether paper prospectuses should also be sent to other investors (e.g., recent purchasers).

-[51]- 17 CFR 274.11A.

-------------------- BEGINNING OF PAGE #25 -------------------

release a number of technical amendments to its rules. -[52]-

IV. ELECTRONIC FILING ISSUES

As emphasized previously, this release addresses only issues relating to electronic delivery of required disclosure documents and does not affect the Commission's electronic filing requirements. However, the Commission recognizes that the same rapid development of electronic communications in recent years that has led to the issuance of this release also has implications for how the Commission should receive, process and make publicly available the documents filed with it pursuant to the federal securities laws. Currently, filings are accepted by the Commission only in the electronic formats prescribed by the EDGAR system, or in paper, where the filer has not yet become subject to mandated electronic filing requirements or where there is an exemption pursuant to the electronic filing rules. While EDGAR may be modified in the future to accept and process a broader array of electronic formats, there may be ways to allow the filing of documents prepared and delivered in other electronic media on a more expedited timetable. As the Commission continues with its review of this area, it intends to issue additional releases. Comment on the costs and benefits to filers and the federal government with respect to these issues should be provided by persons submitting comment on these issues.

V. SOLICITATION OF COMMENT

Any interested persons wishing to submit written comments relating to the views expressed in this release, or with respect to the rule proposals in the companion release, are invited to do so by submitting them in triplicate to Jonathan G. Katz, Secretary, U.S. Securities and Exchange Commission, 450 Fifth Street, N.W., Washington, D.C., 20549. Commenters should refer to File Number S7-31-95. Comment is requested not only on the specific issues discussed on the release, but on any other approaches or issues that should be considered in connection with facilitating the use of electronic media to further the disclosure purposes of the federal securities laws. Comment is sought from the point of view of both parties providing the disclosure, such as issuers and those acting on behalf of issuers, and parties receiving and using the disclosure, such as investors and shareholders. The Commission further requests comment on any competitive burdens that might result from the adoption of the proposals. Comments on this inquiry will be

--------- FOOTNOTES ---------

-[52]- See Release No. 33-7234 for the text of those amendments. Rule changes are proposed to be made to the following rules and forms: Rule 253 of Regulation A [17 CFR 230.253]; Rule 420 of Regulation C [17 CFR 230.420]; Rules 481 and 482 of Regulation C [17 CFR 230.481, 230.482]; Rule 605 of Regulation E [17 CFR 230.605]; Rule 304 of Regulation S-T [17 CFR 232.304]; Forms F-7 [17 CFR 239.37], F-8 [17 CFR 239.38], F-9 [17 CFR 239.39]; F-10 [17 CFR 239.40] and F-80 [17 CFR 239.41]; Rule 12b-12 [17 CFR 240.12b-12]; Rule 13e-3 [17 CFR 240.13e-3]; Rule 13e-4 [17 CFR 240.13e-4]; Schedule 13E-4F [17 CFR 240.13e-102]; Rule 14a-3 [17 CFR 240.14a-3]; Rule 14a-5 [17 CFR 240.14a-5]; Rule 14a-7 [17 CFR 240.14a-7]; Rule 14c-4 [17 CFR 240.14c-4]; Rule 14c-7 [17 CFR 240.14c-7]; Rule 14d-5 [17 CFR 240.14d-5]; Schedule 14D-1F [17 CFR 240.14d-102]; Schedule 14D-9F [17 CFR 240.14d-103]; and Rule 8b-12 [17 CFR 270.8b-12]; Rule 30d-1 [17 CFR 270.30d-1] and Rule 30d-2 [17 CFR 270.30d-2].

-------------------- BEGINNING OF PAGE #26 -------------------

considered by the Commission in complying with its responsibilities under Section 23(a) of the Exchange Act. -[53]-

AMENDMENT OF THE CODE OF FEDERAL REGULATIONS

For the reasons set out in the preamble, Title 17 Chapter II of the Code of Federal Regulations is amended as set forth below:

PART 231 - INTERPRETIVE RELEASES RELATING TO THE SECURITIES ACT OF 1933 AND GENERAL RULES AND REGULATIONS THEREUNDER

1. Part 231 is amended by adding Release No. 33-7233 and the release date of October 6, 1995, to the list of interpretive releases.

PART 241 - INTERPRETIVE RELEASES RELATING TO THE SECURITIES EXCHANGE ACT OF 1934 AND GENERAL RULES AND REGULATIONS THEREUNDER

2. Part 241 is amended by adding Release No. 34-36345 and the release date of October 6, 1995, to the list of interpretive releases.

PART 271 - INTERPRETIVE RELEASES RELATING TO THE INVESTMENT COMPANY ACT OF 1940 AND GENERAL RULES AND REGULATIONS THEREUNDER

3. Part 271 is amended by adding Release No. IC-21399 and the release date of October 6, 1995, to the list of interpretive releases.

By the Commission.

NOTES

13

INVESTMENT ADVISERS AND INVESTMENT COMPANIES ON THE INTERNET

Matthew A. Chambers

Investment Advisers and Investment Companies on the Internet

Table of Contents

Investment Advisers and Investment Companies on the Internet

by Matthew A. Chambers*

I. Registered Investment Companies.

A. Effect of the Securities Act of 1993 on Investment Companies. The Securities Act creates special problems for investment companies, particularly mutual funds, because of the nature of their business and of their securities offerings. Mutual funds almost invariably are engaged in continuous offerings of their securities, meaning that the advertising restrictions of the Securities Act never go away. Moreover, unlike other companies, the only products offered by mutual funds are their securities. Thus, almost any advertisement about a fund is an offer to sell its securities that must meet the requirements of that Act. *See* Division of Investment Management, SEC, PROTECTING INVESTORS: A HALF CENTURY OF INVESTOR PROTECTION (1992) (Chapter 9: Investment Company Advertising). For that reason, the Internet offers mutual funds a very convenient and efficient medium for advertising and selling fund shares (or, in industry vernacular, distribution).

B. The SEC's 1995 Interpretive Release. In 1995, the Securities and Exchange Commission issued an interpretive release setting forth general principles for applying the federal securities laws to electronic delivery of financial services, including the Internet and the Web. Securities Act Release No. 7233 (October 6, 1995) (addressing primarily issues concerning securities issuers under the Securities Act, the Securities Exchange Act of 1934, and the Investment Company Act of 1940) (the "1995 Release"). The principles announced by the SEC in the 1995 Release include:

1. The "use of electronic media should be at least an equal alternative to the use of paper-based media. Accordingly, issuer or third party information that can be delivered in paper under the federal securities laws may be delivered in electronic format."

2. Distribution of information by electronic media meets the prospectus and other delivery requirements of the federal securities

---

* Matthew A. Chambers is counsel in the Washington, D.C. office of Debevoise & Plimpton.

laws if the distribution results in the delivery to the intended recipients of substantially equivalent information as they would have received in paper documents.

3. Persons using electronic delivery of information should have reason to believe that the electronic means will result in satisfaction of the delivery requirements, such as confirmation of an investor's accessing, downloading, or printing information.

4. The "liability provisions of the federal securities laws apply equally to electronic and paper-based media." Put plainly, common sense rules apply to material placed on a Web site. Compliance staff should review all such material before its inclusion.

5. Where a person has a right to receive a document under the federal securities laws and chooses to receive it electronically, the sender should provide a paper copy if the person revokes his or her consent to electronic distribution or specifically requests a paper copy.

6. The 1995 Release also included 52 examples illustrating the securities law implications of use of electronic media by issuers and others.

C. The 1996 Interpretive Release. In 1996, the SEC issued a second interpretive release addressing the use of electronic media by broker-dealers, transfer agents, and investment advisers to satisfy their delivery obligations under the Exchange Act and the Investment Advisers Act of 1940. Securities Act Release No. 7288 (May 9, 1996). The SEC also noted that broker-dealers and advisers must supervise use of electronic media and safeguard their customers' personal financial information. Finally, the SEC supplemented the examples it gave in the 1995 Release with seven additional examples.

D. Mutual Fund Prospectus Delivery. Most significantly for mutual funds, they may provide their prospectuses to investors by electronic download from a Web site. Some regulatory issues remain, however.

1. An issuer must have a reasonable basis for believing that an investor can access a prospectus. Mutual fund sponsors offer their

prospectus in a variety of formats, including Adobe Acrobat™ format (designated by a file name ending with the extension "pdf"), with a link to a free download of that software (*e.g.*, Fidelity -- *www.fidelity.com*); Windows help (*.hlp) (Vanguard -- *www.vanguard.com*); and Macintosh (*.bin) (also Vanguard).

2. Some commenters have suggested that issuers should place the prospectuses on Web pages that do not contain hypertext links to other Web pages, out of concern that the SEC or courts will view the linked material as incorporated by reference into the prospectus. *See Highlights of the 28th Annual Institute on Securities Regulation,* 30 Sec. & Comm. Reg. 109, 112 (1997) (statement of Professor Grundfest, Stanford Law School). The SEC staff has not yet addressed this issue, although it has said that including the address of an issuer's Web site in a registration statement under the Securities Act would not result in the material on that site, or linked to that site, being deemed to be incorporated by reference into the registration statement. *See, e.g.,* Baltimore Gas & Electric, SEC No-Action Letter (January 6, 1997).

3. In addition, most, but not all, mutual fund issuers require prospective investors to provide their name, address, electronic mail address, and phone numbers before permitting downloading, so that they may maintain records indicating who has received a prospectus.

E. Advertisements and Sales Literature.

1. Advertising Rules. To allow mutual funds to advertise, the SEC has adopted two safe harbor rules: Rule 482, which allow funds to advertise performance data, and Rule 134, the so-called "tombstone" rule, which allows almost any kind of information other than performance data. Both rules have certain legend and related requirements. Also, any advertising under those rules, or sales literature of a fund that a registered broker-dealer distributes must comply with the rules of the NASD Regulation, Inc. (the "NASDR"). (In particular, Conduct Rules 2210, 2210-2, and 2210-3 address mutual fund advertisements and sales literature.) Those rules include requirements concerning filings with the NASDR and strict requirements concerning rankings and ratings.

The NASDR's rules apply to electronic delivery of advertising and sales materials. (The Conduct Rules were amended in 1995 to make clear that electronic communications were covered. NASD Notice to Members 95-74 (September 1995).)

2. Sales Literature. The term "sales literature" generally is used to refer to advertising material that accompanies or is preceded by a prospectus and thus is not subject to the requirements of Rules 134 or 482. Such material is still subject to antifraud rules and to NASDR filing and review requirements, and also to Rule 34b-1 under the Investment Company Act, which imposes certain requirements regarding the use of performance information. The SEC has agreed that material on a Web site that also includes "comparable access" to a fund's prospectus is accompanied or preceded by that prospectus and thus is not subject to the requirements of Rules 482 and 134. 1995 Release at Examples 14, 15, and 35; 1996 Release at Example 4.

a. Because sales literature tends to consist of shorter, simpler documents, fund sponsors may determine that it is unnecessary to present it in a format such as Acrobat. It is not clear, however, whether providing a prospectus in a format, such as Acrobat, that requires special software to access (even if the fund sponsor provides a link to the Adobe site offering the software for a free download) while offering direct view of the sales literature without the need for that software, is comparable access. In the 1995 Release, the SEC said that comparable access means that the investor does not need any *additional software* or to take any burdensome steps to view or print the prospectus and thus has reasonably comparable access to both documents. 1995 Release at Example 35.

b. If providing sales literature that may be viewed directly from any Web browser with a prospectus accessible only in Adobe Acrobat format does not constitute comparable access, then a mutual fund sponsor has three options. It may (i) put all sales literature in the Acrobat format; (ii) ensure that all such sales literature meets the content requirements of the SEC's advertising rules under the

Securities Act; or (iii) provide access to a version of the prospectus that can be viewed directly from the Web browser. (One way for a fund sponsor to provide such access is to include a link to the fund's prospectus at the SEC's own Web site (*www.sec.gov*).) Ironically, the EDGAR versions of prospectuses are in unsightly ASCII text.) In passing, it should be noted that although Acrobat is not a standard feature of Web browsers, it has gained widespread acceptance and is used by many Web sites, including that of the Internal Revenue Service.

F. Status of Hyperlinks.

1. What are Hyperlinks? Hyperlinks are portions of text or graphics on a Web page that refer to other pages, either at the same site or at another site. If a user places his or her cursor on the hyperlink and clicks with the mouse (or other pointing device) the linked document appears on the user's computer screen. Hyperlinks are a key feature of the World Wide Web because they make it easy and enjoyable to use.

2. Mutual Fund Use. Mutual fund sponsors use hyperlinks in a variety of ways. For example, they may want to link to Web sites maintained by mutual fund rating services, such as Morningstar, media articles about their funds, or Web sites of affiliates.

3. Original NASD Position. In 1996, the NASD indicated its view that hyperlinks to independent Web sites were, in effect, reprints of the material on those sites requiring NASD filings and review of the linked material. NASD Regulatory & Compliance Alert, April 1996. ("The NASD is still considering the extent of the member's responsibility for sites to which that member has chosen to link . . . If a member's site must be filed with the NASD and the member's site includes information promoting a link to another site, or urging the user to view a linked site, the NASD will likely require that the member provide the linked information for review.") NASDR Conduct Rule 2210 expressly provides that reprints are subject to the NASDR's filing and review requirements. Given that a hyperlink serves to connect the computer user to the new site, and the person linking to that site has no editorial control over its

content, a hyperlink seems to be more akin to an instruction about how to obtain the information on the linked site, rather than a reprint of that material.

4. New NASD Position. In 1997, in response to the urging of the Investment Company Institute (the "ICI"), the NASDR modified its position. Letter from Thomas M. Selman, Director, Advertising/Investment Companies Regulation, NASD Regulation, Inc. to Craig S. Tyle, General Counsel, ICI (November 11, 1997). The NASDR stated that when a member links to a Web site of an independent third party, the member is generally not responsible for the content or filing of the information on that site. In the letter, the NASDR also stated that members were not responsible for links to independent sites that provide general reference and educational materials. A condition for the NASDR's position, however, is that an NASD member not remove a link if the linked site is revised so that it has unfavorable information about the member or its products. Because this standard turns on subjective intent, it likely will prove impossible to enforce. The NASDR also cautioned that a member may not link to a third party's site if the member knows that the site has false or misleading information about the member's products. Presumably, a member could link to that site if it placed correcting disclosure at the link, although the NASDR did not address this.

5. Implications of New NASDR Position. The new NASDR position removes a major impediment to the flow of information to investors. Mutual funds may link to Morningstar reviews and to articles in the financial press without having to file that third party information with the NASDR, or to comply with the NASDR's rules on the content of advertising. For a thoughtful discussion of the implications of the NASD's position, see Gavis, "Hyperlinks in Mutual Fund Advertising," wallstreetlawyer.com, Vol. 1, No. 8. (January 1998).

6. SEC Position Unclear. The SEC has not yet addressed the status of links. Its position is important because of the rules on the advertising of fund investment performance. Under Rule 34b-1 under the Investment Company Act, if a fund includes any information regarding fund performance in either advertisements or

sales literature, the fund also must present its standardized total return for the last one, five and ten year periods, up through the most recently completed calendar quarter. Thus, if the SEC deems links to independent sites to be the equivalent of reprints, funds that link to sites such as Morningstar would have to include standardized performance data with the links and would have to update that data promptly at the end of each quarter.

G. Effecting Purchases and Sales of Fund Shares on the Internet. Allowing investors to buy and sell fund shares through a Web site is more a matter of security and consumer acceptance than a legal matter.

1. Current Practices. Some fund groups allow investors to buy and sell fund shares through the Internet, but only to reallocate money already invested in the fund complex.

2. Margin Rules. Many non-securities Web sites allow for purchases of commercial goods over the Internet, using credit cards. The margin provisions of the Securities Exchange Act would seem to prohibit the use of credit cards to buy most types of investment company securities, however.

3. Likely Changes. Many parties are racing to establish payment mechanisms for transactions over the Internet. As one or more of these mechanisms gain consumer acceptance, fund shares will be bought and sold over the Internet.

H. Shareholders' Meetings. Most registered investment companies are mutual funds that are not required by state law to hold annual meetings of shareholders. For those companies, the ability to conduct solicitations and hold meetings electronically is less important than for typical operating companies and closed-end funds. Nevertheless, in some circumstances, such as the sale of the fund's investment adviser, shareholders' meetings are necessary.

1. General Principles for Information Delivery. Delivery of annual reports and proxy statements may be made electronically. 1995 Release at Examples 23, 25, 26, 28, 30 and 45.

2. Electronic Voting. Proxies generally may be voted electronically, but *only if permitted under state law.* The SEC staff has suggested that issuers employing electronic (or telephonic) voting must (i) adopt a reasonable means of verifying the authenticity of the proxies, (ii) provide shareholders with the opportunity to validate their electronic votes, (iii) determine that electronic voting is permissible under state law, (iv) and retain voting records. *See* Letter to Investment Company Registrants from Carolyn B. Lewis and Barry D. Miller, Assistant Directors, Division of Investment Management at 4 (February 15, 1996). One may question why the Division believed conditions (i), (ii) and (iv) were necessary, but they are not particularly burdensome.

3. Dissident Web Sites. Web sites provide dissident shareholders with an inexpensive way to disseminate their views. *See* Friedman, "Proxy Solicitations and the Cyberspace Revolution," Insights, Vol. 11, No. 12 (December 1997).

4. Electronic Meetings. At least one corporate issuer has held an electronic meeting, allowing shareholders to participate in the question and answer part of the meeting via e-mail. *See id.*

II. Private Investment Companies on the Internet.

A. Exceptions from Investment Company Act. As a result of the National Securities Markets Improvements Act of 1996, there are now two exceptions from the Investment Company Act for private funds.

1. Section 3(c)(1). This exception dates from 1940 and is available for any issuer that is not making or proposing to make a public offering and has no more than 100 shareholders.

2. Section 3(c)(7). This exception was added by Congress in 1996 and is available for any issuer that is not making or proposing to make a public offering and whose securities are owned exclusively by "qualified purchasers." The term "qualified purchaser" is defined in Section 2(a)(51) and in some complex rules.

B. Private Offerings over the Internet. In Lamp Technologies, Inc., SEC No-Action Letter (May 29, 1997), the SEC staff agreed that private investment companies relying on Section 3(c)(1) may offer their securities through a Web site that is password-protected and restricted to persons that have qualified as accredited investors.

C. Secondary Markets? Although the SEC has not considered whether private funds may allow secondary trading in their securities through a password-protected Web site, it has said that ordinary private issuers may do so, if the site is restricted to "qualified institutional buyers" as defined in Rule 144A under the Securities Act. Net Roadshow, Inc., SEC No-Action Letter (January 30, 1998). While such an approach would not be possible for funds relying on Investment Company Act Section 3(c)(1), because of the 100 securityholder limit, it would be possible for Section 3(c)(7) funds, if the site also were restricted to qualified purchasers. In setting up such a system, a fund would need to bear in mind that not all qualified institutional buyers are qualified purchasers.

III. Investment Advisers and the Internet.

A. The 1996 Release. In 1996, the SEC made clear that investment advisers may satisfy their information delivery obligations under the federal securities laws by electronic distribution. The 1996 Release listed the adviser delivery obligations that could be satisfied electronically; the SEC did not list any adviser delivery obligations that could *not* be satisfied electronically. In using electronic media, however,

1. Advisers should consider the extent to which electronic communication provides timely and adequate notice that information is available electronically.

2. Advisers also must consider whether customers who receive information electronically have access to that information comparable to what they would have if the information were provided in paper form.

3. Advisers should consider the need to establish procedures to ensure that applicable delivery obligations are met.

4. Advisers should consider the need for systems and procedures to supervise firm personnel using electronic media.

5. A person who has the right under the federal securities laws to receive a document and chooses to receive it electronically also should be given the information in paper form upon request.

6. Advisers sending personal financial information electronically should take precautions to ensure the integrity, confidentiality, and security of that information and should obtain the client's "informed consent" before sending the information electronically.

B. Rule 206(4)-1 -- Past Specific Recommendations. Investment Advisers Act Rule 206(4)-1(a)(2) restricts the ability of investment advisers to advertise past specific recommendations. The SEC has agreed that an investment adviser to investment companies could provide information about the funds' recent purchases and sales without running afoul of the Advisers Act's restrictions on advertising past specific recommendations. Munder Capital Management, SEC No-Action Letter (May 17, 1996).

C. Recordkeeping Requirements. Materials concerning an adviser that are potentially available to ten or more persons through an electronic system would be considered subject to the recordkeeping requirements applicable to such communications. Thus, all material posted on a Web site and any material sent via e-mail to ten or more persons should be preserved under paragraph (a)(11) of Investment Advisers Act Rule 204-2.

D. Holding Oneself Out as an Adviser. In the 1996 Release, the SEC said that "if an adviser uses a publicly available electronic medium such as a World Wide Web site to provide information about its services, the adviser would not qualify for the exemption from registration" in Section 203(b)(3). That Section exempts advisers with fewer than fifteen clients that do not hold themselves out generally to the public as investment advisers. While the SEC's position seems generally correct, there are circumstances where it may have overly broad application. For example, an adviser that advises only private venture capital funds may have a Web site intended for issuers seeking capital, rather than advisory clients. Also, foreign advisers with fewer than fifteen clients should be allowed to have public Web sites for their non-United States clients without jeopardizing their ability to rely on Section 203(b)(3).

E. State Regulation of SEC-Registered Advisers. Investment advisers registered with the SEC are not subject to state investment adviser registration. Investment Advisers Act Section 203A(b)(1). Moreover, although states retain jurisdiction over "investment adviser representatives," the SEC has said that employees who conduct business through a Web site to clients in various states do not subject themselves to state jurisdiction, except through physical offices. Thus, the mere fact that an employee might conduct business with a client in State Z through a Web site maintained on a Web server located in State Y does not subject the employee to the jurisdiction of either State Z or State Y. *See* Investment Advisers Act Release No. 1633 (May 15, 1997) at n.129.

IV. Financial Planning Software and the Investment Advisers Act.

A. Types of Financial Planning Software. In the 1990s, a wide variety of financial planning software has emerged. The most well-known example is the Quicken Financial Planner, but there are several other prominent examples. In addition, some Web sites include interactive worksheets that allow the user to plan for his or her retirement. Fidelity offers retirement planning software for free downloads from its Web site.

B. Definition of "Investment Adviser". Section 202(a) (11) defines "investment adviser" to include, with certain exceptions, "any person who, for compensation, engages in the business of advising others, either directly or through publications or writings, as to the value of securities or as to the advisability of investing in, purchasing, or selling securities, or who, for compensation and as part of a regular business, issues or promulgates analyses or reports concerning securities."

1. Advice about Securities. This element has been interpreted very broadly by SEC. For example, the SEC has said that a "person who, in the course of developing a financial program for a client, advises a client as to the desirability of investing in securities as opposed to, or in relation to, stamps, coins, direct ownership of commodities, or any other investment vehicle would also be "advising" others within the meaning of Section 202(a)(11)." Investment Advisers Act Release No. 770 (August 13, 1981). Thus, an adviser's advice need not be about specific securities;

simply providing advice about the advisability of investing in securities generally is enough.

2. Is the Person "in the Business"? Again, the SEC has interpreted this element expansively. In the SEC's words, "the giving of advice or issuing of reports or analyses concerning securities for compensation need not constitute the principal business activity or any particular portion of the business activities of a person in order for the person to be an investment adviser * * * . Whether or not a person's activities constitute being engaged in the business of advising others as to the value of securities or the advisability of investing in securities or issuing reports or analyses concerning securities as part of a regular business will depend on (1) whether the investment advice being provided is solely incidental to a non-investment advisory, primary business of the person providing the advice; (2) the specificity of the advice being given; and (3) whether the provider of the advice is receiving, directly or indirectly, any special compensation therefor." *Id.*

   See also Applicability of the Investment Advisers Act to Financial Planners, Pension Consultants, and Other Persons Who Provide Investment Advisory Services as a Component of Other Financial Services, Investment Advisers Act Release No. 1092 (October 8, 1987) (investment advice would include "a recommendation that a client allocate certain percentages of his assets to life insurance, high yielding bonds, and mutual funds or particular types of mutual funds such as growth stock funds or money market funds. However, specific investment advice does not include advice limited to a general recommendation to allocate assets in securities, life insurance, and tangible assets.").

3. Advice Must be Provided "for Compensation". According to the SEC, the "compensation element is satisfied by the receipt of any economic benefit, whether in the form of an advisory fee, some other fee relating to the total services rendered, commissions, or some combination of the foregoing. It is not necessary that a person who provides investment advisory and other services to a client charge a separate fee for the investment advisory portion of the total services." *Id.* Moreover, it "is not necessary that an adviser's compensation be paid directly by the person receiving

investment advisory services, but only that the investment adviser receive compensation from some source for his services." Id. Thus, free advice, such as that provided by Fidelity's downloadable software, or Vanguard's Web site, is not covered by the Act.

C. Availability of Publisher Exclusion.

1. Section 202(a)(11) (D). This section literally excludes from definition of investment adviser "the publisher of any bona fide newspaper, news magazine or business or financial publication of general and regular circulation."

2. History of Interpretation by SEC. For many years, the SEC interpreted the exclusion overly narrowly, holding that it was not available to anyone that provided advice about specific securities. For example, in 1977, the SEC said:

> Upon reconsideration of its past positions, the staff has concluded that registration under the Act should not be required solely because a publication contains one or more formulae or guidelines intended to be used by investors in making determinations as to what securities to buy or sell or when to buy or sell them. From an administrative standpoint, difficulties have arisen in distinguishing between essentially mechanical formulae or guidelines, and those more general investment philosophies, techniques or analytical approaches for which registration under the Act has not normally been required in the absence of other factors. Also, the staff believes that, even as to publications within the former category, the benefits to investors from registration under the Act of an author or publisher may be slight. For example, "scalping" or similar fraudulent and manipulative practices would not present a real danger.
>
> The staff has concluded, therefore, that the definition of investment adviser should not be construed to include the author or publisher of any

book, pamphlet, or article (1) which does not contain recommendations, reports, analyses, or other advisory information relating to specific securities or issuers and (2) which is not one of a series of publications by such person or intended to be supplemented or updated, *provided that* the author or publisher has not and does not intend to engage in any other activities which would bring him within the definition of investment adviser. Applicability of Investment Advisers Act to Certain Publications, Investment Advisers Act Release No. 563 (January 10, 1977).

3. Lowe v. SEC, 105 S. Ct. 2557 (1985). In 1985, the Supreme Court ruled that the SEC had no authority over *bona fide* publishers, even if they provided advice as to particular securities. Although the justices were divided 5 to 3, all 8 agreed that the SEC had no authority. Five justices based their opinion on the statutory exclusion for publishers; three relied on the First Amendment.

4. Application of Publisher Exclusion to Financial Planning Software.

   a. Are sellers of software "publishers"? Literally, the term "publish" is used for software creators.

   b. Do software publishers publish "regular(ly) and continuous(ly)"? This has been interpreted to mean that the published material not be timed to specific market activity or to events affecting or having the ability to affect the securities industry. Financial planning software certainly meets this test.

   c. Are sellers of software "bona fide"? This has been interpreted to mean that the advice contain disinterested commentary and analysis as opposed to promotional material. Again, financial planning software meets this test.

   d. Is the advice provided by financial planning software "impersonal"?

(1) On the one hand, the marketing for that type of software often promotes it as providing personalized investment advice -- that is, advice tailored to the user's particular financial circumstances.

(2) On the other hand, interaction with a computer can hardly be described as a "personalized relationship". Moreover, the advice provided by software depends entirely on its quantitative analysis of the responses provided by the user.

e. Applying the Supreme Court's analysis in Lowe is not entirely conclusive. Of course, since the opinion was written in 1986, in the very early days of the computer revolution, the Court could not have anticipated today's software industry.

(1) At points, the majority opinion can be read to indicate that financial planning software could be regulated. For example, the majority wrote that the "Act was designed to apply to those persons in the investment-advisory profession -- those who provide personalized advice attuned to a client's concerns, whether by written or verbal communication." 105 S. Ct. at 2572.

(2) At other points, however, the wording of the Court's opinion very strongly suggests that software should not be regulated. For example, the majority said that "[a]s long as the communications between petitioners and their subscribers remain entirely impersonal and do not develop into the kind of fiduciary, person-to-person relationships that were discussed at length in the legislative history of the Act and that were discussed at length in the legislative history of the Act and that are characteristic of investment adviser-client relationships, we believe the publications are at least presumptively, within the exclusion and thus not subject to registration under the Act." 105 S. Ct.

2573. In a footnote, the Court noted that "[i]t is significant that the Commission has not established that petitioners have had authority over the funds of subscribers; that petitioners have been delegated decisionmaking authority to handle subscribers' portfolios or accounts; or that there have been individualized investment-related interactions between petitioners and subscribers." *Id.* at n.57.

(3) In the legislative history of the Advisers Act cited by the majority, there are references that support the idea that software should not be regulated. *E.g.*, H.R. Rep. No. 2639, 76th Cong., 3rd Sess. 28 (1940) (bill "recognizes the *personalized character* of the services of investment advisers and especial care has been taken in the drafting of the bill to respect this relationship between investment advisers and their clients").

(4) Of course, even if the publisher's exclusion is not available, the First Amendment might preclude regulation of financial planning software. In this regard, at least one court has held that software is speech entitled to First Amendment protection. Bernstein v. United States Department of State, 922 F. Supp. 1426, 1434-36 (N.D. Cal. 1996). *Cf.* Karn v. United States Department of State, 925 F. Supp. 1, 9-14 (D.D.C. 1996) (assuming that operating code is speech, but finding export controls on cryptographic algorithms to be consistent with the First Amendment).

f. It is difficult to see the utility of applying the Investment Advisers Act to software. For example, would a consumer (or the SEC) expect a software retailer to provide the cash disclosure statement required under Rule 206(4)-3?

g. Unfortunately, since Lowe, the SEC staff has been reluctant to address whether a particular person qualifies for the publisher's exclusion "because of the fact-specific analysis required to make this determination." Louis Russo, SEC No-Action Letter (June 16, 1994).

h. Moreover, the SEC staff's letters following the Lowe decision say that the staff believes that the publishers' exclusion applies only where the software does not address a user's particular financial needs and circumstances. *See, e.g.,* Datastream International, Inc., SEC No-Action Letter (March 15, 1993). Moreover, at least once, the SEC sent a letter to ask why a software publisher had not registered in connection with selling financial planning software. Many books and magazines, however, provide similar advice as to financial planning, in that they may offer equations or worksheets for individuals to make investment decisions. The difference between such publications and software is one of degree and not of kind.

i. At least one software publisher registered a subsidiary as an investment adviser. *See* Form ADV of Quicken Investment Services, Inc. (File No. 801-48822).

D. Effect of National Securities Markets Improvements Act of 1996. In 1996, Congress amended the Investment Advisers Act to divide primary regulatory responsibility between the SEC and the states. With few exceptions, the only advisers that may register with the SEC are (1) advisers to registered investment companies, (2) foreign advisers, and (3) advisers with at $25 million in assets under management (meaning that they provide "continuous and regular supervisory or management services"). As a result, publishers of financial planning software, if they are investment advisers, may not register with the SEC, but may be subject to state regulation. Quicken Financial Services withdrew its registration with the SEC in July 1997. See Form ADV-T (File No. 801-48822).

E. Uniform Securities Act. The Uniform Securities Act's definition of investment adviser is substantially similar to that in the Investment Advisers Act. It contains an exclusion for "a publisher of any bona fide newspaper, news column, newsletter, news magazine, or business or financial publication or service, whether communicated in hard copy form, or by electronic means, or otherwise, that does not consist of the rendering of advice on the basis of the specific investment situation of each client." *See*

§ 401(f)(5) of the Uniform Securities Act, as amended by NASAA, *reprinted in* NASAA Reports ¶ 4978 (CCH). One would hope that the state regulators would read this provision consistently with the Lowe opinion.

NOTES

NOTES

14

THE OFFERING AND DISTRIBUTION OF SECURITIES IN CYBERSPACE: A REVIEW OF REGULATORY AND INDUSTRY INITIATIVES

Alexander C. Gavis

The Offering and Distribution of Securities in Cyberspace: A Review of Regulatory and Industry Initiatives

*By Alexander C. Gavis**

Early in the next millennium your right and left cuff links or earrings may communicate with each other by low-orbiting satellites and have more computer power than your present PC. Your telephone won't ring indiscriminately; it will receive, sort, and perhaps respond to your incoming calls like a well-trained butler. . . . The digital planet will look and feel like the head of a pin.

—Nicholas Negroponte[1]

INTRODUCTION

Hardly a day passes without the newspapers and other media publishing stories about how a digital age is about to envelop the world. Soon, it is forecast, traditional forms of communication—paper-based mail and telephone use—will give way to electronic communications over computer networks[2] such as the Internet,[3] and particularly the World Wide Web

*Assistant Counsel, Investment Company Institute. B.A. 1986, Swarthmore College; J.D. 1991, University of Pennsylvania. This Article was completed as of mid-summer 1996 and is generally intended to provide interested readers with a review of recent regulatory and industry developments in the area of electronic communications and securities law and a discussion of emerging issues. As a general disclaimer, the views and opinions expressed in this Article are those of the author and do not necessarily reflect or represent those of the Investment Company Institute or its members.

1. NICHOLAS NEGROPONTE, BEING DIGITAL 6 (1995).

2. *See* Peter Coy, Faster, Smaller, Cheaper, BUS. WK., Fall 1994 Bonus Issue, at 54; Richard W. Wiggins, *The Unfolding Net,* INTERNET WORLD, Nov. 1995, at 43 (stating that, with respect to the Internet, "[m]illions of people worldwide use it daily to communicate and fetch information. Major newspapers carry page-one articles about it. Fortune 500 companies rush to use it to tell their story. . . . It's even the subject of feature films."); Elizabeth Corcoran, *On the Internet, a Worldwide Information Explosion Beyond Words,* WASH. POST, June 30, 1996, at A1; Peter Leyden, *Hitting Home—Just as motors transformed our homes in the 20th Century, microprocessors promise to liberate our personal lives,* STAR TRIB., June 11, 1995, at T1.

3. The Internet is the name for an extensive worldwide network of computers. The Internet's "roots lie in a project called ARPANET which was sponsored by the United States Department of Defense Advanced Research Projects Agency (ARPA)." HARLEY HAHN, THE INTERNET COMPLETE REFERENCE 2 (2d ed. 1996). The Department of Defense was interested in building a decentralized network of computers that could maintain itself under

(Web).[4] By the end of the decade—if not sooner—we are told, consumers will be able to purchase everything from toothpaste to municipal bonds from their homes by using computer based-networks.[5] The public will

adverse conditions, particularly in the event of a nuclear war. The project began in 1968 and eventually evolved into a more general goal of developing techniques to build a large-scale national computer network. *Id.*; NEGROPONTE, *supra* note 1, at 233-34. It is generally believed that the modern version of the Internet was not born until 1987, when the National Science Foundation upgraded its nationwide supercomputer network to speeds that supported real-time collaboration between users. In addition, it was not until the early 1990s that the Internet became widely recognized outside the educational and research communities. *See* Jeffrey Payne & David Pool, *Forging Ahead*, INTERNET WORLD, Nov. 1995, at 55. Today, the Internet connects over 45,000 independent computer networks, comprising approximately five million host computers. *See Mutual Funds on the Internet*, MUTUAL FUND OVERVIEW (Stategic Insight, New York, N.Y.), Nov. 1995, at i.

In general, the public can access the Internet either by obtaining a modem connection from their personal computer to an Internet service provider or through a commercial online computer network. The Internet provides for file transfer, remote log-in, electronic mail, news, and other services. Commercial online networks are distinct from the Internet. Examples of these services include America Online, CompuServe, Prodigy, and the Microsoft Network. These services offer the public access to a proprietary network of information that is usually maintained and compiled by the service. A fee is generally charged for access to the service. Most of the major online computer network services offer access to the Web portion of the Internet through a "gateway." *See* Mike Mills, *The Tangle Behind an Easy-to-Use Tool*, WASH. POST, July 2, 1996, at A1.

4. For the purposes of this Article, the author uses the term "Internet" to refer to all computer networks, including the Web and proprietary online computer services. The Web is the name for that portion of the Internet that is used for the transmission of "hypermedia documents" (i.e., documents containing pictures, graphics, sound files, or other multimedia based information) between computer users internationally. *See* Kevin Hughes, *A Guide to Cyberspace* (last modified May 1994) <http://www.eit.com/web/www.guide> (on file with *The Business Lawyer*, University of Maryland School of Law). It is "a specialized portion of the Internet that is generally recognized as the most user-friendly and easily searched portion of the Internet." Woodrow W. Campbell et al., *Mutual Funds in Cyberspace*, INV. LAW., Nov. 1995, at 14. The "Web uses hypertext markup language (HTML), which enables navigation by pointing and clicking on various options. The Web supports multimedia applications with data, audio, and image, and hence is quickly becoming the predominant choice for commercial applications with the Internet." *Mutual Fund Overview*, *supra* note 3, at i; *see also* Kara Swisher, *There's No Place Like a Home Page*, WASH. POST, July 1, 1996, at A1.

The Web officially began in early 1989 when researchers at the European Particle Physics Laboratory (known as CERN) developed a project that involved a network capable of transmitting linked documents among members of the world-wide, high-energy physics community. At the end of 1990, software was introduced on a NeXT computer system (developed by Steven Jobs, formerly of Apple Computer), which had the capability to view and transmit hypertext documents to other people on the Internet. Since that time, other Web-based software has been developed and widely disseminated for use with the Internet. *See* HAHN, *supra* note 3, at 163-66.

5. *See* Debora Spar & Jeffrey J. Bussgang, *Ruling the Net*, HARV. BUS. REV., May-June 1996, at 125 ("The promise is of a radical new world of business—a friction-free arena where millions of buyers and sellers complete their transactions cheaply, instantaneously, and anonymously."); John Schwartz, *The Site-Seers' Guide to Some Way-Out Internet Futures*, WASH. POST, July 3, 1996, at A1.

"surf" through "cyberspace,"[6] locating the products or services they want, and purchase them with a few keystrokes or the click of a mouse.[7] The pace of technological change supposedly is so quick that a more detailed description in this Article is likely to be out of date by the time of publication.

Hyperbole aside,[8] the popular accounts of the coming digital age serve to highlight several important developments that will affect commerce in the United States directly, including the distribution and sale of securities and other financial instruments. As of this writing, although not yet as ubiquitous as the toaster oven in every home, personal computers (PCs) are owned by an estimated thirty million households in the United States (or about twenty-five percent of all households in the country).[9] This number has tripled since the late 1980s, and it is expected that approximately

6. One commentator defines "cyberspace" as "the conceptual 'location' of the electronic interactivity available using one's computer," and "a place 'without physical walls or even physical dimensions' in which interaction occurs as if it happened in the real world and in real time, but constitutes only a 'virtual reality.' " William S. Byassee, *Jurisdiction of Cyberspace: Applying Real World Precedent to the Virtual Community*, 30 WAKE FOREST L. REV. 197, 198 n.5 (1995) (quoting Lawrence H. Tribe, *The Constitution in Cyberspace: Law and Liberty Beyond the Electronic Frontier*, HUMANIST, Mar. 26, 1991, at 15). Another commentator defines cyberspace as:

> 1) A word coined by William Gibson, in his popular science fiction novel *Neuromancer*, to describe the realm and cultural dynamics of people and machines working within the confines of computer-based networks. 2) An entirely meaningless buzzword that *might* have been related to the Gibson term, once, but has since been sucked into the reality distortion field that surrounds Hollywood, Madison Avenue, and pop culture.

G. BURGESS ALLISON, THE LAWYER'S GUIDE TO THE INTERNET 331 (1995). Finally, the author's favorite definition of "cyberspace" is "that place you are in when you are talking on the telephone." Jay G. Baris, Current Disclosure Issues, Remarks at the 1996 Mutual Funds and Investment Management Conference (Mar. 25-28, 1996) (quoting John Perry Barlow, former cowboy, rancher, Grateful Dead lyricist, and cofounder of the Electronic Frontier Foundation) (on file with *The Business Lawyer*, University of Maryland School of Law).

7. Because many terms and words related to computers have become part of the general vernacular through their use in press articles, the author will not attempt to define all such terms or words used in this article (e.g., mouse or modem), except with respect to those terms or words that may not generally be understood by the public. *See generally* HAHN, *supra* note 3.

8. *See* Peter Coy, *Has the Net Finally Reached the Wall?*, BUS. WK., Aug. 26, 1996, at 62 ("The Internet is a highway that stays congested no matter how many lanes are added."); Walter S. Mossberg, *Cable Technology May Make Internet As Accessible as TV*, WALL ST. J., Apr. 18, 1996, at B1 ("The Internet will simply never become a mass medium until every user has access to high-speed, no-hassle connections that are always available without placing a call."); G. Pascal Zachary, *Digital Age Spawns 'Neo-Luddite' Movement*, WALL ST. J., Apr. 12, 1996, at B1 ("Today, few homes offer refuge from digital intruders: pagers, fax machines, call-waiting signals and cell phones. In some quarters, that's led to a growing willingness to 'poke fun at technology, to point out the gap between its promise and the reality.' ").

9. *See* Robert A. Robertson, *Personal Investing in Cyberspace and the Federal Securities Laws*, 23 SEC. REG. L.J. 347, 349 (1996).

forty million households will own PCs by 1997.[10] Moreover, a recent survey found that approximately thirty-seven million people in the United States and Canada have access to the Internet, either through work, home, friends, or a commercial online service, such as America Online.[11]

The growing use of PCs and the Internet by the public has not been lost on the business community. In fact, the Web portion of the Internet has developed into a virtual electronic bazaar of advertisements and announcements focused on the consumer marketplace. As of this writing, thousands of electronic "Web sites"[12] have been created by various corporations and businesses to provide the public with information and advertisements about new products and services.[13] In fact, the Internet's commercial domain[14] has been the fastest growing segment over the past several years, and is now the largest domain.[15] Companies as diverse as

10. *Id.*

11. This number represents about 17% of the total population over the age of 16. In addition, the survey reported that approximately one-third of users are women and that more than half of Internet users are between the ages of 16 and 34. *Id.; see, e.g.,* Rajiv Chandrasekaran, *Usage of the Internet Surges in U.S., Canada, Survey Finds,* WASH. POST, Aug. 14, 1996, at F1 (reporting on follow-up survey by Nielson Media Research for CommerceNet); Bruce L. MacLaughlan, *Wired Nation: Half of U.S. Homes Now Have a Computer,* DET. NEWS, July 21, 1995, at D3 (stating that nearly half of all American households own at least one PC); Jim Morrison, *Hot Modems, Cold Lives: Refugees From Cyberspace,* N.Y. TIMES, Apr. 30, 1995, at 45 (estimating that 31% of American households own a PC); Kara Swisher, *Internet's Reach In Society Grows, Survey Finds,* WASH. POST, Oct. 31, 1995, at A1 (reporting on the Internet Demographics Survey conducted by Nielsen Media Research for CommerceNet).

12. A Web site is the particular data communications link that is established with the Internet. For example, when a company establishes a Web site, it generally designates a computer (often called a "server") that is linked to the Internet and that allows for access by the public via the Internet. The site usually can be accessed by anyone who has access to the Internet and has appropriate "browser" (e.g., Netscape or Mosaic) software that assists in viewing various Internet sites. The Web site's "home page" is analogous to the cover page and table of contents of a book. If someone were to access the corporation's Web site, he or she would first see the home page, which would then provide links (usually called hyperlinks) to other parts of the corporation's Web site or to other Web sites. *See generally* HAHN, *supra* note 3, at 181-85; Mills, *supra* note 3, at A1; Swisher, *supra* note 4, at A1.

13. *But see* Spar & Bussgang, *supra* note 5, at 125 ("For many . . . companies . . . the Internet has yet to deliver on its promises. Although doing business in cyberspace may be novel and exhilarating, it can also be frustrating, confusing, and even unprofitable.").

14. The "domain" is the part of a standard Internet address that indicates the origin of the computer. In general, the domain part of the Internet address of an entity will fall into one of several different categories depending upon the type of entity that is operating the computer. For example, most commercial businesses that have Web sites use the suffix ".com" at the end of their domain name, most educational institutions use ".edu" at the end of their domain name, and most governmental agencies use ".gov" at the end of their domain name. *See generally* David Hilzenrath, *Group Plans Challenge to Net Address Monopoly,* WASH. POST, Aug. 23, 1996, at F1.

15. It is estimated that there were approximately 76,000 commercial Internet addresses registered with InterNIC (the organization responsible for registering Internet domain names) as of July 1995, compared to 29,000 in December 1994, and 17,200 in July 1994. *See* Cynthia Bournellis, *Internet '95: The Internet's Phenomenal Growth is Mirrored in Startling Statistics,* INTERNET WORLD, Nov. 1995, at 47.

CNN, Coca-Cola, Merck, and Disney, for example, have established Web sites and, in many cases, heavily advertise that they have done so.[16] Thus far, such companies are using the Internet as a new distribution channel in which to disseminate advertisements and product and consumer information to millions of consumers around the world.

Concurrent with corporate America's realization that the Internet provides a new distribution channel for communicating with the public, financial service industries, including the banking, mutual fund, and securities industries, have all begun to incorporate the Internet into their strategic plans. Although, over the past fifteen years, these industries have embraced new technologies with respect to their operations,[17] the Internet presents an entirely new mechanism for the interaction of these entities with the public. This Article will examine the tremendous growth in the use of the Internet by market participants, including mutual funds, broker-dealers, investment advisers, and corporate issuers to communicate electronically with the public, and the federal and regulatory initiatives related to that growth.

At last count, for example, over seventy mutual fund companies have created online "investor centers" on the Internet that provide detailed information on funds and their portfolio managers.[18] One of the important features of these "investor centers" is the public's ability to download prospectuses and applications, eliminating the traditional wait for mail.[19] A number of brokerage firms and investment banks also have established Web sites on the Internet.[20] Investment advisers and financial planners are beginning to explore ways in which the Internet might assist them in pro-

16. The Web site address for CNN is <http://www.cnn.com> (visited Sept. 10, 1996); for Coca-Cola, <http://www.coca-cola.com> (visited Sept. 10, 1996); for Merck, <http://www.merck.com> (visited Sept. 10, 1996); for Disney, <http://www.disney.com> (visited Sept. 10, 1996). *See* Swisher, *supra* note 4, at A1.

17. For example, the U.S. securities industry has developed some of the most sophisticated electronic trading systems in the world.

18. *See* Kimberly Weisul, *The Cyberspace Rush,* Inv. Dealers' Dig., Feb. 26, 1996, at 3 (listing many of the mutual fund Web sites available as of February 1996).

19. Fund investors also can access a variety of other information at these sites, including investment primers, worksheets, sales literature, and share price and fund performance information. *See* Sana Siwolop, *Now, The Superhighway Leads to Mutual Funds,* N.Y. Times, Aug. 13, 1995, at F5; Kimberly Weisul, *Mutual fund sites mushroom on Internet's World Wide Web,* Inv. Dealers' Dig., Dec. 18, 1995, at 9; *see also infra* notes 229-257 and accompanying text.

20. The sites established by brokerage firms usually provide investor information about the securities markets, and some provide for the electronic trading of securities over the Internet. The investment banking firm sites generally provide information concerning the firms' various activities. See *infra* notes 258-277 and accompanying text for further discussion of these activities; *see also* Hal Lux, *Wall Street Wires Into the Web,* Inv. Dealers' Dig., June 26, 1995, at S2 (listing many brokerage and investment bank sites on the Internet).

viding information and services to their clients.[21] In at least one instance, a corporate issuer has recognized that the Internet may be a useful medium in which to distribute and make a market for its securities, and has established an electronic trading forum for the purchase and sale of its securities by the public.[22]

When the federal securities laws were enacted over fifty years ago—during a time of paper-based communication—the growth of electronic communication could not have been anticipated.[23] Nonetheless, the drafters established a basic set of objectives for securities disclosure that could be achieved regardless of the type of communication used to distribute or offer those securities. In addition, the other objectives of the securities laws—preventing fraud in the securities markets,[24] maintaining fair and honest markets,[25] and improving the breadth of capital available to securities markets[26]—also are not dependent upon any particular form of communication.

The Securities and Exchange Commission (SEC) has regulated the distribution and sale of securities over the past fifty years, beginning with the time in which securities were sold primarily through face-to-face communication to more recent times when they are sold primarily through telephone transactions.[27] Throughout this time, the SEC has not insti-

21. Also of note, a number of commercial publications, such as *Money Magazine*, and financial information service providers, such as Morningstar, advertise their services and offer investor information concerning investments on the Internet. *See* James Aley, *How Investors Can Use the Internet*, FORTUNE, Apr. 17, 1995, at 154 (providing information on how and where to obtain financial information on the Internet); *Mutual Fund Related Web Sites*, SAN DIEGO UNION TRIB., Jan. 4, 1996, at 1 (listing Web sites for investment newsletters and other financial information providers).

22. *S.E.C. Clears Trades of Stocks on Internet*, N.Y. TIMES, Mar. 26, 1996, at D4 (stating that the SEC has "cleared the way for a New York brewer to resume a pioneering Internet trading system for its stock"); *see also infra* notes 103-24 and accompanying text.

23. It is interesting to note that the leading securities law treatise, LOUIS LOSS & JOEL SELIGMAN, SECURITIES REGULATION (3d ed. 1989-1994), does not yet mention electronic communication or technology in its index. *See id.*

24. For example, the Securities Act of 1933 (Securities Act), which regulates the distribution of securities, has the objectives of providing the investing public with "full and fair disclosure of the character of securities" and of "preventing fraud" in the sale of securities. Securities Act, Preamble, Pub. L. No. 73-22, 48 Stat. 74 (1933).

25. LOSS & SELIGMAN, *supra* note 23, at 3-50.

26. *Id.*

27. *See* Investment Company Filing Guidance, SEC Generic Comment Letter, 1994 WL 808442 (S.E.C.) (Feb. 25, 1994) (describing procedures for mutual fund telephone transactions); Investment Company Institute, SEC No-Action Letter, [1987-1988] Transfer Binder Fed. Sec. L. Rep. ¶ 78,691 (Apr. 27, 1988) (applying SEC rules to automated telephone systems).

tuted,[28] nor sought from Congress,[29] fundamental changes to the federal securities laws in response to changing uses of technology by market participants. Instead, it has updated and revised its rules and regulations incrementally to address new forms of communication and technologies. Most recently, the SEC has undertaken several initiatives that address the use of the Internet and other electronic media by market participants.[30]

Among the federal self-regulatory organizations (SROs),[31] the NASD has taken the lead in addressing issues related to the Internet. As of this writing, twenty-three states have begun to address the issue of when an offer of securities made over the Internet or other electronic media would

28. For example, since 1975, the SEC has generally overseen the development of the structure of a "national market system for securities." *See* 15 U.S.C. § 78k-1 (1994). The SEC's role in this regard generally has been to facilitate market participants' development and use of new technologies in the trading of securities, rather than to mandate a specific market structure. *See generally* SUBCOMM. ON OVERSIGHT AND INVESTIGATIONS OF THE HOUSE COMM. ON INTERSTATE AND FOREIGN COMMERCE, 96TH CONG., 2D SESS., NATIONAL MARKET SYSTEM: FIVE YEAR STATUS REPORT (Comm. Print 1980); Development of a National Market System, Exchange Act Release No. 14,416 [1978 Transfer Binder] Fed. Sec. L Rep. (CCH) ¶ 81,502, at 80,024 (Jan. 26, 1978); Development of a National Market System, Exchange Act Release No. 15,671 [1979 Transfer Binder] Fed. Sec. L. Rep. (CCH) ¶ 82,016, at 81,561 (Mar. 22, 1979) (Status Report); JOEL SELIGMAN, TRANSFORMATION OF WALL STREET 439-568 (1982).

29. On occasion, however, the securities laws have been amended by Congress as a result, in part, of the development of new technologies. For example, in 1975, Congress added §§ 11A and 17A to the Securities Exchange Act of 1934 (Exchange Act) in order to promote technological advances in the securities markets and in the systems for clearing and settling securities. Pub. L. No. 94-29, 89 Stat. 97 (1975) (codified at 15 U.S.C. §§ 78k-1, 78q-1 (1994)); *see* 15 U.S.C. §§ 78k-1(a)(1)(B) (1994) ("The Congress finds that—. . . (B) New data processing and communications techniques create the opportunity for more efficient and effective market operations."); 78q-1(a)(1)(C) (1994) (The Congress finds that—. . . (C) New data processing and communications techniques create the opportunity for more efficient, effective, and safe procedures for clearance and settlement."). In 1990, Congress added § 17B to the Exchange Act to assist the SEC in policing fraudulent activity in the Penny Stock market. Pub. L. No. 101-429, 104 Stat. 955 (1990) (codified at 15 U.S.C. § 78q-2 (1994)); *see* 15 U.S.C.A. § 78q-2(a)(3) (1994) ("[A] fully implemented automated quotation system for penny stocks would meet the information needs of investors and market participants and would add visibility and regulatory and surveillance data to that market.").

30. *See* Use of Electronic Media for Delivery Purposes, Securities Act Release No. 7233, 60 Fed. Reg. 53,458 (Oct. 13, 1995) [hereinafter October Interpretive Release]; Use of Electronic Media for Delivery Purposes, Securities Act Release No. 7234, 60 Fed. Reg. 53,468 (Oct. 13, 1995) (accompanying release proposing technical amendments to existing regulations that do not contemplate distribution of electronic prospectuses); Use of Electronic Media for Delivery Purposes, Securities Act Release No. 7289, 1996 WL 242455 (S.E.C.) (May 9, 1996) [hereinafter Adopting Release]; Use of Electronic Media by Broker-Dealers, Transfer Agents, and Investment Advisers for Delivery of Information; Additional Examples under the Securities Act of 1933, Securities Exchange Act of 1934, and Investment Company Act of 1940, Securities Act Release 7288, 61 Fed. Reg. 24,644 (May 15, 1996) [hereinafter May Interpretive Release].

31. These organizations include the New York Stock Exchange, Inc. (NYSE), the American Stock Exchange, Inc. (AMEX), and the National Association of Securities Dealers, Inc. (NASD).

fall under the purview of the state's securities laws. In addition, several states have begun to consider how the Internet will fit into their securities enforcement programs. Recently enacted federal legislation, however, will directly affect the ability of states to regulate the offering and distribution of securities through the Internet. The National Securities Markets Improvement Act of 1996 (NSMIA),[32] among other things, precludes the states from directly or indirectly imposing any registration requirements on securities issued by investment companies and securities that are listed on a national exchange.[33] States may continue to be able to require investment companies to make notice filings, to assess fees, and to bring antifraud actions.[34] The legislation also divides regulation of investment advisers between the states and the SEC. Advisers with $25 million or more in assets under management must register exclusively with the SEC and all other advisers must be registered exclusively with the states.[35] The states retain antifraud authority over all advisers.[36] Thus, the legislation significantly changes the regulatory landscape with respect to the offering of securities through the Internet because it precludes the states from imposing registration requirements on investment companies, corporate issuers, and large investment advisers who use the Internet to offer and distribute securities. The states are not be precluded, however, from bringing antifraud enforcement actions with respect to such offerings.[37]

The first section of this Article will review the initiatives by federal regulators, including the SEC and SROs, to address the use of the Internet by market participants. The second section will review the response to Internet activities by state securities regulators. The third section will review how the Internet currently is being used for the offering and distribution of securities by market participants including mutual funds, broker-dealers, and investment advisers. Finally, the last section will discuss some

32. Pub. L. No. 104-290, 110 Stat. 3416 (1996). The NSMIA took effect on October 11, 1996.

33. *Id.* § 303.

34. Specifically, the legislation vests in the SEC exclusive authority for the registration or qualification of investment company offerings and offerings listed on the NYSE, AMEX, NASDAQ-NMS, or other exchanges that the SEC determines to have substantially similar listing standards, as well as for securities offered or sold to qualified purchasers. *See id* §§ 201-10. With respect to investment company offerings, the states may (i) continue to require the filing of any document filed with the SEC for notice purposes only, along with a consent to service of process; (ii) continue to charge fees in connection with such filings, require additional reports as necessary to assess such fees, and impose penalties for the failure to pay fees; and (iii) retain jurisdiction with respect to fraud and deceit and unlawful broker-dealer conduct in connection with securities or securities transactions. *Id.* § 102.

35. *Id.* §§ 301-08.

36. States can continue to receive filings and fees from advisers that are registered with the SEC and may require the registration of representatives of such advisers if the representatives have a place of business in the state. *See id.*

37. *Id.*

of the emerging securities law issues that confront federal and state regulators.

FEDERAL INITIATIVES

THE SECURITIES AND EXCHANGE COMMISSION

The regulatory initiatives of the SEC related to market participants' use of the Internet to distribute and offer securities fall into five principal categories. First, the SEC has provided interpretive guidance to corporate issuers, mutual funds, and other market participants concerning how these entities can use the Internet and other electronic media to provide information, such as prospectuses and shareholder reports, to investors while complying with the federal securities laws. Second, the SEC has provided interpretive guidance to broker-dealers, investment advisers, and transfer agents about how these entities can use the Internet and other electronic media to provide investment services and information to their clients and customers while complying with federal securities laws. Third, the SEC has provided guidance to both corporate issuers and broker-dealers who have proposed to operate trading systems for securities on the Internet. Fourth, the SEC has established a system in which corporate issuers and mutual funds can submit their filings in electronic format to the SEC and in which the public can access those documents through the Internet. Finally, the SEC has devoted a portion of its enforcement resources to monitoring the Internet to detect and prosecute cases involving the fraudulent offering of securities over the Internet.[38]

SEC Guidance on the Use of Electronic Media to Deliver Information

The first pronouncements by the SEC and its staff concerning the use of electronic media by corporate issuers, mutual funds, and other market participants to deliver information to investors were made through the SEC's no-action letter process. Market participants sought specific advice from the SEC staff on how to meet their obligations under the securities laws, while providing clients with enhanced and more timely delivery of information. The SEC followed its no-action guidance with an interpretive release.

38. The recently enacted federal legislation, see *supra* note 32 and accompanying text, requires the SEC to conduct a study of "(i) the impact of technological advances and the use of on-line information systems on the securities markets, including steps that the Commission has taken to facilitate the electronic delivery of prospectuses to institutional and other investors; (ii) how such technologies have changed the way in which the securities markets operate; and (iii) any steps taken by the Commission to address such changes." *Id.* § 510.

No-Action Guidance

In February 1995, the staff of the SEC's Division of Corporation Finance issued a response to a request for interpretive advice from a law firm on behalf of several broker-dealer clients which would allow the broker-dealers to deliver prospectuses in electronic format to their customers.[39] The *Brown & Wood* requesting letter "was prompted by the logistical problems encountered by the securities industry in providing a final prospectus to customers prior to or at the same time as delivery of a confirmation in connection with underwritten transactions."[40] According to the requesting letter, "[t]he staff and the Commission have been aware for many years of the serious logistical problems encountered by the securities industry in providing a final prospectus to customers prior to or contemporaneously with delivery of a confirmation in connection with underwritten transactions."[41] Moreover, the letter stated that these problems had become especially acute as a result of several recent developments, including the SEC's adoption of a shortened, three-day settlement period for most securities transactions[42] and the staff's granting of no-action relief to allow for the electronic transmission of confirmations.[43]

The requesting letter argued that a prospectus encoded in an electronic format should be considered a "prospectus" as defined and referenced

39. Brown & Wood, SEC No-Action Letter, 1995 SEC No-Act. LEXIS 281 (Feb. 17, 1995).

40. Joseph McLaughlin, *SEC Approves Use of Electronic Prospectuses and Proposes T + 3 Relief*, INSIGHTS, Apr. 1995, at 3 (written by the lawyer from the law firm Brown & Wood, who submitted the no-action letter to the SEC).

41. *Brown & Wood*, 1995 SEC No-Act. LEXIS 281, at *7 (footnote omitted). " 'Final prospectus' . . . refers to a prospectus that meets the requirements of Section 10(a) of the [Securities] Act, whether as a stand-alone document as in the case of traditional offerings or as a combined base prospectus and prospectus supplement as is common in the case of shelf-registered offerings." *Id.* at *7 n.1.

42. The SEC adopted Exchange Act Rule 15c6-1 in February 1995, under which most securities transactions effected on or after June 7, 1995, are required to settle on the third business day (T + 3) after the transaction is executed. Prospectus Delivery; Securities Transactions Settlement, Exchange Act Release No. 35,396, 60 Fed. Reg. 10,724 (Feb. 27, 1995) (adopting releases and amendments for T + 3 settlement requirement). According to the requesting letter:

> [W]hile the rule currently exempts 'initial' sales by a broker-dealer participating in a firm commitment underwriting registered under the Act, the operational difficulties associated with a two-tiered settlement cycle will likely lead the Commission eventually to repeal this exemption. At that time the T + 3 requirement will place further pressure on the underwriter or dealer to find a means of delivering a prospectus that will enable him to deliver the required confirmation.

Brown & Wood, 1995 SEC No-Act. LEXIS 281, at *8.

43. The letter also noted that "the terms of modern securities transactions are frequently so complex as to cause the customer to desire as much as the underwriter or dealer that the transaction be confirmed as promptly as possible to reduce the risk of error and to expedite prompt settlement." *Id.* at *9.

under the various provisions of the Securities Act of 1933 (Securities Act).[44] Because the Securities Act does not specifically define or address the use of electronic prospectuses, the requesting letter derived its argument from the existing definition and interpretations of the word "prospectus" under the securities laws and by the SEC. Accordingly, the letter argued that an electronic prospectus should be considered a "written" prospectus inasmuch as the definition of "written" in section 2(9) of the Securities Act includes "graphic communications," and which the SEC, in Rule 405, has defined to include "magnetic impulses or other forms of computer data compilation."[45] The requesting letter also suggested that the requirement under the Securities Act that conditions the furnishing of a confirmation or supplemental sales literature to a customer on his or her being "sent or given" a prospectus was intended by Congress to focus on the transmittal, rather than receipt, of the prospectus.[46] It was argued, therefore, that an electronic prospectus that is transmitted to a customer's computer should be deemed to be "sent or given" without requisite proof that the customer actually received the envelope or read the prospectus.[47]

In its response letter, the SEC staff agreed that the term "prospectus" as defined and used in the Securities Act includes an electronic prospectus.[48] The staff also agreed that the transmission of an electronic prospectus to a customer would satisfy the Securities Act requirement that a prospectus be "sent or given" to a customer.[49] The response required, however, that users of electronic prospectuses include therein the same information found in the paper version of the prospectus, establish procedures to provide investors with an election to receive a prospectus (or future prospectuses) in electronic form, notify investors who have elected to receive an electronic prospectus of its availability, and provide investors with contin-

44. *Id.* at *10. In particular, it should be considered a prospectus as defined in § 2(10) and as referred to in §§ 5 and 10 of the Securities Act. Section 2(10) of the Securities Act defines prospectus, in part, as "any prospectus, notice, circular, advertisement, letter, or communication, written or by radio or television, which offers any security for sale or confirms the sale of any security." 15 U.S.C. § 77b(10) (1994).

45. *Brown & Wood*, 1995 SEC No-Act. LEXIS 281, at *11. Section 2(9) of the Securities Act states: "The term 'write' or 'written' shall include printed, lithographed, or any means of graphic communication." 15 U.S.C. § 77b(9) (1994). SEC Rule 405 (Definition of Terms) states: "The term *graphic communication*, which appears in the definition of 'write, written' in section 2(9) of the Securities Act, shall include magnetic impulses or other forms of computer data compilation." 17 C.F.R. § 230.405 (1996).

46. *Brown & Wood*, 1995 SEC No-Act. LEXIS 281, at *13. Section 2(10)(a) of the Securities Act conditions the furnishing of a confirmation or supplemental sale material upon a customer being sent or given a § 10 prospectus. 15 U.S.C. § 77b(10)(a) (1994); *see* McLaughlin, *supra* note 40, at 3.

47. *Brown & Wood*, 1995 SEC No-Act. LEXIS 281, at *13.

48. *Id.* at *4.

49. *Id.*

uous access to the electronic prospectus.[50] At the time of the staff's response to the *Brown & Wood* letter, the SEC stated its intent to review issues related to electronic delivery of prospectuses and other shareholder information in greater detail with a view toward providing further interpretive advice or proposed rulemaking.[51]

Interpretive Release

In October 1995, the SEC issued an interpretive release (October Interpretive Release)[52] that expressed its views on the electronic delivery of documents such as prospectuses, annual and semiannual reports, and proxy solicitation materials under the Securities Act, the Exchange Act,[53] and the Investment Company Act of 1940 (Investment Company Act).[54] In the interpretive release, which became effective upon its publication in the *Federal Register*, and expressly superseded the *Brown & Wood* no-action letter,[55] the SEC provided guidance to issuers (including corporations and mutual funds) and other market participants (including broker-dealers) on how they can meet their securities law obligations while delivering various types of documents to investors through electronic means. The release was intended to address the use by market participants of a broad range of electronic media, including audiotapes, videotapes, facsimiles, CD-ROM, electronic mail, electronic bulletin boards, and Internet Web sites.[56] It

50. *Id.* Although neither the requesting nor responding letters were specific to investment companies, the SEC staff indicated that the response letter applied to them. In the response letter, the staff specifically noted that investment companies should consider including an "item to be completed by the investor confirming that a prospectus has been sent or given to the investor electronically" in any application for the purchase of shares that is based on an electronically transmitted prospectus. *Id.* at *5. If the item is answered negatively by the purchaser, the investment company should immediately send a paper prospectus to the investor. *Id.*

51. *Id.*

52. October Interpretive Release, *supra* note 30, at 53,458.

53. 15 U.S.C. §§ 78a-78*ll* (1994 & West Supp. 1996).

54. *Id.* §§ 80a-1 to -64.

55. With respect to the continued application of the *Brown & Wood* letter, the SEC stated, "[w]hile the Commission anticipates that issuers and others will rely upon the guidance of this release, continued reliance on the generally more stringent requirements of the *Brown & Wood* letter is no longer required, but would be permissible." October Interpretive Release, *supra* note 30, at 53,459.

56. *Id.* at 53,458 n.9. Electronic bulletin board systems (BBSs) are available either inside or outside of the Internet. Internet BBSs are generally sites where various computer users can post a message or information free of charge on a particular subject. Other computer users can access the site and post responses or other information. In addition, the Internet supports the USENET system, which is like "a global message center. The messages are 'posted' in thousands of 'newsgroups' that are electronic versions of the old-fashioned pegboard bulletin boards." Gary Weiss, *Online Investing*, BUS. WK., June 5, 1995, at 64; *see also* ED KROL, THE WHOLE INTERNET USER'S GUIDE, SPECIAL EDITION 209-28 (1994). For non-Internet BBSs, one computer dials another similarly equipped computer, establishes a communications connection, and operates as a guest to that host computer. BBS software

covered a broad range of documents including prospectuses, annual reports, semiannual and quarterly reports, proxy and information statements, sales literature, advertisements, and tender offer materials.[57]

The SEC premised the interpretive release on several specific, well-grounded principles. The SEC acknowledged that federal securities laws do not preclude electronic delivery of prospectuses and other information.[58] As such, the SEC indicated that the interpretive release addressed *procedural* rather than substantive aspects of the federal securities laws.[59] Thus, according to the release, the interpretation does not affect rights and responsibilities of issuers and other market participants.[60] The SEC indicated in the release that it believed the use of electronic media should be at least an equal alternative to the use of paper-based media and "given the numerous benefits of electronic distribution of information and the fact that in many respects it may be more useful to investors than paper, its use should not be disfavored."[61] The SEC stated that the "release does not affect any applicable state laws or self-regulatory organization rules. Consequently, issuers and others need to consider the potential application of state law (e.g., state securities laws and business corporation laws) and other rules."[62]

In providing guidance and a degree of certainty with respect to electronic delivery of information for compliance with the federal securities laws, the SEC identified three factors that should be considered by market participants when providing electronic delivery.[63] The SEC indicated, however, that the identified factors "are not the *only* factors relevant to determining whether the legal requirements pertaining to delivery or transmission of documents have been satisfied."[64]

allows guests to access and run certain programs, read files, and download files directly to their computer over the telephone connection. The host's BBS software typically establishes the screen format, a menu of available capabilities/services, and limits access to parts of the host system to maintain a secure operating environment.

57. October Interpretive Release, *supra* note 30, at 53,458 n.9.

58. *Id.* at 53,460.

59. *Id.* at 53,459.

60. As an example, the SEC indicated that liability under the antifraud provisions of § 10(b) of the Securities Act would apply equally to information delivered in paper or electronic format. *Id.* at n.11. "As another example, section 17(b) of the Securities Act . . . would apply to any report circulated on the Internet just as if the report were provided in paper." *Id.* (citation omitted).

61. *Id.* at 53,458. The SEC also stated that it "appreciates the promise of electronic distribution of information in enhancing investors' ability to access, research, and analyze information, and in facilitating the provision of information by issuers and others." *Id.*

62. *Id,* at 53,459 n.11.

63. *Id.* at 53,460-61.

64. *Id.* at 53,460 (emphasis added). In addition, the SEC stated, "[i]f an issuer or third-party develops a method of electronic delivery that differs from those discussed below, but provides assurance comparable to paper delivery that the required information will be delivered, that method may satisfy delivery or transmission obligations." *Id.* Thus, "the ultimate responsibility for satisfying the applicable statutory requirements remains with the issuer or other party to whom the law assigns the responsibility." *Id.*

The first factor involved *notice of delivery*. The SEC stated that market participants who provide electronic delivery of information "should consider the extent to which the electronic communication provides timely and adequate notice to investors that information for them is available."[65] Moreover, electronic delivery requires that investors receive virtually the same level of notice that would be provided by paper delivery.[66] For example, the delivery of a document on a computer disk, CD-ROM, videotape, or electronic mail message to an investor would provide the investor with adequate notice.[67] If the document is provided on an Internet site, however, separate notice most likely would be necessary to inform the investor that the document is available at the site.[68]

The second factor constituted *access to electronic documents*. The SEC stated that investors who are provided information through electronic delivery should be provided with comparable access to the information as would be provided in the paper context.[69] Thus:

> the use of a particular medium [by a market participant] should not be so burdensome that intended recipients cannot effectively access the information provided. Moreover, as is the case with a paper document, a recipient should have the opportunity to retain the information or have ongoing access equivalent to personal retention.[70]

The third factor constituted *evidence of delivery*, i.e., evidence that the investor actually received the information in electronic format.[71] The release provided several examples of methods that could be used to satisfy the evidence of delivery requirement. For example, the receipt of a revocable informed consent from an investor to receive the electronic information through a particular electronic medium, coupled with assurances of appropriate notice and access, would satisfy the delivery requirement.[72] Accordingly, the consent should inform the investor that the information provided is available through a specified electronic medium or source, of the possibility that the investor might incur an expense, and of the period during and the documents for which the consent will be effective.[73] Market

65. *Id.*
66. *Id.*
67. *Id.*
68. *Id.*
69. *Id.*
70. *Id.* (footnotes omitted). Also, as part of its guidance, the SEC cautioned that paper versions of electronic documents should be kept on hand by issuers, given the possibilities of systems failures, computer incompatibilities, and situations in which investors who had requested electronic documents change their mind and request paper versions. *Id.* at 53,461.
71. *Id.*
72. *Id.* n.29.
73. *Id.* The October Interpretive Release also notes that

> [i]nformation may be provided through more than one medium; for example, proxy

participants could also establish a reasonable belief that investors received electronic information by using a delivery system which involves an electronic mail return receipt or a confirmation that the investors actually have accessed, downloaded, or printed the information. Furthermore, market participants could disseminate information through certain facsimile methods in order to satisfy evidence of delivery. Finally, the evidence of delivery requirement could be satisfied by allowing investors to access a document through a "hyperlink"[74] from another document.[75]

The release provided a series of fifty-two examples in the form of hypothetical fact situations to illustrate various applications of the SEC's concepts.[76] Twenty-two of the examples specifically related to mutual funds.[77] In a follow-up interpretive release, published in May 1996, the SEC provided seven additional examples clarifying certain examples in the October Interpretive Release in response to comments from industry groups and mutual funds.[78]

> statements and proxy cards might continue to be delivered in paper while prospectuses might be delivered electronically. If the recipient of information provides a general consent to receive *all* documents electronically, it would be permissible for a provider of information to attempt to accommodate that request if the provider so desired.

Id.

74. The term "hyperlink" generally means a link from one electronic document to another. Hyperlinks usually are indicated on an Internet site by colored text. If the person selects (i.e., points his or her mouse to, and clicks on) a hyperlink, he or she will be automatically transported to the material or site that is the object of the hyperlink. *See* KROL, *supra* note 56, at 53.

75. October Interpretive Release, *supra* note 30, at 53,461. The October Interpretive Release provides an example in which a company places its sales literature in a discussion forum located on the Internet and the sales literature contains a hyperlink to the company's final prospectus. *Id.* at 53,463. An investor who views the sales literature can use the hyperlink to instantaneously access the prospectus. According to the SEC, the final prospectus would be considered to have accompanied the sales literature and, consequently, the placing of sales literature in the Internet discussion forum would satisfy the company's delivery obligations, as long as the hyperlink provides direct access to the final prospectus. *Id.*

76. *Id.* at 53,461-67. Comment was specifically requested on whether other examples might be appropriate for publication in a subsequent release, on issues raised by the release, and on any other approaches or issues that should be considered in connection with facilitating the use of electronic media under the federal securities laws. *Id.* at 53,467.

77. *Id.* at 53,461-67.

78. May Interpretive Release, *supra* note 30, at 24,650-51; *see, e.g.,* Letter from Alexander C. Gavis, Assistant Counsel, Investment Company Institute to Jonathan G. Katz, Secretary, SEC (Nov. 22, 1995) [hereinafter Gavis Letter] (on file with *The Business Lawyer*, University of Maryland School of Law); Letter from S. Elliot Cohan, Senior Vice President, Federated Administrative Services, to Jonathan G. Katz, Secretary, SEC (Dec. 6, 1995) (on file with *The Business Lawyer*, University of Maryland School of Law); Letter from Sullivan & Cromwell to Jonathan G. Katz, Secretary, SEC (Dec. 4, 1995) (on file with *The Business Lawyer*, University of Maryland School of Law); Letter from Paula Drake, Legal Counsel, Fidelity Investments, to Jonathan G. Katz, Secretary, SEC (Nov. 21, 1995) (on file with *The Business Lawyer*, University of Maryland School of Law); Letter from John J. Brennan, President, The Vanguard Group, to Jonathan G. Katz, Secretary, SEC (Nov. 20, 1995) (on file with *The Business Lawyer*, University of Maryland School of Law).

SEC Guidance on Use of Electronic Media by Broker-Dealers, Investment Advisers, and Transfer Agents

SEC guidance with respect to broker-dealers', investment advisers', and transfer agents' use of electronic media also first occurred through the no-action process. The first two no-action letter responses in this area were issued by the SEC's Division of Market Regulation and involved the electronic delivery of confirmations for the purchase or sale of securities. These letters were followed by an interpretive release.

No-Action Guidance

In 1983, the staff was asked by the Depository Trust Corporation (DTC), a clearing agency for securities transactions registered under the Exchange Act, to provide no-action assurances that DTC could comply with the securities laws by transmitting copies of securities trading confirmations to institutional clients electronically.[79] Previously, DTC had transmitted confirmations for the purchase or sale of securities in paper format to its clients in compliance with Exchange Act Rule 10b-10.[80] The Division of Market Regulation staff granted DTC's request with few specific comments.[81]

Ten years later, a broker-dealer sought similar no-action relief for the electronic transmission of confirmations for the purchase or sale of securities to institutional clients. The requesting letter, submitted by a law firm on behalf of Thomson Financial Services, sought assurance from the SEC staff that it would not recommend enforcement action with respect to Thomson's electronic trade confirmation system, known as "OASYS Global."[82] OASYS was a post-trade confirmation network, whose subscribers included domestic and foreign broker-dealers and their institutional clients. The system provided broker-dealers and institutional investors with a means of electronically communicating from the time a securities order was executed to the time the trade was settled.

The requesting letter sought two specific types of relief. First, assurances were sought that OASYS Global's electronic confirmation messages could be treated as confirmations in accordance with Rule 10b-10 under the Exchange Act.[83] Second, the letter requested that electronic storage of

79. Depository Trust Co., SEC No-Action Letter, 1983 WL 30797 (S.E.C.), at *6, (Feb. 28, 1983) ("DTC is a clearing agency registered with the Commission under Section 17A of the [Exchange] Act. Among other things, DTC effects the transfer and pledge of securities by book-entry for participants and engages in the settlement of transactions in securities.").

80. Rule 10b-10 "requires broker-dealers to disclose specified information *in writing* to customers at or before the completion of a [securities] transaction." 17 C.F.R. § 240.10b-10 (1996) (emphasis added).

81. *Depository Trust Co.*, 1983 WL 30797 (S.E.C.) at *6.

82. Thompson Fin. Serv., Inc., SEC No-Action Letter, 1993 SEC No-Act. LEXIS 1241 (Oct. 8, 1993).

83. *Id.* at *20-*23.

such confirmation messages by broker-dealers and their clients be consistent with the recordkeeping requirements of the Exchange Act and the Investment Advisers Act of 1940 (Advisers Act).[84]

In granting the no-action request with respect to the delivery of electronic confirmations under Rule 10b-10, the Division of Market Regulation articulated several conditions of OASYS Global that were important to its decision, including: (i) an electronic confirmation could be printed or downloaded by the institutional customer, (ii) an institutional customer could respond affirmatively through the system to affirm or reject a trade, (iii) an electronic confirmation could not be deleted automatically by the system, and (iv) the system ensured that both sides of a securities transaction had the capacity to receive an electronic confirmation.[85] The response represented the first articulation by the SEC staff of the necessity of establishing procedural elements to be adhered to by market participants when delivering documents to investors through an electronic communications system.[86]

With respect to the request that electronic confirmation be allowed to be stored in electronic rather than in paper format, the staff of the Division of Market Regulation responded in a different fashion from the staff of the Division of Investment Management. The Division of Market Regulation staff stated that it was unable to assure that it would not recommend enforcement action if participants in the OASYS Global system electronically stored confirmations as a method of compliance with the Exchange Act's recordkeeping requirements.[87] The Division of Investment Management staff, however, granted no-action relief to investment advisers under

84. *Id.* Specifically, relief was sought under Exchange Act Rules 17a-3 and 17a-4, which provide a list of the various records that must be made and kept by certain exchange members and broker-dealers. 17 C.F.R. §§ 240.17a-3, 17a-4 (1996). Relief was also sought under Advisers Act Rule 204-2(a)(7), which provides, in relevant part, that a registered investment adviser shall keep and maintain true, accurate, and current originals of all written communications it receives relating to any receipt, disbursement, or delivery of funds or securities, or the placing or execution of any order to purchase or sell any security. 17 C.F.R. § 275.204-2(a)(7) (1996).

85. *Thomson Fin. Serv.*, 1993 SEC No-Act. LEXIS 1241, at *7-*8.

86. The SEC's views on the electronic delivery of confirmations stated in *Thomson Fin. Serv.* have been superseded by later interpretive pronouncements by the SEC. *See infra* notes 89-102 and accompanying text.

87. *Thomson Fin. Serv.*, 1993 SEC No-Act. LEXIS 1241, at *8. Since that time, the staff has granted no-action relief allowing for certain types of electronic storage of records by broker-dealers. *See* Optical Storage Tech., SEC No-Action Letter, 1993 WL 246230 (S.E.C.) (June 18, 1993) (permitting the optical storage of all paper records, including handwritten records, except those records required to be made under paragraphs (a)(6) and (a)(7) of Exchange Act Rule 17a-3, 17 C.F.R. § 240.17a-3(a)(6), (7) (1996) (proprietary and customer order tickets)). The Commission has proposed for comment amendments to the broker-dealer record preservation rules, which would permit broker-dealers to use, under certain conditions, optical storage technology to maintain records. *See* Reporting Requirements for Brokers or Dealers Under the Securities Exchange Act of 1934, Exchange Act Release No. 32,609, 58 Fed. Reg. 38,092 (July 15, 1993); May Interpretive Release, *supra* note 30, at 24,651.

the Advisers Act, and also went beyond the original request and granted relief to investment companies under the Investment Company Act, allowing them to maintain electronic confirmations when complying with recordkeeping requirements.[88]

Interpretive Release

Most recently, in May 1996, the SEC issued an interpretive release that provides broker-dealers, investment advisers, and transfer agents with further guidance in using various types of electronic media to satisfy their delivery requirements under the Exchange Act and the Advisers Act.[89] The release was intended to provide these entities with guidance on how they may deliver information electronically to clients and customers.[90] While the release became effective upon publication in the *Federal Register*, it also solicited comments from the public concerning the issues that it raised.[91]

Although the release does not specify the electronic medium that broker-dealers, investment advisers, or transfer agents may use, it provides a list of what it terms "Covered Delivery Requirements"—those rules or requirements under the Exchange Act and the Advisers Act allowing for the distribution of documents by broker-dealers, investment advisers, or trans-

88. *Thomson Fin. Serv.*, 1993 SEC No-Act. LEXIS 1241, at *3. With respect to investment advisers, the staff stated, "[r]egistered investment advisers that participate in OASYS Global must preserve [confirmations], whether received electronically or otherwise, in an accessible form in a manner that complies in all respects with rules under the Advisers Act." *Id.* at *10 n.7. The staff specifically cited Rule 204-2(g), 17 C.F.R. § 275.204-2(g) (1996), which allows investment advisers to produce or reproduce records in computer storage medium, and allows them to maintain and preserve records created or received on electronic media in a computer storage medium. *Thomson Fin. Serv.*, 1993 SEC No-Act. LEXIS 1241, at *10 n.7. With respect to investment companies, the staff noted that "registered investment companies . . . must preserve [the confirmations], whether received electronically or otherwise, in an accessible form in a manner that complies in all respects with rules under the 1940 Act." *Id.* at *10. The staff cited Rule 31a-2(f), 17 C.F.R. § 270.31a-2(f) (1996), which allows registered investment companies to produce or reproduce records on magnetic tape, disk, or other computer storage medium, and to maintain and preserve records created or received by or on behalf of investment companies on electronic media in a computer storage medium. *Thomson Fin. Serv.*, 1993 SEC No-Act. LEXIS 1241, at *10. For further background on the storage of electronic records by investment advisers, see First Call Corp., SEC No-Action Letter, 1995 SEC No-Act. LEXIS 693 (Sept. 6, 1995); Disclosure, Inc., SEC No-Action Letter, 1996 SEC No-Act. LEXIS (Aug. 22, 1996).

89. May Interpretive Release, *supra* note 30.

90. The release states that, because the SEC does not have the technological capacity to receive electronic transmissions of information from broker-dealers, transfer agents, or investment advisers, the interpretation does not apply to other requirements to file information with the SEC under the Exchange Act and the Advisers Act. *Id.* at 24,645 n.8.

91. *Id.*

fer agents—that may be subject to electronic delivery.[92] Of particular note, the release allows for the electronic delivery of confirmation statements under Exchange Act Rule 10b-10.[93]

The SEC generally applied the same basic principles that were articulated in the October Interpretive Release with respect to the activities of broker-dealers, investment advisers, and transfer agents. According to the SEC, these entities first should consider the extent to which electronic communication provides timely and adequate notice that such information is available electronically.[94] Second, similar to the October Interpretive Release, the release indicated that persons to whom information is sent electronically should be given access to information comparable to that which would have been provided if the information were delivered in paper form.[95] Third, if electronic delivery is used by broker-dealers, investment advisers, or transfer agents, they should have reason to believe that the electronically delivered information actually was received by the intended recipients.[96] According to the SEC, this can be achieved by (i) obtaining the intended recipient's informed consent to electronic delivery, and assuring that he or she has appropriate access and notice; (ii) obtaining actual evidence of receipt through, for example, a return receipt electronic mail message; or (iii) disseminating information through certain facsimile methods.[97]

The release also addressed the unique informational requirements of broker-dealers and investment advisers. The SEC indicated that, with respect to certain information that is specific to a person's "personal financial matters" (e.g., confirmation and account statements), broker-dealers and investment advisers "should take reasonable precautions to ensure the integrity, confidentiality, and security of that information, regardless of whether it is delivered through electronic means or in paper form."[98] In particular, the release requires that, before personal financial information can be transmitted electronically, an informed consent be obtained from

92. *Id.* at 24,649. The release lists the specific requirements that are covered. With respect to broker-dealers, it covers: (i) confirmations; (ii) account statements disclosing policies on payment for order flow; (iii) consents to hypothecation or pledge of customer securities; (iv) disclosure of control relationships with, or interests in, an issuer; and (v) in penny stock transactions, disclosure of bid and ask quotations, and broker-dealer and associated persons compensation. *Id.* at 24,648-49. With respect to investment advisers, it covers: (i) adviser brochures (Part II of Form ADV); (ii) consents to the assignment of advisory contracts; (iii) disclosure and consents for principal and agency cross transactions; (iv) disclosure about performance fee arrangements; (v) disclosure about custody of client assets; and (vi) disclosure and consent relating to cash solicitation arrangements. *Id.* at 24,649.

93. *Id.* at 24,648.

94. *Id.* at 24,646.

95. *Id.*

96. *Id.* at 24,647.

97. *Id.*

98. *Id.*

the investor.[99] The SEC apparently believes that a consent is necessary to ensure the intended recipient is willing to accept the delivery of such information through electronic media and has actual notice that the personal financial information will be delivered electronically.[100]

The electronic delivery of information that, in some cases, is being provided voluntarily by broker-dealers or investment advisers to customers and clients is not covered by the release and therefore does not have to comply with it. In this regard, the release stated that it is permissible for investment advisers to use various electronic media to disseminate advertisements for an investment adviser's services. The release noted, however, that, if an adviser uses a publicly available electronic medium, such as a Web site, to provide information about its services, the adviser may not qualify for the exemption from federal registration for persons with fewer than fifteen clients who do not hold themselves out to the public as advisers.[101]

In the release, the SEC did not address directly issues related to the uses of electronic mail by broker-dealers or investment advisers to communicate with clients and customers. Instead, the SEC indicated that regulation of these electronic communications should be based on the content and audience of the message, and not merely on the electronic form of the communication, and noted that the SROs should provide guidance in this area.[102]

SEC Guidance on Use of Electronic Media for Bulletin Board-Based Trading Systems

Thousands of public corporations have established Internet sites that generally advertise their products, provide customer information, and, on occasion, mention information related to the issuers' publicly traded stock. As of this writing, two corporate issuers have used the Internet for another purpose that is both innovative and far-reaching under the federal securities laws. Each issuer has developed an electronic bulletin board trading

99. *Id.* The consent may be made either by a manual signature or by electronic means. *Id.* at 24,647 n.23.

100. *Id.*

101. *Id.* at 15-16. Section 203(b)(3) of the Advisers Act exempts from registration requirements "any investment adviser who during the course of the preceding twelve months has had fewer than fifteen clients and who neither holds himself out generally to the public as an investment adviser nor acts as an investment adviser to any investment company registered under subchapter I of this Act." 15 U.S.C. § 80b-3(b)(3) (1994).

102. May Interpretive Release, *supra* note 30, at 24,645 n.5. For a discussion of industry concerns with respect to the SEC's May Interpretive Release, and the regulation of electronic mail, see Letter from Alexander C. Gavis, Assistant Counsel, Investment Company Institute, to Jonathan G. Katz, Secretary, SEC (June 10, 1996) (on file with *The Business Lawyer*, University of Maryland School of Law); Letter from C. Evan Stewart and Kenneth S. Spirer, Securities Industry Association to Jonathan G. Katz, Secretary, SEC (July 26, 1996) (on file with *The Business Lawyer*, University of Maryland School of Law).

system that allows the public to trade shares in the issuer over the Internet. In both cases, the SEC issued no-action letters to the issuers that specified a series of conditions that must be met in order for the issuers' trading systems to comply with federal securities laws.

In February 1995, Spring Street Brewing Company, a small New York-based microbrewery,[103] sponsored an initial public offering that raised approximately $1.6 million. The publicly offered shares were registered with the SEC and with twenty-two states. What was unique about the offering was that the company established an Internet site in which investors could review the offering documents and place an order to purchase shares. In order to complete a purchase transaction, however, investors were required to send a check and a signed agreement to purchase the shares by regular mail. Subsequent to the public offering, Spring Street launched an electronic bulletin board system at its Internet site, called Wit-Trade, that allows buyers and sellers to meet and sell shares of the company.[104] Wit-Trade is comprised of two bulletin boards, one that contains listings of buyers and the prices they are willing to pay for shares of Spring Street, and one that contains sellers with the prices they are willing to accept to sell their shares. Trading occurs when buyers and sellers contact each other via electronic mail and agree to a trade, which is then documented on a contract, digitally provided by Spring Street.[105] The parties to a trade then send a check and stock certificates through regular mail to Spring Street, which completes the transaction.[106] Within several weeks of operation, the SEC asked Spring Street to suspend its trading system until the SEC staff had an opportunity to determine whether the system complied with the federal securities laws.[107]

103. The company manufactures and sells Wit, Amber Wit, and Black Wit Beer, a Belgian-type beer. *See* Hal Lux, *Beer brewer now plans on-line investment bank*, INV. DEALERS' DIG., Apr. 8, 1996, at 10; *Firm Halts Trading Stock on Internet—Experiment Shelved Pending SEC Study*, WASH. POST, Mar. 21, 1996, at B11; Harriett Magee, *Investors Belly Up to Net* (visited May 15, 1996) <http://www.corpfinet.com>.

104. Spring Street Brewing Co., *Wit-Trade* (visited Apr. 24, 1996) <http://plaza.interport.net/witbeer/index.html> ("This site contains Wit-Trade, the bulletin board based market mechanism through which the Common Stock of Spring Street Brewing Company publicly trades.").

105. "Wit-Trade provides an Offer and Acceptance Form so that parties who have agreed to trade can easily document their agreement. In addition, the Offer and Acceptance Form carefully spells out a simple procedure by which parties can conclude their trading transactions." *Id.*

106. *Id.* According to Wit-Trade's Internet site as of June 1, 1996:

> [A]lthough the stock market mechanism enables prospective buyers and sellers to meet, it is not a matching service. On the contrary, under the mechanism prospective traders must initiate direct communication with prospective trading parties they find on the bulletin boards. Through e-mail, telephone or otherwise, the parties must then negotiate directly until they agree to buy or sell shares at a particular price or not at all.

Id.

107. *Firm Halts Trading Stock on Internet*, *supra* note 103, at B11.

In a letter made available publicly in April 1996, the staff of the SEC's Divisions of Corporation Finance and Market Regulation detailed concerns about the operation of Wit-Trade.[108] The letter recognized that "Wit-Trading is an innovative mechanism that has the potential to provide Company shareholders with greater liquidity in their investments."[109] The letter went on to state several concerns with the trading system, however, including "that investors' funds and securities be handled appropriately, that investors understand the risks involved in purchasing illiquid and speculative securities, that buyers are aware of last sale prices and that investors are provided with ongoing disclosure about the Company."[110]

With respect to these concerns, the staff set forth a series of conditions that it believed to be appropriate for Spring Street and Wit-Trade to follow in order to comply with federal securities laws. First, the staff indicated that "[a]ccess to and control of investor funds must be handled carefully to provide investors using [the system] with adequate protections."[111] Because Wit-Trade was not registered as a broker-dealer under the federal securities laws, it should modify its system to eliminate the company's control over these funds and allow for an independent agent, such as a bank or escrow agent, to receive checks from payors.[112] Second, the staff stated that, to prevent customer confusion about the role of the system, Wit-Trade should supplement the information currently provided by adding information that is particularly relevant to first-time investors, including information about the risks of investing in inherently illiquid securities.[113] Third, "[u]sers of the system should be informed that if they choose to post quotations simultaneously on both the Buyer and Seller Bulletin Boards they may be considered a 'dealer' that is required to register and comply with broker-dealer requirements under the federal securities laws."[114] Finally, the staff indicated that it views the sale of securities through the Wit-Trade system as involving an offer or sale by Spring Street for the purposes of the Securities Act, and absent an exemption,

108. Spring Street Brewing Co., SEC No-Action Letter, 1996 SEC No-Act. LEXIS 435 (Apr. 17, 1996).

109. The staff also stated that "[i]nnovation and creativity are the hallmark of our nation's securities markets, contributing enormously to the most efficient capital formation system in the world." *Id.* at *1. It cautioned, however, that although the staff tries to encourage such modernization, "it is our job, first and foremost, to insure protections for public investors." *Id.*

110. *Id.* at *2.

111. *Id.*

112. *Id.* at *2-*3 In addition, investors should send their checks directly to the independent agent, rather than to Spring Street. *Id.*

113. *Id.* at *3.

114. *Id.* The staff also stated its opinion that "a transaction history would allow investors to make more informed investment decisions [and that] the price and number of shares for recent transactions should be disclosed through the system." *Id.* at *3-*4.

the system should register under the Securities Act.[115] The staff indicated, however, that the system might be eligible to use the Regulation A exemption from registering.[116] Spring Street has stated in a press release that it will modify the Wit-Trading system in order to conform its activities with the positions expressed in the SEC staff letter and submit a no-action letter request for regulatory clearance.[117]

In June 1996, a second issuer submitted a no-action request to the SEC that proposed the formation of an Internet trading system for the issuer's stock. In its letter to the SEC, Real Goods Trading Corporation (RGTC), a California mail-order retailer of conservation products including solar-powered devices, sought no-action relief to be permitted to establish a passive "bulletin board" trading system on the Internet for its publicly traded stock.[118] The proposed trading system would make certain information available to the public via RGTC's Internet site, including the identities of interested purchasers and sellers of stock and number of shares and prices offered for sale or desired to be purchased. RGTC would not have any role in effecting transactions between participants in the system; instead, participants would transmit their trading information to RGTC's Internet site by electronic mail and would then negotiate and complete transactions through direct contact.[119] RGTC requested that the SEC allow it to operate the electronic trading system without:

> (i) RGTC registering as an "investment adviser" under Section 203(a) of the Advisers Act; (ii) RGTC . . . registering as a "broker" and/or "dealer" under Section 15(a) of the Exchange Act; (iii) the registration of the System as a "national securities exchange" under Section 6 of

115. Specifically, the staff stated, "Absent an available exemption, Spring Street would be required to register under the Securities Act and undertake to keep the registration statement 'evergreen' during the existence of Wit-Trade." *Id.*

116. Regulation A generally provides an exemption for certain issuers who conduct securities offerings that have an aggregate offering price of less than $5 million. *See* Regulation A—Conditional Small Issuer Exemption, 17 C.F.R. § 230.251 to -263 (1996).

117. *See SEC Addresses Concerns Tied to Spring Street Brewing's Wit-Trade,* NO-ACTION LETTER WEEKLY, Apr. 22, 1996, at 1.

118. The letter stated that trading in RGTC's stock "is extremely light and the market for it is very illiquid." Real Goods Trading Corp., SEC No-Action Letter, 1996 WL 422670 (S.E.C.) (June 24, 1996); *see also* Jeffrey Taylor, *SEC to Allow Firm to Run Market for Its Own Shares on the Web Bulletin Board,* WALL ST. J., June 27, 1996, at B12.

119. The letter also stated that

> Neither RGTC nor any affiliate of RGTC will (i) receive any compensation for creating or maintaining the System; (ii) receive any compensation for the use of the System; (iii) be involved in any purchase or sale negotiations arising from the System; (iv) give advice regarding the merits or shortcomings of any particular trade; (v) use the System, directly or indirectly, to offer to buy or sell securities, except in compliance with the securities laws[;] . . . or (vi) receive, transfer or hold funds or securities as an incident of operating the System.

Real Goods Trading Corp., 1996 WL 422670 (S.E.C.), at *2.

the Exchange Act; or (iv) registering offers and sales made through the System under the Securities Act.[120]

In granting no-action relief from these provisions, staff of the SEC's Divisions of Corporation Finance, Market Regulation, and Investment Management specified certain conditions that must be followed by RGTC. Accordingly, RGTC must not, among other things, (i) receive any compensation for the creation, maintenance, or use of the system; (ii) become involved in any purchase or sale negotiations arising from the system; (iii) provide information regarding the advisability of buying or selling securities; or (iv) receive, transfer, or hold funds or securities as an incident of operating the system.

Since issuing the *Spring Street* and *Real Goods Trading Corporation* no-action letters, the SEC staff has granted similar no-action relief to another corporate issuer[121] and to a brokerage firm that has proposed to establish a trading system to sell private placement securities through an Internet site called "IPONet."[122] In each case to date, the SEC staff has required that the issuer or brokerage firm comply with a rigorous set of conditions in order to obtain no-action relief—the most important of which appears to be that the issuer or brokerage firm not participate actively in the trading system. It is also interesting to note that each of the proposed Internet trading systems has involved the trading of relatively illiquid securities. The SEC staff letters appear to be a good first step in providing guidance to corporate issuers who seek to facilitate trading in their securities. If other (perhaps larger) issuers, however, find that it is beneficial to establish Internet trading systems for their own securities,[123] it may be worthwhile for the SEC to publish an interpretive regulatory release, as opposed to responding to no-action requests, in order to establish appropriate regulatory standards.[124]

120. *Id.* at *4.

121. Perfect Data Corp., SEC No-Action Letter, 1996 SEC No-Act. LEXIS (Aug. 5, 1996). Perfect Data Corp. is a public company that sells computer cleaning products and accessories.

122. IPONET, SEC No-Action Letter, 1996 SEC No-Act. LEXIS 642 (July 26, 1996); *see also* Hal Lux, *Another start-up looks to do IPOs on the Internet*, INV. DEALERS' DIG., July 22, 1996, at 7 ("Web IPO-Capital Formation Group joins a growing group of online companies that plan to use the World Wide Web to sell initial public offerings to investors."); Kimberly Weisul, *Web-based underwriters form trade association*, INV. DEALERS' DIG., July 22, 1996, at 9.

123. Larger issuers might, for example, establish a bulletin board trading system in conjunction with a dividend reinvestment program.

124. The recently enacted NSMIA contains a section that provides the SEC with authority to exempt any person, security, or transactions from the Securities Act and Exchange Act and the rules thereunder (except for provisions regarding government securities broker-dealers) to the extent that such exemption is necessary or appropriate in the public interest and consistent with the protections of investors. *See* H.R. 3005, 104th Cong. § 105 (1996). It is possible that the SEC could use its new authority to provide exemptive relief under the Securities Act and the Exchange Act to certain issuer-sponsored Internet trading systems, instead of responding to no-action letters.

Electronic Filing and Retrieval of SEC Documents

For the past ten years, the SEC has overseen the development of a massive electronic database of documents that have been filed publicly by corporate issuers under the federal securities laws. Today, practically every issuer registered under the federal securities laws must file its documents through the Electronic Data Gathering and Analysis (EDGAR) system.[125] In addition, the SEC now makes the vast EDGAR database of corporate filings available to the public through the Internet. By making EDGAR filings available to the public, the SEC has essentially created a new distribution channel for publicly filed documents. It is now possible, for example, for investors to obtain, without much difficulty,[126] a copy of a prospectus or annual report of a public company without ever contacting the company.

The EDGAR system has had a relatively bumpy history, one that has been punctuated by delayed implementation, cost overruns, and criticism by Congress and corporate issuers. Over the past year, the EDGAR system has come under increased scrutiny by the SEC[127] and Congress.[128] This has been a result of several factors, including the 1997 expiration of the contract to implement the EDGAR system and the recent increase in use

125. *Final Registrant Phase-in of EDGAR Nears Completion,* MUTUAL FUNDS GUIDE (CCH) 705 (Apr. 29, 1996). According to one source, "The SEC receives more than 2.5 million documents in a heavy year. . . . [T]he number of filers in 1996 will be approximately 15,000. The average size of document filed on EDGAR is 42 pages long. Approximately 10 million pages per year are filed on EDGAR." REPORT PREPARED BY REPRESENTATIVE DAN FRISA FOR REPRESENTATIVE JACK FIELDS, CHAIRMAN SUBCOMMITTEE ON TELECOMMUNICATIONS AND FINANCE, WHAT'S UP WITH EDGAR? THE PROSPECTS FOR PRIVATIZING THE SEC'S ELECTRONIC DATA GATHERING, ANALYSIS, AND RETRIEVAL SYSTEM (EDGAR) 25 (Feb. 28, 1996) [hereinafter FRISA REPORT] (on file with *The Business Lawyer*, University of Maryland School of Law).

126. Before the EDGAR database became available on the Internet, an investor could have obtained a copy of a publicly filed document either from the SEC's public reference room or through a commercial information service provider.

127. The SEC has undertaken three major initiatives to solicit ideas on how it should proceed with EDGAR, including: (i) holding an SEC EDGAR Technology Conference in August 1995, in which it solicited private sector views on how EDGAR can be improved; (ii) arranging a panel in December 1995 of nationally recognized industry and academic experts to examine a wide range of ways to redesign EDGAR; and (iii) publishing two Requests for Information in the Federal Register that solicited public comments on how to improve the EDGAR filing process. EDGAR Request For Information, Exchange Act Release No. 36,683, 61 Fed. Reg. 740 (Jan. 10, 1996).

128. Significant congressional attention to EDGAR occurred recently when Congressman Jack Fields, Chairman of the House Subcommittee on Telecommunications and Finance, introduced securities legislation that, among other things, directed the SEC to request proposals for the privatization of EDGAR and to submit a report to Congress on its findings. *See* H.R. 2131, 104th Cong. § 10 (1995); H.R. 3005, 104th Cong. § 107 (1996). Congressman Jack Fields also requested that Congressman Dan Frisa conduct an investigation and report on the EDGAR system. *See* FRISA REPORT, *supra* note 125.

of electronic communications systems such as the Internet by corporate issuers and the public.

Upon the adoption of an integrated disclosure system for corporate issuers in 1982,[129] the SEC began focusing its attention on how electronic technologies might be applied in the context of the filing and retrieval of corporate filings. The integrated disclosure system, which provided for a uniform disclosure system under the Securities Act and Exchange Act, established a new database framework for filed information. By the early 1980s, a number of document retrieval companies were employed by investors to retrieve documents from the SEC's Public Document Room, which resulted in a cumbersome and costly process. The SEC came to the conclusion that it should develop an electronic system that would automate the filing, analysis, and dissemination of documents filed with the SEC.[130] Accordingly, it was determined that the emerging database of corporate filings should be made easily and cheaply available to the public. The SEC established a task force to study the various means by which the SEC could achieve electronic acceptance, processing, and dissemination of corporate filings and, in March 1984, it published a release requesting comments on a pilot program to establish EDGAR.[131]

The EDGAR system was developed through a series of contracts between the SEC and private sector firms. The system originally was designed and implemented through a two-year pilot program (from 1984 to 1986), which lasted until 1989 and cost the SEC, according to one esti-

129. *See* Adoption of Integrated Disclosure System, Securities Act Release No. 6383, 47 Fed. Reg. 11,380 (Mar. 3, 1982).

130. According to SEC Chairman John Shad, who oversaw the initial development of the EDGAR system, the four principle reasons for EDGAR were:

> First, to enhance investor protections through broad, quick access to corporate information. Second, to accelerate the preparation and transmission of such information by companies to the Commission. Third, to reduce errors by eliminating the frequent need to transfer data manually from one format to another. And fourth, to enable the Commission staff to process and analyze filings more efficiently at computer work stations.

FRISA REPORT, *supra* note 125, at 13-14 (quoting testimony of SEC Chairman John Shad).

131. Electronic Filing, Processing and Information Dissemination System, Securities Act Release No. 6519, [1983-1984 Transfer Binder] Fed. Sec. L. Rep. (CCH) ¶ 83,600, at 86,684 (Mar. 22, 1984). In its release, the SEC boldly stated:

> Technological developments have revolutionized information analysis and distribution in the financial community. The traditional paper-supported system of data processing and reporting is being replaced by sophisticated electronic communication and data management systems. Computer literacy, instant data retrieval and electronic mail are having a profound impact on information gathering and dissemination.

Id. at 86,685. The central component of the SEC's EDGAR rules is Regulation S-T, 17 C.F.R. §§ 232.10 to .903 (1996), a separate regulation containing rules prescribing requirements for filing electronically and the procedures for making such filings. Rulemaking for EDGAR System, Securities Act Release No. 6977, 58 Fed. Reg. 14,628 (Mar. 18, 1993).

mate, over $28 million.[132] The SEC next entered an eight-year operational contract in 1989. As of May 1996, all domestic registrants were required to file electronically through EDGAR. Thus, it has taken twelve years for the SEC to develop a stand-alone computer filing system that includes all the necessary hardware, software, applications, maintenance, and assistance.[133]

As a practical matter, the EDGAR system consists of three major subsystems: (i) receipt and acceptance of filings, (ii) internal SEC analysis and review of the filings, and (iii) dissemination of the filings to the public. With respect to the receipt and acceptance of filings, the EDGAR system has been criticized as significantly lagging behind developments in electronic communications. Presently, in order to file a document with the SEC through EDGAR, an issuer must conduct a series of steps to put the document in "EDGARized format." This involves converting the document into ASCII[134] text and inserting special "marker tags," which flag key format and content information for EDGAR processing. The filing is then transmitted by tape, diskette, or a direct modem link to the SEC or to an account designated for filings with CompuServe.

The EDGAR system cannot currently accommodate graphics or multimedia information that has been incorporated into a document. For the purpose of filing, issuers must describe, in text, the content of any such information that may be contained in a document provided to the public.[135] Many mutual funds, for example, include pictures, symbols, and charts in their paper documents that describe their investment programs and related risks.[136] The use of the Internet by funds and other market participants further enhances their ability to display such material in

132. *See* U.S. General Accounting Office, Pub. No. IMTEC87-31, Lessons Learned from SEC's EDGAR Pilot Test (Aug. 1987).

133. Frisa Report, *supra* note 125, at 6.

134. ASCII is the abbreviation for "American Standard Code for Information Interchange." According to one source, it "is a comparatively standard scheme for translating bytes—represented in a computer as a string of ones and zeros—into the characters of an alphabet. It's a lowest-common-denominator standard for exchanging simple text files." Allison, *supra* note 6, at 329.

135. Along with the May Interpretive Release, the SEC also issued final rule amendments that made technical changes to certain SEC rules and forms to address the use of electronic media by issuers. The SEC's rules that prescribe the physical appearance of a paper document were amended to provide that an issuer, when delivering an electronic document, may comply with the requirements by presenting the information in a format readily communicated to investors. In addition, the SEC amended Rule 304 of Regulation S-T, 17 C.F.R. § 232.304 (1996), to provide that whenever a document delivered to investors or others includes graphic, image, or audio information that cannot be reproduced in an EDGAR filing, the EDGAR filing must include a fair and accurate narrative description, tabular presentation, or transcript of the omitted material. *See* Adopting Release, *supra* note 30.

136. In addition, all mutual funds are required to include a performance graph in their annual report or prospectus comparing total return of the fund to a broad-based securities market index over a specified time period. *See* SEC Form N-1A, Item 5A(b).

graphic format and to include multimedia information (e.g., video and audio images) in documents. Because the EDGAR system only accepts filings in ASCII text format, many issuers must prepare at least two versions of every filed document—the version produced for publication and dissemination to investors and the ASCII version for filing. Thus, current requirements that all EDGAR documents be formatted in ASCII text, and that graphic and multimedia material be summarized, pose significant problems for issuers as they begin to develop sophisticated documents for use on the Internet.[137]

The irony is that virtually all of the types of documents that must be reformatted and filed on EDGAR are landing on the Internet.[138] With increasing use of the Internet by issuers, it will become especially important that the SEC address issues related to the EDGAR system technology. If the EDGAR system is not capable of keeping pace with advances in electronic communications, it will pose a significant technological drag on issuers and ultimately will harm investors.

The process in which documents are disseminated to the public by the EDGAR system also has been criticized by Congress and the public. Under the current dissemination system, two private firms have been awarded the sole contractual rights to disseminate SEC filings on a real-time basis: one owns the exclusive rights to disseminate EDGAR data,[139] and the other owns the sole commercial rights to provide microfiche, CD-ROM, and an online, value-added EDGAR service.[140] The SEC's Web site provides public access to EDGAR filings; however, dissemination of data is

137. For a more detailed discussion of these issues, see, for example, Gavis Letter, *supra* note 78; Letter from Alexander C. Gavis, Assistant Counsel, Investment Company Institute, to Jonathan G. Katz, Secretary, SEC (Mar. 11, 1996) (comment letter on SEC's request for information on EDGAR filing system) (on file with *The Business Lawyer*, University of Maryland School of Law).

138. This is especially evident with a recent rule adopted by the SEC. If a mutual fund intends to disseminate its prospectus electronically and is an electronic filer, it must now include a statement on the cover of its prospectus that the SEC "maintains a Web site (http://www.sec.gov) that contains the Statement of Additional Information, material incorporated by reference, and other information regarding registrants that file electronically with the Commission." Adopting Release, *supra* note 30, at *12.

139. The *Frisa Report* noted:

> After Receipt and Acceptance, filings automatically become public and are passed from the SEC Operations Center to *Lexis-Nexis* who use a subcontractor, *General Electronic* to provide the approved electronic filings to anyone who subscribes. . . . Prices are set by *Lexis*, but they are regulated by the SEC to ensure there is no cross subsidization between *Lexis'* commercial activities and the Dissemination subsystem. . . . There are at least 14 companies who resell EDGAR data as part of a value added package.

FRISA REPORT, *supra* note 125, at 28.

140. "*Disclosure* enjoys a monopoly on the history of all filings before EDGAR's electronic filings began in 1993. *Disclosure* turns all the documents filed in the public document room into a CD ROM product which it leases to clients, and it also sells an electronic online feed." *Id.*

on a twenty-four hour-delayed basis.[141] It has been suggested, among other things, that the SEC allow for competition between several private companies to provide both filing and dissemination services, or that it consider the feasibility of allowing a dissemination free-for-all in which the SEC provides real-time, free Internet access to EDGAR data and any person could then process and package the information in any way they chose.[142] Finally, recently passed federal legislation requires the SEC to examine proposals for the privatization of EDGAR and to submit a report on this examination not later than 180 days after the enactment of the legislation.[143]

SEC Enforcement Initiatives

With increasing use of the Internet by market participants to offer and distribute securities, the SEC has devoted a portion of its enforcement resources to monitoring the Internet for instances of securities law violations. Several SEC enforcement lawyers have been assigned to "surf" the Internet and various electronic bulletin boards on a part-time basis to search for possible securities law violations.[144] In addition, the SEC has established an "Enforcement Complaint Center" (Center) on its Web site. The Center allows the public to communicate through electronic mail with the SEC's Division of Enforcement regarding possible instances of secu-

141. In 1993, the National Science Foundation gave a grant to New York University and Internet Multicasting to set up a free Web site for EDGAR data. In October 1995, as a result of insufficient funds to keep the project going, the SEC took over responsibility for making EDGAR data available on the Internet and incorporated the database into its Web site, <http://www.sec.gov>. *See* Mark H. Anderson & Jared Sandberg, *SEC Unveils Internet Site To Give Access to Filings,* WALL ST. J., Aug. 28, 1995, at C15; *SEC Unveils Internet Site To Give Access to Filings,* WALL ST. J., Sept. 29, 1995, at B4. With respect to public access to EDGAR data through the Internet, SEC Chairman Levitt stated:

> One of the main reasons the SEC was created was to act as a library for corporate information and make it available to investors. . . . Technology is so advanced that the cost to the Commission is quite modest. With a personal computer and modem, you'll be able to have the entire SEC Public Reference Room in your own living room.

Arthur Levitt, Jr., Chairman, SEC, An Address to the National Association of Investors Corp. (Aug. 27, 1995), *reprinted in SEC Chairman Arthur Levitt Details Agency Plans to Make Database Widely Available,* SEC PRESS RELEASE 95-175, 1995 WL 505904, Aug. 27, 1995, at *1.

142. FRISA REPORT, *supra* note 125, at 7.

143. H.R. 3005, 104th Cong. § 106 (1996).

144. *See* Susan Antilla, *Has Cyberspace Got a Deal for You!,* N.Y. TIMES, Mar. 19, 1995, at 5; Patrick McGeehan, *Business Deals on the Internet Hard to Regulate,* USA TODAY, Jan. 31, 1996, at A1. Other regulators have also begun to patrol the Internet actively for securities scams, including the NASD and state securities regulators. Kimberly Blanton, *SEC Targets Investment Claim in On-Line Probe,* BOSTON GLOBE, Aug. 8, 1995, at 39; Jerry Knight, *Tracking Stock Cyberscams—NASD Regulators Go On-Line to Warn Investors of Dangers,* WASH. POST., Aug. 23, 1996, at F1. For a discussion of the enforcement activities by state securities regulators, see *infra* notes 211-222.

rities fraud. The SEC also has published a series of public bulletins at its Web site that warn investors of various emerging securities fraud schemes via the Internet, including pyramid schemes and "pump and dump" scams.[145] As of this writing, the SEC's enforcement actions related to the Internet generally have involved defendants who used the Internet to sell nonexistent, unregistered, or worthless securities.

One of the earliest Internet enforcement actions was brought by the SEC in March 1995. The SEC filed a complaint in federal court against Pleasure Time, Inc., and several of its employees, requesting a temporary restraining order, a permanent injunction, and civil penalties. The SEC's complaint alleged that the defendants participated in a fraudulent sales scheme involving unregistered securities that were offered and sold to approximately 20,000 investors raising over $3 million. According to the SEC, investors were recruited through a pyramid scheme which involved solicitations by telephone, facsimile, the Internet, and other computer networks. Investors allegedly were told they would reap enormous profits from a worldwide telephone lottery run by a Native American tribe, with projected receipts of $300 million, and which supposedly was going to use a 900 telephone number to attract players. The SEC alleged that the defendants violated the antifraud and registration provisions of the federal securities laws[146] because they "understated and failed to disclose legal, regulatory and technical obstacles to starting a lottery" to potential investors.[147] The federal district court entered a temporary restraining order, which included a freeze of assets.[148]

A second case involving the Internet was brought in August 1995 and concerned an attempt by Daniel Odulo, a nineteen year-old "entrepreneur," to use the Internet to sell bonds in an allegedly legitimate business that would capture baby eels off the eastern United States, raise them in captivity, and then sell them to the public.[149] Odulo called his business "Golden Waters Productions" and estimated the business would need $500,000 in start-up capital. He wrote and posted a solicitation for inves-

145. *See* U.S. Sec. & Exch. Comm'n, *Commission Opens Enforcement Complaint Center on the Internet* (last modified June 14, 1996) <http://www.sec.gov/news/newenf.html>; U.S. Sec. & Exch. Comm'n, *Investment Fraud and Abuse Travel to . . . Cyberspace* (last modified June 12, 1996) <http://www.sec.gov/consumer/cyberfr.html>.

146. In particular, the company was charged with violating §§ 5(a), 5(c), and 17(a) of the Securities Act, 15 U.S.C. §§ 77e(a), 77e(c), 77q(a) (1994), and §§ 10(b), 15(a)(1), and 15(c)(1) of the Exchange Act, 15 U.S.C. §§ 78j(b), 78*o*(a)(1), 78*o*(c)(1) (1994), and Rules 10b-5 and 15c1-2, 17 C.F.R. §§ 240.10b-5, 240.15c1-2 (1995), thereunder. SEC v. Pleasure Time, Inc., Litigation Release No. 14,825, 1996 SEC No-Act. LEXIS 510 (S.D. Ohio Feb. 26, 1996).

147. *Pleasure Time*, 1996 SEC No-Act. LEXIS, at *1.

148. *Id.*

149. SEC v. Odulo, Civ. Action No. 95-424P, 1995 WL 505138 (D.R.I. Aug. 24, 1995); *see* Robertson, *supra* note 9, at 402-03.

tors with two Internet newsgroups.[150] The solicitation sought investors for a $500,000 offering of $1000 denomination bonds and stated the bonds would yield a "whopping 20% rate of return" and were a "very low risk investment."[151] The solicitation also stated that interest on the bonds would be compounded semiannually, that payment on the bonds would not be made until three years after their purchase by investors, and that Golden Waters "insures all of its products against any possible loss."[152] Finally, it provided the names and endorsements of several fictitious investment advisers. Odulo apparently never sold any of the bonds.

The SEC's complaint alleged that Odulo's solicitation and business plan contained false and misleading statements, including the fact that Golden Waters was not an ongoing business, that Odulo had no experience in raising eels, that there was no insurance against loss, and that the endorsements were fabricated. The SEC sought a permanent injunction and civil penalties against Odulo for violating the antifraud and registration provisions of the federal securities laws. Without admitting or denying the allegations, Odulo consented to an injunction against violating the securities laws.[153]

The SEC has brought several other enforcement actions against individuals who have used Internet bulletin boards or newsgroups to solicit investors for fraudulent offering schemes. These cases include the offering of prime bank instruments, "hard currency" bonds, and shares in Costa Rican businesses through the Internet.[154] The Costa Rican case, for example, involved a defendant who allegedly posted numerous messages on bulletin boards to lure investors with the promise of riskless profits and above-average returns from investments in two Costa Rican coconut plantations. As part of the scheme, the defendant apparently falsely represented that one of the companies had a major distribution contract for its products with A&P Supermarkets and that a bank had guaranteed investors' prin-

150. "Newsgroups" are "discussion groups [that are] similar to public bulletin boards—in which participants come to a common location to read and post messages. There are newsgroups on thousands of topics." ALLISON, *supra* note 6, at 336. Odulo posted the solicitations on the "misc.invest" (a newsgroup devoted to the discussion of investing) and "alt.make.money.fast" newsgroups (a newsgroup devoted to describing schemes in which to make money).

151. *Odulo,* 1995 WL 505138, at *1.

152. *Id.*

153. The payment of civil penalties by Odulo, however, were waived by the court due to his inability to pay. *Id.*

154. *See* SEC v. Frye, Litigation Release No. 14,720, 60 S.E.C. Docket (CCH) 1787 (S.D.N.Y. Nov. 15, 1995) (Costa Rican business); SEC v. Block, Litigation Release No. 14,598, 59 S.E.C. Docket (CCH) 2543 (D. Mass. Aug. 10, 1995); SEC v. Block, Litigation Release No. 14,711, 60 S.E.C. Docket (CCH) 1608 (D. Mass. Nov. 2, 1995); SEC v. Block, Litigation Release No. 14,804, 61 S.E.C. Docket (CCH) 579 (D. Mass. Jan. 30, 1996); SEC v. Block, Litigation Release No. 14,828, 61 S.E.C. Docket (CCH) 971 (D. Mass. Feb. 27, 1996) ("Prime bank" instruments); SEC v. Octagon Tech. Group, Litigation Release No. 14,942, 62 S.E.C. Docket (CCH) 380 (D.D.C. June 11, 1996) ("Hard currency" bonds).

cipal and fifteen percent interest for a one-year investment. The SEC sought and obtained a federal district court order against the defendant for violating the antifraud provisions of the federal securities laws; a preliminary injunction and asset freeze were imposed.[155]

SELF REGULATORY ORGANIZATIONS

Among the SROs, the NASD[156] has taken the lead[157] in addressing issues related to its member firms' use of the Internet to offer and distribute securities and the enforcement of securities fraud and manipulation on the Internet.[158] The NASD's initiatives have fallen into three general categories. First, it has amended the rules governing the activity of its members to apply specifically to electronic communications, in addition to paper-based communications. Second, it has provided informal interpretive advice to broker-dealers and investment companies as to how the NASD's rules apply to electronic communications. Finally, it has attempted to remind its broker-dealer members of their obligations under the NASD's rules with respect to their promoting and selling securities using the Internet.

155. *Frye,* 60 S.E.C. Docket (CCH) at 1787; Ryan J. Donmoyer, *Net Scams*, INTERNET WORLD, May 1996, at 95, 96.

156. The NASD is a self-regulatory organization comprised of brokers and dealers who are registered under the Exchange Act. In addition, the NASD governs the regulation of advertising by registered investment companies. Similar to the other U.S. securities exchanges, the NASD is subject to SEC regulatory oversight and can issue rules (subject to SEC review and approval) that are applicable to its members. *See* 15 U.S.C. §§ 78a-78jj (1994); NASD Manual (CCH), at 151 (1996).

157. Of the other SROs, the NYSE surveyed its membership in early 1996 concerning current and planned uses of technology in their businesses. *See* NYSE Information Memorandum 96-1 (Jan. 2, 1996) (on file with *The Business Lawyer*, University of Maryland School of Law). In addition, as of this writing, the NYSE submitted a rule proposal to the SEC that addresses its members' use of electronic communication such as e-mail. The proposal awaits publication by the SEC for public comments. *See NYSE News*, NYSE PRESS RELEASE, Sept. 5, 1996 (on file with *The Business Lawyer*, University of Maryland School of Law).

158. As a preliminary initiative, the NASD established an internal task force to consider the use of new technologies by member firms and to develop ways in which the NASD itself can use these technologies to provide enhanced services to its members. NASD Regulation, Inc., the regulatory and enforcement arm of the NASD, has established a Web site that includes, among other things, information warning investors of online investment schemes. It will also eventually include information on the disciplinary history of securities brokers and their firms. *See Airing CRD Over the Internet Raises Industry's Hackles*, COMPLIANCE REP., Apr. 1, 1996, at 6; *NASD Says Broker Information Could Be On Internet As Soon As 1997*, SEC. REG. L. REP. (BNA), Mar. 22, 1996, at 412; *NYSE and Nasdaq will join other exchanges on Internet*, INV. DEALERS' DIG., Jan. 15, 1996, at 11; Jerry Knight, *Tracking Stock Cyberscams*, WASH. POST, Aug. 23, 1996, at F1; NASD Regulation, Inc., Homepage (visited Oct. 8, 1996) <http://www.nasdr.com>.

NASD Rule Changes to Address Electronic Communications

The NASD's Conduct Rules[159] (Conduct Rules) generally set forth basic standards with respect to its member firms' communications with the public.[160] The Conduct Rules apply to various types of communications, including advertisements and sales literature, and prescribe the review, recordkeeping, and filing requirements members must adhere to in making such communications. With respect to members' use of advertisements and sales literature, the Conduct Rules specify both general and specific standards. The general standards prohibit members from using fraudulent or misleading statements in advertisements and sales literature. The specific standards provide various restrictions on the content of advertisements and sales literature, including the type of data, recommendations, claims and opinions, testimonials, and predictions.[161]

As part of an effort to address the increasing use of communication such as electronic mail and the Internet by its members, the NASD has included the term "electronic" in the definitions of "Advertisement" and "Sales Literature" in the Conduct Rules.[162] According to the NASD, the amend-

159. Rule 2210, Conduct Rules, NASD Manual (CCH), at 4171 (1996) (Communications with the Public). The NASD's Conduct Rules were formerly called the Rules of Fair Practice.

160. Rule 2210 of the NASD Manual is the primary rule regulating members' communications with the public. *Id.*

161. The Conduct Rules also generally require that NASD members (and persons associated with the members) adhere to high standards of commercial honor when dealing with members of the public. *See* Rule 2110, Conduct Rules, *id.* at 4105 (Standards of Commercial Honor and Principles of Trade).

162. National Ass'n of Sec. Dealers, Inc., Notice to Members 95-74, SEC Approves Amendments to Advertising and Sales Literature Filing And Review Requirements (Sept. 1995) [hereinafter NASD Notice to Members 95-74] (on file with *The Business Lawyer*, University of Maryland School of Law). The amendments to the definitions read as follows:

> (1) Advertisement—For purposes of this section and any interpretation thereof, "advertisement" means material published, or designed for use in, a newspaper, magazine or other periodical, radio, television, telephone or tape recording, videotape display, signs or billboards, motion picture, telephone directories (or other routine listings), *electronic*, or other public media.
>
> (2) Sales Literature—For purposes of this section and any interpretation thereof, "sales literature" means any written *or electronic* communication distributed or made generally available to customers or the public, which communication does not meet the foregoing definition of "advertisement." Sales literature includes, but is not limited to, circulars, research reports, market letters, performance reports or summaries, form letters, *telemarketing scripts*, seminar texts, and reprints or excerpts of any other advertisement, sales literature or published article.

See also Self Regulatory Organizations, Exchange Act Release No. 35,801, 60 Fed. Reg. 30,618 (June 9, 1995); Order Approving Proposed Rule Change Relating to Advertising and Sales Literature Filing and Review Requirements Under the Rules of Fair Practice and the Government Securities Rules, Exchange Act Release No. 36,076, 60 Fed. Reg. 42,200 (Aug. 15, 1995). The amendments to the definitions were effective as of their date in the *Federal Register* on August 9, 1995.

ments served to clarify that NASD members have the same obligations under the Conduct Rules with respect to communications with the public sent electronically via computer as they do with regard to other types of communications, such as those sent in paper form.[163]

With respect to the definitional change of the term "Advertisement," the NASD stated that the rule change "clarifies the applicability of the [Conduct] Rules to communications available to all computer or electronic network subscribers, including items displayed over network bulletin boards."[164] With respect to the change in definition of "Sales Literature," the NASD stated that the rule change "is intended to clarify the applicability of the Rules to messages sent directly to targeted individuals or groups."[165]

NASD Guidance on Electronic Communications

Although the NASD stated that its amendments to the definitions of "Advertisement" and "Sales Literature" were intended to clarify the application of its rules to electronic communications, several commentators have requested that the NASD (or SEC) provide further guidance to members as to how the Conduct Rules apply to specific situations involving electronic communications.[166] The NASD recently provided informal guidance by publishing a column entitled "Ask The Analyst About Electronic Communications," in a publication circulated to its members.[167]

The column, among other things, provided the NASD's answers to a number of important interpretive questions under the Conduct Rules. For example, the NASD provided its views on how the rules apply to several types of electronic communications. First, with respect to electronic bulletin boards, the NASD stated that "[c]ommunications posted by members or their associated persons on electronic bulletin boards and/or message boards would be considered advertisements because such material can be viewed by anyone with access to these services."[168] Second, with respect to electronic mail, the NASD distinguished between "group electronic mail"—identical messages sent to multiple individuals—and "individual

163. National Ass'n of Sec. Dealers, Inc., Notice to Members 95-80, NASD Further Explains Members Obligations and Responsibilities Regarding Mutual Fund Sales Practices (Sept. 26, 1995) (on file with *The Business Lawyer*, University of Maryland School of Law).

164. NASD Notice to Members 95-74, *supra* note 162, at 467.

165. *Id.*

166. *See* Gavis Letter, *supra* note 78, at 4-5; Letter from Craig S. Tyle, Vice President & Senior Counsel, Investment Company Institute, to Jonathan G. Katz, Secretary, SEC (June 30, 1995) (on file with *The Business Lawyer*, University of Maryland School of Law).

167. *See Ask The Analyst About Electronic Communications,* NASD REGULATORY & COMPLIANCE ALERT, Apr. 1996, at 4-6.

168. *Id.* at 4. Therefore, under the Conduct Rules, a registered principal within the member firm must review and approve all such communications on a bulletin board before they are used in public. *See id.*

e-mail"—personalized messages sent in lieu of written correspondence. The NASD considers group electronic mail to be "sales literature" and therefore covered by the Conduct Rules. For individual e-mail, the NASD believes that, if it pertains to the solicitation or execution of securities transactions, the e-mail is subject to the Conduct Rules;[169] if it pertains to other matters, it may not be subject to the Rules. Finally, the NASD indicated that statements made by a member firm in a "chat room"[170] would be analogous to oral statements made in a public forum, and therefore would generally not be subject to the Conduct Rules.[171] In addition to electronic mail issues, the NASD has addressed several other emerging and important issues, including the filing obligations of members who use Internet sites, the use by member firms of "broker-dealer use only"[172] materials on the Internet, and the obligations of member firms when "hyperlinking" materials from other Internet sites to their sites.

NASD Statements on Broker-Dealers' Responsibilities

Both the NASD and SEC recently have recognized a correlation, in certain circumstances, between the volatility of thinly-traded securities and the amount of "discussion" (or "chatter") about these securities on Internet bulletin boards devoted to investment topics.[173] In response to this development, the NASD recently published a notice to its members reminding

169. According to the NASD, "[w]hen . . . electronic letters pertain to the solicitation or execution of securities transactions, the rules require their review and endorsement by a registered principle." *Id.*

170. A "chat room" is an interactive electronic forum that is operated on a real-time basis. Computer users can post messages through the chat room. The messages are displayed on a bulletin board that is updated every few minutes and can be seen by all users who have access to the chat room. *See* HAHN, *supra* note 3, at 492.

171. The NASD cautioned, however, that "as with other oral communications, registered persons and member firms are accountable under the [Conduct Rules] and the federal securities laws for what they say regarding securities products or services when participating in chat rooms." *Ask the Analyst About Electronic Communications*, *supra* note 167, at 4.

172. The NASD stated that a member cannot put broker-dealer materials on its Internet site unless it can ensure that only broker-dealers, and not the public, obtain access to the materials. With respect to the linking of materials, the NASD indicated that it has not yet resolved these issues, but that "a member must not link to a site that the member knows contains misleading information about the member's products or services." *Id.*

173. In at least one instance, the SEC has begun an investigation to determine whether certain individuals may have attempted to manipulate the price of a particular security through comments made on an electronic bulletin board. In addition, the NASD has joined with the Motley Fool, an online investment forum on American Online, to warn investors of the possibility that certain statements (or "investment tips") posted anonymously on electronic bulletin boards may be intended to manipulate the prices of certain securities. *See Wallman Concerned That Chat Rooms On Internet Can Be Used to Move Markets*, SEC. REG. & L. REP. (BNA), June 14, 1996, at 751; Judith Burns, *NASD Regulators Warn Internet Users to View Investment Tips With Caution*, WALL ST. J., Aug. 23, 1996, at B8; Deborah Lohse, *Stock Regulators are Worried Dangers Lurk for Investors in On-Line Chat Sites*, WALL ST. J., Sept. 12, 1996.

them of their regulatory responsibilities and obligations to customers when dealing with securities promoted on the Internet.[174]

With respect to recommendations made by brokers to their customers, the notice states that "special care should be taken where a member . . . transmits via e-mail, television, radio, or other electronic medium messages concerning a particular security to a broad universe of investors of varying financial sophistication, experience, and resources."[175] In such cases, brokers should determine the suitability of a security with respect to each customer who responds to the electronic message and should consider notifying customers of suitability issues. The notice also indicates that brokers should take particular care with respect to the accuracy and completeness of information they give out regarding securities that have been promoted on the Internet or other electronic media.[176] The notice warns that brokerage firms should ensure they have appropriate supervisory procedures to cover brokers in their firms who use electronic media to communicate with investors.[177] The need for supervision is particularly acute, the notice states, with respect to the Internet because brokers may be able to transmit anonymous messages about the securities they sell to chat rooms or bulletin boards on the Internet.[178]

STATE INITIATIVES

BACKGROUND

The Internet operates as an interstate and international network of computers, and it can be accessed by investors from virtually every state in the United States. An investor sitting in his or her living room in Austin, Texas, for example, using a PC and modem, easily can access the home page of an investment company located in Portland, Maine. Moreover, an "entrepreneur," such as Mr. Odulo, for example, can solicit investors for bonds in his eel farming operation in Rhode Island by posting messages on Internet bulletin boards that can be read by investors in all fifty states and beyond. This phenomenon has been recognized by state securities regulators who have begun to consider how the framework of the state securities

174. National Ass'n of Sec. Dealers, Inc., Notice to Members 96-50, Supervisory and Other Obligations Related to Use of Electronic Media (July 1996) (on file with *The Business Lawyer*, University of Maryland School of Law). The notice also solicits NASD members' comments on their current practices in the use of electronic media to communicate with customers and the investing public, and on their use of compliance policies and procedures with respect to the use of electronic media. The NASD will apparently use these comments to determine whether there is a need for further specific guidance or regulatory action concerning supervisory responsibilities. *Id.*

175. *Id.*

176. *Id.*

177. *Id.*

178. *Id.*

laws can fit within the emerging use of the Internet as a means to offer and distribute securities.

Initiatives by state regulators have fallen into three general areas. First, a number of state securities regulators, along with the North American Securities Administrators Association, Inc. (NASAA),[179] have begun to examine the regulatory issues implicated by the offering of securities through the Internet. As will be discussed, however, the recent passage of federal legislation will eliminate the necessity of states' efforts in this area. Second, several state regulators have brought administrative enforcement actions involving offers of securities via the Internet. Finally, NASAA, along with a handful of states, has been working to develop an electronic filing system for registrants similar to the EDGAR system.

REGULATORY EFFORTS

In early 1994, NASAA established a committee to address regulatory issues arising from the use of electronic media for securities offerings.[180] The committee has consulted with other NASAA committees, federal regulators, SROs, and various industry representatives in an attempt to develop policy initiatives relating to electronic communications.[181] In addition to commenting on the SEC's initiatives on electronic communication,[182] the committee has considered regulatory issues arising from the placement of offering circulars and prospectuses on the Internet and the use of the Internet by investment advisers.

Guidance on Offering of Securities Through the Internet

A number of states have been active in considering whether an issuer that offers securities through the Internet should be subject to the securities registration requirements of the states because any person in any of the states could obtain access to the offering. These states have concluded that an offering of securities via the Internet would constitute an offer of securities within their borders and therefore would be subject to the states' registration requirements, unless an exemption or exclusion from registra-

179. NASAA, headquartered in Washington, D.C., is the trade association for the 50 state securities regulatory agencies.

180. *See* Letter from Ben Lewis, Chair, Offers on the Internet Committee, and Diane Young-Spitzer, Chair, Investment Companies Committee, to Jonathan G. Katz, Secretary, SEC, at 1 (Dec. 14, 1995) (on file with *The Business Lawyer*, University of Maryland School of Law).

181. On March 23, 1996, for example, the NASAA Offers on the Internet Committee sponsored a one-day roundtable discussion on Internet issues. Attendees included state and federal regulators and mutual fund and securities industry representatives. Securities Offerings and Financial Services for the 21st Century via the Internet, Roundtable Discussion (Mar. 23, 1996) (on file with *The Business Lawyer*, University of Maryland School of Law).

182. *See* Letter from Ben Lewis, *supra* note 180.

tion is available.[183] The states' efforts in this area may be short-lived, however. The recently enacted NSMIA effectively lodges exclusive authority for the registration of investment company offerings and securities offerings listed on a national exchange with the SEC. Accordingly, under the legislation, state regulators will no longer retain the authority to subject investment companies and other issuers that offer their securities through the Internet to registration requirements.

It is useful, however, to examine how the states have addressed the issue of the application of their securities laws to the offerings of securities through the Internet because a similar issue will confront the SEC with respect to the application of federal securities laws and foreign securities laws to the offerings of securities through the Internet by U.S.-based and foreign issuers. Pennsylvania was the first state to address this issue. With respect to whether a communication through the Internet concerning securities constitutes an offer to Pennsylvania citizens, the Deputy Chief Counsel of the Pennsylvania Securities Commission stated:

> Based on the fact that materials appearing on Internet are available to anyone in Pennsylvania who has access to a computer, a modem and a phone line, the Commission's Division of Corporation Finance (Division) has taken the position that a communication on the Internet designed to raise capital for an issuer would constitute an offer for the purchase or sale of a security . . . under Section 102(r) of the 1972 [Pennsylvania Securities] Act[184] and an advertisement under Section 102(a) of the 1972 Act[185] and, for purposes of the 1972 Act,

183. In general, a state's securities laws apply when three conditions are met: "(A) there must be a security, (B) offered and sold[,] and (C) the transaction must have some nexus to the state in question." K. Robert Bertram, *Advanced Technology Issues—The Internet, and State Securities Regulation—A Primer*, PA. BAR ASS'N Q., July 1996, at 133, 136 (footnote omitted); *see also* A. Jared Silverman, *Make Me an Offer Online*, LEGAL TIMES, July 8, 1996, at 20, 23.

184. Section 102(r) of the Pennsylvania Securities Act of 1972 states, in pertinent part:

> (r)(i) "Sale" or "sell" includes every sale, disposition or exchange, and every contract of sale of, or contract to sell, a security or interest in a security for value or any issuance of securities [for value]. . . .
> (ii) "Offer" or "offer to sell" includes every direct or indirect attempt or offer to sell or dispose of, or solicitation of an offer to purchase, a security or interest in a security for value.

PA. STAT. ANN. tit. 70 § 1-102(r) (West 1994). The UNIF. SECURITIES ACT (1956) is substantially similar to this provision.

185. Section 102(a) of the Pennsylvania Securities Act states, in pertinent part: " 'Advertisement' means any publicly disseminated, written or printed communication, including without limitation, communication by radio, television, other public media, used in connection with a sale or purchase or an offer to sell or purchase a security." PA. STAT. ANN. tit. 70 § 1-102(a) (West 1994).

> constitute a mass mailing, public media advertisement and general solicitation.[186]

Thus, the Pennsylvania Division of Corporation Finance developed the view that "a communication on the Internet designed to raise capital" would be an "offer" of securities and an advertisement, and, therefore would constitute a "mass mailing, public media advertisement and general solicitation" under Pennsylvania's securities laws. Implicit in this conclusion was the assumption that an Internet communication originating outside the state would have some nexus to persons within the state. The regulators appeared to believe that a communication via the Internet, involving either an offer to sell or purchase securities, would presumptively be directed to investors within the state for purposes of the scope of Pennsylvania law.[187]

In recognizing the significance of its interpretation, which would deem all communications on the Internet that relate to the selling of securities of an issuer as offerings of securities within Pennsylvania, the Deputy Chief Counsel went on to state:

> While the Division believes its position to be correct on jurisdictional issues, it did recognize, that the position could result in placing persons in violation of the registration requirement of Section 201 of the 1972 Act[188] solely by using Internet where the person did not intend to offer or sell securities in Pennsylvania. The Division therefore recommended that the Commission . . . issue an order exempting In-

186. G. Philip Rutledge, Deputy Chief Counsel, Pennsylvania Securities Commission, *Securities Commission Addresses Internet Offerings* (last modified July 22, 1996) <http://www.state.pa.us/PA_Exec/securities/corpfin/internet1.html> (internal footnotes added).

187. With respect to jurisdiction over the offer and acceptance of securities, §§ 702(b) & (c) of the Pennsylvania Securities Act state:

> (b) For the purposes of this section, an offer to sell or to purchase is made in this State, whether or not either party is then present in this State, when the offer originates from this State or is directed by the offeror to this State and received by the offeree in this State; provided, however, for the purpose of section 201 an offer to sell which is not directed to or received by the offeree in this State is not made in this State.
> (c) For the purposes of this section, an offer to purchase or to sell is accepted in this State when acceptance is communicated to the offeror in this State, and has not previously been communicated to the offeror, orally or in writing, outside this State; and acceptance is communicated to the offeror in this State, whether or not either party is then present in this State, when the offeree directs it to the offeror in this State reasonably believing the offeror to be in this State, and it is received by the offeror in this State.

PA. STAT. ANN. tit. 70, § 702(b), (c) (West 1994) (footnote omitted). The Uniform Securities Act of 1956 is substantially similar with respect to these two provisions. UNIF. SECURITIES ACT §§ 414(c), 414(d) (1956).

188. Section 201 of the Pennsylvania Securities Act states, in pertinent part: "It is unlawful for any person to offer or sell any security in this State unless the security is registered under this act or the security or transaction is exempted under [another section]." PA. STAT. ANN. tit. 70, § 1-201 (West 1994).

> ternet Offers from section 201 of the 1972 Act where the Internet Offer indicates either directly or indirectly, that the securities are not being offered to persons in Pennsylvania. . . .[189]

In August 1995, Pennsylvania issued a discretionary order providing an exemption from registration for offerings made on the Internet.[190] The order exempts the offer, but not the sale, of securities by an issuer that does not intend to offer and sell securities in Pennsylvania.[191] The order preserves the antifraud jurisdiction of the Pennsylvania Securities Commission, however, with respect to all offers and sales of securities through the Internet. The exemption is self-executing provided that an issuer meets three conditions specified in the order.[192] First, the exemption is conditioned upon an issuer indicating, through either direct or indirect language, that no offer or sale of the securities is intended to take place in Pennsylvania. The order does not indicate how an issuer should communicate this language or whether it should be in the form of a legend.[193] Second, the exemption is conditioned on an issuer, or anyone on behalf of the issuer, not directing an offering of securities to any person in Pennsylvania.[194] The final condition of the order is that no sales of an issuer's securities must be made in Pennsylvania as a result of the Internet offer.[195]

189. Rutledge, *supra* note 186 (internal footnote added).

190. *In re Offers But Not Sales Effected Through The Internet That Do Not Result In Sales In Pennsylvania*, Commonwealth of Pennsylvania, Before the Pennsylvania Securities Commission (Aug. 31, 1995) (last modified Sept. 6, 1996) <http://www.state.pa.us./PA_Exec/Securities/corpfin/interord.html> [hereinafter *Pennsylvania Order*].

191. *Id.* The order recognizes that:

> [p]roprietary or 'common carrier' [electronic] delivery system[s], the Internet and the World Wide Web or similar medium . . . [have greatly facilitated the ability] to communicate with a great number of people; and . . . [a] communication made on the Internet generally is available to anyone who is able to access Internet including persons in Pennsylvania.

Id.

192. In addition, the application of Pennsylvania's securities advertising requirements are waived with respect to issuers who comply with the conditions of the order. *Id.*

193. "[A]n indication that the offering is being made only in those jurisdictions where they may be offered legally or where the securities have been registered generally would be considered sufficient notice." Rutledge, *supra* note 186, at 1.

194. Mr. Rutledge stated:

> For instance, an issuer that receives an e-mail message from a Pennsylvania resident indicating an interest in purchasing the issuer's securities as a result of the Internet Offer cannot direct further information concerning the securities that are subject of the Internet Offer (or any other securities of the issuer) to that Pennsylvania resident.

Id.

195. "This includes sales of securities that are the subject of the Internet Offer or any other securities of the issuer." *Id.* It is not clear whether this means that an issuer cannot conduct sales of *any* of its securities within the state, even if some of them have been registered in the state, or that an issuer cannot sell only those unregistered securities that are the subject of the Internet offering.

Following the adoption of the order and in recognition of potentially inconsistent state regulation that could unduly hamper use of the Internet, NASAA adopted a resolution in January 1996 that encourages all "state securities regulators to develop a uniform policy concerning offers of securities on the Internet that is consistent with the goals of investor protection and access to capital markets."[196] The resolution provides the framework for an exemption that is substantially similar to the Pennsylvania order, but with one additional feature. As adopted, the Pennsylvania order does not allow an issuer that relied on the Internet exemption to register and sell its securities within the state at a later date.[197] The rationale for this prohibition was apparently to prevent the exemption from being "utilized by a issuer as a universal 'Test the Waters' procedure"[198] within the state without registering its securities.

The NASAA resolution addresses this issue by encouraging states to allow sales of securities that were the subject of an Internet offer as long as one of two conditions is met: "(A) No sales of the securities [are] made in any state until the offering has been registered and declared effective and the final prospectus . . . has been delivered to the investor prior to such sale; or (B) The sales are exempt from registration."[199] As of this writing, approximately twenty-two states have adopted Internet offering exemptions,[200] including Alaska, Arkansas, Connecticut, Idaho, Indiana, Iowa, Kansas, Maryland, Michigan, Mississippi, Montana, Nebraska, North Dakota, Pennsylvania, South Carolina, South Dakota, Texas, Utah, Vermont, Washington, West Virginia, and Wisconsin.[201] In addition, New Jersey has provided a no-action letter describing such an exemption.[202]

196. NASAA Resolution (Jan. 1996) (on file with *The Business Lawyer*, University of Maryland School of Law). The resolution also states that NASAA will develop a pilot program to monitor Internet offers and subsequent sales resulting from such offers. *Id.*

197. *Pennsylvania Order*, *supra* 190.

198. Bertram, *supra* note 183, at 137 n.24. One Pennsylvania regulator noted:

> Testing the Waters programs have been developed, and continue to develop, through the SEC and pilot programs in several NASAA states to allow an issuer to gauge the level of interest in their securities before the issuer undertakes to file for registration. *See, e.g.,* PA. Sec. Comm. Division of Corporation Finance Release No. 94-CF-1.

Id.

199. NASAA Resolution, *supra* note 196.

200. Each of these states have come to a conclusion similar to Pennsylvania's that a communication on the Internet designed to raise capital would be an "offer" of securities and/or an advertisement, and, therefore, constitutes a mass mailing, public media advertisement, and general solicitation under securities laws.

201. *See* University of Maryland School of Law, Thurgood Marshall Law Library, *State Orders Regulating Internet Securities Offerings* (visited Oct. 7, 1996) <http://www.law.ab.umd.edu/marshall/bluesky/table2.htm> [hereinafter *State Orders*].

202. *See* Letter from Joseph J. Allessie, Regulatory Officer, State of New Jersey, Department of Law Public Safety, Division of Consumer Affairs, Bureau of Securities to Jennifer Aracri, Senior Vice President, Securities Consultants, Inc. (Nov. 29, 1995) (on file with *The Business Lawyer*, University of Maryland School of Law).

Because many state securities commissions do not have the authority to issue orders or rules exempting issuers from the securities laws, uniform adoption of the NASAA resolution would be gradual at best. In addition, the states that do provide exemptions vary from each other and from the NASAA resolution. For example, South Dakota's order does not include the phrase "directly or indirectly" with respect to the condition that the offer indicate the securities that are the subject of the Internet offer are not being offered to residents of South Dakota.[203] Moreover, Alaska's order appears to contemplate that, as a condition for an exemption, an issuer must disclose both in its offer *and in its advertisements* that its securities are not being offered to persons in Alaska.[204]

Guidance on Internet Use by Broker-Dealers and Investment Advisers

While a number of states have addressed the issue of registration of securities offered over the Internet, one state has addressed the issue of registration of broker-dealers and investment advisers who use the Internet to advertise and communicate with clients. The New Jersey Bureau of Securities recently issued a no-action letter allowing brokers of a national broker-dealer, who are not registered to do business in New Jersey, to establish sites on the Internet that provide information on the services the brokers offer.[205]

Because the Internet is accessible from all fifty states, the broker-dealer originally had adopted a policy that its brokers were only authorized to use the Internet to discuss the services they offer if they were registered in all fifty states. In addition, the brokers were only permitted to use the Internet to discuss securities that are registered in all fifty states. In its no-action request, the broker-dealer requested that New Jersey allow brokers who are not registered in the state to establish Internet sites that provide information about their services, so long as the sites contain a series of interactive messages and disclaimers that prevent residents of New Jersey from accessing the site.[206]

According to the Bureau of Securities's no-action letter, the broker-dealer could allow its brokers who are not registered in New Jersey to

203. *State Orders*, *supra* note 201.

204. *Id.* The Alaska order states that, as a condition for an exemption, the Internet offer must disclose, "directly or indirectly, in a format and at a prominent place in the offer and *in any advertisement of the offer* on the Internet that the securities are not being offered to persons in the State of Alaska." *Id.* (emphasis added).

205. Letter from Michael J. Dolan, Bureau of Securities, State of New Jersey, to Don Runkle, Assistant Compliance Officer, Investment Management and Research, Inc., (May 29, 1964) (on file with *The Business Lawyer*, University of Maryland School of Law). The no-action letter was apparently sent to all fifty states. As of this writing, the author is unaware of any other states that have granted similar no-action relief.

206. *Id.*

establish Internet sites, provided that the sites contain a "gateway" which would permit access only to investors residing in states in which a broker is registered.[207] The letter indicated that a broker could establish a "gateway" on his or her Internet site by providing an interactive message at the beginning of the site that asks the investor to identify his or her state of residence.[208] If the investor resides in a state in which the broker is properly registered, he or she could be allowed to access other portions of the broker's site. If the investor identifies him or herself as residing in a state where the broker is not registered, the investor should be denied access to the rest of the Internet site, and should see a message indicating that the broker is not registered in the state and the investor can call the broker-dealer for further information.

The letter also indicated that, once an investor has been permitted to access a broker's Internet site, the investor should not be able to obtain information on a particular security unless the security is registered in the investor's state of residence.[209] This could be accomplished with a site that contains another set of menus asking the investor to identify his or her state of residence. Depending upon the answer, the investor would either be given access to the information or be provided with a disclaimer that the securities have not been registered in the investor's state. Finally, the letter indicated that brokers who are also registered as investment advisers may use a similar set of messages and disclaimers when providing investment advisory services via the Internet.[210] The letter appears to be an interesting approach that uses interactive technology to address the issue of whether a broker who is not registered in all fifty states can use the Internet because it is a system that is open to residents of all states.

ENFORCEMENT INITIATIVES

The most significant issue being considered by state securities regulators today is the enforcement of states' securities laws against those who use the Internet to defraud or mislead investors located within a particular state.[211] State regulators apparently have seen a surge in the number of illicit investment schemes on the Internet, including stock manipulations, pyramid scams, and Ponzi schemes. One state regulator has succinctly described his office's efforts to track and prosecute cases of securities fraud involving the Internet:

> We read postings off various services. Those that sound too good to be true are flagged. We then check registration of the seller and the

207. *Id.*
208. *Id.*
209. *Id.*
210. *Id.*
211. *See, e.g.,* Letter from Ben Lewis, *supra* note 180.

> securities. There is a national computer database on all persons registered to sell securities. If the seller is not registered, we make contact either over the phone or by email. We then wait for a response. If the person responds with information about the investment or encourages its purchase, we send out a target letter requesting information. If we receive a response, including investor lists, we may do a questionnaire to determine what investors were told. If we do not get a response, we can issue a cease-and-desist order, which must be disclosed in future dealings or the seller would be in violation of the fraud provisions of the securities laws.[212]

Another state securities regulator indicates that, since the beginning of 1995, technology-based investment frauds—including those involving more traditional scams promoted through the Internet—have grown dramatically and threaten to become more prevalent with public acceptance of these emerging technologies.[213] A growing number of state securities commissions have established Internet pages or sites on which they have published, among other things, notices that are intended to advise and warn consumers within the state of Internet fraud schemes.[214]

In an Investor Bulletin published at its Web site,[215] NASAA indicated that state securities regulators have identified four types of investment schemes as being among the most common investment fraud and abuse problems on the Internet. NASAA first indicated that commercial bulletin board services may be used to manipulate obscure, thinly-traded stocks.

212. Abbot Chambers, *An Interview with John Perkins (former Securities Commissioner of Missouri, and former NASAA President)* (visited Sept. 10, 1996) <http://www.gnn.com/gnn/meta/finance/feat/archives.interview/perkins/jperkins.2.html>.

213. *1995 Investment Scam Predictions Released: Top Five Securities Enforcement Cases for 1994 Listed,* Before the Department of Finance of the State of Idaho, 1995 Id. Sec. LEXIS 1 (Jan. 1, 1995).

214. State securities commissions have published various materials on the Internet (including state securities codes, orders from administrative proceedings, consumer advisories or warnings, and general information concerning the securities commission). For example, the Oklahoma Securities Commission has published an Investor Bulletin describing the growth of "Information Superhighway" scams and describing recent efforts of state regulators to combine enforcement efforts with the Federal Trade Commission to investigate page licensing and "900" numbers scams." *See* Oklahoma Department of Securities, *The New Generation of Information Superhighway Scams* (visited Sept. 10, 1996) <http://www.state.ok.us/~osc/info_sup.html>; Connecticut Department of Banking, Securities and Business Investments Division (visited Sept. 10, 1996) <http://www.state.ct.us./dob/pages/secdiv.html>; Securities Division, Department of the Secretary of State, North Carolina (visited Sept. 10, 1996) <http://www.secstate.state.nc.us/secstate/sec.html>; Utah Division of Securities (visited Sept. 10, 1996) <http://www.commerce.state.ut.us/web/commerce/securit/sec.html>; West Virginia State Auditor's Office, Securities Division (visited Sept. 10, 1996) <http://www.wvauditor.com/sec/secintro.html>.

215. GNN Personal Finance Center, *Online Investment Schemes: Fraud and Abuse in Cyberspace* (visited Sept. 10, 1996) <http://www.gnn.com/gnn/meta/finance/feat/archives.inrest/nasaa.html> [hereinafter NASAA Investor Bulletin].

According to NASAA, because most commercial electronic bulletin board services[216] allow individuals to post messages anonymously or under different aliases, "a company insider, broker, public relations executive or even just a large shareholder can leave numerous messages calculated to spark interest in an obscure stock . . . [and thus,] there is enormous potential for manipulation of little-known companies that have a small float."[217] In addition, messages promoting an issuer's stock might be posted by "agents" of the issuer who do not disclose that they are being paid a fee to do so and, thus, are violating state and federal securities laws.[218]

NASAA also indicated that state regulators are concerned that brokers may be attempting to obtain new business "without the supervision of their employers and while making liberal use of illegal assurances about the potential for profit in certain investments."[219] This supposedly can be accomplished by a broker using the Internet outside of his or her work environment to solicit and contact clients. In addition, NASAA states that regulators are worried not only about oral statements made to individual clients by brokers, but about the broad distribution of statements to many investors through electronic mail.

As a final warning, NASAA states that

> [h]undreds of messages have been posted in cyberspace promoting a wide variety of highly suspect, unregistered investment deals (e.g., wireless cable television "build-out" schemes, ostrich farming, and viatical settlements), as well as flat-out rip-offs (e.g., pyramid schemes, including a number of twists on "chain e-mail letters," and Ponzi scams).[220]

State regulators have investigated a number of such schemes, including one by a company that allegedly sought $7.7 million in "private placement" capital through the Internet newsgroup, "misc.invest," in order to manufacture battery-powered cleaning devices, and another by a Hawaiian farmer who allegedly advertised on an Internet bulletin board for

216. See *supra* note 56 for a description of electronic bulletin boards. In a similar vein, another commentator states:

> [t]here is a great deal of hype on the stock boards, some of which undoubtedly comes from brokers trying to pump up stock, and a great deal of trash talking, some of which just as surely comes from shortsellers trying to talk stocks down. And because [America Online] employs a system of screen names, giving its subscribers the option of anonymity, viewers have no idea of the private agendas of any of the participants in the online discussion. They don't even know whether the information being posted is true.

Joseph Nocera, *Investing in Fool's Paradise*, FORTUNE, Apr. 15, 1996, at 86.

217. NASAA Investor Bulletin, *supra* note 215, at 1-2.

218. *Id.* at 2.

219. *Id.*

220. *Id.*

$250,000 in capital in order to sell his invention, a "vibrating condom."[221] As of this writing, several states have brought administrative enforcement actions against individuals who have offered unregistered securities on Internet bulletin boards and on which, in some of the cases, investors residing in the state actually purchased the securities.[222]

ELECTRONIC FILING INITIATIVES

In a similar vein to the EDGAR filing system, in 1994, state securities regulators created the Securities Registration Depository (SRD). Its purported mission is to establish and operate an electronic securities registration system for use by participating states and industry filers. As originally developed, the SRD was designed to accept filings on behalf of the states through a closed computer network.[223] Accordingly, it was proposed that issuers would be able to use the SRD to route registration materials to all regulators starting with a single electronic submission to the SEC's EDGAR Program; submit registration renewal notices to participating states; consolidate registration fee payments to the states; receive permits, comments and other state generated notices automatically; and access state registration information online.[224]

The SRD began operating a ten-state pilot program for mutual fund

221. *See Gary Weiss, Online Investing,* BUS. WK., June 5, 1995, at 64 (discussing Pocket Made, Inc., a company allegedly manufacturing battery-powered cleaning devices that sought $7.7 million in capital by advertising in the "misc.invest" newsgroup on Usenet); Philip A. Feigin, Colorado Securities Commissioner, *The Internet and Securities Regulation,* Outline of Presentation to Colorado Association of Corporate Counsel, at 12-13 (Feb. 22, 1996) (on file with *The Business Lawyer,* University of Maryland School of Law) (reporting that, as of September 1995, four states (North Carolina, New Jersey, Kansas, and Missouri) had taken administrative enforcement action against offerings noted on Internet bulletin boards).

222. *See In re* Octagon Tech. Group, Inc., No. 9500578, 1995 Il. Sec. LEXIS 284 (Nov. 2, 1995) (involving an action by Illinois Securities Department against Octagon Technology Group resulting in a temporary cease-and-desist order for offering unregistered securities to Illinois residents by means of the Internet; Octagon sought investors to purchase Inter-American Hard Currency Bonds described as fully insured and earning a 12.28 annual percentage rate); *In re* Tower Consulting, Inc., No. CD-96-05, 1996 Mo. Sec. LEXIS 6 (Jan. 29, 1996) (involving an action by the Missouri Securities Commission which resulted in a cease-and-desist order against the defendants who allegedly marketed and sold unregistered securities to Missouri investors concerning an Internet shopping mall); *In re* the Offer For Sale of Securities by Sarah S. Cooke and Sarah S. Cook d/b/a TSC International, Order No. CDO-1087, 1996 Tex. Sec. LEXIS 18 (Mar. 4, 1996) (involving an action by the Texas Securities Commission which resulted in a cease-and-desist order against the defendants who allegedly offered interests in Spa Time, Inc., a New Jersey company, in connection with efforts to raise $3 million in equity capital through a public newsgroup posting on the Internet).

223. *See* SRD Homepage (under construction) (visited June 1, 1996) <http://www.srd.com>. The original plan for the SRD involved a proprietary network system that would be operated by General Electric Information Services (GEIS). GEIS would have accepted filings and processed them over a closed system.

224. *Id.*

filings and renewals in January 1996. The program, however, attracted few issuers[225] and an industry advisory group to the SRD expressed a number of concerns with respect to the operation of the SRD. These included concerns that the industry will have little input into such issues as filing costs and the operation of the SRD, worries about the security of documents filed with the system, and redundancy issues, such as the possibility that some states may still require paper filings.[226] In response to these concerns and to the possibility of federal legislation that would realign federal/state registration requirements with respect to mutual funds, NASAA announced that it would privatize the SRD. In May 1996, NASAA signed a letter of intent with Mark Holderman, the Ohio Commissioner of Securities, which provided for the sale of the SRD to Holderman for $2.75 million. Holderman subsequently resigned his position as Commissioner in order to start a corporation that would operate the SRD as a filing system using the Internet.[227] According to NASAA, Holderman estimates that his cost of providing the filing system would be "approximately 25 percent" less than estimates of the fees previously proposed for NASAA's SRD. As of this writing, Holderman's corporation has established an Internet site (that is not currently functional) and will apparently begin testing the filing system in November 1996 and accept live filings beginning in January 1997.[228]

THE GROWING USE OF THE INTERNET BY MARKET PARTICIPANTS

Use of the Internet by market participants, including mutual funds, investment advisers, broker-dealers, and corporate issuers has increased dramatically within the past two years. At last count, over seventy U.S. mutual fund companies,[229] over fifty U.S. broker-dealer firms, and a handful of investment advisers and financial planners have established sites on the Internet.[230] In addition, one corporate issuer has conducted its own

225. *See* Tim Cavanaugh, *State Regulators Unveil Central Depository for Fund Filings,* REDEMPTION DIG. & SEC. INDUST. DAILY, Jan. 24, 1996, at 1.

226. *Id.* The industry advisory group includes representatives from the Securities Industry Association and the Investment Company Institute.

227. *See Seeking Uniformity, Best High-Tech and Lowest Cost, States Privatize Electronic Filing for Securities,* NASAA PRESS RELEASE, May 17, 1996 (on file with *The Business Lawyer,* University of Maryland School of Law).

228. *See* Letter from Mark Holderman, President, SRD, Inc., to Tamara Cain, Esq., Investment Company Institute (Sept. 20, 1996) (on file with *The Business Lawyer,* University of Maryland School of Law).

229. *See* Weisul, *supra* note 18, at 1; Qualisteam, *Mutual Funds in the United States* (visited Sept. 10, 1996) <http://www.qualisteam.com/aopcvmusa.html> (listing mutual fund Internet addresses by country).

230. *See* Hal Lux, *Wall Street Wires Into the Web,* INV. DEALERS' DIG., June 26, 1995, at S2; CorpFiNet, *Directory of Brokerage Firms* (visited Sept. 10, 1996) <http://www.corpfinet.com/BrokerageFirms.html>.

initial public offering via the Internet and several issuers and underwriters have established online exchanges for trading shares of stock.[231]

The growing use of the Internet by market participants is a result of two significant developments: the emerging use of the Internet as a new distribution channel for services and products and the recent interpretive guidance by the SEC, which has provided certainty to market participants when developing their strategy to use the Internet.

USE OF THE INTERNET BY MUTUAL FUNDS

Mutual funds registered under the Investment Company Act[232] are particularly well-suited to use the Internet. They continuously offer their shares to the public and, in order to meet their obligations under the securities laws, must provide investors with a host of documents, including prospectuses, annual reports, and confirmation statements. Moreover, mutual fund shares generally are owned by individual investors who, studies show, increasingly are using computers in their everyday life. A recent survey by the Investment Company Institute, for example, concluded that PC ownership among mutual fund shareholders consistently has outpaced the national average, growing from twenty-eight percent in 1990 to fifty-six percent in 1995.[233] It was estimated that nearly seventeen million fund-owning households have PCs, representing slightly more than half of all personal computing households nationwide. Thirty-one percent of these fund-owning households subscribe to online services and therefore have access to the Internet.[234]

Mutual fund companies that sell their funds directly to the public (direct-marketed mutual fund companies)[235] were the first among fund companies

231. See *supra* notes 103-24 for a discussion of these developments.

232. A mutual fund is a type of:

> [i]nvestment company that pools money from shareholders and invests in a variety of securities, including stocks, bonds, and money market instruments. A mutual fund stands ready to buy back (redeem) its shares at their current net asset value, which depends on the total market value of the fund's investment portfolio at the time of redemption. As open-end investments, most mutual funds continuously offer new shares to investors.

INVESTMENT CO. INST., 1996 MUTUAL FUND FACT BOOK 110 (3d ed. 1996). This Article will focus only on how mutual fund companies are using the Internet, and not on closed-end funds that, unlike mutual funds, issue a limited number of shares that trade in the secondary market, or unit investment trusts that maintain a fixed portfolio of income-producing securities with a specific maturity date.

233. INVESTMENT CO. INST., FUNDAMENTALS, MUTUAL FUND RESEARCH IN BRIEF (Nov./Dec. 1995).

234. *Id.*

235. Direct Marketing is "[a] method of distribution whereby a fund company sells shares directly to the public without involving a salesperson. Investors purchase fund shares through the mail or by telephone in response to advertising or other direct solicitations." INVESTMENT CO. INST., *supra* note 232, at 108.

to make use of the Internet. For these fund companies, a presence on the Internet serves several purposes. It allows the fund companies to establish an additional, or fourth, distribution channel for the advertisement and sale of funds. In addition to using U.S. mail, the telephone, and investor centers, these fund companies have created electronic "investor centers" where potential shareholders can obtain detailed information about the companies' various funds and their managers, general information about investing, prospectuses, and applications.[236] Fund companies appear to be using the Internet to test new interactive sales and marketing materials. The Internet also provides a low-cost means for fund companies to distribute documents and information to shareholders. The larger direct-marketed mutual fund companies were the first to establish Internet sites.[237] Since the beginning of 1995,[238] a number of Internet sites of direct-marketed mutual fund companies provide for the downloading of prospectuses and applications.

Fund companies that have decided to establish Internet sites have encountered two options, either to develop their own, independent site or to participate on a site that features funds from many fund companies. Internet sites that allow for participation by many fund companies are often called "intermediary service providers."[239] As of this writing, over sixty direct-marketed mutual fund companies provide information about their funds and prospectuses that can be downloaded through an intermediary service provider.[240]

236. One account of the first wave of mutual fund Web sites states:

> [m]uddy goals produced mediocre results. Early sites relied heavily on the funds' existing marketing materials—already NASD-approved and easily adaptable to the Web. The first exploratory homepages typically consisted of a slowly-loading picture of the chairman, a treatise on the wonders of mutual fund investing, and an 800 number for more information.

Weisul, *supra* note 18, at 1.

237. *See* Fidelity Investments, *Online Investor Center* (visited Sept. 10, 1996) <http://www.fid-inv.com>; The Vanguard Group, *What's New at Vanguard* (visited Sept. 10, 1996) <http://www.vanguard.com>.

238. The SEC's Division of Corporation Finance issued the *Brown & Wood* no-action letter, which allowed for the electronic distribution of prospectuses, in February 1995. See *supra* notes 39-51 and accompanying text for a discussion of the SEC's no-action letter.

239. *See Mutual Funds on the Internet, supra* note 3, at i. NETworth is a leading intermediary service provider. *See* Quicken Financial Network (visited Sept. 9, 1996) <http://networth.galt.com>. On November 8, 1995, Intuit Corporation, maker of "Quicken"—a leading personal software finance program—agreed to purchase GALT Technologies. *See Digest*, WASH. POST, Nov. 9, 1995, at B12.

240. One commentator has described the attraction of using an intermediary service provider such as NETworth:

> Fund companies, especially smaller ones, hope to gain access to the online traffic of potential fund buyers that such sites attract. While an independent site on the Web offers a fund company control over content and user-interface, the site may not receive sub-

A small, but growing, group of fund companies that sell their funds through broker-dealers have also established Internet sites. These sites usually provide two types of information: (i) general information about the company's funds to retail investors, and (ii) specific information that is tailored for brokers who sell the funds. The information for brokers usually is maintained in a password-protected portion of the site,[241] which allows brokers who know the password to access that part of the site and obtain information related to selling the funds.[242] In addition, at least one broker-sold fund company provides retail investors access to account information through its Internet site.[243] Several leading national banks have established comprehensive Internet sites, portions of which contain information about mutual funds of the banks and other companies.[244]

It appears that a growing number of fund companies that are located and sell their shares outside of the United States have established Web sites.[245] These sites can be easily accessed by U.S. residents. Most of these sites contain prominent legends, which warn investors that the funds may be registered and sold only in certain jurisdictions.[246]

There have been a number of interesting and innovative developments with respect to fund companies' use of the Internet. Practically all fund companies that have an Internet site allow investors to contact the com-

> stantial traffic from non-committed fund shoppers if the company lacks strong brand recognition.

Mutual Funds on the Internet, supra note 3, at i.

241. *See* Weisul, *supra* note 18.

242. This allows the fund company to provide its representatives with "broker-only" materials, as defined under the NASD's Conduct Rules. *See* Rule 2210, Conduct Rules, NASD Manual (CCH), at 4171 (1996).

243. Kimberly Weisul, *Calvert becomes first fund to offer account info on-line—Mutual fund company dodges the security issue,* INV. DEALERS' DIG., Jan. 22, 1996, at 9.

244. *See* Nationsbank, *Nations Fund Home Page* (visited Sept. 9, 1996) <http://www.nationsbank.com>; Wells Fargo Bank Homepage (visited Sept. 9, 1996) <http://www.wellsfargo.com>.

245. *See* Fortitude Funds Homepage (visited Sept. 10, 1996) <http://www.fortitude.com.> (U.K. investment company); Sagit Investment Management Homepage (visited Sept. 10, 1996) <http://www.direct.ca/funds/> (Canadian investment company); Trimark Investment Management, Inc. (visited Sept. 10, 1996) <http://www.trimark.com/> (Canadian investment company).

246. For example, the legend for the Fortitude Funds states:

> The distribution of the information contained in this service and the offering of shares in the Funds is restricted in certain jurisdictions. No action has been taken to permit either the distribution of this information or the offering of any of the shares of the Funds in any jurisdiction where action would be required for such purposes. In particular, *neither the shares in the Funds nor the Funds themselves have been registered under any United States securities legislation* and, except in a transaction which does not violate such legislation or require the registration of the Funds, they are not being offered, directly or indirectly, in the United States of America. . . .

Fortitude Funds Homepage, *supra* note 245.

pany through electronic mail, either to ask a question or to request further information.[247] One fund company sponsors an online "Meet the Experts" forum, which allows investors to ask questions of fund managers or market experts via electronic mail. Answers to questions are posted on a delayed basis.[248] Another fund company has created a bulletin board system where investors can post messages or share ideas with other investors.[249]

In addition to electronic mail-based services, fund companies offer various investment services and even games at their Internet sites, which are designed to encourage investors to return to the site. The investment services include: (i) allowing investors to view a recent list of a funds' portfolio holdings;[250] (ii) allowing investors to create customized portfolio reports of various funds they own (updated daily);[251] (iii) interactive calculators that allow investors to determine their appropriate savings strategy for retirement;[252] and (iv) information concerning the status of legislation on Individual Retirement Accounts. Other items offered at Internet sites include a "Guess the Dow Contest" and a ticker showing the daily net asset values of various funds.[253] In addition to using the Internet, some fund companies

247. *See* Susan Bishop, *Fund firms replace snail mail with e-mail,* MUTUAL FUND MAG., May 3, 1995, at 1.

248. *See* Bobbi Nodell, *Montgomery's hot investment,* OAKLAND TRIB., Mar. 11, 1995, at 1 ("[O]ne of Montgomery's seven portfolio managers will make periodic statements about the market and invite comments from any one of the millions of Internet users. Photos and bios of the portfolio managers are provided."); Montgomery Homepage (visited Sept. 10, 1996) <http://xperts.montgomery.com/>.

249. *See* Carol Gould, *Expanding On-Line Services,* N.Y. TIMES, Apr. 23, 1995, at F9.

250. For example, the Internet sites for GIT Investment Funds and Munder Funds list the portfolio holdings for their funds. *See* Harriett Magee, *Mutual Funds Post Holdings on the Net* (visited Sept. 9, 1996) <http://www.corpfinet.com/electric.html>. GIT updates its funds' holdings on a daily basis and provides the names of the securities and number of shares held. *See* GIT Homepage (visited Sept. 10, 1996) <http://www.gitfunds.com>. Munder Funds provides a list of its funds' portfolio holdings on a monthly basis, a list of the funds' securities trades (buys and sells) for the previous month, and what percentage each security represents of the entire portfolio. *See* Munder Funds Homepage (visited Sept. 10, 1996) <http://www.munder.com>. The SEC recently granted no-action relief to Munder, allowing it to publish such portfolio information on its Internet site. Munder Capital Management, SEC No-Action Letter, *reprinted in* SECURITIES LAW PRACTICE IN CYBERSPACE, at 79 (Aug. 5, 1996).

251. *See* Weisul, *supra* note 18 ("T. Rowe Price's family of funds can specify which fund information they would like to see when they first open into the T. Rowe Price site. [http://www.troweprice.com]"); Carole Gould, *News on the Web,* N.Y. TIMES, Apr. 7, 1996, at K1 ("The Vanguard Group has added a feature called 'Custom Mutual Fund Report' to its World Wide Web site to help investors monitor their funds.").

252. *See* Gould, *supra* note 249, at K1; Federated Investors Homepage (visited Sept. 10, 1996) <http://networth.galt.com/www/home/mutual/federate>.

253. *See* Weisul, *supra* note 18 ("Fidelity keeps visitors informed about upcoming IRA legislation; it also runs a popular 'Guess the Dow' contest. The Strong Funds have a ticker showing the daily Net Asset Values of each of their funds running across the top of their site."); Kathleen Gallagher, *Strong sets up page on Web to give investors latest listings,* MILWAUKEE J. & SENTINEL, Jan. 23, 1996, at 1 (Strong Capital Management <http://www

have developed software programs that allow customers to access the company's proprietary electronic bulletin board services.[254] This software allows customers to access fund companies through a direct telephone/modem connection, which allows for a more secure connection. As such, several of these software packages allow customers to conduct transactions.[255]

Finally, there has been much discussion in the press concerning the purchase and sale of mutual fund shares through the Internet.[256] As of this writing, however, most fund companies generally do not offer this option to their customers. Although the SEC stated in its May Interpretive Release that issuers may distribute confirmations for the purchase or sale of securities electronically—thus paving the way for electronic trading of mutual fund shares—fund companies must nonetheless address a host of issues related to the security of online transactions.[257] It is likely that mutual funds will intially provide their existing shareholders with the ability to check account balances and conduct transfers and purchases between preexisting fund accounts electronically through the Internet.

USE OF THE INTERNET BY BROKER-DEALERS AND INVESTMENT BANKS

Brokerage and investment banking firms have been pioneers in using electronic technology to communicate with various stock exchanges and institutional customers. Two of the earliest no-action letters submitted to the SEC regarding electronic communications, for example, concerned

.strong-funds.com>). It has also been reported that both Prudential Securities and Fidelity Investments intend to offer Internet service access to their customers. Interested customers, for example, can obtain software and access to the Internet through Prudential or Fidelity, bypassing traditional Internet service providers. *See* Kimberly Weisul, *Wall Street brokers become Internet service providers—Pru and Fidelity sign agreements with AT&T and MCI,* INV. DEALERS' DIG., Apr. 29, 1996, at 8.

254. *See Mutual Funds on the Internet, supra* note 3, at iii ("Major providers with such software include Fidelity's Online Xpress (FOX), Schwab's StreetSmart, and T. Rowe Price's PCAccess."). In addition, several fund companies have begun to provide electronic access to customers of 401(k) retirement accounts. *See also Fund titans spearhead 401(k) initiatives in cyberspace and advertising,* FUND DECODER, Apr. 1, 1996, at 1.

255. *See Fund titans, supra* note 254.

256. *See Dreyfus, National Financial gear up for fund transactions over the Internet,* FUND DECODER, Mar. 4, 1996, at 1; *Internet Fund Transactions Arrive,* FUND ACTION, Oct. 9, 1995, at 2; Hal Lux, *TIAA-CREF may soon offer transactions over Internet,* INV. DEALERS' DIG., Jan. 15, 1996, at 10; John Waggoner, *Mutual fund trading hits the Internet,* USA TODAY, Mar. 29, 1996, at A1; Kimberly Weisul, *Jack White & Co. is the first to sell mutual funds on Web,* INV. DEALERS' DIG., Apr. 15, 1996, at 1; Russ Wiles, *On the Horizon: Internet Mutual Fund Transactions,* CHICAGO SUN-TIMES, Jan. 28, 1996, at 43.

257. *See* Elizabeth Roy, *Internet Must Still Prove Itself to Three Mutual Fund Leaders,* BOND BUYER, May 24, 1996, at 7; *Some fund groups wait for insurance before doing cyberspace transactions,* FUND DECODER, May 13, 1996, at 1 ("Fund complexes seeking to generate sales over the Internet have discovered to their chagrin that transactions in cyberspace are not insured.").

the electronic delivery of confirmations from broker-dealers to their clients.[258] Proprietary electronic communications networks between large brokerage firms and their clients for the purposes of executing trades have been in existence for at least ten years. More recently, however, discount brokerage firms have brought electronic communications to the retail level.[259]

The use of the Internet by brokerage firms generally differs depending on whether it is being used by a discount or full-service brokerage firm. There are more than a dozen discount brokerage firms that offer electronic-based services either through their own proprietary software, one of the online computer services, or through the Internet.[260] The larger discount brokers began their foray into electronic communications in the late 1980s by offering proprietary software to customers, which involved customers installing the software on their home computer and then accessing the firms' computers through a modem.[261] Through these systems, customers can obtain information about account balances, buy and sell securities, and send inquiries to the firm through electronic mail.[262] As of this writing, the larger discount brokers are beginning to offer online trading through the Internet,[263] and several smaller discount brokerage firms have offered such trading of securities since early 1996.[264] Many of the brokerage firms that provide trading either through a proprietary system, an online service, or the Internet also provide customers with access to information on various types of investments, historical price charts, and

258. *See supra* text accompanying notes 79-88.

259. According to one estimate, "Presently, there are about 624,000 brokerage accounts that trade through PCs, and, by 1998, there are expected to be 1.3 million. Some analysts who study computer services expect on-line trading to grow much faster than on-line banking primarily because more brokerage customers than banking customers have PCs." Robertson, *supra* note 9, at 376 (footnotes omitted).

260. For a listing of such firms, see CorpFiNet, *supra* note 230; Lux, *supra* note 20.

261. "For example, PC Financial Network, part of the Pershing Division of Donaldson, Lufkin & Jenrette, has offered on-line trading through Prodigy since 1988 and recently started offering the service through America Online." Robertson, *supra* note 9, at 377.

262. Robertson notes:

> With each of these services, an order goes from the client's PC to the on-line service's computer to the brokerage's computer and is executed, usually immediately if placed during the trading day. The confirmation is sent back along the same electronic path. The services typically permit customers to place stop-limit orders, cancel unexecuted orders, cover short positions, and sell securities purchased earlier in the day.

Id. at 377-78 (footnotes omitted).

263. *See* Vanessa O'Connell, *On-Line Investing Flourishes as Brokers Slash Commissions on Computer Trades*, WALL ST. J., Sept. 27, 1996, at C1; Kimberly Weisul, *Schwab gives go-ahead for trading on Internet—Brokerage launches pilot program this month*, INV. DEALERS' DIG., Mar. 18, 1996, at 12.

264. *See* E*Trade Securities Homepage (visited Sept. 10, 1996) <http://www.etrade.com/>; National Discount Homepage (visited Sept. 10, 1996) <http://pawws.secapl.com/>.

research reports.[265] In addition, most of the firms offer lower commissions to customers who use electronic communications, mostly because the transmission is at a lower cost to the firm.[266]

Although many full-service brokerage firms have established sites on the Internet,[267] the purpose of their sites appears to be primarily for advertising and client development, rather than for the provision of direct trading services. The firms are, among other things, developing systems whereby clients will be able to access account information via the Internet. In addition, they are developing "private" (i.e., accessed by a password) Internet sites that will disseminate information for use by brokers.[268]

There remain several unresolved and outstanding issues with respect to the use of the Internet by full-service brokers. First, without appropriate built-in security protections on the Internet, neither full-service nor discount brokers are entirely comfortable providing their clients with access to personal account information or the ability to trade securities through the Internet.[269] Accordingly, these firms are more likely to develop and use proprietary computer systems or online computer systems that offer a high degree of security.[270] Second, electronic mail through the Internet would appear to be a potentially useful method of communication between full-service brokers and their clients. The regulation of electronic mail between brokers and their clients under the federal securities laws is still being developed.[271] Accordingly, the brokerage industry appears to be re-

265. Practically all of the current Internet securities trading systems have been designed to allow preexisting customers to trade securities. New customers are not generally allowed to conduct trading until they have established a trading account. *See* Laurent Belsie, *On-line Investing Lures Stockbrokers, Customers,* CHRISTIAN SCI. MONITOR, June 30, 1995, at 8; Vanessa R. O'Connell, *Brokerage Firms Are Moving Into Cyberspace,* WALL ST. J., July 7, 1995, at C1.

266. *See* Kevin McManus, *Investing in a Personal Computer,* WASH. POST, July 26, 1995, at R11; O'Connell, *supra* note 263, at C1.

267. "On June 1, Merrill Lynch became the first nationwide full-service firm to put up a home page for its retail group." Lux, *supra* note 20, at S6. The address for Merrill Lynch's site is <http://www.ml.com> (visited Sept. 10, 1996); *see also* Prudential Securities Homepage (visited Sept. 10, 1996) <http://www.pru.sec.com>.

268. *See* Hal Lux, *Brokerage industry officials crowd Internet conference—Firms see potential, but no profits yet, on the Web,* INV. DEALERS' DIG., Feb. 5, 1996, at 9; Hal Lux, *Broker Chat forum debuts on the World Wide Web,* INV. DEALERS' DIG., Feb. 5, 1996, at 9. One large brokerage firm hosted a "chat" forum on America Online, in which one of its senior officials discussed the importance of financial planning. *See Steffens to Host Cyberchat,* WALL ST. LETTER, Apr. 8, 1996, at 1.

269. *See Firms rule out on-line trading but push to expand services,* FUND DECODER, May 27, 1996, at 5.

270. Kieran Beer, *The Future of Cyberfinance: Should Broker-Dealers Fear It or Embrace It?,* BOND BUYER, May 6, 1996, at 35; Michael Stanton, *Bloomberg: Technology Is No Cure-All, And it Won't Replace Broker-Dealers,* BOND BUYER, Apr. 30, 1996, at 10.

271. The SEC's May Interpretive Release concerning broker-dealers did not directly address issues related to electronic mail. Instead, the SEC indicated that issues related to brokers' use of electronic mail are matters for the self-regulatory organizations to consider. For example, NASD Conduct Rule 2210 and NYSE Rule 472 generally govern member firm

luctant to embrace the use of such communications without further guidance from federal regulators.[272]

Finally, with respect to investment banking services, several of the major Wall Street investment banks, and a few smaller firms, have established Internet sites.[273] As of this writing, these sites have been primarily confined to advertising investment banking firms' services, providing information on recruitment, and occasionally reprinting financial commentary or research reports. In May 1996, Salomon Brothers was the first investment bank to post a client's preliminary prospectus on its Internet site.[274] Salomon posted the preliminary prospectus for the sale of Class B shares by Berkshire Hathaway. While the Salomon posting was unique for a major investment banking firm, several smaller issuers had already conducted public offerings of their securities and provided offering documents to the public via the Internet.[275] In addition, the Salomon posting did not allow for the electronic distribution of the final prospectus, which is clearly contemplated under the SEC's October Interpretive Release.[276] Another investment bank has established an electronic bulletin board on its Internet site that lists companies looking to buy, sell, or restructure.[277]

responsibilities relating to communications with the public, including electronic communications. The SEC indicated, however, that rules concerning the supervisory requirements for electronic communications should be based on the content and audience of the message, and not merely on the electronic form of the communication, and suggested that the SROs should provide guidance in this area. *See* May Interpretive Release, *supra* note 30, at 24,645 n.5; *Ask the Analyst About Electronic Communication*, *supra* note 167; *NYSE News*, *supra* note 157.

272. *See* Letter from Stuart J. Kaswell, Senior Vice President and General Counsel, Securities Industry Association to The Honorable Steven M.H. Wallman, Commissioner, at 3 (Jan. 25, 1996) (on file with *The Business Lawyer*, University of Maryland School of Law).

> We firmly believe that the regulatory treatment of electronic messages should be governed by the *content* of the message rather than the *form of delivery*. In other words, regulations must look beyond the envelope to the words on the letter inside the envelope. Regulatory analysis should not end merely with a determination that a message was sent to a customer via e-mail—it should factor in the nature of the message transmitted.

Id.

273. *See* Lux, *supra* note 20, at S10; JP Morgan Homepage (visited Sept. 10, 1996) <http://www.jpmorgan.com/>; World M&A Network (visited Sept. 10, 1996) <http://www.cqi.com:80/MandA/cando.html>.

274. Eric Hüber, *Salomon Posts Historic But Quirky Offering on the Web*, REDEMPTION DIG. & SEC. INDUST. DAILY, May 2, 1996, at 1, 4-5 (describing the offering and Salomon's site at <http://brk.salomon.com>).

275. One commentator notes that "the Internet may be useful for small deals . . . but makes little sense for large transactions." John Elsen & Hal Lux, *New Strategy hits merger market: surfing for M&A deals online*, INV. DEALERS' DIG., Feb. 12, 1996, at 9.

276. *See* October Interpretive Release, *supra* note 30, at 53,461 (examples 1-2).

277. Elsen & Lux, *supra* note 275, at 9 (describing Yamaichi Securities site (<http://www.yamaichi.com/>), which has an electronic bulletin board listing various companies looking to buy, sell, or restructure).

USE OF THE INTERNET BY INVESTMENT ADVISERS AND FINANCIAL PLANNERS

Although many mutual funds and broker-dealers now have a presence on the Internet, there has not been a similar development of investment advisers and financial planners[278] establishing sites on the Internet. In fact, the author is aware of only a handful of investment advisers that have established Internet sites.[279]

It is likely that many small investment advisers and financial planners are inhibited from using the Internet. Smaller advisers and planners, who advise fewer than fifteen clients, do not hold themselves out generally to the public, and do not act as advisers to investment companies, are generally exempt from federal registration requirements under the Investment Advisers Act.[280] A small investment adviser who establishes an Internet site may lose its registration exemption if it is deemed to be holding itself out to the public. The SEC has indicated it believes that if an adviser uses the Internet to provide information about its services, then it no longer may qualify for an exemption from registration.[281]

A similar issue may arise with respect to an investment adviser's or financial planner's registration requirements under state laws. For example, if an investment adviser establishes an Internet site and is registered under the securities laws of a handful of states (and did not limit access of its site to actual or potential clients within those states)[282] and investors from other

278. Under the federal securities laws, an

> 'investment adviser' means any person who, for compensation, engages in the business of advising others, either directly or through publications or writings, as to the value of securities or as to the advisability of investing in, purchasing, or selling securities, or who, for compensation and as part of a regular business, issues or promulgates analyses or reports concerning securities.

15 U.S.C. § 80b-2(a)(11) (1994). "Financial planners" typically are persons who provide a variety of services, principally advisory in nature, to individuals or families regarding the management of their financial resources based upon an analysis of individual client needs. It is "not a precise term and includes a wide spectrum of advisory activity." Financial Planners, SEC Ruling, [1987-1988 Transfer Binder] Fed. Sec. L. Rep. (CCH) ¶ 84,220, at 89,008 (Mar. 9, 1988).

279. *See* American Express Financial Advisors Homepage (visited Sept. 10, 1996) <http://www.americanexpress.com.>; Turner Investment Partners, Inc. Homepage (visited Sept. 10, 1996) <http://www.turner-invest.com/>.

280. *See* Advisers Act § 203(b)(3), 15 U.S.C. § 80b-3(b)(3) (1994).

281. The SEC has also indicated that "[m]aterials concerning an adviser that are potentially available to ten or more persons through an electronic system would be considered subject to the record-keeping requirements applicable to such communications." May Interpretive Release, *supra* note 30, at 24,648; *see also* 17 C.F.R. § 275.204(a)(11) (record-keeping requirements).

282. For example, it might be possible for the adviser to limit access to its Internet site only to those clients who have obtained a password. Although the members of the public might be able to access the first page of the adviser's site, they would not be able to navigate

states can access the adviser's site, the adviser may run the risk of being found by a state in which it is not registered to have held itself out to the public in that state.[283]

Finally, although there are few larger multistate investment advisers that have established their own sites on the Internet, there are a few intermediary service providers attempting to attract investment advisers and financial planners to participate on their Internet site. At least one intermediary service provider offers a site targeted at financial planners, advisers, and broker-dealers.[284] The site contains, among other things, fund information updated by Morningstar, daily net asset value quotes and graphs for certain funds, downloadable prospectuses, a directory of financial service providers, and links to various financial planner magazines.[285]

EMERGING FEDERAL AND STATE SECURITIES LAW ISSUES

As the Internet becomes increasingly used by market participants, federal and state securities regulators will be faced with new and novel regulatory issues. They will also, no doubt, be called upon to provide clear and coherent solutions or guidance concerning unresolved securities law issues.[286] As of this writing, several important issues stand out as needing appropriate guidance by these securities regulators.

First, federal regulators must address the issue of jurisdiction. The Internet is a global medium. Virtually any person around the world with a personal computer, a modem, and access to an Internet service provider or computer that is connected to the Internet can gain entrance to the Internet. When a market participant offers its securities over the Internet, its audience is not simply located in those states (or countries) where the

beyond that point without providing user identification and a password. Such a system might be similar to those that have been established by broker-dealers and mutual funds that are sold through broker-dealers.

283. One adviser has attempted to deal with this issue by using the following disclaimer language on its Internet site:

> Turner Investment Partners, Inc. is licensed to provide advisory services in the following states, and may only provide services to residents of these states: Florida, Georgia, Illinois, Indiana, Massachusetts, New Jersey, Pennsylvania, Texas, Virginia, and Wisconsin. This information is furnished for the benefit of existing Turner clients. Nothing in this information should be construed as an invitation for residents in states other than those listed to seek advisory services from Turner.

Turner Investment Partners, Inc., Homepage, *supra* note 279.

284. *See* Quicken Financial Network Homepage (visited Sept. 9, 1996) <http://www.networth.galt.com\pro>.

285. *Id.*; *Mutual Funds on the Internet, supra* note 3, at ii.

286. *See* Spar & Bussgang, *supra* note 5, at 125 ("The commercial promise of the Internet, in short, requires rules for its fulfillment.").

participant may be registered to sell securities. Thus, use of the Internet to sell securities has become a global proposition.

Federal securities law requires that securities be registered before an issuer can use any means of communication in interstate commerce to make an offer to buy or sell securities through a prospectus or other document.[287] Does this mean that a United Kingdom company, wishing to offer and sell its securities using the Internet, must register its securities in the United States, even if the company does not intend to offer its securities outside the United Kingdom? As a practical matter, requiring the U.K. company to register its securities might place a heavy burden on its capital-raising efforts and might be difficult for the SEC to enforce (especially without retaliation from other countries). It is not altogether silly, however, to think that U.S. regulators have an interest in regulating offshore offerings that reach this country through the Internet in order to provide U.S. investors with the same protections that they receive when purchasing securities issued by a registered public company.[288]

Fortunately, although much has been made of the issue of jurisdiction with respect to communications over the Internet,[289] both federal and state securities regulators have already begun developing a reasonable approach

287. See Securities Act § 5, which states, in part, "[i]t shall be unlawful for any person, directly or indirectly, to make use of any means or instruments of transportation or communication in interstate commerce . . . to offer or to sell or offer to buy through the use or medium of any prospectus or otherwise any security, unless a registration statement has been filed as to such security." 15 U.S.C. § 77e(c) (1994). Section 2(10) of the Securities Act defines a "prospectus" as "any prospectus, notice, circular, advertisement, letter, or communication, written or by radio or television, which offers any security for sale or confirms the sale of any security." 15 U.S.C. § 77b(10) (1994).

288. This issue of jurisdiction of securities laws and the Internet is not restricted to the offering of securities. Commissioner Steven Wallman has characterized this issue with respect to the trading of securities:

> For example, the Commission has extensive and detailed regulations regarding the operation of securities exchanges. How then would the Commission regulate—and should the Commission regulate—the posting of quotations on the Internet by a foreign stock exchange, when those quotes inevitably become available to investors in the U.S.? And how long will it be after that before there is a simple mechanism for an Iowa resident to buy, for example, Frankfurt Stock Exchange listed stocks over the Internet? Obvious are the enforcement difficulties, and the policy issues arising from the operation of disparate regulatory regimes, if one were to determine that U.S. jurisdictions exists as a result of this conduct.

Steven M.H. Wallman, Commissioner, Remarks Before the Institute of International Bankers Annual Washington Conference, at 14-15 (Mar. 4, 1996) (on file with *The Business Lawyer*, University of Maryland School of Law).

289. The metaphysics of Internet-based jurisdiction has been explored in a number of contexts. *See* William S. Byassee, *Jurisdiction of Cyberspace: Applying Real World Precedent to the Virtual Community*, 30 WAKE FOREST L. REV. 197 (1995); Mark Eckenwiler, *States Get Entangled in the Web*, LEGAL TIMES, Jan. 22, 1996, at S35; *see generally* Darren McDermott, *Singapore Unveils Sweeping Measures to Control Words, Images on Internet*, WALL ST. J., Mar. 6, 1996, at B6; Paul M. Barrett, *Suit Involving Internet Site is Dismissed*, WALL ST. J., Sept. 10, 1996, at B10.

to this issue. The SEC has already started to grapple with these issues with respect to its exemption from registration for certain offerings made outside the United States under Regulation S.[290] Moreover, as previously described, a handful of states have developed an approach to this issue that focuses on the actual "sale" rather than "offer" of securities.[291] These states accept that the use of the Internet by issuers to sell securities may result in "offers" being made within a state; as long as the issuers indicate, either directly or indirectly, that offers are not directed to individuals within the state and no actual sales are made, however, then the issuer can be exempt from registration where it does not wish to be registered. The shifting of emphasis to "sales" rather than "offers" appears to be a logical distinction that may also work in the federal context and is worth exploring.

Second, regulators must be willing to address the blurring of distinctions between various types of market participants that may occur as they increasingly use the Internet. The development of the Wit-Trading System by Spring Street Brewing demonstrates that the Internet may facilitate novel activities by various types of market participants.[292] In the near future, it is likely that the Internet will blur the distinctions between other market participants. For example, the "interactivity" of the Internet may allow those entities who provide investment information to the public to become more like those who provide investment advice, such as broker-dealers and investment advisers.

Currently, it is estimated that as many as ten million people in the United States use personal finance software.[293] This type of software is often interactive, allowing customers to input various scenarios and to obtain advice on appropriate investment strategies and investments. By using the Internet, various market participants can make such interactive software available to investors all over the country (and the world).[294] As the software becomes more sophisticated, it is possible that the advice given to investors will resemble that of an investment adviser or broker-dealer, thus raising registration issues under federal and state securities laws. In addition, the growing use by market participants of electronic mail, bulletin boards, and chat forums to communicate with the public may also result in the blurring distinctions among market participants.[295] Accordingly, fed-

290. *See* Regulation S—Rules Governing Offers and Sales Made Outside the United States Without Registration under the Securities Act of 1933, 17 C.F.R. § 230.901 (1996).

291. *See supra* notes 180-204 and accompanying text.

292. *See* Wallman, *supra* note 288, at 5.

293. Robertson, *supra* note 9, at 357 ("This market is dominated by Intuit and its software package Quicken.").

294. Mutual fund companies also provide such software to investors outside of the Internet. *See* T. Rowe Price Investment Services, Inc., SEC No-Action Letter, 1995 SEC No.-Act LEXIS 694, at *25 (Sept. 8, 1995).

295. For example, if a corporate issuer sponsors a bulletin board concerning its securities and posts answers to various questions from investors, would the issuer be deemed to be providing investment advice to the public?

eral regulators must be willing to reexamine traditional roles that market participants play in the context of new technology which may facilitate a broader range of activities by such participants.[296] Once again, it is likely that there will be a tension between facilitating innovation and protecting investors.

Third, securities regulators must be willing to develop new approaches to corporate disclosure. The Internet will allow issuers to deliver corporate documents to investors rapidly and at low cost. In a purely electronic world, investors may no longer receive paper documents, but will receive documents through their computers in bytes.[297] Unlike the paper context, electronic media can allow for use of multimedia presentations that integrate text, graphics, sound, and video. In addition, it can allow for greater interaction between the reader of an electronic document and the document. For example, the Internet allows for hyperlinks that allow users to move around within documents or to link to other documents with the click of a mouse. These developments will provide market participants with significant tools to structure new presentations for their corporate disclosure documents that meet the needs of various types of investors.[298]

Both federal and state regulators should be willing to embrace technology in their plans for corporate disclosure. In addition, they should be willing to facilitate use of technology by market participants by addressing incompatibilities between filing and distribution systems. In this regard, both filed and distributed documents are winding up at the same place, on the Internet. The filed documents available through the EDGAR system (and possibly the SRD system), however, are often in a different format than the distributed documents. Because there appears to be a confluence of electronic documents on the Internet, both federal and state regulators should examine whether it is feasible to unify the routes by which documents appear on the Internet.

Finally, federal and state regulators should continue to be vigilant in their enforcement efforts. In addition to providing a new channel for the proliferation of traditional investment schemes, including chain letter, pyramid, and Ponzi schemes, the Internet presents new opportunities for securities fraud. For example, it may be possible for someone to build a fake Internet site that looks and feels like a legitimate site of a mutual fund.

296. For example, trading systems such as Wit-Trade may prompt securities regulators to reexamine who should be deemed a "dealer" and subject to the registration requirements of the Exchange Act.

297. *See generally* NEGROPONTE, *supra* note 1.

298. For example, by using electronic media, an issuer might be able to construct a prospectus that meets the needs of several different types of investors. The prospectus might contain key information for experienced investors and a number of hyperlinks to multimedia presentations that explain certain investment information to novice or new investors. *See* Michael J. Downer, *The Regulation of Disclosure in the Computerized Age*, FINANCIAL SERVICES REVOLUTION 303, 306 (forthcoming 1996); Donald C. Langevoort, *Information Technology and the Structure of Securities Regulation*, 98 HARV. L. REV. 747, 803 (1985).

When investors visit the site, they may have no way of determining the site is not legitimate and may thus decide to conduct business at the site. If the site were to accept transactions, it is possible that investors might unknowingly transmit personal information and money to the illegitimate site. This type of scheme might be difficult for regulators to detect without some advanced notice of its existence. It is likely that other, even more nefarious schemes will develop as technology evolves. Federal and state regulators must be experienced in the latest technologies in order to investigate and prosecute securities law violations on the Internet.

CONCLUSION

The growing use of the Internet by market participants has been facilitated by the recent regulatory actions by both federal and state regulators. In part, what has driven this development has been the *certainty* and *uniformity* of these actions, especially with respect to articulation of clear goals for regulation.

The SEC's approach to regulating the offering and distribution of securities through the Internet falls between incrementalism and innovation. On one hand, the SEC has recognized that there is no need to depart radically from current regulatory principles in order to accommodate the use of electronic media in securities distributions and transactions, as long as it is possible to find analogies to the use of electronic media in the paper-based context. This "regulation by analogy" provides the SEC with a firm intellectual basis for its treatment of "cyberspace" issues, given the fact that regulations applicable to paper-based media have developed over many years and are generally considered effective in achieving the objectives of the securities laws. To a large extent, the NASD has followed this approach.

On the other hand, the SEC has recognized that, in instances where no relevant analogy to regulation of paper-based media can be found, it must provide innovative and untested guidance on how the securities laws apply to the use of electronic media. In this regard, the SEC has been willing to adopt a somewhat different regulatory approach than it has in the past, adopting what Commissioner Steven Wallman has termed, a "*goal-oriented* [approach] as opposed to dictating specific processes that must be followed."[299]

Many states and the NASAA have taken a good first step in providing exemptive relief to market participants who offer securities through the Internet. State regulators must be especially mindful of the global nature of the Internet and the implications of adopting varying regulations. In addition, several states have undertaken useful efforts to educate the public and to investigate "cyberfraud" schemes.

299. Wallman, *supra* note 288, at 12.

What appears to be most clear at this time is that use of the Internet by market participants can be appropriately accommodated under the existing federal and state securities laws.[300] Where there are new or novel issues that arise with the Internet, both federal and state regulators should work to adopt uniform and reasonable approaches under the securities laws. It is important that regulators respond to novel issues quickly and provide a *consistent* and *uniform* response. Given the swiftness of change in technology, market participants highly value the certainty and quickness of response from regulators, often as much as the particular response that is given.

300. I. Trotter Hardy, *The Proper Legal Regime for "Cyberspace,"* 55 U. PITT. L. REV. 993 (1994) ("The article [concludes] that popular concern over the legal questions of cyberspace arises in some instances when, in fact, there is no 'new' issue worth discussing.").

NOTES

15

HYPERLINKS IN MUTUAL FUND ADVERTISING

Alexander C. Gavis

JANUARY 1998

wallstreetlawyer.com

Securities in the Electronic Age

Volume 1 / Number 8

contents

Hyperlinks in Mutual Fund Advertising

by Alexander C. Gavis*

Of all the innovations related to the Internet (and particularly, the World Wide Web), one of the most fundamental is the "hyperlink." Hyperlinks allow for the interconnecting of information and materials within and between Internet sites. They are the thread of the Internet, tying together millions of Internet pages and sites. Moreover, hyperlinks within an Internet site ("internal hyperlinks") promote efficiency in the presentation of information by allowing for the tiering of information displayed. Hyperlinks between Internet sites ("external hyperlinks") promote information sharing and create proximity between information sources that could not have been available in the paper context.

Mutual fund companies were pioneers among financial services companies in using the Internet and the concept of hyperlinks. To date, a large number of fund companies have developed "online investor centers" for the advertisement and sale of their funds. Hyperlinks serve an integral role within these sites, threading together fund advertisements, research, and trading functions.

The National Association of Securities Dealers, Inc. ("NASD") has primary responsibility for regulating mutual fund advertisements and sales literature

(continued on page 3)

* Alexander C. Gavis is Senior Legal Counsel in the Corporate Legal Department of Fidelity Investments.

(contined from page 1)

on Internet sites.[1] Among the self-regulatory organizations, the NASD has taken the lead in addressing issues related to its members' use of the Internet to advertise and distribute securities. With respect to hyperlinks, NASD provided early guidance to its members on their responsibility for the content and filing of the information on an Internet site to which it was linked. Moreover, as discussed below, the NASD recently revised its guidance in response to comments from the Investment Company Institute ("ICI").

NASD Guidance: Misleading, Urging or Promoting

The NASD first raised the issue of hyperlinking in an April 1996 "Ask the Analyst" column.[2] The column probed whether NASD members were responsible under the NASD's Conduct Rules for the content and filing of information on Internet sites to which they were linked. The column's informal advice stated that, "[t]he NASD is still considering the extent of a member's responsibility for sites to which that member has chosen to link. However, a member must not link to a site that the member knows contains misleading information about the member's products and services." The column further indicated that, "[i]f a member's site must be filed with the NASD and the member's site includes information promoting a link to another's site or urging the user to view a linked site, the NASD will likely require that the member provide the linked information for review."

Mutual fund companies found the NASD's informal guidance on external hyperlinks difficult to administer for several reasons and thus, few fund companies used them. First, the condition that members cannot link to sites which they know are misleading would appear to place member firms who used them in a difficult situation. If a member firm were to establish a link to an independent third-party's site, it might be able to establish that, at the time the link was established, there was no misleading information within the third-party's site. However, once established, given the constantly changing nature of Internet sites, it would be virtually impossible for a member firm to ensure that the third-party's site was free from misleading information. The member firm might argue, of course, that it had no knowledge of any new misleading information; but it could not argue that it did not have knowledge that such information might occur.

Second, the NASD's position that, if a member firm's site "promotes or urges" a user to view a linked site, the linked material may have to be filed with the NASD, would be extremely difficult to administer. The NASD's guidance offered no clear guidance as to how much of the linked information would have to be filed such as a whole Internet site, a page, or other hyperlinks, and how a member firm might interpret (or the NASD define) the terms "promoting" or "urging."

ICI's Request for Further Guidance

In October 1996, the Investment Company Institute ("ICI") submitted a letter to the NASD requesting further guidance with respect to electronic advertisements and sales literature. The letter recommended, among other things, that the NASD develop a new regulatory standard for the regulation of hyperlinks.[3] The letter also recommended that the NASD allow members to file the contents in electronic, rather than in paper, format and develop a special service charge schedule tailored to the nature of these filings. This past November the NASD replied to the ICI's letter, agreeing to some recommendations and leaving some issues open.[4]

On the issue of hyperlinks, the ICI argued that the linking together of Internet sites is a new and innovative technology. Although the NASD has looked to its regulations regarding the paper-based communication as precedent for addressing electronic media issues, the ICI argued that it is not possible to rely entirely on the former to establish standards for the use of hyperlinks by NASD members. If, for example, a mutual fund were to include a reprint of a favorable magazine article about the fund in a mailing to investors, the reprint would be subject to the NASD's content and filing requirements. Conversely, if the fund's newsletter included a description of the same magazine article along with the publication citation or information about how the investor might obtain a copy from someone other than the distributor of the mutual fund, the fund would not be responsible for the content and filing of the article.

The ICI argued that hyperlinks do not fall squarely within either category. On the one hand, they make it much easier for investors to view the referenced site (as opposed to having to go to a public library or newsstand). On the other hand, a hyperlink by itself does not provide the article in question directly to investors. Instead, it simply provides an investor with the option of accessing another Internet site. If the investor uses the hyperlink, he or she moves from an area within a NASD member's site to an area that contains the hyperlinked material. Because hyperlinks cannot simply be analogized to either a paper-based reprint or a citation, the ICI recommended that the NASD adopt new standards in this area, along the lines set forth below.

The ICI stated that there are three particular circumstances in which a NASD member should not be responsible for the content and filing of the information on an Internet site to which the member's site has been linked:

- If the hyperlink is "ongoing." An ongoing hyperlink allows investors to view a third party's site whether the material is favorable or unfavorable to the member. Moreover, the linked site can be updated or changed by the third party at any time, but investors would still be able to access it. An ongoing hyperlink would therefore not allow the NASD member the ability to promote or urge investors to access a site that contains only favorable information.
- If a NASD member provided a hyperlink to a third party's home page. A hyperlink to the home page of another Internet site would not generally provide investors with a specific and directed advertisement or sales literature concerning the NASD member. Moreover, investors would have the option of hyperlinking to various parts of the third party's site.
- If an NASD member provided one or more hyperlinks to non-member specific information at Internet sites that are intended for use by the public for general reference and education purposes. These types of hyperlinks provide investors with the ability to obtain further information about investing and thus should not be subject to content and filing requirements because they do not specifically promote or recommend the members' products or services.

NASD's Response

The NASD responded to the ICI's request for guidance on the issue of hyperlinks and reserved its response to the issues of electronic filing and fees for a later date. In its response, the NASD addressed each of the three circumstances in which, in the ICI's view, an NASD member should not be responsible for the content and filing of material to which the member's Internet site has been linked. The NASD's letter appears to create a safe harbor from content and filing requirements in two limited circumstances, as long as NASD members follow certain guidelines outlined in the letter.

Ongoing Hyperlinks

The first safe harbor is available for what the ICI described as "ongoing hyperlinks." The NASD restated the ICI's description of an ongoing external hyperlink:

- the hyperlink is continuously available to investors who visit the member's site;
- the member has no discretion to alter the information on the third-party site;
- investors have access to the hyperlinked site whether or not it contains favorable material about the member, and
- the linked site could be updated or changed by the third party and investors would, nonetheless, be able to use the hyperlink.

When a member's Internet site contains such an ongoing hyperlink to an independent third party, the NASD staff would not hold the member responsible for the content or filing of information contained in the site. The NASD retained the "misleading information" standard in its guidance, stating that a member may not establish a hyperlink to a site that "the member knows or has reason to know contains false or misleading information about the member's products or services." In addition, the NASD stated, somewhat ambiguously, that "if the third party site has been produced by another member, then that member would be responsible for the contents of its site."

The ICI's letter had indicated that a member should be allowed to suspend or terminate the hyperlink due to mechanical or technical difficulties or similar problems. In response, the NASD stated its belief that a member's ability to suspend or terminate the hyperlink due to mechanical or technical difficulties, and not the presentation of unfavorable information (or absence of unfavorable information) about the member's products and services, would not, by itself, vest the NASD member with content and filing responsibility. The member firm must be able to demonstrate that the termination was due to mechanical or technical difficulties.

Educational Material Hyperlinks

The NASD also agreed with the ICI that, if a member provides a hyperlink to information in an Internet site that is intended for use by the public for "general reference and education purposes" and the information does not refer to the member, the member should not be responsible for the content or filing of the information at the linked site. If a member firm hyperlinks to any independent third party site that does not refer to the member or any of its affiliates and is meant to educate investors about principles of investing or economic, tax, or financial issues, then the NASD would not hold the member responsible for the content or filing of the information found at that site. Again, the NASD ambiguously stated that "if the third party site has been produced by another member, then that member would be responsible for the contents of its site."

Home Page Hyperlinks

The ICI had recommended that, if a member provided an external hyperlink to a third party's home page that did not meet the conditions of an "ongoing" or "educational" hyperlink, the member should not be responsible for the content or filing of information at the entire linked site. The NASD disagreed with the ICI's position on such "home page" hyperlinks. The NASD indicated that, under the ICI's recommendation, "a member could hyperlink to the home page of an investment newsletter that contains a misleading article about the member's mutual fund." Even though the investor could hyperlink to other articles in the newsletter, the NASD did not believe that this would discharge the member from responsibility for the misleading one. The NASD also stated, somewhat vaguely, that "nor would the fact that the investors must click a mouse or otherwise undertake a simple additional step to reach the misleading article from the home page create such a barrier between the home page and the misleading article as to justify the [ICI's] recommendation."

Open Issues

The NASD's response was narrowly crafted, addressing only those issues raised in the ICI's letter. Nevertheless, it represents a positive step by the NASD and should be useful to NASD members. Going forward, the NASD should consider developing further interpretive guidance on hyperlinks. The following identifies a number of open issues in this area.

First, the ICI's letter attempted to provide general parameters for the term "ongoing hyperlink," however, it was not exhaustive in its analysis and left several issues unresolved. Although the ICI's letter argued, and the NASD agreed, that an ongoing link may be suspended due to mechanical or technical difficulties, it is not difficult to imagine other situations in which an ongoing hyperlink may need to be altered. For example, if a fund company establishes an ongoing hyperlink as part of its Internet site and then, at a later date, undertakes to redesign the site or undergoes a business model change for the site, would the fund company have to maintain the ongoing hyperlink, even if the link no longer made sense in the context of the redesign or new business model?

In addition, with respect to misleading information, the NASD's response letter stated, "we are not commenting on a member's possible responsibility to suspend or terminate a hyperlink when it has come to the member's attention that the hyperlinked site contains false or misleading information." It is unclear what is meant by the phrase, "come to the member's attention." One reading could imply that members may have an obligation to continuously monitor an ongoing hyperlink for false and misleading information. A continuous monitoring requirement, however, would be extremely burdensome for fund companies to administer and would work against the concept and spirit of ongoing hyperlinks to independent third party sites. A reasonable standard might not require monitoring, but would allow fund companies to discontinue an ongoing hyperlink if they become, or are made, aware of false or misleading information.

Under a literal reading of the NASD's response letter, an ongoing hyperlink would have to be maintained under practically all circumstances. Perhaps a more balanced approach might include allowing fund companies to terminate an ongoing hyperlink for (1) mechanical or technical reasons, (2) if the member's site undergoes a reasonable business model change or redesign that is unrelated to the establishment of the hyperlink, or (3) if the fund company becomes, or is made, aware of false or misleading information.

Second, the NASD's letter provides a safe harbor for ongoing hyperlinks to sites of an *independent third party*, which is defined as "any entity that is independent of the member and its affiliates, and whose services are not procured by the member or any of its affiliates to develop or provide information on the third-party site." Many companies that have established Internet sites have begun to scrutinize third party hyperlinks to their sites, as a result of recent litigation between Ticketmaster Group, Inc. and Microsoft.[5] In a lawsuit filed in U.S. District Court in Los Angeles, Ticketmaster charged that Microsoft's Seattle Sidewalk Web site illegally uses the Ticketmaster name and trademark by linking directly to pages within the Ticketmaster site, rather than to Ticketmaster's homepage. It is becoming increasingly common for companies with Internet sites to request that any hyperlinks to their sites be the subject of a linking agreement. These agreements attempt to spell out the terms and conditions under which a third-party will hyperlink to a company's site. Although not entirely free from doubt, it appears that the NASD's definition of independent third party would exclude situations in which a member firm entered into a linking agreement with a third-party, as long as the agreement is not related to the member firm's developing or providing information on the third-party site.

Third, a number of fund companies have established programs in which they distribute their funds along with funds from other fund companies. These programs — or fund supermarkets as they are commonly named — involve agreements between the sponsor of the program ("sponsor") and the funds distributed through the program ("participants"). As the Internet becomes increasingly useful as a means of distributing information about funds to the public, it is likely that the sponsors of such fund supermarkets will wish to establish hyperlinks between their sites and the sites of supermarket fund participants. Such hyperlinks do not appear to fit squarely within the NASD's ongoing or educational hyperlinks categories.

According to the NASD's letter, ongoing hyperlinks require that the third party be independent of the member or its affiliates, and educational hyperlinks may not be produced by another member. Nevertheless, the author believes that the ongoing hyperlink safe harbor should be allowed for an ongoing link between the sponsor's site and a participant's site, as long as the sponsor has not procured the participant's services to develop or provide information on the participant's site. In addition, on two occasions in the letter, the NASD states that "if a third party site has been produced by another member, then that member would be responsible for the contents of its site." It is not clear which party is being referred to in this sentence as having content responsibility. It appears that the sentence may indicate that the third party member firm has responsibility for content and filing and not the member who has established the hyperlink.

Finally, the NASD's letter did not address the concept of internal hyperlinks. Internal hyperlinks help investors navigate a fund company's site or display information that may be relevant to a particular area of the site but that cannot be accommodated due to space or size limitations. Such hyperlinks are enormously useful both to fund companies (because they conserve space within Internet sites and allow for links between related items) and to investors (because they provide access to multiple layers of information).

The advertising rules contain specific requirements for the content and placement of disclosure. For example, when a fund company advertises performance information about a particular fund, the information must contain average annual total returns for the one, five and ten year period for the fund in equal prominence to any other performance numbers.[6] A fund company could perhaps display non-standard performance on one page of its Internet site and provide a hyperlink to standard performance. It is unclear, however, whether the hyperlink would meet the "equal prominence" standard of the advertising rules. The concept of equal prominence was established as a paper-based concept in large measure to ensure that investors who see fund advertisements containing performance of a fund also see standardized (1, 5 and 10 year) measures.

With any new technology that enhances the delivery of information to investor, there is a need to take a fresh look at rules that affect the delivery. For example, in the late 1980's, the SEC reexamined the equal prominence requirement with respect to automated telephone response systems used by fund companies.[7] In that context, under certain circumstances fund companies are permitted to provide investors with nonstandardized performance on one telephone menu selection and standardized performance on another menu selection.[8]

Hyperlinks clearly allow for new and innovative forms of disclosure of information. Accordingly, the NASD should take a close look at the disclosure requirements under the advertising rules and determine whether there are situations in which the rules should be reinterpreted or updated in order to address this new technology.

footnotes

1. Most mutual fund sales material originates from NASD member firms and is therefore subject to the NASD's Conduct Rules, which include content and filing requirements. The NASD has included the term "electronic" in the definitions of "Advertisement" and "Sales Literature" under the Conduct Rules. NASD Notice to Members 95-74 (Sept. 1995).
2. Ask the Analyst About Electronic Communications, NASD Regulatory & Compliance Alert (April 1996) at 5.
3. Letter from Alexander C. Gavis, Assistant Counsel, Investment Company Institute, to R. Clark Hooper, Senior Vice President, Office of Disclosure and Investor Protection, NASD Regulation, Inc., dated October 15, 1996.
4. Letter from Thomas M. Selman, Director, Advertising/Investment Companies Regulation, NASD Regulation, Inc., to Craig S. Tyle, General Counsel, Investment Company Institute, dated November 11,1997. A copy of the letter can be accessed at the NASD's Web site: http://www.nasdr.com/2910/2210_01.htm.
5. *See, e.g.*, Rebecca Quick, Can't Get There From Here May be the Web's New Motto—Companies Start to Curb Links to Their Sites, Wall St. J. (July 2, 1997).
6. *See* Securities and Exchange Commission Rule 482(e)(3)(iii).
7. Investment Company Institute (pub. avail. April 27, 1988).
8. The SEC has indicated that its guidance regarding legal prominence is not intended to cover the use of automated telephone response systems for marketing purposes.

NOTES

16

THE YEAR 2000 PROBLEM: A TECHNOLOGICAL TIME BOMB

Stephen J. Schulte

The author thanks William F. Sullivan for his assistance in writing this article.

TABLE OF CONTENTS

INTRODUCTION

A technological time bomb is ticking in a vast number of computer systems throughout the world; it is known as the "Year 2000 Problem" and is also sometimes referred to as "Y2K" or the "Millennium Bug." The problem is that many older computer programs were designed so that years are expressed with two digits rather than four.[1] These programs assume that the first two digits of a year are "19", meaning that when the year 2000 arrives, many computer systems are going to interpret the date as 1900.[2] This flaw is not limited to software and may also be present in older hardware and embedded chips.[3] Because many computer functions are date-sensitive (such as sorting, validating and comparing), this glitch may result in serious miscalculations and, in some cases, complete system failures.[4]

This article focuses on the Year 2000 Problem in the context of the federal securities laws. Part I examines the general scope of the Year 2000 Problem; Part II discusses current regulatory and legislative initiatives; Part III explores certain accounting considerations associated with the Year 2000 Problem; Part IV summarizes a survey of disclosure trends in annual reports that have been recently filed with the SEC; and Part V sets forth a model strategic plan to address a company's Year 2000 issues.

PART I. GENERAL SCOPE OF THE PROBLEM

The scope and severity of the Year 2000 Problem cannot be overstated. Experts predict that it will result in a variety of catastrophes, including the malfunction of traffic lights, elevators and pacemakers,[5] failures in the nation's air traffic control systems,[6] and possibly even a worldwide recession.[7] Because of its high level of computer dependency, the business world will be particularly affected by the Millennium Bug. The Securities Industry Association (the

"SIA") has declared that "the transition into the Year 2000 is the biggest business and technology effort that the world has ever experienced."[8] Similarly, the NASD has stated that the Year 2000 Problem "is a significant, world-wide challenge across all business and industry lines for any company, social or government agency, institution, or individual using computers or other certain automated application/systems to accomplish a task."[9]

For financial institutions, the Year 2000 Problem may readily translate into severe business disruptions. The range of potential problems is vast, including errors in checking account transactions, interest calculations, payment schedules, bank recordkeeping, and currency and securities transfers.[10] Some of these concerns are already starting to emerge. For example, thousands of credit cards with expiration dates past December 1999 have recently been rendered invalid because many validating computers are not Year 2000 compliant.[11]

The securities industry is also particularly vulnerable to the Millennium Bug because "[e]very securities transaction depends for proper execution on the correct sequencing of events and calculations based on dates."[12] For example, if there is a Y2K malfunction or failure in a securities firm's computer system it could undermine the firm's ability to settle trades, calculate positions/exposures, and meet regulatory requirements.[13] Thus, if the Year 2000 Problem causes malfunctions in automated transactions, it will be difficult or impossible for many securities firms to conduct business.[14]

Even those entities which are able to remedy their Year 2000 Problems may nevertheless face severe business disruptions as a result of the system failures of third parties ("counter-parties"), such as suppliers, service providers or partners which may not have remedied their own Year 2000 Problems – in other words, the chain will only be as strong as its weakest link. Given the high level of interconnectedness that exists in the securities and financial industries, "a default in any one of a multitude of areas could trigger a system-wide crisis that ultimately could threaten even businesses fully prepared to address the Millennium Bug."[15] This may result in "potential business collapses and even bankruptcies due to companies not receiving payments; possible market collapses due to failed transactions, failed payments, and the inability of manual clearing to catch up with the backlog; and severe capital strain on even healthy businesses."[16] A recent study has indicated that a "Y2K snafu at a single firm, clearinghouse and exchange could cost the global financial markets as much as $10 million in one week . . . ."[17]

Fixing the Year 2000 Problem will be extremely costly and time consuming. Although experts differ on the extent of the projected damage and disruption, in all cases, the estimates are staggering. The projected costs to fix the problem range from $600 to $900 billion worldwide,[18] and a substantial portion of these expenses will be absorbed by the financial institutions and Wall Street firms. For example, the cost of Year 2000 projects for U.S. commercial banks is estimated at $7.2 billion[19] and Wall Street firms are expected to spend $3 to $4 billion.[20] For individual firms, these numbers translate into huge cash outlays. One large commercial bank recently reported that it expects to spend $600 million to remedy its Year 2000 Problems.[21] Similarly, many large investment banks generally expect to spend between $200 to $300 million in remediation expenses.[22] Moreover, these costs do not include the expense and consequences of litigation likely to arise from Year 2000 related claims, which some experts predict will "equal the cumulative costs of tobacco, pollution cleanup, [and] asbestosis . . . ."[23] Others have predicted that litigation costs could amount to $2 to $3 for every dollar spent trying to fix the problem.[24]

The Year 2000 Problem is, of course, exacerbated by the time pressure. There are only 21 months left, and, unlike many deadlines, there will be no extensions. The task of becoming Y2K compliant is daunting for many businesses and industries, especially given the time constraints and size and complexity of many of the software programs that must be updated or replaced and the related costs.[25] The magnitude of the problem is reflected in the number of entities that lag in addressing their Year 2000 issues. For example, one study has indicated that 71% of U.S. private and public entities have a formal Year 2000 program in place, while in Asia that number drops to 63%, and in Europe it drops even further to 57%.[26]

PART II. REGULATORY AND LEGISLATIVE INITIATIVES

A. Staff Legal Bulletin No. 5

In Staff Legal Bulletin No. 5, issued October 8, 1997, and revised on January 12, 1998 (the "Bulletin" or "Revised Bulletin"), the Divisions of Corporation Finance and Investment Management provided interpretive guidance on Year 2000 disclosure issues. The first part of the Bulletin focuses on the disclosure requirements for public companies and the second part focuses on the requirements for investment companies and investment advisers.[27]

The following is a summary of the key points of the Revised Bulletin. As a prelude, it should be noted that the Staff of the SEC has recently warned that (1) filings that do not include any Y2K disclosure will automatically trigger inquiry as to the reasons for the absence thereof, and (2) the Staff will not be sympathetic to securities law or other regulatory violations resulting from failure to become Y2K compliant.[28]

1. Disclosure by Public Companies

The section on public companies begins by noting that "[e]ach company's potential costs and uncertainties will depend on a number of factors, including its software and hardware and the nature of the industry. Companies must coordinate with other entities with which they electronically interact, both domestically and globally, including suppliers, customers, creditors, borrowers, and financial service organizations."[29]

The Revised Bulletin warns that "[c]ompanies should review, on an ongoing basis, whether they need to disclose anticipated costs, problems and uncertainties associated with Year 2000 consequences, particularly in their filings with the Commission."[30] Before outlining the specific areas in which Year 2000 issues must be disclosed, the Bulletin explains that public companies may have to disclose this information in SEC filings because:

- the form or report may require disclosure, or
- in addition to the information that the company is specifically required to disclose, the disclosure rules require disclosure of any additional material information necessary to make the required disclosure not misleading.[31]

In this connection, the Bulletin warns that companies should also "consider the anti-fraud provisions of the Securities Act and the Exchange Act . . . . [which] apply to statements and omissions both in Commission filings and outside of Commission filings."[32]

a. MD&A

MD&A (the acronym for "Management's Discussion and Analysis of Financial Condition and Results of Operations") is considered by the Securities and Exchange Commission to be one of the most important components of disclosure. The MD&A guidelines, set forth in Item 303 of Regulation S-K,[33] are intended to require management to provide a narrative analysis of a company's financial statements and prospects, with the focus on liquidity, capital resources, and results of operations, including a discussion of known trends, events or uncertainties that are likely to have a material impact.[34]

The Revised Bulletin emphasizes that companies should include Year 2000 disclosure in their MD&A section if:

- the cost of addressing the Year 2000 issue is a material event or uncertainty that would cause reported financial information not to be necessarily indicative of future operating results or financial condition, or

- the costs or the consequences of incomplete or untimely resolution of their Year 2000 issue represent a known material event or uncertainty that is reasonably expected to affect their future financial results, or cause their reported financial information not to be necessarily indicative of future operating results or future financial condition.[35]

b. Description of Business

Description of Business is a section required to be included in various filings under the Securities Act and Exchange Act pursuant to Item 101 of Regulation S-K.[36] The Revised Bulletin warns that public companies may need to report Year 2000 issues in the Description of Business section of Commission filings if such issues "materially affect [the] company's products, services, or competitive conditions . . . ."[37] Moreover, in deciding whether to disclose Year 2000 issues, "companies should consider the effects of the Year 2000 issue on each of their reportable segments."[38]

c. Form 8-K

Form 8-K is a current report under Sections 13 or 15(d) of the Exchange Act. Companies generally are required to file this form upon the occurrence of a significant corporate change.[39] Item 5 of Form 8-K is where a company may report any events that it "deems of importance to security holders."[40] Regarding Y2K, the Revised Bulletin states that a "company's Year 2000 costs or consequences may reach a level of importance that prompts it to consider filing a Form 8-K."[41] It further advises that in considering whether to file a Form 8-K, "companies should be particularly mindful of the accuracy and completeness of information in registration statements filed under the Securities Act that incorporate by reference Exchange Act reports, including Form 8-Ks."[42]

d. Accounting Considerations[43]

The Revised Bulletin provides some guidance to companies for determining how to properly reflect the costs of modifying computer software for Year 2000 projects. Citing a release promulgated by the Emerging Issues Task Force,[44] the Bulletin notes that "these costs should be charged to expense as they are incurred."[45] This standard applies only to modifications and not to replacements which may be capitalized and amortized.

e. Specific Disclosure Considerations

The Revised Bulletin was issued to provide more specific guidance regarding Year 2000 issues and includes a section titled "Specific Disclosure Considerations." That section states that disclosure is required if a company "has not made an assessment of its Year 2000 issues or has not determined whether it has material Year 2000 issues . . . ."[46] In addition, the Revised Bulletin states:

> the determination as to whether a company's Year 2000 issues should be disclosed should be based on whether the Year 2000 issues are material to a company's business, operations, or financial condition, without regard to related countervailing circumstances (such as Year 2000 remediation programs or contingency plans). If the Year 2000 issues are determined to be material . . . the nature and potential impact of the Year 2000 issues as well as the countervailing circumstances should be disclosed.[47]

The Bulletin notes that as part of this disclosure at least the following topics should be addressed:

- the company's general plans to address the Year 2000 issues relating to its business, its operations (including operating systems) and, if material, its relationships with customers, suppliers, and other constituents; and its timetable for carrying out those plans; and

- the total dollar amount that the company estimates will be spent to remediate its Year 2000 issues, if such amount is expected to be

> material to the company's business, operations or financial condition, and any material impact these expenditures are expected to have on the company's results of operations, liquidity and capital resources.[48]

The Revised Bulletin also warns that "disclosure must be reasonably specific and meaningful, rather than standard boilerplate."[49]

f. Foreign Companies

The Bulletin also contains a brief section pertaining to foreign private issuers, advising that they also should follow the Bulletin's guidance. In particular, they should consider the disclosure requirements of Form 20-F, Item 1 ("Description of Business") and Item 9 ("MD&A").[50]

2. Investment Companies and Investment Advisers

The Revised Bulletin provides that Year 2000 disclosure may also be required under the Investment Company Act of 1940 and the Investment Advisers Act of 1940 "if operational or financial obstacles are presented by the Year 2000 issue."[51] In this connection, the Bulletin states that "[d]isclosure of the Year 2000 issue is necessary if it is materially misleading to shareholders to omit the information."[52] Investment companies and investment advisers that determine that Year 2000 disclosure is required should follow the guidelines under "Specific Disclosure Considerations" discussed above.[53]

a. Investment Companies

Regarding investment companies, the Revised Bulletin notes that it is unlawful for them to omit from their public filings "any fact necessary in order to prevent the statements made therein, in light of the circumstances under which they were made, from being materially misleading."[54] The Bulletin also notes that Item 5(b) of Form N-1A requires that mutual funds describe in their registration statements the experience of their investment advisers and the services that the advisers provide.[55] In this connection, the Revised Bulletin states: "In response to [Item 5(b)], investment companies may need to disclose the effect that the Year 2000 issue would have on their advisers' ability to provide the services described in their registration statements."[56]

b. Investment Advisers

The Bulletin cites the anti-fraud provisions of the Investment Advisers Act of 1940 and reminds investment advisers of their "affirmative duty, consistent with their fiduciary obligations, to disclose to clients or prospective clients, material facts concerning their advisory or proposed advisory relationships."[57] In this connection, if an adviser's failure to address its Year 2000 issues could materially affect its ability to deliver its services (or create an uncertainty in that regard), the Bulletin warns that the adviser has an obligation to disclose that information in a timely manner so that clients and prospective clients may take steps to protect their interests.[58]

B. Recent SEC Broker-Dealer Proposal

The SEC is considering a proposal that would require larger broker-dealers and non-bank transfer agents to report to the Commission on their efforts to address Year 2000 Problems.[59] "The rules are intended to ensure senior management is paying attention to the Year 2000 problem," according to Robert L. Colby, Deputy Director of the SEC's Division of Market Regulation.[60] The proposed rules would go further than the guidance in the Revised Bulletin.[61] They would be specific and mandatory and would require firms to submit reports separate from regular filings.[62] Some of the more controversial issues are whether the reports should be public or private and whether an auditor's attestation should be required.[63]

C. NASD Initiatives

Since mid-1996, the NASD has issued a number of statements relating to Year 2000 compliance.[64] In late 1997, a Special NASD Notice to Members 97-96 (the "Special Notice") was sent to all member firms and included a compliance survey to be completed and returned to the NASD. The Special Notice states that the Year 2000 Problem "is particularly acute in the securities industry, due to its heavy reliance on information technology."[65] In this connection, the Special Notice reminds every member to analyze the readiness of its own computer systems, as well as other computer systems that each member relies upon.[66] Citing an earlier Notice to Members,[67] the Special Notice states: "computer failures related to Y2K problems generally will be considered neither a defense to violations of firms' regulatory compliance responsibilities nor a mitigation of sanctions for such violations."[68]

To ensure that its member firms are prepared to meet the challenges of the Year 2000 Problem, the NASD has instituted a Year 2000 Program.[69] In this connection, a special NASD Office has been established, which is responsible for the development of metrics and reporting, oversight for standardization of testing and certification, and development of various processes (*i.e.*, correspondence tracking and different types of reporting).[70] The program will require that later this year members certify to NASD Regulation the status of their Year 2000 compliance program and their readiness for testing.[71] NASD Regulation also plans to require that each member certify that its systems have been remediated and other necessary steps have been taken to address systems compliance for Year 2000.[72] More information about the NASD's Year 2000 Program is available on its web sites at "http://www.nasd.com" and "http://www.nasdr.com."

In addition to its own initiatives, the NASD is also a founding member of the

Y2K Exchange and Utility Subcommittee of the SIA, along with the New York Stock Exchange, the American Stock Exchange, the National Securities Clearing Corporation, the Depository Trust Corporation, and the Securities Industry Automation Corporation.[73] The NASD is working with these organizations to establish data interchange guidelines and to plan for three stages of Year 2000 testing: unit, bilateral, and industry-wide.[74]

The first stage, known as "unit testing," involves one-on-one testing between an exchange and its participants.[75] The second stage of testing is "bilateral testing," which involves one-on-one testing between exchanges.[76] The first two stages of testing are expected to be completed by the end of 1998.[77] The final stage of testing is "industry-wide testing," which will provide the securities industry with a test market environment to perform transaction cycle testing, and allow industry participants to synchronize their computers to simulate a particular trading date.[78] This testing is tentatively scheduled throughout 1999 and will allow the industry participants to ensure that their systems will continue to operate in a Y2K environment.[79]

D. Proposed Federal Legislation

1. Senate Proposal

In late November 1997, Senator Robert Bennett (R-Utah) introduced a bill (S. 1518) entitled, the Year 2000 Computer Remediation and Shareholder Protection Act of 1997 (the "CRASH Act").[80] The proposed bill would require extensive disclosure by public companies of their Y2K status.

In light of the subsequent release of the Revised Bulletin, however, it is not clear whether the proposed legislation will move forward.[81] Senator Bennett has recently said, "[t]he SEC chose to incorporate key components of my legislation in their revised bulletin . . . . I commend Chairman Levitt for his leadership and his courage in taking this initiative."[82]

Moreover, Senator Bennett stated that "[t]he information I will receive from reviewing the results of this new bulletin will be very valuable in determining how to proceed with my own legislation . . . . I'm more concerned that we bring about this important change than how we do it."[83] On February 10, 1998, Senator Bennett's staff announced that the CRASH Act has been put on hold until he reviews the wave of 10-Q reports that are filed in mid-February.[84]

2. House Proposal

The House Banking Committee recently voted "to give federal regulators of thrifts and credit unions new authority to monitor the companies that sell services to those institutions to make them ready [for the year 2000]."[85] The bill (H.R. 3116) is being sponsored by Banking Committee Chairman, James Leach (R-Iowa), who stated that "[t]his bill will be an ally to the smaller, more vulnerable institutions that need help the most."[86] Supporters said that the bill "would put S&L and credit union regulators on an equal footing with bank regulatory agencies such as the Federal Reserve, the Comptroller of the Currency and the Federal Deposit Insurance Corp."[87] Although a date has not yet been scheduled, the bill will soon go before the full House "where its passage appears assured."[88]

E. President Clinton's Year 2000 Council

President Clinton recently issued an executive order creating a "Year 2000 Conversion Council" that will be headed by John Koskinen, former Deputy Director of the Office of Management and Budget.[89] The purpose of the council "is to coordinate executive branch agencies on Year 2000 preparations, including their interactions with state and local governments."[90] In addition, the executive order directs agencies to "cooperate with the private sector operators of critical national and local systems, including the banking and financial system . . . in addressing the Y2K problem."[91]

PART III. CERTAIN ACCOUNTING CONSIDERATIONS

Generally Accepted Accounting Principles ("GAAP") are the accounting rules that govern the preparation of financial statements used in SEC filings. The standards are promulgated by the Financial Accounting Standards Board ("FASB") and the American Institute of Certified Public Accountants ("AICPA").

Under GAAP, the costs associated with Year 2000 repairs generally should be charged to expense as incurred, while costs of replacement may be capitalized and amortized. This accounting principle will cover the majority of cases involving Y2K remediation efforts. However, some companies may need to address FASB Statement No. 5, *Accounting for Contingencies* ("SFAS 5"), in situations when they are faced with Year 2000 issues at a particular reporting date that are contingent in nature (*e.g.*, litigation).

SFAS 5 requires that contingencies which are reasonably possible, whether or not their amounts can be calculated or estimated, must be disclosed in a note to the financial statements. The Statement provides that a "contingency" is an existing condition, situation, or set of circumstances involving uncertainty as to possible gain or loss to an enterprise that will ultimately be resolved when one or more future events occur or fail to occur.[92] SFAS 5 defines "reasonably possible" as more than remote, but less than probable.[93] Thus, if under these standards it is reasonably possible that a company will not become Year 2000 compliant on time, then that contingency must be disclosed in a note to the financial statements.

In some cases, Year 2000 related losses may be required to be included in the body of the financial statements. In particular, SFAS 5 provides that a related loss should be included if: (1) it is probable[94] that the company will not become Year 2000 compliant in time; (2) an asset has been impaired or a liability incurred as of the date of the financial statements;

and (3) the amount of the loss can be reasonably estimated. If a company's Year 2000 Problem meets the three prong test, then the estimated loss must be charged against earnings and reported in the body of the financial statements.

Auditors must also be concerned about the impact of Year 2000 issues when conducting audits of a company's financial statements. In this connection, auditors must comply with Generally Accepted Auditing Standards ("GAAS"), including Statements on Auditing Standards ("SAS"). SAS No. 53, *The Auditor's Responsibility to Detect and Report Errors and Irregularities*, requires that auditors provide reasonable assurance for detecting errors and irregularities. It defines "errors" as unintentional misstatements or omissions, and "irregularities" as intentionally false or misleading statements that reach a financial statement level of materiality.

The AICPA has issued a summary of accounting guidance entitled, "The Year 2000 Issue—Current Accounting and Auditing Guidance" (October 31, 1997). The document provides an overview of the Year 2000 Problem and summarizes the applicable accounting, disclosure, and auditing standards. The summary is available on the AICPA's Web Site at "http://www.aicpa.org/members/y2000/intro.htm."

PART IV. CURRENT DISCLOSURE TRENDS IN ANNUAL REPORTS

This section reflects Year 2000 disclosure trends in 10-Ks, based on a sample of 10-K reports that were filed by 40 registrants after the issuance of the Revised Bulletin (the "Survey").[95] The principal areas of disclosure are: (A) actual or estimated costs of Year 2000 remediation; (B) impact of Year 2000 remediation costs on financial position and results of operations; (C) whether the company has investigated the level of Year 2000 readiness of its counter-parties; (D) whether the costs or consequences of unresolved Year 2000 issues are a material known event or uncertainty; (E) projected date of completion of remedial efforts; (F) whether the remediation efforts are being handled internally or with outside assistance; and (G) the manner in which remediation costs are handled from an accounting perspective.

A. Remediation Costs

Of those annual reports surveyed, 17.5% included the actual or projected cost of Year 2000 remediation projects; the remainder were silent in this regard. Below are examples of typical disclosures that specify the projected or actual costs of remediation.

- [The Company] estimates that the total cumulative cost of the project will be approximately $40 million, which includes both internal and external personnel costs related to modifying the systems as well as the cost of purchasing or leasing certain hardware and software.

- The Company incurred $1.0 million in costs attributable to the Year 2000 project in fiscal 1997 and expects to incur $2.6 million in such costs in fiscal 1998.

B. Impact of Remediation Costs on Financial Position and Results of Operations

Of the annual reports surveyed, 70% discussed whether Year 2000 remediation costs would have a material impact on the company's financial position or results of operation. All of these companies indicated that they did not expect these costs to be material. The following examples illustrate the manner in which companies made these disclosures.

- The estimated cost of these efforts are not expected to be material to the Company's financial position or any year's results of operations.

- The total cost associated with the required modifications and conversions is not expected to be material to [the Company's] consolidated results of operations and financial position . . . .

C. Inquiry of Year 2000 Status of Counter-Parties

"Counter-parties" refers to third parties on which a company relies in the ordinary course of its business (*e.g.*, suppliers, service providers, and partners). Both the Revised Bulletin and the NASD Special Notice to Members warn that companies must coordinate their Year 2000 remediation projects with their counter-parties. In the Survey, 22.5% of the registrants indicated that they had or would communicate with counter-parties as part of their Year 2000 remediation programs. The following excerpts provide examples of the way in which companies disclosed the issue.

- The Company is also monitoring the progress its major service providers are making to prepare their systems for operations for the year 2000. The Company does not anticipate that it or its major service providers will be unable to meet year 2000 operation commitments.

- The Company will initiate formal communications with all of its significant suppliers and large customers to determine the extent to which the Company is vulnerable to those third parties' failure to remediate their own Year 2000 Issue.

- In an effort to evaluate and reduce its exposure in this area, the Company has inquired of its vendors and other parties about their progress in identifying and addressing problems that their computer systems may face in correctly processing date information related to the year 2000. In particular, the Company has obtained written statements from a substantial majority of its suppliers that certain of their products are year 2000 compliant, can be upgraded to meeting year 2000 demands, or do not affect "date sensitive" information.

D. Impact of Year 2000 Issues as a Known Event or Uncertainty

The Revised Bulletin directs companies to disclose if "the costs or consequences of incomplete or untimely resolution of their Year 2000 issue represent a known material event or uncertainty that is reasonably expected to affect their future financial results . . ." In the

Survey, 20% of the companies addressed the topic. Below are examples of such disclosures:

- The 'Year 2000 Issue' creates risk for the Company from unforeseen problems in its own computer systems and from third parties with whom the Company deals on financial transactions worldwide. Such failures of the Company's and/or third parties' computer systems could have a material impact on the Company's ability to conduct its business, and especially to process and account for the transfer of funds electronically.

- Any of the Company's computer programs that have date-sensitive software may recognize a date using '00' as the year 1900 rather than as the year 2000. This could result in a system failure or miscalculations causing disruptions of operations, including, among other things, a temporary inability to process transactions, send invoices, or engage in similar normal business activities.

E. Anticipated or Actual Date of Completion

According to the Revised Bulletin, if a company determines that its Year 2000 issues are material, then it must disclose, among other things, a timetable for carrying out remediation plans. Of the companies surveyed, 30% provided such a timetable. The following examples illustrate the manner in which companies disclosed this information.

- The Company anticipates maintaining its hardware platform but replacing or upgrading most of the software. In addition, all PCs, HVAC, test equipment and external providers will be reviewed and acted on accordingly. It is anticipated that the Company will be fully Year 2000 compliant by April 30, 1999.

- Management expects to have substantially all of the system and application changes completed by the end of 1998 and believes that its level of preparedness is appropriate.

F. Internal v. External "Fixes"

Although there is no formal requirement that companies disclose whether they are using internal or external resources to resolve Year 2000 Problems, 22.5% of the companies in the Survey included this information in their annual reports. The following are examples:

- [The Company] estimates that the total cumulative cost of the project will be approximately $40 million, which includes both internal and external personnel costs related to modifying the systems as well as the cost of purchasing or leasing certain hardware and software.

- The Company will utilize both internal and external resources to reprogram, or replace, and test the software for Year 2000 modifications.

G. Accounting Treatment of Year 2000 Remediation Costs

Although the Revised Bulletin provides limited guidance on the accounting treatment of software modification costs, it does not address whether supplemental disclosure is necessary outside the financial statements. In the Survey, 20% of the companies disclosed their accounting methodology. Below are two examples:

- Purchased hardware and software will be capitalized in accordance with normal policy. Personnel and all other costs related to the project are being expensed as incurred.

- The Company continues to evaluate appropriate courses of corrective action, including replacement of certain systems whose associated costs would be recorded as assets and amortized.

In closing, it should be noted that most companies today include in their SEC filings disclaimers designed to invoke the protection of the safe harbor provision of the Private Securities Litigation Reform Act of 1995. Although there has not yet been a trend of specifically identifying Year 2000 issues in connection with these disclaimers, some companies are moving in that direction. The following are two examples from the Survey:

- The discussion above incorporates the Company's best estimates of the costs and completion date of the Year 2000 project. The Company derived these estimates using numerous assumptions of future events, including the continued availability of certain resources and other factors. There can be no guarantee that the Company will achieve these estimates. Therefore, actual results could differ materially from those plans. Specific factors that might cause such material differences include, but are not limited to, the availability and cost of personnel trained in this area, the ability to locate and correct all relevant computer codes, and similar uncertainties.

- Certain statements contained in this Item may be "forward-looking statements" within the meaning of The Private Securities Litigation Reform Act of 1995. Forward-looking statements are inherently subject to risks and uncertainties . . . . Some of the important factors that could cause the Company's actual results to differ materially from those projected in forward-looking statements made by the Company include, but are not limited to, the following: . . . year 2000 issues. . . Exhibit 99.1 to this Annual Report on Form 10-K, which is attached hereto and incorporated by reference herein, discusses these important factors in greater detail.

-Corresponding Excerpt from Exhibit 99.1

Many currently installed computer systems and software products, including several used by the Company, are coded to accept only two digit entries in the date code field. Beginning in the year 2000, these date code fields will need to accept four digit entries to distinguish 21st Century dates from 20th Century dates. Therefore, the Company's date critical functions related to the year 2000 and beyond, such as sales, distribution, purchasing, inventory control, merchandise, planning and replenishment, facilities and financial systems may be adversely affected unless these computer systems are or become year 2000 compliant. The Company began work several years ago to prepare its computer-based systems for the year 2000 and is utilizing both internal and external resources to identify, correct, or reprogram, and test its systems for year 2000 compliance. The Company is in the final stages of implementing the required changes to its internal computer systems and has recently begun a review of the computer systems used in recently acquired businesses and operations. The Company continues to evaluate the estimated costs associated with these efforts based on actual experience and does not expect the future costs of resolving its internal year 2000 issues to materially exceed the year 2000 related costs incurred in recent years. However, no assurance can be given that the Company's computer systems will be year 2000 compliant in a timely manner or that the Company will not incur significant additional expenses pursuing year 2000 compliance. Furthermore, even if the Company's systems are year 2000 compliant, there can be no assurance that the Company will not be

> adversely affected by the failure of others to become year 2000 compliant or by the failure of the Company's venders to provide year 2000 compliant products for resale or configuration by the Company. For example, the Company may be adversely affected by, among other things, warranty and other claims made by the company's customers related to product failures caused by the year 2000 problem, the description or inaccuracy of data provided to the Company by non-year 2000 compliant third parties, and the failure of the Company's service providers, such as security, data processing, and independent shipping companies to become year 2000 compliant. . . . However, despite the Company's efforts to date, there can be no assurance that the year 2000 problem will not have a material adverse effect on the Company in the future.

PART V. HOW COMPANIES SHOULD PREPARE - A STRATEGIC PLAN

As discussed earlier in this article, in addition to remediation costs, the potential legal exposure relating to Year 2000 failures is extensive. In the securities field alone, corporations, officers, directors and others will be subject to a broad array of suits ranging from corporate mismanagement and attendant loss of business and stock price declines, to fraud actions and enforcement proceedings for deficient disclosures.[96] Accordingly, as the year 2000 swiftly approaches, companies must take measures to protect themselves; and it is clear that management and the Board bear the primary responsibility in this area.

The centerpiece of any remediation assessment program should be adoption by the Board of Directors, in conjunction with senior management and after input from technical personnel, of a strategic plan with clearly defined objectives and deadlines. Although each company must tailor its approach to its needs and circumstances, the following is a general outline of a strategic plan.[97]

Strategic Plan

- Assemble the appropriate personnel to conduct, and promptly complete, a detailed written analysis of the company's internal and external Y2K exposure, which should include:

    - identification (through management, technical, financial and legal audits) of the areas of risk and exposure, including the prospective impact of counter-party failures;

    - a step-by-step prioritized remediation plan and timeline to address each of these areas, including an analysis comparing time and cost efficiencies of replacement versus repair, and a testing schedule;

    - identification of resource requirements (including specified internal/external personnel) necessary to complete the remediation plan;

    - analysis and strategy of funding or otherwise obtaining the necessary resource requirements;

    - assessment of the adequacy of D&O, business interruption and other insurance coverage, as well as relevant indemnification arrangements, relating to potential Y2K Problems; and

    - a contingency plan for addressing unanticipated Y2K Problems or remediation failures.

- Develop a due diligence strategy (based on an "all reasonable efforts" approach) to assess the Y2K status of counter-parties and software supplied by vendors, including written inquiry of counter-parties and "certification" requests from software vendors.

- Expand the company's disclosure review process for the preparation of SEC filings to include Y2K disclosure considerations.

- Prepare a strategy for educating corporate personnel of the company's Y2K status and plans, and for responding to all outside inquiries regarding these matters.

- Develop a reporting schedule to keep the Board of Directors fully and timely informed of the company's Y2K status, including satisfaction of the strategic plan's timeline.

CONCLUSION

Ready or not, here it comes – Year 2000 is around the corner, and you better be prepared. It is important to remember that although the Year 2000 Problem presents significant technical and legal considerations, it is primarily a business issue. Accordingly, in preparing for the new millennium, entities should focus on survival and not on potential legal remedies. As a legal officer of a major investment bank recently said: "Do you want to be in business in year 2000, or do you want to have the right to sue in year 2000? I assume you'd rather be in business."[98]

ENDNOTES

[1] Edward Yardeni, *A Race Against the Calendar*, New York Times, December 7, 1997.

[2] *Id.*

[3] "Embedded chips" are used in a number of devices including traffic lights and elevators. *See* Gary E. Clayton, *Trends in Computer Law: First Comes the Year 2000, Then the Lawyers*, Texas Lawyer, November 10, 1997. These chips can also be found in security systems, vaults, telephones, fax machines, and heating and air conditioning systems. Andrew M. Reidy & Robert L. Carter, *Year 2000 Bug May Create Securities Law Risks But Insurance Policies Could Provide Protection*, National Law Journal, November 3, 1997, at B13.

[4] NASD Notice to Members – "For Your Information" section (July 1996).

[5] Clayton, *supra* note 3.

[6] Matthew L. Wald, *Warning Issued on Air Traffic Computers*, New York Times, January 13, 1998, at A16.

[7] Yardeni, *supra* note 1.

[8] *SIA Year 2000 Web Site* (visited February 15, 1998) <http://www.sia.com/year_2000/index.html>.

[9] NASD Notice to Members 98-22 (February 1998).

[10] *Hearing on the Millennium Bug: Banking and the Year 2000 Computer Problem*, Congressional Press Release, November 4, 1997.

[11] Daniel R. Mummery & Thomas A. Unger, *Year-2000 Bug May Create Securities Law Risks*, National Law Journal, November 3, 1997, at B12.

[12] Vivian A. Maese *et al.*, *Year 2000: Contending With and Disclosing the Risks to Markets and Firms*, Insights, Vol. 12, No. 2, February 1998, at 4.

[13] *Id.*

[14] *Id.*

[15] *Id.*

[16] *Id.*

[17] Joshua Hallford, *Y2K Report Warns of $10 Billion Threat to Industry*, Securities Industry News, January 19, 1998.

[18] NASD Notice to Members, *supra* note 4.

[19] *The Year 2000 Bug can Pack a Lethal Legal Sting*, Bank Network News, November 21, 1997.

[20] NASD Notice to Members 98-22, *supra* note 9.

[21] Citicorp, Annual Report (filing date: February 25, 1998).

[22] Jed Horowitz, *"Year 2000" Budgets Surface, And the Numbers Are Big: Biggest firms to spend $300 million each– probably more*, Investment Dealers Digest, November 10, 1997, at 3.

[23] Lisa S. Howard, *Y2K May Spur U.K. D&O, E&O Sales*, National Underwriter, Property & Casualty/Risk & Benefits Management Edition, November 10, 1997, at 10.

[24] *The Year 2000 Bug can Pack a Lethal Legal Sting*, *supra* note 19.

[25] For example, the IRS's Year 2000 project involves examining over 62 million lines of computer code at an estimated cost of $900 million. Rob Wells, *IRS Faces Three Computer Hurdles*, Chattanooga Free Press, December 22, 1997, at A1. Similarly, the Prudential Insurance Company anticipates correcting 125 million lines of computer

code. Roger Lowenstein, *The Year 2000 and the CEO's Big Secret*, Wall Street Journal, July 25, 1996, at C1.

[26] Borzou Daragahi, *Survey: Firms Outside U.S. Lag in Y2K Readiness*, Securities Industry News, December 22, 1997, at 3.

[27] In addition, the SEC Chairman, Arthur Levitt, has sent letters to all registered investment advisers, transfer agents, broker-dealers, and utility holding companies stressing the importance of all securities firms implementing plans and devoting sufficient resources to modify their computers to be ready for the Year 2000. Also, in June 1997, the SEC issued a report to Congress in which the Commission noted the readiness of the securities industry and public companies to meet the challenge of Year 2000 issues.

The Canadian Securities Administrators have also issued a similar notice which calls on boards of directors and senior management of all reporting issuers in Canada to give serious consideration to the Millennium Bug issue, and to make appropriate disclosure in Management's Discussion and Analysis. Similarly, the Toronto Stock Exchange has passed a by-law which requires all listed companies to disclose material information concerning the information systems issues and related business implications and uncertainties resulting from the year 2000 century change, and any remedial action the issuer is taking in this regard. *TSE Requires Year 2000 Reporting By Listed Companies*, Edmonton Journal, February 5, 1998.

Similarly, the International Organization of Securities Commissions has taken an active role in expressing concern that participants in securities markets adequately address the risks associated with the Year 2000. Maese, *supra* note 12, at 6.

[28] Brian Lane, Remarks at the Practising Law Institute's Conference, *The SEC Speaks* (February 27, 1998).

[29] Revised Staff Legal Bulletin No. 5 (the "Revised Bulletin"), January 12, 1998, at 1.

[30] *Id.*

[31] *Id.*

[32] *Id.* at 2 n.3 (citing Section 17(a) of the Securities Act of 1933 (the "Securities Act") and Section 10(b) of the Securities Exchange Act of 1934 (the "Exchange Act")).

[33] Item 10(a)(1)-(2) of Regulation S-K makes the regulation applicable to the following reports and filings:

> (1) Registration statements under the Securities Act to the extent provided in the forms to be used for registration under such Act; and
>
> (2) Registration statements under Section 12, annual or other reports under Sections 13 and 15(d), annual reports to security holders and proxy and information statements under Section 14 of the Exchange Act, and any other documents required to be filed under the Exchange Act, to the extent provided in the forms and rules under such Act.

[34] Item 303 of Regulation S-B, which governs the disclosure requirements for small businesses, is the analog of Item 303 of Regulation S-K.

[35] Revised Bulletin, at 2.

[36] For small businesses the analogous provision is Item 101 of Regulation S-B.

[37] Revised Bulletin, at 2.

[38] *Id.*

[39] General Instructions to Form 8-K. For example, companies must file a Form 8-K upon changes in control, acquisition or disposition of assets, bankruptcy or receivership, changes in the company's certifying accountant, resignation of the company's directors, and changes in the fiscal year.

[40] *Id.*

[41] Revised Bulletin, at 2.

[42] *Id.*

[43] *See* discussion *infra* Part III of this article for a more thorough discussion of the accounting considerations associated with Y2K.

[44] Emerging Issues Task Force of the Financial Accounting Standards Board Issue No. 96-14, *Accounting for the Costs Associated with Modifying Computer Software for the Year 2000*, July 18, 1996.

[45] Revised Bulletin, at 2.

[46] *Id.*

[47] *Id.*

[48] *Id.* at 3.

[49] *Id.*

[50] *Id.*

[51] *Id.*

[52] *Id.*

[53] *Id.*

[54] *Id.* (citing Section 34(b) of the Investment Company Act of 1940).

[55] *Id.*

[56] *Id.*

[57] *Id.*

[58] *Id.*

[59] *SEC to Consider Proposal on B-D Year 2000 Reports*, Federal News, Vol. 30, No. 9, February 27, 1998.

[60] *SEC to Require Reports on "Year 2000" Fixes*, The Arizona Republic, March 3, 1998.

[61] *Id.*

[62] *Id.*

[63] *SEC to Consider Proposal on B-D Year 2000 Reports*, *supra* note 59.

[64] In connection with Year 2000 compliance, the NASD has issued a number of statements, including: NASD Regulatory & Compliance Alert (September 1997); NASD Notice to Members – "For Your Information" section (July 1996); NASD Notice to Members 97-16 (March 1997); NASDR Memorandum to all International NASD Member Firms (January 2, 1998); and Nasdaq's Subscriber Bulletin (June 1997). Also, in May 1997, Nasdaq Trading and Market Services began including Year 2000 as a topic at its quarterly vendor focus groups. In addition, there are Year 2000 web pages on both the NASD web site <http://www.nasd.com> and the NASD Regulation web site <http://www.nasdr.com>.

[65] Special NASD Notice to Members 97-96, at 1.

[66] *Id.*

[67] Notice to Members 97-16.

[68] Special NASD Notice, *supra* note 65.

[69] Notice to Members 98-22, *supra* note 9, at 130.

[70] *Id.*

[71] *Id.*

[72] *Id.*

[73] NASD Regulatory & Compliance Alert (September 1997).

[74] *Id.*

[75] *Id.*

[76] *Id.*

[77] *Id.*

[78] *Id.*

[79] *Id.*

[80] *See* Beth Duncan, *Companies That Don't Correct Year 2000 Computer Glitch, Disclose Correction Costs, May be Marked as Malefactors*, BNA's Corporate Counsel Weekly, December 3, 1997, at 4.

[81] Mark Hendrickson, *Senator's Y2K Disclosure Bill Put on Hold*, Securities Industry News, February 16, 1998.

[82] *Disclosure Rules*, Congressional Press Release, January 12, 1998.

[83] *Id.*

[84] *In Brief*, BNA's Corporate Counsel Weekly, February 18, 1998, at 7.

[85] Marcy Gordon, *House Panel Votes to Give Regulators New Authority*, The Boston Globe Online (dated February 6, 1998) <http://www.boston.com/dailynews/wirehtml/037_lr/House-panel_votes-to-give-regulators.htm>.

[86] Mary Mosquera, *Committee OKs Regulators to Assist Banks in Year 2000 Changeover*, TechWeb News (February 6, 1998) <http://www.techweb.com/wire/story/y2k/TWB19980206S0013>.

[87] Marcy Gordon, *supra* note 85.

[88] *Id.*

[89] Brian Friel, *The Year 2000 Czar* (dated February 5, 1998) <http://www.govexec.com/dailyfed/0298/020598b1.htm>.

[90] *Clinton Creates Year 2000 Council; House, SEC Act on Other Fronts*, Washington Update, February 1998, Vol. 6, No. 2, at 3.

[91] *Id.*

[92] Statement of Financial Accounting Standards 5 ("SFAS 5").

[93] *Id.*

[94] SFAS 5 defines "probable" as meaning "the future contingent event is likely to occur."

[95] The Survey was conducted by Schulte, Roth & Zabel, LLP, based on a selection companies that had filed annual reports between January 15 and February 15, 1998. The Survey was limited to companies that included Year 2000 disclosures in their annual reports. Half of the companies are listed on the New York Stock Exchange and half are traded on Nasdaq (14 on the National Market System, 5 on the SmallCap Market, and 1 on the OTC market). The companies in the Survey are of varying sizes and reflect a broad range of industries.

[96] For a good general discussion of these issues, see Dennis J. Block & Stephen A. Radin, *Year 2000 Director Liability Issues, Parts I & II*, New York Law Journal, Outside Counsel Section, January 13 & 20, 1998.

[97] The strategic plan is directed to companies that may be using non-compliant products and does not address the special legal concerns of vendors of such products.

[98] Justin Dini, *Year 2000 Compliance*, Institutional Investor Compliance Reporter, Vol. IV, No. 26, December 22, 1997, at 14 (quoting Oliver Herzfeld, Assistant General Counsel at J.P. Morgan and Chairman of the SIA's Legal

and Regulatory Subcommittee on Year 2000).

EXHIBIT A

STAFF LEGAL BULLETIN NO. 5
(REVISED ON JAN. 12, 1998)

Staff Legal Bulletin No. 5 (CF/IM)

Revised January 12, 1998

Action: Publication of Divisions of Corporation Finance and Investment Management Staff Legal Bulletin

Summary: The Divisions remind public operating companies, investment advisers, and investment companies to consider their disclosure obligations relating to anticipated costs, problems and uncertainties associated with the Year 2000 issue. This Bulletin, originally issued on October 8, 1997, is revised to provide more specific guidance under the existing Commission rules and regulations due to the importance of the Year 2000 issue and some uncertainty expressed by members of the accounting and legal professions regarding what should be disclosed.[1]

Supplementary Information: This legal bulletin represents the Divisions' staff views. This bulletin is not a rule, regulation, or statement of the Securities and Exchange Commission. Further, the Commission has not approved or disapproved its content.

Contact Person: For further information, please contact Broc Romanek regarding public operating companies at (202) 942-2900 and Anthony Vertuno regarding investment companies and investment advisers at (202) 942-0591.

I. The Year 2000 Issue

Many existing computer programs use only two digits to identify a year in the date field. These programs were designed and developed without considering the impact of the upcoming change in the century. If not corrected, many computer applications could fail or create erroneous results by or at the Year 2000. The Year 2000 issue affects virtually all companies and organizations.[2]

II. Disclosure by Public Companies Regarding the Year 2000 Issue

Many companies must undertake major projects to address the Year 2000 issue. Each company's potential costs and uncertainties will depend on a number of factors, including its software and hardware and the nature of its industry. Companies also must coordinate with other entities with which they electronically interact, both domestically and globally, including suppliers, customers, creditors, borrowers, and financial service organizations. If a company does not successfully address its Year 2000 issues, it may face material adverse consequences. Companies should review, on an ongoing basis, whether they need to disclose anticipated costs, problems and uncertainties associated with Year 2000 consequences, particularly in their filings with the Commission. Public companies may have to disclose this information in Commission filings because:

- the form or report may require the disclosure, or
- in addition to the information that the company is specifically required to disclose, the

disclosure rules require disclosure of any additional material information necessary to make the required disclosure not misleading.[3]

The following is a discussion of certain requirements.

Management's Discussion and Analysis of Financial Condition and Results of Operations

Companies should include disclosure in their "Management's Discussion and Analysis of Financial Condition and Results of Operations" [4] if:

- the cost of addressing the Year 2000 issue is a material event or uncertainty that would cause reported financial information not to be necessarily indicative of future operating results or financial condition, or
- the costs or the consequences of incomplete or untimely resolution of their Year 2000 issue represent a known material event or uncertainty that is reasonably expected to affect their future financial results, or cause their reported financial information not to be necessarily indicative of future operating results or future financial condition.

Description of Business

If Year 2000 issues materially affect a company's products, services, or competitive conditions, companies may need to disclose this in their "Description of Business."[5] In determining whether to include disclosure, companies should consider the effects of the Year 2000 issue on each of their reportable segments.

Form 8-K

A company's Year 2000 costs or consequences may reach a level of importance that prompts it to consider filing a Form 8-K. At their option, companies would file these reports under Item 5 of Form 8-K. In considering whether to file a Form 8-K, companies should be particularly mindful of the accuracy and completeness of information in registration statements filed under the Securities Act that incorporate by reference Exchange Act reports, including Form 8-Ks.[6]

Accounting Considerations

The Emerging Issues Task Force considered the issue of how to properly reflect the costs of modifying computer software for Year 2000 projects in the financial statements. In July 1996, the EITF concluded that these costs should be charged to expense as they are incurred.[7]

Specific Disclosure Considerations

If a company determines that it should make Year 2000 disclosure, the applicable rules or regulations should be followed. If a company has not made an assessment of its Year 2000 issues or has not determined whether it has material Year 2000 issues, the staff believes that disclosure of this known uncertainty is required. In addition, the staff believes that the determination as to whether a company's Year 2000 issues should be disclosed should be based on whether the Year 2000 issues are material to a company's business, operations, or financial condition, without regard to related countervailing circumstances (such as Year 2000 remediation programs or contingency plans). If the Year 2000 issues are determined to be material, without regard to countervailing circumstances, the nature and potential impact of the Year 2000 issues as well as the countervailing circumstances should be disclosed. As part of this disclosure, the staff expects, at the least, the following topics will be addressed:

- the company's general plans to address the Year 2000 issues relating to its business, its operations (including operating systems) and, if material, its relationships with customers, suppliers, and other constituents; and its timetable for carrying out those plans; and
- the total dollar amount that the company estimates will be spent to remediate its Year 2000 issues, if such amount is expected to be material to the company's business, operations or financial condition, and any material impact these expenditures are expected to have on the company's results of operations, liquidity and capital resources.

The disclosure must be reasonably specific and meaningful, rather than standard boilerplate.

Foreign Companies

Foreign private issuers also should follow this guidance. In particular, these issuers should consider the disclosure requirements of Form 20-F, Item 1 ("Description of Business") and Item 9 ("Management's Discussion and Analysis of Financial Condition and Results of Operations").

III. Disclosure by Investment Companies and Investment AdvisersRegarding the Year 2000 Issue

Under the Investment Advisers Act of 1940 and the Investment Company Act of 1940, investment advisers and investment companies may be required to make appropriate disclosure to clients and shareholders if operational or financial obstacles are presented by the Year 2000 issue. Disclosure of the Year 2000 issue is necessary if it is materially misleading to shareholders to omit the information.

The Investment Company Act provides that it is unlawful for investment companies to omit from registration statements and other public filings "any fact necessary in order to prevent the statements made therein, in light of the circumstances under which they were made, from being materially misleading."[8] Open-end investment companies ("mutual funds") are required by Item 5(b) of Form N-1A to describe in their registration statements the experience of their investment advisers and the services that the advisers provide. In response to this item, investment companies may need to disclose the effect that the Year 2000 issue would have on their advisers' ability to provide the services described in their registration statements.

The anti-fraud provisions of the Investment Advisers Act generally impose on investment advisers an affirmative duty, consistent with their fiduciary obligations, to disclose to clients or prospective clients, material facts concerning their advisory or proposed advisory relationships. [9] If the failure to address the Year 2000 issue could materially affect the advisory services provided to clients, an adviser that will not be able to or is uncertain about its ability to address Year 2000 issues has an obligation to disclose such information to its clients and prospective clients. This disclosure must be made in a timely manner so that the clients and prospective clients may take steps to protect their interests.

Investment companies and investment advisers that determine that Year 2000 disclosure is required also should follow the guidelines under "Specific Disclosure Considerations" discussed above.

Footnotes

1 Recently, Senate Financial Services and Technology Subcommittee Chairman Robert Bennett introduced legislation, the Year 2000 Computer Remediation and Shareholder Protection Act of 1997 (S.1518).

2 In a June 1997 report to Congress, the Commission noted the readiness of the securities industry and public companies to meet the challenges of the Year 2000 issue. This report is available on the Commission's web site at http://www.sec.gov/news/studies/yr2000.htm.

3 Securities Act Rule 408, Exchange Act Rule 12b-20, and Exchange Act Rule 14a-9. Companies also should consider the anti-fraud provisions of the Securities Act and the Exchange Act. These anti-fraud requirements apply to statements and omissions both in Commission filings and outside of Commission's filings. Securities Act Section 17(a), Exchange Act Section 10(b), and Exchange Act Rule 10b-5.

4 Item 303 of Regulations S-K and S-B. The Commission provided interpretive guidance regarding the disclosure required by Item 303 in Securities Act Release No. 6835.

5 Item 101 of Regulations S-K and S-B.

6 General Instruction B.4 of Form 8-K.

7 Emerging Issues Task Force of the Financial Accounting Standards Board Issue No. 96-14: Accounting for the Costs Associated with Modifying Computer Software for the Year 2000, July 18, 1996.

8 Section 34(b) of the Investment Company Act of 1940.

9 Sections 206(1) and (2) of the Investment Advisers Act of 1940. See SEC v. Capital Gains Research Bureau, Inc. 375 U.S. 180 (1963).

http://www.sec.gov/rules/othern/slbcf5.htm
Last update: 01/12/98

Return to previous screen (Other Commission Notices)

Return to SEC Home Page

NOTES

NOTES

17

THE YEAR 2000 ISSUE – ACCOUNTING, FINANCIAL REPORTING AND AUDITING IMPLICATIONS

Allen I. Young

Reprinted from the PLI Course Handbook, Preparation of Annual Disclosure Documents 1998. Order No. B4-7230

The Year 2000 Issue - Accounting, Financial Reporting and Auditing Implications

A. The Year 2000 Issue has both accounting, financial reporting and auditing implications.

1. Because complications arising from the inability of a company's information system to operate in the new century can affect a company's financial condition and results of operations, the company may need to address the accounting for such complications in its financial statements if the effects of that inability are material.

2. To the extent that the effects are material, the company may also need to consider appropriate disclosure in footnotes to the financial statements.

3. Because the financial statements and the footnotes to those statements may have to reflect the effects of Year 2000 problems on a company, the independent accountant may have to adjust audit procedures to assess the appropriateness of the accounting for, and related disclosure of, those problems.

4. In October 1997, a special task force of practitioners in public practice and the staff of the AICPA issued a study which included current accounting and auditing guidance which can be helpful to companies and their auditors when addressing Year 2000 issues.

B. Companies may need to consider accounting questions relating to treatment of the costs of modifying computer software for the Year 2000, and product warranty obligations of software and hardware vendors and software providers as well as of other vendors who sell products containing software, and possible impairment of fixed assets containing software or hardware components and capitalized costs of software developed for internal use that have not been modified to be Year 2000 compliant.

1. In 1996, the Emerging Issues Task Force issued guidance on accounting for the costs of modifying computer software for the Year 2000.

a. The EITF reached a consensus that external and internal costs specifically associated with modifying internal-use software for the Year 2000 should be charged to expense as incurred.

b. The EITF statement (EITF Issue 96-14) was specifically limited to the upgrading of existing internal-use software and did not address purchases of hardware or software that replace existing software that is not Year 2000 compliant.

c. In July 1997 the SEC representative on the EITF reaffirmed the SEC's concurrence in this position and specifically confirmed that references to FASB 5 in the SEC Report to Congress regarding the Year 2000 was not intended to suggest that the Staff would permit accrual of expected future costs to modify software for Year 2000 problems.

2. In its October 1997 release, the AICPA task force reminded companies involved in the sale of computer hardware and software and their independent accountants that Year 2000 problems could have an unexpected effect on the timing of revenue recognition because of factors such as the uncertainty of customer acceptance, customer cancellation privileges and postcontract customer support.

3. Computer hardware and software manufacturers need to consider the implications of FASB 5 if there are product-warranty or product-defect liability issues as well as other guidance relating to the issue of product return.

4. Because Year 2000 problems may be an indicator of impairment of fixed assets containing software or hardware components such as microchips, companies need to consider whether there are impairment losses relating to those assets which require the values of such assets to be written down or off.

5. In addition, Year 2000 problems could affect the estimated useful lives used to calculate the depreciation and amortization of those assets.

C. SOP 94-6 may require additional disclosures related to the Year 2000 Issue if it is reasonably possible that the amounts reported in the financial statements could change by a material amount within one year from the date of the financial statements.

1. Disclosure may be required in areas such as impairment or amortization of capitalized software costs, inventory valuation, long-term-contract accounting, warranty reserves, reserves for sales returns and allowances and litigation.

2. The disclosures required in the footnotes to the financial statements by SOP 94-6 may be similar to the disclosures of these problems in the MD&A.

D. In October 1997, the AITF issued several interpretations to the auditing standards that address how independent accountants are to deal with the Year 2000 Issue in the course of their examinations of the financial statements of their clients.

1. The interpretations make it clear that an auditor's responsibility relates to the detection of material misstatements of the financial statements being audited, whether caused by the Year 2000 Issue or by some other cause.

2. By the same token, the interpretations provide that an auditor does not have a responsibility to detect current or future effects of the Year 2000 Issue on operational matters that do not affect the client's ability to prepare the financial statements being audited in accordance with GAAP.

3. In other words, an audit of financial statements conducted in accordance with generally accepted auditing standards does not contemplate that the auditor would need to assess whether data processing errors caused by the Year 2000 Issue could result in material misstatements of financial statements in periods subsequent to the period being audited.

4. Furthermore, if during the course of an audit, the auditor becomes aware that the Year 2000 Issue could adversely affect the client's accounting systems in some period after the period being audited, the potential significant internal control deficiency is not a current "reportable condition" which the auditor is obligated to report to management and the board of directors currently.

5. The October 1997 interpretations state that the potential internal control deficiency becomes a "reportable condition" only when, in the auditor's judgment, it could adversely affect the client's ability to process financial data currently.

6. While the auditor is not obligated currently to report its findings concerning possible future computer problems to the client's board of directors or management, the interpretation states that the auditor may nevertheless wish to communicate this concern for the benefit of management even though this problem is not a reportable condition.

E. The auditors will have certain responsibilities concerning public disclosures that the client may make of its Year 2000 problems.

1. To the extent that a publicly held client includes disclosures on that subject in its MD&A, the auditor will have the responsibility to read management's disclosures and to consider whether such information, or the manner of its presentation, is materially consistent with information, or the manner of its presentation, in the financial statements.

2. If the auditor concludes that there is a material inconsistency, or if the auditor becomes aware of information that he or she believes is a material misstatement of fact, the auditor is required to take certain actions, which may include withdrawal from the engagement.

3. Responsibility for such MD&A disclosures is no different than the auditor's responsibilities for other disclosures presented outside the financial statements in a document issued publicly which contains an auditor's opinion on client financial

statements.

F. If voluntary disclosures about the Year 2000 Issue are included in the notes to the audited financial statements of a nonpublic entity, the auditor should determine whether sufficient competent evidential matters exist regarding the information that the client has disclosed.

G. The October 1997 AICPA report suggests that, to avoid misunderstandings about the auditors' responsibilities with respect to the Year 2000 Issue, the auditor may specifically set forth the responsibilities of the auditor under current auditing standards in communications with the client during audits leading up to the Year 2000.

1. Such communications may take the form of statements in audit engagement letters, management letters or discussions with management and the audit committee.

2. The report stresses the importance for auditors to communicate with clients about the auditor's professional responsibility with respect to the Year 2000 Issue.

3. For example, management and the audit committee may not understand that potential future internal control problems are not required to be reported as "reportable conditions" if they do not affect the period under audit.

4. Likewise the definition of a "reportable condition" may differ from what management expects an auditor to communicate based on the content of past management letters or other reasons.

5. Since the Year 2000 Issue may affect an entity's internal controls, an auditor may want to advise the client's audit committee that because an audit is not intended to provide assurances on the effectiveness of internal control, an audit of financial statements does not provide any assurance with respect to the Year 2000 Issue.

6. The October 1997 AICPA report suggests a number of situations relating to the Year 2000 Issue that the auditor may wish to address in the management letter typically provided to management at the completion of the audit, including situations where:

a. The client has not begun to address the Year 2000 Issue;

b. The client recognizes the issue, but needs to develop a Year 2000 compliance program;

c. The client recognizes the issue, but needs to assess the effect of the Year 2000 Issue on its systems;

d. The client needs to consider the budget/resource implications of the plan; and

e. The client is not currently meeting its Year 2000 compliance project's timetable.

NOTES

18

'BOOTING' THE FEDERAL SECURITIES LAWS INTO THE 21ST CENTURY

Joseph McLaughlin

Reprinted from the PLI Course Handbook,
International Securities Markets 1997.
Order No. B4-7215

This article previously appear in INSIGHTS,
Volume 11, Number 7, July 1997.

THE FUTURE

'Booting' the Federal Securities Laws into the 21st Century

While the SEC has taken a number of steps to adapt the federal securities laws to the new era of electronic communications, much more remains to be done. A noted practitioner offers his "Top Ten" list of electronic fixes.

By Joseph McLaughlin

We live in a time that even Arthur Levitt, the Chairman of the Securities and Exchange Commission (SEC), calls the "age of information."

If the SEC believes this, why is it that its whole regulatory approach under the Securities Act of 1933 (Securities Act) towards the offering of securities continues to be based on *restricting* the flow of information to investors?

Nothing illuminates the fault lines in the SEC's regulation of securities offerings better than the impact of electronic communications media. Indeed, the ABA's Federal Regulation of Securities Committee recently cited the growing role of electronic communications media as the single most important reason why the SEC should get out of the business of regulating *offers* of securities (as opposed to the conditions under which actual *sales* take place).[1]

Of course, the SEC and its staff have hardly ignored the impact of electronic communications media. Indeed, the SEC has been a trailblazer in its establishment of, and continuing efforts to improve, its EDGAR system. In addition, the SEC less than two years ago adopted a policy that the use of electronic media should be at least an equal alternative to the use of paper-based media.[2]

But there is a lot more that needs to be done, and time is running out. In shaping its priorities, the SEC would do well to pay attention to recent remarks by John R. Walter, the new president of AT&T Corporation. Mr. Walter notes that it is not possible to "have a three- to five-year rollout of a new process when the enabling technology is doubling in speed and power every 18 months." The speed of technological change requires a "culture in which we expect to make mistakes, learn from them and quickly apply everything we learn."

Mr. Walter illustrated his point as follows:

> We used to make changes in business according to this command: Ready. Aim. Fire! Today, the command has to be: Fire. Aim. Fire. Aim. Fire. Aim! You fire in order to aim. Fire a burst. See what happens. Make corrections. Fire another burst. Build speed into everything you do and measure yourself against the speed of the world around you.

I do not know any securities lawyers who would imagine that Mr. Walter is describing the SEC's usual approach to problem-solving.

As an agency charged with investor protection, of course, the SEC's caution is understandable. There is an urgent need, however, to find ways to adapt the Securities Act to today's changed circumstances. Delay will only discourage innovation in our capital markets, particularly as compared to what is going on in other countries.

I continue to believe that the SEC must eventually move in the direction of deregulating "offers" of securities, as urged by the ABA's Federal Regulation of Securities Committee. In the meantime, however, there are concrete steps the SEC could take to liberate electronic communications media and free up the flow of information in connection with new securities offerings.

With all this as preface, here is my "Top Ten" list of electronic fixes.

Email Communications

A broker may, of course, discuss a new public offering on the telephone with a customer. Prior to the effective date, however, the Securities Act requires that "written" communications be limited to the preliminary prospectus. The SEC defines "written" as including "magnetic impulses or other forms of computer data compilation." Notwithstanding this definition, most lawyers—not all—would agree that a broker could nevertheless leave a voicemail message for the customer.

What about an email communication? This method of communication surely offers much more accuracy and efficiency than multiple telephone calls, but there

Joseph McLaughlin is a partner at Brown & Wood LLP in New York, N.Y.

is great uncertainty about its status under the Securities Act. The SEC noted last year that the status of a communication should depend less on its form and more on its substance and audience and on whether it "replace[s] or substitute[s] for telephone conversations."[3] The SEC needs to follow up on this eminently sensible observation by applying it in an objective fashion to the Securities Act.

I suggest that the SEC exempt from the definition of "prospectus" any electronic message limited to 200 words or less. Alternatively, I suggest that the SEC permit email messages limited in content to that permitted by Rule 134 but without the lengthy "red herring" legend.

Electronic Roadshows

The SEC has worried for years that all investors are not invited to roadshows. It may not be feasible for all investors to be invited to lunch at the Waldorf, but the technology exists to make it perfectly possible for any investor to log on to a designated site and enjoy—at a time of the investor's own choosing—an audio and video playback of the road show. Again, many lawyers worry that this is a "written" communication that amounts to an illegal prospectus.

The SEC staff recently issued a no-action letter that permits an electronic road show if the presentation is not "inconsistent" with the prospectus.[4] (*Editor's note: For future discussion of this letter and electronic roadshows, see p. 3*) Of course, this leaves open the status of information that is presented at a road show that is simply not included in the prospectus. Also, a no-action letter is less desirable than a rule for purposes of protection from civil liability.

I suggest that the SEC adopt a rule to exempt from the definition of "prospectus" any electronic version of a presentation made by an issuer or underwriter at a meeting attended by prospective investors. If the SEC thought it desirable, a "red herring" legend could be included as part of the playback.

Issuers' Web Sites

According to the National Investors Relations Institute, some 55 percent of that organization's membership have an Internet page and another 29 percent say that they have one under development. The SEC should welcome this development, which promises to provide issuers and investors with opportunities for the exchange of information that could not have been imagined only a few years ago.

Problems arise, however, when such an issuer becomes involved in a public or private securities offering. Does the Web site become an illegal prospectus? Does it constitute "gun-jumping" or a "general solicitation"? In the event of a merger, does information on the Web site violate the proxy rules?

I suggest that the SEC exempt from the definition of 'prospectus' any electronic message limited to 200 words or less.

Traditional statements by the SEC to the effect that issuers may continue "normal publicity" does not help much in deciding whether an issuer should purge its Web site of recent reports filed under the Securities Exchange Act of 1934 (Exchange Act), annual and quarterly reports to shareholders, transcripts of officers' speeches, broker-dealer research reports, new product announcements, press releases, or transcripts or summaries or electronic versions of shareholders' or analysts meetings.

Of course, the issuer *could* purge its Web site of this information. But why? Investors' need for the information does not disappear just because there is a public or private offering in the works. Moreover, much of the information may be available from other sources, ***e.g.***, the SEC's own Web site, private databases or even the local library, albeit at greater effort and expense.

The SEC should exempt from the definitions of "offer," "prospectus," and "general solicitation" any material included on an issuer's Web site maintained in the regular course of business. If necessary, the exemption could apply only after the Web site had been in operation for some period of time (*e.g.*, three months).

Research Published Before Public or Private Offerings

There has been a tremendous expansion of research in recent years, in the U.S. and abroad, on the fixed-income side as well as in equities. Broker-dealers and their customers are finding tremendous advantages in the electronic dissemination of this research. As in the case of an issuer's Web site, should a broker-dealer purge its Internet site of relevant research when it becomes involved in a public or private offering of its securities? Again, the research has been distributed and is available from other sources. Why should the customer who has downloaded the research or retained hard copies have an advantage over the customer who has not?

Rule 139 and similar rules exempt certain kind of research in the context of registered public offerings, but the exemptions are not nearly adequate to the task.

The SEC should exempt from the definitions of "offer," "prospectus," and "general solicitation" any research published prior to the commencement of an underwriter's or dealer's participation in a public or private offering, whether or not the research continues to be disseminated after the commencement of such participation.

Research Published During Public or Private Offerings

The previous suggestion would help, but it really does not go far enough. In public offerings today, everyone has a viewpoint, and everyone wants to express it. Investors want to hear diverse opinions about issuers and their securities, *especially* at the time of a public offering. In many areas of the world, such viewpoints can be freely expressed before, during, and after an offering. They are frequently carried on the Internet.

In connection with the same offering, however, U.S. investors are allowed to see only the official view—*i.e.*, the view expressed in the prospectus filed with the SEC. Research may be provided to prospective U.S. investors if the offering is being made in the United States as a private placement, but then steps must be taken to limit the distribution of the research so that it does not constitute a "general solicitation."

The problem also arises in connection with large mergers and acquisitions. Foreign investors can receive an uninterrupted flow of information, opinions and recommendations relating to announced transactions; U.S. investors must rely on firms not involved in the transaction or in subsequent public financing transactions.

Again, Rule 139 and similar rules exempt certain kind of research in the context of public offerings. The exemptions do not apply to initial public offerings, however, or to certain other categories of issuer or types of research.

The SEC should exempt from the definitions of "offer," "prospectus," "general solicitation," and "directed selling efforts" any information, opinions and recommendations distributed in the ordinary course of business by a registered broker-dealer.

Asset-Backed and Foreign Sovereign Securities

Rule 139 and related "safe harbor" rules are limited to research that covers companies that report under the Exchange Act. Certain foreign private issuers are also covered by Rule 139 if they have had securities traded in a designated market for 12 months. By contrast, the safe harbor does not permit U.S. investors to receive research even on investment-grade asset-backed securities (because these are not usually issued by "reporting" entities). Nor does it permit U.S. investors to receive research on foreign sovereign debt transactions.

Investors' need for the information does not disappear just because there is a public or private offering in the works.

The SEC recently issued interpretive advice in the asset-backed area, but subject to numerous conditions.[5] What is needed is an exemption from the definition of "prospectus" for any information, opinions, and recommendations distributed in the ordinary course of business and relating to investment-grade asset-backed securities or to securities registered pursuant to Schedule B under the Securities Act.

Screen-Based Information on Restricted Securities

Some privately-placed securities that are traded in the marketplace may be traded only among "qualified institutional buyers" (QIBs); others may also be traded among accredited investors. Investors frequently benefit from the electronic posting of information on such securities. In addition, the availability of information sometimes encourages additional broker-dealers to make bids and offers for the security.

After the completion of a private placement (whether under Rule 144A or Regulation D), it should be possible for relevant information about the security to be posted for the benefit of those investors eligible to purchase the security. There is uncertainty, however, whether a public posting of such information might somehow destroy the exemption for the initial offering.

The SEC should exempt from the definition of "offer" for Rule 144A purposes and "general solicitation" for Regulation D purposes any communication regarding an outstanding restricted security if the communication states that it is not directed to any person who would not be eligible to purchase the restricted security.

Screen-Based Information on Offshore Offerings

Foreign banks and brokers are also making use of the Internet in connection with offerings in foreign countries or on the international markets. These communications may be viewed by persons in the United States, and there is concern that they may be "directed selling efforts" under Regulation S or "offers" or "general solicitations" under the private placement rules. In addition, some organizations of dealers are trying to establish a reliable electronic data base for the dissemination of information on the terms and conditions of international offerings.

It may be assumed that any screen-based communication will contain a legend to the effect that it is not intended as an offer to any person in any jurisdiction where such an offer is not permitted.

The SEC should act as an example for foreign securities regulators and U.S. blue sky authorities by adopting an exemption for "Internet offers" originating outside the United States where sales are not made in the United States.

Internet Messages and Blue Sky Laws

Some major underwriters are beginning to put up preliminary and final prospectuses on a Web site. A limiting factor here is the blue sky concern if the security is not a "covered security" under the National Securities Markets Improvements Act of 1996. Such securities would include asset-backed securities and foreign sovereign debt offerings. Passwords could be used to limit access to institutions, but passwords are complicated to administer and the definition of exempt "institution" varies form state to state.

Some 20 states have exempted "Internet offers" from their registration and advertising requirements. It is simply unacceptable, however, that an issuer or underwriter that posts on a Web site a preliminary or final prospectus for a non-covered security in conformity with SEC rules should still be exposed to administrative, civil or even criminal penalties under state law. The SEC needs to take action, not only to make uniform the definition of "qualified purchaser," but also to encourage all remaining states to adopt similar exemptions for "Internet offers."

Internet Messages and Secondary Market Transactions

Foreign banks and brokers who make use of the Internet in order to provide their clients with research and quotes run the risk of being deemed to have "solicited" brokerage business from U.S. persons. Many lawyers believe that a foreign bank or broker that receives an order from a U.S. person who has viewed the relevant Internet page may still rely on the "unsolicited transaction" exemption in Rule 15a-6(a)(1). Clarification of this point would be desirable.

Conclusion

In conclusion, I would like again to quote John Walter of AT&T. He noted that "it has been said that digital technology eats everything and tramples anyone who tries to oppose it," He believed, however, that this understated the case:

> You don't have to oppose digital technology to be trampled; innocent bystanders will be flattened, too. . . . You must become a digital revolutionary or risk losing everything.

NOTES

1. Letter dated December 11, 1996 (File No. S7-19-96).

2. Release No. 33-7233 (October 6, 1995).

3. Release No. 33-7288 (May 9, 1996).

4. SEC No-Action Letter, *Private Financial Network* (available March 12, 1997).

5. SEC No-Action Letter, *Dissemination of Research Materials Relating to Asset-Backed Securities (PSA The Bond Market Trade Association* (available February 7, 1997).

NOTES

19

THE USE OF ELECTRONIC MEDIA IN CONNECTION WITH SHAREHOLDERS' MEETINGS

Bonnie J. Roe

THE USE OF ELECTRONIC MEDIA IN CONNECTION WITH SHAREHOLDERS' MEETINGS

Bonnie J. Roe

I. INTRODUCTION

A. Advantages of Using Electronic Media
1. Efficient dissemination of information to shareholders.
2. Permits greater participation among shareholders who may not be able to participate in person.
3. Potential savings on printing, mailing and processing costs.

B. Corporate Governance Concerns
1. Shareholders' meetings originated to bring shareholders together to communicate corporate decision making and to provide a forum for shareholders to express their concerns.
2. In modern corporations, shareholders are dispersed geographically and generally do not depend on the annual meeting to learn about the corporation or to express concerns.
3. Consequently, corporations spend time, effort and money on shareholders meetings that are sparsely attended and often have little effect on corporate governance.
4. The use of electronic media in connection with shareholders meetings promises in the long run to make a cumbersome process more efficient and to increase shareholder democracy. In the short run, however, there are both legal and technological hurdles. The use of any particular medium for any particular purpose needs to be scrutinized to make sure that it meets federal securities law disclosure requirements and does not present other practical or legal problems.

II. FEDERAL SECURITIES LAW REQUIREMENTS

A. The Securities and Exchange Commission (the "SEC") has issued two principal releases relating to electronic disclosure, in October 1995 (SEC Release Nos. 33-7233; 34-36345) (the "October Release") and May 1996 (SEC Release No. 33-7288; 34-37182) (the "May Release"). These releases did not establish new disclosure and delivery requirements, but explain how the existing standards can be applied to electronic communications.

1. The October Release states that delivery of information through an electronic medium can generally satisfy delivery or transmission obligations under the federal securities laws.

2. The May Release addresses, among other things, the use of electronic media by broker-dealers, transfer agents and investment advisers and states that broker-dealers' obligations to deliver information can be satisfied through electronic communications. The SEC reminded broker-dealers, transfer agents and investment advisers to consider their obligations under applicable self-regulatory organization rules and state law, and to pay particular attention to questions concerning the validity of customer consents to the receipt of electronically transmitted information.

3. The general principle articulated in the October and May Releases is that federal securities law delivery and disclosure requirements can be met through electronic deliveries.
   a. Federal securities laws require the disclosure of material information that enables investors to make informed investment and voting decisions, but does not specify the means.
   b. No federal securities laws prevent use of electronic communications for a shareholder meeting.
   c. Electronic communications must be prepared, updated and delivered consistent with the provisions of federal securities laws in the same manner as paper documents.

4. The October and May Releases establish four general requirements:
   a. Notice of electronic delivery: notice must be given to investors in a "timely and adequate" fashion to inform them information is available electronically.
   b. Consent for electronic delivery: a company must obtain informed consent from a shareholder to receive information through a specified electronic medium.
   c. Access to electronic documents: the recipient should have an easy method for obtaining information and maintaining it.
   d. Evidence of electronic delivery: the sender must reasonably believe that the information arrived, for example through e-mail return receipt or confirmation of access, downloading or printing or an investor's accessing a document with hyperlinking to a required document, or using forms or other material available only by accessing the information.

5. The October and May Releases give several examples of the application of these four general requirements. The following examples pertain specifically to shareholders' meetings.

a. Generally, delivery of an e-mail, disk or tape would be sufficient to provide notice that a document is available, but posting a document on the company's web site is by itself insufficient and companies should send separate notice. See Example 24 in the October Release:

> in January, a company places a copy of its final prospectus on its web site. Prior to viewing the prospectus, an investor provides express consent to the delivery of the prospectus and all final documents related to the offering via the web site. The investor then purchases the securities. In connection with its May annual meeting, the company places proxy soliciting materials on its web site and places an advertisement in the Wall Street Journal indicating its proxy materials are available on its web site. The advertisement, even coupled with the express consent relating to the offering documents, is insufficient delivery relating to the proxy statement. The company must provide more direct delivery or notice of the proxy materials.

b. Notice must be in close proximity to the time that the shareholder's action is requested, unless a history of shareholder communications creates a reasonable expectation that delivery in advance is sufficient. See Example (25) in the October Release:

> in September 1997, a shareholder of a company requests all future corporate communications, including proxy statements and annual reports, be delivered electronically through the company's web site. The consent form states that the company expects that its proxy statement and annual report for its annual meeting will be available on April 1, 1998. On April 1, 1998, the company places the material on its web site. In this case, advance request, without more, may not be close enough in time to the requested action to be effective. However if the company reasonably expects for other specific reasons, such as a history of communications with the shareholder, that delivery of information through the web site would be effective delivery, then the procedure would be acceptable.

c. Consent to receive: a document may be furnished electronically only where shareholders have given informed consent to receive it or where evidence exists that shareholders actually accessed the proxy statement electronically. See Example (23) in the October Release:

> a company places its annual report and proxy soliciting material on its Internet web site and sends a notice to all its record holders that this material is available on its web site, along with an address. This is inadequate delivery because the company may not presume that all record holders have access to the Internet. Therefore, the company must get a consent form or other evidence of shareholder consent or access.

d. Shareholders must be able to request a paper copy of a document even if they have previously consented to electronic delivery. See Example (26) in the October Release:

> a record holder consents to delivery of all documents via company's web site. On April 1, the company provides notice to the record holder that its annual report and proxy solicitation materials for its annual meeting scheduled for May 1 are available on the web site. On April 5, the record holder notifies the company that her computer is broken and requires a paper copy. Because the record holder's notice indicates that electronic delivery will be ineffective, the company should provide paper copies. The record holder does not need to withdraw her consent to receive paper copies.

e. A company should maintain access for as long as delivery requirement applies. See Part II(B), n. 26 in the October Release:

> Annual reports should be available electronically for a sufficient length of time for delivery to be satisfied. In the case of proxy soliciting materials regarding the election of directors, investors might reasonably expect the proxy soliciting materials and annual report to be available on the web site until their votes have been cast and the meeting adjourned.

f. Brokerage firms may transmit documents electronically, subject to the same general rules, and both the brokerage firm and the company may rely on consents furnished to the other. See Example (29) in the October Release:

> a brokerage firm solicits its customers who are beneficial owners of a company to determine whether they would like to receive that company's annual report and proxy solicitation materials via the Internet. The brokerage firm informs the company that 100 beneficial owners prefer the Internet and 200 beneficial owners prefer paper documents. The company provides the brokerage firm the location of the electronic materials to those who prefer electronic delivery and paper materials for those who prefer paper documents. This would be consistent with the proxy rules.

g. Sending documents by using various methods is acceptable. A company can deliver one document either by electronic means or normal mail and deliver a second document by another form (see Example (12) in the October Release), or send one document both by electronic means or normal mail. See Example (30) in the October Release:

> a company wishes to produce its annual report on videotape, CD-ROM and in paper form. The company sends a letter asking shareholders in what form they would like to receive the annual report. The company then sends the annual report on videotape to shareholders who preferred this form, by CD-ROM to shareholders who preferred this form and by paper form to shareholders who preferred this form. This is satisfactory delivery.

h. Beneficial owners may transmit voting instructions electronically to a brokerage firm that is the record owner. See Example 3 of the May Release:

> a brokerage firm, a record holder of a company's common stock, received consents from beneficial owners of the company's common stock for electronic delivery of the company's annual report and proxy materials and for electronic processing of voting instructions. These customers

are provided with the Internet web site address where the shareholders can provide their voting instructions to the brokerage firm. The electronic processing of voting instructions from beneficial holders and the electronic voting of proxies would be consistent with the proxy rules. Issuers and others are reminded to consider any applicable state laws or self-regulatory organization rules.

i. Shareholders may download a form of proxy from an electronic transmission and return it by mail to the company with a manual signature. See Example 28 from the October Release:

a company places its annual report and proxy solicitation materials on the Internet and provides sufficient notice to shareholders. The record holders are instructed to print the proxy cards, execute the proxy and send it back to the company. This would be consistent with the proxy rules.

For a discussion of state law limitations on the electronic transmission of proxies see Section III of this outline.

B. Other Federal Securities Law Concerns for Issuers.

1. Issuers can post a preliminary proxy on their web site to elicit shareholder comment, although issuers must not furnish a proxy card until after delivery of the definitive proxy statement.

2. Because the annual report must accompany or precede an annual meeting at which directors will be elected, care must be taken to coordinate the timing of delivery of the annual report and the definitive proxy statement and proxy card.

Since annual reports often contain elaborate graphics and other material that are difficult to transmit electronically, an issuer may choose to continue to deliver the annual report in paper format. An appropriate period of time should elapse between the date of mailing the annual report and the date the definitive proxy statement is posted on the issuer's web site or otherwise transmitted electronically to shareholders.

3. Issuers may use their electronic mail system to disseminate proxy statement to employee shareholders and participants in 401(k) plans and similar stock-

based plans who are expected to log-on to electronic mail routinely in the course of performing their duties. Distribution of proxy cards or electronic transmission of completed proxy cards through the issuer's e-mail system may raise confidentiality concerns.

4. Particularly in sensitive or contested elections, issuers need to separate proxy material from other material posted on their web site so as to avoid the implication that such other material is other soliciting material.

C. Use of Electronic Communications by Shareholders.

1. Shareholders submitting a shareholder proposal under Rule 14a-8 under the Securities Exchange Act of 1934, as amended (the "Exchange Act") may use a web site to communicate with other shareholders. There does not seem to be any reason why the shareholders could not include the address of the web site in the materials submitted by it for inclusion in the issuer's proxy statement. The material included in the shareholder's web site could also presumably exceed the 500 word limit imposed by Rule 14a-8(b)(i).

   A proponent of a shareholder proposal who did not seek a proxy to vote on the proposal but who held over $5 million in market value of the issuer's shares would be required to file a notice of exempt solicitation with the SEC and each exchange on which the issuer's shares were listed. See Rule 14a-6(g). The notice would include a copy of the materials posted on the web site.

2. Issuers that have filed a proxy statement and persons filing a proxy statement in opposition to management may use a web site to post soliciting material, subject to the normal filing requirements for such soliciting material.

III. STATE LAW

A. State law governs manner of shareholder voting and specifies whether a proxy is valid and confers the authority to cast someone else's vote.

B. State statutes usually require that a shareholder may vote at a meeting "in person or by proxy."

1. State statutes do not prohibit electronic attendance for shareholders.
2. Electronic attendance may satisfy the "in person" requirement, but further clarification is necessary. A provision similar to the typical provision for

participation in a directors meeting through "any means of communication by which all directors may simultaneously hear each other during the meeting" would be helpful.

3. Bylaw provisions may provide some support for electronic attendance constituting presence in person, but they are not conclusive in the absence of statutory or case law authority.
4. As a result, proxies should be collected for shareholders who plan to attend a meeting by electronic communication.

C. Delaware law permits stockholders to affix a signature to a proxy "by any reasonable means including, but not limited to, by facsimile signature" and to transmit a proxy by "telegram, cablegram or other means of electronic transmission to the person who will be the holder of the proxy or to a proxy solicitation firm, proxy service organization or like agent. . . ." The electronic transmission must either set forth or be submitted with information from which it can be determined that the electronic transmission was authored by the stockholder. See Delaware General Corporation Law § 212(c). A similar provision has recently been added to New York law. See New York Bus. Corp. Law § 609(i).

D. Many states have not made allowances for electronic communication and require proxy cards to be signed by shareholder's signature.

1. May throw validity of an electronically submitted proxy into doubt.
2. Efforts exist to make definition of "signature" include a "digital signature."

NOTES

20

SUPERVISION OF ELECTRONIC COMMUNICATIONS

Kenneth S. Spirer

Portions of this outline have been or may be used in connection with other legal education programs.

I. SUPERVISION - STATUTORY AND REGULATORY BASIS

A. Federal Securities Laws

1. Section 15(b)(4)(E) of the Securities Exchange Act of 1934 authorizes the Securities and Exchange Commission ("SEC") to impose sanctions on a broker-dealer if the Commission finds that the broker-dealer or any of its associated persons have "failed reasonably to supervise, with a view to preventing violations of the provisions of [certain enumerated provisions of the federal securities and commodities laws by] another person who commits such a violation, if such other person is subject to his supervision."

2. Section 15(b)(4)(E) contains a safe harbor which allows broker-dealers to raise the defense that there have been "established procedures, and a system for applying such procedures, which would reasonably be expected to prevent and detect, insofar as practicable, violations of the securities laws by their supervised persons, and that the person with supervisory responsibilities has reasonably discharged his obligations under these procedures."

B. Self-Regulatory Organization Rules

1. National Association of Securities Dealers, Inc. (the "NASD") - - Conduct Rule 3010 ("Supervision")

   a. Each member shall establish and maintain a system to supervise the activities of each registered representative and associated person.

   b. The member's supervisory system must be reasonably designed to achieve compliance with applicable securities laws and regulations and NASD rules.

   c. At a minimum, a member's supervisory system shall provide for:

   - a written supervisory plan
   - the designation of appropriate offices of supervisory jurisdiction (OSJs), each with a registered principal
   - the designation of a registered principal with supervisory authority
   - the conduct of an annual inspection of all OSJs
   - the maintenance of written records of the dates upon which each review and inspection was conducted

2. National Association of Securities Dealers, Inc. Conduct Rule 2210 ("Communications with Customers and the Public")

a. Rule 2210(b)(1) - "[e]ach item of advertising and sales literature shall be approved by signature or initial, prior to use or filing with the Association, by a registered principal of the member."

b. In 1995 the NASD amended the definitions of "advertisement" and "sales literature" in NASD Conduct Rule 2210 to include electronic messages (NASD Notice to Members 95-74) (Sept., 1995).

- Rule 2210(a)(1) - "advertisement" means material published, or designed for use in, a newspaper, magazine or other periodical, radio, television, telephone or tape recording, video tape display, signs or billboards, motion pictures, telephone directories (other than routine listings), electronic or other public media (emphasis added).

- Rule 2210 (a)(2) - "sales literature" means any written or electronic communication distributed or made generally available to customers or the public" which does not meet the definition of "advertisement" (emphasis added).

3. New York Stock Exchange, Inc. (the "NYSE")

a. NYSE Rule 405 (the "Know Your Customer" rule) as it is interpreted with respect to supervision, provides that a broker-dealer must:

- learn essential facts relative to every customer order and account
- diligently supervise all accounts

b. NYSE Rule 342 ("Offices - Approval, Supervision and Control")

- each office of a member shall be under the supervision and control of the member
- the general partners or directors of each member shall designate a general partner or principal executive officer to assume overall responsibility for supervision
- the appointment of a compliance officer to direct day-to-day compliance activities
- conducting an annual inspection of each branch office

II. RECENT REGULATORY CHANGES - SUPERVISION OF ELECTRONIC COMMUNICATIONS

A. Securities and Exchange Commission

a. In its May, 1996 release addressing the use of electronic media by broker-dealers, transfer agents and investment advisors, the SEC "strongly" encouraged the SROs "to continue to work with broker-dealers to adapt SRO supervisory review requirements governing communications with customers to accommodate the use of electronic communications by broker-dealers", *see*, Exchange Act Release No. 37182; May 5, 1996 at footnote 5.

B. New York Stock Exchange, Inc.

a. NYSE created an Electronic Communications Committee in May, 1996 to review existing NYSE rules governing communications with the public and to recommend revisions to accommodate emerging technology. This Committee met numerous times from May - July 1996 and made recommendations to the NYSE staff.

b. On September 5, 1996, the NYSE Board of Directors approved amendments to NYSE Rules 342, 440 and 472. On September 12, 1996, the NYSE filed these proposed rule amendments with the SEC (File No. SR-NYSE-96-26) and on November 13, 1996 the SEC published them for comment (Exchange Act Release No. 37941) (61 FR 58919)(November 19, 1996).

c. On November 6, 1996 the NYSE filed Amendment No. 1 to the rule filing which revised the original rule filing to include language changes to NYSE Rules 440 and 472(c) with respect to recordkeeping requirements for member organization communications with the public suggested by the SEC staff.

d. On November 3, 1997 the NYSE filed Amendment No. 2 to its rule filing (SR-NYSE-96-26). This amendment provides that supervisory review will continue to be required of all incoming communications directed to registered representatives in nonelectronic format. According to the NYSE filing, "[t]his review is necessary as a way to provide that incoming customer complaints are handled and monitored in accordance with firm policies and Exchange rules and that customer funds or securities are directed to the appropriate area/department for processing."

e. On November 25, 1997 the NYSE filed Amendment No. 3 to its rule filing (SR-NYSE-96-26). This filing consisted of a proposed NYSE Information Memo that would be issued upon SEC approval of the rule changes and is intended to provide guidelines and parameters for assistance in complying with the rule amendments.

f. On December 31, 1997, the SEC approved the NYSE's rule amendments (Exchange Act Release No. 39511) (63 FR 1135; January 8, 1998). The rules were amended as follows:

- NYSE Rule 342 ("Offices - Approval, Supervision and Control")

  (1) Section .16 of the Supplementary Material was revised to delete the references to the 1982 NYSE guidelines, "Patterns of Supervision", which stated that pre-use review of outgoing correspondence and a supervisor's initialing of the outgoing correspondence to evidence his review were appropriate methods of supervision.

  (2) Section .16 was revised to require that member firms have "reasonable procedures for review of registered representatives' communications with the public relating to their business . . . . Such policies and procedures should be in writing and be designed to reasonably supervise each registered representative."

  (3) A new Section .17 captioned "Review of Communications With the Public" was added requiring member firms to "develop written policies and procedures that are appropriate for their business, their size, structure and customers . . . ." These policies and procedures must include provision for the education and training of employees, documentation of such education and training and surveillance and follow-up to ensure that such policies and procedures are implemented and adhered to.

- NYSE Rule 440 ("Books and Records")

  (1) The NYSE books and records rule was revised to reflect that books and records should be maintained in a "format or medium" that complies with SEC Rule 17a-4.

  (2) This is intended to allow for flexibility in record retention as the SEC permits new technologies to be utilized for retention of records.

- NYSE Rule 472 ("Communications with the Public")

  (1) Rule 472 was amended to clarify the specific types of communications that continue to require pre-use approval, e.g., advertisements, market letters, sales literature and research reports.

  (2) The record retention requirements were revised to require that the names of persons who prepared, reviewed and approved communications must be "readily ascertainable" from the retained records. This is intended to permit electronic approvals rather than requiring initials on the actual document or a copy.

g. The NYSE issued NYSE Information Memo No. 98-3 (January 14, 1998) to provide guidance to members on how to implement the new and amended rules. This Information Memo is discussed in Section II, D.

C. The National Association of Securities Dealers, Inc.

a. In December, 1996 the NASD issued Notice to Members 96-82 in which it solicited comment on proposed amendments to Conduct Rules 3010 ("Supervision") and 3110 ("Books and Records").

b. The NASD proposal was designed to be consistent with the approach taken by the NYSE to provide broker-dealers firms with flexibility in developing reasonable procedures for the review of correspondence. It is intended to help ensure a coordinated regulatory framework for supervision of manual and electronic correspondence.

c. The NASD filed its proposed rule changes with the SEC on April 11, 1997 (SR-NASD-97-24) Exchange Act Rel. No. 38548 (62 FR 24147; May 2, 1997).

d. On December 1, 1997 the NASD filed Amendment No. 1 to its rule filing. The Amendment consisted of a draft Notice to Members that would be issued following the approval by the SEC of the proposal.

e. On December 31, 1997 the SEC approved the NASD's proposed rule changes (Exchange Act Release No. 39510) (63 FR 1131; January 8, 1998). The rule were amended as follows:

- Rule 3010(d)(1) requires firms to establish written procedures for review of outgoing and incoming manual and electronic correspondence of its registered representatives relating to the business of the member.

  (1) the supervisory procedures should specify what is to be pre or post reviewed, the level and qualifications of persons who will conduct the reviews, the frequency of review, and how the review will be evidenced.

  (2) NASD member firms will no longer be required to review each item of correspondence. NASD Regulation indicated, however, that reasonable procedures could entail review of all correspondence of particular individuals.

  (3) although written approval of correspondence would no longer be required, firms should specify the means for evidencing review. Firms can electronically record evidence of supervisory review.

- Rule 3010(d)(2), as amended, requires each member to develop written procedures for review of incoming and outgoing correspondence tailored to its structure and the nature and size of its business and customer base. If a firm does not conduct a prior review of correspondence it must:

  (1) regularly educate and train registered representatives as to the firm's procedures for review of communications;

  (2) document such education and training; and

  (3) monitor to assure implementation and compliance with the procedures.

- Rule 3010(d)(3), as amended, requires each member to retain correspondence in accordance with the NASD's amended books and records rule (Rule 3110). The names of the persons who prepared and reviewed the correspondence must be ascertainable from the retained records.

f. The NASD issued Notice to Members 98-11 (January 1998) that provided guidance to members on how to implement the new rules. This Notice to Members is discussed in Section II, D.

D. Overview of the SRO Interpretative Releases

1. Immediately after the SEC approved the rule filings, the NYSE and NASD issued interpretive releases (NYSE Information Memo No. 98-3 (January 14, 1998) and NASD Notice to Members 98-11 (January 1998) that, while purporting to offer "Guidelines for Supervision and Review" of communications with customers, nonetheless state that members must:

- specify, in writing, the firm's policies and procedures for reviewing different types of communication;
- identify how supervisory reviews will be conducted and documented;
- identify what types of communication will be pre-reviewed or post-reviewed;
- identify the organizational position(s) responsible for conducting reviews of the different types of communications;
- specify the minimum frequency of the reviews for different types of communications;
- monitor the implementation of and compliance with the firm's procedures for reviewing public communications;
- periodically re-evaluate the effectiveness of the firm's procedures for reviewing public communications and consider any necessary revisions.

2. In their interpretive releases, the NYSE and NASD, at the urging of the SEC, are very specific about the minimum review procedures that must be followed by member firms. These require that the member:

- specify procedures for reviewing registered representatives' recommendations to customers;
- require supervisory review of some of each registered representative's public communications, including recommendations to customers;
- consider the complaint and overall disciplinary history, if any, of registered representatives and other employees (with particular emphasis on complaints regarding written or oral communications with clients);
- consider the nature and extent of training provided registered representatives and other employees, as well as their experienced levels in using communications media, (although a firm's procedures may not eliminate or provide for minimal supervisory reviews based on an employee's training or level of experience in using communications media).

3. The NYSE and NASD have made it clear that these factors are not exclusive and members must consider all appropriate factors when developing their supervisory procedures and implementing their supervisory reviews. Finally, the interpretive releases expressly stated that supervisory policies and procedures must also:

- provide that all customer complaints, whether received via e-mail or in written form from the customer, are reported in compliance with SRO rules;
- describe any firm standards for the content of different types of communications;
- address permitted and prohibited activities (e.g., lectures, seminars, mass media appearances, etc.);
- prohibit registered representatives and other employees use of electronic communications to the public unless such communications are subject to supervisory and review procedures developed by the member. (For example, members and member organizations are expected to prohibit communications with the public from employees' home computers or through third party computer systems unless the member is capable of monitoring such communication.)

E. Open Issues

1. The effective date of the NASD rules, which was originally scheduled for February 15, 1998, has been postponed at the request of the NASD because of concerns raised by certain members after the amendments were approved by the SEC, *see*, "Postponement of Rule Relating to Supervision of Correspondence," <http://www.nasdr.com/2690.htm>.

2. These concerns, articulated in comment letters to the SEC, are:

- the requirement that NASD members review all non-electronic correspondence received from customers.

- the manner in which NASD members are expected to monitor communications with customers from employees' home computers or through third party system.

3. The NASD has noted that joint members of the NYSE and NASD would be permitted to rely on the procedures now permitted by the amended NYSE rules.

NOTES

NOTES

21

CHAT ROOMS AND RELATED ISSUES

Scott W. Campbell

Portions of this outline are drawn from other outlines prepared by Mr. Campbell.

Chat Rooms and Related Issues
by
Scott W. Campbell

I. CHAT ROOMS

Introduction. The development and operation of bulletin boards or chat rooms by broker-dealers presents any number of issues, including (i) civil liability, (ii) "Communications with the Public" considerations, (iii) risk profiles of topics, and (iv) operations. Guidelines are beginning to emerge that should enable firms to move beyond fairly limited online forums that are actively moderated by firms towards unmoderated chat room models that are prevalent in non-financial online communities. Until the legal and regulatory aspects associated with chat rooms become more developed, however, firms should proceed with caution.

A. Civil Liability Exposure for Defamatory Content. The two leading cases that address the potential liability of a bulletin board or chat room operator for alleged defamatory statements posted by a third party (a visitor) suggest that an operator should exercise little or no editorial control over, or monitoring of, content. Compare Cubby v. CompuServe, Inc., 776 F. Supp. 135 (S.D.N.Y. 1991) ("Cubby") and Stratton Oakmont, Inc. v. Prodigy Services Co., (63USLW 2765 New York 1995) ("Stratton Oakmont") [(not approved for publication by State Reporter of Decisions)].

(i) Content Distributor/"Bookstore". In Cubby, the court granted CompuServe's motion for summary judgment that is was not liable as a publisher because CompuServe exercised no editorial control over the content available through its online forum. CompuServe argued successfully that it was merely a distributor of content, much like a bookstore.

(ii) "Publisher". In contrast, the court in Stratton Oakmont determined that Prodigy could be held vicariously liable as a "publisher" of several alleged defamatory statements about a securities firm and its president that had been posted by a third party on the "Money Talk" bulletin board operated by Prodigy. Key factors cited by the court included:

(1) Editorial Control. Prodigy held itself out to the public as a service that exercised editorial control over the content of messages posted on its bulletin boards.

(2) "Offensive Language" Screening Software. Prodigy prescreened all bulletin board postings for offensive language using a word screening software program.

(3) Content Guidelines. Prodigy created and posted guidelines for its bulletin boards that prohibited certain conduct, including the posting of harassing messages.

Potential Defenses Under The Communications Decency Act of 1996.

(1) "Interactive Computer Service Providers" (ICSPs) are not publishers.

(2) "Good Samaritan" defense is available to provider or user of interactive computer service that attempts to remove content that it considers to be objectionable.

Open issues:

- Impact of constitutional challenges
- Scope of ICSPs (includes all firms operating chat rooms?)
- Application beyond alleged defamatory statements

B. "Communications with the Public" Considerations. In its April 1996 "Ask the Analyst" publication, the NASD indicated that it viewed chat rooms as interactive, extemporaneous public forums.

(i) Statements of Registered Representatives and Member Firms. Such statements are not generally subject to the NASD's rules regarding correspondence, sales literature or advertising. When participating in chat rooms, however, member firms and their registered representatives are accountable under the Rules of Fair Practice and the federal securities laws (e.g. anti-fraud prohibitions).

(ii) Statements of the Public. In its Notice to Members 95-74 (August 1995), the NASD stated that the term "advertisement" as used in the NASD rules does not include communications by members of the public. Consequently, member firms generally would not have review or filing obligations with respect to such statements.

(iii) False or Misleading Statements regarding Products and Services. In recent interpretive guidance of the NASD, the NASD indicated that it may hold member firms responsible for content on a third-party site linked to by a member firm where the member firm knew or had reason to know that the third party site contained false or misleading information relating to the member firm's products or services. See November 11, 1997 letter of the NASD to the Investment Company Institute (regarding third-party links). The NASD expressly noted that it was "not commenting on a member's possible responsibility to suspend or terminate a hyperlink when it comes to the member's attention that the hyperlinked site contains [any] false or misleading information [not necessarily information about the member's products or services.]" See footnote 3 of the ICI letter.

C. Risk Profiles of Chat Room Topics. Recent enforcement action of the Commission related to Internet fraud indicates that chat rooms can be an attractive forum for unscrupulous stock promoters or others engaged in speculative, fraudulent or illegal activities. See generally John Reed Stark, "Tombstones: The Internet's Impact Upon SEC Rules of Engagements," Insights, Vol. 12, No. 2 (February 1998). See also Joseph J. Cella III and John Reed Stark, "SEC Enforcement and the Internet: Meeting the Challenge of the Next Millennium A Program for the Eagle and the Internet," 52 Bus. Law. 815 (May 1997).

To reduce risks associated from such activity, chat room operators may wish to consider the following:

- Narrowly Define Chat Room Topics (e.g. no penny stocks),
- Limit Access to Customers,
- Require Chat Room Participants to Identify Themselves,
- Actively Moderate Rooms,
- Invite Regulatory Participation,
- Encourage Self-Policing within the Online Community.

D. Operations.

1. Supervision of Firm Communications. Recently approved NYSE and NASDR rule changes regarding supervision and review of communications with the public, particularly electronic communications, offer additional guidance in designing procedures with respect to initial postings and re-use of statements by registered representatives of member firms. See SEC Release 34-39511 (December 31, 1997) (NYSE) and SEC Release No. 34-39510 (December 31, 1997) (NASDR).

2. Records. Depending on the nature of the communications appearing in a chat room or bulletin board, firms likely will want to consider record retention and other issues related to chat room communications. For example, see Reid & Co., SEC No-Action Letter (available December 22, 1997) (maintain records of indications of interest posted to bulletin board of Internet Capital Corporation for not less than three (3) years and make them available to the staff of the Commission and any organized market on which the securities are traded or quoted upon reasonable request).

3. Complaints. Firms will want to consider procedures relating to certain postings by customers that may constitute "complaints" for regulatory purposes. For example, see NYSE Rule 351(d).

4. User Rules and Disclosures. Chat rooms frequently have rules that provide:

- Prohibit the posting of unlawful, defamatory or indecent communications;
- State that the operator reserves the right to review and remove any communication in its sole discretion;
- Require users to register, using their real names, to participate in chat room discussions or otherwise limit participation to specific users;
- Require that communications be limited to the chat room topic, if any;
- Require that participants disclose their affiliations;
- State that the operator reserves the right to bar future participation if rules are not observed;
- Reserve the operator's right to distribute or disclose chat room discussions with or without participant attribution and without any duty, obligation or liability to the participant; and
- Warn chat room participants that all postings represent the views of the individual contributors, should not be relied upon as accurate and do not represent the opinions, advice or recommendations of the operator or its affiliates.

II. CONFIDENTIALITY, SECURITY AND PRIVACY

A. Confidentiality and Security.

Personal Financial Information. According to the Commission's Interpretive Release on electronic media issued in May 1996, personal financial information is that which is "specific to a particular person's personal financial matters." SEC Release 33-7288, 34-37182, IC-21945, IA-1562 (May 9, 1996) at page 14. Examples may include: (i) Rule 10b-10, confirmations of securities transactions; and (ii) Rule 10b-16, quarterly statements of interest charges (frequently incorporated into account statements).

Reasonable Precautions. According to the Commission, broker-dealers, transfer agents and investment advisors who use electronic media to communicate with investors are "required by federal securities law" to take "reasonable precautions" to ensure:

- Integrity
- Confidentiality
- Security

See page 14 of the May 1996 Release. See also SEC Release No. 34-39025 (September 5, 1997) (NASD Notice to Members Regarding Electronic Delivery of

Information Between Members and their Customers) (NASDR will permit electronic delivery provided member firms adhere to standards of the Commission).

Security Measures. Measures taken must be tailored to the medium to insure that the information is reasonably secure from tampering or alteration. Examples cited by the Commission in the May 1996 Release include:

- Firewalls
- Passwords
- Encryption
- Monitoring of Intruders
- Frequent Periodic Notice to Customers of Account Activity
- Transaction Limits and Reviews
- System Alerts of Unusual Activity
- Warnings or other Notices of Measures Employed

Consent. Subject to facts and circumstances, financial firms generally should obtain a recipient's consent to electronic delivery of personal financial information. Consent may be either manual or by electronic means. The Commission has said that consent may not be required where a broker-dealer is (i) responding to a request for information that is made through electronic media, or (ii) the person making the request specifies delivery through a particular media. "[I]n most cases in which a request for information is made through an electronic medium, consent to receive the requested information by means of electronic delivery may be presumed." See fn. 23 at page 13 of the May 1996 Release.

B. Privacy.

Privacy and Internet Commerce. The concept of privacy can be considered somewhat broader than confidentiality and security since it relates to consumer awareness and choice regarding use of their personally-identifying information. With the rapid growth of electronic commerce and the technological ease of collecting personal information from users, privacy concerns are attracting more attention both domestically and internationally.

1. Federal Policy. In its "White Paper" released in July 1997, titled "A Framework for Global Electronic Commerce," the Clinton Administration noted growing concern of privacy as it relates to electronic commerce. Citing the 1995 and 1997 reports of the Privacy Working Group of the U.S. government Information Infrastructure Task Force, the Administration stated that privacy principles should incorporate principles of fair information practices and rest on fundamental precepts of awareness and choice.

Awareness and Choice. In particular, the White Paper stated that privacy principles of "data-gatherers" should:

- Inform consumers about (i) what information they are collecting, and (ii) how they intend to use such data; and

- Provide consumers with a meaningful way to limit use and reuse of personal information.

Private Industry Self-Regulation Preferred. Rather than dictate privacy standards, the White Paper said:

> If privacy concerns are not addressed by industry through self regulation and technology, the Administration will face increasing pressure to play a more direct role in safeguarding consumer choice regarding privacy online.
>
> [The Administration] believes that private efforts of industry working in cooperation with consumer groups are preferable to government regulation, but if effective privacy protection cannot be provided this way, we will reevaluate policy.

Federal Trade Commission's "Sweep". The FTC has announced it is conducting a "sweep" of e-commerce sites in March 1998 to review the progress of private industry in developing initiatives on data protection as urged by the Administration. The FTC is expected to report its findings to Congress on June 1, 1998.

2. European Union's Directive on Data Protection. In October 1995, the European Parliament adopted the Directive on the Protection of Individuals with regard to the Processing of Personal Data and on the Free Movement of such Data (the "Directive") scheduled to take effect in October 1998, which establishes European standards for the gathering, use and disclosure of personal information.

Prohibition on Data Transfers to Jurisdictions Without "Adequate" Protection. Importantly, Article 25 of the Directive prohibits the transfer of personal information of anyone from the EU to other countries that the EU determines do not provide "adequate" levels of privacy protection.

Notice, Use, Correction. Since it is unclear at this time whether U.S. law is adequate for purposes of the Directive, EU commentators have suggested that U.S. industries establish "privacy codes of conduct" that, at a minimum:

- Afford notice to consumers of what data is collected about them and how it is intended to be used,

- Provide meaningful opportunity for consumers to limit the use and re-use of their personal data, and

- Allow the correction of errors that may exist in company files.

Current U.S. Law. In addition to privacy protections emanating out of federal and state constitutional "penumbras" and common law torts, U.S. law has been described as a "patchwork" of federal and state statutory and regulatory authority governing collection, use and distribution of information by government and private parties. See Mark F. Radcliffe and Mary E. Shallman, "Privacy and Internet Commerce" (March 1996)(prepared with funding from CommerceNet, www.commerce.net). Of the more significant federal statutes relating to privacy issues, the above article describes the following in some detail:

- Electronic Communications Privacy Act, 18 USC 2510
- Privacy Act, 5 USC 552 (a)
- Cable Communications Policy Act, 47 USC 551
- Video Privacy Act of 1988, 18 USC 2710
- Telephone Consumer Protection Act of 1991, 47 USC 227
- Fair Credit Reporting Act, 15 USC 1681

Protective Measures. All industries that engage in electronic commerce are encouraged by the Administration and privacy advocates to tell customers and visitors who visit their Web site how data is collected and used. A growing number of e-commerce sites include web pages that describe practices and policies.

For additional information, the following Web sites contain current information and links to other resources:

- Direct Marketing Association at www.the-dma.org
- CommerceNet at www.commerce.net
- Federal Trade Commission at www.ftc.gov
- Center for Democracy and Technology at www.cdt.org

III. CROSS-BORDER CONSIDERATIONS

Global Access, Local Regulation. Information that an issuer or financial institution puts on a Web site may be accessed globally and, thus, subject the firm to local laws and regulations neither intended nor contemplated.

A. NASAA Resolution on Internet Offers. In January 1996, the North America Securities Administrators Association adopted a board resolution (modeled after an earlier Pennsylvania position) to exempt "Internet Offers" from state registration under the following conditions:

- The Internet Offer indicates, directly or indirectly, that the securities are not being offered to the residents of a particular state; and

- The offer is not otherwise specifically directed to any person in a state by, or on behalf of, an issuer of securities.

Prevent Unlawful Sales. Issuers may satisfy the exemption if securities are sold only to residents of states in which the offering is registered or qualified or otherwise exempt.

Adoption by States. To date, 31 states and the District of Columbia have adopted the NASAA Resolution on Internet Offers, including California and New York.

B. Securities and Exchange Commission. Informally, the Commission has indicated that it will not bring enforcement action against foreign issuers who use Web sites for offerings, if:

- Prominent legends state that the securities are not being offered in the United States, and

- In fact, the securities are not sold publicly to persons in the United States.

The Commission is expected to issue an interpretive release soon regarding foreign offerings of securities on the Internet. The Commission is expected to take the position that if a message is posted by a foreign issuer on a Web site that is not directed to a specific individual in the U.S., the offering is not subject to U.S. registration requirements. See D. Moray, "SEC Worries About Investors' Expectations", Wall Street Journal, at page B5A (March 9, 1998).

C. International Regulators.

1. United Kingdom. In positions announced last spring, UK regulators (SFA, IMRO, and SIB) have said that Web sites located outside of the UK that are accessible by persons in the UK could violate current UK statutes if the Web sites offer investment services. The Securities and Futures Authority, Board Notice 416 (April 25, 1997). UK regulators have since indicated informally that before considering enforcement proceedings, they will consider facts and

circumstances to determine whether offers of investment services are being directed at persons in the UK.

2. IOSCO. The Technical Committee of the International Organization of Securities Commissions (IOSCO) has established an Internet Task Force that, as a part of its work plan, is working on the issue of "what constitutes an offer of a collective investment scheme (CIS) or open-end mutual funds within a particular jurisdiction." See Glorianne Stromberg, "Coming to Grips with the Internet - IOSCO Initiatives," Wallstreetlawyer.com, Vol. 1, No. 7 (December 1997). The Internet Task Force will consider and advise on issues such as:

   - Use of Disclaimers
   - Password-Protected Sites
   - Blocking Devices
   - Other Comparable Measures

   See also www.iosco.org.

D. Protective Measures. To reduce exposure to enforcement or regulatory proceedings in foreign jurisdictions, an issuer or financial institution should institute measures to prevent shares from being deemed offered or sold in jurisdictions where the firm or activity is not qualified or otherwise exempt.

- Disclaimers and Legends. Prominent disclosures should be used to make it understood that shares, products and services are only being offered in those jurisdictions where they are registered or qualified or otherwise exempt.

- Procedures to Restrict Actual Sales. Firms and issuers should institute reasonable procedures to prevent unlawful sales from occurring.

- Review All Content and Functionality for Consistency. In addition to disclaimers and legends, the overall content and functionality of the Web site should be reviewed periodically for consistency with the disclaimers and legends. For example, a fund group posting its daily NAVs in British pound sterling would not appear to be acting consistently if its legends specifically state that it is not selling to residents of the United Kingdom.

NOTES

22

LEGAL DEVELOPMENTS IN THE ELECTRONIC SECURITIES MARKETS: ONLINE TRADING SYSTEMS AND THE USE OF WEBSITES FOR OFFSHORE INTERNET OFFERS

Brandon Becker
David Westbrook
Lyle Roberts

PART ONE
ONLINE TRADING SYSTEMS[1]

I. Overview

A. Introduction

1. **Impact on SEC**. The implementation of new technology in the secondary markets[2] presents the Securities and Exchange Commission ("SEC" or "Commission") with three challenges: a) to accommodate innovative applications of technology; b) to ensure investor confidence in the marketplace as it is transformed by the application of technology; and c) to minimize the disruption of existing markets.

2. **Components of online trading systems**. This outline uses the term "online trading system" to encompass a range of data communication systems that facilitate the secondary trading of securities. Viewed schematically, online trading systems share three basic components: a) computer terminals that allow users to send and receive transaction communications; b) a central processing host facility that receives orders and either displays, matches, crosses or otherwise facilitates trade executions; and c) a network that serves as a communications link between the users and the central processing host.[3] In practice, different online trading systems have different capabilities. Their regulatory status under the Securities Exchange Act of 1934 ("Exchange Act") is an evolving issue and the subject of this outline.

B. Characterizing Online Trading Systems

1. **Regulatory Categories**. In fulfilling its investor protection and market oversight roles, the SEC traditionally has focused its efforts on the regulation of broker-dealers and organized markets. Online trading systems do not

---

[1] Part One of this outline summarizes and updates the material in Brandon Becker, David A. Westbrook, Soo J. Yim, *Online Trading: Issuers, Broker-Dealers and SROs*, in SECURITIES IN THE ELECTRONIC AGE: A PRACTICAL GUIDE, 3-1 (John F. Olson & Harvey Pitt, eds., 1998).

[2] Securities, of course, may be offered as well as traded online. Indeed, the same system may be used for both issuance and secondary trading. *See, e.g.*, Niphix Investments Inc., SEC No-Action Letter, 1997 WL 209335 (Apr. 18, 1997).

[3] *See* Michael B. Sundel & Lystra G. Blake, *Good Concept, Bad Executions: The Regulation and Self-Regulation of Automated Trading Systems in United States Futures Markets*, 85 Nw. U. L. Rev. 748, 749-54 (1991).

completely fit into either category. Consequently, the SEC long has wrestled with the issue of whether the operation of various online trading systems constitutes a) broker-dealer activity, or b) operating an exchange, or c) some other regulated activity.

a. **Broker-Dealer Activity**. To date, the question of whether the sponsorship of a particular online trading system is broker-dealer activity generally has been answered in the affirmative. In most cases, it is a straightforward issue: whether a person is facilitating securities transactions for the account of others in return for transaction-based compensation. Many online trading systems are designed to facilitate just this business. Moreover, the vast majority of online trading systems have been sponsored by entities that already are registered broker-dealers, or are SROs composed of broker-dealers. The primary exception to such arrangements has been the sponsorship of issuer bulletin boards.

b. **Operating an Exchange**. The second and third questions, however, have been far more problematic.[4/]

i. **Delta Release**. Following a court case over the regulatory status of the Delta System, an online trading system for the trading of options contracts written on U.S. Treasury debt obligations, the SEC issued the Delta Release.[5/] The Commission examined a variety of characteristics of traditional exchanges, many of which the Delta System included. Ultimately, however, the Commission decided that "the central focus of the Commission's inquiry should be whether the system is designed . . . to centralize trading and provide buy and sell quotations on a regular or continuous basis so that purchasers and sellers have a reasonable expectation that they can regularly execute their orders at those price quotations."[6/] In short, under the logic of the Delta Release, a reasonable expectation of regular executions at quoted prices is the key to exchange status.

4/ The third question raised by online trading systems, *i.e.*, whether the system should be characterized as some other type of regulated entities, such as a clearing agency or information processor, generally has been addressed in the context of determining whether or not exchange regulation is necessary.

5/ Exchange Act Release No. 27611 (Jan. 12, 1990), 55 Fed. Reg. 1890 ("Delta Release").

6/ *Id.* at 1900.

ii. **Concept Release**. In its Concept Release,[7] however, the Commission suggested that it should "expand its current interpretation of 'exchange' to encompass many more trading systems than are currently considered 'exchanges.'"[8] The Commission noted that the narrow definition of exchange adopted in the Delta Release "effectively excluded most alternative trading systems from exchange regulation."[9] Instead, the Commission proposed that an exchange should be defined as "any organization that both (1) consolidates orders of multiple parties and (2) provides a facility through which, or sets material conditions under which, participants entering such orders may agree to the terms of a trade."[10]

3. **Functional Analysis**. The proliferation of online trading systems requires functional -- as opposed to institutional -- thinking about how securities regulation works. Approaching regulation of online trading systems from a functional perspective, this outline devotes considerable attention to the technical capabilities of various online trading systems. Operational information about online trading systems will be important in understanding the nature of communications made through the medium of online trading system. For many years, the SEC has regulated some, but not all, communications concerning the secondary trading of securities. Online trading systems are regulated only insofar as they facilitate such regulated communications. Accordingly, understanding regulatory obligations requires understanding the nature of communication carried by online trading systems.[11]

7/ *See* Securities Exchange Act Release No. 38672 (May 28, 1997), 62 Fed. Reg. 30485 (June 4, 1997) ("Concept Release").

8/ *See id.* at 30505.

9/ *Id.*

10/ *Id.* at 30507. At the same time, however, as discussed below, the Concept Release also makes it clear that broadening the definition of exchange as suggested is likely to raise substantial market structure concerns.

11/ We have some doubt about the durability of this approach. Contemporary regulation of online trading assumes that a given system will be regulated in one way or another because of functional limitations in the online trading system -- *e.g.*, a system will not fulfill some link(s) in the transactional chain. Such limitations have no technical basis. It seems unlikely to expect a business culture that is growing increasingly accustomed to

(continued...)

II. Online Trading Systems Sponsored by Entities Not Registered Under the Exchange Act

A. Electronic Bulletin Boards

The most straightforward example of an online trading system is an electronic bulletin board, accessible via the Internet, used to communicate trading interest.

B. Issuer Bulletin Boards

So-called "issuer bulletin boards" allow stockholders to advertise interest in buying or selling securities of the issuer sponsoring the bulletin board. A number of issuers have received SEC confirmation that their proposed bulletin boards do not require the issuer to register as a broker-dealer, or the bulletin board to be registered as an exchange.[12/] Such bulletin boards generally facilitate trading of the sponsoring issuer's securities by providing information about prospective buyers and sellers. Actual transactions, however, are effected outside the system by interested parties who contact each other directly.

C. Internet Capital Corporation

The SEC granted no-action assurance to Internet Capital Corporation that establishment of its passive bulletin board would not subject Internet Capital to enforcement actions. [13/]

Internet Capital sought to charge registered but thinly-traded companies for posting information about themselves on the site. The bulletin board would allow parties, not affiliated with Internet Capital, to post messages regarding trading interest. Actual trades would be consummated off-site. Postings would not be deemed to be offers or firm quotes; two-sided quotes would be prohibited. Internet Capital successfully argued that it was not offering or trading securities, it was not acting as a broker, dealer, or investment adviser, and the site itself was not an exchange.

Internet Capital escapes the bifurcation between broker-dealer activity and the conduct of an exchange that has structured so much trading regulation.

11/ (...continued)
perfect communication to accept such limitations.

12/ *See, e.g.*, Real Goods Trading Corp., SEC No-Action Letter (publicly available June 24, 1996).

13/ Internet Capital Corporation, SEC No-Action Letter (publicly available January 13, 1998).

III. Online Trading Systems Sponsored by Broker-Dealers

A. Overview

1. **Terminology**. The Commission has used a number of overlapping terms to refer to the various online trading systems sponsored by broker-dealers.

a. **Proprietary Trading System ("PTS")**. The term "PTS" has come to mean an online trading system sponsored by a broker-dealer that does not have to register as an exchange.

b. **Broker-Dealer Trading System ("BDTS")**. The term "BDTS" is defined by Exchange Act Rule 17a-23 (requiring reporting by broker-dealers who sponsor certain online trading systems) as any "facility that provides a mechanism, automated in full or in part, for: (i) collecting, receiving, or displaying system orders; and (ii) matching, crossing, or executing system orders, or otherwise facilitating agreement to the basic terms of a purchase or sale of a security between system participants, or between a system participant and the system sponsor, through use of the system or the system sponsor."[14]

c. **Electronic Communications Network ("ECN")**. The term ECN is defined by Exchange Act Rule 11Ac1-1 ("Quote Rule") as "[a]ny electronic system that widely disseminates to third parties orders entered therein by an exchange market maker or [over-the-counter] market maker, and permits such orders to be executed against in whole or in part," with some exceptions. The term "ECN" does not include crossing systems or broker-dealer internal order routing systems.[15]

d. **Alternative Trading System**. The term Alternative Trading System is used in the Commission's recent Concept Release "to refer generally to automated systems that centralize, display, match, cross, or otherwise execute trading interest, but that are not currently registered

---

[14] *See* 17 C.F.R. § 240.17a-23.

[15] These systems are not deemed ECNs because they do not communicate to multiple market participants the prices at which system subscribers are willing to trade. *See* Exchange Act Release No. 37619A (Sept. 6, 1996), 61 Fed. Reg. 48290, 48313 (September 12, 1996) ("Order Handling Release").

with the Commission as national securities exchanges or operated by a registered securities association."[16]

2. **Order Routing**. Electronic order routing systems are most commonly used by institutional investors. Over the last few years, however, a number of broker-dealers have begun to offer electronic order routing services to retail investors. These systems generally have been viewed by the SEC as an extension of broker-dealer services, rather than as new electronic marketplaces that replicate an exchange marketplace, because they perform traditional brokerage activities (*i.e.*, routing orders to a market of which the broker-dealer is a member for execution), thereby obviating the need to handle customer orders manually.[17]

3. **Schwab No-Action Letters**. The discount broker Charles Schwab & Co., Inc. ("Schwab") sought to sponsor an online trading system that would include certain linkages with three well-established Internet service providers ("ISP"). [18] Schwab proposed to have the ISPs provide limited communication services (in particular order transmission) between investors and Schwab and sought no-action assurance from the Commission staff that this arrangement would not subject the ISPs to regulation as broker-dealers. In Schwab I, the Commission indicated it would not recommend enforcement action if Schwab paid the ISPs a nominal, flat, per order fee in return for the communication services. Schwab later sought to provide its customers, through Schwab's website, with data and research from Standard & Poor's and First Call Individual Investor Services (the "content providers").[19] Schwab sought similar no-action assurance from the Commission staff that this arrangement would not subject the content providers to regulation as broker-dealers. In Schwab II, the Commission indicated it would not recommend enforcement action if Schwab paid the content providers the greater of a base monthly fee or a variable fee calculated by multiplying the number of active customer households times a nominal fixed-dollar amount. A customer household is viewed as active if it has engaged in at least one on-line securities trade in a

---

16/ *See* Concept Release, 62 Fed. Reg. at 30487 n. 3.

17/ *See* Exchange Act Release No. 21383 (Oct. 9, 1984), 49 Fed. Reg. 40159 (Oct. 14, 1984) ("Computer Brokerage Release") (creating general guidelines for broker-dealers sponsoring such systems).

18/ Charles Schwab & Co., Inc., SEC No-Action Letter, 1996 WL 762999 (Nov. 27, 1996) ("Schwab I").

19/ Charles Schwab & Co., Inc., SEC No-Action Letter (July 17, 1997) ("Schwab II").

given month. The main point of concern in Schwab I and II was the fee arrangement, because transaction-based compensation is traditionally one of the factors assessed in requiring an entity to register as a broker-dealer. In granting no-action assurance, the Commission focused on the absence of significant contact between Schwab's customers and the ISPs and content providers.

4. **Automatic Execution**. Some electronic order routing systems sponsored by broker-dealers include automatic execution functions, usually for small orders. Typically, transactions are executed by the sponsoring broker-dealer against its own account on a principal basis, causing these systems to be viewed as broker-dealer activity. As recently described by the SEC, these types of automatic execution systems "merely provide a more efficient means of communicating the trading interest of separate customers to one dealer and thus would not be considered exchange activities."[20]

5. **Blind Brokerage Systems**. Some online trading systems offer so-called "blind brokerage" services to participants in the government and municipal securities markets. Also known as inter-dealer brokers, these blind brokerage systems permit the sponsoring broker-dealer (commonly referred to as a "broker's broker") to receive indications of trading interest from other broker-dealers or institutional customers and re-broadcast such interest over its network.[21] Until recently, the SEC has regarded these systems as distinct from the securities business conducted on exchanges or over-the-counter. In the Concept Release, however, the Commission suggests that, depending on the degree of automation and centralization, some blind brokerage or inter-dealer broker systems may be encompassed in the more functional understanding of the term "exchange."[22] The Concept Release further suggests that even if these systems were characterized as exchanges, the Commission would exempt them from many of the regulatory burdens associated with that status.[23]

20/ Concept Release, 62 Fed. Reg. at 30508.

21/ The Delta Government Options System also provides clearing and settlement services. *See* Delta Release, 55 Fed. Reg. at 1898.

22/ *See* Concept Release, 62 Fed. Reg. at 30510.

23/ *See id.* at 30511.

B. Broker-Dealer Trading Systems

1. Exchange Act Rule 17a-23. Rule 17a-23 imposes certain recordkeeping and reporting requirements on broker-dealers that sponsor a BDTS.[24] The Rule is intended to help the Commission monitor and assess the effect of BDTSs on the secondary market; it does not address the issue whether a particular BDTS is required to register as an exchange. Through the Rule's definitional terms, the SEC has sought to prevent any circumvention of the Rule's requirements by those that seek to operate a BDTS without registering as a broker-dealer.[25]

2. Recordkeeping Requirements. The sponsoring broker-dealer must maintain the following records: a) daily summaries of trading, including the number of "system orders," that provide the most accurate assessment of participant trading interest; b) identity of the parties using the system (including any affiliations between those participants and the sponsor; c) time-sequenced records of each transaction executed; and d) notices from the sponsor disseminated to users in general.

3. Reporting Requirements. The sponsoring broker-dealer must file Form 17A-23, which calls for the following information: a) operation reports describing the system and its procedures for reviewing capacity, security and contingency planning, which must be filed at least 20 days prior to initial operation or subsequent implementation of a material change; b) quarterly reports of summary trading information; and c) a final report after terminating the system.

4. Exemptions. The SEC has granted an exemption, pursuant to paragraph (i) of Rule 17a-23, to four major broker-dealers (Merrill Lynch, PaineWebber, Prudential Securities, and Smith Barney) in connection with operating certain automated order routing and inventory systems.[26] The Commission took the position that, when operated together, these systems can

---

[24] *See* Exchange Act Release No. 35124 (Dec. 20, 1994), 59 Fed. Reg. 66702 (Dec. 28, 1994) ("BDTS Release"). Note that the Rule does not apply to order-routing systems that deliver orders to an exchange or another market for execution <u>outside</u> the system.

[25] *See* Exchange Act Release No. 33605 (Feb. 9, 1994), 59 Fed. Reg. 8368, 8371 (Feb. 18, 1994).

[26] *See* Merrill Lynch, Pierce, Fenner & Smith, Inc.; PaineWebber Inc.; Prudential Securities, Inc.; and Smith Barney, Inc., SEC No-Action Letter, 1995 WL 704997 (Dec. 1, 1995).

comprise a BDTS as defined by Rule 17a-23. Nevertheless, because a trader must view each order prior to its execution, and because the order has opportunities for price improvement as does an order transmitted through more traditional means, the Commission determined that these particular systems do not significantly alter traditional trading functions or the manner of execution of trades, affect the market structure, or pose novel surveillance issues.

C. Proprietary Trading Systems

1. In General. Certain online trading systems that are currently subject to the BDTS recordkeeping and reporting requirements under Rule 17a-23 are also commonly referred to as PTSs. This sub-group of BDTSs link together third parties who may trade among one another, via the system, in an anonymous and confidential manner. PTSs collect indications of interest, quotations, or orders to purchase or sell securities, and also provide procedures for executing or settling transactions. Access is limited to subscribers of the system, who typically are required to be creditworthy market professionals such as institutional investors, broker-dealers, and specialists.[27]

2. Nature of Regulation. The SEC has been confronted with the question of whether sponsorship of a PTS should be regulated as a broker-dealer activity, or whether the PTS should be deemed to constitute an exchange and be regulated accordingly. Under the most recent version of Rule 15c2-10 proposed by the SEC in 1989, certain "proprietary trading systems such as Instinet and POSIT" would not be considered exchanges because they were "not inter-dealer quotation or transaction mechanisms, in which participants enter two-sided quotations on a regular or continuous basis, thus ensuring a liquid market."[28] Although Rule 15c2-10 was not adopted, it remains influential, because it reflects the policy rationale behind the no-action letters issued by the Division of Market Regulation to the sponsors of PTSs for the last twenty years.[29]

27/ *See* SEC Division of Market Regulation, Market 2000: An Examination of Current Equity Market Development, Study V (1994) ("Market 2000 Study"), Appendix IV.

28/ Exchange Act Release No. 26708 (April 11, 1989), 54 Fed. Reg. 15429 (re-proposing Rule 15c2-10 to regulate proprietary trading systems) ("1989 Release"); and Exchange Act Release No. 33621 (Feb. 14, 1994), 59 Fed. Reg. 8379 (withdrawing re-proposed Rule 15c2-10).

29/ Since the early 1980s, the Division of Market Regulation has issued over 20 letters to the sponsors of PTSs, assuring them that the staff would not recommend (continued...)

3. PTSs in Use. Below are brief discussions of four PTSs currently in use: Instinet, Portfolio System for Institutional Trading ("POSIT"), the Arizona Stock Exchange ("AZX"), and the most recent addition, TradeWeb.

a. Instinet

i. Description. The real-time trading service operated by Instinet Corporation ("Instinet") provides an alternative to dealer-intermediated trades for both Nasdaq and exchange listed securities by permitting subscribers to enter buy and sell orders into a network of computer terminals.[30/] Limit orders of subscribers are maintained in the Instinet book, where potential buyers and sellers can find each other and either negotiate electronically in private or trade automatically against the best contra side order displayed throughout the system.[31/] Acting as agent, Instinet, a registered broker-dealer, executes matched orders on behalf of the buyer and the seller and then reports the security price and size of the transaction to both subscribers and to the clearing broker or bank.[32/] More trading volume now occurs on Instinet than on any organized U.S. stock market other than the NYSE and Nasdaq.[33/]

ii. Regulatory Status. In requesting no-action relief, the company contended that it essentially does what many broker-dealer firms do in the upstairs block market, except that Instinet performs these tasks electronically. Faced with the alternative of regulating Instinet as another SRO, the SEC concluded that

---

29/ (...continued)
enforcement action if they did not register as exchanges. *See* Market 2000 Study, Appendix IV.

30/ *See* Instinet, SEC No-Action Letter [1989 Transfer Binder] Fed. Sec. L. Rep. (CCH) ¶ 78,997, at 78,938 (Sept. 8, 1986) ("Instinet Letter").

31/ The interactive nature of price setting on Instinet contrasts sharply with the passive pricing of systems, such as POSIT, in which orders are executed at predetermined prices.

32/ *See* Instinet Letter.

33/ *See* Order Handling Release, 62 Fed. Reg. at 48308.

Instinet could be regulated properly as a broker-dealer, subject to certain reporting requirements.[34]

b. POSIT

i. Description. POSIT is an electronic crossing system in which subscribers may buy and sell securities at a price derived from the primary market in which the security is traded.[35] Although originally designed to accommodate portfolio trading, POSIT now also handles orders consisting of only a single stock. POSIT currently matches orders four times during the trading day. Investment Technology Group ("ITG"), a registered broker-dealer, executes orders matched by POSIT at the mid-point between the best bid quotation and the best ask quotation prevailing in the security's primary market at the predetermined time. Any "residual" unmatched portion of customer orders may be either canceled, retained for future crossing in POSIT, or sent to other markets such as the New York Stock Exchange.[36]

ii. Regulatory Status. In seeking a no-action position from the SEC, POSIT argued that it merely acts as a facility for efficient order routing. The Commission concluded that POSIT, whose sponsor is already regulated as a broker-dealer, need not register as a national exchange. As in the case of Instinet, the staff's response was conditional on POSIT's compliance with certain requirements to provide information to the SEC.[37]

---

[34] More recently, however, the SEC has noted that "Instinet (and similar systems) provides to its customers ECN services that are significantly different from the services provided by other broker-dealers to their customers. Specifically, Instinet, without discretion, publicizes subscriber orders and enables other subscribers to trade with these orders at their stated price." *See* Order Handling Release, 61 Fed. Reg. at 48310 n.239.

[35] *See* Jefferies & Co., Inc., SEC No-Action Letter [1987-1988 Transfer Binder] Fed. Sec. L. Rep. (CCH) ¶ 78,515 at 77,660 (Jul. 28, 1987) ("POSIT Letter").

[36] *See* Market 2000 Study, Appendix IV.

[37] *See* POSIT Letter.

c. **AZX**

i. **Description**. AZX is an electronic call market facility that brings together supply and demand for a security at a particular point in time and finds an equilibrium price.[38] AZX currently operates two auctions a day, at 9:15 a.m (EST) for all Nasdaq issues and at 5:00 p.m. (EST), after the close of normal trading hours, for both listed and over-the-counter stocks.[39] A registered broker-dealer (formerly BT Brokerage Corporation, currently ITG) executes orders that are electronically matched by AZX at the auction price.[40]

ii. **Regulatory Status**. Because the price at which orders are executed is set by the interaction of the buy and sell orders entered by AZX's participants (both broker-dealers and institutional investors), the Commission determined that AZX is an exchange under Section 3(a)(1) of the Exchange Act.[41] Because of its limited volume, however, the Commission exempted AZX from the requirement to register as a national securities exchange, subject to a number of terms and conditions.[42] To date, AZX is the only recent exchange to qualify for the limited volume exemption. In approving AZX's continuing operations on that basis, the Commission emphasized that AZX's exemption depends on having an average daily

---

38/ *See* Exchange Act Release No. 28899 (Feb. 20, 1991), 56 Fed. Reg. 8377 (Feb. 28, 1991) ("AZX Release I"); Exchange Act Release No. 37272 (June 3, 1996), 61 Fed. Reg. 29145 (June 7, 1996) ("AZX Release II").

39/ *See* Phyllis Plitch, *Arizona Stock Exchange Plans Auction in Morning to Reignite Trading System*, Wall St. J., Oct. 13, 1997, at B8. *See also* AZX Release II (SEC authorization to conduct intra-day call).

40/ *See* Wunsch Auction Systems, Inc. SEC No-Action Letter [1990-1991 Transfer Binder] Fed. Sec. L. Rep. (CCH) ¶ 79,662, at 78,037 (Feb. 28, 1991) (AZX was formerly owned by Wunsch Auction Systems).

41/ *See* AZX Release I.

42/ Under Section 5 of the Exchange Act, the Commission has the authority to exempt any exchange with a limited volume of transactions from registration as a national securities exchange, provided that it is not practicable and not necessary or appropriate in the public interest or for the protection of investors to require registration. *See* 15 U.S.C. § 78e.

volume less than the average daily volume of any of the fully regulated national securities exchanges.[43]

d. **TradeWeb**

i. **Description**. TradeWeb allows its users, which consist of government securities dealers and the institutional and broker-dealer customers of those dealers, to simultaneously access information and request bids and offers concerning money market instruments, United States Treasury securities, other United States Government Securities, and repurchase agreements relating to these instruments.[44] The system is accessible via dedicated telephone line or over the Internet. Customers must meet certain criteria and are only authorized to transact with and receive research information from dealers with whom they have a customer agreement. TradeWeb does not participate in the clearance or settlement of trades facilitated by its system.

ii. **Regulatory Status**. The Commission granted no-action relief to TradeWeb, concluding that TradeWeb, whose sponsor is regulated as a broker-dealer, need not register as a national exchange. As in the case of Instinet and POSIT, the staff's response was conditional on TradeWeb's compliance with certain requirements to provide information to the SEC.[45]

D. **Electronic Communications Networks (ECNs)**

1. **In General**. All ECNs are BDTSs, as defined in Rule 17a-23. For example, Instinet, which is the most important ECN in terms of its size, continues to be regulated as a broker-dealer. As a particular type of BDTS, each ECN is designed to disseminate widely market maker trading interest and facilitate execution against such interest. In recently adopting the Order Handling Rules, the SEC recognized that, although ECNs are regulated as broker-dealers, "in providing a mechanism by which system subscribers can (1) broadcast prices to other system subscribers and (2) trade with one another

---

43/ *See* AZX Release II, 61 Fed. Reg. at 29147 n.21 (stating that the Phlx is currently the lowest volume national securities exchange and finding that AZX's average daily volume is "well below" that of the Phlx).

44/ TradeWeb, LLC, SEC No-Action Letter, 1997 WL 65960 (Oct. 23, 1997) ("TradeWeb Letter")

45/ *Id.*

at those prices, these systems also *function as securities markets*."[46] This statement suggests that while ECNs may not be required to register as exchanges under the existing framework governing the operation of PTSs, the SEC is concerned about any regulatory gaps created as a result.[47]

2. **Examples of ECNs.** In the past year, several new ECNs have been launched to compete with Instinet in the secondary trading of Nasdaq securities. They include the Bloomberg Tradebook,[48] Island,[49] TONTO,[50] and REDI.[51] These ECNs operate in a manner similar to Instinet, providing their subscribers with the means for wide dissemination of their trading interest and execution against displayed interest on a "hit-or-take" basis. Trading on these systems accounts for about 20% of daily Nasdaq executions.[52]

3. **ECN Display Alternative.** Under the Order Handling Rules, an ECN is permitted to submit, on behalf of participant market makers, the best bids and offers entered into the ECN by these participants to an SRO for inclusion into the public quotation stream ("ECN Display Alternative"). Specifically, the revised Quote Rule provides that the ECN Display Alternative will be deemed to satisfy the obligations of market makers to include all superior prices shown through an ECN in their quotes if the price entered into the ECN is provided by the ECN to an exchange or association for inclusion in the public quotation system and if the ECN provides access to non-subscriber

---

46/ *See* Order Handling Release, 61 Fed. Reg. at 48307 n.217 (emphasis added).

47/ *See* Concept Release, 62 Fed. Reg. at 30490 (discussing various inadequacies of the existing regulatory approach). Note that while all ECNs may be viewed as PTSs, there are PTSs, such as POSIT or AZX, which do not qualify as ECNs, because they do not widely disseminate priced orders entered by their subscribers and permit such orders to be executed through the system.

48/ *See* Bloomberg Tradebook LLC, SEC No-Action Letter, 1996 WL 711206 (Dec. 12, 1996).

49/ *See* Datek Inc., SEC No-Action Letter, 1997 WL 18338 (Jan. 17, 1997).

50/ *See* Terra Nova Trading, LLC, SEC No-Action Letter, 1997 WL 18333 (Jan. 17, 1997).

51/ *See* Spear, Leeds, & Kellog, SEC No-Action Letter, (Oct. 6, 1997) ("REDI Letter").

52/ *Spear, Leeds Begins Rolling Out New Redi-Plus System*, Securities Week, Dec. 1, 1997, at 1.

broker-dealers to trade at that price.[53] Note that the ECN Display Alternative addresses trading conducted by market makers and specialists only, and not trading by institutional investors.[54] Activity of these participants on ECNs is disclosed to the public market on a voluntary basis.

4. ECNs Satisfying Requirements of ECN Display Alternative. As of December 31, 1997, five online trading systems have received temporary no-action assurance from the SEC staff that, by virtue of their linkage to Nasdaq, they are in compliance with the ECN Display Alternative: Instinet, Island System, TONTO, Bloomberg Tradebook, and REDI.[55] These ECNs differ in how they handle orders entered into the system by non-market makers. Instinet, for example, displays to the public only orders of market makers and those institutional customers that affirmatively choose to have their orders so displayed, while Island displays to the public the best prices of any orders entered into their systems (whether from market makers or institutional customers). All four ECNs, however, share various operational features. Each utilizes an electronic communication linkage with Nasdaq via the SelectNet system.[56] In the SEC staff's letters to these ECNs, they have all been reminded of their obligation to provide equal access to both subscribers that enter orders directly into the ECN and non-subscribers that enter orders through the SelectNet system.[57]

53/ SEC Rule 11Ac1-1(c)(5)(ii).

54/ *See* Concept Release, 62 Fed. Reg. at 30493.

55/ *See* Instinet Real-Time Trading Service, SEC No-Action Letter, 1997 WL 528239 (August 28, 1997) (extending temporary no-action position until January 16, 1998); Island System, SEC No-Action Letter, 1997 WL 528231 (August 28, 1997) (same); Terra Nova Trading, LLC, SEC No-Action Letter, 1997 WL 528234, (August 28, 1997) (same); Bloomberg Tradebook, LLC, SEC No-Action Letter, 1997 WL 528238 (August 28, 1997) (same). *See also* REDI Letter (granting temporary no-action position until January 16, 1998).

56/ SelectNet is an online trading service offered by the NASD to its members that may be utilized to buy or sell purchase or sell Nasdaq-listed securities.

57/ *See* Instinet Real-Time Trading Service, SEC No-Action Letter, 1997 WL 361033 (June 30, 1997); Tradebook System, SEC No-Action Letter, 1997 WL 361006 (June 30, 1997); Datek Inc., SEC No-Action Letter, 1997 WL 361011 (June 30, 1997); Terra Nova Trading, LLC, SEC No-Action Letter, 1997 WL 361000 (June 30, 1997).

IV. Online Trading Systems Sponsored by Self-Regulatory Organizations

A. General

While the use of online systems to handle execution, market information and comparison services has improved substantially the efficiency of SRO markets, the SEC has been concerned about the vulnerability of these systems to operational problems during periods of extremely high volume, such as the October 1987 Market Break. Accordingly, in 1989, the SEC adopted an Automation Review Policy ("ARP") recommending that SROs should, on a voluntary basis, establish comprehensive planning and assessment programs to determine the capacity and vulnerability of online trading systems sponsored by the SRO.[58/]

B. Exchanges

1. Primary Exchanges

a. **SuperDot.** The NYSE operates an electronic order routing system initially called the Designated Order Turnaround System, now known as "SuperDot," which allows member firms and institutional investors to send orders to the trading floor via computers.[59/] SuperDot routes market and limit orders directly to the specialist post where each stock is traded, or to the member firm's booth on the trading floors. SuperDot also streamlines the post-trade reconciliation process. Once an order is executed, the trade is submitted to the comparison cycle on a locked-in basis, thereby reducing the manual processing costs associated with post-trade clearing and settlement.[60/] While SuperDot represents a significant step toward computerizing the exchange's order routing and delivery processes, it does not provide for automatic execution of orders. Once orders are delivered electronically via SuperDot to the trading floor, they still require manual action by the specialist at the point of trade.

58/ *See* Exchange Act Release No. 27445 (Nov. 15, 1989), 54 Fed. Reg. 48703 (Nov. 24, 1989) ("ARP Release I").

59/ *See generally* SuperDot 250: The Electronic Pathway to the New York Stock Exchange, New York Stock Exchange (1992).

60/ The Amex operates an electronic order routing system called Automated Post Execution Reporting System, or AutoPERs. *See* ARP Release I.

b. Regional Exchange Order Systems. The four regional exchanges each operate systems, similar to SuperDot, that route and also execute small-size retail customer orders.[61]

c. After-Hours Trading. The NYSE's Off-Hours Trading ("OHT") facility automates the execution of single stock orders and baskets of securities, based on prices derived from the exchange's closing price. The OHT facility operates through two trading sessions. "Crossing Session I," which executes single-stock, single-sided closing-price orders and crosses of single-stock, coupled closing-price buy and sell orders, and "Crossing Session II," which executes crosses of multiple-stock aggregate-price buy and sell orders. The NYSE's OHT facility currently generates only a limited amount of volume, well below that of POSIT.[62] The Amex offers a similar after-hours automated trade execution service.[63] In response to these after-hours trading systems, the regional exchanges have adopted programs that provide for executions of securities at prices that reflect after-hours trading activity on the NYSE and Amex.

d. Cincinnati Stock Exchange. The CSE is a fully automated exchange on which members effect transactions from computers located in their offices. CSE members enter agency or principal orders into the National Securities Trading System, which are stored, queued, and executed by the system according to price and time priorities.

e. Pacific Exchange ("PCX") OptiMark System. The SEC recently approved the PCX's OptiMark system.[64] The system will allow PCX members and their customers to submit certain visual depictions of trading interest known as "Profiles" to the OptiMark

---

61/ The BSE, CHX, Phlx, and PCX (commonly known as regional exchanges) operate, respectively, BEACON, MAX, PACE, and P/COAST. *See* ARP Release I.

62/ *See* Concept Release, 62 Fed. Reg. at 30518 n. 204.

63/ *See* Exchange Act Release No. 29515 (Aug. 2, 1991), 56 Fed. Reg. 37736 (Aug. 8, 1991).

64/ *See* Exchange Act Release No. 29515 (Aug. 2, 1991), 56 Fed. Reg. 37736 (Aug. 8, 1991). The OptiMark System is an electronic communication and information system developed by OptiMark Technologies, Inc. ("OTI"). Mr. Becker has represented OTI in connection with the development of the PCX Application.

System from their own computer terminals.[65] At specified times throughout the trading day, the system will conduct trade optimization calculations against such expressions of interest in order to specify orders capable of execution. Unless routed to other markets as Intermarket Trading System commitments, the resulting orders will be executed on the PCX.

2. National Association of Securities Dealers

a. Nasdaq. The Nasdaq system consolidates the trading interest of market makers registered with the NASD and displays such interest in real-time to the NASD member subscribers on a computer screen. The system also permits market makers to update their displayed quotations. The Nasdaq system does not, however, provide for automatic execution of orders within the system itself. Transactions in the Nasdaq stock market typically are executed by calling a market maker and arranging the terms over the telephone.

b. SelectNet. SelectNet allows market makers and other order-entry firms to negotiate securities transactions in NASDAQ securities through computer communications rather than relying on the telephone.[66] To enter an order in SelectNet, a participant directs the usual trade information (security symbol, transaction size, and price) to a particular market maker, or broadcasts it to others on an anonymous basis. By permitting participants to enter orders above or below the inside bid or ask, SelectNet provides an opportunity to negotiate electronically for a price superior to the current quote through an exchange of counter-offers until an agreement is reached. Once agreement is reached, the execution is "locked-in" and reported to the tape.

c. Small Order Execution System ("SOES"). The NASD sponsors an automated trade execution system for transactions of limited size in active Nasdaq securities called the Small Order Execution System ("SOES").[67] A qualifying SOES order is executed

---

65/ The system will provide automatic order formulation, matching and execution capabilities in the equity securities listed or traded on the PCX.

66/ *See* Exchange Act Release No. 25263 (Jan. 11, 1988), 53 Fed. Reg. 1430 (Jan. 19, 1988).

67/ *See* Exchange Act Release No. 21433 (Oct. 29, 1984), 49 Fed. Reg. 44042 (continued...)

against the account of a participating market maker at the Nasdaq inside price -- that is, the execution price of a buy order is set equal to the lowest offer price while a sell order's execution price is set equal to the highest bid price. Notification of each trade execution is sent immediately to both the order entry and market maker firm.

d. Proposed System

(i) In general. On March 12, 1998, the SEC published for comment a proposal by the NASD to build a new integrated order delivery and execution system ("System") for Nasdaq.[68/] As proposed, the System (which has no official name yet) would replace completely the two electronic trading mechanisms currently in place, SOES and SelectNet, and provide one integrated trading platform instead.

(ii) Double execution risk. Operating SOES and SelectNet side-by-side creates problems for market makers. Because a market maker is generally obligated to execute orders presented at its displayed quote under the firm quote rule, the market maker may be subject to double execution when faced simultaneously with automatic executions from SOES and delivery of orders from SelectNet. The proposed System seeks to reduce this exposure through an integrated trading platform.

(iii) Level playing field. The NASD is also concerned that ECNs may enjoy a competitive advantage over market makers, which are required to participate in SOES. Quotes of ECNs linked to SelectNet under the ECN Display Alternative are accessible through SelectNet only, and are not accessible through SOES. The System is intended to place all providers of liquidity in the Nasdaq market on the same footing for purposes of order execution.

(iv) Enhanced Access. In addition, the System would feature a voluntary limit order book ("Limit Order File") and

---

67/ (...continued)
(Nov. 1, 1984).

68/ Exchange Act Rel. No. 39718 (Mar. 4, 1998), 63 Fed. Reg. 12124 (Mar. 12, 1998) ("Rule Filing").

permit direct access by non-members under qualifying market makers' sponsorship.

(v) **Comment**. It seems inevitable that the Nasdaq systems evolve in order to meet the trading community's need to respond to the proliferation of electronic communications technology. In addition, regulatory experiences over the past few years, particularly implementation of the order handling and firm quote rules, have contributed to the impetus for change. While regulators and market participants seem to agree that the current operation of SelectNet and SOES is less than optimal, there is much room for disagreement as to what sort of changes are needed, and how fast. As of the date of this writing, comments are officially due May 5, 1998.

V. The Concept Release

A. Alternative Trading Systems

1. **Inadequacies of the Current Regulatory Structure**. The Commission's recent Concept Release examines, and solicits comments on, various areas in which current regulation is perceived to be inadequate.[69] The Commission maintains that the regulation of ATSs as broker-dealers on an *ad hoc* basis has had unintended and deleterious effects on three fundamental policies. First, the broker-dealer regulatory scheme, at least as it currently exists, is not well suited to ATSs, and consequently secondary market activity conducted within ATSs is underregulated in some ways, and overregulated in others.[70] Second, broker-dealers are themselves regulated by the SROs of which they are members. Competition among trading systems may be stifled

---

69/ One of the areas discussed in the Concept Release is the proposed regulation of U.S. investor participation in foreign securities markets, which falls outside the scope of this outline. We note in passing, however, that national regulation of activity conducted via the Internet is likely to be difficult, and perhaps impossible, without substantial international consensus.

70/ *See* Concept Release, 62 Fed. Reg. at 30490. A potential example of the consequences of underregulation is the Chicago Partnership Board ("CPB"), an ATS for limited partnership interests. *See* Chicago Partnership Board, Inc., SEC No-Action Letter, 1988 WL 234698 (Aug. 18, 1988). The Commission recently obtained a final judgment and order of permanent injunction against CPB and its owner based on violations of the antifraud, customer protection, and books and records provisions of the federal securities laws. SEC News Digest 98-4, 1998 WL 2697 (Jan. 7, 1998).

by the interests of the SROs.[71] Third, the proliferation of ATSs "has impeded effective integration, surveillance, enforcement, and regulation of the U.S. markets as a whole"[72] -- that is, ATS activities under the existing regulatory framework may undermine the Commission's effort to build a National Market System. To address these concerns, the Concept Release invites comment on two possible approaches to regulating alternative trading systems: expanding the scope of broker-dealer regulation, or expanding the scope of exchange regulation.

2. **Broker-Dealer Regulation of ATSs ("Broker-Dealer Plus").** The Concept Release suggests the possibility of extending broker-dealer regulation to address the market, as opposed to brokerage, activities of ATSs. Under this approach, these systems would continue to be regulated as broker-dealers. The broker-dealer regulatory regime, however, would be modified to achieve the goals of exchange regulation. The SEC is doubtful, however, about this approach. Insofar as ATSs are proprietary systems, with customers rather than members, it will be difficult to achieve the same levels of procedural fairness and transparency that membership organizations can attain. Moreover, ATSs may continue to be subject to brokerage regulation that is costly but irrelevant to their business.[73]

3. **Regulation of ATSs as Exchanges ("Exchange Minus").** The Concept Release also solicits views on expanding the definition of the term "exchange" to include "any organization that both (1) consolidates orders of multiple parties and (2) provides a facility through which, or sets material conditions under which, participants entering such orders may agree to the terms of a trade."[74] Depending on the degree of centralization and automation of their business, established broker-dealers, organized dealer markets, information vendors and bulletin boards, and broker's brokers could all be deemed exchanges. The Commission does not envision that all of these entities would be regulated in the same way. It has suggested a "three-tiered" approach based on the volume of trading and level of price discovery for some systems (first and second tier) and a third tier for systems sponsored by existing exchanges, or the NASD, with traditional SRO structures. The Commission also recognized, however, that broadening the definition of

---

71/ *See* Concept Release, 62 Fed. Reg. at 30490.

72/ *Id.*

73/ *Id.* at 30497-30499.

74/ *Id.* at 30507.

"exchange" in order to regulate ATSs creates a host of conflicts between the business of ATSs and the requirements imposed on exchanges.[75]

B. Regulation of Online Trading Systems Sponsored by SROs

The Concept Release solicits comment on how regulatory requirements for SROs might be expedited or reduced to allow greater flexibility for innovation. It also asks for suggestions on how to reduce the costs associated with SRO surveillance and enforcement by permitting certain allocations of oversight obligations among the registered exchanges and any newly created automated exchanges.[76]

75/ *Id.* at 30511-30516.

76/ *Id.* at 30516.

PART TWO
SEC INTERPRETIVE RELEASE ON
THE USE OF WEBSITES FOR OFFSHORE INTERNET OFFERS[77]

I. Overview

A. The Question. To what extent do the registration requirements of the federal securities laws apply to "offshore Internet offers"[78] made over websites?

B. The Problem. In general, the various registration requirements of the federal securities laws apply when an offer of a security or financial service is offered in the United States, or to U.S. persons.[79]

The posting of information on a website can constitute an offer.

Because an Internet communication is globally accessible, it is unclear when the posting of offering or solicitation materials on a website would be considered to be made within the United States, and hence subject to registration.

C. Scope

1. **Communication assumed to be offer in substance**. For the purpose of this interpretation, the Commission assumed a website containing material that, if publicly communicated in the United States, would be subject to regulation as an offer.

2. **Law**. The Commission made an effort to take a position consistent across the federal securities laws, specifically the Securities Act, the Investment Company Act, the Investment Adviser Act, and the Exchange Act.

---

[77] International Series Release No. 1125 (March 23, 1998), "Statement of the Commission regarding use of Internet websites to offer securities, solicit securities transactions, or advertise investment services offshore," ("Release").

[78] "[O]ffers over Internet Websites of securities or investment services that by their terms are not made to U.S. persons". *Id.* at 2. For convenience, this outline refers to the various offers, solicitations, and related materials discussed by the Release, *see id.* at 6-7, 13, collectively as "offers."

[79] The Release uses the term "U.S. person" as defined in Rule 902(k) of Regulation S. *See id.* at n.20.

This Release does not affect the scope of the personal jurisdiction that a U.S. Court might exercise.

Fraud and manipulation provisions of the securities laws apply to all cases that meet the applicable jurisdictional tests, in general, that originate in the U.S., or put U.S. investors at risk.

3. **Evolving Issue**. The Commission stated that it might revisit these and related issues because the technology and practice at issue continue to develop.

D. **General Answer**. Under the Release, the Commission will not view securities industry professionals "that implement measures that are reasonably designed to guard against sales or the provision of services to U.S. persons to have targeted persons in the United States with their Internet offers. Under these circumstances, Internet postings would not, by themselves, result in a registration obligation under the U.S. securities laws."[80/]

The Release thus places the burden on securities industry professionals to take responsible steps to prevent ineligible U.S. persons from obtaining access to offshore Internet offerings.

II. Analysis

A. **Targeted and non-targeted communications**. The Commission distinguished "targeted" communications from non-targeted communications. Targeted communications are "comparable to traditional mail because the sender directs the information to a particular person, group, or entity."[81/] Information posted on a website is not so directed.

B. **E-mail**. The Commission stated without discussion that the sender of targeted communication is responsible for the substance of the communication. Therefore, communication that constituted an offer would, if targeted at the United States, subject the sender and the offer to the applicable U.S. registration requirements.

E-mail, whether individually addressed or sent to a mass audience, is a targeted communication. Presumably, therefore, e-mail communication that constitutes an offer or solicitation that is sent to the United States would be an offer, and would be governed by the registration requirements of the securities laws accordingly.

80/ *Id.* at 3.

81/ *Id.* at 5-6.

C. **Websites**. Unlike more targeted modes of communication, access to a website is sought rather than received. It is therefore unclear to whom an offer, posted on a website, is directed.

The issue, then, is when would an offer made on a website be deemed targeted at U.S. persons, and so subject to registration with the Commission? The Release addressed the obverse: what could offerors do to ensure that the Commission would *not* regard the offshore offering as targeted at U.S. persons, and so *not* subject to registration under the federal securities laws?

The Commission recommended specific steps "to guard against sales to U.S. persons,"[82/] thereby ensuring that the communication would not be deemed targeted at U.S. persons.

D. Protecting offshore Internet offerings from access by U.S. persons

1. In general

a. Procedural safeguards. The Commission adopted a three part structure through which offshore offers would avoid enforcement acts for failing to meet U.S. registration requirements: (i) the websites must contain a disclaimer indicating that the offer was not being made to U.S. persons, *and* (ii) the offeror must have "procedures that are reasonably designed to guard against sales to U.S. persons."[83/] In addition, if the offeror is itself a U.S. person, the Commission requires the adoption of additional safeguards.[84/]

b. Substantive exception. Offers which are substantively targeted at U.S. persons, *e.g.*, advertising U.S. income tax benefits, would be regarded as made in the United States, regardless of the measures taken to prevent sales to U.S. persons.

82/ *Id.* at 3.

83/ *Id.* at 10.

84/ Discussed below in the context of specific Acts.

2. **Disclaimers**. Disclaimers must:

- be "prominent". The disclaimer must be displayed "on the same screen as the offering material," or "must be viewed before a person can view the offering materials."[85]

- exclude the United States. The disclaimer may either state that it is not being made in the United States or to U.S. persons, or may list the jurisdictions, excluding the United States, in which the offer is being made.

- be "meaningful". In addition to the foregoing, the disclaimer cannot limit the reach of the offer by stating that the offer is not made in any jurisdiction where such an offer might be illegal.

3. **Procedures**. In order to ensure that an offer made on a website is not deemed targeted at U.S. persons, offerors must have in place procedures reasonably designed to guard against sales to U.S. persons. Such procedures might include checking residence addresses, phone numbers, bank information, and so forth for indications that a prospective purchaser is a U.S. person.

4. **Evasion of safeguards**

a. **Actual sale not dispositive**. Offshore Internet offers which result in sales to U.S. persons, despite such precautions, are not retroactively deemed to have been targeted at U.S. persons, "absent indications that would put the issuer on notice the purchaser is a U.S. person."[86]

b. **Verification**. If an offeror has reason to believe that a given purchaser is a U.S. person, the offeror should seek to verify that this is not the case prior to consummating a sale.

c. **Assessment of adequate safeguards**. Discovery of sales to U.S. persons pursuant to offshore offers may necessitate reassessment of the offeror's safeguards.

85/ Release at n. 21.

86/ *Ib.* at 11.

5. Third-party websites

a. In general. A third party service provider, used to post an offer, would not be deemed to have targeted the offer to U.S. persons so long as the third party service provider used safeguards that would be adequate if used by the offeror.

b. Access by U.S. persons. If offering material is posted on a third party website to which significant numbers of U.S. persons may be expected to obtain access, then additional safeguards may be necessary.

c. Hyperlinks. If offering material is posted on a website which is hyperlinked to a third-party site, such as an investment site, then additional safeguards may be necessary.

III. Regulation of Offerings Under the Securities Act

A. Regulation S. Subject to certain provisions, a purchaser of offshore securities pursuant to Regulation S would not be barred from reselling such securities into the United States because the offering was made over the Internet.

B. Concurrent Offshore and Private Placement Offerings

1. No linkage. Websites may not be used to locate investors for private placement. Consequently, publicly accessible websites used to make offshore offerings may not be linked to concurrent private placements, or other offerings exempt from registration, made in the United States.

2. Separation of offerings. Foreign issuers should ensure that those who obtain access to the offshore offering do not participate in the U.S. exempt offering. Such issuers may make the website:

- protected by passwords issued only after verifying that a prospective investor was not a U.S. person; or
- publicly accessible, if participants in the U.S. exempt offering are required to represent that they had not accessed the website; or
- publicly accessible, if the issuer keeps records of who had accessed the website, thereby preventing those who had seen the offshore offering materials from participating in the private exempt offering.

3. Website content limitation. The website should contain materials relating only to the offshore offering, not to the U.S. offering.

C. Offerings by U.S. Issuers

1. In General. The Commission distinguishes between offshore securities issued by U.S. entities from similar offerings by non-U.S. entities. U.S. issuers are required to be more careful than their foreign counterparts.

2. Policy. Offshore offerings by U.S. issuers are more highly regulated than similar offerings by non-U.S. issuers for the following reasons:

- A U.S. issuer has substantial contacts with the United States;
- Securities of a U.S. issuer, albeit initially issued offshore, are likely to enter the U.S. market; and
- U.S. issuers and investors expect that securities issued by a U.S. entity will be governed by the federal securities laws.

3. Password required. A U.S. issuer using a website to make an unregistered offshore offering will not be considered "to have implemented reasonable measures to prevent sales to U.S. persons unless, in addition to general precautions discussed [above], the U.S. issuer implements password-type procedures that are reasonably designed to ensure that only non-U.S. persons can obtain access to the offer."[87]

4. Policy under consideration. The restrictions on offering communications will be reconsidered in conjunction with broader Securities Act reform.

D. Concurrent Offshore and U.S. Registered Offerings

The Commission is concerned that an offshore offering on a website may constitute an offer made prior to, or otherwise outside of, the statutory prospectus. The Commission is currently considering whether further guidance on this topic is merited.

---

[87] *Id.* at 16-17 (footnote omitted).

E. Underwriters

Underwriters and distributors stand in place of the issuers. "Thus, regardless of whether the underwriter is foreign or domestic, what constitutes measures reasonably designed to prevent sales to U.S. persons will depend on the status of the issuer."[88]

Underwriters of U.S. offshore offerings will have to meet the requirements for websites sponsored by U.S. issuers.

IV. Investment Company Act

A. In General

The registration requirements of the Investment Company Act will not apply to a foreign fund that makes an offshore offering of its securities, via a website, so long as the fund "implements measures reasonably designed to guard against sales to U.S. persons."[89]

B. Exception

A foreign fund's offering may be deemed to be a public offering in the U.S., and hence subject to registration, if the fund makes attempts "to attract U.S. persons to the Internet offer, such as advertising the existence of the foreign fund's Website in a U.S. publication."[90]

C. Concurrent Offshore and U.S. Private Offers made by Foreign Funds

1. In general. A foreign fund will not be considered to be making a public offering in the United States if it uses a website to make an offshore offering, so long as:

- the foreign fund takes measures reasonably intended to guard against sales of the offshore offering to U.S. persons;
- the offshore offering is not used as a solicitation for the private domestic offering.

88/ *Id.* at 18.

89/ *Id.* at 20.

90/ *Id.* at 21.

2. Disclaimer. The disclaimer on the website, stating that the offshore offering is not made to U.S. persons, may:

- allude to the existence of the U.S. private offering; and
- disclose as much about the U.S. private offering, beyond its existence, as is required by law.

3. Deemed directed toward U.S. persons. A website (on which the offshore offering is made) may be considered to target the United States if it, for example:

- provides information regarding the types of persons eligible for the concurrent private offering;
- explains how information on the private offering may be obtained; or
- has a hyperlink to a website providing information on the private offering, or otherwise provides directions to sales information on the concurrent offering.

4. Password protection for concurrent offering. If a foreign fund wishes to disseminate information about the concurrent domestic private offering on its website, it may adopt password protected procedures to ensure that only persons eligible to purchase such securities receive the information.

D. Offshore offers made by U.S. funds

As under the Securities Act, under the Investment Company Act the Commission requires more care from U.S. entities than from non-U.S. entities in ensuring that ineligible U.S. persons do not purchase offshore securities.

However, a U.S. fund may make a private offshore offer pursuant to one of the exclusions from the Investment Company Act if it "uses procedures, such as password-protected sites, reasonably designed to ensure the private nature of the offer."[91]

Again as under the Securities Act, other forms of marketing may give rise to more exacting requirements to ensure that U.S. persons do not purchase offshore securities.

91/ *Id.* at 25 (footnote omitted).

V. Investment Advisers Act. A foreign investment adviser must register with the Commission, unless it has (i) fewer than 15 U.S. clients in the past year, and (ii) is not holding itself out as an investment adviser in the United States.

An investment adviser providing advisory services over the Internet is holding itself out to be an investment adviser in the United States, unless it has taken measures reasonably intended to guard against such holding out. Such measures might include:

- a prominent disclaimer, explaining to whom the materials are, or are not, directed; and
- procedures reasonably intended to prevent the direction of information to non-U.S. persons, such as checks against residency information or telephone numbers.[92]

VI. Exchange Act

A. Broker Dealer Activities

1. The problem. A broker-dealer must register with the Commission if it is physically present in the United States, or if its activities result, or are intended to result, in securities transactions in the United States. The question is whether a foreign broker-dealer's website is an attempt to induce securities transactions in the United States.

2. Exemption. The Commission will not require the registration of a broker-dealer on account of its website so long as the broker-dealer takes reasonable precautions to ensure that its website does not induce securities transactions by U.S. persons. Such precautions may include:

- a disclaimer explaining that the broker-dealer's services are available in listed jurisdictions apart from the United States, or that the services are not available in the United States; and
- refusal to offer brokerage services to any potential customer that the broker-dealer has reason to believe is, or indicates that it is, a U.S. person, based on residence, mailing address, payment method, or other grounds.

---

[92] These procedures would not prevent the direction of information to the 14 or fewer U.S. clients which the investment adviser is permitted to advise without being obliged to register with the Commission.

These precautions are not exclusive.

3. **Unsolicited Exemption**. Foreign broker-dealers that transact with U.S. persons, but who did not solicit the business, have been exempted from the Commission's registration requirements pursuant to Exchange Act Rule 15a-6. A broker-dealer's website is a solicitation. Therefore, foreign broker dealers that wish to rely on the unsolicited exemption must ensure that the transaction was not, in fact, solicited through the website. This may be done by procedures such as:

- requiring affirmative representations from potential U.S. clients that they had not obtained access to the website; or
- maintaining records sufficiently detailed to determine that U.S. clients had not obtained access to the website.

B. Exchange Activities

1. **In General**. The Commission is considering, but has made no definitive statement regarding, the circumstances under which a foreign securities exchange that provides the ability for U.S. persons to trade, either directly or indirectly, via the Internet, must take measures to exclude such persons, or must register as a U.S. exchange.

2. **Preliminary View**. The Commission nonetheless took the view that a foreign exchange will not be considered to be subject to U.S. regulation so long as it takes reasonable steps to prevent the sale to U.S. persons of securities unregistered in the U.S.

3. **Disclaimer**. The exchange must post a disclaimer either (i) listing the jurisdictions in which the exchange's services are available (excluding the United States), or (ii) stating that the exchange's services are not available in the United States.

4. **Procedures designed to guard against sales to U.S. persons.**

a. **Direct access**. The exchange must require members or other direct participants to state their address, and refuses participation to those believed to be U.S. persons.

b. **Indirect access**. In addition to preventing direct access, the exchange must attempt to prevent U.S. persons from gaining access to the exchange via Internet communication with members of the exchange.

NOTES

23

STATEMENT OF THE COMMISSION REGARDING USE OF INTERNET WEB SITES TO OFFER SECURITIES, SOLICIT SECURITIES TRANSACTIONS OR ADVERTISE INVESTMENT SERVICES OFFSHORE (RELEASE NOS. 33-7516, 34-39779, IA-1710, IC-23071)

SECURITIES AND EXCHANGE COMMISSION

17 CFR Parts 231, 241, 271, 276

[Release Nos. 33-7516, 34-39779, IA-1710, IC-23071]

International Series Release No. 1125

STATEMENT OF THE COMMISSION REGARDING USE OF INTERNET WEB SITES TO OFFER SECURITIES, SOLICIT SECURITIES TRANSACTIONS OR ADVERTISE INVESTMENT SERVICES OFFSHORE

AGENCY: Securities and Exchange Commission

ACTION: Interpretation

SUMMARY: The Securities and Exchange Commission is publishing its views on the application of the registration obligations under the U.S. federal securities laws to the use of Internet Web sites to disseminate offering and solicitation materials for offshore sales of securities and investment services.

EFFECTIVE DATE: March 23, 1998

FOR FURTHER INFORMATION CONTACT: Paul Dudek, Chief, and Rani Doyle, Attorney, Office of International Corporate Finance at 202-942-2990 (with respect to Securities Act issues); Paula Jenson, Deputy Chief Counsel, Division of Market Regulation, at 202-942-0073 (with respect to broker-dealer registration issues), Elizabeth King, Senior Special Counsel, Division of Market Regulation, at 202-942-0140 (with respect to exchange registration issues); and Karrie McMillan, Assistant Chief Counsel, Sarah A. Wagman, Special Counsel, and Brendan C. Fox, Attorney, Division of Investment Management, at 202-942-0660 (with respect to matters relating to investment companies and investment advisers).

SUPPLEMENTARY INFORMATION

I. EXECUTIVE SUMMARY

The Internet permits market participants to disseminate advertisements and other information regarding securities and investment services across national borders. Because persons in the United States have access to this securities-related information, market participants have expressed uncertainty about the application of the registration requirements of the U.S. securities laws to their offshore Internet offers (i.e., offers over Internet Web sites of securities or investment services that by their terms are not made to U.S. persons). Today, we are providing our views on how issuers, investment companies, broker-dealers, exchanges and investment advisers may use Internet Web sites to solicit offshore securities transactions and clients without the securities or investment company being registered with the Commission under the Securities Act of 1933[1] or the Investment Company Act of 1940,[2] or without the investment service provider registering under the Investment Advisers Act of 1940,[3] or the broker-dealer or exchange registering under the broker-dealer and exchange registration provisions under the Securities Exchange Act of 1934.[4]

The purpose of this interpretation is to clarify when the posting of offering or solicitation materials on Internet Web sites would not be considered activity taking

---

[1] 15 U.S.C. 77a, et seq. (the "Securities Act").

[2] 15 U.S.C. 80a-1, et seq. (the "Investment Company Act").

[3] 15 U.S.C. 80b-1, et seq. (the "Advisers Act").

[4] 15 U.S.C. 78a, et seq. (the "Exchange Act").

place "in the United States." We are only providing clarification on this aspect of the registration requirements and are not altering the fundamental requirement that all offers and sales in the United States be registered under the U.S. securities laws or made under an applicable exemption.

Under this interpretation, application of the registration provisions of the U.S. securities laws depends on whether Internet offers, solicitations or other communications are targeted to the United States. We would not view issuers, broker-dealers, exchanges, and investment advisers that implement measures that are reasonably designed to guard against sales or the provision of services to U.S. persons to have targeted persons in the United States with their Internet offers. Under these circumstances, Internet postings would not, by themselves, result in a registration obligation under the U.S. securities laws.

The determination of whether measures reasonably designed to guard against sales to U.S. persons have been implemented depends on the facts and circumstances, and can be satisfied through different means. We discuss in this release examples of measures that are adequate to serve this purpose for both U.S. and foreign entities. We also discuss why measures that are adequate for foreign issuers would not necessarily be adequate measures for U.S. issuers. U.S. issuers should undertake more restrictive measures when using the Internet to solicit offshore securities transactions.

This interpretation does not address the anti-fraud and anti-manipulation provisions of the securities laws, which will continue to reach all Internet activities that satisfy the relevant jurisdictional tests.[5] Even in the absence of sales in the United States, we will take appropriate enforcement action whenever we believe that fraudulent or manipulative Internet activities have originated in the United States or placed U.S. investors at risk. Further, we are not addressing the circumstances under which a U.S. court could exercise personal jurisdiction over a non-U.S. person with respect to that person's offshore Internet offer.

The interaction between the U.S. securities laws and the Internet can be expected to continue to evolve. As technology and practice develop, we may revisit these and related issues.

II. BACKGROUND

A. The Global Reach of the Internet

The development of the Internet presents numerous opportunities and benefits for consumers and investors throughout the world. It also presents significant challenges for regulators charged with protecting consumers and investors. Regulators in many countries are attempting to administer their respective laws to preserve

---

[5] The courts have recognized U.S. jurisdiction over fraudulent conduct where substantial conduct or effects occur in the United States. See generally Itoba Ltd. v. LEP Group PLC, 54 F.3d 118 (2d Cir. 1995), cert. denied, 516 U.S. 1044 (1996) and Robinson v. TCI/US West Communications Inc., 117 F.3d 900 (5th Cir. 1997) (citing Schoenbaum v. Firstbrook, 405 F.2d 200 (2d Cir.), rev'd on other grounds on rehrg. en banc, 405 F.2d 215 (2d Cir. 1968), cert. denied, 395 U.S. 906 (1969) (effects test)); Bersch v. Drexel Firestone Inc., 519 F.2d 974 (2d Cir.), cert. denied, 423 U.S. 1018 (1975) (conduct test); Leasco Data Processing Equipment Corp. v. Maxwell, 468 F.2d 1326 (2d Cir. 1972) (conduct test).

important protections provided by their regulatory schemes without stifling the Internet's vast communications potential.[6] We share this goal in our administration of the U.S. securities laws.[7]

Information posted on Internet Web sites concerning securities and investments can be made readily available without regard to geographic and political boundaries.[8] Additionally, the interactive nature of the Internet makes it possible for investors to purchase electronically the securities or services offered. For these and other reasons, we believe that the use of the Internet by market participants and investors presents significant issues under the U.S. securities laws.

Although this release focuses on Internet Web sites, the Internet offers a variety of forms of communication. We distinguish between Web site postings and more targeted Internet communication methods. More targeted communication methods are comparable to traditional mail because the sender directs the information to a particular

---

6 See President William J. Clinton and Vice President Albert Gore, Jr., A Framework for Global Electronic Commerce (1997), <http://www.iitf.nist.gov/eleccomm/ecomm.htm>; European Ministerial Conference, "Global Information Networks: Realizing the Potential," July 6-8, 1997, Ministerial Declaration, Global Informational Networks, <http://www2.echo.lu/bonn/final.html>.

7 For a discussion of recent Commission actions addressing the Internet, see The Impact of Recent Technological Advances on the Securities Markets, Report prepared by the Staff of the U.S. Securities and Exchange Commission pursuant to Section 510(a) of the National Securities Markets Improvements Act of 1996 (Oct. 1997) <http://www.sec.gov/news/studies/techrp97.htm>.

8 Wilske and Schiller, International Jurisdiction in Cyberspace: Which States May Regulate the Internet?, <http://www.law.indiana.edu/fcj/pubs/v50/no1/wilske.html>, Section II.A.2.(c).

person, group or entity. These methods include e-mail and technology that allows mass e-mailing or "spamming." Information posted on a Web site, however, is not sent to any particular person, although it is available for anyone to search for and retrieve.[9] Offerors using those more targeted technologies must assume the responsibility of identifying when their offering materials are being sent to persons in the United States and must comply fully with the U.S. securities laws.

B. Regulation of Offers

Many registration requirements under the U.S. securities laws are triggered when an offer of securities or financial services, such as brokerage or investment advisory services, is made to the general public.

- Under the Securities Act, absent an exemption, an issuer that offers or sells securities in the United States through use of the mails or other means of interstate commerce must register the offering with the Commission.[10] An offering of securities may be exempt from registration if it is conducted as a "private placement," without any general solicitation of investors.[11]

- Under the Investment Company Act, a foreign investment company may not use the mails or other means of interstate commerce to publicly offer its securities in the United States or to U.S. persons unless the investment company receives an order from the Commission permitting it to register under the Investment Company Act.[12] A foreign investment company may,

---

[9] The Web site sponsor can aid Internet searches by adding "tags" to its Web site that facilitate a search engine identifying the site as containing information relating to targeted topics. Generally, we will not view the use of tags relating to securities or investments as transforming the Web site into a targeted communication that would require additional measures to assure against sales to U.S. persons, such as blocking access by U.S. persons to the offering materials.

[10] Section 5 of the Securities Act, 15 U.S.C. 77e.

[11] See, e.g., Section 4(2) of the Securities Act, 15 U.S.C. 77d(2); Regulation D [17 CFR 230.501-508].

[12] Section 7(d) of the Investment Company Act, 15 U.S.C. 80a-7(d).

however, make a private offer of its securities in the United States or to U.S. persons in reliance on one of the exclusions from the definition of "investment company" under the Investment Company Act.[13]

- Under the Advisers Act, an adviser is prohibited from using the mails or other means of interstate commerce in connection with its business as an investment adviser, unless the adviser is registered with the Commission, or is exempted or excluded from the requirement to register.[14]

- Under the Exchange Act, a broker or dealer generally must register with the Commission if it uses the mails or any means of interstate commerce to effect transactions in, or to induce or attempt to induce the purchase or sale of, any security.[15]

- Under the Exchange Act, an exchange generally must register with the Commission if it uses the mails or any means of interstate commerce for the purpose of using its facilities to effect any transaction in a security or to report any such transaction.[16]

The posting of information on a Web site may constitute an offer of securities or investment services for purposes of the U.S. securities laws.[17] Our discussion of these issues will proceed on the assumption that the Web site contains information that constitutes an "offer" of securities or investment services under the U.S. securities

---

13 See Section 3(c)(1) and Section 3(c)(7) of the Investment Company Act, 15 U.S.C. 80a-3(c)(1), 15 U.S.C. 80a-3(c)(7). See also Staff no-action letter, Goodwin, Procter & Hoar (available Feb. 28, 1997) ("Goodwin Procter").

14 Section 203(a) of the Advisers Act, 15 U.S.C. 80b-3(a).

15 Section 15(a) of the Exchange Act, 15 U.S.C. 78o(a).

16 Section 6 of the Exchange Act, 15 U.S.C. 78f.

17 See, e.g., Securities Act Release No. 7233, Question 20 (Oct. 6, 1995) [60 FR 53458] ("The placing of the offering materials on the Internet would not be consistent with the prohibition against general solicitation or advertising in Rule 502(c) of Regulation D.").

laws.[18] Because anyone who has access to the Internet can obtain access to a Web site unless the Web site sponsor adopts special procedures to restrict access, the pertinent legal issue is whether those Web site postings are offers in the United States that must be registered.

III. OFFSHORE OFFERS AND SOLICITATIONS ON THE INTERNET

A. General Approach

Some may argue that regulators could best protect investors by requiring registration or licensing for any Internet offer of securities or investment services that their residents could access. As a practical matter, however, the adoption of such an approach by securities regulators could preclude some of the most promising Internet applications by investors, issuers, and financial service providers.

The regulation of offers is a fundamental element of federal and some U.S. state securities regulatory schemes. Absent the transaction of business in the United States or with U.S. persons, however, our interest in regulating solicitation activity is less compelling.[19] We believe that our investor protection concerns are best addressed

---

18 We also assume that the Internet is an instrument of interstate commerce and that its use satisfies the "jurisdictional means" requirements of the federal securities laws. See American Library Ass'n v. Pataki, 969 F. Supp. 160, 161 (S.D.N.Y. 1997).

19 Under a resolution adopted by the North American Securities Administrators Association ("NASAA"), states are encouraged to take appropriate steps to exempt Internet offers from the registration provisions of their securities laws when the offers indicate that the securities are not being offered to residents of their state and the offers are not otherwise specifically made to any persons in their state. Sales of the securities that were the subject of the Internet offer could be made in that state after the offering has been registered and the final prospectus has been delivered to investors, or where the sales are exempt from registration. NASAA, Resolution Regarding Securities Offered on the Internet (adopted Jan. 7, 1996), 1996 CCH Par. 7040 (Jan. 1996).

through the implementation by issuers and financial service providers of precautionary measures that are reasonably designed to ensure that offshore Internet offers are not targeted to persons in the United States or to U.S. persons.[20]

B. Procedures Reasonably Designed to Avoid Targeting the United States

When offerors implement adequate measures to prevent U.S. persons from participating in an offshore Internet offer, we would not view the offer as targeted at the United States and thus would not treat it as occurring in the United States for registration purposes. What constitutes adequate measures will depend on all the facts and circumstances of any particular situation. We generally would not consider an offshore Internet offer made by a non-U.S. offeror as targeted at the United States, however, if:

- The Web site includes a prominent disclaimer making it clear that the offer is directed only to countries other than the United States. For

---

According to NASAA, 32 states have implemented the resolution and 15 states have indicated an intent to do so.

Several foreign authorities have provided guidance on Internet and securities related issues. See, e.g., Policy Statement 107 on Electronic Prospectuses (Sept. 1996) <http://www.asc.gov.au> (Australia); Notice and Interpretation Note, Trading Securities and Providing Advice Respecting Securities on the Internet (Mar. 3, 1997), NIN #97/9 (British Columbia, Canada).

20 We use the term "U.S. person" as it is defined in Rule 902(k) of Regulation S under the Securities Act [17 CFR 230.902(k)], which is premised on residence in the United States, regardless of any temporary presence outside the United States. See Securities Act Release No. 7505 (Feb. 18, 1998) [63 FR 9632 (Feb. 25, 1998)] (renumbering CFR sections). "U.S. person" generally has the same meaning for purposes of Section 7(d) of the Investment Company Act as under Rule 902(k) of Regulation S under the Securities Act. See Goodwin Procter, supra note 13. For purposes of this release, we deem Internet offers "targeted at the United States" to include Internet offers targeted to U.S. persons. Cf. Rule 902(h)(2) of Regulation S [17 CFR 230.902(h)(2)] (offers targeting identifiable groups of U.S. persons offshore are not offshore transactions).

example, the Web site could state that the securities or services are not being offered in the United States or to U.S. persons, or it could specify those jurisdictions (other than the United States) in which the offer is being made;[21] and

- The Web site offeror implements procedures that are reasonably designed to guard against sales to U.S. persons in the offshore offering. For example, the offeror could ascertain the purchaser's residence by obtaining such information as mailing addresses or telephone numbers (or area code) prior to the sale. This measure will allow the offeror to avoid sending or delivering securities, offering materials, services or products to a person at a U.S. address or telephone number.

These procedures are not exclusive; other procedures that suffice to guard against sales to U.S. persons also can be used to demonstrate that the offer is not targeted at the United States. Regardless of the precautions adopted, however, we would view solicitations that appear by their content to be targeted at U.S. persons as made in the United States. Examples of this type of solicitation include purportedly offshore offers that emphasize the investor's ability to avoid U.S. income taxes on the investments.[22] We are concerned that the advice that we provide to assist those who attempt to comply with both the letter and spirit of the securities laws will be used by

---

21 The disclaimer would have to be meaningful. For example, the disclaimer could state, "This offering is intended only to be available to residents of countries within the European Union." Because of the global reach of the Internet, a disclaimer that simply states, "The offer is not being made in any jurisdiction in which the offer would or could be illegal," however, would not be meaningful. In addition, if the disclaimer is not on the same screen as the offering material, or is not on a screen that must be viewed before a person can view the offering materials, it would not be meaningful.

22 In our view, while a relevant factor, the fact that an Internet offeror posts offering materials in English even though it is based in a non-English speaking country will not, by itself, demonstrate that the offer is targeted at the United States.

others as a pretext to violate those laws. Sham offshore offerings or procedures, or other schemes will not allow issuers or promoters to escape their registration obligations under the U.S. securities laws.

C. Effect of Attempts by U.S. Persons to Evade Restrictions

We recognize that U.S. persons may respond falsely to residence questions, disguise their country of residence by using non-resident addresses, or use other devices, such as offshore nominees, in order to participate in offshore offerings of securities or investment services. Thus, even if the foreign market participant has taken measures reasonably designed to guard against sales to U.S. persons, a U.S. person nevertheless could circumvent those measures.

In our view, if a U.S. person purchases securities or investment services notwithstanding adequate procedures reasonably designed to prevent the purchase, we would not view the Internet offer after the fact as having been targeted at the United States, absent indications that would put the issuer on notice that the purchaser was a U.S. person. This information might include (but is not limited to): receipt of payment drawn on a U.S. bank; provision of a U.S. taxpayer identification or social security number; or, statements by the purchaser indicating that, notwithstanding a foreign address, he or she is a U.S. resident. Confronted with such information, we would expect offerors to take steps to verify that the purchaser is not a U.S. person before selling to that person.[23] Additionally, if despite its use of measures that appear to be reasonably designed to prevent sales to U.S. persons, the offeror discovers that it has

---

23 These additional steps could include a request for further evidence (e.g., a copy of a passport or driver's license).

sold to U.S. persons, it may need to evaluate whether other measures may be necessary to provide reasonable assurance against future sales to U.S. persons.

D. Third-Party Web Services

An issuer, underwriter or other type of offshore Internet offeror may seek to have its offering materials posted on a third-party's Web site. In that event, if the offeror uses a third-party Web service that employs at least the same level of precautions against sales to U.S. persons as would be adequate for the offshore Internet offeror to employ, we would not view the third-party's Web site as an offer that is targeted to the United States. [24]

When an offeror, or those acting on its behalf, uses a third-party's Web site to generate interest in the Internet offer, more stringent precautions by the offeror than those outlined in Section III.B. may be warranted. These precautions may include limiting access to its Internet offering materials to persons who can demonstrate that they are not U.S. persons. For example, additional precautions may be called for when the Internet offeror:

- Posts offering or solicitation material or otherwise causes the offer to be listed on an investment-oriented Web site that has a significant number of U.S. clients or subscribers, or where U.S. investors could be expected to search for information about investment opportunities or services; or

- Arranges for direct or indirect hyperlinks from a third-party investment-oriented page to its own Web page containing the offering material.

---

[24] Governmental authorities or securities exchanges could post issuer information that is required by law to be filed with them, including prospectuses, on their Web sites without restriction. Securities exchanges, however, should consider the U.S. registration implications of their Web sites as a whole. <u>See infra</u> Section VII.B.

IV. ADDITIONAL ISSUES UNDER THE SECURITIES ACT

Our Securities Act analysis assumes that the information posted on a Web site would, were we to deem it to occur in the United States, constitute an "offer" within the meaning of Section 5(c) of the Securities Act and Regulation S, a "public offering" prohibited under Section 4(2) of the Act, a "general solicitation or general advertising" prohibited under Rule 502(c) of Regulation D,[25] and a "directed selling effort" prohibited under Regulation S.[26] The focus of our analysis, then, is under what circumstances should we deem offshore Internet offers to which U.S. persons can gain access not to occur in the United States.

A. Offshore Offerings by Foreign Issuers

1. Regulation S

When a foreign issuer is making an unregistered offshore Internet offer and does not plan to sell securities in the United States as part of the offering, it should implement the general measures outlined in Section III.B. to avoid targeting the United States. Assuming that the offering is made pursuant to Regulation S, the offering must comply with all of the applicable requirements under that regulation, including the requirement that all offers and sales be made in "offshore transactions."[27]

---

25 Rule 502(c) under the Securities Act [17 CFR 240.502(c)].

26 Rule 902(c) [17 CFR 230.902(c)].

27 Rule 902(h) and Rule 903 of Regulation S [17 CFR 230.902(h) and 230.903]. The issuer's or underwriter's use of an Internet Web site to offer securities will not, by itself, prevent bona fide offshore purchasers in a Regulation S offering from reselling into the United States pursuant to registration or an exemption, such as Rule 144A [17 CFR 230.144A], provided that: (1) those purchasers are not part of the selling group; (2) those purchasers are not affiliated with the issuer or any member of the selling group; and (3)

2. U.S. Exempt Component

Foreign issuers commonly make offshore offerings concurrently with private offerings to U.S. institutional buyers. An offering exempt under Section 4(2) of the Securities Act may not involve "any public offering." Regulation D specifically prohibits the offer or sale of securities through a "general solicitation or general advertising." Publicly accessible Web site postings may not be used as a means to locate investors to participate in a pending or imminent U.S. offering relying on those provisions. If a Web site posting would be inappropriate for a U.S. private placement, an issuer should not attempt to accomplish the same result indirectly through the posting of an offshore Internet offer.

In addition to implementing the type of precautionary measures previously discussed, foreign issuers could implement other procedures to prevent their offshore Internet offers from being used to solicit participants for their U.S.-based exempt offerings, including:

- The Internet offeror could allow unrestricted access to its offshore Internet offering materials, but not permit persons responding to the offshore Internet offering to participate in its exempt U.S. offering, even if otherwise qualified to do so. In that situation, the offeror would keep a record of all persons responding over the Internet and all persons who otherwise indicate that they are responding to the offshore Internet offering;[28] or

---

the issuer's or underwriter's use of the Web site was not undertaken as part of an arrangement with, or on behalf of, such offshore purchasers.

[28] To identify those persons who are responding to the Internet offer, the Web site could provide telephone numbers, contact persons, or addresses that differ from those used in the offeror's other, more traditional offering materials. Under an approach suggested in staff no-action letters, the offeror could communicate with U.S. persons on the list to determine whether they are accredited investors with a view towards permitting their participation in separate, future exempt U.S. offerings by the issuer or, where the Web site offeror is an intermediary, other issuers. See Staff no-action

- The Web site offeror could ensure that access to the posted offering materials is limited to those viewers who first provide their residence information and, in doing so, do not provide information such as a U.S. area code or address that indicates that they are a U.S. person.[29] Thus, U.S. persons could obtain access only by misrepresenting their residence information.[30]

We believe that it would not be advisable for us to dictate the use of any one particular technology or screening method to protect against general solicitation in these instances. Any less costly, less intrusive method that is equally or more effective than those that we have suggested would be adequate as well.

In addition, the posted offering materials should relate only to the offshore offering.[31] The materials should contain only that information (if any) concerning the

---

letters, Royce Exchange Fund (available Aug. 28, 1996); Bateman Eichler (available Dec. 3, 1985); E.F. Hutton & Co. (available Dec. 3, 1985); Woodtrails-Seattle (available Aug. 9, 1982). Likewise, any investor solicited by the issuer or underwriter prior to or independent of the Web site posting could participate in the private offer, regardless of whether the investor may have viewed the posted offshore offering materials.

29 This step could be accomplished in multiple ways. For example, when a person reaches the Web site and then attempts to move to a section that includes offering information, a screen could ask for the required residence information. After the user enters the information, the area code and address could be automatically and immediately screened to eliminate further access to those who match a U.S. area code or address. Alternatively, the offeror could require a password and not assign a password until it verifies that address information, or it could block access by using technology that recognizes the country from which the Web site is being accessed.

30 Web site offerors must act in good faith to screen U.S. persons from viewing offering information. A screening mechanism that suggests ways of easy bypass would not be evidence of good faith.

31 A foreign issuer that wishes to use an Internet Web site to conduct the concurrent private placement in the United States could follow the general procedures developed in the domestic context for private placements on the Internet. See, e.g., Staff no-action letters, IPONET (available July 26, 1996); Lamp Technologies, Inc.

private U.S. offering that is required by foreign law to be provided to investors participating in the offshore public offering.[32]

B. Offshore Offerings by U.S. Issuers

Our approach to the use of Web sites to post offshore securities offerings distinguishes between domestic and foreign issuers.[33] For the following reasons, additional precautions are justified for Web sites operated by domestic issuers purporting not to make a public offering in the United States:

- The substantial contacts that a U.S. issuer has with the United States justifies our exercise of more extensive regulatory jurisdiction over its securities-related activities;

- There is a strong likelihood that securities of U.S. issuers initially offered and sold offshore will enter the U.S. trading markets; and

- U.S. issuers and investors have a much greater expectation that securities offerings by domestic issuers will be subject to the U.S. securities laws.

Our experience with abusive practices under Regulation S indicates that we should proceed cautiously when giving guidance to U.S. issuers in the area of unregistered offshore offerings. As a result, we would not consider a U.S. issuer using a Web site to make an unregistered offer to have implemented reasonable measures to

---

(available May 29, 1997). Under these procedures, the public offer posted on the Web site may not provide a hyperlink or otherwise alert the viewer to any Web site containing private placement offering materials.

32 Rule 135c under the Securities Act [17 CFR 230.135c] provides useful guidance on what limited information could be included on the Web site under these circumstances.

33 We use the term "foreign issuer" as it is defined in Rule 902(e) of Regulation S [17 CFR 230.902(e)]. See Securities Act Release No. 7505.

prevent sales to U.S. persons unless, in addition to the general precautions discussed above in Section III.B., the U.S. issuer implements password-type procedures that are reasonably designed to ensure that only non-U.S. persons can obtain access to the offer.[34] Under this procedure, persons seeking access to the Internet offer would have to demonstrate to the issuer or intermediary that they are not U.S. persons before obtaining the password for the site.[35]

In the context of broader Securities Act reform, we have been considering whether the current general solicitation and other offering communications restrictions on issuers and other offering participants should be modified to create greater flexibility.[36] To the extent that we reform those restrictions on offering communications in the future, we also will consider the implications of those changes for unregistered offshore Internet offerings.

---

34 See, e.g., IPONET and Lamp Technologies, Inc., supra note 31. Our interpretation therefore would allow for the creation of limited-access systems. Eventually, closed systems may develop that target only non-U.S. persons and qualified U.S. investors.

35 See Securities Act Release No. 7392 at n.31 (Feb. 28, 1997) [62 FR 9258] (issuer cannot accept at face value representations by investors regarding their residence). See also IPONET, supra note 31(IPONET's activities were supervised by an entity that verified information provided to IPONET by people who filled out IPONET's on-line questionnaire. Information from the questionnaires was used to determine whether respondents qualified as accredited investors and therefore were eligible to obtain password to access password-protected Web pages where IPONET posted private offerings).

36 Securities Act Release No. 7314 (July 25, 1996) [61 FR 40044]; Securities Act Release No. 7187 (July 10, 1995) [60 FR 35645].

C. Concurrent U.S. Registered Offering

A registered offering in the United States that takes place concurrently with an unregistered offshore Internet offer presents concerns because of the Securities Act's restrictions on making offers prior to the filing of a registration statement or, in the case of written or published offers, outside of the statutory prospectus. Consistent with these requirements, therefore, premature posting of offering information must be avoided. Existing Commission rules that provide a safe harbor for announcements of anticipated offerings provide guidance in this respect.[37] The Commission is considering whether to provide further guidance or to make further changes concerning concurrent U.S. registered offerings and offshore Internet offers in the context of broader Securities Act reforms.

D. Underwriters

Just as an issuer must take reasonable steps to avoid offers of unregistered securities in the United States, so too must persons acting on behalf of the issuer, such as underwriters or distributors. These persons, for purposes of the Securities Act, stand in the place of the issuer. Thus, regardless of whether the underwriter is foreign or domestic, what constitutes measures reasonably designed to prevent sales to U.S. persons will depend on the status of the issuer. For example, if the issuer is domestic and precautionary measures would call for its Web site containing offshore offering

---

[37] See, e.g., Rule 135 under the Securities Act [17 CFR 230.135].

information to be password-protected, so too should the information be protected on the underwriter's Web site.[38]

V. ADDITIONAL ISSUES UNDER THE INVESTMENT COMPANY ACT

This portion of the release addresses certain issues that arise under the Investment Company Act when a foreign fund (that is, an investment company that is organized under the laws of a jurisdiction other than the United States) makes an offshore Internet offer of its securities. In general, as with other types of securities offerings, we would not consider an Internet offer by a foreign fund to cause the fund to be subject to regulation or registration under the Investment Company Act if the foreign fund implements measures reasonably designed to guard against sales to U.S. persons.

The issue raised by the use of the Internet is whether a foreign fund's Internet offer that can be accessed by U.S. persons should be considered a public offer in the United States.[39] Consistent with our position under the Securities Act, if a foreign fund

---

[38] This, however, would not include bona fide research that complies with the Commission's safe harbor rules for research reports. See Rules 137 - 139 under the Securities Act [17 CFR 230.137 - 230.139]. Cf. Exchange Act Rule 15a-6(a)(2) [17 CFR 240.15a-6(a)(2)](conditional exemption from U.S. broker-dealer registration for foreign broker-dealers that furnish research reports to "major institutional investors" as defined in the rule).

[39] Section 7(d) of the Investment Company Act generally prohibits a foreign fund from using U.S. jurisdictional means to make a public offer of its securities in the United States or to U.S. persons, unless the fund receives an order from the Commission permitting it to register under the Investment Company Act. The Commission may issue such an order only if it finds that it is legally and practically feasible to enforce the provisions of the Investment Company Act effectively against the foreign fund, and that the issuance of the order is consistent with the public interest and the protection of investors.

implements measures reasonably designed to guard against sales to U.S. persons, we would not consider the foreign fund's Internet offer to be targeted to U.S. persons, and therefore would not consider the Internet offer to constitute a public offer in the United States subjecting the foreign fund to regulation and registration under the Investment Company Act.

An Internet offer by a foreign fund may arise in a number of situations. For example, a foreign fund could conduct an Internet offer that is targeted exclusively offshore. A foreign fund also could conduct an offshore Internet offer in addition to a private U.S. offer.[40] We discuss these situations separately below. We also address the use of the Internet by unregistered U.S. funds making private offshore offers, and the use of other forms of Internet marketing of investment company securities.

A. Internet Offers by a Foreign Fund

1. Offers Targeted Exclusively Offshore

When a foreign fund is making an unregistered offshore Internet offer and does not intend to sell securities in the United States as part of the offering, our general

---

For purposes of Section V, references to offers and sales to U.S. persons include offers or sales in the United States. Similarly, references to offers or sales in the United States include offers or sales to U.S. persons.

[40] In addition, a foreign fund also may use the Internet exclusively to conduct a private U.S. offer. This release does not address the ability of a foreign fund to conduct a private U.S. offer over the Internet, except to the extent that it is relevant to the foreign fund's ability to simultaneously conduct an offshore Internet offer. See infra note 45 and accompanying text. As discussed above in Section I, the statements made in this release do not alter the requirement that all offers and sales in the United States must be pursuant to registration under the U.S. securities laws or an applicable exemption.

statements in Section III.B. outlining the need for precautionary measures to avoid targeting the United States apply here as well. We may view an Internet offer as being targeted to U.S. persons, however, if the foreign fund is engaged in activities, either as a part of or in addition to its Internet offer, that are designed to attract U.S. persons to the Internet offer, such as advertising the existence of the foreign fund's Web site in a U.S. publication.

2. Foreign Funds Conducting Offshore and Private U.S. Offers

Next, we address offshore Internet offers by foreign funds that also are conducting private U.S. offers.[41] We would not consider a foreign fund that is concurrently conducting both a private U.S. offer and an offshore Internet offer to be making a public offer of its securities in the United States if the foreign fund implements measures reasonably designed to guard against public sales of its securities

---

[41] The staff previously took the position that under certain circumstances a foreign fund that is conducting an offshore offer also may make a private U.S. offer in reliance on the exclusion from the definition of "investment company" in Section 3(c)(1) of the Investment Company Act consistent with the public offering prohibition contained in Section 7(d). See Staff no-action letter, Touche Remnant & Co. (available Aug. 27, 1984) ("Touche Remnant"). In Goodwin Procter, supra note 13, the staff similarly took the position that under certain circumstances a foreign fund that is conducting an offshore offer also may make a private U.S. offer in reliance on the exclusion from the definition of "investment company" in Section 3(c)(7) of the Investment Company Act consistent with the public offering prohibition contained in Section 7(d). The staff also has stated that if U.S. persons become shareholders of a foreign fund for reasons beyond the control of the fund or persons acting on its behalf, the fund would not be required to count those shareholders as U.S. persons for purposes of determining whether the fund may rely on the exception from the definition of "investment company" in Section 3(c)(1) of the Investment Company Act. See Staff no-action letter, Investment Funds Institute of Canada (available Mar. 4, 1996). The same position applies to foreign funds relying on Section 3(c)(7) of the Investment Company Act. See generally Goodwin Procter, supra note 13. We take the position that Touche Remnant is superseded to the extent that it is inconsistent with these positions.

to U.S. persons, and the Internet offer is not indirectly used as a general solicitation for participants in the private U.S. offer. As stated above, what constitutes adequate measures will depend on all of the facts and circumstances. In addition to implementing the type of precautionary measures discussed in Section III.B. (with one modification noted below), a foreign fund could use any procedures reasonably designed to guard against use of its Internet offer to generally solicit participants in the U.S. private offer.[42]

If a foreign fund that is concurrently conducting a private U.S. offer and an Internet offer uses a disclaimer that reflects the existence of two separate offers and indicates that the Internet offer is not being made in the United States, we would view this action as an indication that the fund has taken measures reasonably designed to guard against publicly selling its securities to U.S. persons. The disclaimer could state, for example, that this offer (the offshore Internet offer) is not being made in the United States (or identify the jurisdictions in which the Internet offer is being made) and that the offer and sale of securities in the United States is not permitted except pursuant to an exemption from registration.

If, however, a foreign fund directly or indirectly provides any additional information on its Web site about the types of persons to whom offers and sales can be made pursuant to an exemption under U.S. law, or provides guidance on how U.S. persons may obtain this or other purchasing information, we would view this action as an indication that the foreign fund is using its Internet offer to target the United States,

---

[42] See notes 28-32 supra and accompanying text.

except to the extent that foreign law requires that the information be disclosed.[43] Moreover, if the foreign fund provides a hyperlink, or otherwise directs U.S. persons, to another source that provides information about the private offering, we would view this action as an indication that the foreign fund is targeting the United States. In our view, either of these actions could result in the foreign fund making a public offer in the United States.

A foreign fund also may be making a public offer in the United States if it provides any other information about the private U.S. offer on its Web site, except to the extent that foreign law requires that the information be disclosed.[44] If the foreign fund wishes to provide information on its Web site relating to its private U.S. offer (other than information required by foreign law), it generally may do so without registering under the Investment Company Act if it adopts and implements password-type procedures with respect to that information.[45]

---

[43] Although Rule 135c by its terms applies only to Section 5 of the Securities Act, we would take a similar approach with respect to the type of information that a foreign fund may, if required by foreign law, provide on its Internet site about a U.S. private offer without violating the public offering prohibition contained in Section 7(d) of the Investment Company Act. See supra note 32 and accompanying text.

[44] An adviser to a foreign fund conducting an offshore Internet offer that also sponsors a U.S.-registered investment company with the same investment objectives and policies as the foreign fund may provide information about, or direct the viewer to, the registered U.S. offer without the Internet offer being considered to be a public offer of the foreign fund's securities in the United States.

[45] See Lamp Technologies, Inc. and IPONET, supra note 31. Prequalification and password-type procedures are intended to ensure that only persons eligible to privately purchase the securities can obtain access to a Web site used in connection with a private offer and that the dissemination of information through the Internet site does not constitute a "general solicitation" under Rule 502(c) of Regulation D under the Securities Act. In addition to the procedures discussed in Lamp Technologies, there

As with our position under the Securities Act, we are concerned that our guidance with respect to the Investment Company Act may be used by some foreign funds that are conducting Internet offers to engage in activities that are part of a plan or scheme to make public offers in the United States. None of our statements in this release is intended to suggest that any foreign fund could do indirectly what it could not lawfully do directly.[46]

B. Offshore Offers by U.S. Funds

As previously noted, the Commission's position on the use of the Internet for unregistered offshore offers generally distinguishes between U.S. and foreign issuers, based upon the Commission's greater interest in regulating the conduct of U.S. issuers in the United States. As noted in Section IV.B., we will not require a U.S. issuer making an offshore offer over the Internet to register the offer under the Securities Act if it uses procedures reasonably designed to ensure that only non-U.S. persons may view the offer. We conclude that the same approach should apply under the Investment Company Act to U.S. funds making offshore Internet offers. Thus, we would not consider a U.S. fund making a private offshore offer in reliance on one of the exclusions from the definition of "investment company" in Section 3(c)(1) or Section 3(c)(7) of the Investment Company Act to be making a public offer in the United States

---

may be other, equally effective procedures designed to restrict access to information on the Internet to those persons who are eligible to purchase securities in a private U.S. offer.

46 See Section 48(a) of the Investment Company Act.

if the fund uses procedures, such as password-protected web sites, reasonably designed to ensure the private nature of the offer.[47]

As noted above, we are considering whether the current restrictions on general solicitations in connection with private offers under the Securities Act should be modified.[48] In the event that we revise current Securities Act restrictions on exempt private offers and unregistered offshore offers, we anticipate that we would consider parallel revisions under the Investment Company Act.

C. Other Forms of Internet Marketing of Investment Company Securities

We analyze Internet offers made by or on behalf of a foreign fund in generally the same manner as offers by other types of issuers.[49] If a foreign fund or persons acting on its behalf seek to use a third-party Web site to generate interest in an offshore offer, the implementation of more stringent restrictions on the offshore Internet offer may be necessary to ensure that the offer is not being directed into the United States, including limiting access to the Internet offering materials to persons who can demonstrate that they are not U.S. persons.[50]

VI. OFFERS OF ADVISORY SERVICES UNDER THE ADVISERS ACT

This portion of the release addresses issues that arise under the Advisers Act when a foreign adviser (that is, an investment adviser that is organized under the laws

---

47 See supra notes 34-35 and accompanying text.

48 See supra note 36 and accompanying text.

49 See Section III.D., supra.

50 Id.

of a jurisdiction other than the United States) offers its advisory services over the Internet. In general, a foreign adviser may be able to rely on an exemption from registration under the Advisers Act if it has fewer than fifteen U.S. clients and implements measures reasonably designed to ensure that, based on its Internet activities, the adviser is not holding itself out as an investment adviser in the United States.[51]

The issue raised by a foreign investment adviser's use of the Internet is whether and, if so, under what circumstances, the foreign adviser may provide information about its advisory services over the Internet without being considered to be holding itself out as an investment adviser in the United States. We conclude that a foreign adviser providing advisory services over the Internet generally would be holding itself out as an investment adviser. Specifically, we have stated that we generally will consider an adviser who uses a publicly available electronic medium, such as the Internet, to provide information about its services to be holding itself out to the public as an adviser, and to not qualify for the exemption from registration contained in

---

[51] Section 203(a) of the Advisers Act generally prohibits any investment adviser from using U.S. jurisdictional means in connection with its business as an investment adviser, unless the adviser is registered with the Commission, or is exempted or excluded from the requirement to register. Section 203(b)(3) of the Advisers Act provides for an exemption from registration for any adviser who during the course of the preceding twelve months has had fewer than fifteen clients and who neither holds itself out generally to the public as an investment adviser nor acts as an adviser to a U.S.-registered investment company or business development company. The staff has taken the position that foreign advisers are required to count only their U.S. clients for purposes of determining whether they are exempt from registration under Section 203(b)(3). See Protecting Investors: A Half Century of Investment Company Regulation, at 223 n.6 (1992); Staff no-action letter, Murray Johnstone Ltd. (available Oct. 7, 1994).

Section 203(b)(3) of the Advisers Act.[52] If, however, the adviser implements measures reasonably designed to guard against directing information provided on the Internet about its advisory services to U.S. persons, we would not consider the foreign adviser to be holding itself out as an investment adviser in the United States for purposes of Section 203(b)(3).

What constitutes measures reasonably designed to guard against an adviser holding itself out as an investment adviser in the United States will depend on all of the facts and circumstances. We generally would consider an adviser to have implemented measures reasonably designed to guard against holding itself out as an investment adviser in the United States if:

- The Web site includes a prominent disclaimer making it clear to whom the site materials are (or are not) directed.[53]
- The adviser implements procedures reasonably designed to guard against directing information about its advisory services to U.S. persons (e.g., obtaining sufficient residency information such as mailing addresses or telephone numbers prior to sending further information), other than to its fourteen or fewer U.S. clients.[54]

Other measures also may provide adequate assurance that a foreign adviser is not holding itself out as an investment adviser in the United States.

---

52 See Use of Electronic Media by Broker-Dealers, Transfer Agents, and Investment Advisers for Delivery of Information, Securities Act Release No. 7288 (May 9, 1996) at text accompanying n. 32. But see Lamp Technologies, Inc., supra note 31.

53 See supra note 21 and accompanying text.

54 See text following supra note 21.

VII. EXCHANGE ACT REGISTRATION ISSUES

The Internet activities of broker-dealers and markets (including exchanges) also raise issues under the Exchange Act. Foreign entities that perform these functions should consider whether their Internet activities would subject them to registration under the Exchange Act.

A. Broker-Dealer Activities

Broker-dealers must register with the Commission if they are physically present in the United States, or if, regardless of their location, they effect, induce, or attempt to induce securities transactions with investors in the United States. The issue, therefore, is whether the Commission would deem a broker-dealer's Web site to be an attempt to induce securities transactions with U.S. persons. Broker-dealer Web sites may offer market information and investment tools, real-time or delayed quote information, market summaries, research, portfolio management tools, and analytic programs. Some sites also include information on commissions and other fees, branch office locations, and instructions on how to contact the broker-dealer. In essence, Web sites advertise the broker-dealers' services to potential investors with the intent of attracting securities business.

In keeping with the general principles outlined above (Section III.B.), the Commission will not consider a foreign broker-dealer's advertising on an Internet Web site to constitute an attempt to induce a securities transaction with U.S. persons if the foreign broker-dealer takes measures reasonably designed to ensure that it does not effect securities transactions with U.S. persons as a result of its Internet activities.

Under our general principles, as applied in the broker-dealer context, a foreign broker-dealer generally would be considered to have taken measures reasonably designed to ensure it does not effect securities transactions with U.S. persons as a result of its Internet activities if it:

- Posts a prominent disclaimer on the Web site either affirmatively delineating the countries in which the broker-dealer's services are available, or stating that the services are not available to U.S. persons; and

- Refuses to provide brokerage services to any potential customer that the broker-dealer has reason to believe is, or that indicates that it is, a U.S. person, based on residence, mailing address, payment method, or other grounds.

As a means to implement the latter procedure, the broker-dealer should require potential customers to provide sufficient residence information.

These procedures are not exclusive. Adoption of other equally or more effective precautions can also suffice to demonstrate that the broker-dealer does not effect securities transactions with U.S. persons as a result of its Internet activities.

The Commission has exempted foreign broker-dealers that effect transactions with U.S. customers from registering in the United States if these customers initiated transactions with the foreign broker-dealers outside of the United States without solicitation. Specifically, Exchange Act Rule 15a-6 currently provides an exemption from U.S. broker-dealer registration for foreign broker-dealers that effect transactions in securities with or for persons that they have not solicited.[55] Foreign broker-dealers

---

55 Exchange Act Rule 15a-6(a)(1) [17 CFR 240.15a-6(a)(1)].

that solicit transactions with U.S. persons, however, are required to register as broker-dealers in the United States.

Foreign broker-dealers that have Internet Web sites and that intend to rely on Rule 15a-6's "unsolicited" exemption should ensure that the "unsolicited" customer's transactions are not in fact solicited, either directly or indirectly, through customers accessing their Web sites.[56] In particular, these broker-dealers could obtain, as a precaution reasonably designed to prevent that result, affirmative representations from potential U.S. customers that they deem unsolicited that those customers have not previously accessed their Web sites. Alternatively, a broker-dealer could maintain records that are sufficiently detailed and verifiable to reliably determine that such U.S. customers had not obtained access to its Web site.

B. <u>Exchange Activities</u>

Until recently, in order to obtain current market information about, and to purchase or sell securities on, a foreign market, a U.S. investor typically contacted a U.S. broker-dealer by telephone or facsimile. Alternatively, the U.S. investor could directly contact a foreign broker-dealer that is a member of the foreign market. Today, however, the technology exists for investors to obtain real-time information about trading on foreign markets from a number of different sources, and to enter and execute orders on those markets electronically from the United States. Many exchanges, for example, offer Web sites through which they provide real-time quotes and other market information, e-mail addresses for questions, general contact and

---

[56] Because a securities firm's Web site itself typically is a solicitation, orders routed through the Web site would not be considered "unsolicited."

membership information (including the names and addresses of members), and other investing tools.

The U.S. securities laws require exchanges to register with the Commission if they (or any broker or dealer) "make use of the mails or any means or instrumentality of interstate commerce for the purpose of using any facility of an exchange within or subject to the jurisdiction of the United States to effect any transaction in a security, or to report any such transaction."[57] The Commission currently is considering the question of under what circumstances a foreign market that provides the ability in the United States for U.S. persons to trade directly in the market must register as a U.S. exchange.[58]

At this time, however, the Commission will not apply the exchange registration requirements to a foreign market that sponsors a Web site generally advertising the foreign exchange, disseminating quotes (including real-time quotes with counterparty identification), or allowing orders to be directed to the market through its Web site, so long as the exchange takes steps reasonably designed to prevent U.S. persons from directing orders to the market through its Web site. In our view, an exchange generally would be considered to have taken steps reasonably designed to prevent U.S. persons from accessing the market through its Web site if it:

- Posts a disclaimer on the Web site affirmatively stating either the countries in which the exchange's services are directly available, or that the exchange's services are not directly available to U.S. persons;

---

57 Section 5 of the Exchange Act, 15 U.S.C. 78e.

58 Exchange Act Release No. 38672 (May 23, 1997).

- Requires potential members or direct participants in the exchange to state their residence and mailing address;

- Refuses to allow trading on the exchange through the Web site by any person that the exchange has reason to believe, or that indicates it, is a U.S. person; and

- Refrains from making arrangements to provide U.S. persons with access to the exchange over the Internet indirectly through its members.[59]

LIST OF SUBJECTS

17 CFR Parts 231, 241 and 276

Securities.

17 CFR Part 271

Investment companies, Securities.

AMENDMENTS TO THE CODE OF FEDERAL REGULATIONS

For the reasons set forth in the preamble, the Commission is amending Title 17, Chapter II of the Code of Federal Regulations as follows:

PART 231 - INTERPRETATIVE RELEASES RELATING TO THE SECURITIES ACT OF 1933 AND GENERAL RULES AND REGULATIONS THEREUNDER

1. Part 231 is amended by adding Release No. 33-7516 and the release date of March 23, 1998, to the list of interpretative releases.

PART 241 - INTERPRETATIVE RELEASES RELATING TO THE SECURITIES EXCHANGE ACT OF 1934 AND GENERAL RULES AND REGULATIONS THEREUNDER

---

[59] This last step would preclude an exchange from relying on this release if it, for example, sets the terms under which exchange members provide Internet access to the exchange, or makes arrangements for U.S. persons to directly clear and settle trades conducted on the exchange through the Internet. Foreign exchanges that knowingly provide U.S. persons with access to their trading facilities through the Internet would not be able to rely on this interpretation, and may be required to register with the Commission.

2. Part 241 is amended by adding Release No. 34-39779 and the release date of March 23, 1998, to the list of interpretative releases.

PART 271 - INTERPRETATIVE RELEASES RELATING TO THE INVESTMENT COMPANY ACT OF 1940 AND GENERAL RULES AND REGULATIONS THEREUNDER

3. Part 271 is amended by adding Release No. IC-23071 and the release date of March 23, 1998, to the list of interpretative releases.

PART 276 - INTERPRETATIVE RELEASES RELATING TO THE INVESTMENT ADVISERS ACT OF 1940 AND GENERAL RULES AND REGULATIONS THEREUNDER

4. Part 276 is amended by adding Release No. IA-1710 and the release date of March 23, 1998, to the list of interpretative releases.

By the Commission.

Jonathan G. Katz
Secretary

Dated: March 23, 1998

NOTES

24

SECURITIES REGULATION AND THE USE OF ELECTRONIC MEDIA

Linda C. Quinn
Ottilie L. Jarmel

SECURITIES REGULATION AND THE USE OF ELECTRONIC MEDIA

I. Introduction

The Securities and Exchange Commission (the "Commission") has issued two interpretive releases providing guidance as to the use of electronic distribution to meet information delivery obligations mandated under the federal securities laws.[1] The releases reflect the Commission's commitment to encouraging and facilitating electronic media to communicate with investors. This commitment is based on the Commission's view that the use of electronic media also enhances the efficiency of the securities markets, by allowing for the rapid dissemination of information to investors and principal markets in a more cost-efficient, widespread and equitable manner than traditional paper-based methods.

The releases outline a process that requires (1) electronic documents be prepared, updated and delivered consistent with the federal securities laws; (2) electronic delivery be as certain as paper delivery; and (3) investors be given effective access to information required to be disclosed and the opportunity to retain it.

In general, the Commission to date has approached the use of electronic media by analogy to paper, rather than adapting various concepts and requirements to reflect the special nature of electronic communications:

> The Commission believes the question of whether delivery through electronic media has been achieved is most easily examined by analogy to paper delivery procedures. The Commission would view information distributed through electronic means as satisfying the delivery or transmission requirements of the federal securities laws if such distribution results in the delivery to the intended recipients of substantially equivalent information as these recipients would have had if the information were delivered to them in paper form.[2]

However, the ubiquity of information on the Internet presents challenges to regulatory regimes that base jurisdiction on geographical considerations and that place restrictions on the free flow of information. In March 1998, the Commission took an important step in addressing these issues and published an interpretative release with respect to its views on the application of registration obligations under the federal securities laws to the use of Internet Web sites to disseminate offering and soliciting materials for offshore

Linda C. Quinn is a partner and Ottilie L. Jarmel is an associate with Shearman & Sterling in New York, New York. They can be reached at (212) 848-4000. Their Internet address is http.//www.shearman.com. These materials present their own views and do not necessarily reflect the views of others at their firm.

sales of securities and investment services. The Web Site Release provides guidance, principally for non-U.S. issuers, that will allow the use of Web site communications in connection with certain offshore offerings.[3] The Commission has not provided general guidance on the status of nonmandated general corporate communications through electronic media—most notably, Web sites—and has not yet attempted to address potential liability issues relating to the content of information placed on a Web site—except to remind companies that the liability provisions of the federal securities laws apply equally to electronic-based media. In the absence of Commission guidance, analogizing to paper, as the interpretive releases on electronic delivery do, may be the best way to approach the issue, although it may lead to an unintended result of limiting the use of the Internet in ways that the Commission may ultimately not endorse, or that neither serve the public interest nor are consistent with investor protection. In addition, to the extent that the Commission acts to exempt offers from registration, allows communications other than statutory prospectuses during the offering period or relaxes the general solicitation prohibitions on certain private offerings made under Regulation D, as discussed in its Securities Act Concept Release,[4] many of the open issues will be resolved.

II. What Is Electronic Media?

Electronic media includes audiotapes, videotapes, facsimiles, CD-ROM, electronic mail ("e-mail"), bulletin boards, Internet Web sites and computer networks. The "Internet" includes the World Wide Web or a proprietary or common carrier electronic delivery system. A document may be delivered through any medium so long as the conditions for notice, consent and access are satisfied. Moreover, a company may elect to deliver its information through any number of such media.

III. Guidelines on Electronic Delivery

The releases address the wide range of disclosure delivery obligations applicable to companies engaged in financings and those subject to the Securities Exchange Act of 1934 (the "Exchange Act") reporting requirements, *e.g.*, prospectuses, annual reports and proxy statements. In order to discharge its disclosure obligations, a company must take reasonable steps to ensure that the dissemination of information will result in actual delivery to investors. When the dissemination is through electronic means, it is not enough, as a senior SEC staffer stated at the 1996 annual ABA meeting, to "just put stuff on the Web and have people know it's there." The move to electronic media at this point does not reflect a move by the Commission from delivery to an access model of regulation.

On October 6, 1995, the Commission published a release which addresses the electronic delivery of documents, such as prospectuses, annual reports to shareholders and proxy solicitations under the Securities Act of 1933 (the "Securities Act"), the Exchange Act and the Investment Company Act of 1940.[5] The Commission's main concern with the use of electronic media to deliver information is to ensure that the disclosure made by companies complies with the requirements of the securities laws. Specifically, the October Release addressed three aspects of the delivery requirements: notice, access, and evidence to show delivery.

Notice

Electronic communication should provide timely and adequate notice to investors that information is available. The key is that investors receive the same measure of notice that would be provided by paper delivery. Providing an electronic document itself (*e.g.*, on computer disk, CD-ROM, audiotape, videotape or e-mail) will suffice for such purpose; however, the mere posting of a document on a Web site will not, unless there is evidence of actual delivery. In such case, separate notice (*e.g.*, through e-mail, letter or postcard) would be required to satisfy the delivery requirements. If an investor consents to electronic delivery via a Web site but does not provide an e-mail address, the issuer may post its final prospectus on the Internet and make the investor aware of the availability and location of the final prospectus by having the underwriter mail a notice of the location of the Web site with the confirmation.[6]

Access

The October Release requires that investors be given both effective access through an unburdensome medium and the ability to retain a document by downloading it or maintaining continued on-line access. The October Release makes clear that there must be the opportunity to retain a permanent record of the information and have "ongoing access equivalent to personal retention."[7] Downloading a document from an electronic medium would be sufficient to satisfy this requirement.[8] If a document is posted on a Web site or made available through an on-line service, it should remain accessible for so long as any delivery requirement applies.

The Commission has cautioned that companies should always be prepared to provide paper versions of their documents in the event computers are incompatible, computer systems fail or investors revoke their consent to receive documents electronically.

While the Commission permits an offering to be limited entirely to persons that consent to receive a prospectus electronically, if the offering is not so limited, paper versions of the prospectus must be given to broker-dealers to be made available to investors who do not have electronic access.[9] In addition, the secondary market prospectus delivery requirements of the Securities Act in an initial public offering would require that an issuer make paper versions available to after-market purchasers.[10]

Evidence to Show Delivery

Companies should have reasonable assurance analogous to that provided by the U.S. Postal Service that the electronic medium they use will satisfy the delivery requirements. Assurance of this nature may be derived from (i) e-mail, return receipt, or confirmation that a document has been accessed, downloaded or printed; (ii) transmission of the document by fax; (iii) an investor's accessing of the document by hyperlinking to a document incorporated by reference; and (iv) using forms or other material available only by accessing the document. A company will be deemed to have satisfied the delivery requirements "if such distribution results in the delivery to the intended recipients of substantially equivalent information as these recipients would have had if the information were delivered to them in paper form."[11]

In addition, a company may meet its delivery requirements by obtaining informed consent to receive specified information through a specified electronic medium. Consent delivered to one person can be relied upon by another. For example, if an investor agreed with an investment banking firm to receive prospectuses electronically, a company could rely on that consent for purposes of its own prospectus delivery obligations. The consent should indicate the particular electronic medium that may be used, and that costs may be incurred. Consent to one medium does not imply consent to another. Consent is revocable at any time, but must be given a reasonable time before electronic delivery of a particular document has commenced for the issuer to be on notice that continued delivery using such means will not be effective.[12] If an investor revokes consent, continued electronic delivery by the company will not satisfy its delivery requirements.

Notwithstanding the established guidelines, the Commission has expressly recognized that alternate methods of electronic delivery not contemplated by the October Release may satisfy the applicable statutory requirements if they provide "assurance comparable to paper delivery that the required information will be delivered. . . ."[13] Thus, "[t]he ultimate responsibility for satisfying the applicable statutory requirements remains with the issuer or other party to whom the law assigns the responsibility."[14]

The Commission has also reminded companies that the October Release "does not affect any applicable state laws or self-regulatory organization rules. Consequently, issuers and others need to consider the potential application of state law (*e.g.*, state securities laws and business corporation laws) and other rules."[15]

IV. Publicity Guidelines During the Offering Process: Web Sites and Other Communications

Companies should be aware that any information they post on their Web sites, whether in the context of an offering or otherwise, may be construed as a corporate communication upon which investment decisions may be made and, therefore, as to which the Company may have potential liability. Web site communications will be evaluated in this context whether or not they are intended for such purpose and whether they are related to product, marketing, business or financial information.[16] All Web site communications should be reviewed regularly, dated, evaluated for continued accuracy and relevance, and removed as they become stale or irrelevant.

In addition, when a company is offering securities or conducting a proxy solicitation or a tender offer, care must be taken that any information that is posted on the Web site during that period, particularly information commenting on such offer, proxy solicitation or tender offer, is consistent with the statutory and regulatory requirements. In the absence of specific Commission guidance concerning publicity and the use of electronic media, traditional regulatory publicity guidelines would apply to the use of Web sites by companies contemplating or engaged in a securities offering or proxy solicitation.

Since the Internet is, in the simplest sense, a publicity vehicle, the publicity guidelines in the context of registered offerings are directly relevant to the question of the permissible use of Web sites by companies contemplating or engaged in a securities offering.

A. Registered Offerings: Securities Act Framework

The Securities Act imposes significant restrictions on publicity that "conditions the market" for proposed securities offerings and on offers of securities. One basic premise of the Securities Act is that investment decisions should be based principally on a prospectus meeting the statutory requirements of Section 10 of the Securities Act.

Under Section 5(c) of the Securities Act, no offers, written or oral, can be made before a registration statement is on file with the Commission. The Commission interprets "offer" broadly to include any communication that conditions the market or arouses public interest in the securities.[17] Thus, the publication of information by a company of information on its Web site may be an illegal offer of securities and thus constitute "gun-jumping"—which could delay effectiveness—if it is found to condition the market for an upcoming securities offering. Rule 135(a) and (b) allow limited announcements of upcoming offerings prior to the registration statement; inclusion of such announcements on the company's Web site should not be a problem.[18]

Once a registration statement is filed, there is no restriction on oral offers, although they remain subject to Section 12(a)(2)[19] liabilities and antifraud prohibitions. However, no "prospectus" other than one conforming to the requirements of Section 10 of the Securities Act may be used in connection with the offering.[20] The Securities Act defines the term "prospectus" broadly to encompass any written communication, and specifically includes any communication by radio or television.[21] By its terms, the definition of "prospectus" excludes:

- a limited notice of an offering that identifies the security and its price; from whom a Section 10 prospectus may be obtained; by whom the orders will be executed; and such other information as permitted by the Commission;[22] and

- written materials used after the effective date of a registration statement, *provided* a written prospectus meeting the requirements of

Section 10(a) (*i.e.*, a final prospectus) is sent or given to the person prior to or with such materials.[23]

Once the registration statement is effective, sales may be made under Section 5(a). However, a final prospectus is required to be delivered to an investor before or accompanying a confirmation of the sale.[24]

Publication of information on a Web site or by e-mail is viewed by the Commission as a written communication (with some exception for electronic roadshow).[25] Therefore, such communication, if found to condition the market or offer for sale the securities covered by the registration statement, would constitute a prospectus and would be subject to the same limitations during the offering process as any other written communication.

Since the Commission has not yet addressed how Web site communications outside the four corners of formal offering documents will be viewed for liability purposes, heightened sensitivity needs to be paid to Web site management during the registration process. Companies should put in place procedures to assure that no information that can be viewed as conditioning the market for their securities in violation of Section 5 is disseminated over their Web sites. As a guideline, companies should:

- Forgo establishing a new Web site or materially expanding the scope of an existing Web site until the offering is completed.

- Continue to use their Web sites consistent with past practice for ordinary course corporate communications, product marketing and advertising, but should not launch or substantially expand an image campaign.

- Limit any discussion of the offering outside the prospectus to those communications permitted by Rules 134 and 135 under the Securities Act.

- Review all information before it is posted; the review should include legal review to address compliance issues.

- Assure information is current and remove information that is no longer factually correct; continued publication on the Web site may suggest continued relevance or accuracy, or constitute republication.

- Avoid posting documents containing overly enthusiastic statements, or hype, regarding current or anticipated performance.

- Beware of hyperlinking, especially from a posted prospectus. Any information hyperlinked to a prospectus may be considered to be delivered with the prospectus and may be viewed as incorporated by reference into the prospectus.

- Avoid posting or hyperlinking to an analyst's report; a company may be viewed as adopting the report and may become responsible for its contents.

In general, the publication of ordinary course press releases relating to business developments, advertising, product and marketing information and, if it is a reporting company, Exchange Act reports should not be viewed as conditioning the market in violation of Section 5. In addition, preliminary prospectuses and final prospectuses may be published on a company's Web site.[26] There has been concern, however, regarding whether publication of a prospectus on a Web site would be viewed as importing other Web site information into the prospectus or render it part of the offering effort. Although the Commission has not spoken directly to the issue, its recent no-action position that placing an issuer's Web site address in the prospectus does not, by itself, include or incorporate by reference the contents of its Web site would appear to support the view that posting the prospectus on the Web site should not implicate other communications on the Web site. The prospectus and other offering communications should be on its own home page and clearly segregated from other information. Lack of Commission guidance on this point is one of the factors inhibiting greater use of electronic communications to meet disclosure requirements.

B. Private Placements/Regulation D Offerings

The basic rationale underlying the private placement exemption available under Section 4(2) of the Securities Act is the absence of general solicitation or advertising. The October Release makes it clear that, without implementing procedures to restrict access to a class of permitted purchasers, the Commission views placement of private offering materials on a company's Web site as clearly violating the prohibition against general solicitation or advertising.[27]

The Commission has taken the position in a recent no-action letter that the qualification of accredited or sophisticated investors, and the posting of a notice of a private offering in a password-protected page on the company's Web site accessible only to IPONET members who have so qualified, would not involve a "general solicitation."[28] (IPONET has a home page and other linked pages on the World Wide Web through which companies and their underwriters distribute tombstone advertisements and preliminary prospectuses.)

In taking this position, the Commission noted that (1) the invitation to complete a qualifying investor questionnaire would be generic and would not refer to any specific transaction posted or to be posted on the password-protected page of IPONET;

(2) the password-protected page of IPONET would be available only after the investor was determined by the underwriter to be accredited; and (3) a potential investor could purchase securities only after qualification and only in transactions posted on the password-protected page of IPONET.

Of course, private offering materials may be transmitted to prospective purchasers who have been identified without a general solicitation and who have given proper consent to electronic delivery.[29]

Companies proposing to conduct an unregistered offering (whether a private placement or an offshore offering) may believe they have a duty to announce the proposed offering. Rule 135c permits an issuer reporting under the Exchange Act (and certain foreign private issuers exempt from Exchange Act reporting under Rule 12g3-2(b) of the Exchange Act) to publish a notice of an unregistered offering of securities, *provided* that such notice meets certain specified conditions.[30] Rule 135c provides that such a notice will not be deemed to be an "offer" of securities for purposes of Section 5 of the Securities Act; Rule 502(c) of Regulation D provides that such a notice will not be deemed to constitute a general solicitation or general advertising under Regulation D; and Regulation S provides that such a notice will not be deemed to be a directed selling effort. It is likely that the Commission would permit a Rule 135c notice to be posted on an issuer's Web site.

C. Electronic and Internet Road Shows

1. Background

Introduced in the 1970s, roadshows today are an integral part of a securities offering, whether a public offering registered under the Securities Act or an exempt Rule 144A quasi-public style distribution.[31] In addition to marketing the specific securities being offered, the roadshow helps the issuer develop strong and ongoing investor interest in the company. Depending on the size and nature of the offering, the roadshow can consist of a series of meetings in the United States and frequently abroad, lasting from several days to several weeks, at which management makes presentations to potential investors and provides them with the opportunity to ask questions. Driven by institutional demand and a desire on the part of issuers to develop long-term relationships with institutional investors, roadshows today commonly include one-on-one meetings between key management and major potential institutional investors. More interactive, and less scripted than the more traditional group sessions, these meetings enable investors to explore more fully, in a question and answer format, the prospects of an issuer and the merits of an offering. They also give management an opportunity to adapt its presentation accordingly and gauge investor interest more quickly. These one-on-one meetings are subject to the same regulatory regime as the more traditional group roadshow presentations.

The SEC staff has issued several no-action letters addressing the issues raised by electronic roadshows as discussed below. Cathy Dixon, Chief Counsel of the Division of

Corporation Finance, speaking at the February 1998 "SEC Speaks" conference advised that persons, in addition to the requesting parties, may rely on the no-action letters.

2. Roadshows and the Statutory Framework under the Securities Act

a. *Registered Offerings*.

As discussed above, communications by radio or television in connection with an offering are treated as written communications under Section 5. The term "prospectus" is defined broadly under Section 2(a)(10) as "any notice, advertisement, or communication, written or by radio or television, which offers a security for sale or confirms the sale of a security" (emphasis added). It is this reference to radio and television in Section 2(a)(10)'s definition of "prospectus" that has, until recently, largely foreclosed the use of electronic communications to conduct roadshows.

b. *Rule 144A Offerings*.

Roadshows also are frequently used in exempt Rule 144A offerings. In these offerings, the critical concern is to assure that the roadshow is conducted in a manner consistent with the prohibition on general solicitation and general advertising. Thus, the principal focus will be on assuring that those invited to, and attending, the roadshow are sophisticated investors to whom the issuer may appropriately offer the securities under Section 4(2) of the Securities Act. Unlike in the context of a registered offering, there is no statutory restriction on the use and distribution of written materials at a Rule 144A roadshow. Steps should be taken, however, to keep any such materials confidential and preclude their public distribution which could result in a general solicitation. Typically, because of concerns that such materials run the risk of being viewed as offering material for liability purposes, only the offering circular will be distributed at the Rule 144A roadshow. The SEC staff issued a no-action letter to Net Roadshow involving the use of electronic roadshows in a Rule 144A placement.[32]

3. Electronic Roadshow No-Action Letters

a. *Private Financial Network No-Action Letter*

In March 1997, reflecting the Commission's policy of encouraging the use of electronic media to communicate with investors,[33] the Commission staff issued a no-action letter to Private Financial Network ("PFN") to allow it to broadcast road shows electronically to its subscribers.[34] While on its face a modest first step, the PFN no-action letter lays the groundwork for allowing the road show process to take full advantage of the electronic communications technology that is radically changing the capital markets. It also potentially opens road shows to the investing public.

PFN, a private network and wholly owned subsidiary of MSNBC Interactive LLC, a joint venture of the National Broadcasting Co., Inc. and Microsoft Corporation, provides business and financial coverage in multimedia format and was established as a companion to a textual research service. PFN requested that the Commission staff issue a no-action letter that would permit it to broadcast road shows electronically, either live or on a delayed basis, over a private network to its subscribers. PFN noted that it currently has fewer than 100 subscribers, principally broker-dealers and investment advisers. In its request for no-action relief, PFN undertook to (i) limit the availability of the video transmission of the road show to PFN subscribers who agreed not to videotape, copy or distribute the broadcast; (ii) ensure that each subscriber receives a copy of the prospectus, as filed with the Commission, prior to any transmission of the road show; (iii) require issuers and underwriters to take reasonable steps to ensure that information disclosed in the road show was not inconsistent with the filed prospectus; and (iv) include in each transmission a text "crawl" referring viewers to the filed prospectus for more information about the offering and containing a prohibition on videotaping, copying, distribution or use in the sale of securities to the general public; road shows broadcast prior to effectiveness were required to include a visual presentation of the legend required by Rule 134(b) under the Securities Act.

In requesting relief, PFN posited that its proposed controlled transmissions by KU satellite, T1 telephone circuits and fiber optic and other cable were not within the scope of the reference to radio or television in Section 2(a)(10)'s definition of "prospectus"[35] and therefore were not prospectuses. PFN contended that the statutory reference to radio and television is to broadcasting, not to the use of radio or television technology for closed circuit or other controlled retransmission of non-prospectus materials.[36] Citing *Gustafson v. Alloyd Co., Inc.*,[37] PFN reasoned that "prospectus" as used in Section 2(a)(10) is "intended to reach only those documents or communications that are widely disseminated to an undifferentiated public rather than to a discreet, invited audience."[38]

Without discussion, the Commission staff agreed that it would not recommend enforcement action to the Commission if PFN transmitted a company's road show to PFN's subscribers for the purposes and pursuant to the procedures described in the letter and in reliance on company counsel's opinion that such transmissions are not prospectuses within the meaning of Section 2(a)(10). While PFN's request cites a number of factors upon which the staff could have based its no-action response, the staff did not give any guidance in its response as to its analysis of the issue or the rationale for its no-action position. Based on the statutory framework and the facts presented by PFN, it would appear that there were two key factors underlying the staff's no-action position. First is PFN's assurance that all persons to whom the road show was broadcast would have a copy of the prospectus at the time of the broadcast. Second is PFN's undertaking to incorporate into the broadcast effective reminders to the investor of the availability of detailed information about the issuer and the offering in the prospectus.

b. *Net Road Show, Inc. No-Action Letter*

On September 9, 1997, the Commission's staff issued a no-action letter authorizing the transmission of a road show over the Internet. The letter goes beyond PFN largely by clarifying that the Internet is a permissible medium for road show transmissions. It also indicates that electronic access need not be based on a subscription process. Like PFN, the Commission staff's no-action position continues to reflect concern that viewers (i) have available to them, and appreciate the importance of, the filed prospectus, (ii) not have unlimited opportunities to view the road show and (iii) not have the ability to tape or distribute it. Also, like PFN, the Commission's position is narrowly drawn.

In its request for no-action relief, Net Roadshow, Inc. ("Net Roadshow"), a company proposing to provide road shows for public offerings over the Internet, represented the following:

- The road shows would not be transmitted prior to the filing of a registration statement with the Commission.
- The transmission would be restricted to institutional investors having an access code that would be changed each day, and viewing would be permitted for one day only.
- The Internet road show would be the "exact same road show" as the live road show (*i.e.*, the live road show would have to be filmed in its entirety, including the entire question and answer ("Q&A") segment).
- A periodic text "crawl" would alert viewers to any material developments arising between the taping of the road show and its Internet transmission.
- Viewers would be advised on-screen, and required to agree to not copy, distribute or download the road show.
- A periodic text "crawl" would remind viewers of the importance of viewing the filed prospectus.
- Viewers would have continuous access during the transmission to the filed prospectus and would be able to print it at any time.
- Issuers and underwriters would be required to assure that information presented in the road show was not inconsistent with either the filed prospectus or the live road show.

- Editing would not be permitted. Nor would viewers be permitted to access selected segments of the road show; it would have to be viewed in its entirety.

c. *Bloomberg L.P. No-Action Letter*

In October 1997, a third electronic roadshow letter was issued by SEC staff to Bloomberg; the letter generally contained comparable conditions to the earlier letters. However, the submission by Bloomberg makes clear that viewers will be able to view less than the entire roadshow if they wish, and the presentation may be organized in such a fashion to provide an agenda of specific segments of the roadshow. Given the extensive subscriber base for Bloomberg, one can fairly assume that the SEC staff has determined that the number of viewers is not an issue, provided that each viewer is an "institutional investors, investment adviser or other person of a type the underwriter would customarily invite to a roadshow . . .". The Bloomberg letter also makes clear that the required delivery of the preliminary prospectus to viewers could be effected by a hyperlink to the preliminary prospectus filed on Edgar; paper delivery would not be required if the viewer had consented to electronic delivery.

d. *Net Roadshow, Inc. No-Action Letter*. Most recently, the SEC staff provided a no-action letter that addressed the use of electronic roadshows in the context of a Rule 144A placement.[39] The letter provides for electronic roadshows on the following basis:

- viewers limited to QIBs;

- confidential password unique to the specific roadshow and will expire at the termination of the offering;

- representations from the seller that the viewers are QIBs, the offering is exempt and only QIBs have received a password; and

- the Company broadcasting the roadshow is not affiliated with the seller or the issuer.

Given the IPONET no-action letter[40] that permitted electronic communications with private placees, counsel may conclude that so long as access to the roadshow is properly limited to avoid a general solicitation, electronic roadshows may be used in a variety of contexts outside the parameters of the 144A Net Roadshow letter.

D. Proxy Solicitations and Annual Meetings

U.S. companies with securities registered under Section 12 of the Exchange Act are subject to the Commission's proxy rules. Rule 14a-3 prohibits the solicitation of proxies unless the shareholder being solicited is furnished a proxy statement containing the information specified in Schedule 14A regarding matters to be considered at the meeting. The company has to file all proxy soliciting material with the Commission.[41] Solicitation of a proxy is broadly defined to include any "communication to security holders under circumstances reasonably calculated to result in the procurement, withholding or revocation of a proxy."[42] Thus, care must be taken that any communication posted on a Web site that would be viewed as a solicitation is filed with the Commission. In addition, Rule 14a-9 imposes liability on any person who solicits a proxy "by means of any proxy statement, form of proxy, notice of meeting or other communication, written or oral," containing any false or misleading statements, or omission of any material fact.

Internet technology also facilitates communications among shareholders with regard to shareholder proposals and provides them with an inexpensive means of soliciting shareholder support for their proposals.[43] Internet communications will enable shareholders to realize the full potential of the Commission's 1992 proxy reform which sought to remove the regulatory barriers and lower the costs of shareholder communications by exempting such communications from the proxy statement filing and disclosure requirements.[44]

The Internet also could enable shareholders to disseminate on a cost-effective basis more information than would otherwise be permitted under the shareholder proposal rule. While a shareholder proposal is limited to no more than 500 words, a shareholder could include in its proposal a statement that additional information regarding the proposal may be found either on its Web site, giving its Web site address, or if it does not have its own Web site, on the Web site of a independent Internet newsgroup to which it subscribes.

E. Use of Web Sites in Offshore Offerings

Issues with respect to the use of Web sites by non-U.S. companies are more complex and require heightened sensitivity as to how to manage an offshore Web site in the context of an offering. In international and global offerings, securities are frequently offered in jurisdictions in which the customary practice is to broadly disseminate publicity as a means of generating investor interest. Further, including offering documents and other publicity about an offering on a company's Web site is not uncommon. In its release adopting Regulation S, the Commission specifically provides for these offshore publicity practices stating that:

> The Regulation generally will not interfere with activities conducted outside the United States, if such activities are legal and customary in the foreign jurisdiction. Such activities may relate to a foreign distribution or to the ordinary course of an issuer's business. In this regard, activities carried out abroad such as advertising in newspapers or magazines with no general circulation in the United States or granting interviews or conducting promotional seminars outside the United States and not targeted to the United States will not preclude reliance on the Regulation's safe harbor.[45]

Typically, non-U.S. issuers regard publication on their Web sites as conduct outside the United States. In its new Web Site Release, the Commission has provided guidance as to the circumstances in which it would view Web site communications with respect to offshore offerings as activity outside the United States for purposes of Section 5 of the Securities Act. The basic principle underlying the Commission's interpretation is that Web site communications not targeted to the United States should be viewed as activity outside the United States. Key to demonstrating that the communications are not targeted to the United States is the implementation of "measures that are reasonably designed to guard against sales . . . to U.S. persons."

The Commission notes that the adequacy of measures will depend on the facts and circumstances, and can be satisfied through different means. U.S. issuers are specifically cautioned by the Commission to undertake more restrictive measures than would be required of non-U.S. issuers when using the Internet to solicit offshore securities transactions. In general, the Web Site Release seems to suggest that U.S. issuers would likely have to resort to some means to limit U.S. investors access to the Web site offering communications. Non-U.S. issuers on the other hand may rely on procedures to protect against sales and the use of disclosures to make clear offer is not being made in the United States.

Antifraud prohibitions will still apply to the Web site offerings. The Commission warns in the Web Site Release "even in the absence of sales in the United States, we will take appropriate enforcement action whenever we believe that fraudulent or manipulative Internet activities have originated in the United States or placed U.S. investors at risk."

The Commission states in the Web Site Release that it would generally not consider an offshore Internet offer made by a non-U.S. offeror as targeted at the United States, if:

- the Web site includes a prominent disclaimer making it clear that the offer is directed only to countries other than the United States; and

- the offeror and underwriters implement procedures that are reasonably designed to guard against sales to U.S. persons in the offshore offering.

Notwithstanding the foregoing, solicitations that appear by their content to be targeted at U.S. persons will be viewed as being made in the U.S.; for example, if the solicitation included a discussion of the U.S. tax benefits of the investment.

In the event that notwithstanding the issuer's implementation of reasonable procedures, a U.S. person circumvents the procedures and buys the securities, the Commission makes clear that the circumvention would not, in and of itself, cause the Commission to consider the offer to be targeted at U.S. persons so long as the issuer did not have reason to believe the buyer was a U.S. person. However, frequent circumventions may cause the reasonableness of the procedures to be questioned.

If the non-U.S. offeror is undertaking a private offering in the United States at the same time it is conducting an offshore offering using an Internet solicitation, the Commission suggests that additional procedures should be implemented to protect against the Internet communications resulting in the solicitation of investors in the exempt offering. The Web Site Release makes clear, however, that ". . . any investor solicited by the issuer or underwriter prior to or independent of the Web site posting could participate in the private offer, regardless of whether the investor may have viewed the posted offshore offering materials."[46] The Internet posting should only relate to the offshore offering.

The Web Site Release offers little guidance as to appropriate procedures in the context of a registered U.S. offering and a concurrent Internet offshore offering by a non-U.S. issuer. In fact, the only guidance provided is a warning that "premature posting of offering information must be avoided" and a cite to Rule 135.

Similar issues arise under the laws of other jurisdictions. For example, under the U.K. Financial Services Act of 1986 (the "FSA"), material posted on a Web site could be regarded as an "investment advertisement," or offering material, which is prohibited from being issued in the United Kingdom if it has not been approved by a person authorized under the FSA.[47] The U.K. Securities and Investment Board (the "SIB") views any advertisement issued outside the United Kingdom as having been issued in the United Kingdom if it is directed at persons in the United Kingdom or made available to them other than by way of a periodical published or circulated principally outside the United Kingdom.[48] This policy reportedly is under review.

For this reason, material posted on the Internet by U.S. issuers could subject such issuers to liability under the FSA depending on the extent to which U.K. investors need the protections of the SIB, whether any offer was, in fact, directed at prospective U.K. investors and the degree to which the issuer took steps to prevent persons in the United Kingdom from gaining access to the material. Accordingly, the SIB has advised that issuers control access to their sites to avoid breaching the FSA.[49] The SIB has also stated that disclaimers to the effect that the material is not aimed at, or intended to be viewed by, persons in the United Kingdom, although they may discourage inquiries, are not sufficient to avoid the advertisement being issued in the United Kingdom if, as a matter of fact, it is received by persons in the United Kingdom.[50]

V. SEC Guidance on Specific Uses of Web Sites

Preliminary Prospectuses

A company may post a preliminary prospectus on its Web site. It should be updated in the same respects as would a paper version, although the company need only send notice of updates to persons who are expected to purchase securities in the offering.[51] The Web site should also be made available to all persons to whom the company expects to sell securities in reliance on electronic delivery.[52]

Final Prospectuses

A company will satisfy its prospectus delivery obligations via electronic media with respect to investors who have either consented to electronic delivery or actually accessed the document on the Web site if it places its final prospectus on a Web site and confirms sales by mail with a notice that states that the final prospectus is available on the Web site and provides the Internet address.[53] In the case of a continuous offering, the prospectus should remain available for as long as the company will rely on its delivery through the electronic medium.[54]

Mixed-Medium Prospectus

A company may also satisfy its prospectus delivery obligations by delivering a "mixed-medium final prospectus." Accordingly, even if a preliminary prospectus is placed on a company's Web site, the company may, upon effectiveness of its registration statement, deliver in paper format (most likely with confirmations) a term sheet pursuant to Securities Act Rule 434.[55]

Graphic, Image and Audio Information

If a company produces more than one version of a prospectus and one version contains material graphic, image or audio information, either version can be used to satisfy the company's delivery requirements so long as each complies with the applicable provisions of the securities laws and the company discloses the availability of the other version. The company, however, is under no obligation to deliver the other version.[56] Nor is it required to include in the delivered version a fair and accurate description or transcript of the omitted information, as was originally proposed.[57] Each version must be filed with the Commission as part of the company's registration statement or separately pursuant to Rule 497. Alternatively, the company may file with the Commission, as an appendix to the prospectus, a script of a movie, for example, together with a fair and accurate narrative description of the image material.[58]

CD-ROM Prospectuses

Companies are beginning to distribute CD-ROM with their prospectuses. Recent examples include Ameritrade Holdings Corporation ("Ameritrade"), an Omaha, Nebraska discount brokerage that offers securities trading on the Internet, and Sulzer Medica, a Swiss medical technology company that recently conducted an initial public offering of registered shares and American Depositary Receipts. Each company included a CD-ROM demonstration of its products and services, and Sulzer Medica included a description of its facilities. Ameritrade included its whole prospectus on the CD-ROM; Sulzer Medica did not. Each company filed a screen-by-screen script of the accompanying narrative with the Commission. Sulzer Medica also filed copies of the screens themselves. Ameritrade included the script as an appendix in its prospectus; Sulzer Medica included it as an exhibit to the registration statement.

In both cases, the CD-ROM was part of the prospectus and so stated; this is necessary to allow it to be used prior to distribution of a final prospectus.

Given the logistics and the expenses of production, and the fact that production delays are not built into the registered offering process, companies wishing to distribute a CD-ROM are advised to:

- Plan ahead and provide for advanced production.

- Include the CD-ROM, together with the script, at the time the preliminary prospectus is filed. The Commission will want to view it as part of the initial filing.

- Note that the Commission staff may have comments on the CD-ROM or prospectus which might necessitate changes to the CD-ROM. If time is of the essence, the content of the CD-ROM could be simplified to minimize the possibility of having to make last minute changes, rehire actors and production crew and reshoot any segments.

The logistical problems associated with CD-ROM production are exacerbated for EDGAR filers who, under current Commission requirements, are obligated to file electronically a detailed description of each screen comprising the CD-ROM.[59] Although Ameritrade is an EDGAR filer, its visuals were modest in comparison to the film and graphics techniques that technology affords, and it was permitted to satisfy this requirement by including within the script a simple narrative description of each visual image. With more complex visuals and voiceovers, montages and fast-paced editing, an unqualified obligation to describe each frame will be onerous, if not substantively useless. Whether the Commission will grant relief in these circumstances remains to be seen.

Sales Literature[60]

Just as sales literature may be used to market securities after a registration statement is declared effective, *provided* it is preceded or accompanied by a final prospectus,[61] sales literature may be linked to a final prospectus[62] on a company's Web site so long as the prospectus and the sales literature are accessible from the same menu on the Web site, and are clearly identified and appear in close proximity to each other in the menu.[63] The sales literature may be accessed before viewing or downloading the prospectus, and may take the form of any medium, including graphics, pictures and multimedia.

A company may mail sales literature to investors who receive effective delivery of the final prospectus via the Internet so long as notice of the availability of the final prospectus and its Web site location are clearly highlighted in the forepart of the literature.[64]

The prospectus delivery obligation may also be satisfied by placing sales literature in a discussion forum on a Web site, *provided* that a hyperlink to the final prospectus is included.[65] The hyperlink function enables the final prospectus to be viewed as if it were packaged in the same envelope as the sales literature.[66]

Hyperlinking to Other Web Sites

The hyperlink function provides direct and immediate access from one Web site to another. The October Release has taken the position that "provid[ing] the ability to access information located on another Web site almost instantaneously"[67] through hyperlinking associates the two Web pages as a single electronic document (as would mailing two documents in a single envelope), for which the company may be potentially liable. In discussing access to mandated disclosure, the Commission has stated that "if an investor must proceed through a confusing series of ever changing menus to access a required document so that it is not reasonable to expect that access would generally occur, this procedure would likely be viewed as unduly burdensome."[68] So, too, would requiring "additional software."[69] Although the Commission has not specifically addressed the extent or parameters of potential liability to which a company may be subject in connection with statements made by a third party in a hyperlinked document, a number of its examples suggests that there may be potential liability; in essence, the company may be viewed as having adopted or ratified the information by the hyperlink. The Commission staff has applied the same theory where a company sends out third party information.

Until the Commission addresses the issue, companies should be aware that they are potentially liable for third party hyperlinked statements. Accordingly, they may wish to consider qualifying a hyperlinked document with a disclaimer of responsibility for, or endorsement of, its contents, even in the absence of precedent on the legal effect of such a disclaimer.

Research Reports[70]

A hyperlink to a research report may be viewed as analogous to including a paper version of the report in the same envelope used to mail a preliminary prospectus. Since, during the waiting period, a company may make offers only through the use of a preliminary prospectus, posting a research report on the company's Web site or providing access to it through a hyperlink to an analyst's Web site during this period could run afoul of Section 5 of the Securities Act, unless the research report were made part of the prospectus.[71]

Hyperlinking to an analyst's report, or perhaps even referencing the report on the company's Web site, may be viewed as adoption by the company of the report, thereby making the company responsible for its contents. If the company elects to list on its Web site analysts who follow it, it should list all analysts, not just those publishing favorable reports, and should not list them in order of the strength of their favorable recommendation.

Tombstone Advertisements

Tombstone advertisements that otherwise comply with Securities Act Rule 134 may be placed on the company's Web site.[72] It is also permissible to place the electronic address of the underwriter from whom a paper version of a prospectus can be obtained on a printed tombstone for the purpose of obtaining materials.[73]

Rule 135 and Rule 135c Announcements

Like Rule 134 announcements, Rule 135 and Rule 135c announcements would be permitted to be posted on a Web site; the rules do not draw any distinction with respect to the medium of communication among the several types of announcements.

Fund Prospectuses and Prospectus Updates

When a fund materially amends a prospectus, an electronic version of which has been placed on its Web site, the fund may satisfy its prospectus delivery obligations by (i) sending a postcard or e-mail to persons to whom a prospectus has been delivered through electronic means or who have consented to electronic delivery, notifying them of the availability of the amended prospectus, or (ii) sending a paper copy of the amended prospectus to investors, including those who consented to receive documents electronically.[74] With respect to a scheduled prospectus update, the use of a newsletter or statement would constitute sufficient notice for effective delivery.[75] (Similarly, a fund that transmits annual and semiannual reports electronically can satisfy its notice and delivery obligation each time a shareholder report is posted by including notification in the preceding quarterly account statement informing investors of the date by which the report will be available.)[76]

Annual Reports and Proxy Statements

A company may deliver its annual reports and proxy statements to consenting shareholders by posting them on its Web site and providing effective notice of their availability. Mere posting alone would not be sufficient to constitute delivery to all shareholders.

Annual reports should remain available electronically for a sufficient length of time for the delivery requirements to be satisfied, and both they and proxy soliciting materials should be made available on the Web site until votes have been cast and the meeting to which they relate has been adjourned.[77]

If a company places its annual report and proxy solicitation on its Web site and provides investors timely and appropriate notice, an investor who has consented to electronic delivery via the Web site may print the proxy card from the Web site, execute it and mail it to the company.[78] Instructing the record holders to electronically vote their proxies would also conform to the proxy rule requirements. Exercising the proxy would show that the shareholder had actual access to the information, thereby satisfying the delivery requirements. The proxy statement should be placed on the Web site in time to permit compliance with the requirements of applicable corporation law, the proxy rules, the rules of the exchanges on which the company's securities are listed and the company's bylaws.

A printed advertisement in accordance with Exchange Act Rule 14a-2(a)(6) may also be used to indicate the availability of proxy soliciting materials and the location of an Internet Web site.

E-Mail to Employees as Delivery Option

The placing by a company of a prospectus for its securities on its internal e-mail system would satisfy delivery obligations with respect to employees who use the company's e-mail system in the course of performing their duties, or who are expected to have an alternative means made available to receive e-mail messages.[79]

Press Releases and Other Communications

A company may wish to provide its shareholders and investors with copies of the reports it files with the Commission, such as quarterly reports on Form 10-Q and current reports on Form 8-K. It may also wish to provide access to press releases about the company. The company can put this information on its Web site if it chooses to do so, without any requirement for ensuring notice or access, as there is no requirement to deliver such materials to shareholders. However, as discussed below, posting of such information may raise concerns under Section 5 of the Securities Act, as well as under the proxy or tender offer rules.

Web Site Address

A company may place its Web site address in its prospectus; its appearance will not, by itself, incorporate by reference into the prospectus information posted on its Web site[80] or render everything published on its Web site as part of the selling effort. In two recent no-action letters, the Commission stated that:

> [T]he identification by a company of its Web site address and the statement "[o]ur SEC filings are also available to the public from our Web site" will not, by itself, include or incorporate by reference any information into the registration statement that is included or hot linked to the issuer's regular Web site that is not

otherwise incorporated by reference into the registration statement.[81]

Moreover, the Commission, in its Proposed Rule on Plain English Disclosure,[82] is encouraging companies to give their Internet address in offering documents, if one is available. The Commission specifically stated in its recent no-action letters, however, that its position "does not address any other federal securities law issues that may arise through publication of information on the Web site."[83]

DRIPS

A company may announce its unregistered Dividend Reinvestment Plan (the "DRIP") on its Web site so long as the information is limited to the announcement of the DRIP and the name and address of the independent agent from whom additional information can be obtained. As with paper, a company may not use its Web site to advertise the DRIP, nor may it provide a hyperlink to DRIP materials.

ESOPS

Putting prospectuses for employee stock option plans ("ESOPS") on a Web site will satisfy the delivery requirements to employees if they have access to computers in the normal course of performing their duties as employees, and would be expected to be able to access the information. The consent of these employees would not be necessary; however, they would need to be provided with notice. The notice must include information on how to access the document through the local area network, and on how to obtain a paper version of the document. The notice could be distributed over e-mail if the employees have access to it, and would be expected to log on routinely.

Optional Documents

A company may wish to provide its shareholders and investors with copies of the reports it files with the Commission, such as quarterly reports on Form 10-Q and current reports on Form 8-K. It may also wish to provide access to press releases about the company. The company can put this information on-line if it chooses to do so, without any requirement for ensuring notice or access, as there is no requirement to deliver such materials to shareholders.

VI. Open Issues

The October Release addresses only the procedural aspects of electronic delivery. Although the Commission has stated that "the liability provisions of the federal securities laws (namely, the antifraud provisions in Section 10(b) of the Exchange Act and Rule 10b-5 thereunder and Section 17(b) of the Securities Act) apply equally to electronic and paper-based media," it has not yet addressed potential securities law liability.

Accordingly, the scope of potential liability for information disseminated by a company on the Internet, whether through its own Web site or via hyperlinks to documents on another Web site, remains to be seen.

Issuers now have the benefit of reassurance from the Commission that information posted on their Web sites is not incorporated by reference into a prospectus containing their Web site address. Nonetheless, unless the Commission exempts from the definition of "offer," "prospectus" and "general solicitation" material that is included on a Web site in the ordinary course of business, there remains a basis for concern as to how Web site information not constituting part of the offering materials will be viewed for liability purposes and how, during the registration process, documents routinely published on an issuer's Web site (including ordinary course marketing materials) should be handled.

The following questions illustrate the nature of issues requiring Commission guidance:

- Are hyperlinks a part of the document such that issuers must take responsibility for the information contained in them? Does it matter whether the hyperlinked material is proprietary to the issuer or not?

- Can a company be said to adopt an analyst's report if the report is available on the company's Web site? What if the analyst's report is accessible only through a hyperlink to the analyst's Web site? What if the company only gives the name and Web site address of the analyst?

- Would a company be viewed as continuing to publish a document by virtue of not taking it off the Web site?

- Is continued access to information on the Internet a republication? Does a company have a duty to update such information?

- Are forums such as "chat rooms" deemed to be advertisements or sales literature subject to the advertising rules, given that they may be recorded or transcribed and used as advertisements or sales literature at a later date?

- Can a company respond to an inquiry or statement made in a chat room during the waiting period? Can the response include statements not contained in the statutory preliminary prospectus or would such statements constitute gun- jumping?

VII. Blue Sky Implications

The sweep of the Internet raises questions about the scope of state securities or "Blue Sky" laws in Internet offerings. Blue Sky laws impose registration or qualification requirements as a condition to the offer and sale of certain securities. The recently enacted National Securities Markets Improvement Act of 1996 preempts state regulation of securities listed on the New York Stock Exchange, the American Stock Exchange and the National Market System of the Nasdaq Stock Market, securities sold in certain exempt offerings and mutual funds. With respect to securities that fall outside the scope of preemption, however, an Internet offering will be subject to state regulation if it is accessible within the state, leaving open the question whether, absent an exemption, the offered securities would have to be registered in every state. In the absence of guidance, it may be prudent for issuers to include in any Internet prospectus a general legend to the effect that no offers or sales will be made in any jurisdiction in which such offer or sale is not qualified or otherwise exempt from regulation.

Not wanting to discourage the use of the Internet for offerings, Pennsylvania became the first state to address the regulatory issues in this context. Taking the position that "a communication on the Internet designed to raise capital for an issuer would constitute an offer for the purchase or sale of a security,"[84] as well as an advertisement, and thus "constitute a mass mailing, public media advertisement and general solicitation,"[85] the Pennsylvania Division of Corporation Finance issued an order exempting Internet offerings from state registration when (i) the issuer indicates that the securities are not being offered to persons in Pennsylvania, and that no offer or sale is intended to take place there; (ii) an offer is not being made or directed to persons in Pennsylvania by any other means (thus, an issuer could not send information about the offer in response to an e-mail message from a Pennsylvania resident); and (iii) no sales are made in Pennsylvania as a result of the Internet offer, including sales of securities that are the subject of the Internet offer or any other securities of the issuer.[86] A number of states are pursuing a similar course.

Concerned that potential inconsistency among the states could thwart the use of the Internet, NASAA passed a resolution in January 1996 (the "NASAA Internet Resolution") that provided relief from registration requirements for communications that might otherwise be regarded as "offers." NASAA has encouraged the adoption of the resolution by all states. Specifically, the NASAA Internet Resolution encourages states to allow sales of securities that are the subject of an Internet offer where one of two conditions is met: (i) no sale is made in any state until the offering has been registered and declared effective and the final prospectus has been delivered to the investor prior to such sale; or (ii) the sales are exempt from registration. Notably, the NASAA Internet Resolution provides that, in limited instances, an issuer who posts an offer to sell securities on the Internet may sell in a jurisdiction other than the one in which the offer was originally registered or exempt from registration. According to NASAA, thirty-one states have adopted the NASAA Internet Resolution and 16 states have indicated that they intend to adopt it.[87]

On March 9, 1997, NASAA proposed for public comment a model interpretive order under the Uniform Securities Act (the "Act")[88] regarding general advertising of products and services through the Internet by broker-dealers, investment advisers, agents and investment advisor representatives. The purpose of the proposed order is to clarify that broker-dealers and the like "who use the Internet to distribute information on available products and services will not be deemed to be 'transacting business' in [the] state for purposes of [those sections of the Act that prohibit persons from transacting business in the state as a broker-dealer or investment advisor unless they are registered under the Act]" if the following conditions are met: (i) the Internet communication (A) contains a legend stating that the person may only transact business in those states where he is registered or exempted, (B) contains a mechanism reasonably ensuring that any subsequent interaction with a prospective customer residing in a state where the person is not registered is limited so as not to trigger state licensing requirements and (C) does not involve the actual effecting of securities trades, or the rendering of advice, but is limited to the dissemination of information on products and services; and (ii) in the case of agents or representatives of a broker-dealer or investment advisor, (A) the broker-dealer or investment advisor affiliation is disclosed within the Internet communication, (B) the broker-dealer or investment advisor authorizes the Internet communication and retains responsibility for reviewing and approving its contents and (C) the agent is acting within the scope of its authority.

VIII. SEC Guidance for Broker-Dealers, Transfer Agents and Investment Advisers; Technical Rule Amendments

In May 1996, the Commission issued two releases, the "May Release,"[89] confirming that the principles of the October Release apply equally to communications by broker-dealers, transfer agents and investment advisers and providing additional illustrative examples, and a second release adopting technical rule amendments that adapted requirements premised on printed material to the use of electronic media.[90]

The May Release is intended to provide broker-dealers, transfer agents and investment advisers with guidance on how they may use electronic media to meet their delivery obligations to customers, securities holders and clients. The release provides a list of "Covered Delivery Requirements"; rules and requirements under the Exchange Act and the Investment Advisers Act that may be subject to electronic delivery. Among other things, the Release allows for the electronic delivery of confirmations under the Exchange Act. It also cautions broker-dealers and investment advisers to "take reasonable precautions to ensure the integrity, confidentiality and security of [personal financial] information, regardless of whether it is delivered through electronic means or in paper form."[91] In addition, to ensure that personal financial information can be delivered confidentially, informed consent must be obtained from the investor prior to electronic delivery. This consent ensures that the investor is willing to accept delivery of personal financial information electronically and has actual notice that it will be delivered in such manner.

The electronic transmission of non-mandated disclosure that is being provided to customers and clients voluntarily is not covered by the May Release and, therefore, need not conform to its guidance. Electronic advertising is also permitted under this Release provided it complies with the same requirements that apply to paper advertisements, such as the prohibition against misleading disclosure and applicable rules of the National Association of Securities Dealers, Inc. (the "NASD"), which were amended in 1995 specifically to include electronic communications.[92] According to the NASD, communications posted by members or their associates on electronic bulletin boards are considered advertisements subject to review by a registered principal, and filing with the NASD.[93]

Like the October Release, the May Release explicitly states that it does not affect the applicability of any self-regulatory organization rules or of any state laws.

The Technical Rules Release reflects the Commission's view that "the use of electronic media should be at least an equal alternative to the use of paper-based media."[94] Most importantly,

- When a document includes graphic, image or audio information that cannot be reproduced on EDGAR, the EDGAR filing must include a fair and accurate narrative description, tabular presentation or transcript of the omitted material.

- Rules requiring legends to be printed in red or bold-faced type may be satisfied by any presentation "reasonably calculated to draw attention to them."

- Rules identifying mailing as the delivery method should be read to allow the use of reasonably prompt alternative methods.

- The Commission makes electronic filings publicly available on the Internet within 24 hours of acceptance. Registrants are now required to include a statement that electronic filings are publicly available on the Commission's Web site.

- Registrants are also required to include a statement in the prospectus that the Commission maintains a Web site that contains reports, proxy and information statements and other information regarding registrants that file electronically with the Commission.

IX. Offerings on the Internet

Real Goods Trading Corporation

In June 1996, the Commission issued its first no-action letter with respect to Internet "bulletin board" stock trading.[95] Real Goods Trading Corporation ("Real Goods"), a California corporation that sells alternative energy and conservation products primarily through mail order, proposed to establish an on-line trading system for its common stock, which is registered under Section 12 of the Exchange Act and traded on the Pacific Stock Exchange. The on-line system would serve as an informational bulletin board and would include contact information for prospective buyers and sellers of Real Goods' common stock. In its letter to the Commission, Real Goods described the system as follows:

- Transactions would be effected wholly independent of the system.
- Real Goods would play no role in effecting such transactions and would receive no compensation for creating or maintaining the system.
- Real Goods' operation of the system would not constitute an offer to sell or solicitation of an offer to buy Real Goods stock.
- Real Goods would provide an on-line disclaimer that it was not a registered national securities exchange, securities information processor, broker-dealer or investment adviser.
- Real Goods would inform users that federal and state securities laws would apply to offers and sales and that registration requirements would apply absent an exemption.

The Commission granted Real Goods the no-action relief requested, stating that offers and sales of securities made through an on-line trading system of the type described by Real Goods were not required to be registered under the Securities Act and that Real Goods may maintain the system without registering as an investment advisor under the Investment Advisers Act of 1940, or as a broker-dealer or securities exchange under the Exchange Act. In taking this position, the Commission noted the foregoing representations made by Real Goods and set forth the following additional requirements, among others:

- Real Goods would be required to keep records of all quotes entered into the system and make them available to the Commission and any exchange on which the securities were listed.
- Real Goods would not participate in any purchase or sale negotiations and would not provide any information regarding the advisability of buying or selling the stock.

- Real Goods would not receive, transfer or hold funds or securities as part of its operation of the system.

The Real Goods no-action letter reflects the Commission's support for Internet trading.

PerfectData Corporation & The Flamemaster Corporation

In August and October 1996, the Commission issued no-action letters concerning other Internet "off the grid" trading systems proposed to be established by PerfectData Corporation ("PERF")[96] and The Flamemaster Corporation ("Flamemaster"),[97] respectively. Like Real Goods' trading system, these systems would function as passive "bulletin boards" providing information to prospective sellers and buyers of common stock. Each system was described as being functionally identical to that of Real Goods, and the Commission staff granted the no-action relief requested based on conditions comparable to those on which Real Goods' no-action relief was based.

Spring Street Brewing Company

Spring Street Brewing Company ("Spring Street"), a New York microbrewery, conducted its initial public offering through the use of the Internet without the involvement of an underwriter. Spring Street's offering was made pursuant to Regulation A, which provides an exemption from registration under the Securities Act for public offerings by nonreporting companies of up to $5 million. Spring Street solicited investors by transmitting its offering circular on its Web site.

Following the offering, Spring Street's president and chief executive officer received more than 600 calls from companies seeking information about the Internet offering process and subsequently established Wit Capital, a new company that offers investment banking services in connection with Internet-based offerings. In an informal letter from the Commission's Divisions of Market Regulation and Corporation Finance to Spring Street,[98] the Commission addressed regulatory issues raised by Wit Trade, Wit Capital's bulletin board-based stock-trading mechanism, and suggested that the following steps be taken:

- Spring Street should eliminate any control it has over investor funds by having a bank or escrow agent receive checks from buyers. The checks should be payable to, and sent directly to, the seller of the security or the bank, rather than to Spring Street.

- Spring Street should inform investors that the shares are not traded on any registered securities exchange or through Nasdaq, that the shares are highly illiquid, and of the risks inherent in investing in illiquid securities.

- Spring Street should inform users of the system that if they post quotations simultaneously on both the buyer and seller Wit Trade bulletin boards, they may be considered a "dealer" subject to broker-dealer registration requirements under the federal securities laws.

- Spring Street should disclose price and volume quotations for recent transactions and maintain records of all quotations posted on Wit Trade and all transactions effected through the use of the system.

The Commission also noted that the sale of securities through Wit Trade appeared to involve an offer or sale by Spring Street for purposes of the Securities Act and that absent an available exemption—in this case, Regulation A—Spring Street would be required to register under the Securities Act and to keep its registration statement "evergreen" for so long as quotations are posted through Wit Trade. The Commission staff, citing the company's apparent continued reliance on Regulation A, indicated that delivery of an updated Regulation A offering circular would be appropriate.

Munder Capital Management/The Munder Funds

In February 1996, Munder Capital Management ("Munder Capital"), a registered investment adviser, and the Munder Funds (the "Funds"), registered open-end investment companies, requested confirmation by the Commission that the publication of certain information regarding recent purchase and sale information by the Funds did not result in a violation of Rule 206(4)-1 under the Investment Advisers Act of 1940.[99]

Munder Capital and the Funds have developed their own Web site to provide users with access to information that was previously available in printed form only. The information includes basic information about Munder's advisory organization, including information about the firm's history and investment philosophy, as well as background information on key personnel. The information regarding the Funds includes the prospectuses of the Funds, information regarding Fund size, portfolio turnover rate, number of portfolio holdings, industry diversification and top ten holdings, as well as advertising and supplemental sales literature. In addition, Munder provides portfolio transaction information on a fund-by-fund basis. The portfolio transaction information reflects all new portfolio positions added or eliminated during the month. The presentation of the portfolio transaction information also discusses each portfolio company's business, along with the reasons the investment adviser found the security attractive or the adviser's rationale for selling the security.

Munder Capital and the Funds argued that providing portfolio transaction information is useful to existing fund shareholders, brokers and potential investors, and is consistent with the Commission's efforts to provide mutual fund investors with material information regarding mutual funds and their investment performance. Further, they asserted that the disclosure of these transactions was not a recommendation by the Funds or their adviser to purchase or sell a particular security, but simply factual information regarding recent purchases and sales by the Funds, particularly because it was not presented on a selective basis, but reflected all transactions for a given period. They further argued that the information provided constituted investment company sales literature and was not an advertisement for advisory services under Rule 206(4)-1(b).

The Commission granted Munder Capital and the Funds the requested relief, permitting use of the Internet Web site for such purpose. The Commission also agreed that the portfolio transaction information, which reflected only services provided to the Funds and did not refer to services provided to Munder's other clients, should not be considered an advertisement for Munder's advisory services.

X. SEC Enforcement

Recognizing the potential for fraud in the use of the Internet, both in the offering of securities without registration and in the promotion of illegal investment schemes, securities regulators have undertaken active surveillance of the Internet.[100] Illegal investment schemes through the use of the Internet are reportedly growing, most commonly through the use of the commercial bulletin board systems to manipulate thinly traded securities, through the solicitation of investors by brokers acting outside the scope of their employment and making baseless assurances about the potential for profit, and through such traditional investment scams as pyramid schemes, Ponzi schemes and the like.

The Commission is vigorously seeking to bolster enforcement to ensure that the Internet is not exploited as a means of avoiding the federal securities laws. In June 1996, the Commission established the Enforcement Complaint Center (the "Complaint Center") on its Web site. The Complaint Center allows investors to communicate directly with the Commission through the Internet about potential violations of securities laws. The Complaint Center directs complaints to the Division of Enforcement and the Office of Investor Assistance and Education for review and further action.

The NASD has emphasized to members their supervisory and regulatory responsibilities, as well as responsibility to customers, when dealing with stocks promoted on the Internet or other electronic media. It has also reminded members that "all communication with the public, regardless of the medium, are subject to the antifraud provisions of the federal securities laws, Commission rules and NASD rules."[101]

The Commission has brought the following enforcement actions alleging violations of the securities laws by means of the use of the Internet:

Securities and Exchange Commission v. George Chelekis, KGC, Inc. and Hot Stocks Review, Inc.[102] The Commission filed a complaint against Chelekis and Hot Stocks Review alleging that Chelekis, who publishes an on-line investment newsletter, knowingly or recklessly made false and misleading statements regarding six publicly traded companies, failed to disclose that he controls KGC and Hot Stocks Review and received over $1 million from more than 150 issuers for recommending their stocks. Chelekis and Hot Stocks Review consented to the entry of a final judgment ordering them to pay $162,000, representing $75,000 in disgorgement, $12,000 in prejudgment interest and $75,000 in civil penalties.

Securities and Exchange Commission v. Charles O. Huttoe, et al.[103] At the request of the Commission, the court froze the assets of Charles O. Huttoe ("Huttoe"), chairman of Systems of Excellence, Inc. ("SOE") and agreed to impose a temporary restraining order enjoining SOE's failure to file with the Commission required reports, failing to maintain records, and failing to maintain a system of internal accounting controls, all in violation of the Exchange Act. Thousands of messages regarding SOE were posted on Internet investment-related bulletin boards, many of which cited SGA Goldstar's frequent reports on the stock, which were alleged by the Commission to be "highly promotional, strongly urging accumulation of the stock, discouraging sales and even discouraging investors from independently verifying SGA's information." The Commission alleged, among other things, that Huttoe promoted the stock by issuing misleading news releases, including one in May that reported a $3.4 million order that did not exist; that SGA Goldstar Research Inc. promoted SOE in return for unregistered shares in SOE, which it sold when the stock reached new highs in May and June; and that SOE filed false documents with the Commission in an effort to conceal the fraud.

Securities and Exchange Commission v. Western Executive Group, Inc., et al.[104] The Commission obtained a temporary restraining order enjoining the continued offer and sale by Western Executive Group, Inc. ("Western") of investment contracts for the sale and leaseback of privately owned automated teller machines (ATMs). Defendants misrepresented the number of ATMs actually operating and failed to disclose that the ATMs were not generating sufficient funds to yield returns in the form of lease payments. Western solicited investors through private investment seminars, mass mailings, cold calls and the Internet and raised over $3 million from at least 132 investors. The Commission seeks preliminary and permanent injunctions and disgorgement and civil penalties. The action is pending.

Securities and Exchange Commission v. Wye Resources, Inc. and Rehan Malik.[105] Wye Resources, Inc. ("Wye"), a Canadian corporation, engaged in a fraudulent promotional campaign targeted towards U.S. investors by placing advertisements in U.S. publications and messages over the Internet through a computer bulletin board in which it misrepresented the status of Wye's ongoing exploitation of certain Zairian mining properties. In May 1997, the U.S. District Court for the District of Columbia issued a Default Judgment against Wye Resources.

Securities and Exchange Commission v. William B. Sellin, II, et al.[106] William Sellin ("Sellin") conducted a fraudulent offering of securities through at least 21 newsgroup bulletin board postings on the Internet and through advertisements placed on

CompuServe, an Internet access provider. Sellin represented that he could deliver "guaranteed" annual returns of 12% to 22% even though the securities were neither secured nor collateralized by U.S. government securities. Sellin also failed to disclose a long history of regulatory violations and criminal sanctions.

Securities and Exchange Commission v. Octagon Technology Group, Inc., et al.[107] Octagon Technology Group, Inc. ("Octagon") linked to the Internet a Web site for the Agency for Interamerican Finance, a Panamanian shell subsidiary offering Interamerican hard currency bonds, a sham security. The Web pages promised a risk-free investment with guaranteed returns of 11.75% annually and instructed that payment be sent to a rented mail drop in Antigua. The Commission entered a Final Judgment enjoining Octagon, its chief executive officer and vice president from future violations of the antifraud provisions of the Securities Act. In addition, the chief executive officer agreed to pay a $5,000 penalty.

Securities and Exchange Commission v. Donald B. Spencer and IVT Systems, Inc.[108] The Commission filed a complaint seeking to permanently enjoin Donald B. Spencer ("Spencer") and IVT Systems, Inc. ("IVT") from violating the federal securities laws and requesting the disgorgement of all funds that were misappropriated by Spencer and IVT. Spencer solicited investors through the use of the Internet, among other means, for the construction of a proposed ethanol plant in the Dominican Republic, promising a potential 50% return without any reasonable basis.

Securities and Exchange Commission v. Pleasure Time, Inc. d/b/a Telephone Information Systems, et al.[109] A permanent injunction was entered against Pleasure Time, Inc. ("Pleasure Time"). Pleasure Time sold over $3 million in unregistered securities to approximately 20,000 persons through a multilevel marketing system in which investors were recruited by telephone, fax and the Internet and promised enormous profits from a worldwide telephone lottery.

Securities and Exchange Commission v. Gene Block, et al.[110] Gene Block ("Block") used the Internet to induce potential investors to buy "prime Bank Guarantees," a fake security, promising to "double" investors' funds in as little as four months. The Commission enjoined Block from continuing his fraudulent offering on the Internet and froze certain of his assets.

Securities and Exchange Commission v. Daniel Odulo, et al.[111] Daniel Odulo was enjoined from soliciting investors for a proposed eel farm and promising them a "whopping 20% return" and a "low risk" investment.

Securities and Exchange Commission v. Scott A. Frye.[112] A federal court permanent injunction was entered against Scott A. Frye ("Frye"). Frye posted numerous messages on the Internet seeking investors for two Costa Rican enterprises. Frye promised riskless profits, above-average returns and represented falsely that one of the companies had a distribution contract with A&P Supermarkets.

OmniGene Diagnostics, Inc.[113] On November 20, 1996, in its first use of an electronic bulletin board for such purpose, the Commission announced, on an America Online message board that discussed OmniGene Diagnostics, Inc. ("ODI") stock, the temporary suspension, pursuant to Section 12(k) of the Exchange Act, of over-the-counter trading of the securities of ODI, which it terminated on December 4, 1996. The Commission suspended trading because of questions about the accuracy and adequacy of publicly disseminated information concerning, among other things, ODI's alleged ownership and other rights as to certain patents and trademarks, ODI's sales, past and projected, ODI's operations and facilities and the number of freely traded shares of ODI common stock. ODI's stock was posted on the Internet's electronic bulletin boards in October 1996, and at the same time, several messages praising the company appeared on different boards. When ODI's problems first became apparent, some concerned investors posted their information on the bulletin boards as well. The Commission has announced that it intends to use the Internet to alert investors to potential problems with specific securities when circumstances warrant.

Securities and Exchange Commission v. Comparator Systems Corporation ("Comparator"), et al.[114] Comparator set the record for having the most actively traded stock of all time. Driven in large part by the hyping of Comparator's stock on Motley Fool, a reputable on-line educational investment Web site which hosts an on-line talk forum, Comparator's stock—traditionally, a penny stock—soared to a high of $1.87 per share during three days of record trading on the Nasdaq stock market in May 1996, despite the fact that Comparator had not reported a profit in over 20 years, rarely had a sale, and had no identifiable product. The Commission suspended trading in the stock, which was delisted in June 1996 and now sells for about a penny per share in informal trading.[115] The National Association of Securities Dealers now routinely investigates on-line talk forums to see if they are contributing to otherwise inexplicable stock movements.

Motley Fool, which has relied on volunteers to moderate its on-line discussion groups and write investment articles, has decided to hire a full-time staff of moderators instead.[116] Although there were no allegations of wrongdoing by Motley Fool in connection with the Comparator scandal, Motley Fool's chief executive said that its lawyers, ostensibly concerned with potential liability, may begin requiring Motley Fool representatives to disclose whether they have an interest in the companies they are discussing, a requirement that would be difficult to enforce with respect to volunteer staff.[117]

77439/NYL3A

ENDNOTES

1. *See* Use of Electronic Media for Delivery Purposes, Securities Act Release No. 33-7233; 34-36345 (October 6, 1995) (the "October Release") and Use of Electronic Media by Broker-Dealers, Transfer Agents and Investment Advisors for Delivery of Information; Additional Examples Under the Securities Act of 1933, Securities Exchange Act of 1934 and Investment Company Act of 1940, Securities Act Release No. 33-7288 (May 9, 1996) (the "May Release").

2. *See* October Release, *supra* note 1, Section II.A.

3. *See* Statement of the Commission Regarding Use of Internet Web sites to Offer Securities, Solicit Securities Transactions or Advertise Investment Services Offshore, Securities Act Release No. 33-7516 (March 23, 1998) (the "Web Site Release").

4. Securities Act Concepts and Their Effect on Capital Formation, Securities Act Release No. 33-7314 (July 25, 1996).

5. *See* October Release, *supra* note 1.

6. *See id.*, Section II.D, example 10.

7. *Id.*, Section II.B.

8. *Id.*, Section II.B, n.25.

9. 17 C.F.R. 240.15c2-8.

10. 17 C.F.R. 230.174.

11. *See* October Release, *supra* note 1, Section II.A.

12. *See* id., Section II.D, example 5.

13. *Id.*, Section II.B

14. *Id.*

15. *Id.*, Section I, n.11.

16. *See Public Statements by Corporate Representatives*, Securities Act Release No. 33-6504 (Jan. 20, 1984) ("The antifraud provisions of the federal securities laws apply to all company statements that can reasonably be expected to reach investors and the trading markets, whatever the intended primary audience"). *See also In re Ames Dept. Stores Inc. Stock Litigation*, 991 F.2d 953 (2d Cir. 1993).

17. *See, e.g.,* SEC Release No. 33-5180 (August 16, 1971); SEC Release No. 33-5009 (October 7, 1969); and SEC Release No. 33-3844 (October 8, 1957).

18. *See* October Release, *supra* note 1, Section II.D, example 14.

19. Section 12(a)(2) under the Securities Act imposes civil liability, for rescission or for damages if the security is no longer owned, on any person who offers or sells a security, whether or not it is registered, by means of a prospectus or oral communication "which includes an untrue statement of a material fact or omits to state a material fact necessary in order to make the statements in the light of the circumstances under which they were made, not misleading."

20. *See* Securities Act, Section 5(b)(1).

21. *See* Securities Act, Section 2(a)(10). Until recently, the reference to radio and television in Section 2(a)(10)'s definition of "prospectus" largely foreclosed, as a legal matter, the use of electronic communications to conduct roadshows. However, the Commission staff recently issued three no-action letters with respect to electronic road shows. *See* Private Financial Network ("PFN"), 1997 SEC No- Act. LEXIS 406 (avail. Mar. 12, 1997) and Net Roadshow, Inc., 1997 SEC No-Act. LEXIS 864 (avail. Sept. 8, 1997), Bloomberg L.P. (avail. Oct. 22, 1997).

22. For a discussion of Rule 135c announcements, *see* note 27, *infra*.

23. The Commission adopted Rule 134 under this provision. It allows an announcement about the offering that contains somewhat more information, including the name of the underwriters, than that permitted by Rule 135. Note that Rule 134 announcements are still deemed to be offers and, therefore, are not permitted before the filing of the registration statement; Rule 134 simply takes the announcement outside of the definition of "prospectus."

24. This is because Section 2(a)(10) specifically defines a confirmation to be a prospectus; since the confirmation does not meet the requirements of Section 10(a), its delivery would violate Section 5(b)(1) unless it comes within an exception from the definition of "prospectus." Thus, the final prospectus needs to be sent or given to the customer at the same time as or prior to the delivery of the confirmation. In such case, the confirmation will fall within the exception from the definition of "prospectus" for certain written communications after effectiveness. Note that other written materials (*e.g.*, sales literature) may also be used under the same exception to the definition of "prospectus" subject to the same requirement that the final prospectus has been sent or given to the person receiving the sales literature at or prior to the sales literature communication offering.

25. *See* discussion, however, of no-action letters permitting use of electronic or internet roadshows.

26. If Web site publication of a prospectus is selected as the method for delivery, the company should comply with the Commission's electronic delivery guidance discussed in Part III, above.

27. *See* October Release, *supra* note 1, Section II.D, example 20.

28. *See* IPONET, 1996 SEC No-Act. LEXIS 642, July 26, 1996. *See also* Lamp Technologies, Inc., 1997 SEC No-Act. LEXIS 638, May 29, 1997.

29. *See id.*

30. Under Rule 135c, the notice (1) cannot be for the purpose of conditioning the market; (2) cannot contain more than the following additional information: "the name of the issuer, the title, amount and basic terms of the securities to be offered, the amount of the offering, if any, to be made by selling security holders, the anticipated time of the offering and a brief statement of the manner and purpose of the offering without naming the underwriters"; (3) must include a legend stating that the securities are not registered and may not be sold in the United States absent registration or an applicable exemption; and (4) must be filed with or furnished to the Commission on a Form 8-K or 6-K, or pursuant to Rule 12g3-2(b), as the case may be.

31. *See Road Shows on the Internet through MSNBC Desktop Video*, The Georgeson Reporter 5 (May 1997) (an interview with Victoria Crane, former Georgeson Vice President, describing MSNBC's internet roadshow service entitled, "Virtual Roadshow"). *See How Seat-of-the-Pants IPO's Turned Into Global Events: In Today's Huge Deals, There's No Room For Error*, Investment Dealers Digest (May 22, 1995); *On The Road Again . . . ; With Few Exceptions Wall Street Road Shows Are Larger and More Grueling Than Ever*, Investment Dealers Digest (Sept. 20, 1993); S. Schulte, *IPO Road Shows—A Primer for the Practitioner*, 962 PLI/Corp 93 (1996).

32. *See* Net Roadshow (avail. Jan. 30, 1998).

33. *See* Chairman Arthur Levitt, "Corporate Finance in the Information Age," Securities Regulation Institute, San Diego, California (January 23, 1997)) SEC Web site www.sec.gov/news/speeches/spch 135; *see also* Securities Act Release No. 33-7233 (October 13, 1995) in which the Commission articulates its policy to encourage and facilitate the use of electronic distribution of information based on its potential to enhance investors' ability to access, research and analyze information and to facilitate, expedite and lower the costs of issuers informing the markets.

34. *See supra* note 19.

35. *See* supra text accompanying note 19.

36. *See id.*

37. 115 S. Ct. 1061 (1995) (holding that Section 12(a)(2) of the Securities Act, which imposes liability for material misstatements or omissions in prospectuses or oral communications in the offer or sale of securities, does not apply to private placements or secondary market transactions).

38. *See* PFN No-Action letter, *supra* note 19.

39. *See* Net Roadshow (avail. Jan. 30, 1998).

40. *See* IPONET (avail. July 26, 1996).

41. *See* Exchange Act, Rule 14a-6.

42. *See* Exchange Act, Rule 14a-1(l).

43. Rule 14a-8 under the Exchange Act permits eligible shareholders to have included in the company's proxy statement a proposal for action at the shareholder meeting. Eligible shareholders include those who have held, for at least one year, at least 1%, or $1,000 in market value, of voting securities of the company. *See* Exchange Act, Rule 14a-8(a)(1).

44. *See* Exchange Act Release No. 34-31326 (October 16, 1992).

45. Offshore Offers and Sales, Securities Act Release No. 33-6863 (April 24, 1990).

46. *See* Web Site Release, fn. 28.

47. *See* U.K. Financial Services Act of 1986, Section 57 (Halsbury's Statutes, 4th Ed.).

48. *See id.*, Section 207(3).

49. *See* Investment Advertising Over the Internet, http://www.sib.co.uk/enf/adverts.

50. *See id.*

51. *See* October Release, *supra* note 1, Section II.D, example 9.

52. *See id.*, Section II.B, n.26.

53. If a company's stock is traded on the New York Stock Exchange (the "NYSE"), the company must supply paper copies of its final prospectus to the NYSE pursuant to Securities Act Rule 153 so that the NYSE can provide paper versions of prospectuses to investors who do not use electronic means to receive information. *See id.*, Section II.D, example 11.

54. *See id.*, Section II.B, n.26.

55. *See id.*, Section II.D, example 12.

56. *See* May Release, *supra* note 1, Section IV, example 7.

57. *See* Technical Rules Release, *infra* note 83, I.B.1, citing May Release, Section IV, example 7.

58. *See* October Release, *supra* note 1, Section II.D, example 13.

59. Id. Sulzer Medica was allowed to file copies of the graphic images rather than describe them because as a foreign private issuer it is not required to file electronically.

60. During the "waiting period" between the filing of a registration statement and its effectiveness, sales are prohibited and written offers may be made only by means of a preliminary prospectus. No "free writings" are permitted to be distributed during this time even if they are accompanied by a preliminary prospectus. Once the registration statement is declared effective, however, sales are permitted and other sales literature may be used to market the securities, as long as such literature is preceded or accompanied by a final prospectus.

61. *See* Part IV, *infra, Registered Offerings: Statutory Framework.*

62. *See* October Release, *supra* note 1, Section II.D, examples 14, 15 and 17; and May Release, *supra* note 1, Section IV, example 4.

63. *See* October Release, *supra* note 1, Section II.D, example 14.

64. *See id.*, example 17.

65. *See id.*, example 15.

66. *Id.*

67. *Id.*

68. *Id.*, Section II.B, n.24. The Commission acknowledges that there are certain circumstances where burdensome procedures may be appropriate. *See id.*, example 42.

69. See id., example 14.

70. The publication and distribution of research reports in connection with a proposed offering of securities present additional concerns with respect to publicity rules. Because research reports may fall within the definition of "offer" as broadly defined under Section 2(3) of the Securities Act, they represent a risk of violating the "gun-jumping" prohibition of Section 5(c) of the Securities Act. Because research reports are written documents, they also represent a risk of violating Section 5(b)(1) or 5(b)(2) during the waiting and

quiet periods, in that they are prospectuses (as broadly defined under Section 2(a)(10) of the Securities Act) not complying with the requirements of Section 10 under the Securities Act.

71. *See* October Release, *supra* note 1, Section II.D, example 16.

72. *See id.*, example 18.

73. *See id.*, example 19.

74. *See id.*, example 43.

75. *See* May Release, *supra* note 1, Section IV, example 5.

76. *See* October Release, *supra* note 1, Section II.D, n.46.

77. *See id.*, Section II.D, n.26. *See also* Part IV.D, *infra, Proxy Solicitations and Annual Meetings.*

78. *See id.*, example 28.

79. *See* May Release, *supra* note 1, Section IV, example 1.

80. *See* Section VI, *infra.*

81. *See* ITT Corporation, SEC No-Action Letter (December 6, 1996) and Baltimore Gas and Electric, SEC No-Action Letter (January 6, 1997).

82. SEC Release Nos. 33-7380; 34-38164 (January 14, 1997). The Proposed Rule also requires that, if a registrant is an electronic filer, it must disclose in plain English, as required by Rule 421(d) of Regulation C, that the reports it is required to file with the Commission may be viewed on the SEC's Internet site (*e.g.*, by stating that "Our SEC filings are also available to the public on the SEC Internet site (http://www.sec.gov).") or that copies may be obtained by writing to the SEC's Public Reference Section.

83. *See supra* note 74.

84. G. Philip Rutledge, Deputy Chief Counsel, Pennsylvania Securities Commission, *Securities Commission Addresses Internet Offerings* (July 22, 1996), http://www.state.pa.us/PA.

85. *Id.*

86. *In re Offers But Not Sales Effected Through the Internet That Do Not Result in Sales in Pennsylvania*, Commonwealth of Pennsylvania, Before the Pennsylvania Securities Commission (August 31, 1995). The Order captures the state's view that a "communication made on the Internet generally is available to anyone who is able to access the Internet including persons in Pennsylvania."

87. This information is based on the NASAA's most recent survey, dated October 3, 1996. As of that date, no information was available regarding Georgia, Hawaii, Nevada or Puerto Rico.

88. Uniform Laws Annotated, §§ 101-429.

89. *See* May Release, *supra* note 1.

90. *See* Use of Electronic Media by Broker-Dealers, Transfer Agents, and Investment Advisers for Delivery of Information, Securities Act Release No. 33-7288 and Use of Electronic Media for Delivery Purposes, Securities Act Release No. 33-7289 (the "Technical Rules Release") (May 9, 1996).

91. *See* May Release, *supra* note 1, Section II.B.1.

92. NASD, Notice to Members 95-74 (September 1995); NASD Notice to Members 95-80 (September 1995).

93. *See* NASD Regulatory Compliance Alert, April 1996.

94. *See* October Release, *supra* note 1, Section I.

95. 1996 SEC No-Act., LEXIS 566, June 24, 1996.

96. 1996 SEC No-Act., LEXIS 700, August 5, 1996.

97. 1996 SEC No-Act., LEXIS 972, October 29, 1996.

98. 1996 SEC No-Act., LEXIS 435, April 17, 1996.

99. 1996 SEC No-Act., LEXIS 518, May 17, 1996.

100. *See* McLucas, William R., *Recent S.E.C. Enforcement Cases*, 28th Ann. Instit. on Sec. Reg., 688 PLI/Corp. 619 (1996), and Mary Revell, *Getting a Handle on NASD and NYSE Oversight of Broker-Dealer Internet Activities*, wallstreetlawyer.com., Vol. 1, No. 1, p. 8 (1997).

101. *See* NASD, Notice to Members, 96-50 (July 1996). For a description of the applicability of NASD Rules to electronic communications, including Web sites, bulletin boards, group and individual e-mail and chat rooms, *see* "Ask the Analyst About Electronic Communications," NASD Regulatory Compliance Alert (April 1996). The NYSE has filed a proposed rule change with the Commission to amend its rules governing supervision of member communications with the public to address issues raised by electronic communications. *See* Self-Regulatory Organizations; Notice of Filing of Proposed Rule Change and Amendment No. 1 to the Proposed Rule Change by the New York Stock Exchange, Inc., Relating to NYSE Rules 342, "Offices--Approval, Supervision and Control," 440, "Books and Records" and 472, "Communications with the Public," Exchange Act Release No. 34-37941 (November 13, 1996).

102. Litigation Release No. 15264 (February 25, 1997).

103. Civil Action No. 96-02543 (November 7, 1996).

104. Litigation Release No. 15134 (October 23, 1996).

105. Litigation Release No. 15073 (September 26, 1996).

106. Litigation Release No. 15004 (August 7, 1996).

107. Litigation Release No. 14942 (June 11, 1996).

108. Litigation Release No. 14856 (March 29, 1996).

109. Litigation Release No. 14825 (February 26, 1996).

110. Litigation Release No. 14598 (August 10, 1995).

111. Litigation Release No. 14591 (August 7, 1995).

112. Litigation Release No. 14720 (November 15, 1995).

113. SEC Release No. 34-37966 (November 20, 1996).

114. Litigation Release No. 14927 (May 31, 1996).

115. In addition to the delisting, the Commission charged that Comparator issued false and misleading financial statements for its fiscal years that ended in June 30, 1994 and June 30, 1995, as well as for the first three quarters of 1996. The Commission also charged that three executives caused Comparator to file misleading financial statements so that the company's shares would remain listed on the Nasdaq SmallCap Market. The Commission also alleged that Comparator made materially false and misleading claims regarding its technology, including that it owned certain patents and licenses that it, in fact, did not own. *See id.* Comparator settled charges of fraud and record-keeping violations with the Commission in September 1996. *See* Litigation Release No. 15056 (September 19, 1996).

116. Deborah Lohse, *Motley Fool is Wising Up Its On-line Forum Staff*, Wall Street Journal Interactive Edition, March 27, 1997.

117. *Id.*

NOTES

Program Schedule and Faculty

First Day: 9:30 a.m. - 5:30 p.m.

Morning Session: 9:30 a.m. - 12:45 p.m.

9:30
Keynote Speaker Alfred R. Berkeley
President, NASDAQ Stock Market:
Forward-Looking Trends and Developments

10:00
Corporate Web Sites
- Usage and content
- Pitfalls for the unwary
  - Hyperlinks and entanglement with analysts' reports
  - Selective disclosure
  - Projections and the "Safe Harbor" of the Private Securities Litigation Reform Act
  - Policing the accuracy of postings - archiving and updating
  - Investor relations and communications with stockholders
  - Disclaimer legends
- Emergence of industry trends
- EDGAR

W. Andersen, S. Bochner, B. Lane, H. Pitt, S. Schulte and J. White

11:30 Break

11:45
Internet Offerings
- Registered and exempt offerings
  - Principal types
  - Conforming historical practice to use of the "Net"
  - General solicitation, "testing the waters" and gun-jumping
  - The "electronic envelope"
    - Incorporation by reference
    - The hyper-prospectus
    - Delinking approaches
  - NASAA position
- Road shows
- DRIPS, ESOPS and other securities purchase plans

A. Klein, B. Lane, C. Neal, S. Schulte and J. White

12:45
Luncheon Speaker Daniel H. Callahan
Managing Director, Morgan Stanley & Co. Incorporated:
Disintermediation / Where is the "Value Add?"
- Investment banking and informational technology
- Research coverage/client links
- Innovations

Afternoon Session: 2:30 p.m. - 5:00 p.m

2:15
Multiple Markets, Multiple Jurisdictions – Weaving the Two Together
- Cross border offerings
- International secondary trading markets
- International enforcement
- Cross-border implications of multiple markets

R. Dinerstein, E. Fleischman, B. Lane, M. Mann and C. Neal

3:00
Use of the Web: Enforcement and Ethical Considerations
- SEC concerns and surveillance techniques
  - Boiler room – manipulation
  - "Surf days"
  - Chat room oversight
  - Coordination with NASD
- Issuer surveillance
  - Identifying third party information on the web
  - Communications with the SEC enforcement staff
- Diligence issues when using the Web for transactions
  - Money laundering issues and monetary systems
  - "Know your customer"

E. Kwalwasser, B. Santangelo and J. R. Stark

Second Day: 9:00 a.m. - 1:00 p.m.

9:00
Corporate America and the "Street" – Industry Practices and Initiatives
- How to marry the regulations with evolving technology
  - Electronic road shows
  - Internet prospectuses
  - CD-ROMs
- Practical advice from the trenches – a spare multimedia presentation
  - Lawyers' perspective
  - Bankers' perspective
  - Investors' perspective
    - Institutional versus retail
- Access, authentication and security issues
  - SRO requirements and other legal considerations
  - Security/encryption systems
  - Payment systems

J. McLaughlin, L. Quinn, J. Rosen, J. Tricarico, Jr. and M. Wallach

10:30
Electronic Stockholder Meetings
- Proxy solicitations and stockholder meetings
  - Voting mechanics
  - The "virtual" meeting – interactive considerations
- Proxy contests
- Stockholder communications

L. Quinn, B. Roe and M. Wallach

11:00 Break

11:15
Internet Trading Systems
- On-line trading systems sponsored by issuers
- On-line trading systems sponsored by broker-dealers
  - Automated trading systems
  - Electronic communications networks
- On-line trading systems sponsored by markets
  - The Exchanges
  - NASDAQ
- The SEC concept release and characterization questions
  - Securities information processor
  - Broker-Dealer
  - Automated trading system
  - Electronic communications network
  - Exchange (including exempt)
  - Clearing agency
- SEC proposals (e.g., broker-dealer plus versus exchange minus)

B. Becker, S. Campbell, R. Ketchum, R. Lindsey and K. Spirer

4:00 Break

4:15
Investment Companies and Investment Advisers
- Private investment companies
- Fund disclosure and marketing materials
  - Prospectus delivery
  - Banner advertisements
  - Status of hyperlinked materials
  - Delivery to electronic "households"
- Financial planning and other interactive tools
- Electronic disclosure to employee benefit plan participants
- Stockholder communications
  - Account information
  - Portfolio holdings and transactions
- On-line transactions

M. Chambers, A. Gavis and N. Jordan

5:00
The Year 2000 Problem – Its Impact on Various Industries
R. Dinerstein, N. Jordan, S. Schulte and A. Young

12:15
E-mail/Chat Rooms
- The legal implications of E-mail
- Supervision of broker-dealer E-mail
  - SEC supervisory requirements
  - NASD and NYSE supervisory rules
- Electronic surveillance tools
- Chat rooms
  - What are the risks?
  - NASD position
  - Supervisory responsibilities
- Employee E-mail usage: policies, monitoring, blocking and ownership?
- Retention of electronic communications

B. Becker, S. Campbell, R. Ketchum, R. Lindsey and K. Spirer

CO-CHAIRS:

Brandon Becker
Wilmer, Culter & Pickering
Washington, D.C.

Stephen J. Schulte
Schulte Roth & Zabel LLP
New York City

Michelle C. Wallach
Vice President and Counsel
Morgan Stanley U.K. Group
London

FACULTY:

Alden S. Adkins
Senior Vice President and General Counsel
NASD Regulation, Inc.
Office of the General Counsel
Washington, D.C.

Warren G. Andersen
General Motors Corporation
Detroit

Alfred R. Berkeley
President
NASDAQ Stock Market
Washington, D.C.

Steven E. Bochner
Wilson Sonsini Goodrich & Rosati
Palo Alto, California

Daniel H. Callahan
Managing Director
Morgan Stanley & Co. Incorporated
New York City

Scott W. Campbell
Vice President and Associate General Counsel
Charles Schwab & Co. Inc.

San Francisco

Matthew A. Chambers
Debevoise & Plimpton
Washington, D.C.

Robert C. Dinerstein
Senior Managing Director and General Counsel
UBS
New York City

Edward H. Fleischman
Linklaters & Paines
New York City

Irving Faught
Administrator
Oklahoma Department of Securities
Oklahoma City

Alexander C. Gavis
Senior Legal Counsel
Fidelity Investments
Boston

Nora M. Jordan
Davis Polk & Wardwell
New York City

Andrew D. Klein
Founder and Chief Strategist
Wit Capital Corporation
New York City

Howard L. Kramer
Senior Associate Director
Division of Market Regulation
Securities and Exchange Commission
Washington, D.C.

Edward A. Kwalwasser
Group Executive Vice President
New York Stock Exchange, Inc.
New York City

Brian J. Lane
Director
Division of Corporation Finance
Securities and Exchange Commission
Washington, D.C.

Michael D. Mann
Richards Spears Kibbe & Orbe
Washington, D.C.

Joseph McLaughlin
Brown & Wood LLP
New York City

Harvey L. Pitt
Fried, Frank, Harris, Shriver & Jacobson
New York City and Washington, D.C.

Linda C. Quinn
Shearman & Sterling
New York City

Victor Rodarte
Assistant Director
Securities Division
State of Arizona Corporate Commissions
Phoenix

Bonnie J. Roe
Proskauer Rose LLP
New York City

Jeffrey D. Rosen
Product Manager, Internet Related Offerings
Morgan Stanley & Co. Incorporated
New York City

Betty Santangelo
Schulte Roth & Zabel LLP
New York City

Kenneth S. Spirer
First Vice President and Assistant General Counsel
Merrill Lynch & Co., Inc.
New York City

John Reed Stark
Special Counsel for Internet Projects
Division of Enforcement
Securities and Exchange Commission
Adjunct Professor of Law
Georgetown University Law Center
Washington, D.C.

James A. Tricarico, Jr.
General Counsel
Executive Vice President
Law Department
Prudential Securities Inc.
New York City

John W. White
Cravath, Swaine & Moore
New York City

Allen I. Young
Deputy General Counsel
Price Waterhouse LLP
New York City